Y0-CRP-605

POWER, POVERTY,

and

URBAN POLICY

Volume 2, URBAN AFFAIRS ANNUAL REVIEWS

INTERNATIONAL EDITORIAL ADVISORY BOARD

CHARLES ABRAMS
Columbia University

HOWARD S. BECKER
Northwestern University

ASA BRIGGS
University of Sussex

JOHN W. DYCKMAN
University of California (Berkeley)

H. J. DYOS
University of Leicester

MARILYN GITTELL
Editor, Urban Affairs Quarterly

JEAN GOTTMANN
Ecole des Hautes Etudes (Sorbonne)

SCOTT GREER
Northwestern University

ROBERT HAVIGHURST
University of Chicago

WERNER Z. HIRSCH
University of California (Los Angeles)

EIICHI ISOMURA
Tokyo Metropolitan University

OSCAR LEWIS
University of Illinois

WILLIAM C. LORING
U.S. Public Health Service

MARTIN MEYERSON
State University of New York (Buffalo)

EDUARDO NEIRA
Interamerican Development Bank

HARVEY S. PERLOFF
Resources for the Future

D. J. ROBERTSON
University of Glasgow

WALLACE SAYRE
Columbia University

P. J. O. SELF
The London School of Political Science and Economics

KENZO TANGE
Tokyo National University

POWER, POVERTY,

and

URBAN POLICY

Edited by

WARNER BLOOMBERG, Jr.
and HENRY J. SCHMANDT

Volume 2   URBAN AFFAIRS ANNUAL REVIEWS

SAGE PUBLICATIONS, INC. / BEVERLY HILLS, CALIFORNIA

HT
108
.47
vol.2

Copyright © 1968 by Sage Publications, Inc.

Printed in the United States of America

All rights reserved. No part of this book may be reproduced or utilized in any form or by any means, electronic or mechanical, including photocopying, recording, or by any information storage and retrieval system, without permission in writing from the Publisher.

Sage Publications, Inc., Beverly Hills, California

Library of Congress Catalog Card Number: 68-24710

Standard Book Number: 8039-0006-6

SECOND PRINTING

Contents

Part IV

KNOWLEDGE, POLICY, AND POVERTY

Prologue

The Issue Is Great and Very Much in Doubt

WARNER BLOOMBERG, JR.
and HENRY J. SCHMANDT

☐ THE JOY AND SORROW of this volume is the great degree of consensus that obtains among its contributors. If one could be only an editor, or only a social scientist, it would be possible to read through the chapters which follow with a feeling of immense satisfaction. Authors who had no communication with one another have written parts that make a whole, that link with one another, relate, reinforce, complement and supplement to a degree one normally dares not hope for. It has not been necessary to create editorial camouflage for gaps, disparities, and incongruities of the sort so often encountered in assemblages of independently written pieces. This suggests that we are beginning to observe and interpret such phenomena of poverty with a more adequate base of social science theory and information.

Though we are still far distant from a kind of science that could adequately bear the demands already placed upon it for answers to questions about social policy, we are at least equally far from the kind of pseudo-science that once allowed every author to develop his own concepts, taxonomies, and data as carriers for preconceived conclusions. The essays which follow display both the "harder" and the "softer" kinds of social science; their diversity makes it clear that we would be foolish to claim the status of a body of exact sciences; their underlying unity indicates that it is equally ridiculous to deny, as some still do, the existence of a social *science*. The function of this volume is to bring to bear such science as we now have upon the perplexing and vexing problem of urban poverty.

And that is the sorrow: whatever the imperfections of this "instrument" at its present stage of development, there are too many consistencies in the readings it has given us to risk rejecting the evident summary observation—we are failing to reduce impoverishment to anywhere near the degree our resources would seem to permit. We could do considerably more than we are now doing, and our failure in this respect is a product, not so much of ignorance or of individual intransigence, but mainly of the very fabric of our social system, our institutions, our political arrangements. By the time one reaches the end of this book it is sadly clear that the poverty we deplore issues from the same source as many of the pleasures enjoyed by those who have written its various chapters and by the varied readers who may consult their contents.

Most of us are in no position to be too self-righteously indignant about poverty amid affluence, for we are beneficiaries of the very institutional arrangements which also produce the deprivation we decry. This volume should make abundantly clear that the world of the urban poor is not some "other America"; it is of one piece with the America of wealth and well-being. There is not one body that is well and another that is sick, but a single social organism. The infection of impoverishment, though it may be most evident in one part or another, in the end spreads its effects through the entire system.

Understanding that this is true enables us to grasp immediately why the present "war on poverty" has had so little success, indeed, why it was foredoomed to achieve only minor successes at the most. A true war on poverty would be a "war against ourselves," a militant campaign to alter the institutions that, quite literally, produce poverty. They would have to be transformed into systems which, as Haworth suggests, would make genuinely accessible to all individuals real, as against merely formal, opportunity to develop themselves as human beings. But the good city cannot be achieved without modification of institutions that today conduce to inequity, injustice, and finally violence—both physical violence against property and person, and psychological violence against individual talents, emotional health, and even the capacity for feelings of relatedness with other human beings.

Yet, we do not want the institutional arrangements with which we are familiar changed, no matter how convinced we may be on objective grounds that even our own lives would be bettered by some sweeping reforms. We are like the fat man who cannot give up his compulsive eating even though he knows that he is dying from his accumulating corporeality. The sickness meets too many of our most immediately felt needs, and good health is only a promise of what lies beyond an utterly painful battle with ourselves to become other than what we have for so long been. Far more than the poor, the affluent in our society are unable to endure such delayed gratification.

Like many of those who are pathologically obese, we tend to assert that our condition is "natural" and really not so bad (in place of "It's my nature to be on the heavy side" read "We are down to a kind of hard-core poor who always will be evident in a free economy")—perhaps in some ways even desirable (translate "Fat people are jolly" into "Our free enterprise system of vigorous incentives has produced the greatest good for the greatest number"). When in moments of realism and troubled conscience we find such generalizations untenable, we turn in a mood of anxiety to one or another nostrum that allegedly will melt away the trouble with fairly little effort and in a relatively short time; thus, much of the war on poverty is patent medicine, a public policy equivalent of reducing pills and faddish diets that promise major results without any serious change in our values or alteration of our modes of conduct ("Lose pounds a week without ever feeling hungry"). But, when even these superficial efforts turn out to be somewhat disturbing and the meager results disillusioning, the impulse grows stronger to abandon the whole effort, to return to the pleasures of our old routines and the comforts of our habitual rationalizations. This book is, in part, a portrait of America as the corpulent man hung up between his awareness of the ineffectiveness of the easy nostrums and his temptation to indulge in the relief of admitting defeat, foregoing any more painful departures from the rich menus that are his main delight.

THE POWER DIMENSION

Those who wish to read more treatises on the economics of poverty will have to consult sources other than this volume. No effort is made here to add to that still accumulating literature in which increasingly sophisticated procedures are used to cost out and estimate the effects of such proposed innovations as provision of a guaranteed annual dollar income for all individuals and families, the creation of employment in the public sector of such an extent and character that the presently poor could earn enough for a decent level of living regardless of their limitations in skill or mental and physical ability, and a drastic increase in the quality and quantity of directly transferred goods and services. It seems quite obvious that the elimination of poverty, or even a very substantial reduction of its incidence, will require some mix of these methods and that the mix will have to vary from one type of community setting to another.

It also seems clear that past and present economic strategies cannot do the job. At best they have amounted to a deliberate allocation of somewhat more of the annual increases in national productivity to lower income people than the mechanisms of the marketplace would otherwise accomplish. Only in this very limited sense can we be said to have engaged in some "redistribution" of wealth, and even here we find evidence that certain segments of the already affluent have enjoyed proportionately greater shares of the national increment than the deprived. In short, we are far from puzzled about the economics of impoverishment in the United States. And while it is always desirable to improve our ability to diagnose and prescribe, today we clearly face an unwillingness or inability of the doctors to apply such knowledge as they possess and of the patients to accept and obey such prescriptions as are made. This is one syndrome that this book seeks to explore.

To conduct such an inquiry we must examine the response to the challenge of poverty in an affluent society evident in many of the institutional systems through which the lifeways of our urban communities are shaped. We travel, as it were, from residence to supermarket, from church to police station, observing what happens to the poor that maintains, increases, or reduces the deprivation they experience. In every institutional sector we discover patterns that deprive the poor of opportunities to become less deprived, that contribute to the likelihood that most of them will remain impoverished. Moreover, the contribution of each institution to the production of poverty in America reinforces the "output" from the others, and this cumulation of consequences helps to explain the refractory nature of the problem when we attempt piecemeal solutions.

The chapters which deal with particular institutions in some detail also reveal that many of the changes in our institutions, which would do most to reverse the prevailing pattern, would also be of benefit to many who are among the more advantaged majority, especially those in the lower ranges of the moderate income strata. As Huber points out, the entrapment of low income people by the easy credit gimmick and by their own lack of skill in shopping is only a distorted reflection of the situation of millions of apparently affluent Americans whose consumer behavior embodies an almost compulsive quest for satiation in a system that keeps raising the criteria for mere satisfaction. And Doctors Roemer and Kisch remind us that the medical "mainstream" in the United States is itself so seriously polluted by inadequacies that only its general reform can hope to bring reasonable opportunity for health to the deprived. Alvin Schorr has a similar message about housing: only when we see the provision of shelter in terms of a wide range of related community goals are we likely to create policies and programs in which the poor man's home will be a resource for improving his lot in life rather than a reminder and reinforcement of his impoverishment.

The second insight gained from these inquiries into discrete institutional sectors has to do with the knowledge, predispositions, and judgments of those with the greatest power and influence over present practices. In every case it becomes apparent that only a small minority in this category are prepared to attempt major institutional reforms. Even if those in the managerial superstructures could be persuaded of the need for substantial changes, they often fear massive resistance by underlings or equally intransigent opposition from constituencies. Moreover, most people, apart from ritual griping, seem relatively content with things as they are. Among the advantaged majority few parents send their children to what they perceive as seriously inadequate schools; few consider that their ills are not properly diagnosed and treated relative to what existing medical knowledge and technology make possible; few have not been able to get a house they can claim to like; few who are innocent have been arrested and sent to jail; and very few consider the churches of their choice obsolete rather than uplifting or view with pleasure pickets in clerical garb or theological debates that question good old-fashioned "morality."

As a result, most successful experiments in institutional innovation fail to diffuse very rapidly, if at all. Doctor, lawyer, merchant, and chief (of police), as well as preacher and teacher, go on doing mainly what they have always done, pretty much convinced that the problems of the poor with respect to health, justice, material deprivation, education and moral conduct result from either flaws of a personal nature or from some other institutional sector's improper policies or irresponsibility. This means, quite simply, that reforms which might have a major impact on present patterns of impoverishment and deprivation will not occur unless the reforming minority within each institutional sector can exert enough influence or wield enough power to overcome the resistance or inertia of the majority. In short, if democracy American-style means only majority rule, then this generation of Americans is not likely to witness or bring about more than very modest gains against the chronic poverty that lingers in the midst of our ever increasing material productivity.

This conclusion leads us to examine the political situation of those who have tried to carry out as vigorously as possible even the mini-war against poverty that the present national administration proposed and steered through Congress. Here the power dimension can be observed most directly, and it is quite obvious that those measures which might increase the power resources of the reformist minority, including those which might further empower the poor themselves, have produced the greatest opposition and have been subject to the most effective countermeasures on behalf of the institutional *status quo*. As Arthur Shostak's review of the whole war indicates, the most acceptable programs have been those which apparently aim only at aiding the poor in overcoming alleged inadequacies such as lack of skills for employment, of home management competences, and of vocabulary and attention span for successful participation in conventional public schools. At the same time, any implications of experience to date for institutional reform, even for changes that would benefit all and not just the poor, tend to be disregarded or rejected. So also the effort in Congress to cut funding and to disassemble the Office of Economic Opportunity and redistribute its pieces among other federal agencies obviously has more to do with political reality than with fiscal responsibility. It is the politics of poverty, as Kravitz points out, that made one title of the Economic Opportunity Act—the community action component—the salient sector for a powerful counterattack against what was in fact a very modest opening campaign for any authentic war against poverty.

THE URBAN DIMENSION

This counterattack originated most of all among certain of the leaders in our large- and middle-sized urban communities, especially those leaders holding top offices in the local government and quasi-private welfare institutions. The nature of this opposition, together with other developments, has made it increasingly clear that many of the programs with the greatest potentiality for diminishing poverty require effective supporting administration at the local level regardless of the proportion of federal funding, and that such support and effectiveness cannot be produced from Washington. National legislators and administrators apparently did not adequately perceive this difference between most of the programs encompassed by the Economic Opportunity Act and those that permit a direct flow of benefits from the national level to the individual (e.g. tax benefits and social security payments), or that may be fielded largely through non-local or supralocal agencies such as the regional and national business corporations and the universities that have been involved in the Job Corps projects. It is those local institutions, in short, on which the federal government has had to depend for implementing a very large part of its antipoverty program—municipal governments and their police forces, country governments and their public welfare agencies, and private welfare systems dominated by wealthy suburbanite leaders of local business and industry —that have done so much to exacerbate the discontent of the black ghettos.

As those who manage these local urban institutions have turned war-on-poverty projects to their own uses and interpreted them in ways congruent with established interests, the federal administration, especially through regional offices, has sought to maintain or regain its control by tightening up on "guidelines" and increasing its intervention as overseer and evaluator. Both reformers within the established institutional sectors and protest leaders among the poor at first sought to bypass the local political and business-welfare leadership by going directly to federal administrators in regional and national offices. But the managers of the urban institutional establishment responded by exerting their influence on Congress. When resulting legislative pressure on the Presidency became great enough, compromises and defensive tactics traveled down the same pipeline through regional offices that previously had carried the impetus for more militant and extensive reforms. As a result, many local agency reformists are now desperately trying to find sources of funds other than the federal government, and many ghetto leaders have decided that their best strategy is to engage the local establishment in a direct confrontation—on the streets of the city, if necessary—rather than trying to sustain a working coalition with what they consider an increasingly compromised and politically cautious federal bureaucracy. Some rural areas are caught up in the same kind of political drama, but the real stage for this part of the play runs almost directly from Washington to the big and middle-sized cities.

There is an even more profound reason than the above for emphasizing the urban dimension of the problem of poverty in the United States. Although it is true that there is much rural poverty, the rural poor are themselves largely symptomatic of the still continuing decline of rural society. In spite of the precipitous decline in the proportion of the population engaged in agriculture in the United States over the past half century, we are still in the process of transferring marginal farmers and unemployed or under-employed and underpaid farm labor from rural residence to places of greater economic opportunity. Although they often remain unemployed, underemployed, and underpaid after moving into town or city, there has been no reverse migration of any significant proportions. Clearly, then, much of "rural poverty" will remain rural only for as long as the rural poor resist moving to the urban area or cannot acquire the means to do so. This, of course, does not mean that they ought to be ignored or underrepresented in present plans to aid the poor; it simply means that deprivation will continue to become more and more an urban problem and that in absolute numbers the rural poor will continue to decline through movements that add to the size of the impoverished segment of urban populations.

Urban areas, moreover, are the locale for most of the more meaningful institutional innovations affecting the poor. This fact simply reflects the greater magnitude and accessibility of both "target populations" and professionals willing to conduct experiments through the agencies to which they are attached. Moral and technical support is available from universities and political support is available from liberal organizations and activists, both of which are usually more evident in the city than in small town or rural countryside. In addition, there has been an increasing tendency for the poor to be Negro, and this development in turn lies behind the emergence of racial conflict as the volatile nexus of urban politics in the mid-1960s. The politics of race and the politics of poverty will continue to merge for at least the next few years, and city ghettos will continue to be the spatial locus of that merger. This ominous and increasingly omnipresent characteristic of our urban milieu has shaken up old political alliances and stimulated entirely new concepts of how urban institutions ought to be organized and what they ought to do. And so we focus the attention of this volume on the cities, not because rural poverty is minimal or unimportant, but because it is here where most of the action is and where the transformation from poor to non-poor must take place.

KNOWLEDGE AND POLICY

Finally, the chapters of this book address themselves, in varying degree, to a somewhat paradoxical situation best epitomized by the assertion that we lack the knowledge needed to accomplish our purposes and at the same time fail to use relevant knowledge presently available to us. The recent spate of articles and books concerned with poverty represents, not that outpouring of new knowledge which the slow cumulation of research and interpretation may produce when it culminates in a real breakthrough in theory and understanding, but an eager (sometimes overeager) response to a rapidly expanding market for both fact and fantasy about "the poor." Some researchers and commentators have found in the present situation a long sought opportunity to devote themselves to a persistent concern for which there was relatively little support in past decades; others are simply academic opportunists jumping on what appears to be a bandwagon for funds and publication. Many articles and essays have been reprinted and even re-reprinted, not because they are brilliant or particularly seminal or somehow definitive, but simply because they are fairly adequate and immediately available. For the past few years those who wanted or were willing to write about poverty have enjoyed a sellers' market.

We are now coming into a more critical period, and that is all to the good. It is increasingly apparent how much hard work lies ahead if research and theory are ever to provide an adequate knowledge base for designing effective institutional responses to the challenge of poverty, rather than merely indicating in often vague and too frequently contradictory terms "the direction" in which those who shape policies and practices ought to go. Gordon Sutton reminds us that even our working definitions of poverty leave much to be desired and may themselves mislead some of our practical efforts. Stephen Pflanczer underscores the glibness that has characterized many rather journalistic comparisons between welfare systems in other industrial countries and our own. Oscar Ornati presents a pioneer effort to relate the spatial dimension of poverty to the understanding of the processes which produce and maintain deprivation, with the hope that others will follow this lead. Kravitz, Bloomberg and Rosenstock, and Haggstrom together disclose how very fuzzy much of our thinking has been about both the purposes and the possibilities of increasing political participation by the poor, revealing how our generalizations and expectations have reflected a low yield mix of ideology, conventional wisdom, and social science. Indeed, not one author has been able to ground his contribution in a field of extensive, validated research and theory. It is a credit to their intellectual honesty that they have been quite explicit about this lack.

But that is only one side of the coin. On the other side is imprinted an obstinate addiction to the "conventional wisdom" on the part of a large segment of governmental officials, both elected and appointed, and of those with authority over private welfare agency programs. This resistance to the new insights and information provided by available, albeit inadequate, social research often precludes any honest hearing for such arguments and evidence as are developed in the chapters dealing with various urban institutions; translation into implemented policies thus is even more unlikely. Equally damaging is the powerful reluctance of many officials, especially some in certain private agencies, to allow use of available research techniques to obtain as rigorous an evaluation of their programs as is possible. There also is a strong predisposition to prevent any public scrutiny of such objective assessments as may be made. In several places in his overview of the "war on poverty" Shostak alludes to the damaging degree of duplication and the exercises in futility that can go on year after year because of this.

Clearly, the ethical imperative for secrecy in charity, intended to protect the poor from being exploited for the sake of the self-aggrandizement of the giver, cannot possibly justify the refusal to submit present efforts by private and public agencies and organizations to the most rigorous and revealing kinds of scrutiny. Indeed, proper social science inquiry carefully preserves the anonymity of those studied. What is now being protected are the images of institutional authorities, the budgets they administer, the professional habits of their staffs, and the self-righteous contentment of their constituencies, whether voters or donors. To put the matter most bluntly, more adequate research is often resisted precisely because it would reveal that the poor are in effect used to maintain and aggrandize organizations and agencies whose expenditures and activities represent less rather than more effective efforts to reduce or eliminate deprivation. And this tends more often to be the case as one moves from national to local levels.

There is another connection between knowledge and policy demonstrated by some of the contributions to this volume. Chapters by Breese, Gutkind, and Mangin deal specifically with aspects of the poverty problem in some of the underdeveloped nations; others —Ornati's, Pflanczer's, and Schorr's, for example—provide a further comparative perspective. Taken together they heavily underscore the difference between the problem of have-not societies and the problem of deprivation within affluent societies. To lump together under uncritically cosmic generalizations the societal impoverishment of the underdeveloped areas and the selective deprivation of certain minority segments of the citizenry within the increasingly productive urban-industrial nations best serves both those whose slogans assert that all poverty is a capitalist plot and those whose comfortable conservatism is psychologically secured by the conviction that the poor shall always be with us. The comparative materials provided in the pages which follow insistently remind us that the kind of deprivation we have in the United States need be with us only for as long as we cannot bring ourselves to make the reforms in our institutions that would bring it to an end. Such reforms, in turn, might well enhance our ability to face more realistically and more creatively the far greater challenge presented by societal impoverishment in Africa, Asia, and Latin America.

THE TEST OF POVERTY

This consideration brings us, once again, to the realization that the national response to poverty in our kind of society is likely to affect far more in the years ahead than simply the amount of deprivation that obtains within our own borders. History may be testing the very viability of what is so often referred to with various kinds of editorial embellishment as "our American way of life." In his book *The Good City,* Haworth has argued that reconstructing urban institutions in technologically advanced societies may well be a necessary step toward the achievement of a peaceful and secure international order. For the latter is likely to remain beyond our reach until we have developed far greater capacities for social commitment and institutional creativity. The opportunity to develop such capacities inheres in the demand that we use our now sufficient technology to establish urban social systems that promote both individual self-development and a full measure of social justice.

Is it likely, or even possible, that we can pass such a test? The contributions to this volume indicate many of the lines of possibility, but the judgments of most of the authors reflect great uncertainty as to the likelihood that such lines will be followed. At least the question remains open. If there are no grounds for great optimism, neither is there justification for defeatism. Perhaps, if there is a more effective effort to make evident how fundamental is the issue of poverty in our kind of society, it may be possible to elicit from those in positions of power and from the citizenry in general, a greater willingness to use the knowledge we already have and to seek the further understanding that is still required. This volume is, hopefully, a contribution to such needed realization, application, and continued inquiry.

Part I

AFFLUENCE AND POVERTY

Some Basic Dimensions of the Problem

Introduction

THE polarity between affluence and poverty, increasingly evident in the modern world, raises fundamental issues of both a normative and a behavioral nature. These issues have become ever more critical to the formation of urban policy—whether at the national, state, or local level—as tension has mounted dangerously between those who enjoy at least material well-being and those who are deprived of it. Policy formulation and execution, no matter of what character, rest upon some conceptualization and evaluation of the problem to be solved, some set of values and attitudes toward it, and some notion of the ends to be sought. Unfortunately, the philosophical and empirical issues involved in the problem of deprivation have been clouded by ill-founded assumptions, emotional polemics, and useless rhetoric; witness the national debate over the "war on poverty."

The three chapters which make up Part I of the present volume address themselves to the nature and dimensions of the poverty problem and the basic issues associated with it. Although the emphasis and approach of each are different, all of them are concerned with the questions of definition and evaluation and their implications for policy-making. For, as they point out in graphic terms, radically different consequences can result from policies grounded on alternative conceptions of the causes of poverty and of remedies for it. Each contribution, in its own way, also stresses the fallacy of easy assumptions in this field, the complexity of the variables involved, the need to be cognizant of differentiations among the poor, and the necessity of basing policy on both normative standards and empirical theory.

Chapter 1 establishes a normative base for much that is to follow in the volume. In it, Lawrence Haworth, one of the few

American philosophers who has concerned himself with the city and its problems, trenchantly poses the ethical and moral issues which lie at the root of the poverty question. As he points out, we are not clear what winning the war on poverty consists of since we are not sure what poverty is or why we should be fighting it. To be adequate for policy guidance, a definition of poverty must serve two purposes: it must be usable in identifying those who are to be the beneficiary of poverty programs, and it must lead to an identification of the conditions to be remedied. The thrust of Haworth's argument is that money is relevant to poverty only insofar as it determines access to institutional opportunities which make humanly significant activity possible. Hence economic definitions or measurements of poverty, standing alone, are insufficient. The object of the fight on deprivation should be to mold the structural conditions of the city so that all individuals are provided with the institutional opportunities for self-realization. This objective requires the alteration of those conditions which have differential impact on the poor, the segment of the population which has least access to whatever opportunities the city has to offer. The point is examined with much empirical detail in Part II.

Poverty, as Haworth notes, is a form of social injustice. The poor are not mere beneficiaries of welfare programs but a group that has been wronged. Here the logic cuts sharp. Urban institutions are unjust to the extent that they systematically deny to some the opportunity for personal growth. This denial may take place either by erecting discriminatory bars to participation or by tolerating incapacitating conditions which effectively disqualify certain individuals or groups from participation. Thus, the perpetuation of an environment—the ghetto, for example—which causes persons not to develop skills and habits necessary for subsequent participation in the life of the city is as much a wrong as the maintenance of discriminatory institutions—segregated housing or education, for example—which simply deny persons admission to the places where opportunities are located.

In Chapter 2, Oscar Ornati distinguishes between two major sets of poverty definitions: one based on the notion of a subsistence level, the other on relative deprivation or income differentials. The first is aimed at measuring the gap between consensually determined needs and the resources available to individuals and families. The second is directed toward measuring the disparity between those who have little and those who have much. All definitions of poverty now used for policy formulation purposes are variations of the subsistence level notion. Yet, as Ornati points out, for wealthy nations such as the United States, poverty is emerging increasingly as a problem of inequality. This development calls for policy and action founded not on definitions embodying the concept of sub-sistence but on those directed at relative deprivation. It means, in Ornati's terms, that we must break away from the current "strategy of services" to the poor to strategies designed to bring about a more equitable income distribution.

The bulk of Ornati's chapter deals with the inter- and intracity dimensions of poverty: the relative importance of poverty in dif-ferent cities and the distribution of the poor within the space of the city. Such variables as size, employment diversity, industrial mix, demographic composition, and migration, are examined for their possible relation to spatial distribution patterns. Comparisons are made with foreign cities to the extent the available data permit. Here, the experience of other countries proves most valuable in the area of redistributive policy, such as transfer payments and tax incidence. (The volume returns to the concern for comparative analysis in Part III and, especially, in Part IV.)

Like Haworth, Ornati holds the existence of poverty to be a failure of one of the city's essential functions. For the urban com-munity is the locus of the great transformation: the place where the poor become not poor. In a closing statement, the author strikes a responsive chord, noting that the long impossible dream of eradi-cating poverty and achieving more egalitarian income distribution has new justification: "the economy is so productive, the subsist-ence requirements are so easily fulfillable, income redistribution so painless to those that have more than enough, the very rich so relatively few and so enlightened, that it can be done cheaply and easily if not quickly and forevermore."

In Chapter 3 Arthur B. Shostak examines the antipoverty effort in the United States and finds that to date it embodies all too little of either Haworth's sense of moral imperative or Ornati's convic-tion of what is now economically and technically feasible. If there is a war against poverty, in resource terms it is thus far a mini-war whose battles have produced neither major victories nor crushing defeats. In his overview of the response to poverty by the established institutions of this most affluent nation, Shostak sets out themes explored in detail in both Part II and Part III.

On the positive side of the ledger Shostak finds that the current campaign has succeeded, among other things, in (1) putting the problem of deprivation emphatically before the public; (2) discouraging premature reform prescriptions and making possible the consideration, and in some instances the small-scale institution, of experimental programs; and (3) encouraging recognition of, and throwing some light on, the substantive linkages between poverty and such other factors as ill health, educational inadequacies, and self-perceived political impotence.

On the debit side, Shostak finds a persistent unwillingness to allocate resources equal to the task, a lack of bold and imaginative leadership, and the suppression of innovative change in the face of opposition from established interests and the unwillingness of a conservative public to accept more than small increments from "safe" programs. The result, as he puts it, has been a "severely limited war on poverty, significant as much for its concerted defense of the non-poor and their favorite institutions as for its undersupported 'band-aide' attempt to help the deprived."

It is evident from Shostak's discussion that the poor have been an *issue* rather than significant *actors* on the political scene and that the "war on poverty" has done little to remedy this situation. Very few of the poor have "gotten in on the act" of shaping and reshaping the poverty program. Neither OEO nor other relevant public and private agencies have been willing to press for basic reforms that would bring the deprived into the political mainstream, nor have they been willing to accept political action and the use of conflict strategies by the disadvantaged as part of the normal governmental process. In fact, few experiments or programs have pressed the case for "participatory democracy" much beyond ensuring the token inclusion of the poor on local CAP boards.

These, then, are the dimensions of deprivation explored in this volume: moral and behavioral, institutional and societal. They must be taken together if we are to understand why we are what we are and how we might yet become something better.

—W. B. Jr. and H. J. S.

1

Deprivation and the Good City

LAWRENCE HAWORTH

☐ LIKE MOST WARS, THE IMPERATIVE that we should fight poverty is more obvious than the reasons why we should. Typically, the question, "Why?" comes up after a war has begun. Yet, asking why we are fighting may seem an indulgence, practiced by those who can contribute little to the course of the battle. Few imagine that what is decided on as the reason for fighting has implications for the way we should fight. In wars our object is to win, and we identify winning with the surrender of the other side. No serious philosophical or moral questions arise. The end is clear, and one will know when it has been reached.

A war on poverty is different. Since not everyone agrees about what overcoming poverty would consist in, we lack a consensus regarding how the fight is going, and we cannot be sure we will know when the battle is won. It is not clear what winning would consist in because it is not clear to us what poverty is. And, paradoxically, we cannot decide what poverty is without having first decided why we should be fighting it.

It follows, then, that the essentially philosophical and moral question, "Why fight poverty?" is also a practical one. The answer has implications for the manner in which the war should be fought: differing views regarding what winning would consist in give rise to corresponding differences regarding what should be done in the interest of winning.

DEFINITION OF POVERTY

The air of paradox which surrounds these initial remarks may be dispelled by considering the implications of the most widely accepted definition of poverty for our attitude toward the effort to eliminate poverty. Commonly, poverty is defined in terms of annual income. This permits identification of a poverty-line. A family of four is said to be, in the relevant sense, "poor" if its annual income falls below the line; $3,000 is the figure currently mentioned. Now, one who accepts the definition should identify victory in the war on poverty with a condition in which no family of the appropriate size has an annual income that falls below the line. Strangely enough, however, by no means all who profess to be satisfied with the definition accept this implication. Not all agree that were no one to fall below the line, there would be no reason for concern about deprivation. Conversely, some envisage the possibility of this reason for concern being dissipated even though many families continue to fall below the line.

One may well wonder how these doubts could arise. If poverty consists in some particular condition, it could not persist after the condition is eliminated; nor could it fail to persist while the condition obtains. Necessarily, then, one who has such doubts is calling into question the aptness of the poverty-line definition. He is putting it to a test of relevance by confronting it with his intuitive sense of why poverty is objectionable and ought to be eliminated. Unless this confrontation occurs, there is danger that we will expend our energy on the wrong enemy. And the confrontation cannot be successful unless we achieve clarity concerning why poverty ought to be eliminated. Our intuitive sense forms a good point of departure, but only that. In the end what we require is an account that formulates in clear language the reasons why we should be concerned enough about poverty to invest a noticeable percentage of our gross national product in the effort to eradicate or at least ameliorate it.

A definition of poverty must perform two major functions. First, it must be usable in the sense of facilitating identification of those who are to be beneficiaries of poverty programs. Were the definition couched in such terms as to lead different investigators to identify different persons or families as forming the relevant group, poverty programs would be marked by chaos. This is a methodological requirement and leads to the demand for an "instrumental" and quantitative definition. The second function of the definition is to identify the relevant group in the relevant way. That is, it should lead us to the group we ought to be concerned about, and it should identify the condition that ought to be corrected.

The poverty-line definition performs the first function admirably. This is understandable, since it was a ruling consideration in its formulation that it should do so. Indeed, the fact that there are census data which enable researchers to determine readily how many individuals fall below the line, where they live, and a variety of other facts about them, is largely responsible for the widespread acceptance of the poverty-line definition.

But this motive—to secure a definition that takes advantage of existing arrangements for gathering data—would lead to ludicrous results if the second function of a definition of poverty were ignored. In any case, we will derive our notions about how to fight poverty and what overcoming it consists in from our understanding of what poverty is. But it is inappropriate, even dangerous, to decide what poverty is by concentrating altogether on the methodological question, "What definition will be useful for purposes of empirical research?" while ignoring the moral question, "Why ought we to be concerned?" The definition should be so drawn that if we allow it to direct the fight against poverty, and use it to help us to decide how the fight is going, we are well served. And being well served in this connection means more than getting answers. It means that the answers are to the point in the sense that they bear on the real issues. To illustrate, present enthusiasm for a negative income tax is probably tied in some way to the poverty-line definition. The argument is disarmingly simple. If poverty consists in falling below the line, the object of a war on poverty must be to raise everyone up to the line. This goal can be accomplished with one stroke by passing a law that provides for supplementing the income of everyone who falls below the line by the required amount.

There are three ways in which a definition of poverty may fail. It may identify what it means to be poor—the condition in which poverty exists—but do this in a way that precludes our discovering who *are* poor. Or, it may provide a ready way of identifying the group who are poor without identifying the condition referred to in calling them poor. Finally, the definition may fail on both counts. It may identify the wrong group and the wrong condition.

We may ignore the third possibility. The distinction between the first and second parallels that between the intension and extension of a term. One may know the symptoms of a disease without knowing what the disease is, and by looking for symptoms may be able to identify every occurrence of it. This would be to know the extension of the term that refers to the disease, but not to know its intension. The analogy with disease makes clear the danger of adopting a definition of poverty that does not tell us what poverty *is* (its intension), and only shows us how to pick out the group who are poor (its extension). It also indicates, indirectly, the danger of taking up the question of what poverty is in isolation from the question, "Why fight poverty?" If one does not notice that the definition of a disease only tells how to find cases of it by identifying its symptoms, one may be led to fight the disease by fighting its symptoms. Cosmetics will hide the signs of measles. In the same way, if our definition of poverty does not tell us what poverty is, but by identifying its symptoms only shows us how to find the group who are "poor," we may be led to adopt poverty programs that, like cosmetics, cover up symptoms without getting to the real problem. For example, some hold that the real problem is inequality. For them, the fact that a portion of incomes falls below the line is only incidentally relevant. If all were above the line, but wide discrepancies remained, they would be as concerned about the problem of poverty as they are now. They might accept the poverty-line definition, but not because it identifies what it means to be poor. For them, poverty consists in having much less than others have, and is independent of how much any one has. But they might accept the poverty-line definition because it directs one to the group who are poor in the relevant sense. If inequality is the heart of the problem—if we ought to be concerned about the poor because they receive much less than others do and not because they receive so little—then a program aimed at raising the level of those who have least would promise to solve the problem of poverty only if it did not eventuate also in higher incomes for those who have most. A negative income tax might or might not be well-advised, depending on its long-range impact on the latter group.

THE GOOD CITY

The reasons people have for fighting urban poverty—and this is the only kind of poverty that shall concern us here—fall under three headings. These correspond with the three basic moral categories: goodness, justice, and prudence. Poverty is sometimes seen as a public problem, a defect in the city itself. So far as there is poverty in a city, it fails of being a good city. Second, poverty is often seen as a form of social injustice, a liability predicated of the people who are poor, not of the city they inhabit. Third, poverty is often objected to by those who are not themselves poor, as a threat to their own well-being. All three present good reasons for combatting poverty. The point of the discussion which follows is to clarify each, and to exhibit the implications it has for a war on poverty. Clarification of these reasons for fighting poverty leads to the conviction that none of the current definitions of poverty identifies the condition we ought to be focusing on in our struggle against it. That condition, it will appear, is not inequality, not low income, not lack of goods and services. It is instead a structural condition of the city, considered as an environment. And, in the last analysis, the object of the fight should be to mold that structure so that it meets the genuine needs of the city's inhabitants. Raising incomes, eliminating gross inequality, and increasing access to goods and services are relevant only insofar as they have impact on that structure.

All cities are beset by numerous problems, each of which forms a particular respect in which they are less than ideal and demand improvement. The object in attacking these problems may be simply to bring into being a good city, one that is on all sides and in all respects satisfactory. When poverty is seen as one such problem, it is viewed as a blemish on a city as a whole. This leads one to regard attempts to eliminate poverty as undertaken not for the benefit of any group within a city, not even the poor themselves, but simply for the good of the city.

Some find this point of view strange. They are accustomed to thinking of traffic and parking problems, congestion, air and water pollution, and urban sprawl and blight as essentially civic problems. Although they realize that it is people who are inconvenienced by such conditions, they have no difficulty in attributing the conditions to the city, so that it is seen as burdened by them and efforts to eliminate them are seen as efforts to improve it. Poverty, by contrast, is thought to involve only people; the city's involvement is thought to be restricted to the fact that the impoverished people reside in a city, though some might extend this to include the possibility that the city contains institutions that contribute to their poverty. But one does not ordinarily suppose that our interest in having a good city, which forms a motive for various efforts on the side of physical planning, might also reasonably constitute a motive for our efforts to eliminate poverty. Only unfamiliarity with the idea stands in the way of its general acceptance. If a person genuinely identifies with the city he inhabits, so that he associates his well-being with it and feels a spontaneous enthusiasm for any activity he perceives as likely to improve it, he is bound to apprehend urban poverty as a civic failing, no different than the failure to provide clean air and water and sufficient space for children to play, pedestrians to walk, motorists to park.

But if our reason for fighting poverty is that we see it as a blemish on the city, forming a particular respect in which the city fails of being a good city, then we shall require an understanding of what a good city would be like. Without clarity concerning our ideal for the city, we lack clarity concerning the objective that poverty programs should focus on, insofar as those programs are undertaken in order to improve the city itself. This result may seem unfortunate. We are asked to decide what a thoroughly good city would be like so that by referring to the conception of such an environment we can be assured that our efforts to eliminate poverty are relevant to the problem at hand. If those efforts have no tendency to make the city more nearly like the ideal, then the time, energy, and money they use up are wasted. There is a natural temptation to reject points of view which complicate matters, but here the complication introduced by the idea that the discussion of poverty must take off from a wide-ranging discussion of social ideals cannot be side-stepped. The situation resembles that which conscientious city planners face. They cannot intelligently decide how to attack any particular problem that falls within their orbit unless they have some conception of the form to be taken by the solution to all their problems. They require, in other words, a plan for the whole before they can plan intelligently for its parts.

I shall only summarize the conclusions to which I have been led in trying to clarify the conception of a good city. The beginning of wisdom in this connection is discovery of the sense in which a city is more than people and artifacts. From many points of view what is more important is that a city is or encompasses a life style or design for living laid down by the complex of urban institutions. In the largest view of the matter, poverty is a condition of the urban life style. Urban poverty consists, in the first instance, in the fact that the urban life style is impoverished;

and people are deprived to the extent that their lives are settled by an impoverished life style. By a life style I mean the objective counterpart to the actual patterns of action an individual's life exhibits. In calling a life style objective I mean to underscore the idea that it is something solidly present, confronting the individual as a milieu that decisively shapes his patterns of action. It is a serious mistake to view a person's life as having been shaped by his own will, considered as an internal faculty that reaches decisions prompted by internal drives and needs, as if the context of action—the world one immediately confronts—were a vacuum open to any manner of entry that the person decides upon. Instead, this world forms a structured environment composed of determinate instrumentalities for action. These are the particular ways in which one's world allows one to act and to live—the institutional opportunities or roles available to him. In detail, this refers to positions in offices and factories, modes of participation in family life, recreational and educational opportunities, one's manner of worshipping God and of functioning as a consumer, and the character of one's involvement in local and national politics.

When these instrumentalities are considered as institutional opportunities, stress is placed on their character of laying out channels within which are located the whole of an individual's chances for developing and expressing himself, and therefore his chances for living what he can regard as a decent life. When they are considered as roles, an additional feature is introduced, namely, that they constrain the individual's activity in the sense of laying down limits beyond which, for all practical purposes, he may not go in taking advantage of the opportunity. The constraints and opportunities are two sides of the same fact. We could not have one without the other. Were our world not an order of institutional constraints, neither would it present us with extensive opportunities for significant action.

The life style an individual confronts is the totality of roles or opportunities open to him, regarded not pluralistically but rather as a unified *way* of living, a design for living. His life style is not his in the sense that he makes it up, but in the same sense that a particular fate is his. So far as his life in society is concerned, indeed, it *is* his fate. To say this, however, is not to assert a deterministic or fatalistic view, if this means that people have no control over their destiny, no purchase for exercise of spontaneity. But the opportunity one has for such control and for exercise of spontaneity is itself settled by his life style. He may or may not be "fated to be free." The serf in a manorial village had less opportunity to control the ground conditions of his life than does the denizen of a small New England town. This did not arise from his lack of initiative or decisiveness, but was an unavoidable consequence of the life style ordered by manorial villages. Similarly, the relative freedom enjoyed by a Yankee is no credit to himself—he meets it. It may be a credit to his predecessors who, one might suppose, had something to do with the fact that those little places settle the life that they do.

It is important not to conceive the elements of a life style—roles or opportunities—in purely mechanical terms. The limits of a role and the breadth of an opportunity are fixed in part, by bare technological conditions, in part by legal arrangements, and, not least, in part by ideas. These are all components of the role. Technological and legal factors set constraints but the ideas people hold about what is proper and improper are often more decisive in determining what they do. The ideas that define roles, however, are not in the first instance the ideas of those who assume the roles. The person does not bring them to the role, but meets them there as elements of his involvement, definite fixed features of the world in which he acts. These ideas are, in an extended sense, a society's moral code. Instead of thinking of this code as a body of moral rules designed to limit the person's "conduct," it is more realistic to think of it as a class name for the set of ideas that define the acceptable and unacceptable manners of functioning in the various institutional positions that give form to a society.

An implication of the view expressed here is that the idea of a good city is a conception concerning the character urban life styles should have. This conception in turn is a view about desirable traits of urban institutions. In asking what a good city would be like, one is asking what life styles are implied by the idea of city dwellers living in a way they would find as satisfactory as the human condition permits. The value of focusing on life styles, or on institutional traits which compose life styles, is that the resulting conception of a good city will be structural. In this way one may gain clues regarding what to do in the interest of reaching the ideal. If instead our thought stopped at the level of the individual by merely delineating a preferred way of acting without translating this into an account of the kind of environment that must exist if this way of acting is to be possible, the ideal would have no *use*.

What traits of institutions are implied by the idea of people living a life they would find on all sides satisfactory? If we are to answer the question by abstracting from all particular cities, so that the answer becomes applicable to any city, then the response must be quite formal and abstract. But it will not for that reason be without use, since by referring to it one who has a particular city in mind will be able to decide what it would take to improve that city by considering ways in which it may incorporate the formal and abstract traits that form the ideal.

The leading idea in pursuing an answer to such a question is that of self-development, self-realization, self-fulfillment. Whatever goals a person holds for himself, satisfaction for him (hence what he can call a good life) appears to consist in his fulfilling these ideals and thereby realizing himself in the sense of developing the potentialities that uniquely define him. These ideals do not ordinarily arise in a vacuum, but are representations in the individual of purposes that do or might characterize the overt institutional order. Everything depends on whether this order institutes opportunities for people to live in the way they must if they are to develop their natures to the fullest. Institutional opportunity—recreational, educational, vocational, artistic, religious, political, and familial—is strictly correlative to personal self-fulfillment. That is, there is nothing more a society can do for a person, from the standpoint of contributing to his chances of living a satisfactory life, than open to him maximal institutional opportunity along the lines suggested. Without this opportunity he has no chance of reaching a notable level of self-realization.

Analysis of the idea of self-realization makes it possible to give content to the correlative notion of institutional opportunity. Self-realization is partly a personal and partly a social affair. On one hand, the individual has a variety of personal capacities, the development and expression of which are indispensable to his own well-being. I have indicated that he must depend on the life style that his city confronts him with for whatever real chance he has to realize those capacities. On the other hand, he is a social creature and hence will not perceive himself to have made very much of his life if the sharpening of his unique capacities occurs in a way that isolates him from affective relations with others. From this second point of view, what the individual requires is a setting in which he is led to find common cause with his neighbors. As a characteristic of the overt, institutional order, this indicates the need for community, a condition in which the fragmentation and divisiveness of present urban life are replaced by a setting made cohesive by the presence of shared purposes. The idea is that each should confront a life style that permits him to come to terms with himself in activity that at the same time brings him into meaningful relations with others. These latter relationships are necessary to an individual's own development as a person.

A good city—considered as a place where the kinds of institutional opportunities that permit people to develop themselves to the fullest are found—must be a community or a group of communities. It is not important whether the basis for these communities is spatial or functional, that is, whether people find the larger social wholes with which they affectively identify to be geographically delimitable areas within which they establish their places of residence (neighborhoods), or functionally defined joint activities (their office, factory, church, or clan).

The other side of the coin is that within an overarching community the individual should find opportunities for his own development as a person. We may analyze this requirement into two parts. Personal growth requires a social environment in which are found extensive opportunities for significant action, a condition that I shall call moral power. It also requires that these opportunities impinge on the person in such a way that in following them out he is active, in short, self-determining or free. These two requirements—that the urban institutions which constitute life styles should ground moral power and freedom—are in turn analyzable into a set of institutional traits, or objective conditions that must obtain if life styles are to have the required impact on the persons who confront them. In the first place, moral power is a function of three institutional traits: richness, openness, and person-centeredness. First, a city's institutions should offer extensive opportunities for significant action, and in this sense should not be barren from a human point of view. This is the requirement of institutional richness. Second, the opportunities should be open to all, not merely in the legal and formal sense that all are allowed access, but in the more profound if informal sense of all being genuinely capable of enjoying this access should they choose to do so. The fact an employer does not discriminate among job applicants on the basis of race makes the job no more accessible or open to Negroes whose family and neighborhood environments have prevented them from developing competence to perform the job than it would be if there were a rule of law that excluded them. Third, moral power involves the ordering of institutional opportunities into a life style that is person-centered in the sense that it contemplates a total way of living consonant with the idea of personal integrity.

Freedom, to the extent that it is grounded in urban life styles, may also be analyzed into three institutional traits. The point of departure here is awareness that a person's capability of living as a free or self-determining agent is conditioned by the manner in which institutional opportunities are ordered. In the first place, it is obviously important whether these opportunities are discretionary or imposed. We may identify the requirement suggested by this fact as voluntariness, the requirement that roles should be so defined that participation in them is discretionary. Second, it is also important that the roles should be flexible. Inflexibility in this connection means a condition in which roles are narrowly defined in the sense that one who takes them up is bound to act in one and only one way, so that in the act he is virtually reduced to the level of a machine. Flexibility, by contrast, is a condition that requires a person who takes up the role to make individual decisions regarding the manner in which it is to be carried out. The role thus leaves scope for alternative interpretations and room for maneuvering. Finally, the freedom encompassed in a way of life is affected by the extent to which the roles defining it are shaped by the persons who take them up. However inflexible and non-discretionary the institutional opportunities one confronts may be, if one has had a real voice in determining their form they are not constraints but they are tools by which one is enabled to shape his social destiny. This introduces the idea of social democracy, which in the present context is the requirement that people should have effective control over the institutional roles they confront, and thereby control over the life styles formed by the interrelationships of these roles.

This account of the good city is unfortunately highly sketchy and abstract. It may be summarized in the proposition that a good city is a community in which the participants are enabled to develop themselves as human beings in consequence of its richness, openness, person-centeredness, voluntariness, flexibility, and controllability.

POVERTY AND THE GOOD CITY

The relevance of the foregoing account to the topic of urban poverty may be seen by considering its bearing on the idea of a decent standard of living. The root idea behind the poverty-line definition is that poverty consists in incapacity to live up to a decent standard. The error in the definition (if it is intended to accomplish anything more significant than provide a ready way of identifying those who are poor) is its assumption that a standard of living consists solely or mainly in some degree of access to goods and services. It is very natural to make such a mistake in a consumption-oriented society. The alternative to defining a standard of living in terms of access to goods and services (the amount one is able to *consume*) is to define it in terms of opportunity to *act*. And the justification for adopting the second alternative—which forms the point of departure for the conception of a good city—is simply this: whatever positive sense one may gain of having lived a good life results not from the number and kinds of goods one has consumed but from the quality of the action one has been enabled to carry out, and from the impact of that action on oneself, in the sense of its effect of developing one's powers and of forming an integral person.

Taking seriously the idea that not consumption but action is the critical element in a standard of living leads one to identify poverty as severe deprivation with respect to capability to act in humanly relevant ways. Since this capability is grounded in urban life styles, the measure of poverty in a city is the extent to which it fails to satisfy the ideal of a good city.

It is possible for an entire city to be deprived, despite the monetary affluence of some of its denizens. This is the case when urban life styles are so constrained that not even the most affluent find opportunities to act in meaningful ways. When all of a city's institutional opportunities are inflexible, trivial, or compulsory, the community itself is poorer than it would be if no one who lived in the place had an annual income above $3,000.

It is obvious that the poverty of a city is unevenly distributed among its inhabitants. Some are poor in the profound sense of confronting a life style that does not offer extensive opportunities for significant action, while in the same sense others are rich indeed. The differences are partly tied to differences in income, a circumstance that gives a poverty-line definition whatever relevance to poverty it has. But there is a hidden danger associated with responding to this fact simply by undertaking to raise incomes. If the life style of the most deprived is one of the major causes of their low incomes, as Oscar Lewis has suggested, the result of raising incomes without altering the life style may well be that instead of eliminating poverty one merely changes the group upon whom it impinges. There are forces that maintain slums and assure full occupancy. When these forces are not tampered with, but through job-retraining and other means we make it possible for present slum-dwellers to vacate the tenements, a vacuum is created in the slums that the outside forces will cause to be filled. The life style is there; others will enter and take it up. Not the amount but only the incidence of poverty will have been changed. This is the logical outcome of treating symptoms rather than causes.

The chief bearing of money on poverty is that it determines access to institutional opportunities and thereby contributes to the openness of institutions and of life styles. One is poor not because he has no money, but because, possibly owing to lack of money, he lacks also access to the social instrumentalities that make humanly significant action possible. In part, it is a simple matter of not having the price of admission—to a theater, university, or recreation area. But in larger part it is a matter of not having the character or competence (e.g. lack of verbal facility, lack of motivation, destructive orientation) that establishes one's capability of taking up an opportunity that is formally open. Often, lack of money is a prime reason why one has failed to form the requisite character or to develop the requisite competence.

The intention of these remarks is to place the financial aspects of the problem of poverty in a perspective that permits us to acknowledge the relevance of money to poverty, and at the same time enables us to avoid the mistake of supposing that being poor *consists in* lacking money or the consumer goods that money can buy. This perspective forces rejection of the view that raising incomes, minimizing inequalities of income, or providing commodities and services in lieu of income is the complete solution to the problem. Any strategy calculated to improve the quality of urban life is relevant to a war on poverty. The role of speaking specifically of such a war—and of a unique problem of "poverty"—rather than of the need and effort simply to shape actual cities so that they more nearly measure up to the ideal of a good city, is that it establishes an order of priority. It indicates that in the effort to improve the quality of urban life it would be humane to begin by altering those conditions that have differential impact on the least affluent, meaning by least affluent, again, those who have least access to whatever opportunities the city offers for people living decent lives.

THE JUST CITY

When we consider poverty as a form of social injustice, however, we cannot so easily assimilate the problem to that of improving the quality of urban life, nor can we so easily assimilate the war on poverty to the general attempt to solve the city's difficulties. This results from the peculiar force of the notion of injustice. The preceding discussion was based on the assumption that the principal beneficiary of a war on poverty is the city as a whole. But the view that recognizes poverty as a form of social injustice leads to the idea that the beneficiaries are the poor themselves, and that the war is being fought in order to improve their condition. Moreover, if we are fighting injustice, then the poor are not merely beneficiaries but they are a group who, as a group, are *wronged*, and in attempting to improve their condition we are undertaking to right the wrong. This circumstance makes the term "beneficiary" somewhat misleading. In any strict sense, if injustice is at issue, a poverty program is not something we do "for" the poor—as if morally we could enact it or not as we chose and as if it were morally indifferent whether we do so or not—but the poor *exact* the program, they demand it as a matter of right. There is no charity in it, anymore so than there is charity in repaying a debt or paying properly exacted damages. Rather, as in repaying a debt or in making restitution (if the view that poverty is a form of social injustice has merit), we are bound to the poor themselves to enact programs aimed at alleviating poverty and to replace presently inadequate programs with more ambitious ones.

Before one can assess the claim that poverty is a form of injustice, he must understand it. And for this purpose one must have an understanding of the concept of justice. The idea of justice is intimately allied with those of desert and equality. We tend to identify just treatment with getting what is deserved, so that paradigm cases of injustice are those of one who has much merit being badly treated, and one who has no merit being well treated. But we also regard markedly unequal treatment as unjust. These two notions of desert and equality are not entirely compatible. Desert is a differentiating concept; by referring to it we justify differential treatment. Since some have more merit than others, justice demands that people be differentially, therefore unequally, treated in a way that reflects their differing degrees of merit. The basis for one's desert is an open question, and fortunately one that need not be decided here. Some suppose that ancestry is the principal desert-basis, others place the emphasis on a person's past conduct, and still others stress competence as the proper measure of desert.

It is possible to associate the ideas of desert and equality by arguing, as Aristotle did, that proportioning rewards to desert involves maintaining equality in the proportions. If one who deserves little receives little, while another who deserves much receives much, then the justice manifested in this differential treatment of the two lies in the fact that the proportion of reward to desert is the same in both cases. But there seems little basis for the view that the idea of justice requires people to be treated equally in an absolute sense, so that it is always unjust for one person to have more of some value, such as money, than others have.

Many, however, hold that the idea of equality introduces a theme not present when justice is associated with desert. Equality suggests the conception of individual *worth*. This refers to a person's value as a person, independently of the differential merit he may possess in consequence of personal characteristics that distinguish him from others. Individual worth is thought of as an intrinsic characteristic. Perhaps it is not wise to ask whether people in this sense *have* worth. Instead, we should ask whether our common life is founded on the practice of ascribing such worth to people. Do we, and is it sensible that we should, treat people in a way that suggests we regard them as having equal worth, despite their differing degrees of merit? Most would say that we do and that we should. Every Western legal system is founded on this idea. Nor is it easy to conceive what our life would be like if it were not ordered around the notions that each person has worth or dignity as a person, and that despite differences in merit, all people have equal worth or dignity, and equally deserve to be treated as ends-in-themselves. One may even say that our capability of identifying human beings as "persons," and distinguishing them in this way from "things," depends on our ascribing to them intrinsic worth, and that the idea of their equality as persons presupposes their equal worth. For, by a "thing" we mean that which may legitimately be used wholly for our own purposes and need not be regarded as itself having ends to which we ought to defer. By a "person," we mean instead that which has ends of its own to which some consideration should be given, so that we do not entirely use it as a means to our own ends. In fact, there seems no difference between treating a person as if he had ends of his own to which we ought to defer, and ascribing to him intrinsic worth.

At this point the fundamental sanity of the legal use of "person," in terms of which persons are regarded as "right and duty bearing units," may be seen. For, we would not attribute rights to an individual without also attributing duties, and to regard him as having rights is the same as to attribute to him ends to which we ought to defer, that is, to refuse to treat him merely as a means to our own purposes.

When the idea of personal worth, and the closely allied idea of the dignity of the person—a dignity he is supposed to have entirely apart from his merit or ill-desert—is stressed, the very principle of justice demands that people be treated in a way that acknowledges their worth and dignity as persons. The idea of equality is, therefore, relevant to justice because of the supposition that all persons are, in respect to worth or dignity, equal. The fundamental right is that one's dignity or worth as a person should be acknowledged. All injustices are forms of violation of this right. And this right is an equal right—all share in it, and equally—in consequence of the fact that none has less worth or dignity than another.

What is involved in acknowledging a person's dignity or worth? It has been argued by Gregory Vlastos ("Justice and Equality," in Richard Brandt [ed.], *Justice*, Englewood Cliffs, N.J.: Prentice-

Hall, 1962) whose account I am following rather closely here, that
what mainly is at stake are well-being and freedom. Both are
caught up in the idea of opportunity to act—opportunity to express
oneself and to develop one's nature. One's worth as a person is
acknowledged insofar as he enjoys an opportunity to develop his
nature and to express that which has been developed. The fundamental right, then, is to enjoy such an opportunity; and social
injustice consists in withholding that opportunity from some or all
of the members of a society.

That all have an equal right to see their dignity or worth
acknowledged means that all ought to enjoy equal opportunity to
develop and express themselves. But in this connection the sense
of the term "opportunity" must be carefully specified. In a rather
superficial way, whether two people enjoy equal opportunity is a
matter of whether they possess equal resources. If one is richer
than the other, his opportunity to have the things money can buy
is greater. But we would not say that this implies injustice.

In a more fundamental sense, the measure of one's opportunity
is the extent to which what he is or has achieved can be chalked
up to luck or his own initiative. The critical issue is whether discrepancies in the degree of well-being and freedom enjoyed by
people are the outcome of remediable conditions which are or were
beyond control of the disadvantaged persons. Slavery is a paradigm
case. The inequality of opportunity between the slave and his
master is not merely the trivial inequality consisting in the fact
that the master enjoys greater freedom now, and is now better
able to satisfy his needs and desires. The inequality is none of the
slave's doing; it is not owing to bad luck, as when one loses a
good bet, nor is it a result of the slave's failure to assert himself.
The difference in their positions is the outcome of remediable conditions that are and were beyond control of the slave himself. Or,
more succinctly, he never had a chance. This is the basic reason
why the institution of slavery is unjust.

An injustice is a case of a stacked deck, and unjust institutions
are unfair in much the same sense that cheating at cards is. If
the deck is not stacked and the deal is honest, then there is no
unfairness in one person being dealt a "jack high" and another a
full house. The inequality of their hands is important to the players,
but morally irrelevant. But if the deck is stacked, or the deal dis-

honest, a slight discrepancy in the strength of the hands means considerable unfairness in the game.

The analogy suggests the two elements that form inequalities of opportunity in this more profound sense. The inequality may result from an initial condition that jeopardized a person's chances of *subsequently* enjoying as much freedom and well-being as others enjoy. Or, it may result from a continuing penalty imposed on him by discriminatory institutions. The first element is analogous to a stacked deck, arrangements that prejudice one's chances from the start, so that however fair the situation he subsequently confronts may be in itself, he is not able to take full advantage of it owing to the initial incapacitating conditions to which he was subjected. The most obvious way in which this occurs is by a person being born and growing up in a milieu that either causes him not to develop skills and habits necessary for subsequent participation in the life of the city, or causes him to develop habits or ideals that channel his energies in other directions. The second element is analogous to a dishonest deal. The person may have had an equal chance at the start, but may find that he is constantly discriminated against when he seeks to make the contacts in the surrounding urban world that would enable him to live in the way his developed faculties contemplate. The obvious example is job discrimination.

Urban institutions are unjust, then, to the extent they systematically deny to some an equal chance to enjoy the opportunities for personal growth that the city contains. This denial may occur when the society either erects discriminatory bars to participation or tolerates conditions that create extreme liabilities in persons which effectively disqualify them for participation, even in cases where there is no formal prohibition. The injustice of these arrangements stems from their bearing on the worth or dignity of the affected persons. Attributing to them equal worth as persons leads to the idea that they have a right to an equal chance to develop and express themselves. The arrangements referred to withhold such a right, and are for this reason and in this sense unjust.

The discussion has a clear bearing on the claim that urban poverty is a form of social injustice. Deprivation in one's standard of living is not as such unjust; consequently, neither is poverty, as such, unjust. But poverty is unjust when it is remediable and results from discriminatory institutions in either of the two ways mentioned above: when it results indirectly from discriminatory institutions that withhold from a person competence to participate in the genuine opportunities for significant action offered by the city, or when it directly results from discriminatory institutions that simply deny a group admission to the places where these opportunities are located.

One implication here is that it is inappropriate to become overly concerned about inequalities between the affluent and the deprived when the energy behind an assault on urban poverty is the sense of poverty as unjust. Mainly, inequality shows that a city possesses sufficient resources to remedy the condition of the deprived. Similarly, one who is responding to the sense that poverty is unjust ought not to be overly concerned about the number of families whose income falls below a poverty-line. Even if their incomes were well above the line, the deprivation they experience might be unjust. And, in any case, where they stand relative to any such line has no bearing on the justice or injustice of their condition. What matters is why they are deprived, not the level of deprivation. Deprivation is unjust only when it results from discriminatory institutions.

There can be no question, then, that the bulk of urban poverty in the United States is unjust. For, as most now agree, the problem of poverty in the American city is largely indistinguishable from the race problem, and more particularly, the problem of the American Negro. And that problem is unquestionably one of institutionalized bias. Those who try to minimize the problem by calling attention to the wretched condition of the majority of people in Asia and by arguing that in the sense in which those people are poor the American Negro is affluent, wholly miss the point. The problem is not that the American Negro has relatively few of the things money can buy; it is, rather, that he has less opportunity to live a decent life than others have in a society which could improve his condition but which imposes this condition on him by maintaining discriminatory institutions. The fact that for the most part the discrimination is informal rather than legal, that it does not occur in violation of law but exists in the interstices of legal rules, neither diminishes nor magnifies its unjust character.

The relation between the conception of poverty one is led to by following out the idea that poverty is a form of social injustice, and the conception that results from regarding poverty as a defect of the city, is close indeed. Poverty-as-injustice is a more restricted condition. Of the six traits identified as constitutive of a good city, only one is relevant to justice. Any defect with respect to the six traits is a mark of deprivation, but what makes the deprivation unjust is lack of openness in a city's institutions. This trait, then, has a peculiar prominence in the conception of a good city. For, on one hand it is, along with the others, essential to the quality of urban life. But also, its absence transforms any defect with respect to the other five from a merely unfortunate situation, which in general ought to be corrected, to an unjust situation that anyone who can is *bound* to correct, in the same way as he is bound to repay his debts and honor his promises. To deny this obligation, as the preceding discussion establishes, is to reject the view that all human beings have equal dignity and worth. Or, more pointedly, it is to take the view that some human beings are not persons at all but things, tools that may be used but need not be respected.

PRUDENCE

The third good and sufficient reason for fighting poverty is prudential. While the second reason indicates much the same strategy in fighting poverty as the first and only implies a difference in emphasis, the prudential reason threatens to be idiosyncratic. If one's only reason for objecting to urban poverty is that it is a threat to oneself, then any way of fighting it which minimizes the threat will do. Then gas chambers will do. But clearly a prudential argument is a good argument only in case the self-protection one is aiming at is compatible with the legitimate well-being of those against whom one would protect oneself. Otherwise arguing for one's own interest would be nothing but a way of insisting on a bias, and bias, as such, cannot be justified.

The real problem, then, is whether those who are not themselves poor *can* find a strategy that responds to the first two reasons for fighting poverty, and at the same time contributes in readily discernible ways to their own well-being. Unless such a strategy is found, we may expect a hardening of the lines in riot-torn cities. It is not difficult for a middle-class white who lives in the vicinity of a race-riot to perceive that the poverty of the Negro is a major cause: people who devote the daylight hours to work they regard as worth doing do not devote the evening to looting stores. But whether the middle-class white responds in a constructive way to his perception depends on whether he feels there is a constructive response that will improve his own situation. And I cannot believe that any strategy will succeed that does not have the felt approval of middle-class whites, since in large measure their attitudes constitute the problem. We have, then, an additional reason for broadening our view of the war on poverty so that it is seen as an aspect of the effort to create a good city. For that effort is in everyone's interest.

2

The Spatial Distribution
of Urban Poverty

OSCAR A. ORNATI

☐ IT IS IN THE CITIES THAT THE great transformation takes place.
It is there, in modern times, that many of the poor become non-poor.
The extent to which many urbanites remain in poverty is a measure
of the failure of one of the cities' essential functions; the poor are
thus a "residuum" or the symptoms of temporary imbalances. They
are not, contrary to the belief of many romantics, a necessary result
of urban organization.

Urban poverty is an anomaly the world over even though there
are many cities that have many poor people. But spatial comparisons require precise definitions. Therefore, this chapter begins
with observations on definitions of poverty. It goes on to discuss
what is known about intercity and intracity characteristics of poverty and ends with a short discussion of policy.

DEFINITIONS OF POVERTY

The wealth of nations determines what their peoples regard as
poverty. In advanced industrialized societies, having or not having
"enough" resources is at the heart of the formal judgment of who
is and who is not called "poor." The judgment that some people do
not have enough implies that at least others do. In some cases it
implies also that others have more than enough.

Many variables go into the definition of poverty: levels of production and income, the existing pattern, rate and direction of
changes in income distribution, the demographic profile and characteristics of the population, social values and expectations, the
population's urban and rural distribution, variation and changes in
the cost of living, and many others. Obviously the weight of these

variables changes with time and place. The multiplicity of determinants and the desire to make over-time comparisons and, therefore, the need to establish varying *contemporary* standards, lends
scientific meaning to the common sense observation that poverty
is relative even though the term "relative," more often than not,
reflects only different individual perceptions of poverty. I have
argued elsewhere that because of this "relativeness" of poverty it is
also necessary that we express discussions about poverty in terms
of a "band" of poverty that recognizes not only different life styles
and different sizes of the poor population but also different patterns
of causation and, consequently, different policy responses and different costs of such responses (Ornati, 1966a, pp. 7-25). Yet, whether
we talk of a band of poverty or of a line of poverty, whether we
note (or do not note) that poverty is relative, all definitions of
poverty used in policy, in the practice of providing relief, or in
measurement, are variations of the notion of "subsistence poverty."

Discussion of the spatial distribution of poverty must recognize
that there are actually at least two major sets of poverty definitions:
(1) those aimed at measuring the gap between "consensually-set"
needs and resources (those discussed so far) and (2) those aimed
at measuring social relative (distributional) deprivation focused
primarily on the knowledge of the disparity between the low access
of the poor to resources and the observable large control over resources of the elite. The first set of poverty definitions, those based
on a notion of subsistence, is troublesome enough even when comparing reasonably similar industrialized nations, to say nothing
about the problem of comparison among different cities in various
industrialized countries. In the *Poor and the Poorest,* for example,
Abel-Smith and Townsend, in comparing the United States and
Great Britain, have shown that the measure of poverty in the former
is of greater purchasing value than the "national assistance"
standard used to measure poverty in the latter even though both
standards have an approximately similar relationship to average
wage rates (Abel-Smith and Townsend, 1965). Thus, by the first
set of definitions we can argue that the poor of Great Britain are,
so to speak, poorer than the poor of the United States, while under
the second set, this conclusion is not necessarily so.

Subsistence-based definitions are much more troublesome in
comparisons of poverty in the developing countries. This difficulty
primarily results from the fact that what is viewed as the "barest

minimum" in one country—and not available there to many—may define for another nation a condition in which almost nobody has "enough." Or it may even define situations in which a theoretical total redistribution of the resources of those who have enough would not elevate significant numbers of the poor above the poverty level. A Poverty Datum Line derived in South Africa, for example, which reflected money equivalents of the "barest minimum upon which subsistence and health can theoretically be achieved," was found inapplicable to both Kenya and Tanganyika since it was much higher than average wages in these two countries (Report of the Territorial Minimum Wages Board, Tanganyika, 1962).

These and similar considerations have recently led Townsend to suggest that *two* standards are required, "national-relational" and "world-relational" (Townsend, 1966, pp. 3-6). What, in fact, is involved, as the reader must have observed, are two standards for two sets of definitions as in the diagram which follows:

TABLE 1

	TYPES OF DEFINITIONS	
SUBSISTENCE-BASED	consensually derived need Nation-Relative	consensually derived need World-Relative
DISTRIBUTIONAL	social-relative deprivation —resources gap	social-relative deprivation —resources gap

The system of definitions presented in Table 1 represents an ideal. With the exception of the definition in the first quadrant, most of the others cannot be made operational for statistical or policy purposes. Indeed, no available data can provide statistical meaning for the "world-relative" set of definitions. On the other hand, almost all governments have some form of policy to alleviate the lot of their poor; therefore, there exist national operative money definitions and, consequently, statistical data on the number of their poor. There exist also data to give some concreteness to nation-relative distributional comparisons. Indeed, indexes of inequality for a number of countries, industrialized or otherwise, have been developed and certain comparisons can be made among them. All statistical measurements of poverty are open to much criticism as data on income distribution for even the industrialized countries are not very reliable. Those of the United States, for instance, with whose shortcomings students have become familiar, have further been weakened recently by the discovery of a sizable Census undercount of the poor population.

VARIATIONS IN INCOME DISTRIBUTION

In spite of the data shortcomings, we must face up to the question of whether there are more or less poor, either in the subsistence-based definitions or in the distributional sense, in one country or in another. Table 2 has been introduced for illustrative purposes and a number of observations on this topic follow.

TABLE 2

INCOME DISTRIBUTION AFTER TAXES: GINI INDEX OF INEQUALITY

Country	Gini Index of Inequality	Year	Per Cent of Income Earned by the Top 10 Per Cent of Earners
West Germany	.432	1950	34
Guatemala	.423	1948	43
Ceylon	.407	1953	37
Denmark	.396	1952	29
El Salvador	.393	1946	43
Netherlands	.388	1950	33
Sweden	.388	1948	29
United States	.373	1956	29
India	.350	1956	33
United Kingdom	.318	1955	26
Norway	.313	1950	26
Australia	.277	1956	30

SOURCE: Russett, et al., 1964, p. 247.

Surely, the first thing to be noted is the importance of regional variations within many countries. As the United States has significant differentials in income distribution and poverty between the North and the South, so do Italy, Yugoslavia, Nigeria, and Pakistan, for example. This is also true, for the United Kingdom where Scotland and Northern Ireland are much poorer than the rest of the nation (Coates and Raustron, 1966). Regional variations are not only reflected in comparisons among nations but go a long way in explaining intercity variations. Thus, for example, the higher proportion of the poor in Edinburgh than in cities of roughly the same size in the Midlands where throughout the region the income distribution is more egalitarian, is better explained by regional influences than by the characteristics of the cities themselves.

The second important generalization to be derived from inspection of Table 2, as well as from many other studies, is that "the distribution of income tends to be more equal the longer and the more thoroughly the country has been exposed to the process of economic and social change associated with the idea of industrialization" (Kravis, 1962). The validity of this proposition has often been challenged by reference to the data of particular countries—India is the classic example (Opha and Bhatt, 1964)—or by comparison at a given point of time. But most challenges to the proposition that the more industrialized the country the more equal its income distribution fall into the fallacy of misplaced concreteness. The Kravis statement does not imply a continuous and unchanging process nor does it imply a high degree of correspondence between the two variables. What takes place is an "accordion-like" movement as observed in wage differentials with the degree of inequality narrowing and widening, but widening less and less with time. In the United States, income differentials narrowed from 1939 to 1953 and, apparently, have stopped narrowing since that date. In England, a sustained tendency toward a reduction in income inequality appears to have stopped by the end of 1957 (Nicholson, 1967). In India, whatever the facts as to its income distribution in comparison with the United States and the United Kingdom, there is much evidence pointing to an increase in inequality since 1961 (Ranodive, 1965). But surely there is no reason to assume no further change.

The third point, which appears quite clearly, is that the political and fiscal structure of the various countries can work with or against the basic economic and developmental forces moving toward income equality. Since it is in this area that developed nations differ most markedly, the experience of other industrialized states is most important in formulating antipoverty policies. All countries have various forms of transfer payments, most of them aimed at alleviating the lot of the poor, but the effect of their transfer payment systems in terms of income redistribution varies considerably.

Whether a system of transfer payments leads to a redistribution of income or not depends on the degree to which the share of income that the recipients obtain differs from their relative share in the financing of the benefits. A recent study by Peterson on the impact of the French system draws certain comparisons with the experiences of the United States and the United Kingdom. The analysis is particularly appropriate at this time because of the experience of the French with family allowances, a device which has been proposed also for the United States either as a form of, or an alternative to, the negative income tax. Peterson shows that transfer payments have made the distribution of income more equal in spite of "the dependence of the system for its financing on taxes which have their incidence on consumption" (Peterson, 1965, p. 21). He also notes that:

> in France taxes imposed directly on the beneficiaries of the system averaged only 17 per cent of the benefits, whereas in Britain slightly over 55 per cent of the cost of the system was borne directly by the beneficiaries. The United States occupies an "in-between" position in that social security taxes paid directly by individuals averaged 31.6 per cent of transfer payments during the period (1956-1961) (*Ibid.*, p. 11).

From the Peterson study and with him, one observes, once again, that economic development is the necessary but not the sufficient condition for eradicating poverty or for bringing about more egalitarian income distributions. What is needed is a commitment to income socialization and, for the United States, this commitment does not appear to be high. These observations on differences in income distribution also point to the fact that, in the long run, changes in the incidence of taxes and in the structure of the United States transfer payment system are more effective than changes in the pattern of outlays affecting the poor in an immediate sense.

INTERCITY DISTRIBUTION OF POVERTY

In order to make good policy formulations it is useful to have some measures of the relative importance of poverty in different cities. Because there are many problems of definition in giving a precise cut-off point, I have found it helpful elsewhere to present some of the appropriate data in terms of a 3x3x3 matrix (Ornati, 1967). Such a matrix looks at poverty in terms of a band of incomes at the level of (1) $3,000, (2) $4,000, and (3) $5,000 of income for a family of four and its equivalents. It analyzes the poverty population within and below this band in terms of (1) the demographic *composition* of the poor population (i.e., how many of the poor are old, females, Negroes, etc.); (2) the incidence of poverty among certain demographic groups (i.e., how many of the young, uneducated, disabled, etc., are poor); and (3) the *risk* of poverty for a number of socio-demographic groups. The "causes" of poverty for the population groups so isolated can be viewed as falling into three broad categories: (1) poverty due to insufficient economic development, as in some of the smaller cities of some of the "core South" states; (2) poverty due to insufficient human resource endowment as with the low levels of education, skills, and health of some of the slum dwellers of the larger Northern cities; and (3) poverty due to the "closedness of our society" which affects primarily members of ethnic minorities. The application of this matrix to data from the United States Census of 1960 for cities of different sizes yields the following:

1. Urban poverty accounts for most of the United States poor;

2. The proportion of the poor in the urban agglomerates is consistently lower than that of rural areas;

3. The proportion of the poor in the total population of urban centers decreases as the size of the urban center increases; the relationship is not monotonic as the link with poverty grows weakest precisely where urban population exceeds one million;

4. Inequalities in income within the city, i.e. the size of the spread between the rich and the poor, increase as the size of the city decreases;

5. Cyclical differences in national economic activities, to the extent that such data can be integrated with the more limited data on income distribution by city size, affect poverty only at the upper level of the band (i.e. those whose family income is between $4,000 and $5,000) and their movement is parallel to that of the cycle. The very poor are not affected by cyclical fluctuations.

When we search for explanations of differences in the proportion of the poor within classes of cities of equal size, the task becomes more complicated and our knowledge more limited. Nevertheless, for the United States, it can be asserted that:

1. Diversity of employment increases with size but, given constant size, the city with greater employment diversity has a smaller proportion of the poor;

2. Cities with a greater proportion of their employees in white collar occupations tend to have fewer poor.

When we search for explanations of the variations in the intercity distribution of poverty according to causes, we can first associate different levels of poverty with different broad systems of causes:

—If we consider $5,000 to be the criterion for poverty, we see that much "poverty" is explained by the presence of low-paying industries.

—If it is $4,000, we find that the different incidences of poverty in different cities are related to their differing labor-capital coefficients and to the occupational (skill-unskilled) ratios of their industries.

—If we use $3,000, then the different incidences of poverty among cities may be better explained by their demographic composition. In this case, wage rates, labor intensivity, or occupational mix have little direct influence. Welfare payments have much more effect on the income distribution below this level.

Much has been said recently about the crisis of American cities in terms of their increased "Negritude"; this is not to be equated with the implied proposition that the demographic mix of cities alone determines their levels of poverty. The increase in the number of Negro city dwellers has had a much more marked effect on the intra- than intercity distribution of poverty. However, since the inflow of Negroes has—on the whole—increased racial residential segregation, it is worthwhile inquiring into the extent to which variations in segregation—per se a cause of poverty—explain variations in poverty among cities. A variety of indexes to measure residential segregation have been developed in recent years (Cowgill, 1956) and from these we have learned that:

1. There is a universally high degree of segregation in all cities of the United States. In the words of two observers, "There is no need for cities to vie with each other for the title of the most

segregated city; there is room at the top for all of them"
(Taeuber and Taeuber, 1965).

2. On the average, segregation has increased between the 1940s
   and 1950s and decreased slightly between 1950 and 1960.

3. What has happened between 1960 and 1967 is not clear. Some
   authorities argue that segregation has in fact increased (Hill,
   1966), and there is good a priori reason—the faster rate of
   growth of the economy—to believe that this has happened.

4. Increases in the degree of segregation do *not* go hand in hand
   with increases in the proportion of people in poverty. While
   no definitive study linking changes in the cities' segregation
   index with changes in their proportion of poverty has been
   carried out, inspection of the data suggests the absence of any
   relationship between these two variables.

We know little else about the causes of urban poverty. The rate
of in-migration from rural areas, the size of the non-native-born
group, their length of residence, the "openness" of the city to the
new in-migrants and the assistance it provides them—all these
determine the incidence of poverty in the various cities. Limitations in our knowledge stem in part from lack of data as well as
from the fact that students of labor economics have not as yet
made great progress with the empirical verification of theoretical
propositions about labor mobility. They are due also to the fact
that demographers concerned with migration tend to ignore the
curiosities of labor economists.

Long concerned with the problems of mobility in the framework
of interfirm, interindustry, and regional wage differentials, labor
economists have not yet inquired into the extent to which the
city's pockets of poverty are due to the level and characteristics
of migration and particularly how they are related to specific characteristics of the labor market. We know that the poverty of the
depressed areas is, to a large extent, a corollary of the out-migration
of the more productive elements of their population. This knowledge aids our understanding of the poverty of the 1950s in some
of the urban communities of the depressed areas, especially the
smaller cities in Appalachia. The opposite is also true: the in-
migration into the cities of the more productive elements from the
rural areas contributes to the cities' development. This fact explains
in part why poverty in Appalachia in the 1960s is almost exclusively
a rural phenomenon. It also indicates that rural poverty in this

region would further be reduced through more out-migration (Miernyk, 1967).

We know little else that bears directly on the relationship between in-migration and the cities' poverty beyond the fact that workers in general and in-migrants in particular are more responsive to the availability of jobs than to their pay level. We do not know, with enough precision, the way in which rural in-migrants are absorbed into the urban labor market, nor what are the adjustment problems they face. There are hints that their labor market behavior is different from that of the bulk of the labor force in terms of job searching patterns, and that they tend to move in fixed patterns (Lurie and Rayack, 1966; MacDonald and MacDonald, 1964). Although the incidence of poverty has decreased throughout the 1960s, both in the nation and in urban areas, the improvement in the economic environment has itself greatly increased the migration of the rural poor to the cities. Therefore, to help these in-migrants in their adjustment to the cities, a great deal more information is required about their labor market behavior and occupational and educational characteristics as well as the rate of migration. It has also been suggested that some of the poverty of the larger cities is due to the slow rate with which information about the labor market moves within it and reaches rural areas of out-migration. At the heart of the problems lies the confusion between the high number of job openings available to the in-migrant (higher in large centers) and their probability of obtaining such jobs (higher in the smaller urban centers).

We are not aware of work dealing with the intercity distribution of poverty in other countries, nor are the data available such that they can be surveyed and reported upon. There is every reason to assume that the generalizations presented above for the United States are valid also for other industrialized nations. However, we must observe certain caveats. First, the findings for the United States are based primarily on data of the last 20 years and therefore reflect, particularly in the relationship between incidence of poverty and size, the peculiarities of the nation's economic growth of recent decades. Significant in this latter regard is the concentration of development during the 1940s and early 1950s in the major urban centers. Even for the United States, the rate of reduction in the incidence of poverty in cities with between 100,000 and 500,000 people can be expected to be higher between 1960 and 1970 than for cities of over a million, for the latter (as a group) are not now developing as fast as the former.

Secondly, American cities are relatively new; most of them were no more than villages less than 100 years ago. This is not the case for the great majority of European and Asian cities whose histories are measured in centuries and millennia. The accretions of history undoubtedly account for differences in the distribution of poverty abroad that makes for an intracity diversity less observable in the United States.

The third cause which leads us to expect departures from the American pattern is the peculiar character, the internal sociopolitical organization of non-American cities, which stems from a specialization not generally considered in economic base analysis. The incidence of poverty in Medina and Benares can be better explained by their specialization as religious centers than by their size; Jogjakarta and Bandung in Indonesia are about the same size but the former is poorer because the latter is the summer capital; and so the listing would go on. American cities do not have a specialization as deeply embedded in history.

Obviously, poverty in the cities of other countries is primarily a reflection of the level of national economic development. However, as is the case in the United States, the cities of the world are not now, never were, nor ever will be, essentially characterized by their poverty but by reference to them as centers of wealth. Hong Kong, Calcutta, Addis Ababa, all have in a nation-relative or in a social-relative sense much poverty but the incidence of it is much lower than in the rural areas that surround them. They have very large "blighted" areas, yet for the mainland Chinese, or the farmer of Assam, or the Anuak tribesman, the city is "where the action is." Obviously, not all cities of the world react successfully to the challenge of different technologies, tastes, and the like. Some die, but most of them do not, giving added value, even if we cannot here provide scientific proof, to the idea that there exists for all cities a pattern of challenge and response similar to that which Thompson found for the United States (Thompson, 1965).

THE INTRACITY LOCATION OF THE POOR

Two ideas dominate our knowledge about the intracity location of the poor: the central city is where the poor congregate, and "birds of a feather flock together." Both are valid and helpful but neither is complete.

The notion that the central city is the repository of the poor population for the United States stems primarily from 1950 and 1960 data, from comparisons of median family incomes in the central city and in the suburbs, and from equating poverty with a subsistence minimum, the bottom of the poverty band expressed in terms of incomes of less than $3,000 per year for families of four or their equivalents. Indeed, the ratio of median family income of the central city to that of the metropolitan statistical area shows a consistent disadvantage for the central city in the case of the major municipalities (Heilbrun, 1967). In 1960 this ratio averaged .83 while it had been .96 as late as 1950. We also know, from the work of Schnore, that the "older" the central city the more often its income is lower (Schnore, 1965).

Moving from an analysis of median incomes to one of distribution, we learn that in 1960, families who lived in a central city of the nation's 213 urbanized areas had nearly twice as great a chance of receiving less than an annual income of $3,000 as those who lived in the suburbs of the same areas. Furthermore, in most of the 16 largest urbanized areas, the city limits contain anywhere from about one and a half to three times as high a ratio of families making under $3,000 as the urban fringes. Typically, one-tenth of suburban families but more than one-sixth of central city families receive less than $3,000 yearly income.

Other measures attest to the central city as the repository of the very poor, as I have pointed out elsewhere (Ornati, 1967). In the central city, poverty extends to educational attainment: the gap between the inner urban core and the suburb is wide. About 51 per cent of those over 25 who live on the urban fringes have completed at least 4 years of high school; only 41 per cent of those over 25 in the city itself are high school graduates. In some areas, the educational gulf is even greater. In Chicago's central city, only 35 per cent of adults over 25 have the equivalent of a high school education. In Chicago's suburbs, about 54 per cent are high school graduates. The ratio varies in different areas but always, the central city lags behind the suburb.

As indicated earlier, the flow of Negroes, Puerto Ricans, Mexican-Americans into our urban population took place within the frozen and debilitating mold of residential segregation which affected the urban-suburban pattern of the location of the poor. Nonwhite overrepresentation in central cities is typical of urbanized areas in general. By 1960, fewer than 5 out of every 100 residents of the fringes of urbanized areas were nonwhites while in the central cities themselves, nearly 1 in 5 was nonwhite. In 1960 already half of the nonwhite population of the country lived in these central cities but only every third white person.

If the suburb is the land of the child, the central city is the land of the aged poor. The "over sixty-five" population of the 16 major central cities ranged from 5.4 per cent in youthful Houston to more than 12 per cent in five major central cities. In 14 out of the 16 major central cities, the proportion over 65 was as high or higher than the national ratio of 9.1 per cent for the urban population in general. Without exception, in each major central city there was a greater proportion of the aged than in its urbanized area as a whole. For example, the 65 and older group constitute 13 per cent of the city of Pittsburgh and only 9.6 per cent of the urbanized area; similarly, they comprise 13.4 per cent of the population of Minneapolis and 9.3 per cent of the Minneapolis urbanized area. The differences would be even more striking if the city and only the urban fringe were compared, since the ratio for the urbanized area is raised by inclusion of the inner core and its elderly.

Predictably, concentration of the very poor in the central city is evidenced in statistics on the locational distribution of recipients of federal welfare programs. Just over half of the families receiving Aid to Dependent Children (ADC)—51.4 per cent—lived in urbanized areas, compared to only 6.8 per cent in the urban fringe. The ADC recipient rate in central cities—63 per 1,000 child residents under 18 years old—was more than three times the rate—17—outside the central cities but within standard metropolitan statistical areas (Mugge, 1963). The majority of Old Age Assistance (OAA) payments still go to non-metropolitan counties. However, within metropolitan counties payments have been increasing while the proportion of the OAA caseload living in cities of under 10,000 population has been declining concurrently with the increasing proportion of caseloads in the larger cities.

The central behavioral hypothesis explaining the concentration of the poor we have described is that people choose to live with their own kind (Hoyt, 1966). This "birds of a feather" theory is attractive for its simplicity and its correspondence to everyday experience. Known also as the "sector theory" of development, it argues that high income consumers move outward from the center of the city to follow fashionable neighborhoods, or better schools, or the panorama. The high income areas set the pattern of development leaving behind them older dilapidated houses which become the heritage of the poor. Land values in the low income districts remain high as the commercial activities of the CBD compete for space. The history and topography of the city, overt and covert discrimination, the power of condemnation in urban renewal-type projects, all reinforce the associative forces posited in the behavioral hypothesis that sets the price of real estate. Selective low status in-migration into the city and high status out-migration to the suburbs (observed also outside the United States) appear to cement the pattern (Goldstein, 1963).

When our observations are raised from city versus suburban income distribution comparisons, from a focus on the 1950-1960 data, from a poverty-line definition, and from the situation in the United States, the picture of the poor concentrating in the central city becomes less convincing. It has often been observed that monocentric gradients are limited in their applicability to locational phenomena. This applies to poverty also. Variations in the pattern of centralization occur simply as a function of size; indeed, increases in the number of poverty centers, and their presence outside the CBD and the central city, correlate positively and closely with increases in the size of urbanized areas. Other variations in the patterns of residence of the poverty populations are the result of "leap frogging" development patterns; still others follow from the scattering of job locations which are in turn due to changes in technology and the characteristics of demand.

Observations of the way of life of the great cities point to the frequent living cheek-by-jowl of rich and poor. Comparisons of income distribution, census tract by census tract, reveal islands of wealth in the middle of the central city and enclaves of poverty in the middle of rich suburban areas. A precise demarcation of where the poor live requires a breakdown of census tracts by blocks but the U. S. Census does not present income data on a block by block basis. Imputations of income distribution from data on average value of homes and from data on average rentals have been made for a limited number of cities (Hoyt, 1955). These do not present conclusive evidence: they do *not* deny that the poor are concentrated in certain neighborhoods nor that these concentrations are large. They suggest that in the larger and older cities there is significant diffusion of low income families in middle and high income areas, and vice versa. Furthermore, they suggest that this diffusion is least marked where the nonwhite population is large.

Income distribution data by city areas are not available for periods before World War II or for other nations. Historical comparisons of the distance between locations of the highest and lowest income groups must therefore be based on sociological studies, the novels of city life, and the work of some urban historians. All these leave the impression that the residential gulf between rich and poor was very large, at least until the beginning of the century. Indeed, living away from where the poor lived was a luxury that the rich of the past could much more easily afford. It is hard to quarrel with the thought that the rise of the middle classes since the thirties has "lessened the precipitous drop in the income contour line between rich and poor" that existed earlier. Nor can one argue that if we look at the distance in the location of rich and poor *irrespective* of patterns of racial segregation, the distance is not decreasing.

If, in studying the spatial distribution of the urban poor, we concern ourselves with those above the minimum subsistence line, the scattering we have observed in the older cities increases. The proportion of the poor outside the central city becomes higher. In the larger urbanized areas we find significant subcenters of poverty extending into the suburbs, a phenomenon which may (or may not) be linked to discriminatory housing patterns. Cities with significant nonwhite populations have suburban subcenters of poverty populations of greater density. All suburban subcenters are characterized by the presence of many aged and unattached individuals.

In the cities of Europe, Latin America, and most Asian nations, the poor in general tend to live in closer proximity to other income groups than in the United States. In London and Paris, the town houses of the rich persist in the poor neighborhoods of the central city. The commercial history of Venice and Amsterdam led to conglomeration of the poor around the palaces of the wealthy merchants (Robson, 1967). The predominance of apartment house living in many of the cities of Europe, and the patio type buildings of Latin America have also contributed to the diminution of the locational isolation of the poor. In other cases, governmental policy has fostered the movement of the poor to the higher income suburbs—as the construction outside the city's periphery of "worker housing" in Paris, Rome, and Milan. The relatively greater intermingling of the poor with the non-poor in the cities of other nations does not, however, mean the absence of slums or the absence of a "ghettoization" of the poor. Paris has its *"bidonville,"* London its East London, Mexico City its *"casa grande"* and its *"vecindad panaderos."* Indeed, the cities of the United States have no monopoly on slums.

African cities display unique characteristics that affect the location of rich and poor. First, many major African cities, excluding those on the Mediterranean, are new, being primarily the gift of colonialism. Second, in former colonial areas, and even today, especially in Francophone Africa, only one real center per colony exists. Provincial capitals such as Enugu in Nigeria or Kumasi in Ghana, or industrial cities like Lubumbashi in the Congo, are obvious exceptions. And although a few traditional African urban centers continue to flourish, most notably Ibadan and Kano in Nigeria, the colonial capital was and continues to be everywhere dominant.

Third, is the overriding fact that in all African cities, both those still ruled by colonials and those now independent, the African continues to live mostly in squalor and at subsistence levels, a condition which makes identification of the location of the poor particularly difficult. The tendency for the poor to cluster in the central city is not clearly defined for Africa and their location cannot be explained in terms of the sector theory or real estate prices. The history of Kano in Nigeria and Nairobi in Kenya exemplify most effectively the forces determining the poor's location. Kano with a population of about 250,000 has the poor living at its center: this stems from the fact that it is made up of a walled city over 1,000 years old, the former seat of a Moslem kingdom, a trading center, and the focus of Housaland. Outside the walls is the township created by the British for government buildings and a European residential area. It is the city's economic nerve center, and with national independence it is the area to which the new indigenous commercial and political elite has moved.

Nairobi in Kenya with more than 285,000 people, shows the opposite pattern. Here the rich live in what could be called the city's CBD, whether they are Europeans owning or managing the bulk of the industrial and commercial firms or the new indigenous managers. Around the CBD, in more of a pie-shaped than a concentric ring-pattern, live the Indians who monopolize and service the retail sector and the poor Africans who are settled in "reserves" of particular tribal or para-tribal groups. The Nairobi pattern reflects the pattern of the European settlements determined by climatic and panoramic attraction more than by differentials in real estate values (Amoye). The Kano and Nairobi patterns exist throughout Tropical Africa and are reflected in such traditional cities as Addis Ababa in Ethiopia; Katsina, Benin City, and Ibadan in Nigeria, and in such new cities as Dakar in Senegal, Dar es Salaam in Tanzania, and Kinshasa in the Congo.

Increased concentration of the poor in the urban core is often explained in terms of the out-migration of the high income, high status population; and much of the crisis of the city—the *erosion* of its tax base, the lack of effective municipal government—is traced to this movement. Indeed, as we have noted above and elsewhere (Ornati, 1966b), the persistence of a large number of the poor in the city in spite of the continued overall reduction of poverty in the United States is clearly traceable to the low income, low status in-migrant. Yet, mostly for the lack of data, there is no systematic documentation of the gross population movements that would verify the hypothesis. Some of the available evidence suggests that reliance on selective out-migration is somewhat inaccurate for white migration and for the largest metropolitan areas. The Taeubers have recently looked in detail at 1955 and 1960 census metropolitan migration data and have assessed the nature of city-to-ring and ring-to-city movement in the larger context of distinguishing migrants from non-migrants (Taeuber and Taeuber, 1964). Their findings shift our attention from the city-to-ring and ring-to-city movers who are "highly similar with regards to average measures of educational and occupational status" to the non-migrant population whose status is found to be lower. The study deals with white migrations and the Taeubers summarized their finding about migration as a "circulation of elites." The hypothesized in-migration of low status Negroes on the average, does not appear to have been significant. One is left with the conclusion that the net out-migration of high status whites, while significant, does not by itself explain enough of the difference between cities and suburbs; the deficit

apparently is due to the immobile low income, low status urban
dweller or immigrant of an earlier year.

This discussion of the net impact of migration is introduced to
note, primarily, the importance of pursuing further this line of
analysis. It is not viewed as denying the contribution of migration
(be it in or out, city-to-ring or ring-to-city) to the clustering of the
poor, since the study is limited as to cities—the twelve largest—
and as to time. It is most probable that the findings of the Taeubers,
particularly as far as in-migrants from outside the metropolitan
areas are concerned, are influenced by the relative decline in the
growth rates of these SMSAs which in turn reflected the relative
economic *stagnation* of the nation in the second half of the last
decade. Surely the impact of migration was different for cities in
the 500,000 to 1 million size class and for the 1960-1965 period
during which both large and small cities contributed more effectively to their traditional function of making the rich richer and
the poor somewhat less poor.

URBAN POVERTY AND THE
"CRISIS OF THE CITIES"

Viewed from the historical and international perspective, the
poverty of urban America does not present a terrifying picture.
The poverty of our cities has been decreasing as our nation's wealth
has increased; the decrease in urban poverty has been more marked
here than in most of the world. American poverty has been declining for generations, though the rate of decrease (probably)
slowed a little during the period 1958-1963. Since during those
years, Germany, Italy, France, and some of the Scandinavian
nations were achieving higher rates of economic growth than the
United States, many European cities thus appeared to have been
more successful in reducing poverty than their American counterparts. The situation seems to have changed since 1963 and, at
least according to preliminary and scattered returns, the American
cities are once again reducing the number of their poor more
rapidly.

Poverty appears to be more concentrated in United States cities
than in foreign cities. There are several reasons for this, most of
them related to the peculiarities of our social and industrial organ-

ization. Our predilection for living in small unattached homes and the discriminatory patterns of housing—particularly outside the South—are central. The organizational structure of the housing industry, the high cost of mortgage money (relative to other forms of credit), and the high wages of construction labor compared with other wages, tell a story of residential construction in the United States very different from that of Europe. The lack of a clear public-housing policy with egalitarian objectives is probably the most important cause of the concentration of the (American) poor in cities. Indeed, besides coming late—public housing became a concern of the national government only in the 1930s while in most of Europe this occurred in the 1890s—public housing, in the final analysis, has really never mattered. An effective low housing program, also aimed at reducing the concentration of poverty within the city, necessarily calls for building in the open spaces surrounding them. But the fractionalization of governmental jurisdiction and the opposition of the urban real estate interest groups have denied our nation this, the most logical of all solutions. What is worse is that at present the drive to do something about public housing seems to have dissipated itself entirely in a search for different rationale—e.g., rent supplements—or for palliatives such as rat control.

Much is being said about the "crisis of the cities," and it is often argued that at the heart of this crisis is the inability of government—local, state, and federal—to cope with poverty (Lowe, 1967). From here the popular argument goes on to speak of the increasing poverty of the cities. Most of it is sheer nonsense. The cities of the United States are not poorer (by any reasonable criteria), and the crisis of the cities involves much more than poverty. We might better ask the reason why the "crisis" label is applied to American cities when their objective standard is at an all-time high as measured by real disposable income, available production and consumption goods, the time and cost of per passenger commutation mile, the real cost of a kilowatt hour of electricity, the quality and availability of water, the number of children of school age in school and the ratio of instructional personnel to students, the number of recipients of welfare benefits, and the real value of these benefits.

What has happened is that the revolution of rising expectations, which in the 1950s was identified with the strivings for the development and independence of foreign nations, has reached our own shores. Spread by a well developed system of communication (to which the poor have full access) and spurred on by the able, careful, and insightful work of a new breed of pundits, pamphleteers, and politicians, rising expectations have spread throughout the nation, fundamentally reducing the political tolerance of inequality. With the support of a verbal, self conscious, and guilt-ridden white liberal elite, the new awareness has led to the finding and launching of a multiplicity of antipoverty action programs.

ANTIPOVERTY ACTION

This is not the place in which to detail and argue for or against specific programs. The manner in which the facts about urban poverty have been organized above should provide sufficient clues for their rational direction. Clearly, the matrix of causes, population groupings, and levels of poverty needed to explain intercity differences of poverty, argues for a multiplicity and a city-by-city tailoring of programs. Clearly, the mass provision of funds for housing programs is a major requirement of policy; and antipoverty action at the neighborhood level, with ample resident participation and involvement, is a requirement even though we do not yet know how this is to be done. There is indeed no adequate theory for neighborhood economic development. At least we can make analogies to the theories of national economic development and international trade to point to the elements of a model for analysis and action.

The model assumes a high degree of local favoritism in the buying pattern of neighborhood residents. It calls for the adoption of essentially "protectionist" policies aimed at reducing the money-flows out of the neighborhood. It also assumes the existence of significant unused cash and labor resources to which (outside) loans, grants, and technical assistance are added. On the basis of such assumptions a system can be developed to band neighborhood people together in a variety of cooperative-type ventures aimed at physical rehabilitation of the area, the creation of locally based small enterprises and, eventually, the development of increased employment and incomes within the neighborhood itself.

The model has much to recommend it. Indeed, we have seen that it is as possible to organize the neighborhood residents for constructive cooperative action in "fighting" City Hall. This has significant benefits since it increases democratic participation. It is also true that poverty neighborhoods have a good deal of cohesiveness and, on occasion, an *elan vital* absent in neighborhoods of higher income. Certainly, labor resources are underutilized. It is possible to assume that either through community involvement or because of the presence of charismatic leaders, such labor resources would be forthcoming for communal activity within the neighborhood even though the supply price of many unemployed workers is higher than what the larger city market is now ready to pay, given their existing skill levels.

Having noted earlier that even within American cities not all poverty is in discrete conglomerates—note again that where this is so, it is primarily due to discriminatory housing patterns—it is here that we can judge antipoverty programs to be of only limited import even when successful. Consequently, one must go to programs of greater scope and spillovers, such as the proposed development of new towns (Perloff and Hanson, 1967), so effective in Great Britain, major employment schemes involving employment guarantees on a city basis, and programs for the improvement of the workings of the labor market.

Antipoverty programs are clearly not enough: not only because they lack coordination, have no overall objective, reflect a piecemeal approach, deal with poverty as due to temporary causes or happenstance, and view the poor as inferior beings. They are not enough because, fundamentally, "programs" imply that poverty can be eradicated through a strategy of services, while poverty is really a problem of income and reducing it calls for an income strategy.

Antipoverty programs are important and indeed many of the poor are poor because of inadequate services: the poor have benefited from them. More fundamentally, one should note that *a strategy of services*—the current thrust of governmental action—*stems from, and is deeply embedded in, a posture derived from the "subsistence based" type definition that we use.* Having defined poverty as the gap between consensually determined needs and available resources, we try to fill the gap by providing services.

For rich nations, and as our own nation becomes richer, poverty emerges increasingly as the problem of inequality. This development in turn forces a shift to action and a policy strategy derived from deprivational (social-relative) definitions and analyses based on them. Obviously, fundamental restructuring of the way incomes are distributed, and of the distributive impact of existing social programs, including antipoverty programs, is called for.

The brief and, albeit, incomplete survey of poverty outside the United States summarized in this article points irrevocably to the fact that it is in the area of redistributive policies—transfer payments, their financing and administration, tax incidence, and the like—that the experience of other countries is most valuable. What the French have done with their family allowances, social security, and housing location schemes must, for example, be juxtaposed against what we have not done in these areas and particularly with the by-products of the relatively little that has been accomplished. To be effective, an income-based strategy of eliminating poverty in the city must recognize, for instance, that currently expenditures on public housing for the poor are less than half the implicit subsidies to the better off which derive from the deductability of interest payments on mortgages.

Relative deprivation, the eradication of poverty, more egalitarian income distribution, have been the impossible dream of good men since the days of Jeremiah. Striving for them has now a new justification: the economy is so productive, the subsistence requirements are so easily fulfillable, income redistribution so painless to those that have more than enough, the very rich so relatively few and so enlightened, that it can be done cheaply and easily if not quickly and forevermore. In antipoverty policy and action, this is the time to right the rightable wrongs.

References

ABEL-SMITH, B. and P. TOWNSEND. *Poor and the Poorest* (London: Bell, 1965).

AMOYE, MAURICE. "A Profile of Two African Cities," Project Labor Market, Graduate School of Business Administration, New York University, unpublished.

COATES, B. E. and E. M. RAUSTRON. "Regional Variations in Incomes," *Westminster Bank Review* (February, 1966), pp. 28-46.

COWGILL, D. O. "Trends in Residential Segregation of Non-Whites in American Cities, 1940-1950," *American Sociological Review*, 21 (February, 1956), pp. 43-47, Note No. 1.

GOLDSTEIN, S. "Some Economic Consequences of Suburbanization in the Copenhagen Metropolitan Area," *American Journal of Sociology*, 68 (March, 1963), pp. 551-64.

HEILBRUN, J. "Poverty and Public Finance in the Older Central Cities," *Urban America: Goals and Problems* (material prepared by the Subcommittee on Urban Affairs of the Joint Economic Committee, U.S. Congress, Washington, D.C.: U.S. Government Printing Office, August, 1967), pp. 141-61.

HILL, H. "Demographic Change and Racial Ghettos: The Crisis of American Cities," *Journal of Urban Law*, 43 (Winter, 1966), pp. 231-85.

HOYT, H. *Economic Survey of Montgomery and Prince George Counties, Maryland* (Washington, D.C.: Hoyt Associates, June, 1955).

——. *Where the Rich and Poor People Live* (Washington, D.C.: Urban Land Institute, 1966).

KRAVIS, I. B. *The Structure of Income* (Philadelphia: University of Pennsylvania Press, 1962), pp. 237-51.

LOWE, J. R. *Cities in a Race with Time* (New York: Random House, 1967).

LURIE, M. and E. RAYACK. "Racial Differences in Migration and Job Search," *Southern Economic Journal*, 33 (July, 1966), pp. 80-95.

MACDONALD, J. S. and L. D. MACDONALD. "Chain Migration, Ethnic Neighborhood Formation and Social Networks," *The Milbank Memorial Fund Quarterly* (January, 1964).

MIERNYK, W. H. "Needed: Appalachian Ghost Town," *Appalachian Review*, 26 (Spring, 1967), pp. 14-20.

MUGGE, ROBERT H. "Aid to Families with Dependent Children: Initial Findings of the 1961 Report on the Characteristics of Recipients," *Social Security Bulletin*, 26 (March, 1963), pp. 3-15.

NICHOLSON, R. J. "The Distribution of Personal Income," *Lloyds Bank Review*, 83 (January, 1967), pp. 11-21.

OPHA, P. D. and V. V. BHATT. "Some Aspects of Income Distribution in India," *Bulletin of the Oxford Institute of Economics and Statistics* (August, 1964), pp. 229-38.

ORNATI, O. A. *Poverty Amid Affluence* (New York: Twentieth Century Fund, 1966a), pp. 7-25.

——. "Program Evaluations and the Definition of Poverty," *IRRA Proceedings* (December, 1966b), pp. 262-64.

——. "Poverty in the Cities," paper prepared for the Conference on Urban Economics, Washington, D.C., January 26-28, 1967.

PERLOFF, H. S. and R. HANSON. "Poverty and Public Finance in the Older Central Cities," *Urban America: Goals and Problems* (material prepared by the Subcommittee on Urban Affairs of the Joint Economic Committee, U.S. Congress, Washington, D.C.: U.S. Government Printing Office. August, 1967).

PETERSON, W. G. "Transfer Expenditures, Taxes and Income Distribution in France," *Economics and Business* (Fall, 1965), pp. 11, 21.

RANODIVE, K. R. "The 'Equality' of Incomes in India," *Bulletin of the Oxford Institute of Economics and Statistics* (May, 1965), pp. 119-34.

ROBSON, W. A. *Great Cities of the World*, 2nd edn. (New York: Macmillan Co., 1967), *passim*.

RUSSETT, B. M., *et al. World Handbook of Political and Social Indicators* (New Haven and London: Yale University Press, 1964), p. 247.

SCHNORE, Leo F. *The Urban Scene* (New York: The Free Press, 1965).

TAEUBER, K. E. and A. F. TAEUBER. "White Migration and Socio-economic Differences Between Cities and Suburbs," *American Sociological Review*, 29 (October, 1964), pp. 718-29.

——— . *Negroes in Cities* (Chicago: Aldine Press, 1965), p. 37.

TERRITORIAL MINIMUM WAGES BOARD. *Report of the Territorial Minimum Wages Board, Tanganyika* (Dar es Salaam, 1962).

THOMPSON, W. R. *A Preface to Urban Economics* (Baltimore: The Johns Hopkins Press, 1965), pp. 18-21.

TOWNSEND, P. "Measures and Explanations of Poverty in High Income and Low Income Countries," paper prepared for the International Seminar on Poverty, University of Essex, April, 1966, pp. 3-6.

3

Old Problems and New Agencies

How Much Change?

ARTHUR B. SHOSTAK

☐ IN OPENING THE LENGTHY AND thorough-going hearings in 1967 on the war on poverty, the chairman of the subcommittee of the Senate Committee on Labor and Public Welfare, Senator Joseph Clark, read a well-known selection from Franklin D. Roosevelt's second inaugural address of 1937 in which reference was made to "one-third of a nation ill-housed, ill-clad, ill-nourished." Citing this passage as the inspirational source or origin of the current war on poverty, the Senator expressed the belief that progress had been made during the ensuing 30 years even though the social and economic problems noted by the deceased president still remain acutely with us. What particularly impressed the Senator was the fact that the old problems were now being subjected to pressure from new kinds of agencies. In his words:

> Because of its very size and diversity, its multiplicity of attacks and the idealism and devotion it has inspired, the war on poverty, young as it is, represents the brightest hope this Nation has ever had to rid itself of the age-old scourge of deprivation and economic suffering (Senate Committee on Labor and Public Welfare, 1967, pp. 1-5).

To keep this hope bright, Senator Clark charged his subcommittee with the exacting task of uncovering "the genuine successes and the obvious failures" of the poverty program. Together the group, made up of Senators Edward and Robert Kennedy, Jacob Javits, and five others, was to produce "constructive criticisms of past performance and constructive recommendations for future action."

It is difficult to imagine a Congressional committee undertaking an effort more politically sensitive or substantively impoverished than this assignment. The reality of the situation was made clear when the majority and minority blocs of the subcommittee, after hearing testimony filling 15 volumes, produced separate and conflicting conclusions. Indeed, the differences between the two factions appeared to have been intensified rather than diminished by their joint exposure to the jumbled mass of uneven data and contradictory opinions uncovered during the investigation. Such a result should not have been surprising since Congressional confusion and conflict have characterized the national antipoverty effort from the very beginning (Graham, 1966; Marris and Rein, 1967; Brager and Purcell, 1967).

Decisive evaluations of facets of the war on poverty, better yet of the entire war itself, are presently premature, as the record of the Clark subcommittee makes plain. For one thing, the war has concentrated on the young; and hardly enough time has passed to know whether such programs as Discovery, Get Set, Head Start, or Upward Bound have really "made a difference." For another, most of the agencies involved have cautiously shied away from evaluation efforts. Researcher Sar Levitan, for example, reports:

> The Bureau of Work Programs in the Department of Labor, responsible for the Neighborhood Youth Corps, and the Bureau of Family Services of the Welfare Administration, responsible for OEO's Work Experience and Training Program have conducted few evaluations. . . . [The officials of both] have not released any serious study evaluating their efforts. Indeed, the Bureau of Family Services has not yet taken steps to assure that an evaluation of its program would be available in the future (1967, pp. 2-3).

Relevant also to the problem of evaluation is the fact that virtually all the programs are in flux. The Job Corps, once vulnerable to the criticism that it "creamed" the best male applicants and ignored its women's corps program, now takes the hardest cases and seeks to meet a Congressional mandate that 23 per cent of the total enrollment be female. Elsewhere the scene is similarly one of almost monthly alterations, some of considerable substance, all serving to make even more difficult the initially difficult task of evaluation.

Congress, possibly influenced by the first-hand trials of those members who have attempted evaluations of the antipoverty efforts, has made some moves to help correct the situation. Senator George

Murphy authored a 1966 amendment to the 1964 Antipoverty Act which requires OEO to undertake an evaluation of the enrollees at various intervals following their departure from the Job Corps program. The Senator complained that not even Head Start, which has generally been regarded as the most successful of the poverty programs, has "produced the information necessary to measure fully its success" (Senate Committee on Labor and Public Welfare, 1967, p. 10). In related action, the Senate has also moved to authorize the first independent audit of antipoverty activities financed in whole *or* in part by the federal government. If carried out, a full report would be available from the Comptroller General's Office by February, 1969.

At present, it is possible to do no more than begin in a tentative way the kind of evaluation necessary if decision-makers are to be put in a position where they can replace hunches, postcard polls of constituents, propaganda from lobbyists, and personal predilections with substantial data and meaningful analysis. In undertaking a general evaluation at this early point in the post-1964 national war on poverty, a number of gains and related setbacks appear particularly significant for analysis. These are treated here in some depth, the exploratory tone of much of the discussion being occasioned by the paucity of relevant information.

ANTIPOVERTY ADVANCES

In assaying how much success the national antipoverty effort has had to date in meeting "old problems," five specific advances stand out. Each is distinguished in terms of reform significance, programmatic sweep, and social impact. The first of these concerns a new-found prominence of certain "old problems" long associated with poverty. The second involves a newly discovered modesty where arrogance once conditioned particular responses to these "old problems." The third focuses on a new recognition of the meaningful interrelationships among many of the same problems. The fourth concerns a new-found sophistication in instances where premature and presumptuous claims of antipoverty successes are involved. And the fifth and last involves the larger lessons, the insights which move above the poverty "border" and which are slowly being secured for the society as a whole. A final comment attempts to trace the possible fate of each advance through the late 1960s.

CREATION OF A VITAL NATIONAL CONCERN

Representative of the vast changes which have occurred recently in the national consciousness of the poverty problem is an appropriate shift in academic utilization of the book often romantically credited with having precipitated the entire "War," Michael Harrington's *The Other America.* Whereas the volume was first assigned as a shocker after its publication in 1962, now, a short six years later, it is more commonly assigned as a dated "classic," happily misleading in its attribution of both invisibility and impotence to the poor.

Thanks in large part to the enormous attention paid the antipoverty effort by characteristically skeptical yet sensationalist mass media, the public in the past four years has had the poverty problem put emphatically before it. Press and television, especially, have personalized the plight of certain "worthy" unfortunates, have woven a sense of brotherhood and community through feature stories on "worthy" self-help efforts, and in other related ways have contributed to the signal American rediscovery of the poor. To be sure, there is also constant harping on OEO setbacks, and there is much harmful distortion in reporting ghetto riots and the efforts of Negro extremists (or, less often, the doings of poor white extremists, such as certain Klansmen). The point remains, however, that the "other America" has finally earned a valuable place in the sun—if only the *Baltimore Sun,* for the present.

National attention has also had the additional virtue of uncovering subjects only previously suspected or whispered about, subjects that deserve the corrective response which cannot occur without disclosure. Typical in this regard are the following:

> On April 10, 1967, at our first field hearing, we [of Senator Clark's Subcommittee] heard testimony in Jackson, Mississippi, that people in the Mississippi Delta were starving. . . . We saw families who, without income with which to buy food or food stamps, were suffering from the effects of acute malnutrition and hunger. . . . Eye-witnesses, including members of this sub-committee, have observed and reported conditions that this sub-committee has de-

scribed as "shocking" and as constituting a national emergency (Senate Committee on Labor and Public Welfare, 1967).

An alleged million-dollar-a-year racket involving kickbacks to welfare supervisors and caseworkers reportedly paid by companies specializing in the moving of Brooklyn relief clients is under investigation. . . . [The Investigation Commissioner] is said to have received an anonymous letter, presumably from a welfare worker, detailing the alleged racket (*New York Times*, October 12, 1967, p. 1).

Three housewives told a Congressional hearing today that Safeway Supermarkets charged poor persons higher prices than they did persons in middle and upper incomes. A lawyer for Safeway denied the charge. . . . [Commissioner of the Bureau of Labor Statistics Arthur Ross] said a major campaign by his Bureau to gather price information would cost $400,000 a year. He said Congress has been reluctant to increase the Bureau's budget (*New York Times,* October 13, 1967, p. 20).

Although exposure of this sort still permits both proponents and opponents of antipoverty measures to bend the material to their own ends, it does compel a public response, as in the case of the subcommittee, the Investigation Commissioner, and the Safeway Company lawyer. In this age of non-existence (the "invisible man" of Ralph Ellison's creation) response-securement alone is a gain.

But the accomplishment or achievement of attention where once there was only a deadly anonymity has a special and underrecognized hazard attached to it. Mass media concern remains a very uncertain and elusive matter. Bayard Rustin, in analyzing the current problems of the Civil Rights movement, makes a sobering point relevant to the possibly fleeting character of faddish national attention:

Because of the drama of the previous period the movement received a great deal of help from the mass media; almost every day for ten years newspapers all across the nation carried news of civil-rights activity on their front pages. In the present period, however, the slow, irksome, and unspectacular work being done does not draw headlines. Much of our present activity is either ignored or relegated to small items on back pages. Perhaps this is why so many people consider the movement dead. In any case, this adds to our problem of developing and sustaining momentum (1967, p. 44).

There is reason to expect a similar decline in coverage of the antipoverty effort. The novelty here will wear thin, innovation

may soon give way to routine, OEO may continue to lose functions
to other federal agencies, and "the action" will likely shift elsewhere
(as, for example, to the "Model Cities" effort in 1968). Already one
academic specialist in the literature notes signs of such a development:

> In June 1966, the tap seems to have been turned down a little,
> and the outpouring of literature on poverty has become a trickle.
> The journals, books, and other sources of literary material may be
> gearing themselves toward new concepts, new ideas, and a new
> topic in the great society (Schlesinger, 1967, p. xi).

Exactly what the impact of diminished media and, thus, public interest might be throughout the late 1960s remains, of course,
unclear.

A letup in supercritical, superfinicky attention may permit new
progress in risk-taking, including more power for the poor, more
margin for reasonable program errors, and more leeway for pro-
fessionally led experimentation. On the other hand, the nation has
a record of assuming that social problems that leave the headlines
are either solved or contained. As a consequence of such a wishful
assumption, national concern turns elsewhere, followed by the
essential energies of federal, regional, state, and local authorities.
Many specialists know better but become too harassed "putting out
new fires" elsewhere to linger long over issues that the apparently
fickle public and mass media have turned from. In due course the
"back-page" problem loses its prominence-fed ability to attract
young innovators and hold onto older experienced hands, while
the relevant programs and agencies settle into self-serving, and too
frequently client-abusing, routines. Funds decline relative to real
needs, programs ossify, and the goal of deep-reaching social change
gives way to one more nearly akin to the maintenance of the social
status quo.

Non-Certainty and Humility

Prior to the 1964 national rediscovery of poverty, and the declaration of a "holy war" against it, three critical questions were too
easily answered by a too casual public. What are the roots of
poverty?—laziness and congenital deficiencies. What should be
done to relieve poverty?—prod some of the poor into action through

welfare inadequacies and lure others into remedial educational and vocational ventures. How long might a "victory" over poverty take?—once consensus has been reached favoring a "victory," however ambiguously defined, it could be secured in a mere ten or so years. Certainly it could be gained in time to grace the 200th anniversary in 1976 of the founding of the Republic (a pledge Congress exacted under enormous pressure from a very reluctant OEO Director, Sargent Shriver).

Four years of a now stalemated war on poverty have shaken public confidence in this conventional wisdom. Human interest profiles in the mass media of innocent enrollees in such programs as Get Set and Head Start have undermined the personal deficiency hypothesis. Horror tales of starvation in the Delta and of rat attacks in Northern ghetto dwellings have somewhat weakened the will to further punish (and prod) the poor. Reliance on some conventional nostrums has been challenged by the ubiquitous inadequacy of such lures as job training allowances and average wage levels in standard post-training employment. And, above all, the expenditure of some $6 billion by OEO and more than fifteen-fold this sum by other governmental agencies between 1964 and 1968 has clearly failed to reduce the problem to anywhere near the extent expected by an impatient general public. Poverty has starkly demonstrated its multifaceted intransigence and its self-regenerating mechanism.

This new uncertainty, however, has opened up the possibility of important programmatic gains. Typical, is abandonment of the certain perception of the poor as a monolith in favor of a new and less certain, but rewarding, perception of significant differences among types of poor people. Current attempts to operationalize the promising four-cell typology advanced by S. M. Miller (copers, skidders, stable, and unstable) hold out promise for guiding the initial allocation of scarce resources among competing programs, and aiding in the later evaluation of program gains (1965, pp. 22-39). If, for example, analysis should establish the presence of more copers and fewer unstable poor in a target area, more counseling services and fewer antidrug, drink, and delinquency efforts might then be prescribed. If none soon leave poverty, but many should shift from being copers to the category of the stable poor, a revealing measure of success is available here to guide further antipoverty efforts. This measure could be used, among other things, to scale down unrealistic expectations of project success and to sensitize all to the value of incremental and otherwise invisible and undervalued changes in the *types* of poor people.

The new national uncertainty has also made possible the serious consideration of antipoverty aids once inconceivable, such as family allowances (popular in Canada and Europe); abortion and birth-control clinics; tax rewards for employers who seek out, train, and retain ex-poor workers; and the use of the 1946 Full Employment Act doctrine of the government as an "employer of last resort." Even more brow-arching are the antipoverty notions embodied in the following projects:

> The Brooklyn chapter of CORE has taken an option on a 900 acre site in the South where it plans a 7,000 person venture in the kibbutz type of communal living. The chapter plans to stop fighting the traditional civil rights-type battles and "retire to the positions of our forefathers—back to the soil." The Project leader explains that this is the "only way that we can save our culture and ourselves." He said that Negroes needed to return to the soil because they were "becoming infected with the same sickness" as white people (*New York Times,* October 15, 1967, p. 51).

> An experimental Headstart Program allows virtually no time for free play. Instead of having a central, motherly teacher for the whole class, the children are split into small groups that move from subject to subject, each with a different instructor. Instead of spending most of their time on non-verbal activities which hardly change from semester to semester, the children and teachers talk, shout, chant in full sentences—following a very specific plan (*New York Times Magazine,* October 15, 1967, p. 70).

> A self-help Negro business organization in New York City maintains that the simplest way to advance against Negro poverty is to "let the Federal Government and private industry give Negro factories contracts for the manufacture of goods." The organization operates a voluntary, nonprofit hospital, a chemical factory, a clothing factory, a laundry, a bakery, a bus line, a construction company and a growing housing program of over 400 units. "We do this without government or philanthropic aid, and we do it training and employing our people whom white America has abandoned as unemployable" (*New York Times,* October 9, 1967, p. 37).

Uncertainty legitimizes criticism of proposed antipoverty measures, as the myth of the expert in antipoverty matters has long since collapsed. Typical here are the following items:

The Negro President of the National Economic Growth and Reconstruction Organization, Dr. T. W. Matthew, assailed Senator R. F. Kennedy's plan to rebuild the nation's slums as "a double fraud, a booby trap for white industry as well as for the black ghetto. . . . " He called Negroes in the slums "clinically sick. . . . [Those] healthy enough to work are already on the subway and are going to work." He said that Senator Kennedy's problem is that he "doesn't understand Negro life," and added: "He is doing a lot of planning without making Negro people a part of it" (*New York Times,* October 9, 1967, p. 37).

Michael Harrington attacked the proposals of Sen. Kennedy and others who would encourage private industry to build low rent housing by giving it tax incentives. He said these proposals were illusory and would not produce housing with rents geared to the poor. Such housing should not be left to private business because it was motivated by profit rather than "social and esthetic goals" (*Tenant News,* 6, September-October, 1967, p. 5).

John Kenneth Galbraith predicted total failure for proposed efforts to solve the problems of American cities with the help of private business. The costs and planning required are beyond the resources and skills of all but government. "Private enterprise and private investment are being aroused to their responsibilities—as they have without result a hundred times before. . . . In the end the results will be invisible" (*New York Times,* October 17, 1967, p. 77).

The dialogue involved in the controversies over these various plans appears exceedingly appropriate at this non-certain stage of the antipoverty effort.

Where the nation will take its new-found non-certainty in the late 1960s is unclear. Conceivably, it might continue to build on the flexibility and humility inherent in the loss of orthodoxy. But many of our citizens are demoralized by uncertainty. With the impetuousness of a rich, young, and enormously well-off country, the nation sometimes prefers the posture of quiet certainty and firm confidence in its attack on topical social problems. When advances in knowledge and the record of experience combine to discourage such a sophomoric posture, the Congress and the problem-related agencies come under enormous pressure to direct the national effort elsewhere, preferably to a more "cooperative" social problem.

Interrelatedness of Poverty Matters

There has been increasing recognition of the mutually reinforcing character of poverty related matters once regarded as only
casually connected. Such items as ill health, educational inadequacy, large family origins, intergenerational welfare histories, and
self-perceived political impotence are now appreciated for their
complementary and cumulative interrelationships. Typical, is the
situation of a representative public housing tenant as analyzed by
sociologist Camille Jeffers:

> Mrs. Todd went from one extreme to another in her housekeeping.
> . . . Her negligence in housekeeping could not be attributed to any
> lack of housekeeping skills; more valid and useful explanations
> would be related to low morale and the lack of incentives. It was
> clear that the solution . . . could be found more readily in dealing
> with reality or situational factors, such as Mrs. Todd's lack of
> money and the prolonged absence of her husband, than, for ex-
> ample, in providing classes in homemaking (1967, p. 26).

Similarly, the interconnectedness of various elements is recognized
by Hansen and Carter in this 1965 comment:

> . . . provision of gainful employment for family heads is an appar-
> ently clear-cut end goal; however, it may be closely associated
> with more immediate and multiple family-life objectives; for the
> family has gained very little if the newly employed man leaves his
> family because his wife persists in her disorganized management
> of home and children (1966, p. 93).

Thus, research, slowly, but surely, has been establishing subtle
and fine interconnections and validating both a call to go beyond
classes in homemaking and to provide exactly such classes.

The concern with substantive linkages also goes beyond such
conventional matters as poverty, jobs, home life, and personal relations to reach out to somewhat fresher and equally significant
connections. A group of Republican House members, for example,
recently argued that the war on poverty would not be won unless
a more vigorous war was also waged against organized crime:

> The Administration has asked Congress for $2.06 billion for the
> War on Poverty in fiscal 1968; the profits of Organized Crime from
> gambling will be three times larger for the same period . . .

and most of the profit will come from those who can least afford
to pay (*New York Times*, August 29, 1967, p. 22).

Similarly, various social scientists, influenced especially by Frank
Riessman, contend that progress in the war is vitally connected with
advances in restructuring and revitalizing the helping professions.
As they point out, millions of poor people could be gainfully employed in new career sequences if the jobs of professionals were
subdivided and indigenous teacher aides, para-medical personnel,
social science research aides, and others given an opportunity to
strengthen client-profession relations (Riessman and Pearl, 1965).
Various amendments currently proposed to major education and
welfare legislation recognize this possibility by extending and expanding the New Careers program in many significant ways.

The new-found concern with substantive linkages also makes
possible the clear espousal of unpopular reform notions, as these
quotations indicate:

> Former Illinois Senator Paul H. Douglas warns that white suburbs
> can no longer afford to "tighten their noose around the necks of the
> central cities," but must permit housing to be constructed for both
> poor people and Negroes (*New York Times,* September 20, 1967,
> p. 31).

> Andrew Heiskell, Chairman of the Board of Time, Inc., called on
> the nation's corporations yesterday to lower employment stand-
> ards, if necessary, to provide thousands of more jobs for people
> living in urban slums. "I urgently suggest that every corporation
> should consider hiring, for every 100 men in its force, one man who
> does not meet their normal standards . . . ." The speech drew only
> brief applause from the audience of about 600 magazine and ad-
> vertising executives. . . . (*New York Times,* September 20, 1967,
> p. 34).

> Gunnar Myrdal made a tentative personal estimate that any proper
> answer [to the poverty challenge] would take "trillions of dollars
> and at least one generation" (*New York Times,* October 4, 1967,
> p. 1).

Whether in shedding light on new relationships or illuminating
old ones we have preferred to ignore, the concern with substantive
linkages moves the antipoverty effort forward.

A new-found sensitivity to interrelationships is further apparent
in the matter of organizational associations. Allied, though often
rival, antipoverty agencies are being brought into a more coordinated and thereby more effective attack on poverty. At the neigh-

borhood level, community aides are busy attempting to link needy neighborhood residents to a custom-tailored array of both better known and little known sources of aid. At the OEO level, representatives of federal, regional, state, and municipal public agencies meet more often now than ever before both with one another and with a range of "Red Feather" agencies from the private sector of the welfare "industry." Indeed, the novelty of direct confrontation on community action agency boards of both spokesmen for the poor and for antipoverty agencies has drawn attention away from the similarly novel and significant confrontation of public and private bodies that have too often in the past attempted too little in order to remain proudly "on their own."

Equally useful have been certain interagency disputes generated by the new-found necessity of groups to work together in one coordinated antipoverty effort. The community action agency in New York City, for example, has been successful in its recent struggle to compel the Board of Education to decentralize certain school matters and authorize a larger role in educational decision-making for neighborhood antipoverty groups. The Council Against Poverty had previously held up $69 million in federal funds with its two-month campaign of protests. Likewise, the antipoverty agency in Newark, New Jersey, has been successful in its vigorous campaign to get the City Council to reverse an earlier decision permitting city police to purchase and employ police dogs. This move had originally been taken against a backdrop of riot and racial tension (New York Times, October 5, 1967, p. 24). Again, in New York City, as elsewhere across the nation, local lawyers employed by OEO-funded antipoverty programs are helping welfare clients press legal claims for increased financial aid against the city government. One such lawyer estimates that two-thirds of New York's 650,000 welfare clients are "just not getting what they are entitled to." And he adds: "We are just trying to force the city to do what by law it is required to do" (New York Times, October 3, 1967, p. 34).

Related here is a classic interagency conflict that now threatens the very existence of the California Rural Legal Assistance Program, the largest legal aid program for the poor in the nation. CRLA has successfully checked the efforts of the state to cut back welfare payments and medical aid to the poor and has fought against the Governor's efforts to import cheap farm labor from Mexico. Few other OEO efforts show as much promise of compelling reforms in the welfare system as does this one—and few are in such serious jeopardy. Indeed, the details of the jeopardy further underline the point of interconnectedness:

Thus far CRLA has been supported by advisory panels at OEO, but the Governor apparently is going to veto the program when it comes up for refunding in December [1967]. OEO can override the veto, but politically this may be difficult for Shriver to do since California's Senator Murphy wants to dump the program, and Congressman Sisk from the farm lands of Fresno is rumbling against CRLA. Mr. Sisk sits on the important House Rules Committee. CRLA will have to muster a strong national lobby soon, or it may go down the drain . . . (*New Republic*, October 21, 1967, pp. 13-14).

The light generated by the friction of these abrasive encounters will hereafter make more difficult the abject exploitation which was all too common previously.

The antipoverty effort's success in drawing in new groups seldom before involved in the same depth and detail provides a further illustration of the increasing appreciation of interconnectedness. Education Commissioner Harold Howe, II, has high expectations of an on-going experiment in Washington, D. C., in which Antioch College is running two inner-city schools as community schools under contract to the board of education. The Job Corps has involved such corporate giants as General Electric, IBM, Litton, RCA, Westinghouse, Philco-Ford, and many others as operators of its centers. OEO has turned to organizations of progressive businessmen and middle-class club-women in its effort to impress Congress with a growing public mandate of support for the antipoverty program. The "out-reach" here has been extraordinary and the new linkages formed invaluable in meeting the many and varied aspects of the problem.

One such linkage deserves special mention both for what it has already exposed and for its special promise. A major problem confronting the nation is how to provide a staggering $300 billion output needed for city housing development in the next years. A partial answer may have been found in the forging of a connection between the need and private investment. This involves, in the present case, a pledge secured from nearly 350 of the country's largest life insurance companies to invest jointly $1 billion (at 6 per cent annual interest) in slum redevelopment (a sum three times the amount allocated for public housing in 1967). In the aftermath of the heralded pledge, a curious *Newsweek* reporter "discovered" that despite hoopla and publicity about earlier business efforts in the low-cost housing field, little has thus far been accomplished:

> The biggest single program by any private company so far has been a slum rehabilitation effort by U. S. Gypsum, which has rebuilt 120 dwelling units in Harlem, plans to re-do 200 others, and is studying similar projects in Cleveland and Chicago. By contrast, the life-insurance industry's $1 billion could create up to 80,000 new dwelling units (*Newsweek,* September 25, 1967, pp. 13-14).

HUD Under Secretary Robert C. Wood hailed the new alliance as providing the "first big-business money involved in low-cost housing." HUD experts were especially cheered by the prospects that the nation's banks, an even more important source of mortgage money than insurance firms, and the nation's fire insurance firms, whose coverage is as essential as mortgages, might soon follow the lead of the life insurance companies.

Nevertheless, the final impact of heightened public recognition of the intricate interconnectedness of poverty and antipoverty components remains unclear. In the late 1960s, such recognition presumably might yield new public support for vast and sweeping social reform efforts, public *and* private, largely urban in focus, and hopefully innovative in character. The expansive "Marshall Plan" proposals of A. Philip Randolph, Whitney Young, Gunnar Myrdal, and others come to mind, as does also the ten-year $100 billion Freedom Budget espoused by Leon Keyserling and Bayard Rustin (Myrdal, 1965, pp. 121-27; Keyserling, 1967). A new coalition of 800 private enterprise leaders, including Henry Ford II, David Rockefeller, Andrew Heiskell, George Meany, and Walter Reuther, is also busy drafting plans for privately sponsored attacks against urban poverty.

On the other hand, the nation has on occasion permitted severe imbalances to develop inside of new and untried interrelationships. Cloward and Piven, for example, warn that a new corporate role in the slums may come at a high price to the Negro's steadily growing political power in urban affairs (*The Nation,* September 5, 1966). While their economic lot might be improved somewhat, Negroes may be reduced to instruments of national corporate power.

In the process, they may lose the opportunity previous ethnic blocs have had to use municipal funds for jobs and services and thereby create a base for power in state and national affairs. Immediate post-riot gains here may be illusory, as the long-term economic prospects of the Negro may really depend instead on their potential political power; and under corporate dominance, that power is likely to be diminished.

The general public also has a record of associating complexity unveiled with effort unhinged. This can often result in a concession of defeat just when the basis for more effective action could be established, with resources being redirected toward something else which seems "simple enough" to "do something about."

Education reporter Fred Hechinger puts the challenge here squarely, using as he does the provocative case of the interconnectedness revealed by the "golden boy" of all of the OEO antipoverty efforts:

> It is doubtful whether either the national mood or the educational expertise is prepared to face the fact at which Head Start merely hinted: that masses of children of the slums may have to be "taken over" by a new education process—not the old-line schools—at two or three years of age, and that they may have to stay in the program from early morning to evening, and perhaps through the night. Unless education can assume the responsibility of home and community for otherwise lost children, the pilot projects, crash programs, and integration gimmicks will be aspirin against an epidemic of the plague (*New York Times,* July 30, 1967, p. E7).

Unsettled by the implications for sweeping change and reform of certain antipoverty relationships, the nation runs the risk of experiencing a critical "failure of nerve." Like declining publicity and the loss of conventional "certainties," increasing revelation of complexity could lead us to turn away from opportunity and settle instead for the meager expedient of seemingly restored security.

CONSTRUCTIVELY-CRITICAL SKEPTICISM

Few interested parties have very much use for White House boasts that two million Americans passed over the poverty income line in 1966. Few take seriously the OEO claim that it "reached" four million Americans in 1966. And fewer still value, on the local level, the commonplace practice whereby the Philadelphia Community Anti-Poverty Board boasts of the several thousand "contacts" recorded annually by each of its twelve neighborhood centers. It is increasingly recognized that the White House statement not only leaves unclear who left poverty and why but also provides no assurance that these near-poor individuals will not soon again be poor. The OEO claim, for example, fails to stipulate just what kind of contact was made, with what effect, and with what related adjustment of the agency's relevant effort. The local level boast of numerous contacts is weak for much the same reasons, and is therefore increasingly sloughed off by a public grown defensive against the widespread effort of agencies to substitute public relations for meaningful information.

Congress, particularly in its investigating subcommittees, has compelled new rigor and honesty in the establishment of project criteria, the measurement of progress, and the evaluation of results. In hearings held in numerous cities, county seats, and even Indian reservation headquarters, skeptical and sometimes hostile members of Congress have closely cross-examined the claims of progress made by local antipoverty professionals and partisans, even as they have provided time for local critics of the antipoverty campaign. However limited the readership of the ultimate produce of such hearings (volumes which encompass thousands of pages) and however small the sum of the actual audiences exposed to them, the local press and television outlets generally cover the hometown hearing with considerable concern.

Certain members of Congress, Senator W. F. Mondale of Minnesota, for one, go even further in urging the creation of a three-man Council of Social Advisors to the President. Much like the Council of Economic Advisors, the proposed CSA could influence government agencies to coordinate research and evaluation efforts, organize data more effectively, and develop law-guiding "social indicators." "Should we have known that Newark was going to explode?" the Senator asks. He goes on to recommend that the CSA issue a yearly Social Report of an evaluative nature which would serve as the focal point of a "searching annual public debate about the condition of the social life of America" (Mondale, 1967).

In a similar fashion both academicians and welfare careerists have sharpened their assessments of both projects and studies. Typical in this regard is the model scrutiny demonstrated by Lowell Gallaway in his exacting review of the Ornati-Twentieth

Century Fund study, *Poverty Amid Affluence* (Gallaway, 1967, pp. 541-42). Equally useful is the critical essay-review of several poverty anthologies that Bernard Beck prepared recently for *Social Problems* (1967, pp. 101-14). The evaluations of OEO programs being completed by Greenleigh Associates, along with those underway at a number of major colleges and universities (Wisconsin, Brandeis, Chicago, and elsewhere), have already contributed to new sophistication in evaluating evaluations. The Brandeis Project, for example, suggests the application of four useful standards to any claim of success by a community action agency:

1. Has it established itself and developed procedures for maintaining itself over time?
2. Has it been effective in improving and coordinating existing services?
3. Has it planned, developed, and delivered a variety of specific services to individuals?
4. Has it insured the participation of the poor in the planning and implementation of its programs? (Brandeis University Project, 1967).

Refinement of this sort, long overdue, makes increasingly foolish the propensity to judge crassly complex undertakings as either entirely successful or utter failures.

It is uncertain what the impact will be of heightened public, professional, and Congressional skepticism regarding claims of anti-poverty success in the late 1960s. On the one hand, such skepticism may compel more old-fashioned honesty and humility in agency-community relations, strengthen the case for new efforts to raise the comprehension quotient of the public where the reality of a social problem is concerned, and reduce both academic and journalistic stereotyping of "the poor" and unconstructive scoffing at inevitable imperfections in both analyses and programs. On the other hand, the nation has a history of running to extremes with its skepticism, so that what begins as a healthy motive force often degenerates into a bleak and corrosive cynicism. There is already a cacophony rising from self-proclaimed analysts on the Left and Right who declare that no claim of success, however qualified, in the antipoverty effort has any "real" merit. The befuddled man-in-the-street, concerned as he is with perceived threats to his own status and rights (job and home ownership) implied by promises of moving 32 million Americans up into the stable working-class, may actually prefer allegations of no gain. The critics of big government and the proponents of decentralization and self-determination, whether on the Left or Right, have their own opportunistic reasons to fan and feed this public cynicism when antipoverty success claims are made by OEO.

All of this could further reinforce the negative tendencies noted in preceding sections, discourage provision of adequate support for the OEO effort, make possible momentary resort to primitive asides (such as antiriot legislation), and provide rationalizations for alterations of dubious merit (such as the proposed disestablishment of an over-agency like OEO). From the growth-potential of close scrutiny of claims of success, the nation may move backward to a pathologic pessimism concerning any and every sort of gain in antipoverty matters, even as some prematurely despair where the challenge of a related urban renaissance is concerned.

New Advances Against Old Problems

When, in the early 1900s, the reformers of the period moved to purify the water and milk supply of tenant dwellers, the social gains accrued far beyond the target boundaries of the ghettos of new immigrants. Extensive recent efforts of similar character have sought to create a tourist industry in Appalachia, to subsidize producer cooperatives of former share-croppers, to lure new light assembly industries into Southern rural communities or Northern urban ghettos, and to salvage draft rejectees previously underutilized and underdeveloped. Such efforts have the possibility of breaking the local "cake of custom" in a far-reaching and constructive way, providing as they do new roles, new sources of status and esteem, and new action and attitude options for all, not just for the poor.

As exciting as the foregoing advances may be, all of them are nevertheless conventional in their fundamental endorsement of the national commonplace. Tourism, agricultural coordination, industry employ, and army eligibility are clearly gains where their local presence or absence spells the difference between area or individual poverty or non-poverty. But an entire region revitalized by highway, motel, and park-and-lake development is not in the least advanced beyond current American standards and taste. Such a region has been helped only to join the mainstream of American society, no more, if surely no less.

What is far more exciting about some of the new agency approaches to the old problems associated with poverty is the promise therein of elevating, rather than only endorsing, certain mainstream conventions of American society. Classroom advances which had their genesis in programs for the disadvantaged and which have been adopted by suburban middle-class schools come immediately to mind. Representative here is the personality enriching innovation reported by a Miami suburban school:

> At the beginning of each day, teachers in the program hold a "verbal sharing experience." As children describe personal experiences, a volunteer stenographer or aide takes the story down in shorthand. She types the stories in large print and makes duplicate copies. The children make books of their favorite stories and these become the basic texts for home reading and class recitation. The teachers had found that commercial texts reduced reading to "abstract exercises and impersonal markings . . . " (Braddock, 1967, p. 4).

A Harvard education specialist predicts that such advances, including the use of para-professional teacher aides, early identification of learning difficulties, the absence of grades and competitive pressures, and the elimination of the artificial breakdown of in-school and out-of-school learning, already form the "vanguard of reform in the education of *all* children and teachers" (*Ibid.*, p. 3).

Coming even closer to home, antipoverty insights hold out special promise where critical intergenerational relations and intrapersonal development patterns are concerned. Typical in this regard is the two-year-old, $250,000 study of the children of 150 poor mothers now underway at the University of Florida. Although the study will seek support to follow the poverty-bound children another ten years through elementary school, it has already produced novel insights into mother-child relations that could reward (and help change) the entire society. For example, the study directors early rejected the convention that naively holds mothers inherently capable of playing constructively with their own children. Instead, they have experimentally developed a program whereby the low-income mothers stimulate the development of their children through a prescribed sequence of talk and innovative infant games.

Invaluable is the gain in self-esteem made possible where a mother feels herself newly important and useful both as part of an educational team and as strategic in the systematic growth of her infant:

> A mother puts her 8-month-old child on the floor beside her, and starts to hand the baby a favorite toy. But she puts the toy down and partly covers it with paper. The baby removes the paper to get the toy, and does so a second time. Through this sequence the child becomes aware of the permanence of objects. Similar games provide the baby with other insights and skills *(Ibid.)*.

Across the nation in Head Start, Get-Set, and Head Start Follow-Through programs, mothers of poor youngsters are working with child development specialists to move beyond certain current American modes of child-rearing and explore the frontiers of personal growth. The steps being taken are generally as small, simple, and cautious as the example above makes plain. But the potential is enormous for social innovation with regard for poor–non-poor distinctions.

Various professions, of course, engage the public in a two-way flow, profiting themselves from the inherent promise in antipoverty efforts of gains that elevate, rather than only endorse the commonplace. "Advocacy planning," for example, is a new approach recently grown popular among certain younger members of the planning profession. The old-style city hall planner took one field trip to the "blighted" area and then worked from statistics and abstract principles. Public hearings were held on his plans only after large sums had already been invested in them. The new approach would have the planner move into the community and work with his neighbors' ideas of what *they* want. He would not only prepare and offer their plans, but he would advocate them as well. The insights gained into the realities of urban life, the particulars of life-style preferences, and the promise of grass-roots participation in life-shaping community decisions should enormously enrich the planning profession—one which has previously had "remarkably little bearing or impact on the enormous, untidy, tragic human problems of an explosive and changing society" (*New York Times*, October 16, 1967).

As the previous illustrations indicate, the teaching profession is an outstanding beneficiary of antipoverty insights that soar above the poverty question. Instructors in the dynamic Philadelphia school system, to cite another instance, are encouraged to buttress their capacity for ghetto classroom work by enrolling themselves in demanding evening courses in group dynamics, sensitivity training, meditation and yoga, body awareness, and other forms of contemporary challenge. Underlying the modernity of this unique advancement program is the heady conclusion that a teacher who is not striving to better understand himself and his times is failing to meet an integral part of the challenge—and responsibility—of being a teacher. Impressionistic data thus far available suggest that ghetto parents who come in direct contact with the staff are all profiting from this vital advance in professional in-service development.

There is reason to hope that many more insights relevant to improving "the mainstream" will be gained from the antipoverty effort. For example, the controversy that now racks the entire Head Start effort, or the question of how to combine cognitive "readiness" with personality enhancement. A wide range of experimental local responses to this challenge is making possible numerous new lessons relevant to child development regardless of social class. Bronfenbrenner writes in this connection:

> The cure for the society as a whole is the same as that for its sickest segment. Head Start, Follow Through, and Parent and Child Centers are all needed by the middle class as much as by the economically deprived. Again, contrary to popular impression, the principal purpose of these programs is not remedial education but the giving to both children and their families of a sense of dignity, purpose, and meaningful activity (1967, p. 66).

Similar involvement with supraclass life prescriptions characterizes the Job Corps, certain VISTA projects, many college tutorial programs, and many special college programs for culturally handicapped matriculants. In every case the project decision-makers are facing the question: Just what kind of *formerly* poor person or persons do we want to help shape? And in every case the subjects themselves are helping to determine the final design and impact of the project, even as the entire effort compels *all* involved to re-examine their own life models.

What will be the impact in the late 1960s of these implications of poverty programs for reform of American institutions in general? Positive reactions could provide the missing extra ingredient necessary to ward off stagnation, routinization, and orthodoxy in the antipoverty effort. But this potential for far-reaching reform may earn only a counterreaction. Already the charge has been made that at least one important Job Corps Center has taken the possibly regressive step of adopting a paramilitary model of life as its socializing vehicle. Similarly, in a choice among containment, cooperation, and codetermination there is reason to fear that the last of these policies—the only one with the potential of helping Americans grow beyond contemporary socio-political conventions— is the policy least honored by the nation's 1,000-odd community action boards (Shostak, 1968). Moreover, the compromise which got the shockingly belated passage of the antipoverty legislation through Congress in December, 1967, will establish city hall and county courthouse politicians in strong, possibly controlling, roles in every CAP agency in the country. The war on poverty has reached the point today in America where it can offer lessons of relevance to all; but since this is far more than many have ever bargained for, the prospects of lesson-taking remain unclear at best, and somewhat bleak.

ANTIPOVERTY SHORTCOMINGS

In assaying the most important of the various shortcomings that mar the national antipoverty effort, it is important to keep in mind certain caveats entered earlier in this chapter: many of the intended beneficiaries need more time to evidence the full impact on themselves of the antipoverty effort; few good evaluations of program components are now available; much remains in flux, turmoil still characterizing the uneasy OEO scene; and, over all, the national antipoverty effort is basically in its infancy. To be sure, the nation has employed an income-supplementation program since the New Deal, but it is only in the last four years that a concerted national effort has been undertaken to replace supplementation through the dole with human capital development programs geared to private labor market demands.

With all of this, three serious shortcomings nevertheless warrant critical attention, and, hopefully, the correction that such attention can sometimes impel. First, new agencies struggling with the old problems intrinsic to poverty have gained the spotlight but not the support appropriate to a national antipoverty effort. Second, the newly developed non-certainty and humility has not led to more systematic planning and implementation of reforms. And, third, the new agencies have failed to keep conspicuous the promise both of national contribution and of national change. These disappointments are briefly discussed below, a final comment in each case attempting to trace the possible course of the shortcoming through the late 1960s.

UNDERSUPPORT OF ANTIPOVERTY EFFORTS

Gunnar Myrdal was quoted earlier to the effect that possibly trillions of dollars and at least one generation might be required to adequately meet the poverty challenge. Leaving aside the time-table of expectations, the contention remains that an annual OEO expenditure of $2 billion is grossly inadequate to the task. In calendar 1965, the new federal outlays against poverty amounted only to about $90 a year per poor person in the country. Since Congress cut the $2.5 billion originally proposed for OEO for fiscal 1967, and again for fiscal 1968, actual expenditures will rise by less than another $9 annually per poor person (Levitan, 1966, p. 43). Even when the extensive supplementation of HEW, HUD, Labor, and other federal projects is taken into account, the fact remains that millions of poor Americans have still not even been "touched," much less engaged and assisted in helping themselves out of poverty.

Despite the advocacy appearance of the OEO Director before Congressional committees considering overdue increases in Social Security, AFDC, minimum wage, and similar income supplementation schemes, little has been won. Benefits continue at levels so low as to leave most recipients below or hazardously close to the poverty line. OEO has also declined to advocate any one of several detailed plans available for direct-income payment or so-called guaranteed annual incomes. Sociologist Bernard Beck comments here:

> . . . it is reassuring that someone had the idea that one way to help people who do not have sufficient resources to live at a prescribed level is to give them those resources. If you go by most of the proposed remedies for poverty, you would never know that these were

people whose basic problem was not having enough money (1967, p. 14).

Indeed, OEO has barely been able to preserve a minimum level of Congressional funding, let alone secure additional aid for the poor. (OEO, increasingly a "poor cousin" in the family of welfare agencies, suffered as much symbolically as it did materially from the recent move [October, 1967] in the House to exclude OEO personnel from a proposed pay raise for federal workers.)

In addition to its inability to win adequate support for the poor, OEO has been conspicuously deficient in "mind-power." Much fanfare surrounded the dramatic Johnson endorsement of the Kennedy-initiated national antipoverty effort. Imaginative, creative assaults on the problems of deprivation were promised. Yet several years later, one finds mainly "business as usual." Long-delayed plans—on the shelf for years in agencies too busy, too understaffed, and too poor to implement them—are just now getting a trial of sorts. Although some are helping in certain valuable ways, as indicated in preceding sections, the overall impression is one of mental stodginess rather than initiative (Levitan, 1966, pp. 43-60; Nicolan, 1967, pp. 77-90).

Beyond separating adolescents from a disadvantageous milieu through Job Corps enrollment, no experiments have considered alterations in the conventional family form. Nor have they explored alterations in conventional labor market forms other than introducing some job factoring and urging the employ of para-professionals. Similarly, no experiments have pressed the case for "participatory democracy" beyond insuring the one-third inclusion of the poor on Community Action Program boards. OEO, in fact, has failed to maintain the general public's curiosity about innovation, an attitude which may be essential if it is even to retain the few innovative features of its own basically conventional programs.

While OEO has solicited research on, and has implemented time-honored projects involving, indigenous homemakers (para-professional home-visiting teachers), it has not publicly considered the rewards possible in children's villages, heavily-subsidized foster care programs, long stay summer camps for poor children, subsidized job-oriented mobility and "new home" support for those over 16, and other such variations on the theme of family form options. Similarly, it has solicited research on and activated projects in the token participation of the poor on policy-shaping boards but it has not effectively pressed for basic political reforms. Hayden offers a provocative plan in this matter:

> Could we visualize, for example, a day when local poverty programs become a framework in which political action and conflict is carried on at the neighborhood level? Instead of area boards being satellites as they are in Newark, what if area boards controlled the poverty program in their communities? Each neighborhood would have its own anti-poverty council, with its own budget, organized and controlled by whoever has effective power in the neighborhood. Representatives from the area boards would dominate the governing body of the entire city's program. All programs —community action, Headstart, training, etc., would be subject to the approval of the city-wide organization and the administrative control of the local board (1966, p. 20).

In these and other substantive areas OEO has sought only more of the same, and even this without very much success. Even the limited participation of the poor facilitated by the original OEO legislation seems likely to be diminished by the latest Congressional action.

Looking ahead, there seems little reason to expect any change in the direction of additional support or more dynamic programming. Pressures today from a conservative and skeptical public seem generally to favor only small increments in "safe" programs. As a *New York Times* editorial warns, "anti-poverty is becoming, like foreign aid, one of those programs which Congress exhaustively studies and studies and wrangles about, out of all proportion to the amount of money being appropriated" (October 10, 1967, p. 46). If OEO, for even a brief period, had the type of claim on the public imagination that might make possible some unique changes (such as the nationalization of exploitative ghetto business or ghetto-serving utilities), the opportunity seems now to have passed.

UNDERCOORDINATION AND WEAK LEADERSHIP

From the very start of the antipoverty program, the relevant federal, state, regional, and municipal agencies jockeyed to defend and advance their interests—almost regardless of the cost involved to the national effort. Sniping among and between OEO and HEW, HUD, Labor, the Appalachian Re-Development Commission, the

Council of Mayors, and others has effectively compromised much of the promise inherent in the creation of such an over-agency and coordinating mechanism as OEO (Graham, 1966, pp. 251-71; Marris and Rein, 1967; Glazer, 1966, pp. 21, 64, 69-73). In consequence, what was intended as a concerted, interrelated, sequential, and systematic national effort has fallen far short of the mark. With half-year or longer Congressional delays in funding OEO projects and the interjection of Congress into the establishment of program priorities, the national effort resembles nothing so much as a cross between a crazy-quilt and a strait-jacket.

Matters are not very much better at the local level. One example, that of a critical educational innovation, should suffice to underline the point of inadequate planning, coordination, and follow-up inside the antipoverty efforts. More Effective Schools (M.E.S.) is an antipoverty compensatory education scheme vigorously championed by the urban-oriented American Federation of Teachers. Employed in 21 New York City schools, M.E.S. holds class size to 22 pupils, provides four teachers for every three classes, and offers intensive educational, remedial, and counseling services. A thoroughgoing independent evaluation credits the program with achieving "an atmosphere and climate characterized by enthusiasm, interest, and hope . . . . " but concludes, overall, that the 21 schools were not as effective as they might be and were certainly far less effective than their enthusiastic supporters would have others believe.

In explaining the seemingly strange failure of near-utopian school conditions to produce better educational results, the evaluation cites two hazards. First, the M.E.S. personnel were inadequately prepared, with teachers handling small classes just as they would large ones. Thus, an opportunity to tailor teaching to the individual child was wasted. Second, the M.E.S. personnel undertook little "in the way of innovation or restructuring in the basic teaching process" (*New York Times*, October 10, 1967, p. 32).

Otherwise put, even the costly securement of structural reforms (the small classes and like measures cost about $500,000 more per school annually) can often prove inadequate. Progress is required on all fronts simultaneously, or, as in the case of the M.E.S. programs soon to go into effect in Baltimore, Detroit, New Orleans, San Diego, and elsewhere, advances are necessary in substantive as well as in structural matters. And, above all, progress is demanded in matters of systematic planning and thoroughgoing leadership, both qualities conspicuous by their all too-common absence from antipoverty endeavors.

Looking ahead, there seems little likelihood that either OEO or local-level authorities will soon lead or plan change in a more effective way. OEO has been effectively neutralized by its political critics, and it continues to run a serious risk of disestablishment. Local-level authorities are caught "up-tight" in their own network of bureaupathologic practices, and regularly press antipoverty programs into a Procrustean bed of inherited lore and practice. Ironically, OEO projects with IBM and other like companies have begun to make available for the first time the simulation models and information-retrieval systems necessary if the national poverty agency is ever to assume a high-level leadership and coordination role (Levitan and Siegel, 1966, pp. 229-88). Similarly, research and evaluation skills (such as those unsparingly, but constructively applied to M.E.S.) are becoming increasingly available to local-level authorities. OEO, however, appears without the Congressional or public confidence necessary for the assumption of new strength. Nor does hope seem justified that local-level authorities will soon feel secure enough to respond to criticism in any but a defensive, and often offensive, way.

PUNITIVE AND MYOPIC FEATURES

In the last analysis, the OEO model of the poor appears a harsh and unrelenting one. Job Corps enrollees must take a sugar-coated loyalty oath, even as OEO employees themselves must sign the pledge. Representatives of the poor on CAP boards must rationalize to their constituents why Congress or the OEO has set this or that national priority in program options, the very kind of decision the CAP board members were originally led to think they would make. All antipoverty workers, poor or otherwise, are obliged to swear fidelity to OEO and its goals, even as members of so-called militant protest groups are barred from antipoverty work. All of this, of course, comes on top of classic welfare legislation with its punitive scale of allowances, its red-tape encumbrances, and its many petty indignities (Shostak, 1965, pp. 128-33). The restrictions enacted by Congress on aid to dependent children ("ADC mothers") is the latest example.

The harsh and unrelenting character of the OEO model goes beyond even this to involve two related failures: the development of the political power of the poor has been sidetracked, and the most fundamental of national linkages have been soft-pedaled, or even denied. It is increasingly apparent that the poor remain politically underrepresented. The record of the invective and scorn annually directed at OEO by bitter Congressional critics is related to the widespread notion that the poor are not yet a meaningful political constituency. In Syracuse, New York City, Chicago, Jackson, and elsewhere OEO has retreated from support of political militants leading efforts to organize the full ballot-box and lobbying potential of the poor. This compromise failed to win the hoped for support of the local political establishment but helped destroy incipient political organization of the poor. One result of this strategy failure was Representative Edith Green's 1967 amendment to the Anti-Poverty Act barring political registration efforts by antipoverty workers.

OEO's capitulation, and more recent emasculation, in this critical matter comes at the poorest possible time. Bayard Rustin, in analyzing the lessons of the long hot summer of 1967, suggests that solutions will be increasingly political:

> ... the previous period was a period of protest; the present period must be one of politics. . . . If Southern Negroes were to register, organize themselves, and enter into alliance with the white liberal and labor movements of the region . . . the effect of such a strategy would be the creation of a two-party South and a consequent erosion of one of the main sources of conservative strength in the United States . . . [this] would make an enormous contribution to solving the problems of the black ghettoes of the North and, indeed, of the entire society (1967, p. 45).

OEO's contribution in this particular matter was not insignificant: CAP boards were the first such community organizations in the South to include Negroes. The agency, however, suffered here as elsewhere from a vital "failure of nerve." Auspicious beginnings quickly petered out, and OEO's ambivalence about augmenting the political power of the poor was soon painfully clear to the poor.

Related is a second major disappointment with the OEO. In the view of some observers, the agency has shied away from the kind of "macro" planning and issue-raising that dares to look critically at the *non*-poor and their favorite social institutions. Schrag explains this where education is concerned:

> The point of the suburban schools is not racial; it may not even be snobbery; it is to give the children of the local residents a head start on everyone else. They exist to keep things unequal. . . . The great question about the Great Society is whether we really wanted it in the first place (1967, p. 63).

Beck extends the point in a useful way:

> We hear the details of store front employment agencies for the poor, but no concrete proposals for effecting necessary changes among the secure. . . . the major problems for poverty warriors are not negotiating with various sectors of the respectable society. . . . there is an irresponsibility in speaking as though poverty were only a problem of the poor, requiring programs only dealing with the poor (1967, p. 112).

OEO has failed thus far to contain or convert those "sectors of the respectable society" that oppose raises in the minimum wage laws, implementation of the doctrine of "government as employer of last resort," or adoption of a plan to put a floor under income.

Since OEO has been unable to surmount its own myopic view of the poverty problem, it has not adequately influenced others to appreciate the need for detailed plans of far-reaching social reform. Criteria for measuring its success reduce themselves to such indices as the number of Job Corps placements or Head Start graduates. At the same time, the agency has moved farther and farther away from such alternatives as collaboration in the specific planning of a nationwide job training, upgrading, and mobility program, or in the specific planning of system-wide educational reforms.

Looking ahead, there seems little reason to expect any change on the part of OEO in the direction of new boldness or depth. On the contrary, the harassment of the organization produces an increasingly conservative reply from it. Congressional and public pressure is likely to seek more refinement in goal-setting, such as a concern that Job Corps graduates obtain not simply jobs but promising ones in which they can develop. However, little pressure of this type can be anticipated for any bold OEO espousal of wide- and deep-reaching challenges to the *status quo*.

SUMMING UP

On balance, America appears to have earned only what it is presently equal to: a severely limited war on poverty, significant as much for its concerted defense of the non-poor and their favorite institutions as for its undersupported "band-aide" attempt to help the deprived. To its credit, the national antipoverty effort has succeeded in publicizing the plight of the disadvantaged, discouraging premature certainty in reform prescriptions, and encouraging recognition of certain system linkages. It has also tutored the nation in a healthy skepticism where claims of program success are involved, even as it has made possible some insights and social advances beneficial to poor and non-poor alike.

On the deficit side the attempt by new agencies to meet the old problems associated with poverty disappoints in three ways: resources secured have never been equal to the task; leadership has never been equal to the challenge; and the appreciation of the case for innovative changes inimical to certain established interests has never been equal to the opposition. Even more discouraging is both the uncertainty of continuance that haunts the precious gains made thus far, and the greater likelihood of persistence that seems to characterize the contemporary deficiencies.

In all, the national antipoverty effort is discouraging as much for what it might have been and for what it seems to be evolving into as for any contemporary shortcomings of a practical character. Some change has been secured, but hardly enough chances have been taken. Some progress has been made, but hardly enough pioneering or planning has been dared. Poverty persists, as well it must, in a rich nation still too spiritually poor and too politically immature to do much about it.

References

BECK, BERNARD. "Bedbugs, Stench, Dampness, and Immortality: A Review Essay on Recent Literature About Poverty," *Social Problems* (Summer, 1967), pp. 101-14.

BRADDOCK, CLAYTON. "The Poor Bring Forth a Boon," *Southern Education Report* (October, 1967).

BRAGER, GEORGE A., and FRANCIS P. PURCELL. *Community Action Against Poverty: Readings from the Mobilization Experience* (New Haven: College and University Press, 1967).

BRANDEIS UNIVERSITY PROJECT. "Study of Community Representation in Community Action Programs," Florence Heller Graduate School for Advanced Studies in Social Welfare, unpublished mimeo, dated July 5, 1967.

BRONFENBRENNER, URIE. "The Split-Level American Family," *Saturday Review* (October 7, 1967).

GALLAWAY, LOWELL E. Review of Oscar Ornati's *Poverty Amid Affluence, Journal of Human Resources* (Fall, 1967), pp. 541-42.

GLAZER, NATHAN. "To Produce a Creative Disorder: The Grand Design of the Poverty Program," *New York Times Magazine* (February 27, 1966).

GRAHAM, ELINOR. "Poverty and the Legislative Process," in Ben B. Seligman (ed.), *Poverty as a Public Issue* (New York: Free Press, 1966), pp. 251-71.

HANSEN, MORRIS H. and GENEVIEVE W. CARTER. "Assessing Effectiveness of Methods for Meeting Social and Economic Problems," in L. H. Goodman, *Economic Progress and Social Welfare* (New York: Columbia University Press, 1966).

HAYDEN, TOM. *A View of the Poverty Program: "When It's Dry You Can't Crack It With a Pick"* (New York: New York University Press, 1966).

JEFFERS, CAMILLE. *Living Poor: A Participant Observer Study of Choices and Priorities* (Ann Arbor: Ann Arbor Publishers, 1967).

KEYSERLING, LEON. *The Freedom Budget* (New York: A. Philip Randolph Foundation, 1967).

LEVITAN, SAR A. "Is This Poverty War Different," in Sar A. Levitan, and Irving H. Siegel (eds.), *Dimensions of Manpower Policy: Programs and Research* (Baltimore: The Johns Hopkins Press, 1966).

———. *Antipoverty Work and Training Efforts: Goals and Reality* (Washington, D.C.: National Manpower Policy Task Force, 1967).

MARRIS, PETER and MARTIN REIN. *Dilemmas of Social Reform: Poverty and Community Action in the United States* (New York: Atherton Press, 1967).

MILLER, S. M. "The American Lower Classes: A Typological Approach," in Arthur B. Shostak, and William Gomberg (eds.), *New Perspectives on Poverty* (Englewood Cliffs, N.J.: Prentice-Hall, 1965), pp. 22-39.

MONDALE, W. F. "Social Indicators as a Method for Forecasting and Planning," (1967 speech available in mimeo from World Future Society, Washington, D.C.).

MYRDAL, GUNNAR. "The War on Poverty," in Arthur B. Shostak and William Gomberg (eds.), *New Perspectives on Poverty* (Englewood Cliffs, N.J.: Prentice-Hall, 1965), pp. 121-27.

NICOLAN, GEORGE. "The War on Poverty," in Robert Theobald (ed.), *Dialogue on Poverty* (New York: Bobbs-Merrill, 1967), pp. 77-90.

RIESSMAN, FRANK and ARTHUR PEARL. *New Careers for the Poor* (New York: Free Press, 1965).

RUSTIN, BAYARD. "The Lessons of the Long Hot Summer," *Commentary* (October, 1967).

SENATE COMMITTEE ON LABOR AND PUBLIC WELFARE. *Examination of the War on Poverty*, Part 1 (Washington, D.C.: U.S. Government Printing Office, 1967).

SCHLESINGER, BENJAMIN. *Poverty in Canada and the United States: Overview and Annotated Bibliography* (Toronto: University of Toronto Press, 1967).

SCHRAG, PETER. "Autopsy for a Great Society," *Saturday Review* (June 17, 1967).

SHOSTAK, ARTHUR B. "Education Reforms and Poverty," in Arthur B. Shostak and William Gomberg (eds.), *New Perspectives on Poverty* (Englewood Cliffs, N.J.: Prentice-Hall, 1965), pp. 62-68.

——. "An Overview of Current Administration Policy," in Arthur B. Shostak and William Gomberg (eds.), *New Perspectives on Poverty* (Englewood Cliffs, N.J.: Prentice-Hall, 1965), pp. 128-33.

——. "Poverty: The Possibilities for Action," in John Kosa *et al.* (eds.), *Poverty and Illness* (Boston: Houghton-Mifflin, 1968, forthcoming).

Part II

URBAN INSTITUTIONS AND THE DEPRIVED

Introduction

MANY features of a social system affect the poor and the disadvantaged in ways quite different than they do the rest of the society. The treatment of the poor by various public and private agencies, the manner in which their legal and political rights are safeguarded, the respect accorded them as human beings, and the opportunities for self betterment available to them consistently fall below the levels enjoyed by other segments of the community. As recent events have so vividly demonstrated, unenlightened and even distorted views toward the poor and their problems are common not only among the general citizen body but also among public officials and institutional caretakers. The social costs of these attitudes and of the policies which flow from them are mounting at an alarming rate.

The situation with respect to the deprived and the differential treatment they receive from the social system is, however, far from static. Under the impact of the civil rights movement, the growing unrest and sporadic outbreaks of violence in the city ghettos, and the national "war on poverty," urban institutions—both public and private—have responded with different mixes of innovation and resistance. Peculiarly, two institutions with relatively little promise as vehicles for needed changes of major dimensions have received the largest amount of attention, at least in journalistic terms: the schools and the social welfare agencies. The schools have held the spotlight partly because of the strategic focus on them in the civil rights struggle against segregation, partly because of the revelation of the massive failure of slum schools to fulfill their obligations to teach the young, partly because of our nation's somewhat illusory conviction that it cares a great deal about children and its equally illusory belief in "education" as a magical cure-all. But there is little evidence that better education would have had more than a vernier effect on the employment-income statistics for many of the poor—the aged, the disabled, the Negro, the resident in economically depressed areas, the mother of many children in a fatherless home, the mentally and physically disabled. Moreover, with educational reform focusing on the younger child, even the limited gains for the poor directly derivable from improved education could not be felt for many years. There are many good reasons for improving education in this country, especially in the urban slums, but a major reduction of poverty in the foreseeable future is not one of them.

Welfare agencies have received much attention for equally misleading reasons: they are officially supposed to "serve the needy" and they have been the targets of dramatic charges of what almost amounts to malfeasance in fulfillment of that duty. At the same time they are used (even by themselves in their own propaganda) to portray a sentiment of charitable concern for the poor with which most Americans disguise the reality of endemic and epidemic social neglect. In point of fact, public welfare agencies operate mainly as dispensaries for inadequate assistance funds. They are generally committed to minimizing the tax load for welfare by doing as *little* as possible to discover qualified people not receiving even the paltry legal benefits and as *much* as possible to spot any reasons for dropping some from the recipient list. Private agencies have similarly demonstrated their incapacity in the face of poverty. Although some, like the Salvation Army and Goodwill Industries, specialize in serving impoverished people, the community chest-united fund welfare organizations taken together devote the larger part of their limited resources to serving those who already fare relatively well.

In any case, welfare agencies and social workers, with very rare exceptions, simply are not prepared to help the poor do anything about securing decent housing, full employment, adequate medical and legal services, and cash incomes with which to achieve a minimally acceptable level of living. In short, the welfare institutions, like the schools, are of little relevance to the task of doing something substantial about poverty in the near future. The impact of the schools at most is indirect, long-range, and uncertain; that of the public and private welfare sector is direct but at best minimally ameliorative and, in psychological consequences, possibly deleterious.

In this volume, therefore, with its focus on the immediacy of the problems of poverty, no chapters are devoted to either education or welfare, although various authors take note of these areas when relevant. Instead, we follow contemporary impoverished American adults as they seek shelter in our cities (Chapter 4), as they come into contact with the market place (Chapter 5), and as they encounter the professions of medicine and law (Chapters 6 and 7). We also ask about the response of the clergy to the life of the urban poor (Chapter 8), since they are in a unique position to raise challenges to the operational values of other societal institutions.

In Chapter 4, Alvin Schorr reviews the problem of housing the urban poor. This, as he shows, is a problem of many dimensions and one that has important consequences for a society and its social order. Inadequate or substandard housing in the urban setting helps both to cause and to maintain poverty. It can contribute to the impoverishment of individuals and families by the attitudes and behavior into which it leads them. It interferes with the development of satisfactory family relations in the home, drives the youngsters into the street, engenders a state of dissatisfaction and cynicism, and leads to pessimism and passivity. The quality of shelter enjoyed by members of a community is, moreover, an important indicator of status: good housing is a mark of affluence, poor housing a badge of deprivation.

Schorr traces the relationship between housing and poverty across a broad range of issues, including those generated by residential segregation, community services, and relocation of displaced families. He examines the efforts put forth in the United States to shelter the poor and analyzes the efficacy of the tools, particularly public assistance and public housing, used for this purpose. In the process, he draws certain comparisons with the housing programs and related practices in Great Britain to show how different traditions and policies in the two countries often lead to differential results. One distinction, for example, stands out here: the extensive and direct involvement of the British national government in the housing field tends to encourage population mixture in the cities rather than the spatial separation of residents by economic level found in the United States.

Schorr makes no attempt to minimize the enormity of the housing problem faced even by nations as affluent and highly developed as the United States. He argues persuasively, however, that existing efforts in this country are insufficient, if not misdirected. As he expresses it, "A simple fact lies at the core of our failure to provide adequate housing for poor people; we have never spent for their housing a sum of money that begins to offset the disadvantage they suffer." Actually, he notes, we have been subsidizing housing for middle and higher income families by much greater sums through income tax deductions allowed for mortgage interest payments. A policy such as this, whatever its merits may be, does little to close the housing gap between those at the bottom and those in the middle. This latter point is particularly important since housing, like poverty in general, is a relative matter. The measure of its adequacy is less biological than cultural; its standard is what most people in the particular society enjoy. Unfortunately, this is the very point that the majority in the population are unable or unwilling to comprehend.

Except for those who are "institutionalized," most of the poor in the United States obtain the bulk of their goods and services in the same manner as other citizens: by purchase in a private enterprise market place. In Chapter 5, Milton Huber examines the place of the poor as consumers in this market and the problems they encounter. Huber writes from the perspective of one who has had wide experience in counseling and working with the disadvantaged in the field of consumer affairs. As he notes, the impoverished areas of American cities are the locus of retail operations and practices that differ radically from those found in the rest of the community—differences which almost always make the situation of the deprived more difficult. He illustrates by vivid examples how the middle class phenomenon of a "credit economy" actually works to the disadvantage of the poor. Denied entrance to the mainstream of the buy-now-pay-later world as "bad risks," they become a captive market for a breed of "easy credit" merchants spawned by the installment buying explosion "to take care of cashless people."

Like poor housing, the practices of the ghetto market contribute to both the causes and maintenance of poverty. Involvement with the "easy credit" merchant often drops the marginal family more deeply and perhaps irretrievably into poverty. For "a price," they receive shoddy merchandise with high mark-ups and they are subjected to unconscionable rates of interest and abusive collection practices. The result, in Huber's words, "is the entrapment of the

poor in a web of financial and legal procedures which they feel
powerless to combat, from which they cannot extricate themselves,
and against which some will eventually strike out in violence."

Huber notes that most programs offered to remedy these conditions—such as teaching the poor how to budget or to buy more
wisely—are designed to help the disadvantaged cope with the
existing system. But these measures are of little help to those for
whom the ghetto merchant is the only available source of credit.
What is needed, Huber contends, is less emphasis on changing the
individual and more on changing the system—a theme frequently
emphasized throughout this volume. Alternative choices to the
"easy credit" merchant must be provided the poor. These include
modifications in the credit policies of major retailers, greater accessibility to credit unions, and the establishment of buying clubs.
Whatever the direction taken, it is important to bear in mind that
the credit world is as important to the poor as it is to individuals
and families of higher incomes. Immersed in an acquisitive and
pecuniary society, those in the poverty category exhibit the same
needs and wants as others in the community. We could hardly
expect otherwise.

In Chapter 6, Drs. Roemer and Kisch focus their attention on
another aspect of the service world as it relates to the poor, that
of health and medical care. As morbidity and mortality statistics
show, the incidence of illness among the economically disadvantaged is greater than among the rest of the society. Both preventive
and general health services available to the poor are inadequate
and often dispensed under circumstances inconvenient or even
demeaning to the recipient. The authors of Chapter 6 discuss and
evaluate the nature and impact of these services; examine the relationship between deprivation and health; and point up the need
for new policies and new approaches to the total health problem.

Drs. Roemer and Kisch emphasize the fact that the unsatisfactory state of medical services to the poor is a reflection of general
deficiencies in medical practice as it has been institutionalized in
the United States. These deficiencies fall most heavily on the economically deprived, but they also affect the total population. The
solution, as they suggest, is not to bring the poor into the presently
inadequate medical mainstream, but to bring about the changes
that will broaden and strengthen the overall health and medical
system of the nation. In other words, the establishment of the kind

of system that would effectively serve the health needs of middle and upper income families would require institutional changes of such nature that the poor, on the principle of "equal protection of the laws," could not be excluded from the same benefits. What is implied here is a distinction between medicine as a profit-making enterprise with its legal entitlement to private gain and medicine as a profession with its multiple responsibilities to mankind.

Another area of concern to the poor, that of the law and legal services, is the subject of Chapter 7. Considerable evidence exists to show that the law falls more heavily upon the deprived than on other segments of the population. In welfare matters it often tolerates unwarranted invasions of privacy and dignity. It permits the occupants of public housing projects to be evicted as "undesirable" after a cursory hearing in which no discernible standard is applied and in which the tenants have no representation by counsel. It provides the creditor with numerous rights and remedies but sets up few safeguards to protect the debtor. The poor, moreover, in their disputes with governmental authorities, merchants, and other citizens are less able than the non-poor to obtain adequate legal services and are less likely to be treated equitably by the police, courts, and related public and private agencies. It is against this background that Edgar S. Cahn and Jean Camper Cahn examine some of the issues and problems involved in the provision of legal services to the poor and the protection of their rights.

The Cahns show how the neighborhood program of legal services, a by-product of the "war on poverty," has helped to generate new legal doctrines for the poor in such fields as welfare, consumer frauds, and public housing. They also show how the legal system is being increasingly utilized by the poor in instances where the political system offers them no hope of redress. Encouraging as these developments are, the "rights explosion" and the "grievance explosion" are challenging the capacity of the legal system as it is presently constituted. This means, the Cahns maintain, that we must think beyond neighborhood law forms to the establishment of more justice-dispensing institutions (e.g., juvenile courts run by juveniles); to altering the makeup of the legal profession so as to include an array of new law-related career positions; to new modes of resolving disputes through such means as arbitration, mediation, and conciliation; and to the development of new doctrines of rights. The legal profession has the key role to play in this process. The critical question is whether it, any more so than the companion professions of religion and medicine, can temper its traditionalism sufficiently to move with dispatch in this direction.

From medicine and law, Chapter 8 turns to a third traditional institution of society, the church. Organized religion has been undergoing intensive self-examination in recent years as to its role and relevancy in an urbanizing world. The institutionalized church, as distinguished from some of its individual prelates and ministers, has traditionally avoided social issues and shown little readiness to become intimately involved with the deprived other than as soul-saver and almsgiver. The force of modern events, however, has increasingly challenged the traditionalism of the churches just as it has that of other societal institutions. The nature of this challenge is made clear by George Webber of Union Theological Seminary who discusses the current relationship between the church and the urban disadvantaged and indicates the direction in which this relationship is evolving.

Webber pulls no punches. For him, the mission of the modern church is to "share in transforming, redirecting, and making manifest the possibilities for all men in a technological society which makes poverty both unnecessary and a denial of God's concern for the good of all men." Organized religion, like law and medicine, exists to serve mankind; and like these two professions, also, it has a special responsibility to see that the disadvantaged receive the assistance they need to lead a full and humane life. This responsibility can be discharged only if the churches recognize such matters as housing, discrimination, and the "war on poverty" as part and parcel of their active concern. Unfortunately, the religious institutions of America, as a result of their historical non-involvement in social issues, are woefully unprepared for this role. Confronted with the reality of poverty and other community problems, they find themselves captives of a middle class culture, caught with the ideological baggage of the past and unable to respond meaningfully and effectively to the needs of the modern urban world.

Webber holds few illusions that an institution as tradition-bound as the church has the capacity for the radical changes such a response requires. So long as the churches maintain their overarching preoccupation with institutional success (and therefore conflict-avoidance) instead of focusing on "obedience to God's claim to participate in public responsibility and involvement at the points of human need," whatever steps are taken will likely be hesitant and feeble. Yet, Webber sees some encouraging signs in the theological reformulations which view the church primarily as a servant body in the world, a development that is causing organized religion to reconsider its present attitudes and practices.

All of these chapters in the end convey the same basic message: the problem of urban poverty is not soluble in the context of our present institutional system. The price for eliminating extreme deprivation, a price Americans are unwilling to pay, is not just billions of dollars but changes in entrenched institutional patterns with which the comfortable and the well-to-do are generally satisfied and in which many of them have vested interests.

—W. B. Jr. and H. J. S.

4

Housing the Poor

ALVIN L. SCHORR

☐ THE URBAN POOR OF THE UNITED STATES tend to be least troubling when moving about in the public places of the community. Few display the easily discernible symptoms of severe malnutrition. Many cannot be distinguished by dress from their less deprived working class peers except, perhaps, upon very close examination. It is when they return home that all question of their impoverishment disappears. Even the most casual observer will recognize that the doorway to the poor American opens into a daily struggle with deprivation, whether it is framed by the wood of a slum tenement or the enameled steel of a public housing project. Whatever he may have seen himself to be on the outside, before the door of his home he faces poverty.

The relationship between housing and poverty ranges across a spectrum of discontinuous issues, from architecture to psychology, from political science to esoteric realms of high finance. This chapter will touch upon a number of these disparate realms, highlighting them briefly in order to trace out the mesh that binds poor people to poor housing. After a broad statement of the problem, we shall ask whether there is a causal relationship between poverty and poor housing. From there we shall turn to the question of

AUTHOR'S NOTE: *This chapter was abstracted from a number of the author's articles, which have appeared elsewhere, in order to provide a general survey and analysis of the housing problem as related to the poor. Recent data are not reported and no effort has been made to take account of such innovations as the model cities and rent subsidies programs. No material has been used, however, if the passage of three or four years has made its point inaccurate. Works that have been drawn upon, by permission, are* Slums and Social Insecurity *(London: Thomas Nelson and Sons, 1964);* "National Community and Housing Policy," The Social Service Review, *XXXIX (December, 1965); and* "The Role of Housing Policies in Reducing Poverty," *International Seminar on Poverty, University of Essex, April, 1966.*

residential separation and its causes and effects, and then move on to the issues involved in providing community services, including the problem of providing suitable relocation. Other aspects will follow in turn: the tools which help the poor to get housed—public assistance and public housing—and the ways in which the poor alter their own living patterns so they can obtain housing. In the process, we shall draw certain comparisons between the United States and Great Britain to show how different policies can indeed be followed by different effects. Finally, we shall look at the overall record in the United States and, in particular, the effort really put forth to house the poor.

AN OVERVIEW OF THE PROBLEM

A number of issues in the field of housing are not susceptible of decision on the basis of evidence alone. They must be decided on the basis of which of several divergent or conflicting goals are seen as primary. If we approach the field of housing with social security in mind, one question stands out: what should housing policy be if wiping out poverty is given primacy? It is by no means settled that wiping out poverty is—everywhere and for everyone—primary, but stating the goal lends clarity to our conclusions.

In a certain hypothetical sense, poverty may be regarded as simple absence of money. Until the implications of automation began to dawn on us we tended to feel that simple poverty would decline with rising wealth and need not concern us. The poverty that has deeply puzzled and troubled us is compounded of such circumstances as poor education; no father or husband, or an inadequate one; relatives who, so far from being able to help, require assistance; a black skin or an offensive accent; poor health; housing that drives one into the streets; a keen perception of barriers to personal opportunity that produces defiance or despair. Simple and compound poverty prove curiously difficult to distinguish from each other. Lack of money may produce poor health as easily as the other way around—the process is mainly a matter of time. Consequently, it is important to think of poverty as a syndrome of mutually reinforcing handicaps. We may attack poverty by elimination of any handicap and make some advance. And advance in one area contributes to advance in others. Similarly, lag in one area holds back progress in others.

It is apparent that there will be difficulties in defining the housing policies that will help to prevent poverty. Policies that contribute to family stability or to an optimistic view of the world also contribute to the prevention of poverty. Therefore, we shall be interested in housing policies that may seem only distantly related to financial adequacy. On the other hand, we shall find that the requirements for housing policies are complex and pervasive. If we are to serve this goal of wiping out poverty, we shall be subordinating other goals.

Some generalizations about the effect of poor housing on behavior are likely to apply in one country as in another. The characteristics of housing that determine people's ability to improve their circumstances should be broadly relevant in any developed country. Broadly relevant, however, does not mean precisely applicable. There are differences between Great Britain and the United States in conditions that are accepted—the absence of central heating, for example—because they are fairly common. In short, our reaction to what we have is colored by what we expect.

What are these elements of housing that affect poor people? Three are largely physical in nature. City space (how generously it is provided and how it is used) affects everyone and affects the poor in special ways. Congestion interferes with their lives. Space that is planned, as it is tending to be planned, for openness and for challenge overlooks their needs. The neighborhood is a second significant physical element. It should provide at least three conditions that are important to self-improvement: it should allow families to choose whom they see and how frequently; it should foster a feeling of local identity; and at least some neighborhoods must be financially and ethnically diverse. The final important physical element is the design and adequacy of the house or apartment itself.

Of the variety of elements of housing that are largely social in nature, some relate to the process of change in which poor people are so often and unwillingly caught up. Though attempts are being made, neighborhood or city plans do not yet adequately integrate social and physical planning. The problem of coordination arises, at least in part, because the housing needs of poor people tend to get left out of planning. When, in the end, their neglect interferes with the execution of a plan, the problem is likely to be defined as one of professional collaboration. Examination shows the problem to be rather one of basic social objective. In the process of change, further, poor people who must move require adequate housing to which to move. They require that the process of change be staged to encourage initiative rather than to produce despair. The evidence does not show that our practice as yet widely reflects such principles.

Other elements of housing that seriously affect poor people are social in nature but not quite so directly connected with change. First, a range of community services must be available to assist them. The methods by which we provide health, welfare, and education services are not precisely suited to the need. Efforts are being made to adjust these and to develop new types of service. Second, segregation by color assists in a variety of ways to keep people poor. Finally, housing codes are probably of greater moment to poor families than the policies under which new standards of housing are set, but they are widely ineffective. Business incentives operate to produce substandard housing, creating pressures against which enforcement proves powerless. A variety of remedies is available, but only those that touch the problem of business incentives are likely to have lasting effect.

THE CAUSAL WEB

Poor housing helps both to cause and to maintain poverty. One would think this conclusion simple and self evident. Yet few people in the United States, whether experts or laymen, subscribe to it. Many of our experts, in fact, believe that poor housing has little effect on poverty. Why do they come to this conclusion?

In the first place, tracing a causal connection from housing to poverty presents an enormously difficult research task. When, infrequently, the task is attempted, conclusions may be frustrated by the singular perversity of human beings. An example of this was the Baltimore study that planned to use a control group in slum housing for comparison with an experimental group that was offered improved housing. In the period of the study, most of the control group moved from one apartment to another on their own initiative —carelessly improving *their* housing in the process (Wilner *et al.*,

1962). And there is the famous depression study that showed that improved housing led to a higher *death rate* (Ferguson and Pettigrew, 1954). It seems that families that moved to better housing found themselves paying higher rents when, catastrophically, everyone's income went down, and so they had less for food and medical care. Inconclusive studies such as these should leave all conclusions still open, but somehow we tend to read "no evidence" as meaning there is no causal connection.

Second, the task of demonstrating a connection lies at the door of social scientists who are, on the whole, uninterested in the problem. In recent decades, they have been more concerned with institutions and interpersonal relationships; these are the stuff of which theories are built. Many social scientists take as an aspersion on their profession the notion that bricks and mortar shape the people they enclose, and therefore the suggestion is not treated seriously. Third, in the United States at any rate, we are in some deep sense antisensual. (This is not to deny that our literature runs heavily to Anglo-Saxon words and our advertising to French pictures. The two observations are not inconsistent.) We see ourselves as manipulators of our physical world rather than at one with it. The idea that poor people are a product of their housing might lead to the thought that we are all products of our environment, and we like to think we are not shaped by anything—least of all by the inanimate world.

Finally, it is widely believed that we have already conducted a grand trial of the relation of housing and poverty, and the verdict is negative—that is, no effect of improved housing on poverty. The public housing program in the United States was begun with high hopes that cleanliness and decent housing would lead to godliness or, anyway, a somewhat more middle-class way of life. It has widely failed to do so; in fact, many housing projects have deteriorated rapidly under the battering of uneducated, disorganized tenants. This grand trial had at least two major defects. First, no one in fact knows the long-term effect of public housing on the families that lived in it. Children may well have grown up freer of disease and better educated than they otherwise would have; we do not know. We only know that the housing itself deteriorated. More important, improved housing was not the only change being tested. Quite often, in addition to improved housing the new situation meant segregation, unfamiliar surroundings and requirements, inadequate schools and police service, and rigid and un-friendly management. It is difficult to sum up in a sentence all the factors that have operated against public housing in the United States; I mean only to indicate that improved housing was not the sole variable in this experiment.

The experiment with public housing has unquestionably had an impact on public opinion. There was once considerable enthusiasm for improving opportunities for poor people through better hous-ing. Now it is fashionable to be cynical about improved housing. Not only ordinary citizens but also sophisticated researchers turn to this history for their view of the relationship of housing and poverty. So quick and dubious a conclusion must betray, more than anything else, a terrible impatience with poor people. If we do not get quick results, we tend to believe that we shall not get any results.

About four years ago, after reviewing all the relevant studies then available about the effect of poor housing on its residents, I came to the conclusion that the following effects may spring from such housing:

> . . . a perception of one's self that leads to pessimism and passivity, stress to which the individual cannot adapt, poor health, and a state of dissatisfaction; pleasure in company but not in solitude, cyni-cism about people and organizations, a high degree of sexual stim-ulation without legitimate outlet, and difficulty in household man-agement and child rearing; and relationships that tend to spread out into the neighborhood rather than deeply into the family (Schorr, 1964, pp. 20-21).

The sequence from poor housing to poor health is readily visualized; but some of the links from cause to effect are more ob-scure. For example, people see themselves in their surroundings and tend to value themselves accordingly. The Princess sleeps on 20 down featherbeds. A pea bothers her through all the featherbeds not because she has royal blood but because she is accustomed to a soft bed and to being indignant about small discomforts. By contrast, if—as surveys have done—you ask a man in a miserable hovel what he needs, he will not speak of an inside toilet, or run-ning water, or electricity. He *may* ask for a new coal stove. Usu-ally, it does not occur to one who is accustomed to very little that he is worth more or can have more. Of late we have papered over this simple observation with pretentious labels, such as "poorly motivated" and "culture of poverty."

Or, consider the matter of child rearing. It is common in the slum areas of our cities to observe how extensively family life is conducted out of doors. Depending on which slum one is considering, the pattern may be attributed to habit brought along from another country or a rural region of one's own country. On the other hand, in a historical Chicago settlement house a daily program for teen-agers kept them away from home every night until curfew at 10 P.M. precisely because these 13- and 14-year-olds live in flats so small that there is no room for them. After they have eaten, sitting on a couch and stools around the table, they drift outside. They will be either at the settlement house or on the streets, but not at home.

A study of poor families in the District of Columbia makes this point quite simply: "In these so-called apartments, there is no place for children . . . The close quarters, the drabness, the lack of something to do drives these children into the street" (R. Lewis, 1964). Elsewhere, the same group of researchers observe that these children escape parental control at quite early ages, some as early as the age of six (H. Lewis, 1961). One can hardly overlook the connection between escaping control and the fact that the children cannot reasonably be kept inside.

Children are, of course, sometimes inside the house. They come home to sleep, for example. A study of working class Negroes at the close of World War II found that the majority slept less than five hours a night. The reason: there simply was not enough space for beds (Davis, 1946). Lack of sleep affects children's growth and health. Implications spring to mind, too, about sexual relations between adults and sexual stimulation of children. Nor can one expect the most patient and permissive child-rearing from a mother who has slept only three or four hours.

When children play inside the house they are, of course, underfoot. I have seen no studies of the tension that arises between parents and children in very crowded quarters, perhaps because researchers are in this case unwilling to dwell upon the obvious. However, a study of families with two children living in apartments with two bedrooms revealed such tension because of inadequate room for the activities of parents and children (Blood, 1952). When children are older, interchange with their parents more directly concerns their careers. A study in Sheffield, England looked into the question of how this interchange with their parents takes place. In crowded housing, even an attempt at parental advice leads to frustration. A youngster is having dinner, somebody is watching television, and a neighbor stops to visit the mother. Guidance takes place in passing and is conducted in shouts. "You can't hang about this summer, boy! Not like last year!" And the boy's irritated answer is swallowed up in the neighbor's story or in a television gun battle (Carter, 1963).

These are two illustrations of the chain from cause to effect— that is, from poor housing to poor self-valuation or to a particular kind of child-rearing. A chain can be described, and in some measures demonstrated, for all the effects that are named in the summary quoted above. In turn, the effects that are ticked off lead to or help to maintain poverty. Poor health, pessimism and passivity, poor household management, and inability to handle stress readily lead to poverty. The child-rearing patterns I have described—the child out of the home and out of control at an early age, poor communication between parents and the children, overly strict demands alternating with no requirements at all—train a child for the poverty his parents have known. Attachment to a neighborhood rather than to one's family interferes with physical and social mobility, thus tending to maintain poverty. Obviously, any of these handicaps can be overcome and can, indeed, take its place in quite another pattern. I am not suggesting a mechanical link between conditions and behavior. Nevertheless, one who looks closely at the lives of poor men or poor families must be struck with the notion that poverty is not merely necessary but overdetermined.

The connections between housing and poverty have been viewed thus far in terms of primordial needs, but people's behavior also reflects the time and place in which they live. For example, it seems quite possible that inside space is less desirable, or even undesirable, when farm land or hunting range stretches all around. An expensive system of disposing of human wastes may be a needless luxury rather than a necessity. Again, poor housing tends to produce a pattern of attachment to one's group and neighborhood, as opposed to a pattern of intimate one-to-one relationships. Attachment to a group and to "turf" may operate against self-advancement in a society where one must be willing to change location in order to seize opportunities, but it may be functional on a farm, or ranch, or feudal holding. In other words, poor housing in the cities we know prepares people for poverty in the cities we know. If a similar causal connection existed in other historic periods or exists in essentially agrarian societies, the content of the connection is certainly different.

People's perception of their housing is, moreover, deeply colored by what they see when they lift their eyes to the television screen or over the rooftop across the street. A squatter's shack is not such a self-indictment in Caracas as in Paris. Conversely, slum dwellings that would be regarded as palatial in South America are not cherished by the residents of Harlem or Watts. We are well aware that the general perception of acceptable *minimum* standards of living bears a direct relationship to the perception of *average* living standards (Schorr, 1966). Therefore, it is hardly surprising that minimally acceptable housing is defined in relation to the average housing that is available. Within a century we have seen the rule of thumb for adequate space, in the United States and Britain, go from one-person-per-bed to one-person-per-room. Similarly, in both countries we have seen official standards for living space suddenly reduced when building materials were short, and raised when materials became available.

RESIDENTIAL SEGREGATION AND SOCIAL SERVICES

We have been a little too willing to assume a universal tendency to lock into the centers of our cities those who are poor, Negro, poorly educated, and inadequately housed. It now appears that this is an accurate profile only of our largest metropolitan areas and those in the Northeast. In many of the metropolitan areas of the South and the West, the classic picture is reversed: poverty and deprivation are characteristics of the suburbs. Thus, our cities do not provide consensus on preferred locations. There is consensus only that people must somehow be classified and separated; inside each town and county we are sorted out into neighborhoods of specified income, or specified color, or specified religion, or specified combinations of all these.

The forces that produce residential separation are familiar. The family cycle plays a role. People with children feel the pull of the suburbs; others may not be so charmed. Racial segregation plays a role, historically at least. A city council or housing authority can assist racial segregation without excess guilt by locating low-cost dwellings in renewal areas or yielding too readily to opposition in higher-cost areas. Local and state tax structures play a role that is often overlooked. Officials become adept at calculating the increase in property tax necessary to provide services to a housing development of specified size, income, and family composition. Eventually, they avoid tax increases by zoning actions to prevent developments that would make increases necessary. The Advisory Commission on Intergovernmental Relations has called this practice "fiscal zoning" (1965). Banks, builders, and real estate brokers, in pursuit of nothing more odious than a secure profit, combine to assure the pure poverty of one neighborhood and the pure wealth of another. Evidently, successful businessmen have misjudged the effect on real estate values when Negroes move into white neighborhoods. It is difficult to know whether they are just as wrong about the outcome if $12,000 houses take their places next to $20,000 houses.

We have constructed a tight myth that feeds from the forces just named and feeds back to strengthen them. The myth is simple: if someone with less money or any other characteristic both exotic and inferior moves next door, then one is not safe in his bed, one's children are not safe in school, and one's mortgage is endangered. The myth is wrapped around an irony, as myths so often are. We have created poor neighborhoods in all our cities, neighborhoods in which people are afraid to live. Not only the people outside are afraid; those who live in the neighborhoods are fearful. They are afraid of being assaulted, of being shamed, of being exploited—by one another and by functionaries of various sorts. From these neighborhoods springs the violence that makes us fearful of walking the streets of our own cities. We created this problem by the myth, and now the problem justifies the myth.

COMMUNITY SERVICES

Coupled with residential segregation, community services are closely related to the problem of housing the poor. In most city centers, these services are in crisis. Many of the agencies see the dimensions of the problem; few find themselves in a position to meet it squarely, with economy of effort and breadth of vision.

Unfortunately, the same trends that increase the problem diminish the services that are available. Physicians and dentists tend to follow their paying patients to the suburbs. Publicly supported schools in the core city tend to be underfinanced and are unable to secure sufficient competent personnel. Voluntary welfare agencies experience difficulty in raising funds. Their income may keep pace with cost of living but not with growing need, and extended waiting periods to receive service are common in certain kinds of agencies (mental health clinics, family service agencies). The solutions for diminished services—increased funds and special incentives for professional personnel—may be hard to achieve but are at least easy to state. The organization of services, on the other hand, poses more difficult problems to which there are as yet no agreed-upon solutions.

Fundamentally, the city has been changing more rapidly than the professions and agencies that cope with its problems. Welfare departments, counseling agencies, health departments, and even schools, have centralized their activities in the interests of efficiency and coordination, only to find that the poorest people do not regard "downtown" as accessible. Recognition of the difficulty produced an impulse to station staff members in neighborhoods or, at least, to have them spend more time out of their offices. However, other changes accompanied centralization of services—agencies have become more professional and more bureaucratic.

Staff time includes heavy elements of reporting, accountability, conferencing, and consultation. It is not only bodily presence in the neighborhood that is required of a health educator or social worker. *Continued* presence is required, that is, he needs to subordinate the calls on his time made by his central office (filling out reports, attending staff meetings). Not all the agencies that press staff members to spend time in the field have, in truth, faced the implication for their own processes. It is not unusual for a professional to spend as much time in auxiliary activities as in providing direct service. With professionalization also has come specialization, that is, greater efficiency in meeting special needs accompanied by an inability to meet varied needs. With professionalization, finally, has come social as well as physical distance from poor people. Professionals have recently been widely concerned that there is not genuine communication between the service worker and the low-income patient or client. It was suggested, for example, that the slum dweller tends "to use agencies and professional personnel *as if* they were legitimate extensions of the kinship unit" (Fried, 1960, p. 11). However, an attempt to be informal—to return gifts for help that has been received, for example—is precisely the sort of advance that professionals have been trained to resist.

The choices faced by community service agencies are far from simple. They are asked to decentralize, which appears to be less efficient and economical, even if additional funds are not in evidence. They are asked to be less specialized, though families are presenting more difficult problems. They are asked to coordinate, though this in itself requires staff time. All these demands were being met—experimentally, at any rate, by at least a few agencies—when the poverty program introduced a totally new element into the cities. Quite apart from operating as an antipoverty measure, community action has been directed precisely to reverse the trends that have been described. They have, in short, launched a direct assault on bureaucratization and professionalization, and have set out to establish neighborhood-based, client-centered services. Whether they can alter the long-run tendency remains to be seen.

New types of services are also developing in relation to the particular needs of families in urban renewal areas and deteriorated housing. Since finding housing for poor families and helping them to use it requires skills in counseling, home economics, and real estate, some services combine these specializations. Out of forces developed by the poverty program and because federal regulations now require it, citizens in renewal areas are being involved in the decisions that are made about their neighborhoods. Obviously, citizen participation rests, in some cases, on firm conviction about individual rights. But it is probably fair to say that management's attempt to involve affected citizens in making decisions is most often perfunctory. Organization of neighborhood residents by city blocks for their own recreational and rehabilitative purposes is, broadly speaking, a type of citizen participation. "Block organization" has, of course, been practiced by neighborhood workers for some time; it is receiving renewed attention as a device for neighborhood improvement. Although it is an attractive concept, its rehabilitative potential should not be overestimated. Some areas require replacement and others require at least code enforcement before people can be expected to hope that their own efforts are worthwhile.

RELOCATION

Relocation is a social service that is critical to housing programs. The failings of relocation efforts are a recurring reminder of the general inadequacies of the housing supply. These inadequacies might tend to be overlooked, but problems of relocation threaten the success of programs to which the cities and the nation are committed. "The kind of housing available for families forced from blighted neighborhoods," former Urban Renewal Commissioner William L. Slayton said, "will make or break the Nation's urban redevelopment program" (Slayton, 1962). When the Commissioner spoke in this fashion, 113,000 families had been displaced by urban renewal in the first 13 years of the program. The estimated number of families to be displaced in the next decade is one million. Moreover, highways and other public works projects are displacing many additional families.

Slum neighborhoods contain a range of families. Some, to be sure, readily move elsewhere; but others face a series of disabilities in terms of moving. Negroes are concentrated in deteriorated areas; consequently clearance is likely to displace them disproportionately —85 per cent of those displaced in one period in Cincinnati, 95 per cent in southwest Washington, 95 per cent in Philadelphia. Thus, finding housing for dislocatees means finding housing for Negroes. Other disabilities include low-income, broken families, large families, unschooled families, old people fearful of change, security that rests in the neighbors and the physical boundaries they know.

Additional aspects of the families' difficulty in accepting relocation remain to be noted. When one looks into the situation of those who most strongly resist moving, it frequently turns out that they own their homes or are paying a low rental. Is it reasonable for them to cling to ownership or low rent? Could they not do as well elsewhere? So far as ownership is concerned, many indeed do not have sufficient equity to purchase elsewhere. Someone has named the owner who cannot move "the white-haired old lady"— a phrase that can be uttered with reverence or with asperity. She is a problem to urban renewal, but only because urban renewal is a problem to her. As for rentals, it seems clear that they rise for the families who relocate. In a Baltimore study of families relocated in private housing, family income remained the same (a little over $2,500 a year) but median rent went from $42.50 to $52.69 a month, that is, from 20 per cent to 25 per cent of income (Baltimore Urban Renewal and Housing Agency, 1961). A review of relocation programs in 41 cities found that about 80 per cent of the families paid higher rent (Reynolds, 1961). It may be argued that families should be willing to pay more for adequate housing; the question is how much they can afford.

A number of studies indicate that people may resist relocation simply because they resist any compulsion. A similar intransigence diminishes the role that public housing might play in relocation. Only a relatively small proportion of families who are eligible for public housing eventually live in such developments. Some are ruled out by management despite their priority. A more important factor, however, appears to be family unwillingness to live in such housing. Local studies in Cincinnati, Philadelphia, and Washington found a majority of those eligible unwilling to apply. One element in this reluctance to live in public housing is a firm and frequently vocal desire to remain in the immediate neighborhood. Such a reaction was readily observed in southwest Washington, D.C., where families saw public housing going up while they were being asked to move to public housing farther away. In any case, it is a quarter-century since Chapin observed that nine out of ten slum residents in Minneapolis relocated within a radius of one mile. A recent study produces virtually the same percentage for families who relocate without help (Reynolds, 1961). Those who are assisted in moving to adequate housing move farther, however, since the immediate neighborhood of an urban renewal site is likely to be blighted.

The problems of relocating families suitably are thus related to housing supply and the location of suitable quarters; to state of education and deep-rooted attitudes about family and neighborhoods; to a resentment of outside interference that might, in other circumstances, be admired; and to all the difficulties that lack of money produces. Special kinds of services are called for under these circumstances. At their best, these include material aids: payment of moving costs, finder's fees for the location of suitable dwellings, and even redecoration of premises to induce owners to rent to displaced families. These services must also include effective arrangements for the location of vacant houses or apartments and for early, professional appraisal of their suitability. Finally, of course, they must provide for patient, realistic, continuous conversations between the displaced family and some helping person. The distinguishing characteristic of successful service programs is that they accept *primary* responsibility for families in designated renewal areas.

How do relocated families make out in general? Upon examination, this fairly simple question turns out to be difficult to answer. Figures regularly collected by the Urban Renewal Administration seem to indicate a very high proportion of families relocated in "locally certified standard housing." These figures, however, appear to be contradicted by a series of local studies (Schorr, 1963, pp. 65-67) and a study of 41 cities made by the School of Public Administration of the University of Southern California (Reynolds, 1961). Following a declaration by the Urban Renewal Administration that it would seek improvements in relocation, a Census survey indicated a better record (Housing and Home Finance Agency, 1965). This latter, however, was a single survey, and its findings have been disputed (Hartman, 1964). As yet, there is not much ground for comfort.

HOW THE POOR GET HOUSED

Among other ways, the poor pay for housing, first, in its poor quality. Whether as owners or renters, it is the poor families that tend to occupy the nation's substandard housing. It is true, of course, that some who are poor acquire standard housing, and not by accident. Analysis of the Chicago population shows that the poor in standard dwellings "typically" pay more rent than those in substandard dwellings (Duncan and Hauser, 1960). Even those who do not manage standard housing make sacrifices for the quality they do achieve.

One step that poor families take is to allocate a high percentage of their income to housing. In 1956 the great majority of families with incomes under $2,000 spent 30 per cent or more of their income on rent. On the other hand, of families with incomes between $8,000 and $10,000, the great majority spent less than 15 per cent.

Current *income* is not always a good indication of a family's financial circumstances. However, relating the amount a family *spends* to the cost of its housing gives a similar picture. In 1950, urban families with incomes under $1,000 a year spent 26 per cent of their total outlay for housing. Families from $1,000 to $2,000 devoted 22 per cent, from $2,000 to $3,000 18 per cent, and so on.

As a private matter, then, poor families get and apply money wherever they can. They use a variety of strategies, some because they come to hand and some in which there is a measure of choice. An aged widow will make different adjustments from a young father, for example. But few of the deliberate choices that are open seem attractive. Families can go without standard housing. They can borrow from food to pay housing. Few who are poor will have saved money; those who have, can use it. They can struggle to buy on installments or to borrow. They can try to buy instead of rent. Those who manage to bring this off may make out better in the end. Others will face additional difficulty because they are borrowing from other budget items and are leaving themselves less room to maneuver in the next emergency. They can extend the size of their households, trading crowdedness and tension for shelter and a measure of financial flexibility. Families can break up or at least give up children. Throughout, they can seek ways to improve their income. Some poor families try all of these. For some, but not for others, purchasing a house and sending additional members to work when possible are constructive steps. For the most part, however, the avenues that are open go around in a tight little circle, enmeshing families deeper and deeper in deprivation.

Public Housing

Public housing and public assistance, in different ways, address themselves directly to the housing needs of poor families. Public housing is not a single program, historically; it is a single vessel that has been used for diverse public purposes. In the 1930s, it was intended for families who voluntarily sought to improve their housing but could not afford private rentals. This group was not regarded as dependent. Indeed, some housing authorities limited the number of public assistance recipients they would accept, and others would not admit any. In the 1940s, the program was redirected to provide housing for war workers. Following the Housing Act of 1949, public housing was oriented again to poor families—with a difference. Partly because postwar amendments gave priority to families having the most urgent housing need, to the aged, and to those displaced by urban renewal, this third generation in public housing contains a high concentration of depressed, untutored, and dependent families.

The alteration in its population also leads to a financial problem for public housing. Tenants' income (in constant dollars) has remained level in the past decade, but each year the tenants' income falls farther below the median for the country. That is, in 1955 the median net income of families admitted to public housing was 46.5 per cent of the median income of all families in the United States. In 1961 it was less than 40 per cent. Consequently, the rents that may be collected from tenants do not rise as rapidly as maintenance costs. Between 1950 and 1958 monthly receipts from rent increased by 25 per cent (from $28.93 to $36.50 per unit per month) but expenditures increased by 52 per cent (from $21.32 to $32.50). Not unexpectedly, then, the federal contribution to local housing authorities has been moving steadily toward its permissible maximum. With the overall federal contribution reaching 87 per cent of the maximum in fiscal 1961, some local housing authorities found themselves still with substantial leeway and others with rather little.

Public housing is not available to more than a small proportion of the low-income families. Though the Housing Act of 1949 authorized 810,000 units, that authorization is as yet far from exhausted. There are in all something over half a million units—roughly 1 per cent of the housing supply. Even if public housing were limited to the lowest incomes, the supply would be wholly inadequate. Half a million units would house only 2 million of 32 million poor people. Since public housing reaches above the very lowest incomes, it houses even a smaller percentage of the poor than these figures indicate.

Since public housing must look to its receipts, it tends to exclude families with the lowest incomes who cannot pay minimum rents. (See Table 1.) The bulk of families entering public housing have

TABLE 1

Percentage of Low-Income 3- and 4-Person Families in Total Population Compared With 3- and 4-Person Families Moving Into Public Housing, 1960

Income for Year	Total Population	Families Moving Into Public Housing
	%	%
Under $1,500	5.8	11.7
$1,500 to $4,000	18.7	83.7

Sources: *Current Population Reports*, P-60, No. 37, Table 5, and *Families Moving Into Low-Rent Housing, Calendar Year 1960*, Housing and Home Finance Agency (Washington, D.C.: October, 1961), Table 6.

incomes under $4,000 a year. Among the families having less than this amount in the total population, roughly one in four has under $1,500 income; but of those who move into public housing, only one in eight has an income under $1,500. Families may also be excluded as undesirable. Although exclusions of this type would doubtless diminish if more public housing were available, such restrictions represent an effort to maintain a degree of acceptability among tenants. Yet, when careful study was made of 82 families excluded as undesirable in New York City, the decision was reversed for 33 of the families (Community Service Society of New York, 1958). Other reviews have produced even higher percentages of reversal. In addition to the limited capacity of the program, many presumably eligible families, as already noted, are not willing to live in public housing. Their reluctance must arise, to some degree, from the program's current difficulties, but it also represents a feeling about living in a managed—particularly in a government-managed—community. As early as 1946, a local study reported that only a third of those eligible were willing to live in public housing (Merton, 1948). In sum, public housing is limited by its quantity, its fixity upon the middle range of low incomes, and by management and tenant views of acceptability.

Public Assistance

Public assistance is the other major program that—in a different manner to be sure—serves to house poor people. It may not be surprising that assistance recipients, having the lowest incomes, are worse off than average. However, it is an impressive figure that four of ten aged recipients and three of ten recipient families with dependent children manage without basic facilities such as hot and cold running water. One can only guess at the proportions of their dwellings that are dilapidated and deteriorated. Measures of crowding suggest that assistance recipients are not improving their housing over time at the same rate as the general population. In the decade from 1950 to 1960, the median number of persons per room in the AFDC household declined from 1.0 to .94. In the same period, the national median declined from .75 to .59. That the median number of persons per room in the AFDC household is now .94 means that almost half the families are crowded. One in five of the AFDC families are, in fact, "critically overcrowded," living in households of 1.5 persons or more per room.

Special state and city studies provide a more intimate appraisal of the housing of public assistance recipients. Florida reviewed 13,000 cases of Aid to Families with Dependent Children to determine whether the homes were suitable for children. The study noted "excessively high rents for unspeakably inadequate slum homes (Florida Department of Public Welfare, 1960). A survey of recipient families with dependent children in the state of Maine found that four out of five did not have central heating (Romany-shyn, 1960). There are variations in the numbers and the degree of detachment with which other studies report, but the same basic situation has been documented for such cities as Chicago, Atlanta, Baltimore, and Philadelphia. Occasionally a study inquires specifically into the housing of recipients who would have special difficulty in finding housing—for example, families with unmarried mothers. The findings are predictable. Of over 3,000 illegitimate children who were receiving AFDC, Cleveland reported that 10 per cent were living in public housing. The remaining 90 per cent lived in housing that was "overcrowded and substandard . . . . The majority live in neighborhoods that are rooming house areas and slums" (Cuyahoga County Welfare Department, 1959).

One may wonder whether, after a period of time, caseworkers remain quite aware how poor is the housing that they are seeing. A national study of families receiving aid for dependent children evaluated housing by both objective standards and caseworker judgments. There was some evidence that the caseworker's judgment of what families are accustomed to or entitled to plays a role in his evaluation. Evidently, too, caseworkers come to evaluate the housing of one recipient by the adulterated standard of what other recipients have. Of the families in the national study who were "critically overcrowded" and lacked running water and any indoor bathroom facilities, only 70 per cent were judged to have inadequate housing. Apparently such housing was thought to be adequate for the other 30 per cent (Burgess and Price, 1963). Thus, the absence of objective standards affects the caseworker's perception of his client's surroundings and has a variety of further consequences. One is that he may not think of helping, even if he can. Another is that any special handicap a recipient has may become built into the system for him. That is, the caseworker sees him as living in poor housing because he is the kind of person who lives in poor housing. A third is that systematic information about recipient housing cannot readily be secured from case records.

Let us turn to the second course open to welfare departments— to arrange for recipients to enter public housing. The proportion of recipients living in public housing has mounted steadily; they are now about 25 per cent of tenant families (Housing and Home Finance Agency, 1961). The converse percentage is more difficult to estimate; roughly, perhaps 7 per cent of public assistance recipients live in public housing. Obviously the policies of each agency are important to the other.

Public housing and public assistance have much in common: their origin, in their present form, in the economic upheaval of the 1930s; their common purpose to assist the poor; and public scepticism about the methods and accomplishments of both. There are also differences between them. The same individual is a client of one agency and a tenant of the other. One may be more philosophical about a client's failure to pay rent than about a tenant's. The assistance agency sees itself as serving a range of family needs. The housing authority is more likely to see itself as providing a single commodity. The assistance agency is interested in finding housing for its clients, but the housing authority thinks of his effect on other tenants. Because of differences such as these a number of issues arise.

Perhaps the oldest, most prevalent issue concerns the rent that a public assistance recipient should pay. To pay according to his income, like those who do not receive aid, would be meaningless for a recipient. The assistance he receives for rent is based on the amount he pays; the rent almost has to be established first. Public assistance agencies may want to pay little; they have many uses for every dollar. On the other hand, public housing authorities face difficulty in meeting their costs and, therefore, want to be paid as much as possible. Other considerations also arise. In states that apply a maximum to assistance payments, higher rentals may mean that recipients have less money left for buying food and other necessary items. Administrators are also mindful that public assistance is, in part, local and state tax money. However, if a public housing authority has more income than its operating expenses and does not use all of the subsidy to which it is entitled, the saving is entirely federal money. Out of such considerations, a variety of agreements are negotiated between public housing and public assistance agencies. In general, localities are tending to establish a fixed rent for all assistance recipients, but a pattern for the level of the rent is not yet apparent.

The issues that exist between public housing and public assistance are predictable by-products of the convergence of two independent programs. The provision of more effective service by public assistance to its clients in public housing should assist in resolving these issues. But with or without issues, public housing is the one dependable resource to which public assistance may turn for acceptable housing for recipients. The help that it finds is limited chiefly because the quantity of public housing is limited.

The British Experience

When we turn to housing for the poor in Great Britain, we find both similarities and differences with the American experience. Without attempting an income definition of poverty in the present British context, we shall compare the housing outcome for those who have more and those who have less. The figure of £10 a week gross household income will often appear to be a significant dividing line (in 1961, 20 per cent of households in the United Kingdom had less than this amount per week).

In the United Kingdom, as in the United States, housing takes a larger percentage of the budgets of those with lower income than of those who are in better circumstances. The majority of households with incomes under £4 allocate over 30 per cent of their spending to rent, power, and heat. Those with incomes between £14 and £20 average 14 per cent. The pattern is familiar; we have counted its costs to the poor. Housing is paid for out of food and clothing. It is paid for in the precise terms that hinder self-improvement—by investing only in immediate needs, by borrowing, by sharing crowded quarters. When these strategies are not sufficient, housing may be paid for with the family's integrity. In recent years, at any given moment, the Children's Department of London County Council has been able to count a thousand "homeless" children in its care. At the other end of the age spectrum, poverty proves to be an important factor leading old people to seek admission to institutions.

Generally speaking, there are three ways to secure housing: purchase, renting from a local housing authority, and renting privately. Though the trend is not yet as far advanced as in the United States, by 1962, owners occupied 42 per cent of all English dwellings. It is not clear whether the change reflects a growing preference for owned housing or constriction of the rental market. Not only is virtually no housing being built for rental; upward of 80,000 rented dwellings a year are demolished or sold to their occupants (Donnison, 1962). In any case, the trend to ownership appears to benefit chiefly those who have, or have had, larger incomes.

Low-income families must, then, turn to rented housing—particularly to Council housing (public housing). Local authority building has provided the larger volume of new housing for rent. As rents are subsidized, there is more hope of getting decent value for comparatively little money. However, the notion that Council housing should benefit the "working classes" was dropped from the law in 1949, and since that time such housing has been intended for those in "housing need." Housing need is an abstract term not clearly related to poverty. It tends to be filled with meaning by shifting government priorities.

Slum clearance has become the first government priority, with much local authority housing allocated to displaced families. In London, in 1962, two-thirds of available housing went for this purpose. Smaller allocations are likely to be devoted to those who are ill, or homeless, or dependent. Various systems of priorities govern the remainder of available dwellings. Simple length of time on a waiting list may be controlling. On the other hand, there

may be complicated assessments of the size of the applicant family
and the housing they occupy. If housing need is defined in terms
that people can arrange, they are apt to arrange it. Therefore,
Councils may ignore such symptoms of need as crowding and
doubling up. Finally, as there has been a good deal of concern
about the aged, units are allocated for them. Many of these priority
circumstances would, of course, tend to arise in low-income families.

Table 2 suggests that the situation of low-income households
in relation to Council housing has improved over time. Although
the income brackets in the two separate years cannot be equated,
the table reflects the fact that incomes were higher in 1961. Nevertheless, it is clear that increased availability of local authority

TABLE 2

PERCENTAGE OF HOUSEHOLDS IN EACH INCOME BRACKET* LIVING IN LOCAL AUTHORITY
HOUSING IN 1953–1954 AND 1961 IN THE UNITED KINGDOM

Weekly Income	1953–1954	1961	Increase
	%	%	%
Under £6	15	24	9
£ 6–£10	24	27	3
£10–£14	26	38	12
£14–£20	22	31	9
Over £20	19	25	6

* Households in free and in furnished housing are excluded
from the calculations.

SOURCES: Calculations from the *Family Expenditure Surveys*,
1953-54 (H.M.S.O., 1957) and 1961, unpublished,
Ministry of Labour.

housing benefited every income group. Those with incomes under
£6 in 1961 represent a category whose income has declined in real
value and in comparison with the average; however, 9 per cent
more of them were in Council housing. National Assistance Board
data confirm this finding. The percentage of its aged recipients
who are tenants of local authorities has risen steadily from 23 per
cent in 1957 to 32 per cent in 1961. Since the government is specially concerned with housing the aged, recipients under pension
age have benefited less. Still, 40 per cent were tenants of local
authorities in 1957 and 44 per cent in 1961.

When one looks beneath general improvements over time, the
view is grimmer. Although the lowest income households benefit
from local authority housing, they do not benefit as much as those
with higher incomes. Approximately one-fourth of the households
with less than £10 a week gross income live in Council housing,

while about a third of the households between £10 and £20 reside in such housing. Household income figures, however, obscure two issues. First, they fail to relate income to size of family. Obviously, a single person with £6 a week is in better circumstances than a family of five with £10. Second, the aged tend to be concentrated in the lowest income groups. Conversely, younger and larger families tend to appear in more nearly average or higher income categories. If Council housing favors families with children, household income figures will suggest only that higher incomes are favored. It is, therefore, useful to isolate a particular family type to see how it fares at various income levels.

Two types of family will repay examination. First is the household of a man and woman, usually but not always a married couple. These families represent a range of circumstances, from newly married youngsters to an elderly brother and sister. Generalizations about this type of family also apply, as it happens, to households of a single adult living alone. Second is the household of a man, woman, and one child. In the respects we are considering, these households are roughly similar to those that include two or several children. Table 3 indicates, for each income bracket, the percentage of families living in Council housing and in other rented housing. One perceives that, so far as local authority housing is concerned, the lowest income man-and-woman families do not fare

TABLE 3

PERCENTAGE OF FAMILIES LIVING IN LOCAL AUTHORITY AND IN OTHER RENTED UNFURNISHED HOUSING, ACCORDING TO INCOME BRACKET AND FAMILY TYPE, THE UNITED KINGDOM, 1961*

Weekly Income	Man and Woman		Man, Woman, and One Child	
	Local Authority Dwellings	Other Unfurnished Dwellings	Local Authority Dwellings	Other Unfurnished Dwellings
	%	%	%	%
Under £6	21	28	⎫	⎫
£ 6–£10	27	42	⎬ 37	⎬ 38
£10–£14	26	32	⎭	⎭
£14–£20	21	30	28	28
£20–£25	9	32	27	26
Over £25	5	18	9	14

* Families in free and furnished dwellings are excluded from the calculations.

SOURCE: Calculations from the *Family Expenditure Survey*, 1961, unpublished, Ministry of Labour.

quite as well as those just above them. For example, 21 per cent of those with less than £6 income are in Council housing compared with 27 and 26 per cent in the next higher brackets. The second and fourth columns in the table, showing families in "other unfurnished" dwellings, are also instructive. Here we see the degree to which Council housing fails to compensate for the low-income family's inability to purchase. For all types of family, the rule is simple: the lower the income bracket, the more that rent privately.

If the system for tenanting local authority housing appears superficially to favor low-income families, hidden factors work against them. As the priority system gives weight to children, adults without children are less likely to be admitted; and many in this category are poor. As length of time on a waiting list is an important factor, families with children will face greater difficulty early than later. After they have waited, growing into their thirties, and seen their incomes rise, they may enter into the kingdom of Council housing. Once admitted, their incomes improve with the passing years. Finally, the poorest families cannot afford Council housing. Half the local authorities do not adjust rents to ability to pay; those that do, adjust them only up to a point.

What of the private rental market to which the lower income families must disproportionately turn? With the social justice which the poor must understand since they experience it so often, they get worse housing in the private rental market and pay as much. This category of rental housing suffers from the fact that virtually none has been built since the war; three-quarters of the stock was built before 1919. Of local authority housing, on the other hand, well over half has been built since World War II and another third between the wars. It is is not surprising then, that in 1958, 56 per cent of all households in privately rented unfurnished dwellings lacked a fixed bath and 53 per cent had no hot water supply.

As Council housing is subsidized, one would expect rents to be lower for equivalent value than in private housing. Rent control appears to have prevented such a differential, but it is now plainly appearing. In 1962, Council tenants were paying a median net rent of 2.2 times the gross value of their dwellings. Private tenants under rent control were paying exactly twice gross value, and decontrolled tenants 2.3 times gross value (Donnison, 1962). The median figure given for decontrolled tenants takes into account expensive as well as cheaper dwellings. It is the latter, valued low enough to have been rent-controlled but freed because of a change in tenancy, which are significant to poor families. In 1960, their net rent was 3.3 times rateable value in Greater London and 2.6 times rateable value in the rest of England and Wales. Thus, for poor families in particular, renting privately represents poor value at high cost.

SOME POLICY DISTINCTIONS

In enacting the Housing Act of 1949, the Congress of the United States made explicit its purpose to provide "a decent home and a suitable living environment for every American family." In introducing the Housing Bill of 1949 to the British Parliament, the Minister of Health paraphrased an earlier White Paper in emphasizing that the Government's first objective was to afford a "good, separate, modern home" for every family which desired to have one. Despite parallel phraseology, it is evident that the United States and British housing programs are markedly different. The divergences may themselves be instructive. Some patterns are rooted in the individual character of each country and would not be transferable. Yet, if one can understand them, distinctive consequences for the two countries are thrown into relief.

We shall start with the most popular distinction—that between a welfare state and a (more nearly) free enterprise state. In principle and in practice, Great Britain funnels a larger proportion of public investment through public channels and places more authority in central government. We shall then be able to understand a second, perhaps more significant difference: British cities tend less than American cities to separate their residents by economic level, like so many cultures of bacteria in a dish of agar.

In Great Britain the central mechanism of housing policy appears to be Council housing—whatever the party in power. The tradition of local authority housing under national legislation goes back unbroken to 1919. After 1951, when materials were still scarce and building licensed, local authorities were permitted to allocate not more than half the licenses to private builders. (The Labor government had advised local authorities to license private enterprise for only one dwelling in five.) In the decade from 1951 to 1960, local authorities built 1.5 million houses and private enterprise 1 million. After determined effort by a Conservative government, by 1958 private enterprise was building more houses annually than the government. From then on, however, the shortage of privately rented housing mounted to a first-class political issue. Under voter pressure and without any effective alternative in sight, Council housing may be expected to move ahead again.

Relatively greater British reliance on government is expressed in other ways. The new towns are administered by development corporations and the New Towns Commission, financed from the Exchequer and appointed by the government. Experimentation with home loans takes the form of local authority lending rather than encouragement of commercial lending. Incentives to private enterprise, when the government seeks them, appear to be neither so grand nor so imaginative as in the United States. The chief incentives are mainly negative, that is, the removal of rent controls and in various ways (controlling numbers, introducing rent rebate schemes) reducing the competition from Council housing. Improvement grants offer an affirmative subsidy to private owners which has so far not moved as rapidly as the government would wish. When even these are clearly lagging the remedy sought is governmental.

It is not only the use of government as a vehicle that distinguishes British from American housing policy, but also the authority lodged in the *central* government. One can discern at least two qualitative differences here. First, the authority of the central government in the United States in the field of housing is essentially negative, resting in the power to withhold grants-in-aid. The British government also exercises control by means of its subsidy program—one does not underestimate the effectiveness of such a device—but it has, besides, explicit authority in the field of housing. It controls standards of space and equipment in Council housing, approves local building regulations, and may withhold permission for local government borrowing. The central government also has broad powers to plan land use; its approval is required for local authority development plans. Second, in the United States, as distinguished from Great Britain, general oversight of municipal functioning lodges in the separate states. In their relations with municipalities, states do not necessarily further federal ends; they may at times appear to interfere with such ends.

These differences do not mean that British government is all-powerful or in every respect more powerful. For example, land values were fixed in 1947, permitting subsequent compulsory purchase at the 1947 value. Legislation in 1954 and 1959 established the right of the owner to receive current value on the private market, returning to a concept much closer to that current in the United States. Another example is provided by comparing the enforcement of codes governing existing housing. Despite the problems of enforcement in the United States, cities do undertake enforcement campaigns from time to time. Violations must be at least as common in Great Britain, but enforcement action appears to be even less frequent. Condemnation has been used, notably in Birmingham, but there has been little attempt to assess penalties when housing fails to meet specified standards. Yet, in spite of countertrends and conflicting evidence, the result of the two qualitative differences—explicit and undiffused central authority in Great Britain—is that government policies, more than those of the United States, are likely to be felt emphatically and across a broad range of housing issues.

Another distinction is also related to the point about central government authority. There is more concern in the United States about the increasing economic stratification of metropolitan populations, aided and abetted by local political fragmentation. A Briton, conscious of the forces which produce residential separation in his own country, tends to minimize such a difference. As comparative studies have not been made, it is difficult to say emphatically that a difference does exist, but an example may make the point. The industrial town of Dagenham is, in Great Britain, widely regarded as a one-class town, having the lowest "social class index" of 157 towns in its population class. Table 4 compares its population with

TABLE 4

Occupational Class of Men in Dagenham and England and Wales

Occupational Class	Dagenham 1958	England and Wales 1951
	%	%
Professional and Managerial (Social Classes I and II)	4	18
Clerical and Shopworkers (portion of Social Class III)	7	8
Skilled manual (remainder of Class III)	49	44
Semi-skilled manual (Class IV)	22	16
Unskilled manual (Class V)	18	14

Source: Willmott, 1963, pp. 14, 112.

the rest of the country. Three-quarters of the potential residents, so to speak, in Classes I and II have elected not to live in Dagenham. The 14 percentiles they fail to occupy are spread among the other three social classes. As the author of the study observes, the residents are "by no means all semi-skilled or unskilled workers." This epitome of a working-class district in England is a full-scale rainbow compared to the single-income, single-class, single-color neighborhoods that are found in the United States.

In whatever respects the two countries do in fact compare, the extensive direct involvement of the British government in housing tends to encourage population mixture. Building at the peripheries of their towns and, more recently, beyond their borders, local authorities have distributed their tenants across the countryside. The London County Council, for example, built over half its prewar dwellings outside the county of London, a process that accelerated after 1946. Council tenancy, moreover, is a fairly diversified cross-section of the population. New and expanded town policy, although aimed at decentralization, has consistently held diversification in its sights.

Partly because they bind houses to employment, new towns tend to select young families with moderate or middle incomes. Special provisions have, therefore, been made to correct the concentration of a single age and family type. Allocating housing to the aged and newly married inevitably introduces some low-income families to new towns, but these are few and the effort is not deliberate. At least, the new towns serve to relocate moderate- and middle-income families beyond the metropolitan suburbs where they would otherwise congregate.

Stratification, moreover, rests not alone on such choices as city center versus suburb. Developments separated by a single city street may house quite different income groups. In the United States, public housing developments suffer from being isolated within their own neighborhoods; their households fall within a narrow income range. The picture is different when one examines United Kingdom Council tenants by income bracket. In every category except the very highest, upward of a fifth of the households are found in Council housing. Thus, in a sector of the housing market representing almost a quarter of the dwellings in Great Britain, a sector conspicuously stratified in the United States, all incomes are substantially represented.

British government housing policy must be credited with operating to some extent counter to a process of stratification. In the United States, the process has been ignored by the national government until very recently and, if anything, actively assisted by local governments. Other factors, although accidental in terms of housing policy, also encourage mixed residential patterns in Great Britain. For one thing, the percentage of its costs which local government must meet out of its own taxation is lower than in the United States. In addition, the general grant which now constitutes about three-quarters of the central government subsidy is heavily weighted in favor of authorities with the largest number of dependent children. Therefore, municipalities are less likely to be concerned about the taxpaying ability of their residents. Furthermore, the British local authority which plans housing is generally different from and smaller than the education authority. (In both countries, education is the largest local government cost.) Hence, the decision to encourage residence and to educate are made and paid for as independent concerns. Finally, families move more readily and often in the United States than in England. Consequently, any wish to fit into a general sorting out of population finds faster expression.

In this chapter, we have dealt with housing supply from the viewpoint of poor people who fail to receive it. When we consider international comparisons, it is necessary also to point to a relative standard, reflecting a relationship between a nation's overall standard of living and its investment in housing. At some balance point, a country can be said to be investing an acceptable portion of its resources in housing. It is possible that housing needs exert more pressure on the world economy in this particular period than at any time in the past. Population increase and migration from rural areas to cities exert crushing pressure for housing in underdeveloped countries and readily perceptible pressure in the developed countries. It has in fact been argued that mankind is now worse housed than at any time in history.

In this circumstance most, if not all, of the nations of the world determine their national investment in housing under the severest pressure. On one hand, need seems to exceed anything that is being done. On the other, even wealthy nations tremble for their economies at the thought of doing everything that is proposed. It is, therefore, possible to have a country that seems poor not solely or chiefly because people are generally poor but because no one but the very rich can afford housing.

Argentina, for example, has a low unemployment rate and an average level of nutrition that must rank fairly high. Although in economic difficulty, Argentina is wealthy in natural resources. Yet, the housing *objective* in Argentina—I do not even speak of the achievement—is only 5 or 6 new units a year per 1,000 population. Because of an assortment of national policies, only the comparatively rich are able to secure housing. Hundreds of thousands of families who would not, by income or other tests, be regarded as poor, live in so-called "towns of misery." They are poor as a matter of national policy.

I have no idea what magic resides in the ratio, but in this period in history it appears that countries must produce roughly 10 housing units a year per 1,000 population. The United Nations has estimated that Africa, Asia, and Latin America need to produce 10 or 11 dwellings per 1,000 per year for the next decade (United Nations, 1965). The needs of underdeveloped areas of the world are well in excess of the needs of the wealthy Western countries. Still, the Western world faces similar, if less acute pressures, and balances them against other domestic needs. It is interesting that western and northern Europe, Canada, and the United States all produce housing at a rate ranging from 5 or 6 units per 1,000 population (Belgium, Austria, Great Britain) to 10 units per 1,000 (Sweden, Germany, Switzerland). Those that fall regularly at the bottom of this scale will find themselves housing-poor, whether they are wealthy or poor in all other ways.

Important to the question of a nation's relative investment in housing is the manner in which it allocates such investment to those who are poor and those who are not. A simple fact lies at the core of our failure to provide adequate housing for poor people: we have never spent for their housing a sum of money that begins to offset the disadvantage they suffer. Two pairs of numbers will establish the dimensions of this situation. In 1962, the U.S. government expended an estimated $820 million to subsidize housing for poor people. (The sum includes public housing, public assistance, and savings because of income tax deductions.) In the same year, the federal government spent an estimated $2.9 billion to subsidize housing for those with middle incomes or more. This sum includes only savings from income tax deductions. (The reasoning on which these estimates are based is found in Schorr, 1965, pp. 442-43.) The federal government, in other words, spent three and one-half times as much for those who were not poor as for those who were, or about as much per person for the poor and non-poor.

These are not conventional and some would say not impeccable statistics. Public assistance, public housing, and income tax are not often combined. There is no doubt, however, that they represent the consequential federal subsidies for housing. Only urban renewal is omitted since it is impossible to divide the federal subsidy between business and residential purposes and to determine what portion of the latter would be for poor people. Loan guaranties are also not included in these figures. Since they do not cost the government money, they are not regarded as subsidies. In any event, both omissions weight the estimates on the conservative side. Neither urban renewal nor mortgage guaranties conspicuously serve poor people. Finally, an income tax deduction is quite as effective a grant of money as a public assistance payment.

The pair of figures offered above does suffer, however, from dealing with the 145 million people who were not poor as if they benefited uniformly from federal subsidies. Closer examination shows that the subsidy is heaviest for the largest incomes. Therefore, a second, rather more refined pair of figures is helpful. In 1962, the federal government spent $820 million to subsidize housing for poor people—roughly 20 per cent of the population. For the uppermost 20 per cent of the population (with incomes over $9,000), the subsidy was $1.7 billion. Thus, a family in the uppermost fifth received about twice as much, on the average, as a poor family.

The composite picture is as follows: The income tax deduction is by far the government's largest direct subsidy for housing. It gives more to those who have more. The two programs that express the national conscience in housing—public assistance and public housing—together manage to raise poor families to per capita equality with the income tax subsidy that goes to all the rest. No more than that is accomplished. Indeed, the result is less, for the poorest fifth receive only half the subsidy that goes to the wealthiest fifth. This policy will not build a sense of community, nor will it build the housing that is needed.

How is it that we do no more for the poor than for the rich? How is it that we think—unless we are faced with the figures—that we are pouring enormous amounts of money into housing for the poor? To begin with, we are chronically afflicted with an impediment of vision called "slum clearance." Eighty years ago a British Royal Commission observed with dismay that poor people rarely benefited when land was cleared and model houses erected (Royal Commission for Inquiring into the Housing of the Working Classes, 1885). Somehow or other, the issue of providing enough dwellings for *all* people fades from the mind when attention is focused on rebuilding streets and neighborhoods. When the total supply remains inadequate, despite conspicuous new working-class districts, it is naturally the poorest who do without.

The situation in the United States is no better. From the Housing Act of 1937 until now, despite everything that experience might teach us, Americans have looked to slum clearance and its metamorphoses—urban renewal and community renewal—to provide housing for poor people. Urban renewal has a responsibility to the poor people whose lives it alters. Judging from the record, it has not taken this responsibility with sufficient seriousness. But the tools given to urban renewal are suited, if anything, to producing a city beautiful or a city prosperous. Although the tools are or must be made adequate to housing dislocated families, they can do little at best for all the others. Urban renewal deals with land which, even when subsidized, is expensive. Therefore it is likely to be regarded as an achievement when it provides housing for families with incomes of $5,000 or $6,000. Despite the current emphasis upon city-wide planning, great sums of money are funneled into one project area or another. This purview is too narrow and the process moves too slowly to produce dwellings by the hundreds of thousands.

Under urban renewal, from the Housing Act of 1949 to the end of 1963 about 100,000 new and rehabilitated units have been completed. Even if all of them had gone to poor people they would have made a very small contribution indeed to solving our national problem. Here the problem is encountered in a single statistic. One must keep in mind the magnitude of the building we see in relation to the magnitude of the problem. Preoccupation with slum clearance, to the exclusion of all else, is a historically proven method of failing poor people to the tune of a rousing campaign song.

If we are to avoid diversions, what alternatives are open? The problems and prospects of public housing are well understood, as

well as the new directions in which it should move. If we assume
a progressive direction, public housing is a vehicle for substantial
increase of dwellings open to poor people. Second, a direct housing subsidy to poor people offers the possibility of dealing directly
with large numbers. Yet, a direct housing subsidy might do little
to improve the supply of housing. If more homes were not built
the subsidy would, in the end, bring poor families little benefit.
Third, the new low-interest-rate program of the Federal Housing
Administration might be given the financing necessary for rapid
expansion. Although only three years old, the program has already
produced as many units as urban renewal. However, this program
carries no federal subsidy and is, indeed, not intended to deal with
the poorest families. Finally, the urban renewal principle of direct
cash subsidy for the production of housing might be extended to
poor people.

These four possibilities indicate the kinds of concepts that are
relevant to producing enough housing for poor people. Obviously,
more space and details are required to propose a program. The
country is spending $2.1 billion less on the housing of poor people
than on the rest of us. If we are to achieve a sense of community,
we might begin by spending equally.

CONCLUSION

Let me make four assertions in conclusion. First, in the city-
culture that we know, housing that falls short of specified standards
rears people for poverty. A longer statement would contain qualifications but I want to leave no doubt about the basic statement:
housing can make a family poor—by the attitudes and behavior
into which it leads them—and it can keep a family poor. If we
want to do away with poverty, we shall provide sufficient housing
of sufficient quality so that our young people may grow up competent to deal with the world they will know.

Second, even housing that is adequate by a biological standard
will seem slum housing if it falls too short of the standard that
most people enjoy. This is a taxing observation and it will leave
us no peace, especially in the wealthy countries. If we want to do
away with poverty, we require mechanisms to see that housing
regarded as minimum is upgraded at a faster rate than average
housing. A faster rate at the bottom is necessary to keep the gap

between those at the bottom and those in the middle from growing.

Third, housing is the most expensive component of a modest standard of living. It appears to be the component that countries postpone, improving only when they are under other pressures. It is impossible to offer a rule for balancing housing needs against other national needs that will apply to rich and poor countries, in peace and war, in crisis and in prosperity. It is, nevertheless, clear that countries that cut their investment in housing too deeply make their populations poor, whatever else they achieve.

Finally, we must perceive that, however simple any particular connection between housing policy and poverty may seem, the network of connections is far from simple and reaches into every aspect of national life. This occurs because poverty is not a discreet phenomenon. It is a shadow cast off by our way of life. If we want to alter it, we shall have to alter everything we do.

References

ADVISORY COMMISSION ON INTERGOVERNMENTAL RELATIONS. *Metropolitan Population Disparities: Their Implications for Intergovernmental Relations* (Washington: 1965).

BALTIMORE URBAN RENEWAL AND HOUSING AGENCY. *The New Locations and Housing Characteristics of Families Displaced from Area 3-C*, March, 1961 (processed).

BLOOD, ROBERT. *Developmental and Traditional Child-Rearing Philosophies and Their Family Situational Consequences* (Doctoral dissertation), University of North Carolina, Chapel Hill, 1952.

BURGESS, ELAINE M. and DANIEL PRICE. *An American Dependency Challenge* (Chicago: American Public Welfare Association, 1963).

CARTER, M. P. *Home, School, and Work* (London: Pergamon Press, 1963).

COMMUNITY SERVICE SOCIETY OF NEW YORK. Committee on Housing, *Not Without Hope* (March, 1958).

CUYAHOGA COUNTY (OHIO) WELFARE DEPARTMENT. "Ill-Starred Children," *Annual Report, 1959.*

DAVIS, ALLISON. "Motivation of the Underprivileged Worker," in William Foote Whyte (ed.), *Industry and Society* (New York: McGraw-Hill, 1946).

DONNISON, D. V. "The Changing Pattern of Housing," *The Guardian* [Manchester, England] (October 5, 1962).

Duncan, Beverly and Philip M. Hauser. *Housing a Metropolis—Chicago* (New York: Free Press of Glencoe, 1960).

Ferguson, Thomas and Mary Pettigrew. "A Study of 718 Slum Families Rehoused For Upwards of Ten Years," *Glasgow Medical Journal*, V (1954), pp. 183-201.

Florida Department of Public Welfare. *Suitable Home Law*, Preliminary Report (September, 1960).

Fried, Marc. "Developments in the West End Research," paper presented at 25th Anniversary of the Department of Psychiatry, Massachusetts General Hospital (Boston: Center for Community Studies Research Memorandum A 3, October, 1960, mimeographed).

Hartman, Chester. "The Housing of Relocated Families," Journal of the American Institute of Planners, XXX (November, 1964).

Housing and Home Finance Agency, Public Housing Administration, *Families in Low Rent Projects* (Washington, August, 1961).

Housing and Home Finance Agency, Office of the Administrator, "The Housing of Relocated Families," March, 1965 (processed).

Lewis, Hylan. "Child Rearing Among Low Income Families," paper presented to the Washington Center for Metropolitan Studies, Washington, D. C., June 8, 1961.

Lewis, Roscoe. Quoted in *The Washington Post*, January 12, 1964.

Merton, Robert K. "The Social Psychology of Housing," in Wayne Dennis *et al.*, *Trends in Social Psychology* (Pittsburgh: University of Pittsburgh Press, 1948), pp. 163-217.

Reynolds, Harry W., Jr. "The Human Element in Urban Renewal," *Public Welfare*, 19 (April, 1961), pp. 71-73.

Romanyshyn, John M. *Aid to Dependent Children* (Augusta, Maine: State of Maine Department of Health and Welfare, June, 1960).

Royal Commission for Inquiry Into the Housing of the Working Classes. *First Report* (London, 1885).

Schorr, Alvin L. *Slums and Social Insecurity* (Washington: U.S. Government Printing Office, 1963).

———. *Slums and Social Insecurity* (London: Thomas Nelson and Sons, 1964).

———. "National Community and Housing Policy," *The Social Service Review*, XXXIX (December, 1965).

———. *Poor Kids* (New York: Basic Books, 1966).

Slayton, William. Quoted in *The Washington Post*, June 7, 1962.

United Nations. *World Housing Conditions and Estimated Requirements*, 1965.

Willmott, Peter. *The Evolution of a Community* (London: Routledge and Kegan Paul, 1963).

Wilner, Daniel L., R. P. Walkley, T. Pinkerton, and M. Taybach. *The Housing Environment and Family Life: A Longitudinal Study of the Effects of Housing on Morbidity and Mental Health* (Baltimore: Johns Hopkins Press, 1962).

5

The Poor in the Market Place

MILTON J. HUBER

□ To PIN DOWN THE PLACE OF THE POOR in the market place at this point in our history is as frustrating as trying to lasso a hurricane. The din of crashing display windows drowns out proclamations of new consumer programs for the poor. The smoke from burning stores blurs economic planning for the ghettos for the foreseeable future. What lies ahead is uncertain. As Andrew Kopkind has observed, it appears that "the continuity of an age has been cut" and that "what comes now will be vastly different from what went before" (1967, p. 3).

The cry for "bread" resounds throughout the ghettos of America. The handmaidens of the Great Society scurry about and respond with a few crumbs. Receiving no "bread," the poor have taken their cue from the queen of an earlier era and have helped themselves to "cake." In the summer of 1967 looting replaced hooting as the economic and political palliative of the ghettos in many large and small cities across the nation. Present prospects are for more of the same in 1968.

There has been method as well as madness in the ghetto uprisings that began in Watts. Looting has been purposeful. "Economic gain was the basis of mass involvement" in Newark, according to Tom Hayden, a community organizer (1967, p. 18). People took what they thought they needed and would be useful. Quality merchandise disappeared first, whether liquor or appliances, and "cheap" merchandise was left behind. Churches and schools accordingly were left unscathed for the most part, not because they were appreciated but because they contained little useful that could be carried off.

More significantly, the targets marked for destruction by the looting masses in city after city have been the same—white merchants in the black community. "Soul Brother" enterprises have most often been spared. Special attention has been given to tearing up the furniture and clothing stores with the tricky credit contracts and shoddy merchandise and the grocery stores, corner or chain variety, noted for inferior or high-priced produce.

THE POOR AS CONSUMERS IN THE UNITED STATES

If nothing else, the summer of 1967 should put to rest with finality the naive notion of past generations that the poor are too poor to occupy any place of consequence in the market place of our American economy. For too many years it has been assumed that the lack of cash or equity held by the poor have exempted them from concerns identified as consumer problems. Until recently professionals in the fields of consumer economics, home economics, and consumer education have given little attention to the consumer problems of low-income families. Even today the market place problems of the poor receive little attention in publications like *Consumer Reports* and *Journal of Home Economics*. As a matter of fact, the initial enabling legislation authorizing the federal antipoverty program did not mention the market place problems of the poor among those requiring attention.

POSSESSIONS AMONG THE IMPOVERISHED

We know better now. America's poor, in Appalachia as well as in the urban ghettos, have found their place in the market place, an ascribed and marginal place, but a place indeed. Even the poor of Harlan County, Kentucky, about as poor a county as can be found in this country, so poor that half the people who lived there in 1950 had left by 1960, claim some of the trappings of American affluence: 88 per cent have washing machines, 67 per cent have TV, and 59 per cent have a car (Miller, 1964, p. 72). Likewise, in our urban ghettos, the material symbols of American affluence within the homes of the poor are readily observable. Among almost 500 low-income families living in public housing projects in New York City, for example, "fully 95 percent owned at least one television set, almost two-thirds owned a phonograph, almost half owned a sewing machine, and almost half owned an automatic washing machine" (Caplovitz, 1966).

Obviously, among the distinctions existing between the American poor and the poor of other lands is the accumulation by the former of costly material goods. From the consumer perspective, poverty here at home is a relative matter. In our mobile, thing-oriented culture, as Herman P. Miller has observed, "Needs stem not so much from what we lack as from what our neighbors have. . . . So long as there are people who have more, others will 'need' more" (1964, p. 55). Where else but in America would the poor's pursuit of "needs" amid the affluence surrounding them result in homes equipped with washing machines but lacking running water, with TV but the electricity turned off, or with cars but no money to keep them running? It is our purpose here to describe the peculiar set of economic institutions that have been devised in the urban ghettos of America that permit poverty and some of the appurtenances of affluence to dwell together under the same roof. What emerges, at least in part, is a rationale for looting that reinforces the sense of purpose that observers have perceived in the ghetto uprisings of recent summers—a legacy for looting, as it were.

THE CONTEXT OF A CREDIT ECONOMY

A prerequisite to understanding the peculiar plight of our ghetto poor in the market place is the recognition of an essential ingredient of the overall economy in which the poor are immersed: ours is a credit economy. "Buy now, pay later" has become a basic part of the American way of life. Currently, at least a hundred million Americans use installment credit to purchase or do anything and everything on the installment plan. Babies are born "on time," later go through college "on time," and at some point, will be buried "on time." Half of all the furniture, TV sets, and outboard motors and more than two-thirds of all new cars are purchased on credit. "The result has been a consumer credit explosion that makes the population explosion seem small by comparison" (Black, 1961, p. 4).

How is all this credit being paid for? The answer is simple: out of future earnings. According to Hillel Black, today "American people must work over two months out of twelve to reimburse their creditors" (1961, p. 5). Consumer credit has become so important to our economy that, if Americans no longer were permitted to buy cars on time, the resulting havoc to our economy "would make any of the post-World War II recessions appear as years of almost unbounded prosperity." In brief, debt buying has become a basic part of our American economy. John Galbraith goes so far as to ponder the possibility that the bill collector is becoming "the central figure in the good society" (1958, p. 201).

The credit world described here is a middle class phenomenon, treatises on the alleged ability of middle class Americans to postpone gratification notwithstanding. The price of admission to the immediate gratification mainstream of this buy-now-pay-later world is a credit rating based on attributes not possessed by the poor: lengthy employment, long residence, home ownership, stable family, and a good credit history. The New York Credit Bureau, for example, has prepared a list of "common danger signals" for credit managers in the city's well-known retail stores to use in refusing credit. They read like a sociological description of the poor family: residence in a rooming house, friend's house, or slovenly home or section; divorced or separated women without financial references; unstable transient employment as dishwasher, day laborer, counterman, laundry worker, maid, housekeeper, waiter, garage worker. Similar guidelines followed by major retail outlets across the nation have the effect of closing their doors to low-income consumers whose only avenue to the good things of life is through installment credit.

However justifiable the exclusion of the poor from charge accounts as unsatisfactory risks by large department stores and other legitimate retailers in our American cities, the consequences for the poor as consumers are serious. Too often they become a captive market for a breed of businessman spawned by the installment credit explosion to take care of cashless people: the "easy credit" merchants whose neon signs of "no money down" or "easy payments" brighten the commercial districts of every urban ghetto. Bombarded by the same daily dose of 1,500 to 2,000 advertisements to which their suburban neighbors are exposed, but less equipped educationally to cope with them or materially to disregard them, a great many of the poor come to view the welcoming door of the credit merchant as their only gateway to the good life (Theobald, 1963, p. 30).

"BUSINESS" IN THE GHETTO

Why is it possible for such ghetto-located enterprises to promote and profit from extension of credit to the very families turned away by reputable merchants as "bad risks"? Regardless of what he professes publicly, the ghetto merchant finds the security for his credit not in the middle class attributes sought by other retailers but in the job held by the poor individual, or someone close to him, and in the high mark-ups on the merchandise he sells. If a poverty area purchaser does have a job and if he defaults on his payments over a period of time, the merchant can fall back upon the state garnishment process to collect his money. Broadly speaking, a garnishment is a legal suit brought against the employer of a customer to require him to withhold a portion of the employee's paycheck for the creditor. Since garnishment is an acceptable grounds for discharge, usually the threat of garnishment by the merchant is sufficient to procure payment from the delinquent account.

GARNISHMENT PRACTICES

Most middle class Americans are largely unaware of the garnishment laws; they have never been their victims. But, then, most middle class Americans still seem to stereotype the poor as too lazy or too incompetent to be employed. Not so the ghetto merchant; he is well aware that poverty and unemployment are not synonymous. Almost half of those classified as poor are employed even though they have insufficient earnings to move them out of the poverty category. A large number of the poor, even many on public welfare, have part-time jobs or find work sporadically for short periods. Finally, those among the poor who constitute the "hard core" unemployed often have members of their family or friends around them who are employed.

In the case of the marginally-employed, part-time employed, or even welfare clients, a stably employed relative or friend is required as a "cosigner" to the credit contract. Upon default of payment, the same garnishment procedure can be instituted against the cosigner to procure payment. In most cases the latter thinks he is merely serving as a character reference and is unaware at the time that he is committing himself to make good on his friend's or relative's contract.

The amount of money that can be garnisheed from a salary paycheck varies from state to state. In Wisconsin, for example, roughly speaking all but 25 per cent of an unmarried worker's paycheck and all but 40 per cent of a married man's can be garnisheed, regardless of the number of dependents. It is not unusual for such an experience to tip a modest-income cosigner's family into the abyss of poverty for the first time. Unexpected deductions from a cosigner's paycheck to pay off another's debt usually leaves such an individual with insufficient funds to meet his own obligations. Delinquencies on his own accounts in turn often result in additional garnishments leading to loss of employment and impoverishment. Garnisheed workers, moreover, are avoided by other employers.

A Typical Case

A recent inquiry provided illustrations of the manner in which many ghetto merchants not only prey upon the poor but also contribute to the impoverishment of ghetto families. Typical is the case of the "Green" family (Hickman *et al.*, 1966), and it is worthwhile to examine some of the details of the process:

> Eight years ago the Greens moved to a northern city from Louisiana to get a fresh start. Limited in education they plodded along for three years raising their large family modestly but contentedly on his income as a church janitor. They walked into trouble one Saturday afternoon.
>
> Window-shopping in the neighborhood business district, they were confronted by a salesman on the sidewalk who invited them into his store. When they turned down his invitation, he took a watch from his pocket and placed it upon Mr. Green's wrist for him to admire. Assuring himself that Mr. Green was working, the salesman encouraged them to keep the watch, no payments until later. All that was required was to enter the store "to sign a few papers." By the time they left, the Greens had been sold, for $12 down, $200 in "high quality" merchandise, including the watch, a $75 coat for Mrs. Green, and $50 for two pairs of trousers. "All we had to pay was $10 every two weeks." Illiterate, Mr. Green signed a credit contract thinking it was a receipt of purchase. Within a month the watch stopped running and within a year the "high quality" clothing was threadbare and discarded—all before the "final" payment was made. Some 13 months and $270 later the Greens received a call from the store informing them that the bill was paid in full, but no "paid in full" statement was ever received.
>
> The following month, another call was received from another clothing store that the Greens had never patronized. They were told that they still owed $60 on the supposedly paid bill and that, as the son of the other store proprietor, he was going to collect it.

Threatened with a garnishment, Mrs. Green became frightened and went to the unfamiliar store and offered to pay $5 every two weeks anyway. Her offer was refused. Within the month, Mr. Green was garnisheed for over $61. Left with only $40 in his biweekly paycheck, he was forced to turn to welfare for supplementary aid to support his family. Two weeks later he was garnisheed again. The Greens had hardly recovered from these garnishments when they were garnisheed a third time by the same store a month or so later.

Meanwhile other obligations left unpaid as a consequence of the above actions resulted in additional garnishments by other creditors. The Greens, subsisting marginally in the first place, have never recovered. Currently, they are obligated to commit $30 of his biweekly take-home pay of $100 to creditors. The balance left to support his family of six still at home makes them a frequent visitor to Welfare for supplementary aid. Interestingly, the Greens still receive mail regularly telling them that their credit is good for new purchases at both of the garnisheeing clothing stores.

An interesting sidelight on the quality and source of the merchandise sold by some ghetto merchants was revealed when the Green family experience was discussed during a training class for a group of community aides attached to poverty programs in the city where the Greens resided. One of the young men remained after class and remarked, "About that watch Green bought. It was probably a 'hot' one. When I was a hustler a few years ago, we used to sell the watches we heisted to that store for about a third of their value."

HIGH MARK-UP, LOW QUALITY, SURE PROFITS

Whatever the source of the merchandise sold by ghetto merchants, the quality of it is best characterized as shoddy. Suits that deteriorate in a year, beds and sofas that collapse after a few months, mattresses that pop their springs within six months after purchase are commonplace experiences. Men's suits, for example, retailed by some credit clothiers in Milwaukee's ghetto for $125, are purchased wholesale by them for $15 to $20. A buyer for one of Milwaukee's largest credit clothiers confided to the author that he never pays more than $20 for any suit in their stores, regardless of the mark-up. Sources of documentation of the prices paid for merchandise sold by ghetto merchants include the police department and claim adjusters for insurance companies. In cases of loss by fire or theft, losses are determined by cost to merchant and so recorded in the police reports and insurance claim files.

It would be difficult to overemphasize the importance of the high mark-ups of poor quality merchandise for the operation of a ghetto merchant's business. While the garnishment process is vital to him as a legal safeguard and backstop in his transactions with low-income consumers, it is the mark-up which absorbs the risks of his credit business. Low quality off-brand items sold at prices equivalent to those of high-quality brand lines permit the merchant to include the credit risk in the price of the merchandise. A $15 man's suit sold at $125 and made available with a "small down-payment" of $20 has the credit risk packed into the selling price. Each weekly payment thereafter, however small, represents the profit margin on such a sale. This is the reason the credit clothier or appliance dealer does not display price tags on his merchandise. It enables him to set a price, not only on the estimated gullibility of the consumer, but also on the basis of his estimate of the risk involved with a particular consumer. The "going price" for the same item among his competitors is only of secondary significance. Indeed, merchants so engaged insist that they do not impose a credit charge; they explain their weekly repayment plans as merely a courtesy to the poor consumer to enable him to obtain merchandise that otherwise would not be available to him.

CONTRACT AND COLLECTION TACTICS

However dubious the shoddy merchandising practices of the ghetto merchants, much more disastrous are their shady credit and collection practices. Through ignorance and fear of the law, the Green family was coerced into paying far beyond a conscionable amount for its installment purchases. The experience was not an uncommon one among ghetto residents. Next to housing, the most important consumer problem of the poor in the market place is installment credit in all its ramifications. Speaker after speaker at the 1965 Consumer Action and the War on Poverty Conference in Washington, D.C., reiterated this position. "The number one problem," Sidney Margolius maintains, "is heavy installment buying at high finance charges" (1965, p. 34).

One factor which favors the ghetto merchant in these dealings is that retailers, unlike banks, consumer finance companies, or credit unions, are not regulated by state banking commissions in terms of maximum rates that can be charged for the use of their money. In contrast to the practice of building the credit risk into the price of low-quality, off-brand items, the ghetto merchant gets the profit margin he requires to justify his risk on brand-name merchandise through the credit package he attaches to a purchase. In the guise of "service" or "carrying" charges, interest rates of over 40 per cent or more true annual interest are not uncommon on appliance purchases. Moreover, special fees are assessed that would be absorbed in the price of the item by reputable appliance dealers. One Milwaukee credit appliance dealer in the ghetto advertises brand-name color TV sets, for example, at competitive prices and then tacks onto the price special charges for delivery, adjustment of set, and factory warranties totalling almost another hundred dollars. The unsophisticated ghetto consumer is unaware that these items are included in the sales price "downtown."

One Detroit "easy credit" furniture dealer has developed such an elaborate scheme of credit procedures to bilk his customers that he has engaged one man, at a very substantial salary for the trade, to operate it. It incorporates a number of credit devices common in the business but less systematically utilized elsewhere. First, following a sale, the credit contract is drawn up deliberately specifying payments that the purchaser will discover after a few weeks are too difficult for him to keep up. Next, upon the purchaser's complaining, the store generously agrees to rewrite the contract requiring smaller payments over a longer period of time, and incidentally at a higher rate of interest and with special refinancing charges added. Again, however, the contract is rewritten requiring payments that the creditor knows are not realistic for the debtor's circumstances. After a few payments are missed, the creditor exercises his right to repossess the appliance. He then "sells" it at a fraction of its value to a "dummy" company which he owns, thereby maintaining possession of the appliance for sale again. Then he hits the delinquent account with a deficiency judgment. This consists of garnisheeing the wages of the debtor for the balance due after the amount gained from resale to the "dummy" company is subtracted from the unpaid balance of the debtor's contract at the time of repossession. After a series of garnishments sufficient to pay off the contract, a coup de grâce is administered. A letter is sent to the debtor indicating with profused embarrassment that the account has been overpaid several dollars. The customer is encouraged to stop by the store to claim his refund. Upon arriving he is informed that the store had anticipated that he would be applying the refund to a new purchase, elaborating upon the many "specials" of the week. Having come full circle the process begins all over again, the debtor grateful that the generous store bears no hard feelings toward him and still desires his patronage after all the trouble he has caused them!

In instances where the situation would make it worthwhile, additional gimmicks can be added to the above scheme. One is a "balloon" clause. It enables a merchant to sell an expensive item to a consumer who is able only to make modest payments. The hooker is that the last payment in the time contract amounts to the remaining balance, a sum always more than the debtor can afford. The "solution" is to rewrite the contract, which involves assessing a series of new fees as well as higher rates of interest.

Another tactic is the "add-on" contract. If, in the course of visiting the store to make his weekly payments, the customer can be induced to purchase another item, the new purchase is simply "added on" to the old contract, using the almost-paid-for merchandise as security for the new. In the event the customer subsequently defaults in paying off the new merchandise, the creditor can repossess all of the items on the old contract as well as the new, even though the original contract had been largely paid off. This device has been employed frequently enough in Milwaukee, for example, to necessitate negotiations between the Milwaukee County Public Welfare Department and representatives of the ghetto stores, with the result that merchants have agreed, in the case of welfare clientele, to limit themselves to repossessing only the last item purchased. Welfare workers had complained that the homes of clients were being stripped bare by ghetto retailers using add-on contracts. Refurnishing such homes was becoming a financial burden for the county.

Consequences for Welfare Clients

Public welfare clients have special problems related to installment credit that deserve more attention than they are presently receiving. Many welfare departments have a policy requiring a family on welfare not to use any of the money granted them for any item not included in the relief budget. In most communities also, there are no provisions in relief grants for the repayment of old debts. Violators of this provision are subject to imprisonment. A policy such as this raises an interesting question: Since installment credit is essentially a contractual relationship between a debtor and creditor, what happens when the borrower subsequently commits himself to another "contract" with the welfare department which, in effect, "tables" his commitment to the creditor?

Some answers to this question are indicated by interviews with 50 families who had recently been general relief recipients and who subsequently had been garnisheed by retailers or consumer finance companies upon obtaining employment (Hickman et al., 1966; also see Huber, 1967, pp. 89-97). Of the 634 general relief families whose cases were closed during the two months under study, 23.3 per cent of them had been subjected to garnishment actions by the time of this pilot inquiry. Of the 50 garnisheed families interviewed intensively, one-fourth of them had been subjected to such action by creditors within two to four weeks after leaving welfare and returning to work. Another quarter were garnisheed within 90 days. Five ghetto credit clothiers and furniture stores and five consumer finance companies with poverty area offices were responsible for almost all of the garnishment problems of the welfare families studied.

Seventy-five per cent of the families interviewed reported that creditors had tried to collect payments while they were on welfare. In almost half of these cases, ignorance of the families' welfare status could not be used as an excuse by creditors for attempting collections since they had been informed by the families of their welfare status. Illustrative of the hounding by creditors of welfare clientele is the case of a deserted 21-year-old Puerto Rican mother of three children (Hickman et al., 1966, p. 46). While on welfare and following a period of hospitalization, the woman was badgered by a finance company to pay off a balance of $250 on a loan to her husband for which she had cosigned at the age of 17. In spite of her protests that welfare regulations and the modest amount of her grant would not permit it, and, in spite of calls to the finance company by her caseworker in her behalf, the collector insisted that she pay $5 every two weeks, welfare or no welfare. For two weeks he went to her home every morning at 6 A.M. and every night at midnight demanding payment. Unable to tolerate his pounding on the door at these unusual hours, she succumbed and paid the amount requested over a two-year period until the loan was paid in full.

Over a third of the families included in the study admitted that they made full or partial payment to creditors while on welfare to "get them off our backs," and a third of the group made payments of $8 per week or more. The average payment was slightly under $21 a month. The average welfare grant at the time of the survey was $115.57 a month. Moreover, 20 per cent of the families reported ghetto merchants and lenders offered them additional credit even though they knew they were on welfare. There was also some indication of families being seduced into making credit purchases while on welfare, only to have the merchant, aware of the client's "no-credit pledge," threaten afterward to expose the family to welfare authorities unless they used their welfare funds to make the payments.

Suggestive of the amount of installment credit available to low-income families was the debt load carried by the respondents included in the study. At the time they were accepted for welfare, the families admitted carrying an average installment debt load of $1,520.50, certainly a sizeable sum for those whose loss or lack of income necessitated welfare assistance. Almost one-third of the families reported more than a $1,600 short-term installment debt; one-third reported owing less than $400. There is every reason to believe that interest on the debts left unpaid continued to accrue during the welfare experiences of the families. Almost half of them felt that the balance the creditors demanded after they were able to obtain work and leave welfare was higher than when they went on welfare. One family was hit with a balance due of $600 on a small loan of $300 contracted before their welfare experience. Given the average amount of indebtedness among the families when they went on welfare, the annual interest rates of 18 to 40 or more per cent charged by ghetto merchants and 24 or 25 per cent charged on the average by small loan companies would increase the debt problems of such families sizeably over a period of a year or more.

THE COSTS OF GHETTO PROFITEERING

For the 50 families in the study, their welfare status appeared closely associated with their garnishment experiences. As intimated earlier, for some of them garnishments proved to be the final straws that broke the backs of their marginal subsistence budgets and put them on welfare, either through loss of job or loss of incentive to continue working. As one family put it, "The money left in the paycheck after garnishment wasn't enough for food money for a family our size." For other families, garnisheed wages reduced their paychecks to the point where they qualified for supplementary aid from welfare. "If I feel any strain I go down to welfare and they make up the difference," was the way one father expressed it. Among civil service workers particularly, there appeared to be a discernible pattern: wage deductions were made to pay creditors; then the workers were sent to welfare for supplemental aid to make up for the creditor's "take."

Thus, it is not only evident that welfare clients have special problems with regard to ghetto merchants but also that their welfare status is no hindrance to their doing business with ghetto lenders and retailers. Something else of significance is just as evident: namely, the stake of the taxpayer in all of this. On the one hand, the ghetto merchant depends upon the state to serve as his bill collector in administering the garnishment procedure. On the other hand, the garnisheed poor have to depend upon the tax funds available through welfare to meet their minimum living expenses and to make up for the wages garnisheed by the ghetto merchants.

Probably the best study in this area is that conducted by George Brunn, attorney and now magistrate in the San Francisco area, for the Center for the Study of Law and Society at the University of California, Berkeley (1965, pp. 1213-53). In Hollywood parlance, Brunn points out how, unlike the cinema version of the western sheriff decked out in ten-gallon hat and outdrawing the black-shirted criminal in the middle of the town's dusty main street, today's deputy-sheriff is likely to wear a business suit, carry a briefcase, and spend his career doing nothing more glamorous than serving papers in civil lawsuits, frequently involving the helpless poor.

The San Francisco sheriff's office, Brunn points out, has a civil department with 11 full deputies and 16 office personnel just for serving papers, the bulk of which relate to wage garnishments; 75 to 80 per cent of the levies served in a recent two months' period were for this purpose. As supervisor of a booming business, the sheriff collects over a million dollars a year for creditors. "Society subsidizes the sheriff's collection work; the cost of operating the civil department runs more than double the amount of fees the department receives" (Brunn, 1965, p. 1217). In Los Angeles County, the cost of operating the Sheriff's Civil Division is about $430,000 per year for which it receives in fees (charged to the debtor) and mileage approximately $220,000. Brunn raises the question, "To what extent should society subsidize the collection process? Raising fees would increase the burden on the debtors unless at the same time creditors are required to pay part of the cost." As he succinctly summarizes the garnishment issue:

> To the deputy, wage levies are mainly a job; to the creditor, a useful collection device; to the employer who must process them, a nuisance and an expense; to the debtor, a humiliating experience that may bring serious hardship in its wake. Society has a major stake in the garnishment process, which is not only a creature of law but an activity of government. Society has a legitimate concern that legal debts be paid; society also has a legitimate concern that the collection tools it fashions and whose use it sanctions do not cause undue distress and hardship (1965, pp. 1214-15).

REDUCING THE REAL INCOME OF THE POOR

Unfortunately, as Brunn is well aware, credit procedures and collection tools are exploited and misused to the disadvantage of the poor. In preparing a debt amortization program for a widow employed by a leather company, the writer was shown a bill for $48.95 owed a ghetto clothier. The merchant claimed the balance was $271.58. An unexpected visit to the store to check the account records clearly disclosed the $48.95 balance in typed numerals. The larger amount was justified "from memory" and penciled notations around the edges of the account statement. The proprietor claimed he made down-payments for her on several appliances she had purchased from other stores to which he had sent her. The widow had no knowledge of this apart from his recommendations of particular stores.

Further investigation revealed that the merchant was charging her for the percentage he normally would have received from the other stores for referring her to them. However, since she could not afford the appliances purchased in the first place, in time they were repossessed. Accordingly, the clothier lost his commission for the "referral." He was trying to reclaim his "cut" by tacking it onto her clothing bill as "down-payments" in her behalf. In referrals, it is customary for the merchant gaining the sale to withhold the "commission" due his referring colleague until most of the payments have been made.

In another case, without warning, a ghetto resident was garnisheed by a credit furniture store for a 15-year-old debt supposedly totalling over $400 on which there had been no action in all that time. In Wisconsin no judgment is required in advance of garnishments. The loss of the paycheck in this instance had disastrous consequences for the victim including the turning off of his electricity, the spoilage of his refrigerated food, and finally eviction from his apartment. Subsequent legal assistance disclosed that all but $40 of the bill had been paid off years before. Legal action brought by the victim's attorney claiming damages against the store resulted in an out-of-court settlement of $1,000 to the individual.

But it was only a chance meeting on the street between the attorney and the ghetto resident, who had known each other through the civil rights movement, that enabled this low-income victim to salvage something for the hardship caused him by the not uncommon practice of over-charging debtors when ghetto merchants instruct their attorneys to bring garnishment action. This is one reason the Inland Steel Corporation in Chicago routinely checks every garnishment suit brought against its employees, a unique policy procedure among major corporations to the writer's knowledge. Dorothy Lascoe, who is in charge of its program, states that more than $10,000 is saved for employees annually by exposing unwarranted claims made by credit merchants and loan companies (1965, pp. 264-66).

One of the most common gimmicks of ghetto merchants, particularly furniture stores, is the "bait and switch" tactic. By means of large signs in the window, or even colorful ads in the comic section of the Sunday paper, three rooms of furniture are advertised for a ridiculously low price, well under $200 in many cases. The merchant has no intention of selling the furniture advertised. Indeed, he might be hard pressed to produce it. It usually consists of cheap, chipped pieces collecting dust in some obscure part of the store. The strategy is to "bait" the customer into the store with the ad and then "switch" him to higher price merchandise.

Two psychological approaches are very effective in this regard. One plays upon flattery, impressing upon the customer that the sales pieces are simply not good enough for one of his tastes. Paradoxically the other technique utilizes ridicule, displaying the cheap sale furniture but expressing regret that the customer is too poor to afford any of the finer merchandise in the store: "Here's a nice set, but it's probably out of your class." The same devices are also very effective in selling used cars. Veteran ghetto salesmen find it relatively easy to bait and switch customers into spending three or four times as much money as they had expected to when they entered the store. One might argue, of course, that the poor person should have the good sense and self-discipline to resist such sales tactics. Unfortunately, it is precisely the poor who are least well armed educationally and psychologically to fend off the blandishments and baitings of the mercantile "pusher."

SITUATION AND MOTIVATION AMONG IMPOVERISHED CONSUMERS

One might also assume from a recital of these illegal or unethical practices that the business of ghetto merchants must be a succession of customers who, "once burned," never return. On the contrary, existing evidence indicates that the poor continue to go back to the same shops for their merchandise. Caplovitz suggests that the personal relationship cultivated by the credit merchant with his customers explains this phenomenon. He credits the intercessory role played by resident peddlers between the poor in Harlem and the debt merchants as important in maintaining relationships. Some peddlers serve as outdoor salesmen who get the poor to the store or take the store to the poor. Others operate independently, selling to the poor themselves; or they act as "brokers" who screen customers and refer them to certain neighborhood stores on the basis of the degree of credit risk and other factors involved. In return for this service, they receive a commission based on the price of the sale. The primary value of the peddler to the ghetto merchants is often his personal relationship with the customers and the knowledge of the individual families he has acquired over years of contact with them. A "Dunn and Bradstreet for the poor," he knows the good and bad risks, how "soft" or stern to be with a family on payments, and when birthdays or other special days occur in different families that can be exploited for additional purchases (Caplovitz, 1966, pp. 25-28).

THE CAPTIVE CONSUMERS

Seemingly more fundamental in explaining the continual return of the poor to the same exploitative merchants is the captive aspect of the relationship between ghetto merchant and customer described earlier. Queries along this line among families being counseled on credit problems usually provoke the response: "With my income and problems, man, where else can I go?" or "I didn't know I had any choice." Implied in these responses is the trapped conditions of the poor in the market place. Given their low income and rejection for credit by the reputable stores, where else are they expected to go to satisfy their needs and wants?

The response of one couple recently counseled by the author points up the interrelated importance of both the captive and personalized aspects of the merchant-customer relationship in the ghetto. Asked how they explained their continued dealings with merchants who sell them shoddy merchandise and then garnishee their paychecks, the reply was, "Who else will let us pick up anything else we need without increasing the amount we pay each week?" Weekly payments made in person to the ghetto merchant furthers the personal relationship between merchant and customer. In turn, the weekly visit regularly exposes the ghetto resident to the enticing wares of the merchant. Relentlessly stimulated by the mass media with a parade of material goods otherwise beyond the reach of their meager incomes, the temptation to succumb to the seemingly "painless surgery" of a modest extraction weekly from their paychecks is almost irresistable to the poor. They become willing victims. Along with the butcher and the baker, the "credit maker" at the neighborhood clothing or furniture store becomes a continuous claimant to the ghetto resident's paycheck.

Moreover, weekly commitments to one store minimize the possibility of doing business elsewhere. Florence Rice of East Harlem, drawing upon her experience as a former saleswoman in ghetto credit stores and as a low-income consumer specialist, states that credit merchants in Harlem will go to extremes to protect the patronage of their "regular" customers from other merchants, including the giving of bad credit reports on good-payers attempting to do business elsewhere. The bad credit reference closes the doors of other merchants and enforces the captive dependency of the ghetto poor upon the original creditor, who looks upon attempted shopping excursions to other merchants as disloyalty. Keeping a customer "in the family" by adding new purchases to his account before old ones are paid off is a common business practice of ghetto merchants and lenders.

COMPENSATORY CONSUMPTION

The experience of one husband interviewed in the public welfare study referred to earlier points up not only the dependency of the ghetto resident upon the same exploitative merchants but also his gullibility for the high price lines of merchandise. While intoxicated he purchased a suit and pair of shoes for $150 from a ghetto clothier. He did not take the suit home nor was there need of altering it. The next day, sobered up, he regretted his purchase and returned to the store to cancel the sale. The merchant refused to nullify the sale and shortly thereafter garnisheed him. Asked whether he would shop there again he replied, "I shop there now. See this 'Gruen' watch. They let me have it for one cent under a hundred dollars." When the interviewer informed him that the name on the face of the watch was Gru*i*n, he remarked, "Who cares about the spelling. It's an expensive watch!"

The eager susceptibility of nonwhite, low-income families for high cost merchandise has been a topic of idle conversation among consumer specialists and the general public as well for years. Reference is frequently made about the "Cadillac complex" among Negro car purchasers, for example. Caplovitz has developed the interesting concept of compensatory consumption, the phrasing of which he credits Robert R. Merton. Just as Veblen observed that the upper classes engaged in conspicuous consumption to display their social superiority, so Caplovitz contends that the low-income family, frustrated in its hopes of greatly improving its low social standing through occupational mobility, turns to consumption as one sphere in which they can make some progress toward the American dream of success. The big car and the expensive appliance or wardrobe can become "compensations for blocked social mobility" (Caplovitz,

1966, p. 16). The Lynds are credited by Caplovitz for giving prominence to this concept in their writings. In *Middletown in Transition,* they observed that the workers compensated for their declining occupational aspirations by shifting them to the realm of consumption, using the installment plan as the means of realization (Lynd and Lynd, 1937, pp. 26, 447-48).

The concept of compensatory consumption merits more attention than it has received. Given the close identification of success with the accumulation of material goods in our American way of life, the temptation of modest income people to use the buy-now-pay-later way to purchase high status durables to bolster their own self-images and to gain favor in the eyes of their associates constitutes an interesting hypothesis. As part of an experimental project in a Milwaukee plant to save the jobs of a group of high seniority employees about to be discharged because of excessive garnishments, a group counseling program was suggested by the author. Participants were "drafted" by management and labor for the weekly sessions as an alternative to discharge. After several such meetings, the participants, all Negroes, began to express their real feelings about becoming involved in the project. Unanimously the members of the group agreed that they would have preferred discharge to being "fingered" and designated for the project. Selection for it had exposed them before all their fellow workers as "frauds." All the expensive installment purchases they had made to impress others that they were "making it big" were now revealed as stuff they could not really afford. They lost "face." They would thus have preferred losing their jobs, even though it meant the loss of accumulated pension and other benefits unlikely to be duplicated in future employment by men of their limited skills.

RIOTS AS CONSUMER RETALIATION

Not emphasized in comments made earlier about the sense of economic purpose and usefulness involved in the looting of recent ghetto upheavals, but an integral part of the looting behavior nonetheless, has been a retaliatory element that suggests a companion concept for Caplovitz's compensatory consumption. Compensatory retaliation would be one way of phrasing it. Any rationale for the looting accompanying all of the major city uprisings draws heavily upon the idea that what was looted was "owed" the looter. Hayden reports the "common claim" by looters in Newark that "this is owed me." The stores "presented the most immediate ways for people to take what they felt was theirs" (1967, p. 18). A similar attitude prevailed in Detroit. Typical of the feelings of the looters there were those expressed to a reporter by a woman observed removing TV sets from a credit furniture store the day before:

> That ain't looting. That's just getting back what they done got from me. I was glad to see that man's store burn. He never did treat black folks nice, always rushing you to make up your mind. And he never wanted to sell you the cheap stuff. Always talking about how another one was better, but it always cost more money (Scott, 1967, p. 10).

The phrase, "they've been robbing us for years; now it's our turn" has been a recurring theme of ghetto uprisings across the country. In Newark, snipers interviewed after the looting and burning revealed that the strategy of the sniping was not to kill or injure but to lure the police from an area to make it vulnerable for looting. In other words, the function of sniping in the Newark riot was to enable the poor to get all the good things that their lack of jobs and poverty kept them from obtaining by more socially acceptable means (*Life*, 63, July 28, 1967, p. 28). Compensatory retaliation for the pent-up frustration of a captive clientele stemming from years of exploitation and injustice at the hands of the ghetto credit merchants thus appears to be a basic part of contemporary ghetto revolts, linked with and reinforced by the pressure for compensatory consumption.

All of the foregoing emphasizes and reiterates the horns of the dilemma of the poor in the ghetto market place. Immersed in an acquisitive pecuniary society in which material possessions symbolize success, the poor exhibit the same needs and wants of others in the community. Far from evidencing a special subculture where material possessions are concerned, their aspirations are typical. Their problem, then, is not one of improper goals; it is one of means. Increasingly, the proper means of obtaining the material symbols of success for the majority of Americans in our mobile society is through consumer credit. Rejected by the larger and more legitimate retailers as unworthy credit risks, the poor constitute a captive market for a variety of merchants of debt who provide the poor with a semblance of the affluence enjoyed by other Americans "for a price." The "price" includes shoddy merchandise, high mark-ups, unconscionable rates of interest, and abusive collection practices in which the process of garnishment is a major ingredient. The result is the entrapment of the poor in a web of financial and legal procedures which they feel powerless to combat, from which they often cannot extricate themselves, and against which some will eventually strike out in violence.

OLD NOSTRUMS AND NEW PRESCRIPTIONS

To phrase it another way, the poor are caught in a vicious circle in the ghetto market place. At one pole are the more legitimate and traditional merchants who reject them as poor credit risks. Thus rejected, they are forced to turn to the credit merchants who constitute the other pole. Once under contract with the merchants of debt and ensnarled in the world of delinquent payments, garnishments, and repossession, the resultant credit record of the poor man, no matter how much he learns from the experience or earns later, prohibits him from doing business with the legitimate merchants to whom he was not acceptable in the first place. For the marginal family, like the Greens discussed earlier, involvement with the ghetto merchants turns the vicious circle into a downward spiral that drops them, perhaps irretrievably, into the poverty syndrome. Any consumer program of significance for the ghetto poor must be prepared to provide alternatives to the present practices which prevail at either pole of this vicious circle.

FAILURE OF TRADITIONAL PROGRAMS

Unfortunately, most of the initial consumer proposals to help the ghetto poor have been limited to helping individuals cope more effectively within the existing system. Traditional consumer programs for the poor strive to teach low-income families how to budget more adequately and to buy more wisely. Emphasis is placed upon changing the individual, not the system. Instruction in the use of consumer credit is illustrative of the limitations of the coping approach. Content in this area usually emphasizes the different rates of interest of various lenders and how to figure true annual interest. This is of little functional value to the poor who have no choice as to where they can get credit or how much they pay for it. Academic knowledge about different interest rates, credit abuses, and the mathematics of figuring interest are of little help to those for whom the only available source of credit is the ghetto merchant.

For this reason newly introduced courses in consumer education being prepared for ghetto youth in New York's schools, for example, might turn out to be frustrating experiences. Unless relevant institutions, such as the larger retail stores, are "trained" as well to receive the new generation of enlightened poor consumers (change their credit-granting procedures for the poor, for example), the end result will be the "same ole bag" of ghetto merchant entrapment. "Where else can I go?" is the legitimate and pressing question of the poor that remains unanswered by consumer education programs which identify the source of the problem as the personal inadequacies of the impoverished.

Given the modest resources of funds and personnel being allotted to consumer programming among the deprived, programs directed at instituting change in the market place system engulfing them will be more rewarding and benefit more poor than the individual rehabilitation emphasis that characterizes most "home economics" programs mounted in poverty areas. For example, programs intended to affect the credit world of the poor must center upon either modifying the conditions at one of the two poles of the vicious circle or providing alternative consumer choices in place of them.

"Third Party" Aid for Poor Consumers

Encouragingly, recent consumer programming in some of the ghettos of our larger cities appears to be moving in this direction. Creative leadership along these lines is coming from outside the ranks of the professionals traditionally identified with money management and consumer education. Modification of the credit policies of several of the large department stores has been achieved to some extent in Milwaukee, to cite one instance. A leather plant, the majority of whose workers are low-skilled ghetto residents, discovered that over 10 per cent of its employees had claims upon their paychecks weekly by garnishments or debt amortizers. University consultation revealed that ghetto credit merchants made up the bulk of the creditors involved and that few, if any, of the employees had been able to obtain credit accounts at the large department stores with locations in the ghetto. A line worker was trained to deal with the money problems of the employees.

One of the achievements of this worker was the negotiating of a policy with the largest department store whereby employees were encouraged to apply for credit accounts. The store agreed not to rely exclusively on the records of the local credit bureau in rejecting an applicant. Applications which normally would be turned down are referred to the trained factory representative for his personal evaluation in the light of his knowledge of the employee's current situation. As a result, accounts at the store are now enjoyed by two-thirds of the plant's employees, most of whom never had them before. Largely because of this program, garnishments and wage assignments at the plant have dropped to the point where the number per year amounts to the number that formerly was experienced each month. Of a similar nature, a community organization agency in Milwaukee negotiated a policy with another department store to open accounts with a group of ADC mothers. In this instance, the retailer left to the agency the entire responsibility for the screening and referring of applicants for accounts. A maximum of $100 credit per account was agreed upon.

What emerges from these programs is a third-party role in the creditor-debtor relationship. Credit is extended on the basis of the status or power of the third party, not the credit rating of the individual. The effectiveness of the third party in its role depends upon personal knowledge of and relationship with the individual debtor, which is, of course, much more encompassing than a mere credit history. For the families affected, these programs provide a vehicle of escape from their entrapment with the ghetto credit vendor. Breaking out of the vicious circle becomes an upward spiral improving and enriching the quality of living. Merchandise of higher quality obtained at a lower total cost extends the purchasing power of the limited dollars of the poor. And the extension to the poor of new shopping alternatives routinely enjoyed by the affluent represents not only a direct modification of the poor's economic environment, but also a meaningful change in terms of self-image.

The experience of these modest third-party programs suggests that the credit rating systems and procedures relied upon by major retailers are not generally applicable to ghetto residents. One of the insights impressed upon the department store by the leather factory representative in evaluating a credit application was the importance of assessing the "record" of the creditor as well as the debtor involved in a garnishment action. Garnishments by ghetto merchants with reputations for excessive use of this procedure were discounted in considering an application. The fact that workers with "bad" payment records with ghetto merchants became reliable accounts at the department store revealed the importance of such evaluation. This experience indicates that if credit accounts are extended with discretion and modest maximums to many low-income families, they are as dependable—even with their limited resources—in making payments as their more affluent counterparts. The refinement of credit-granting procedures by the larger department stores with ghetto locations in our major cities would make credit accounts more accessible to a large proportion of deprived families and contribute substantially to the quality of life in such areas of poverty.

The modest reform in credit merchandising described above illustrates an approach at the "pole of rejection," enabling low-income families to break out of the vicious circle in which they are caught by making available goods and services previously denied them by virtual exclusion from department stores patronized by the mainstream of American consumers. More typical, however, on a national scale are the mounting efforts to help poor consumers by providing local shopping and credit alternatives to the present "pole of acceptance," the "easy credit" ghetto merchant. Most common among the projects of this nature has been the organization of credit unions and buying clubs among the poor.

Credit Unions and "Self Help" Projects

Experience across the country has demonstrated the way buying clubs and credit unions complement one another in serving ghetto residents. In some cities buying clubs have used savings from purchases to start a credit union. In most instances, however, credit unions organized for the poor have provided the cash through loans to enable the poor to bypass the credit merchants and to take advantages of genuine sales at department stores and other mainstream merchants. The main attraction of credit unions for the poor is the availability of loans at 12 per cent simple annual interest, which compares favorably with the 18 per cent permissible on revolving credit accounts at department stores and the 30 to 36 per cent at consumer finance companies.

Suggestive of the sensible approach made by the poor who utilize such credit union facilities is the size of the loans being granted. A survey by the Federal Bureau of Credit Unions in 1965 indicated that anywhere from a quarter to a third of all loans to low-income families were for less than $50 and that over 80 per cent of them were for less than $200. The national average among all income groups for a credit union loan is approximately $850 (*Frontline*, September 23, 1966, pp. 1-2). The modest size of the loans being approved by poverty area credit unions lends support to the hope that some of the small but urgent needs for emergency money by ghetto residents are being met. One of the demoralizing facts of ghetto life is the special monetary demands of the "awful months" of August, December and March, when clothes must be purchased for the opening of school and when Christmas and Easter gifts for the family are in order (Bagdikian, 1964, p. 116). On such occasions credit unions provide a positive alternative to credit merchants, small loan companies, and loan sharks.

Inhibiting the development of ghetto credit unions on a broad scale as an alternative source of credit for the poor is the problem of eligibility for membership. The lack of formal associational ties eliminates large numbers of the poor from credit union services. As membership organizations, credit unions are customarily chartered around a "common bond" of association between potential members such as one's church, labor union, or fraternal organization. While community-based credit unions are possible and more practical for ghetto residents, charter-granting authorities both at the state and federal government levels have been resistant to approve charter requests based upon one's place of residence, particularly neighborhoods within a slum area. Consequently CUNA International, Inc. reports that 99 of the 175 poverty-area credit unions responding to its survey in mid-1967 claimed a grand total of only 22,544 members across the nation.

It would appear that a new instrument to meet the loan needs of the poor will have to be devised if the millions of poor consumers yet unreached are to be helped. Something along the lines of the recent federal money made available for emergency loans at a low rate of interest to victims of the summer uprisings of 1967 should be explored as a basis of an on-going federal program making such low interest loans regularly available to the poor. Housing programs making available mortgage money at 3 per cent to encourage home ownership among low-income families should be seen as another precedent for developing loan programs geared to satisfying other legitimate consumer needs of the poor.

Buying clubs might well be called the poor man's version of a consumers' cooperative. For the most part they have been organized around the buying of groceries from wholesalers. Twenty or more families in a neighborhood pool their food orders weekly and buy items of common interest by the case direct from wholesalers. Goods are ordered early in the week and picked up and paid for at the end of the week. "Ordering" buying clubs of this nature sometimes evolve into "store" buying clubs which stock certain items depending upon customer demand. Paul Katzoff of the East Harlem Tenants Council points out that buying clubs do more than just save money, "They create a sophistication" (1965, p. 27). The insights and learning experience provided by the buying clubs enable participating families to develop the understanding and skills they need to cope more adequately for themselves in the market place.

Probably the most elaborate ghetto consumer action program in the nation had its origin in an egg buying club. What started in Boston in 1966 with a few dozen members grew in seven months to an operation involving six ghetto communities and 2,700 families buying 23,000 dozen eggs a month. Participating families were encouraged to start a credit union and to place in it the cash savings involved from the egg buying club. The accumulation of shares in the credit union in turn provided a source of funds large enough to organize a furniture buying club. With loans from the credit union, members are now able to purchase furniture and appliances for cash direct from factories and wholesalers. Savings range from 30 to 50 per cent less than average retail levels. Fuel oil, petroleum products, and automobile tires are among recent additions to the line of products now available through Boston's "Co-Marts" (Consumer Markets). The only overhead of the Co-Marts is telephone and postage. Developed under the city's anti-poverty agency, the projects are under the control of the various self-help corporations organized at the local level.

Boston's consumer action program demonstrates that the purchasing power of the poor can be organized to provide alternatives to the merchants of debt in the ghetto. But credit unions and buying clubs are strange entities to the ghetto resident. The crux of the challenge is community organization. As the New Haven Buying Club Conference in 1967 concluded, "The most difficult aspect of forming buying clubs is recruiting." Endless energy must be expanded to "spread the buying club gospel and show residents how it can be beneficial to them" (Tucker, 1967). Because of the number of volunteers, the commitment of time, and the business acumen required, the poor who would attempt to launch buying clubs and credit unions in most instances require the assistance of professional organizers. Undoubtedly, a major ingredient in the success of Boston's efforts is the presence on the ABCD staff of three professionals who have parlayed many years of experience in the cooperative movement with an unusual degree of sensitivity about the life-style and problems of ghetto families.

One of the benefits derived from participation in cooperative enterprises by the poor is the acquisition of the ability to maneuver in the middle-class business world of production and distribution. This is a part of the "sophistication" mentioned by Katzoff. The disbanding of a buying club is often another expression of it. Buying from wholesalers, members learn the true costs of merchandise and the profit margins for various items. In time they become "money-wise," skilled at comparative shopping, to the extent that they feel they can cope for themselves more confidently in the open market. They no longer need the buying club. Action-oriented consumer programs obviously appear to be a more rewarding vehicle for consumer education than the traditional content-centered lecture approach. Hard research comparing the relative effectiveness of the two approaches among poor consumers is sorely needed.

Other Lines of Needed Action

A major stipulation of any comprehensive program to enable the ghetto poor to break out of the vicious circle of credit entrapment is more justice before the law. One of the revelations of the antipoverty war has been the paucity of defenses available to the poor in installment credit litigation. Over the years most legislation in this field has been written by creditors or their lobbyists. The conclusion of the chairman of the Human Rights and Constitutional Law Committee of the Milwaukee Junior Bar Association has been reiterated in legal circles across the country: "The law presently is a creditor's paradise" (Jacobson, 1967). Moreover, colleges of law through the years have been teaching credit law largely from the creditor's perspective. The only law school located in metropolitan Milwaukee typically presents its instruction in consumer credit law under the title of "Creditors' Rights." Law graduates accordingly find themselves almost totally unprepared to deal with contractual credit problems of the poor from the perspective of a consumer. Similarly, state legislation, where applicable to the consumer problems of the poor, a rarity in itself, has seldom been utilized in their behalf. In Wisconsin, for example, consumer protection statutes available to the ghetto poor are the responsibility of the Department of Agriculture! Even then, until the Milwaukee ghetto disturbances of 1967, no funds had ever been authorized by the Wisconsin legislature to permit the department to implement those sections of the law which were relevant to the exploitation of the poor in the market place. Consumer protection through the laws and the courts constitutes a vital part of any comprehensive program aimed at enabling ghetto families to break out of their present market place predicament.

Attention has been centered upon the significance of the credit world of the urban poor in comprehending and dealing effectively with the retail market place, as they encounter it; but it should be understood that, though basic, this is not all-encompassing in explaining the consumer plight of the poor. For all practical purposes, fundamental consumer resources and services vital to the pursuit of the good life by American standards are, in general, either closed to the ghetto poor or made available only at premium rates. Adequate housing and retail credit are merely the most obvious examples. Hazard, auto, and term life insurance have been difficult to obtain. The current ghetto upheavals across the nation are serving to dramatize the insurance problems of ghetto businessmen and consumers alike. Insurance cancellations are increasing and are disastrous to property values, accelerating the flight from the ghettos. Place of residence alone has become sufficient grounds for cancellations.

Similarly, there is some evidence that utilities require advance deposits for ghetto residents as a condition of service that are not required in other areas of the city or suburbs. The NET film, *The Poor Pay More,* reveals a series of staged applications by phone for phone services in New York City. Negroes and whites were paired to apply for phones supplying identical application data on vocation, income, savings, and so on, with the exception of home address. One supplied a ghetto address and the other one from a high status neighborhood. Without exception, deposits in advance of service were required by those giving ghetto addresses but were not required of the others. Similar demands of deposits in advance from ghetto residents for gas and electricity services in Milwaukee are commonplace. For poor families, the amounts of the deposits required necessitate in many instances the obtaining of small loans at high rates of interest to pay them. The strategy is often self-defeating. The added monthly loan repayment competes for the limited dollars available to pay the utility bills.

A long summation is unnecessary: it is apparent that the consumer-world of the poor, especially of the ghetto poor, is circumscribed by policies and practices that add both *de facto* and *de jure* discrimination to the normal consequences of inadequate dollar income. Alongside the other civil rights of the day—to secure a job, enter a school, choose a home—should be placed the right to consume equitably, a right that should not be limited by a person's race, culture, creed, or, in this instance, place of residence.

References

BAGDIKIAN, BEN H. *In the Midst of Plenty* (New York: New American Library of World Literature, 1964).

BLACK, HILLEL. *Buy Now, Pay Later* (New York: William Morrow, 1961).

BRUNN, GEORGE. "Wage Garnishment in California," *California Law Review,* LIII (December, 1965), pp. 1213-53.

CAPLOVITZ, DAVID. Testimony before U. S. House of Representatives, Committee on Government Operations, October 10, 1966.

GALBRAITH, JOHN K. *The Affluent Society* (Boston: Houghton Mifflin, 1958).

HAYDEN, THOMAS. *New York Review of Books,* August 24, 1967.

HICKMAN, GERALD, *et al.* "An Exploratory Survey of the Installment Debt Problems of Fifty Milwaukee Families with Public Welfare Histories," unpublished Master's thesis, School of Social Welfare, University of Wisconsin—Milwaukee, 1966.

HUBER, MILTON J. "Installment Credit Problems Among Public Welfare Recipients," *Journal of Consumer Affairs,* I (Summer, 1967), pp. 89-97.

JACOBSON, THOMAS M. "The Poor Pay More," speech before the Milwaukee Junior Bar Association, September 25, 1967.

KATZOFF, PAUL. In *Consumer Action and the War on Poverty: Conference Proceedings,* Office of Economic Opportunity Community Action Program and the President's Committee on Consumer Interests (Washington, D. C.: U. S. Government Printing Office, 1965).

KOPKIND, ANDREW. *New York Review of Books,* August 24, 1967.

LASCOE, DOROTHY. "One Company's Policy on Wage Attachment," *The Legal Aid Briefcase,* XXIII (June, 1965), pp. 264-66.

LYND, ROBERT S. and HELEN M. LYND. *Middletown in Transition* (New York: Harcourt, Brace, 1937).

MARGOLIUS, SIDNEY. "Consumer Information," in *Consumer Action and the War on Poverty: Conference Proceedings* (Washington, D. C.: U. S. Government Printing Office, 1965).

MILLER, HERMAN P. *Rich Man, Poor Man* (New York: Thomas Y. Crowell Co., 1964).

SCOTT, AUSTIN. *Dayton Journal Herald,* July 31, 1967.

THEOBALD, ROBERT. *Free Men and Free Markets* (New York: Potter, 1963).

TUCKER, ROBERT C. *Summary of Proceedings, Buying Club Conference* (New Haven: Community Progress, Inc., 1967).

6

Health, Poverty, and the Medical Mainstream

MILTON I. ROEMER
and ARNOLD I. KISCH

□ OF THE MANY DEPRIVATIONS OF the poor, deficiencies in medical service to heal their ailments and promote their health can be the most distressing. Adequate health service is important not only to cope with pain and suffering, but also to permit work and maintain productivity for the individual and community. It has, moreover, come to be an expected feature of modern civilization. Inaccessibility to medical care can yield resentment toward the whole society in which deprived persons live and further alienation from its norms and values.

In this chapter we will examine briefly the heavier burden of mortality and morbidity among the poor as compared to higher income groups. We will explore the lower level of medical services that they receive and their behavior with respect to such services. Over the centuries, numerous social programs have been launched to provide the poor with services which they would not otherwise get in the open medical market place. These will be briefly described, along with a closer look at several important new governmental health programs inaugurated in the last few years. The net outcome of the operations of both public and private health sectors will be considered. Finally, we will look ahead at the direction of current trends and consider the meaning of the issue emerging on care of the poor inside or outside the mainstream of American medicine.

MORBIDITY AND MORTALITY AMONG THE POOR

The heavier burden of sickness and death among the poor has been observed for centuries. In 1842, when Edwin Chadwick was arguing for public health services in the large cities, he collected data from Liverpool showing the average age at death among families of the gentry to be 35 years, among merchants 22 years, and among laborers 15 years. In the United States, a study of infant mortality (deaths under one year of age) in 1925 disclosed a rate of 59 deaths per 1,000 live births in higher income families (over $1,250 annual income), compared with 167 deaths per 1,000 in lower income families (under $450 annual income) (Stern, 1941).

The higher mortality among the poor is found in all age groups, but the differential is greatest among the young. In the younger years, the hazards of a hostile environment in causing fatal infectious disease and injuries are greater.

The causes of disease are many and complex, but in aggregate they affect the poor more seriously than the well-to-do. The United States National Health Survey conducts periodic interviews on a sample of approximately 42,000 households throughout the nation, and produces a wealth of data on disease and disability. For bouts of acute illness, there is little distinction in the frequency *reported* among different income groups, although it is probable that families of lower income are less likely to remember such events (and report them to an interviewer) simply because they are not so often identified through medical attention. For chronic conditions, however, the heavier burden among the poor is striking. In 1962-1963, chronic disorders, sufficiently serious to cause limitation of normal activity, affected 7.9 per cent of persons in families of $7,000 and over annual income; among poor families of under $2,000 annual income the percentage was 28.6 so disabled (U. S. Public Health Service, 1964).

In terms of aggregate disability, the loss of days from normal activity is greater for the poor by all available measures. Among school children, the upper income families ($7,000 and over) show loss of school days at a rate of 5.9 per child per year, compared with 6.5 days in lower income families (under $2,000). The more solicitous care of the upper income child doubtless reduces the net differential between these figures. In terms of work lost due to sickness, upper income persons suffer 5.4 days per person per year, compared with 8.9 days among the poor. As measured by periods of disability spent in bed, the upper income person has a rate of 5.2 days per year, compared with 12.0 in the poor person. In terms of all types of "restricted activity," the higher income person loses 13.1 days per year, compared with 29.1 days for the poor person.

The diagnoses of diseases causing these various forms of disability are numerous, and they may be classified in different ways. Using broad categories, the National Health Survey found the six leading diagnostic groups to be: heart disease, arthritis and rheumatism, mental and nervous conditions, high blood pressure, visual impairments, and orthopedic impairments (excluding paralyses or amputations, which fit into another rubric). For all six of these leading causes of chronic disorder, the load among the poor is heavier. The common notion that heart disease is a special affliction of the rich is borne out by neither morbidity or mortality data in the United States. As for mental disorder, the intensive New Haven Study by Hollingshead and Redlich suggested not only a higher total prevalence among the poor, but also a greater proportion of the more severe diagnoses leading to hospitalization (Hollingshead and Redlich, 1958).

The hard statistics on mortality and morbidity are necessary to establish the basic disadvantages of the poor, but they tell only a part of the story. Disease means not only pain and distress, but also fear and anxiety. The patient in a poor family is not so often reassured by a doctor, since he has less access to him, and the family may harbor its worries in silence. On the other hand, illness—being a common experience—may be casually regarded and neglected until its progress produces critical symptoms. The loss of time from work caused by disabling disease usually means loss of earnings; in the lowest paid jobs, such absence from work is seldom compensated by disability insurance benefits or "sick-pay" provisions.

The reasons for a greater burden of illness and death among the poor are multiple and complex. Their elaboration, disease by disease, constitutes the vast discipline of epidemiology (MacMahon, Pugh, and Ipsen, 1960). This is not to imply that each and every disease is more prevalent among the poor. Cancer of the lung, for example, is far more common in persons who smoke a great many cigarettes, and the mere cost of the habit reduces this liability among the very poorest persons. But the aggregate impact of the physical and social environment of the poor, including their housing, nutrition, occupations, and whole style of life, contributes to a burden of disease and death that blights their lives much more than among the well-to-do.

The health handicaps of poverty apply to all places, rural and urban. In the urban slum, however, congested living, air pollution, lack of recreational space, and the general squalor are not mitigated even by sunshine and grass. It is true that access to medical care for rich and poor alike is greater in the cities than in rural areas. The urban poor, however, receive much less medical treatment for their illness than the well-to-do, so that a given sickness is more likely to become advanced, disabling, and even fatal. For the Negro and other ethnic minorities, the problems of poverty and ignorance are compounded by the barriers of prejudice and discrimination. The character of the health services received by the poor will be examined below, but first we must consider the organized social programs that have evolved to cope with their sicknesses and ameliorate their hardships.

BASIC PROGRAMS FOR HEALTH CARE OF THE POOR

The serious handicaps of the urban poor, both in the occurrence of disease and the receipt of medical care, have long summoned corrective social actions. Were it not for numerous organized health service programs, health conditions would be far worse. One need only look at the mortality and morbidity of the impoverished masses in underdeveloped countries to see the effects of abject poverty, unalleviated by socio-medical efforts.

Organized health protection of the urban poor has been launched along many paths. Some programs are focused especially on the poor and others, while offered theoretically to everyone, are especially useful for the poor. Some programs are directed to certain specific diseases occurring more commonly among the deprived. In all these programs, there are achievements to report and improvements that have benefited the poor; there are also weaknesses and deficiencies that persist, particularly in comparison with the health services available to the more affluent sections of the population. To record the benefits must not be interpreted as glossing over the defects and gaps.

The modern public health movement had its beginnings in nineteenth-century Europe largely in response to the sordid conditions in big-city slums. The rich in their country manors could, in large degree, take care of themselves, but environmental sanitation to assure clean water and proper sewage disposal was a matter of life-or-death for the urban poor. Up to the present day, the task of the public health sanitarian is heavily concentrated in the tenements of the poor. Health departments throughout the United States operate clinics for prevention of disease in infants and pregnant women. While these "maternal and child health programs" are theoretically open to everyone, in practice they are used—and sometimes deliberately restricted to—families of low income. Higher income families are expected to consult private physicians for preventive as well as curative service. In these clinics, infants receive immunizations and advice is given on diet and child-rearing. Although these programs have demonstrably reduced infant and maternal mortality, they seldom succeed in reaching all the poor and rarely assure the level of service enjoyed by the well-to-do. The funds allocated from general revenues to support such public health clinics are far less than the expenditures made by comfortable families for comparable private care (Hanlon, 1960).

Public health agencies operate other services of special value to the poor. There are clinics for the treatment of venereal disease and tuberculosis. Dental clinics are held for children. Sometimes there are clinics, operated in conjunction with the schools, for treatment of heart conditions, deafness, or other disorders in children. The fact that such public clinics usually lack the gracious setting of a private doctor's office, are often overcrowded and understaffed, and may sometimes give perfunctory attention to patients, does not negate the benefits they do offer. The task is to expand the resources going into such services and to improve their effectiveness.

Public health nurses visit the homes of the poor in connection with communicable disease, advice on newborn baby care, and even bedside service to the chronically ill. The education efforts of health departments are largely directed toward influencing the hygienic behavior of the poor. Screening tests to detect chronic diseases such as diabetes, glaucoma, cancer, or hypertension, are offered by various agencies, and these have special value for lower income groups who lack regular family doctor contacts. One of the frustrating realities, however, is that the very poorest families—alienated by ignorance or apathy—often do not take advantage of such services even when they are made conveniently available (Anderson, 1963).

While public health agency services are, in practice, devoted largely to the poor, welfare department medical services are legally restricted to the poor. The historic development of these services from the Elizabethan Poor Laws, with their sanctimonious distinction between the provident and improvident poor, to the current welfare programs is a saga of evolution in social responsibility, a saga which is still in process. In relation to the past, today's urban slum-dweller is very fortunate, but in relation to the level of services that our current medical resources could provide, the deficiencies remain serious.

The medical and related services financed by welfare agencies for the poor depend on their legal "category." Since the Social Security Act of 1935 and its numerous amendments, federal grants to the states for public assistance are based on a needy person's identification in one of four classes: (1) over 65 years of age; (2) families with children and a lacking or unemployed breadwinner; (3) blind persons; and (4) persons with "total and permanent" disability. Poor persons who do not fit into one of these classes may be eligible for "general assistance," which must be financed entirely from state and local funds, typically meager. In 1962, about 7,500,000 persons received assistance under these programs, constituting about 4 per cent of the national population. These persons are concentrated heavily in the urban slums.

The precise range of medical services available to the poor under public assistance programs varies with their "category," with the state or county in which they live, and with the year under discussion. Recent changes in the Social Security Act, to be discussed below ("Medicaid"), have altered these entitlements greatly. In general, however, medical and hospital services for the "indigent" and the "medically indigent" (see below) are provided under three patterns: (1) the poor person may be seen by a personally chosen physician and hospitalized in an ordinary community hospital, with the expenses being paid by the welfare department; (2) he may be seen in an out-patient clinic of a voluntary hospital and hospitalized in a special ward for the poor in such a hospital; or (3) he may be served in special governmental clinics and hospitals intended exclusively for the poor, and usually operated by special governmental authorities (U. S. Welfare Administration, 1964).

There are special human and technical qualities to each of these patterns of medical care for the urban poor. The public clinics and hospitals are typically crowded places, often badly maintained because of frugal financial support. They have little sensitivity to personal comfort and convenience (long travel time, waiting periods, etc.) although they may give a high technical quality of service—especially if the institution is affiliated with a medical school. The private doctor arrangements, on the other hand, may be more satisfactory on the human side and less on the scientific side. Some busy physicians, however, choose not to see welfare patients at all, so that the poor tend to consult mainly general practitioners in depressed neighborhoods. Here they tend to receive a style of medical care that is deficient both technically and humanistically.

Aside from the governmental hospitals—usually municipal or county—oriented to the poor, there are also state hospitals for mental disorders and tuberculosis, whose patients are largely from the lower income groups. Generally improved living conditions in the United States and effective new drugs (especially streptomycin) have resulted in a great reduction in the census of tuberculosis sanatoria in recent years. These institutions are being converted into facilities for general chronic diseases, predominantly serving the poor. Mental hospitals, on the other hand, are still crowded with patients, mostly from the lower income groups, although there has been a recent slight decline in census due to more effective methods of psychiatric therapy. While mental hospitals have improved their quality of care in recent years, they are still far below the level of maintenance in general hospitals which are supported mainly by the private sector. The large and semi-isolated mental institution remains an unhappy last resort for many senile paupers who, if they had the money, would be cared for at home or in a comfortable local nursing home.

Other special programs of medical care help the urban poor who qualify by reason of certain diagnoses. Crippled children, as defined by various state laws, may obtain service through special clinics or private doctors at governmental expense. Disabled adults may get "vocational rehabilitation," including corrective medical care, if treatment and training would render them employable. These programs typically have a means test, so that they are concentrated in their effects among the poor. They are financed by federal and state funds and maintain high standards of quality for the participating doctors and hospitals. Their quantitative impact, however, is small, because of the restricted medical definitions for eligibility and the relatively meager level of public financial support (Roemer, 1967).

Those urban poor who happen to be dependents of military personnel (wives and children) or veterans of past military service may be the beneficiaries of special governmental medical programs. The dependents can receive care from any physician or hospital, with the bill being paid by the U. S. Department of Defense. Veterans receive care in special governmental hospitals, even for non-service-connected conditions if they are persons of low income. In contrast to the local governmental administration of programs for welfare clients, the federal administration of these services is associated with higher standards of medical performance as well as with preservation of the patient's personal dignity (I. J. Cohen, 1966).

Numerous voluntary health agencies also may serve the urban poor in such fields as home nursing ("visiting nurse associations"); personal assistance to crippled children; treatment of cancer, multiple sclerosis, muscular dystrophy, or other grave diseases; and emergency care after disasters such as floods or fires (Red Cross). Alcoholics may be helped by Alcoholics Anonymous and drug addicts by other bodies. Family planning advice and provisions may be offered in clinics of the Planned Parenthood Association. All these social services help, but they tend to have an impact far below the extent of the need among the poor.

Procurement of medical care by the self-supporting population of the United States has been greatly advanced by the extension of voluntary health insurance. There are many types, under the sponsorship of hospitals (Blue Cross), medical societies (Blue Shield), commercial insurance carriers, and employers or consumer organizations. The principal benefits of this insurance relate to hospitalization and the doctor's services in hospitalized illness, although the range of benefits has been widening. Typically, these programs ease the economic access of persons to private doctors and local hospitals and indirectly they have promoted the quality of care provided. While about 80 per cent of the national population is now protected, at least partially, by hospitalization insurance, the non-protected 20 per cent are heavily concentrated among the unemployed, the casually employed, the migrant, and other persons who make up the urban slum population (Somers and Somers, 1961).

The foregoing provides only a sketchy review of the principal organized social programs involving certain health services for the urban poor. In a nutshell, they all help. They tend to be improvements over the past, but none of them goes far enough. In terms of our medical potentialities, and our democratic expectations, they are generally deficient. The net impact of all these social programs, as well as the effects of actions derived from their own limited private resources, on the health services received by the poor may now be reviewed.

HEALTH SERVICES RECEIVED BY THE POOR

In spite of the variety of health service programs available to help the urban poor, the net volume of health care they receive is lower than that received by the higher income groups in both quantity and quality. This situation exists in the face of the heavier burden of disease and disability which, as we observed earlier, afflicts the poor.

The basic element in medical care is the service of a physician. From an initial contact with the doctor, other services that may be necessary follow, such as prescribed drugs, nursing care, laboratory or x-ray examinations, physical therapy, and hospitalization. Using the basic measure of "physician visits," the average American receives 5.0 such services per person per year (1959 data). For persons in families earning $7,000 or more, however, the rate is 5.7 physician visits, and it declines steadily to 4.5 visits in families earning under $2,000 annually. This relationship characterizes each age group observed separately (U. S. Public Health Service, 1964).

The locales of these physician services reflect the character of medical services received by the affluent and the poor. For both groups, the bulk of services are obtained in the office of a private physician, but the proportions at different sites are revealing. As indicated in Table 1, within the lesser overall rate of doctor's ser-

TABLE 1

Physician Contacts

	Family Income	
Locale of Physician Contacts	$7,000 & Over	Under $2,000
Doctor's office	3.8	2.8
Patient's home	0.6	0.5
Telephone	0.7	0.3
Hospital clinic	0.3	0.7
Other	0.3	0.2
All places	5.7	4.5

vices received by the poor, the rate is lower for all locales of contact, except in hospital clinics where it is much higher. In such clinics, the time allotted per patient is typically much shorter than in a private office.

In spite of conventional notions that the poor are bountifully served in public clinics, it is evident that over 60 per cent of their physician's care is obtained in private offices. Those offices, however, usually belong to general practitioners rather than specialists. Among high income families, for example, a pediatrician was consulted during the year by 29.4 per cent of children (under 15 years of age), compared with 9.6 per cent of low income children. An obstetrician or gynecologist was consulted by 17.1 per cent of women in higher income families, compared with 3.5 per cent of low income women. General physical examinations are a keystone of preventive medicine, but these too are rare among the poor. In 1963, among higher income families ($10,000 and over annually) 54 per cent of youth under 17 years had such check-ups, compared with only 16 per cent of youth from poor families (under $2,000) (U. S. Public Health Service, 1965).

The handicaps for dental service to the poor are even greater than for physician's service. Persons in higher income families ($7,000 and over) have 2.3 dental visits per person per year, compared with 0.7 visits among the poor (under $2,000). The dental services for the higher income groups, moreover, are more likely to consist of fillings and cleanings—preventive in effect—while for the poor they are much more likely to be extractions—the end result of neglect.

Prescribed drugs are also received at lower rates by the poor. Of the total drug consumption of the lower income groups, moreover, a higher proportion consists of self-prescribed or patent medicines. The corner druggist, it has been said, is often the poor man's doctor, offering across-the-counter pills which may only serve to alleviate pains and mask symptoms, thus delaying the procurement of needed diagnosis and therapy (Consumers Union, 1963).

It is only for hospitalization that the record of health services among various income groups shows a different relationship. When prevention has failed, and when early ambulatory medical care has not halted a disease process, admission to a hospital becomes necessary. The basic findings for 1959 are set out in Table 2, but more recent data show the same relationships. As the table demon-

TABLE 2

HOSPITAL DISCHARGES AND STAY, 1959

Family Income	Hospital Discharges per 1,000 Persons	Average Stay (Days)	Aggregate Days per 1,000 Persons
Under $2,000	92.8	11.7	1,086
$2,000–$3,999	103.5	8.5	840
$4,000–$6,999	101.3	7.2	729
$7,000 and over	97.9	7.9	773

strates, the poorest families have admissions to hospitals less than middle-income families, but almost as frequently as the highest income families. Once admitted, however, the average length-of-stay of the poor is much longer, so that the aggregate days of hospital service received by the poor is significantly *higher* than among the well-to-do.

These data reflect a great deal about the disease patterns of the poor and the way in which our society has responded to the general problems of medical care. In a word, our ameliorative social measures have followed a crisis strategy. When health problems get bad enough, we move on them. Thus, the social programs for providing hospitalization are relatively well developed. As noted earlier, there are many municipal and county hospitals for the poor. The extensive Veterans Administration hospital network will serve low income veterans even for non-military disabilities, but such conditions are not eligible for ambulatory treatment. Examining the budgets of welfare departments, we find that about two-thirds of the expenditures go for hospital care of the indigent and one-third for out-of-hospital services; among self-supporting persons, the allocations are almost exactly the opposite. In New York State, the expenditures for welfare medical services in 1963 were $184 million of which nearly $160 million or 87 per cent were for institutional (hospital and nursing home) services (Yerby, 1966).

Once admitted to a hospital, the low income person stays on a longer time than his more affluent counterpart. This differential is due to several reasons. His illness is more likely to be at a far advanced stage, when recovery takes longer. Having a poorer nutritional state, his rate of recovery from surgery or his response to other therapy is likely to be slower. In public hospitals, the actual management of his care is more likely to be assigned to a young resident or intern, whose skills are less than those of a fully trained physician. The non-paying patient is more likely to be "teaching material" in a medical school—kept longer for the education of medical students. On top of all this, the indigent person's home conditions are known to be meager, so that the conscientious physician cannot discharge him as rapidly as he would release the middle-class patient, with a pleasant home in which to convalesce.

All these characteristics of the health services received by the poor are ultimately consequences of their poverty, but this is not to say that lack of money is the total explanation. As we have seen, many programs of financial support have developed over the years and these have compensated to varying degrees for the inability to purchase medical service in the private market. But beyond low purchasing power, as such, the poor suffer other handicaps that obstruct their proper use of modern medical care and their maintenance of health. Having lower levels of education, they are less likely to recognize significant symptoms and seek care. The repeated physical and emotional traumas of poverty make them fatalistic and even apathetic; delays and neglect in seeking care are the result. Even when services for mothers and infants are provided by a public health clinic in a slum neighborhood, it is common for the utilization rate to be low. Initial response to a symptom of illness is more likely to be communication with a neighbor than consultation with a doctor (King, 1962).

Compounding fatalistic attitudes are many practical impediments to medical care like time and transportation. As noted earlier, the low-income worker, unlike the white-collar employee, seldom has "sick-leave" provisions in his job, and a day lost waiting at a public clinic or even seeing a private doctor often means loss of a day's wages. The slum tenement mother cannot take a sick baby to the clinic without making provision for her other small children or dragging them along. Transportation is another problem. Dependence on buses and street cars, rather than a family automobile, is time-consuming, uncomfortable, and often irritating. On top of all this are the insensitivities and long waits in public clinics and even in the private offices of doctors serving a large proportion of the poor.

In the big-city slums, the physicians and dentists located close to the poor are likely to be the least well trained. The Watts area of Los Angeles, for example, has only one-third the doctor-population ratio of the county as a whole and only a handful of specialists. Among the smaller supply of doctors in the Watts area, only 16 per cent are specialists, compared with about 55 per cent in the nation as a whole. Two-thirds of the 16 per cent, moreover, are self-declared specialists, rather than doctors certified by the appropriate American Specialty Boards (Roemer, 1966).

Chiropractors, herbalists, and other cultist practitioners are more likely to be located in the central-city slum than in the fashionable professional sections of a city. They are used more frequently by the poor, not only because they are close at hand, but also because they are less expensive and often more reassuring than scientific physicians. They promise quick cures, about which the unsophisticated or desperate slum-dweller may be gullible. Slick patent medicine and food faddist advertising compound the fraudulence perpetrated on the poor by various profiteers (Deutsch, 1960).

NEW HEALTH PROGRAMS FOR THE POOR

The deficiencies in health services received by the poor have been recognized by socially-minded health leaders for some time. In spite of the numerous categorical programs reviewed earlier, especially the medical services of welfare departments directed to the needs of the indigent, the heavier volume of morbidity among the poor has been far from adequately served. Because of this patent deficiency, a number of new health programs have been launched in recent years by federal legislation. These programs may represent a turning point in America's approach to health services for all the people, poor and affluent (Forgotson, 1967).

Most important of the legislative output were the Social Security Act amendments of 1965 which established the first nationwide social insurance program in the United States for medical care. Known popularly as "Medicare," Title XVIII of the Act provides a series of hospital, medical, and related benefits to virtually all persons in the country 65 years of age and over, whether or not they are entitled to a Social Security old-age pension. The significant point is that there is no means test for these benefits; every aged person receives the same hospital services and related care in an "extended care facility" (nursing home) or at home ("home health services"). For physician's care and certain ancillary services, the aged person must pay (or he may choose to forego these benefits) a small "voluntary" monthly premium ($3 in 1967), which is more than matched by federal subsidy. Moreover, Social Security cash benefits were elevated by over $3 per month to cover this added expenditure (Cohen and Ball, 1965).

Since a major share of the urban poor, especially in slum boarding houses, are over 65 years of age, Medicare will doubtless be of great value to the poor as a social class. As statistics also show, the burden of illness among the aged in all income groups is much greater than in the young, and the aged parent's children must often foot the bills. Voluntary health insurance, as noted earlier, had its least impact among the aged, especially those of low income, so that the Medicare legislation has obviously been a great step forward in social welfare.

The precise benefits of Medicare are far from comprehensive. There are limitations on the number of hospital days payable (90 days in a "spell of illness"), there are cost-sharing requirements (e.g. $40 on hospital admissions and $10 per day after the sixtieth day), and important items are not covered at all, like dental care and out-of-hospital drugs. Limitations on the "voluntary insurance" benefits for physician's care are greater, with a $50 per year deductible and 20 per cent cost-sharing for all services.

In spite of these limitations, imposed in the interests of reducing the total social insurance budget and thereby gaining Congressional approval, Medicare has clearly ushered in a new era for medical care of the poor. For those poor who are aged, the law facilitates access to the same mainstream of community medical care—the private physician and the voluntary general hospital—that serves the well-to-do. In part, even the administration of the law makes use of the existing framework of private insurance plans as "fiscal intermediaries" between the central Social Security Administration and the providers of service. The mainstream entitlements, of course, apply only to those poor who are aged. If any lesson can be learned from the history of social insurance for medical care in other countries, however, it is that with time and experience both population coverage and medical benefits are expanded. There is little doubt that the same will happen to Medicare.

Although Medicare is mainly a "bill-paying" mechanism and accepts the existing framework of private medical practice, it has introduced certain modest influences on the quality of care. Hospitals, to receive payments, must be "certified," and this requires meeting various technical standards. "Utilization review" of cases is one of the most important of these requirements—a measure which should heighten the self-discipline among physicians on hospital staffs. Nursing homes, to be certified, must have a "transfer agreement" with a general hospital, a device which can reduce the previous isolation of these units from professional stimulation. Perhaps most important, the very public visibility of medical care costs—already produced by Medicare—will induce a closer examination of the whole social structure of American medicine. Soaring costs can highlight much of the extravagance and inefficiency of private, solo medical practice, and this publicity in turn can lead to corrective innovations in the patterns of organization. These innovations can have special meaning for the poor.

Along with Medicare for the aged, the Social Security amendments of 1965 also added Title XIX, which involves radical alterations in the whole pattern of medical services for the poor under age 65. "Medicaid," as it has come to be called, is a modification of the long-established public assistance medical care legislation, reviewed earlier, which rests on the principle of federal grants to the states for help to certain demographic categories. Title XIX liberalizes the basis of these federal grants—allowing substantially open-ended matching of state appropriations—and authorizes the states to include among their medical beneficiaries not only the recipients of cash assistance, but also similar persons who are "medically indigent." The latter would include a family with a missing or unemployed breadwinner and dependent children (AFDC) which was not poor enough to qualify for cash assistance but still could not afford private medical care. Theoretically, this provision could reach a substantial proportion of urban slum-dwellers who were not previously receiving medical care. Medicaid also provides that, to receive federal grants, a state must assure a minimum range of five professional and hospitalization benefits to all categorical recipients. Moreover, it must gradually expand its coverage, so that, by 1975, virtually all poor people in the state—whether or not "categorically linked"—must be entitled to financial support for essential medical services (Greenfield, 1966).

How successful Medicaid will actually be in extending good medical care to the nation's poor is a serious question. For one thing, the state government must agree to the federal conditions and, as of this writing two years after enactment of the law, 24 states have still not done so. For another, the definition of in-digency and medical indigency is still left up to each state; many of the poorest states with large numbers of impoverished people draw these lines at very low thresholds. Thirdly, the definitions of health services, even within the federal schedule of five benefits, are subject to varying interpretations; drugs and dental care, more-over, are not even among them. Fourthly, the whole Medicaid program, like Medicare, accepts the "mainstream" approach as un-reservedly desirable; it incorporates no provisions that might modify organizational patterns to better suit the needs of the poor or, for that matter, the efficient application of medical science for persons of any income.

The neutrality of Medicare and Medicaid on the critical issue of patterns of health service organization in America lends special significance to two other pieces of health legislation enacted by the Eighty-ninth (1965-1966) Congress. These are the "Heart Disease, Cancer, and Stroke Amendments of 1965" (PL 89-239) and the "Comprehensive Health Planning and Public Health Service Amendments of 1966" (PL 89-749). Neither of these laws is focused specifically on the poor, but their long-term significance for those in this category may be as great as the milestone of social insurance.

The Heart-Cancer-Stroke law is based on an effort to attack the three leading causes of death in the United States by encouraging improvements in the quality of care for these diseases at the grass roots and in the average urban neighborhood. It provides federal grants for developing "regional medical programs" to improve the diagnosis and treatment of these and related diseases. The regional programs are intended to establish active professional connections between the great medical centers and peripheral hospitals around them. So far, these ties have been largely limited to the organization of postgraduate instruction for practicing physicians, but there is hope that they might be extended to included active consultation and referral services. The goal is to enable every person to receive the best scientific care for his disease, regardless of his geographic location or socioeconomic status. The regionalization concept, embodied in this law, has been applied throughout the world as a mechanism for systematizing medical care and elevating its quality. Whether the Heart-Cancer-Stroke law will evolve into such a full-dress regionalization pattern depends on other political developments in the coming years (Russell, 1966).

The Comprehensive Health Planning amendments have even a broader potential influence on medical care patterns, although the terms of the law are relatively modest. Its immediate purpose is to consolidate federal grants to the states in formerly earmarked fields, such as venereal disease control, chronic illness and aging programs, and "general public health," in order to permit each state to allocate the funds flexibly according to a "state plan" based on its own particular needs. The long-term purpose is much broader; it provides grants to the states for overall planning of health facilities, personnel, and services—in the private as well as the public sector—to best meet the total health needs of the population. If this purpose is taken seriously, the implications are great for improvement of health services to the poor. Any objective description and assessment of our current patterns of medical care, the chaotic multiplicity of agencies, the sovereignty of private, solo medical practice and small autonomous hospitals, and the irrational separation of prevention and therapy can only help to set us on the road to their correction (Stewart, 1967).

Still another federal program, with clear impacts on the health of the urban poor, is the so-called "war on poverty" administered by the Office of Economic Opportunity (OEO). Several projects of this agency, including "Operation Head Start" for preschool youngsters and the Youth Job Corps for unemployed teen-agers have an indirect bearing on health. Most direct and daring of the OEO projects, from the viewpoint of health needs, are the "neighborhood health centers." These are centers for comprehensive ambulatory medical care located in the heart of the slums and open 24 hours a day. In contrast to the out-patient departments of the big municipal hospitals, the neighborhood centers emphasize a personal doctor relationship for each patient and stress participation of the local people in the management of the program and as auxiliary health workers. With such involvement, it is hoped that the poor will make fuller use of the services, instead of distrusting them as the reluctant charity of "the establishment." At this writing, only a half-dozen such centers are in operation, in the central ghettos (mainly Negro) of large cities, but some 40 are being planned. Doctors are engaged in the centers on full-time or part-time salaries, and overall direction is under medical schools, medical societies, local health departments, or other bodies. The neighborhood centers are clearly a deviation from the mainstream concept of medical care for the poor, and it remains to be seen how their character takes shape (Geiger, 1966).

Several other established governmental health programs were expanded or liberalized in 1965-1966 to improve services for the poor. The traditional "maternal and child health" grants to the states were amended to permit comprehensive maternal and child *care* in "high risk" families, meaning essentially families of the poor. The Community Mental Health Amendments of 1965 (PL 89-105) support wider funding of both construction and operation of psychiatric centers oriented mainly to the needs of the poor. The Vocational Rehabilitation Amendments of 1965 (PL 89-290) enlarge the federal share of these grants which, as we noted earlier, help principally low income persons who are disabled but employable. These and other new laws of the last few years, at both federal and state levels, mark an apparent turning point in social concern for the provision of health services to the nation's poor.

THE VIEW AHEAD

Improvement in the health of the urban poor depends, first of all, on their living conditions. Two hundred years ago Johann

Peter Frank wrote that "poverty is the mother of disease." Although there are other progenitors of sickness as well, Frank's axiom is still true. Not only does an insanitary and congested environment contribute to the causation of disease, but the alienation and apathy of poverty discourage behavior that could protect health. Racial and ethnic discriminations compound the difficulties for millions of dwellers in the urban ghetto. The most basic approach to the health of the poor, therefore, must emphasize improvement of their whole standard of living. Adequate employment is obviously essential, associated with proper education, good housing, balanced nutrition, ample recreation, and above all, equal opportunity.

There are two somewhat competing philosophies at play in the current American scene with respect to health services for the indigent. One is to set up special organized facilities for the poor—municipal hospitals and clinics, specially appointed doctors, public health clinics for children, and so on. The latest implementation of this approach is the OEO "neighborhood health center" discussed above. The other philosophy has been called the "mainstream approach"—that is, arrangement for medical care of the poor through existing resources serving the general population, these being principally private physicians and voluntary hospitals. This latter philosophy is embodied in the important Medicare Law of 1965. In either case a public agency pays the costs, but the mainstream approach is thought to have a more democratic quality, because it does not segregate the poor in separate places. And as already noted, the conditions in those separate facilities—whether in massive municipal hospitals or in public health clinics located in the basement of a county courthouse—are often conducive to perfunctory and insensitive medical care (Strauss, 1967).

The issue is not so simple, however, because the quality and accessibility of medical service in the medical mainstream may also be very deficient. Free choice of private doctor, which results in assembly-line treatment in a poorly staffed office of a slum general practitioner is no blessing. Welfare department tabulations reveal shocking mediocrities and abuses of both patients and public moneys in such private practices. In the voluntary community hospital, moreover, the poor may still be segregated in second-class wards, where they do not receive the physician's care, the nursing care, and various amenities accorded to private patients (Rogatz, 1967). On the other hand, the quality and even the human sensitivity of medical care in a special facility may be excellent. The level achieved in most "segregated" Veterans Administration hospitals demonstrates this, as do the standards now being applied in several new OEO neighborhood health centers. Separate facilities for the poor, in other words, may appear to have undemocratic overtones, but they are good or bad depending on the quantity of resources put into them and the policies of management applied.

The root problem is that the mainstream of American medicine has inherent deficiencies that compromise the accessibility and quality of medical care for the affluent as well as the poor. The predominance of solo medical practice, uncoordinated hospitals, self-prescribed drugs, and similar factors represent a heritage from earlier centuries, a heritage which blocks the realization of the full potential of modern medical science. The task, therefore, is to modify the patterns and direction of "mainstream medicine," so that it becomes appropriate to the true requirements of science and the needs of people. This is a long and complex challenge to explain, but it involves essentially *organization* of both preventive and curative health services economically, technologically, and geographically.

If the character of the mainstream in American medical care is appropriately modified—with more imaginative use of comprehensive group practice, with regionalization of hospitals, and with better integration of prevention and treatment—then the care of the poor should certainly be provided within it. In a word, this would mean that certain patterns of health service organization, now applied in a faltering way in the segregated streams, would be improved in their application—through more generous financial support and competent leadership—and incorporated within the mainstream of medicine. The issue posed earlier would then disappear, and all persons, rich and poor, would receive one uniformly high quality of medical care, regardless of the source of financing.

The new legislation for "comprehensive health planning," along with several other developments reviewed above, may help to promote such a better future. If it does, one more blow may be struck against the sordid cycles of poverty and disease that now enchain the dwellers in urban slums.

References

ANDERSON, ODIN W. "The Utilization of Health Services," in H. E. Freeman, S. Levine, and L. G. Reeder (eds.), *Handbook of Medical Sociology* (New York: Prentice-Hall, 1963), pp. 349-67.

COHEN, I. J. "The Veterans Administration Medical Care Program," in L. J. DeGroot (ed.), *Medical Care: Social and Organizational Aspects* (Springfield, Ill.: Charles C. Thomas, 1966), pp. 425-36.

COHEN, WILBUR J. and ROBERT M. BALL. "Social Security Amendments of 1965: Summary and Legislative History," *Social Security Bulletin,* 28, No. 9 (September, 1965), pp. 3-21.

DEUTSCH, R. M. "Nutritional Nonsense and Food Fanatics," in *Proceedings, Third National Congress and Medical Quackery* (Chicago: American Medical Association, 1960), pp. 15-24.

EDITORS OF CONSUMER REPORTS. *The Medicine Show: Some Plain Truths about Popular Remedies for Common Ailments* (Mount Vernon, N.Y.: Consumers Union, 1963).

FORGOTSON, E. H. "1965: The Turning Point in Health Law—1966 Reflections," *American Journal of Public Health,* 57 (June, 1967), pp. 934-46.

GEIGER, H. JACK. "The Poor and the Professional: Who Takes the Handle Off the Broad Street Pump?" paper presented at the Annual Meeting of the American Public Health Association, San Francisco, California, November 1, 1966.

GREENFIELD, MARGARET. "Title XIX and Medi-Cal," *Public Affairs Report* (Bulletin of the Institute of Governmental Studies, University of California, Berkeley), Vol. 7, No. 4, August, 1966.

HANLON, JOHN J. *Principles of Public Health Administration* (St. Louis: C. V. Mosby Company, 1960), "Maternal and Child Health Activities," pp. 470-92.

HOLLINGSHEAD, AUGUST B. and FREDRICK C. REDLICH. *Social Class and Mental Illness* (New York: John Wiley, 1958).

KING, STANLEY H. *Perceptions of Illness and Medical Practice* (New York: Russell Sage Foundation, 1962).

MACMAHON, BRIAN, THOMAS F. PUGH, and JOHANNES IPSEN. *Epidemiologic Methods* (Boston: Little, Brown and Company, 1960).

ROEMER, MILTON I. "Health Resources and Services in the Watts Area of Los Angeles," *California's Health,* 23, Nos. 8-9 (February-March 1966), pp. 123-43.

———. "Governmental Health Programs Affecting the American Family," *Journal of Marriage and the Family,* 29 (February, 1967), pp. 40-63.

Rogatz, Peter. "Our Care of the Poor is a Failure," *Medical Economics*, 29 (May, 1967), pp. 209-17.

Russell, J. M. "New Federal Regional Medical Programs." *New England Journal of Medicine*, 275 (August 11, 1966), pp. 309-12.

Somers, Herman M. and Anne R. Somers. *Doctors, Patients, and Health Insurance* (Washington: The Brookings Institution, 1961).

Stern, Bernhard J. *Society and Medical Progress* (Princeton: Princeton University Press, 1941), "Income and Health," pp. 126-41.

Stewart, William H. *New Dimensions of Health Planning* (The 1967 Michael M. Davis lecture) (Chicago: University of Chicago, Center for Health Administration Studies, 1967).

Strauss, Anselm L. "Medical Ghettos," *Trans-Action*, 4 (May, 1967), pp. 7-15, 62.

U. S. Public Health Service, National Center for Health Statistics. *Medical Care, Health Status, and Family Income*. Series 10, No. 9 (Washington, May, 1964), pp. 52-74.

U. S. Public Health Service, National Center for Health Statistics. *Physician Visits—Interval of Visits and Children's Routine Checkups, United States, July 1963-June 1964*. Series 10, No. 19 (Washington, June, 1965).

U. S. Welfare Administration. *Characteristics of State Public Assistance Plans under the Social Security Act: Provisions for Medical and Remedial Care*. Public Assistance Report, No. 49 (Washington, 1964).

Yerby, Alonzo S. "Public Medical Care for the Needy in the United States," in L. J. DeGroot (ed.), *Medical Care: Social and Organizational Aspects* (Springfield, Ill.: Charles C. Thomas, 1966), pp. 382-401.

7

Justice and the Poor

EDGAR S. CAHN
and JEAN CAMPER CAHN

☐ IN HIS BEST SELLING BOOK, *The Lawyers*, Martin Mayer concludes
his attack on the program of legal services to the poor by warning
that

> The survival of the program requires that it offer legal assistance,
> not a collection of newly manufactured and unseaworthy "rights."
> . . . The battle to improve the condition of the poor as a group
> (as distinguished from the fate of individual poor people individu-
> ally oppressed) must be won in the legislature, not in the courts,
> and it is confusing and cruel to the people to pretend otherwise
> (1967).

We shall focus on this attack by Mayer—not simply, or even chiefly,
because of the notoriety his book has received—or even because
his is the first recent attempt to present a comprehensive overview
of the legal profession to laymen. Rather, Mayer's attack must be
appreciated as expressive of a fundamental school of thought both
within the law and without. In its more familiar form, this position
attacks "judicial activism" of all kinds. In its more pernicious form,
it provides the rationale for the political attacks being mounted
at the local, state, and national levels—attacks which seek to prohibit all federally funded legal service programs from instituting
suit against any government agency such as welfare departments
or public housing authorities.

Mayer's thesis can be summed up by three propositions:

1. the legal theories now being advanced on behalf of the poor
in welfare and related areas are fundamentally "unseaworthy";

2. traditional quality legal representation (as theoretically performed by legal aid agencies in the past) is basically adequate to
handle the purely legal injustices encountered by the poor; and

3. the legal process and the political process are, and ought to remain, entirely distinct.

Each of these propositions will be discussed in turn.

SOUNDNESS OF DEVELOPING LEGAL THEORIES

The first proposition regarding the soundness of the legal theories developed in the poverty area and advanced by neighborhood law firms is best disposed of by looking at the record as reported by the Office of Economic Opportunity and by the *Journal of American Trial Lawyers' Association*. During fiscal year 1967, neighborhood law firms processed over 300,000 cases, and in three-fourths of those which were carried through trial the results were favorable to the poor. As the official publication of the Trial Lawyers' Association comments:

> These are especially remarkable figures for the program's aid is withheld in any case that can be handled on a contingent basis or where there is an available source (as under workmen's compensation) for a poor person to engage a private attorney (*Journal of American Trial Lawyers' Association,* 1967).

The record is even more striking in the area of welfare law where Mayer is particularly skeptical and indeed downright hostile. Fred Graham's summation of recent legal developments in the welfare field shows the significant gains that are being made:

> Taken together, these and other pending cases assert a "bill of rights" for welfare clients.
> The theory is that although the Constitution does not require that the Government provide welfare, once a system is established, clients have a right to receive their benefits without interruption except for good cause and after a fair hearing, free of intrusion by welfare officials into their private lives, and without discrimination.
> These novel assertions, and as the shibboleths of American folklore suggest, are alien to the national traditions of self-reliance and free enterprise.
> Yet, the clients are winning almost all of their cases in the lower courts—perhaps because there are no precedents to bind the judges—and it is already apparent that, barring a stunning series of reversals in the Supreme Court, the welfare clients' "bill of rights" will be transformed from a theory to a fact in a few years (*New York Times,* November 26, 1967, p. IV-14).

Similar triumphs appear to be on the way with respect to medicare, public housing, consumer frauds, bankruptcy, and public education. We shall not attempt here a survey of developments in the poverty law or urban law field. It suffices to say that creative advocacy and legal ingenuity have now proved that they can generate new legal doctrines and new rules of law for the poor as well as for the rich, Mayer's mechanical jurisprudence notwithstanding.

INADEQUACY OF TRADITIONAL LEGAL SERVICES

The second proposition—the adequacy of traditional legal services and of the legal process as we have known it in the past—seems equally difficult to maintain in the wake of recent summers. For it is clearly evident that we face a crisis in the rule of law, a crisis of philosophical as well as logistical dimensions—a crisis to which Mayer appears oblivious. Two of the sources of this crisis are readily discernible. We term them the "rights explosion" and the "grievance explosion."

THE RIGHTS EXPLOSION

Recent years have witnessed the creation of a vast and still growing array of legally vested rights which are enshrined in statutes and court decisions—but which are not honored in practice. The developing case law regarding the rights of juveniles, of tenants in public housing, of persons accused of crimes, of welfare recipients, and of minority group members has challenged the capacity of the legal system.

In the criminal field, the newly expanded right to counsel for those charged with a crime will require, conservatively estimated, a fivefold increase in the number of full-time public defenders. In the civil field, the crisis is even more acute. Cases take longer and longer to come to trial; congestion of the court calendars increases steadily. The capacity—and the inclination—of the profession to supply the requisite quantity and quality of representation recently prompted Justice Douglas to remark:

The supply of lawyer manpower is not nearly large enough. . . .
It may well be that until the goal of free legal assistance to the

indigent in all areas of the law is achieved, the poor are not harmed by well-meaning, charitable assistance of laymen. On the contrary, for the majority of indigents, who are not so fortunate to be served by neighborhood legal offices, lay assistance may be the only hope for achieving equal justice at this time (dissent to dismissal in *Hackin v. Arizona*).

In testimony submitted to Congress, the American Bar Association, the National Legal Aid and Defender Association, and the National Bar Association all take the position that $90 million (triple the amount now expended and nearly 20 times the sum spent in 1964) would be required to assure adequate legal representation to the poor in non-criminal cases. And because of the shortage of lawyers and the high price of justice, the United States Supreme Court only recently struck down a state statute which restricted the supply of lawyers as an unconstitutional infringement on the right to citizens to petition for a redress of grievance as guaranteed by the First Amendment (*United Mine Workers of America v. Illinois State Bar Association*).

THE GRIEVANCE EXPLOSION

Each new right means that a remedy is available for a new class of wrongs. However, a vast quantity of lesser injuries require and deserve redress but fall short of the magnitude necessary to give them the status of legally recognized injuries. In certain situations, such grievances are elevated to constitutional status, as in the case of the Negro who successfully challenged an official for addressing her by her first name. Similarly, in the recent *de facto* school segregation case in the District of Columbia, it was just such trivial differences which together constituted unconstitutionally discriminatory treatment. But, by and large, grievances such as these are neatly dispatched by the aphorism, *de minimis non curat lex.*

The law provides no immunity from the contumely and arrogance of officials: the taunting word "boy" flung in the face of a Negro male, corporal punishment of Mexican-American children for speaking Spanish on school grounds, the continuous insult of being stopped, searched, and humiliatingly interrogated. Nor does the legal system purport to offer remedy for poor garbage collection in slum areas (although recently one legal service program prevailed in its attack on a water company that provided inferior and contaminated water to Mexican-American migrants living on the outskirts of a town). Lawyers cannot stand by to institute legal action every time a child or parent is humiliated by a teacher, every time a taxi refuses to pick up passengers in the ghetto, every time chain stores offer shoddy merchandise in their slum branches. It is just such petty grievances which cumulatively have made tinderboxes of every major urban center and which call into question Mayer's faith in the fundamental adequacy of traditional legal aid.

OFFICIAL IMMUNITY

Finally, we must add a third dimension to this crisis in the rule of law. We have termed it the "new sovereign immunity"— the immunity of officials who administer major government grant programs (poverty, welfare, housing, urban renewal) from any meaningful form of scrutiny, surveillance, criticism, challenge, and accountability. Billions upon billions of dollars are expended by these officials presumably to aid the poor. And yet the poor are still impoverished; their children are still uneducated; their lives are still shorter; and they are told that they must measure government efforts by intention, not by results; by sincerity, not by achievement. The American Indian is most familiar with the beneficent effects of this wardship. The average Indian family has an annual income of $1,200, according to the Bureau of Indian Affairs. If the funds expended by the Bureau were simply distributed to Indians, every Indian family of four would have an income of roughly $4,000. Instead, we have evolved a sovereign bureaucracy which has grown until there is now one well-fed BIA official to watch over every 14 impoverished, starving Indians. We note with interest that the government is now seeking ways to reverse the tide of migration by encouraging the movement from city to farm—perhaps in the hope of repeating (viz. replicating) its success story on the reservation.

Traditional legal representation is unequal to cope with any dimension of this crisis in the rule of law, let alone the three dimensions (rights, grievances, and bureaucratic discretion) in combination. Our best charred cities offer mute testimony to this.

LEGAL AND POLITICAL PROCESSES

As in the case of the others, we must reject Mayer's blanket assertion that the poor must look to the political process and not the legal system for salvation, as if the two were mutually exclusive and at all points distinct. Historically speaking, injured groups have turned to the legal system, and particularly to the courts, when the political system offered them no hope of redress. The reapportionment cases (which so deeply offend Mayer), recent First Amendment cases (where he sides with Justice Frankfurter and against Justice Black), and the school segregation cases (which he alludes to only in passing), are all instances where the legal system, and more particularly the courts, have stepped in to correct seemingly incorrigible defects which appeared immune to political solutions. In fact, it is the relationship between the legal and the political that has made legal services such an extraordinarily potent weapon for the poor.

Legal services for the deprived—at their most effective—have affected the political process through the operation of the "legitimation principle" and the "associational principle." *Brown v. Board of Education* illustrates the former. Once a grievance is legitimated, given legal status, and recognized and acknowledged by the "sovereign," forces are unleashed and set in motion that will not confine themselves to the orderly process of litigation and to the timetable of court calendars. The sit-ins, the marches, the demonstrations are a direct product of the sense of grievance which the court properly legitimated in the Brown case. Similarly, the poverty program, by legitimating a new set of grievances, set another such process in motion. And the new welfare rights cases—those "unseaworthy rights"—have clearly helped spark the formation of welfare rights groups across the country.

Other cases (including the *NAACP v. Alabama* and most recently the *United Mine Workers v. Illinois State Bar Association*) illustrate the significance of the political forces unleashed by protecting the "associational" principle. We saw this most clearly in the Deep South where the Supreme Court safeguarded the rights of Negroes to join the NAACP without harassment and persecution by the state. Although legal service programs have not engaged primarily in group representation, their potential for doing so is great. The Office of Economic Opportunity reports:

> . . . In addition to the 291,000 individuals who received legal services: 834 community action groups, such as tenant associations, welfare mothers groups, and farm worker communities received legal assistance. Members of these organizations, numbering an estimated 50 to 100 thousand poor people received advice and representation to obtain their rights, set up self help institutions, and to win their share of public services, such as health care, street lights, garbage collection, etc.

The most notable and controversial instance of representation to protect the rights of association has been provided by recent actions of the California Rural Legal Assistance Program. In recent months, one attorney, Gary Bellow,

> . . . has been involved in actions against the City of Delano, the Tulare County Housing Authority, the California Department of Motor Vehicles, the Clerk of Kern County, and the grower who is currently the target of Chavez' organizing drive—cases that are, in the words of one McFarland city councilman, "a long way from helping a guy read a contract." During the same period, other C.R.L.A. lawyers,—there are about thirty of them, in ten offices around the state—brought actions on behalf of their clients to enjoin, among others, the Madera County Board of Education (from closing the schools so that the students could help in the fields), the Governor of California (from eliminating some of the services offered by the state's Medi-Cal program), and the United States Secretary of Labor (from issuing a certification for the importing of *braceros*) (*The New Yorker*, November 4, 1967, pp. 173-82).

As *The New Yorker* points out, the C.R.L.A. does not represent the union; in fact, it is prohibited from doing so by the terms of their grant. However:

> . . . the clients and the activities of the two organizations are inevitably intertwined: Chavez' followers are not blue-collar workers but poor people, and, to a large extent, the grape pickers' strike is not a wage dispute but a movement. Obviously, the union profits along with C.R.L.A. clients from legal actions that shut off alternative sources of labor; when Bellow's injunctions kept striking families in Guimarra's labor camp it meant not only that the families would have a place to sleep but also that no non-striker could take over the accommodations (*Ibid.*).

Thus, the C.R.L.A. program is protecting the rights of association by protecting individual members from specific injustices which, unrectified, could have destroyed the union, member by member.

It is within these contexts that we wish to suggest that the legal system and the legal profession have a major contribution to make through legal service programs.

If the crisis now faced by the rules of law is to be met and overcome, it will only be because we are prepared, as a society, to stand each one of Mayer's propositions on its head. This means that we must:

1. develop new doctrines of rights and a new body of law;

2. reshape the legal system by redefining the legal process, by creating new legal institutions, and by restructuring the manpower supply of the legal profession; and

3. begin to redefine the relationship between law and the democratic process so that we may move more rapidly toward a "Just Society."

NEW DOCTRINES OF LAW

Most of the new doctrines of law to which Mayer takes exception are those that have imported concepts of property and due process into public assistance and related programs. The attack on officials has assumed the form not of disputing the substantive policy underlying their decisions but rather of taking issue with the *manner* in which they are made and the *process* by which the final determinations are reached. The right to counsel, the right to a hearing, and the right to be informed of the basis for the decision in welfare cases and eviction from public housing involve essentially procedural questions.

These rights affect the outcome by permitting new facts to enter into the consideration of the decision-maker—by forcing him at least to go through the motions of taking account of previously unintroduced facts in reaching his decision and articulating its basis. This is, however, only a partial and imperfect explanation of why these new procedural rights have been so effective. For due process, in theory, can only require a decision-maker to go through the motions of listening; it cannot invariably guarantee that he will become sympathetic, discard his prejudices, and respond more fairly and wisely. A fuller explanation of the effectiveness of these procedural rights must come from the recognition that they are a form of pressure, by obstruction, on the bureaucracy, including the judicial bureaucracy. For all bureaucracy is undermanned and overworked; and procedural demands, shrewdly employed, can bring a system grinding to a halt because of the extra steps they require administrators to take. Most bureaucracies —regardless of the rules they promulgate—deviate, in fact, must deviate, from their own rules and regulations in order to function efficiently. Hence, they often cut procedural corners in the interest of efficiency and expediency. The sheer press of work, not malice, is responsible for these shortcuts. But holding officials to their own regulations is likely to introduce an additional work load as a form of pressure to more reasoned and more equitable determination.

DIRECTION OF EXPANSION

It is already evident that we will probably witness an enlargement of these procedural rights. The nature of the expansion will come from three directions. First, the newly effective Freedom of Information Act creates, in President Johnson's words, a new "Right to Know." This right is judicially enforceable. It is a right possessed by the ordinary citizen, *qua* citizen, and not (as previously) by a specially and esoterically defined group of those "immediately and directly affected." Full knowledge of decisions, policies, and procedures is an indispensable first step in an effective procedural attack on a decision. It enables one to gain the advantages of "discovery," of pretrial knowledge of the other case, without taking the awesome and sometimes irretrievable step of instituting formal litigation on the merits.

Second, the case law dealing with the question of who has the legal right to bring a suit is undergoing expansion. Under traditional doctrines of "standing" (the technical term used to designate who could and who could not institute suit), only those whose "property" (defined in a traditional manner) has been directly and uniquely injured by some governmental action are permitted to challenge such action. The nature of the injury as alleged would have to amount to an unconstitutional "taking of property" (in the traditional sense) without due process of law before the court would recognize the standing of the party to challenge the governmental action which worked to his detriment. Over the past few years, however, the courts have moved to expand the class of persons who can challenge a government action. They did so most noticeably in the field of race relations—but the commentators have usually assumed that this is a unique class from which it is unsafe and unwise to generalize.

Yet, the change in the law of "standing" is probably a broader one, a change that is being brought about as courts redefine and expand the class of persons who are legally entitled to challenge a government action. The shift may be discerned in the decision in *FCC v. Sanders Bros. Radio Station,* regarding the right of one radio station to challenge whether the grant of a federal license to a potential competitor was "in the public interest." Here the court was not concerned over the possible financial harm that might result from competition. Rather, it permitted the challenge because there was a statutory requirement that radio licenses be awarded "in the public interest." If such a requirement were to take on meaning, it was clear that the challenge would not come from the public in general but rather from those economically motivated to take such action—such as competitors—who would be likely to introduce considerations that would shed light on the meaning of "public interest." Consequently, "standing" was recognized in order to maintain the kind of surveillance necessary to protect the public interest. Most recently, the doctrine was expanded still further to permit an organization representing the audience of a radio station to challenge the renewal of a license. In this case, it was not a competing media but rather the consumers—the audience—which were recognized as a legally appropriate group to police governmental action through the courts.

It is still too early to tell how far these developments will go or whether they are idiosyncratic in nature. But recently, the Supreme Court has agreed to review the classic case in this area, *Frothingham v. Mellon,* which has operated as a blanket prohibition on court challenges brought by taxpayers or other parties lacking a traditional "property interest." It is entirely possible that the case law on "who may properly challenge governmental action" will cease to look solely to whether a definable and traditional property interest has been injured but rather will ask: what is the nature of the public interest involved; and who, if permitted to challenge a governmental decision, is most likely to raise considerations which must receive attention in order to protect the public interest most effectively?

The third discernible expansion of the new body of procedural rights is embodied in the recent poverty law, the Economic Opportunity Act of 1967, legislation which may well be symptomatic of a larger movement. The Act recognizes the right to a hearing of any poverty program whose funds are terminated or suspended. In short, all the procedural rights which, as we earlier noted, had been invoked to protect individual rights to welfare, public housing, and the like, may now be extended to group and organizational interests in instances where government action threatens to damage the vitality or existence of a group striving to achieve broad national goals with federal funds. Even without this new provision in the statute, it is clear that the emergence of new organizational forms among the poor, such as neighborhood corporations, cooperatives, tenant associations, and welfare rights organizations, would shift the focus of legal battles from one of individuals' rights to one of organizational rights.

NEW TRENDS

Yet, if these new procedural rights and the expansions we have predicted are offensive to Mayer, we would make bold to predict that we will shortly see an entirely new body of rights—rights which are not procedural in nature—emerging in the areas of poverty law. For procedural rights have limitations. If, for example, the bureaucracy is willing to expend the effort to go through the proper motions and if it is determined to come up with the wrong results, there is no way to prevent this outcome. Procedural demands can only make such action more difficult. We would suspect, therefore, that a new body of rights will shortly be emerging which go to the substantive grounds of the decisions as well as the way in which they were reached. There are already some indications of this. Although they are only straws in the wind at present, they may well set the pattern. The following four legal examples of recent vintage may clarify what we have in mind.

1. The residence provisions for welfare requiring that a needy person have maintained residence in a community for at least one

year are being struck down on grounds that they both interfere with the constitutional rights to mobility and thwart the underlying purpose of the welfare laws to provide opportunity and upward mobility.

2. A case in the District of Columbia overturned a decision terminating welfare under the "man-in-the-house" rule on grounds of public policy. The welfare department assumes, if it finds a man in the house, that there is a source of income available and, therefore, that the family is no longer in need of public assistance. In this case, the male was the father who had come to visit his children; and the court struck down on policy grounds a welfare ruling that penalized children for seeing their father.

3. An eviction case was reversed where the landlord had evicted a tenant as retaliation for reporting building code violations. The court ruled that such retaliation could not be given the sanction of law in light of the public need to encourage reporting of building code violations.

4. In school system after school system, parents are organizing to demand both equality of resources (as in the successful *de facto* segregation case brought by Hobson in the District of Columbia) and more importantly, equality of results. The demand is formulated (principally politically) as a demand for equality of achievement. The parents insist that the teachers and school administrators stop talking in terms of intentions, motives, sincerity, or even, in terms of educational innovations and gimmickry. Such talk merely describes input whereas the parents want output; they want results and they will leave the method of achieving them up to the professions. The demand takes the form of identifying a core of measurable results; and this new demand on *output* rather than *input* is likely to generate a new kind of accountability, both political and legal.

Thus, if an agency or a public institution sets certain production goals (such as bringing students up to grade level or training a specified number of job applicants), failure to achieve those goals will be scrutinized in new terms. We are not saying, or advocating, that courts will sit in judgment of the policy decisions of officials. Nor are we urging a return to the 1930s and to substantive due process when a judge's biases often determined the constitutionality of a law. What we are saying is that new grounds for judicial scrutinization of results are emerging. First, has the agency articulated any specific measurable goals; second, has it taken steps to collect the information that is needed to determine whether these goals are being reached; and third, has it developed and applied sanctions and incentives suited to penalize deviations from agency policy, rules, regulations, and goals which up until now have been largely ignored as trivial but which cumulatively subvert and thwart a program.

INNOVATIONS IN THE PLANNING PROCESS

A major, and perhaps, indispensable step toward the creation of a new body of substantive rights is to be found in recent innovations in the planning process. The cost effectiveness system, developed by former Secretary of Defense McNamara, is now being applied to social programs. And the Bureau of the Budget is now requiring agencies to treat budget submissions as simply the "financial expression of a program plan." A Bureau of the Budget directive (now in effect for over a year) which has been revolutionizing the planning process states:

> Under present practices, however, program review decision making has frequently been concentrated within too short a period; objectives of agency programs and activities have too often not been specified with enough clarity and concreteness; accomplishments have not always been specified concretely; alternatives have been insufficiently present for consideration for top management; in a number of cases the future year costs of present decisions have not been laid out systematically enough; and formalized planning and systems have had too little effect on budget decisions (Bureau of Budget Bulletin, No. 66-3).

The directive then goes on to require the establishment of a new planning, program, and budget system which includes:

(1) An output-oriented (this term is used interchangeably with mission-oriented or objectives-oriented) program structure (sometimes also called a program format) which presents data on all of the operations and activities of the agency in categories which reflect the agency's end purposes or objectives.

(2) Analyses of possible objectives of the agency and of alternative programs for meeting these objectives. Many different techniques of analysis will be appropriate, but central should be the carrying out of broad systems analyses in which alternative programs will be compared with respect to both their costs and their benefits (Ibid.).

The reason for this new insistence of specificity in planning is to increase accountability—from the chiefs of staff to the Secretary of Defense; from the military to the civilian. Now that this same demand for accountability has been shifted to domestic programs, the "military" in the war on poverty may now find new demands levied on them by neighborhood law firms seeking to implement the civilian perspective.

The very procedures developed to increase accountability *upward* hold promise of vesting accountability *downward* in the ordinary citizen and in groups directly affected by the actions and planning of the bureaucracy. If one couples this demand for specificity of results with the expanded procedural rights (as we have discussed before) something strange results. First, the public will have a right to know about these new goals, standards, and policies. Second, new groups will be recognized as having a legal interest to challenge a governmental action which appears to be at variance with such policies, procedures, and production goals.

Third, and building upon these others, we may begin to see an expansion of the old writ of mandamus (or its equivalent): an order, issuing from the bench to an official ordering him to do his duty. The courts will still refuse to define the nature of that duty; rather they will look to the agencies for guidance as to its character and content. This development has already taken place in the field of desegregation where the relationship of courts to administrative agencies as traditionally conceived has been radically altered. And what has happened in desegregation may well provide a prototype for future developments in the field of poverty law:

> The allocation of responsibilities between the courts and the administrative agency arrived at in *Lee v. Macon County Board of Education* completely reverses the roles originally envisioned for courts and the Office of Education under Title VI. Originally HEW thought that the courts would establish the standards and the government, through Title VI, would be responsible for administering them on a mass basis. In the Alabama opinion the courts are the institution administering the law on a mass basis

and the Office of Education is at best serving in an advisory role helping the courts determine the applicable standards and then helping, in tandem with the Justice Department, to advise the courts on the adequacy of the desegregation plans submitted by the school districts (Comment, *Yale Law Journal*, 1967, p. 364).

Federal agencies that are formulating performance standards in the poverty field may find themselves playing a similar role in the not too distant future.

RESTRUCTURING THE LEGAL SYSTEM

Rights are not self-executing. And creating new rights—on paper —will not necessarily create new realities. It takes manpower to assert rules, manpower in which the legal profession is already sorely deficient. The invoking of a right is not a purely ministerial task as Mayer would tend to imply. He is correct in noting that there was a sense of mission, of zeal, and of purpose which lay behind our original proposal for a neighborhood law firm and which, as first director of the Legal Service Programs, one of the authors of this chapter sought to instill in the program. Neighborhood law firms were intended to be the embodiment of perspective: the perspective of need, of urgency, of grievance and injury as a countervailing force to the empire building, the alliance preserving, and the long range strategic considerations which preoccupy and paralyze bureaucracies.

Yet, if we are to restructure the legal system, we must think beyond neighborhood law firms or other new institutions manned by lawyers. For in truth, the whole legal system is an extraordinarily inefficient production system for providing remedies, for offering guides to conduct, and certainly for protecting life and limb. So long as the law remains the private preserve of a restrictivist guild (all carrying LLB union cards or alternatively, police badges), the rule of law will maintain only the most precarious and partial sway in a society overrun by lawlessness and injustice. The solution is not more lawyers but, in Chaucer's terms, more Men of Law. We not only need more courts and judges; we need more justice-dispensing institutions. We do not need more rules of law; we need more forces to compel decent, humane, compassionate, and equitable behavior.

Elsewhere, we have suggested that at the very least this situation requires an expansion and radical alteration of the makeup of the legal profession to include a whole array of new law-related career positions (Cahn and Cahn, 1964). Equally, it requires the development of new legal procedures and new modes of resolving disputes—through arbitration, through mediation, through conciliation—modes which look not to the past, but to the future, which do not wander into fictional quests for fault but which seek to determine the elements of a constructive and equitable solution. And, most certainly, it requires new institutions—new grievance mechanisms, new ways of maintaining law and order, new forms of sanction, and new kinds of rewards.

Government insurance for all victims of crime and violence seems clearly desirable and increasingly necessary. A radical restructuring of our system of maintaining law and order in ghetto communities is necessary. Programs in this direction might be achieved through the creation of neighborhood security forces akin to those which industry and business use as part of their security system for the protection of property. Youth courts, run by youths, and utilizing new sets of sanctions from ostracism to constructive community work is one alternative to the importation of the full panoply of procedural safeguards into the juvenile courts. Education of the society in the law, not to teach mechanical regurgitation of rules of law but to discipline the basic instinct for fairness and the fundamental sense of justice, might, if begun at age seven or eight, shift both attitudes and conduct.

Suggestions could be proliferated without end. The basic point is that law and lawyers are not an end in themselves. Legal services are basically a trade name product merchandised monopolistically by a small set of producers who jealously guard their profits against all potential competitors. The starting point is to realize that the market is not for legal services; the market is for justice. And the evils of a professional monopoly can only be effectively countered by the combined pressures of increased consumer demand, competition and technological innovation which offers new "inventions" for resolving conflicts, providing remedies, preventing injury, furnishing adequate guides to conduct, and generating pressures which can effectively keep behavior within the perimeters of democratically agreed-upon social norms. The legal system as now structured will not suffice for the needs of modern urban society.

REDEFINING THE RELATION BETWEEN LAW AND POLITICS

We have already noted—in the reapportionment cases, *Brown v. Board of Education,* in *NAACP v. Alabama,* and other cases—how the law has been used effectively for removing obstacles to the effective functioning of the democratic process. When the fundamental mechanisms of change become fouled up, the political process itself may be impotent to purge itself. The courts, by legitimating a grievance or giving an injury legal or constitutional status, can unclog the political mechanism and afford democracy a chance to work through solutions. Then the process once set in motion by legitimating a grievance must be kept in momentum by protecting group associations such as unions and civil rights organizations.

Beyond both the legitimation and associational principles is a third and even more fundamental tenet which Mayer overlooks entirely: the constitutional principle. Historically, lawyers have made their greatest contribution by structuring relationships, institutions, forums, communities, organizations, and nations in such a way that men could proceed effectively to fulfill their desires. Our own Constitution is such a legal structure. Equally, the modern corporation is a product of the legal profession's ingenuity in creating institutional frameworks within which men can function freed of unnecessary encumbrances (including lawyers).

It seems manifest that this nation is now going through a new constitutional phase not, however, in the sense that Senator Dirksen would have it by calling a new constitutional convention. Nor do we have reference to the numerous state constitutions now undergoing revision, though that is a related phenomenon. What we have in mind is the less obvious but profoundly significant redrafting of the social compact between the poor and the rest of society which is underway in community after community. Whether the banner is integration or black power, whether the program is the poverty program or model cities or urban renewal, the modes of citizen participation are changing and expanding to take on constitutional dimensions which equal and even surpass the reapportionment cases as a mode of enfranchising the disenfranchised.

In drawing charters for neighborhood corporations, tenants unions, and welfare rights groups, lawyers are structuring the new units of production and distribution of a "Just Society." In shaping such institutions, in protecting the rights of association, in legitimating new classes of old grievances, lawyers are restructuring the *social* order just as they restructured the *industrial* order in the 1930s when they gave form and content to the right of workers to organize, to bargain collectively, to negotiate in good faith, and to be protected against unfair labor practices.

To advance toward this new goal, the lawyer must be at once a corporate and a constitutional lawyer. For he is redefining citizenship as an equity stake in this society, as an ownership share which carries with it both an obligation to bear risks and a right to share in returns. The poor are now saying: We have long borne the risks without sharing in the profits. We fight the wars, we pay the costs of crime, pollution, urban sprawl and decay, epidemics, depletion of natural resources, inflation, and depression. They are now saying: We want more than welfare and more than a distribution of wages; we want a share in ownership, a share in prosperity, and a share in the growth sector of society, particularly because this sector is in the human services field and most phenomenally in the realm of services and programs aimed at the poor and at minority groups.

Typical of these new demands are two developments recently reported in the *New York Times*. The first involved the establishment of a neighborhood owned and operated enterprise in whose creation a lawyer had clearly played a significant role:

> Six thousand Harlem residents, buying stock at $5 a share, have created "Harlem's gift to Harlem"—a supermarket that will supply "quality food" at fair prices, will train and employ Harlem residents to staff it and will share the profits with the customers.
>
> "This is Harlem's gift to Harlem, where housewives have been overcharged for inferior food for too long," Miss Cora T. Walker, attorney for the sponsors of the new venture, said yesterday.
>
> • • • • • • • • • • • • •
>
> "Ordinary little people" organized the project and obtained loans and expert advice to get it started, Miss Walker said, calling the venture "a solution to the problems we are all talking about."
>
> • • • • • • • • • • • • •

"During the summer," she continued, "17 teenagers went door-to-door in Harlem to sell shares, and in six weeks those kids got $10,000."

. . . .

"We had no balance sheet, no assets, and my board of directors couldn't give them any personal guarantees," she said. "And frankly, if we did give them, they wouldn't mean anything, anyway."

. . . .

"Shareholders who shop in the market will receive an annual rebate of about 5 per cent on their purchases," she said. "Eventually," she said, "the incorporators, who have formed Harlem River Consumer Cooperative, Inc., intend to open five other supermarkets in Harlem" (*New York Times*, December 21, 1967, pp. 1, 42).

The second illustration comes from Newark where Negroes, guided by a law-student–city planner, are resisting the taking of a 150 acre site in the heart of the ghetto:

. . . Junius Williams, a Yale student who heads the recently formed Newark Area Planning Association, . . . said that the effort to get 150 acres in the Negro community was "a land grab" comparable to what happened to the Indians when they were deprived of the land and their one source of wealth.

"The black people cannot slide out of their control that which they can have just by sitting on," he said. "If we are shuffled around, we are rootless and then we are controlled."

Mr. Williams also insisted that his organization was not opposed to the medical college, but only to its size and the failure to meet the needs of the community.

He proposed a 17-acre alternative, designed, he said, by Yale architectural and planning students, which "can provide all the buildings they want without going more than one story above what they have planned."

The youthful head of the Newark planning group also proposed that the medical college double its capacity from the proposed 272 beds to about 500 beds and enlarge its facilities for outpatients.

"Anything coming into the black community must serve the black community," he declared (*Ibid.*, p. 44).

The lawyer today, in drawing up charters for local organizations, poverty programs, unions, citizens groups, and cooperatives, must seek to give the citizen a participating share in the fortunes of this society. A job alone is not their goal. The saying in Harlem is: "We had full employment on the plantation." The poor now want ownership rights and ownership prerogatives. They will bear risk and loss; they will defer present enjoyment and present consumption to invest in the future. But they want a share of the future—the same share which the Founding Fathers promised to all when they wrote:

> We the people of the United States, in Order to form a more perfect Union, establish Justice, insure domestic Tranquility, provide for the common defense, promote the general Welfare, and secure the Blessings of Liberty to ourselves and our Posterity, do ordain and establish this Constitution for the United States of America.

The lawyer has his work cut out. The drafting job must proceed apace.

References

Brown v. Board of Education, 349 U.S. 294 (1955).

CAHN, EDGAR S., and JEAN C. CAHN. "The War on Poverty: A Civilian Perspective," *Yale Law Journal*, 73 (July, 1964), pp. 1317-52.

COMMENT, "The Courts, HEW, and Southern School Desegregation," *Yale Law Journal*, 77 (December, 1967).

Federal Communications Commission v. Sanders Bros. Radio Station, 308 U.S. 546 (1940).

Frothingham v. Mellon, 262 U.S. 447 (1923).

Hackin v. Arizona, 389 U.S. 143 (1967).

MAYER, MARTIN. *The Lawyers* (New York: Harper & Row, Publishers, 1967).

N.A.A.C.P. v. Alabama, 357 U.S. 449 (1958).

United Mine Workers of America v. Illinois State Bar Association, 19 L. ed. 2d 426 (1967).

8

The Clergy, the Laity, and the Issue of Poverty

GEORGE WEBBER

☐ FOR THE RELIGIOUS INSTITUTIONS of the United States, the problem of poverty, along with the crisis in civil rights for minority groups, creates a peculiar urgency and a sense of fatefulness. In the face of this problem, both Jew and Christian have an unambiguous commission to responsible action at the heart of their faith commitments. By the prophet Isaiah, Israel was reminded:

> Is not this the fast that I choose:
>   to loose the bonds of wickedness,
>   to undo the throungs of the yoke,
> to let the oppressed go free,
>   and to break every yoke?
> Is it not to share your bread with the hungry,
>   and bring the homeless poor into your house;
> when you see the naked, to cover him . . . (58:6-7).

And Jesus began his ministry by reading a similar passage from the scriptures as the text for his work:

> The Spirit of the Lord is upon me, because he has anointed me to preach good news to the poor. He has sent me to proclaim release to the captives and recovering of sight to the blind, to set at liberty those who are oppressed, to proclaim the acceptable year of the Lord (Luke 4:18).

Christian and Jew alike are called in faith to express in responsible ways love of neighbor, and in particular, concern for those in poverty or bondage. In the affluence of contemporary society, these demands are often forgotten, casually ignored, or rationalized out of their imperative. On both historical and ideological grounds, the main streams of American religious institutions are unprepared for the challenge of the times. While this chapter will necessarily reflect the Protestant tradition of the writer, it is probable that its general conclusions are largely relevant also to Roman Catholic and Jewish institutions.

THE HISTORICAL PERSPECTIVE

Although the religious institutions of the New World were direct transplants from Europe, they have taken on a distinct flavor that makes them in some ways a new species. To understand the American religious scene, certain unique or unusual facts must be kept in mind. These include the intermixture of church type and sect type, the continued phenomenon of church growth coupled with minimal impact upon the society, and the effects of church success and affluence.

American Denominationalism

Ernst Troeltsch provided significant categories for institutional analysis of the churches when he suggested the distinction between the church type and the sect type. The former is best symbolized by the state churches of Europe such as Lutheran in Scandinavia or Roman Catholic in France where by definition all citizens are part of a parish structure and normally enter the church as infants by baptism. The sect usually arises as a radical protest against the church type, requiring of its members a strong personal commitment and a discipline of life that takes its pattern from the New Testament church. But in the New World, whether in heritage of church type or sect type, all religious institutions in the process of transplantation took on the characteristics of present denominations, a peculiar mixture of both types. The result has been a situation characterized, for our purposes, by several unique features.

In the first place, membership is by choice (in terms of participation in a particular congregation) in almost all Protestant circles, in Jewish life, and in some cases even in Roman Catholic parishes where national churches have cut across the traditional parish pattern. This freedom has led on the one hand to an inevitable competitiveness that weakens the possibility of significant faith commitments. On the other hand, it has made institutional loyalty difficult to achieve since men are quite free simply to move to a more congenial church whenever conflict emerges in a local congregation.

Denominationalism, in the American tradition of tolerance for religious differences, has also produced a strange mixture of sacred and secular. Unlike Europe, where Christian institutions have been rejected by working classes and often viewed as instruments for support of the *status quo,* the churches in the United States have rarely faced any significant antagonism. They are called upon to deal with the religious segment of man's life, one of the 22 departments in *Time Magazine,* and for this purpose they are given respect. At the same time, they are expected to adhere to the doctrine of church-state separation (usually misunderstood) and stay out of politics or other controversial arenas. Since World War II, a serious attempt at dialogue between church and secular world has been undertaken in Europe, in part by the Evangelical Academy movement. No such dialogue has been possible here, for in a secularized church in a pseudo-Christian culture, there is simply no line of demarcation across which a dialogue might emerge. Will Herberg, among many others, has suggested that in fact what has occurred in America is the development of a kind of religion in general, made up of the ideology of the "American way of life," informed by a variety of elements in the Judeo-Christian tradition, and generally acceptable to all (1955).

Finally, denominationalism has meant considerable difficulty in categorizing or analyzing American religious life. For example, Gerhard Lenski in his important study, *The Religious Factor* (1961), concludes that we must deal with four major types: Roman Catholic, Jewish, White Protestant, and Negro Protestant. Other scholars stress the necessity of attention to the "third force" churches, representing the present protest against the main line denominations. For our purposes, however, it is important to underline the clear fact that even this last type does not represent any radical challenge to present social structures or provide a vehicle for social change as did the Protestant churches of the Reformation (McLoughlin, 1967, pp. 43-68). The churches in which the Negro and the poor participate do not gird themselves for battle against either segregation or poverty.

Success Churches and the Secular City

In all of Europe, it has been manifest for more than two decades that Christendom has come to an end. In 1943, a French sociologist-priest called attention to the reality in a book entitled *France, Country of Mission?* Religious participation had fallen to the point where roughly 5 per cent of the population of a so-called Catholic country like France were participating in even minimal church life. For most men, church-going involved only cultic rites of baptism, marriage, and burial—twice they had to be carried in! Observers in other parts of Europe, quick to follow the lead of this initial study, also discovered that similar statistics held true for both Protestant and other Roman Catholic countries. For most men, the church as a significant part of their lives had simply evaporated. A secular era had indeed arrived.

Only in the United States and Canada has the phenomena of church growth and active participation continued and, in fact, grown at a startling rate since the close of World War II. To be a good American was to belong to a church, send one's children to Sunday School, and support the institution financially. Such success was, of course, purchased at the price of almost total irrelevance to social issues. The church was a place for men to leave their problems and discover peace of mind or, in other words, confirmation of their values and goals. Institutional success could only be purchased at the price of washing out all interest in prophetic judgment on issues that might create conflict. As a result, congregations today are woefully unprepared for conflict and deeply disturbed when situations arise which tend to demand actions that antagonize their neighbors or which appear to set the church over against the values of the society. The confusion of the churches in conflict situations was dramatically detailed years ago by Kenneth Underwood in *Protestant and Catholic* (1957).

Thus, we are faced at the present time with an anomalous and disturbing situation. Never in American history has attendance at church and synagogue been so high; yet never has the impact of religious communities upon the society been so minimal. A host of books have reminded Protestants of their failure: *The Suburban Captivity of the Churches, The Noise of Solemn Assemblies, A Private and Public Faith.* Catholics likewise are being sharply reminded of their failures by the reactions of Northern urban communities to integration. In Chicago, for example, the reaction in predominantly Roman Catholic neighborhoods to Martin Luther King has jolted the clergy.

An increasing note in church circles is not to bemoan the emerging fact of secularization and the end of Christendom, but to see in contemporary trends a necessary winnowing of the superficial and uncommitted membership, a development that may lead to a new vitality and relevance for the Christian communities which remain. Without trying to make any firm prophecies, one might hazard the guess that the crest of religious participation in the United States has certainly been passed and a rapid decrease in membership and support in the immediate future may be expected.

Part of the attention received by the "God is Dead" theology can certainly be attributed to the need of a bored middle class for a good excuse to cut out of church attendance. History, of course, does not move at a uniform rate and we shall continue for some time to have sections, such as the Lutheran areas of the midwest, where Christendom lingers on, but this is not likely to be the case in suburban areas. However, the institutional structures, including church buildings, huge and expensive educational plants, and vast denominational organizations, will not easily be shut down or put to alternate uses. One shudders to think of the institutional trauma which may lie ahead as the need for institutional self-preservation is countered by a militant and committed minority who demand that Christians once again take up their role as leaven in the secular society.

THE GAP BETWEEN THE IDEAL AND THE REALITY

By their success and affluence, the religious communities have also thrust themselves into a position that badly compromises the integrity of their statements. An inner city pastor whose salary comes in part from a suburban community in which neither Jew nor Negro Christian can buy a house is in a poor position to explain to his Negro congregation that in Christ all men are brothers. Further, the very success of the churches has obscured time and again the fact that the forms of the religious community have really lost the capacity to bear much life. In seminary, men are still taught to give major attention to preaching, with the pulpit as the base of their proclamation. Yet, a variety of studies indicate the limited impact of such proclamation. In a spectator-oriented, TV-dominated society, preaching from a sacred place, at a sacred hour, to an uninvolved audience is not likely to lead to much response. As an institution, however, the church has been peculiarly able to avoid feedback of any kind. In this way it has been able to escape the necessity of facing the hollowness of its traditional forms in a world far removed from the agricultural society in which such forms made sense. Yet, both the confusion of teenage life in the suburbs and the popularity of a book like *The Feminine Mystique* (Frieden, 1963) ought to force the church to ask what it has been doing all this time in suburbia.

IDEOLOGICAL HANGUPS FOR THE CHURCHES

Confronted with the reality of urban poverty, the churches also find themselves caught with ideological baggage from the past which ill-equips them to respond effectively. This is particularly true in the case of Protestantism with its strong infusion of Puritan ethics in regard to the poor.

Attitude Toward Poverty

As an inner city pastor in an area of an unusually high incidence of urban poverty, I had great difficulty recognizing the dimensions of the problem of deprivation because of my own ideological assumptions. For one thing, I was misled by the myth of upward mobility and kept expecting that East Harlem would experience a continuation of its tradition of constant population mobility characteristic of the immigrant years. Only gradually did it become clear that the melting pot does not function for Puerto Rican and Negro urban poor. Public education, hope of the immigrant child for entry into American society, simply is a massive failure for the non-European newcomer in the urban centers of today.

One of the obvious tragedies at the present time is the fact that so many boards of education and school systems are dominated by first and second generation immigrants for whom the schools did provide an effective means of acculturation. The judgment of such men with respect to the Negro and Puerto Rican, using the standards of their own experience, is devastating. Nor is there much interest in changing the situation among the religious community. Several years ago at the time of a threatened school boycott in New York City, three religious leaders sought to bring about some alternative solution. Only the Jewish member of the team was subjected to any particular attack or criticism. It was quite apparent that the constituency of the Protestant, white, and middle class, had opted out either to private schools or suburbia, while the Catholics were content with parochial education. Only the Jewish community was still involved in urban schools and not about to fight for effective integration.

From the specifically Protestant point of view, of course, the Puritan heritage has left a strong mark. How often in speaking to suburban churches does one face the taunt, "But there are plenty of jobs today. No one has to live in slums unless they want to." The Protestant ideology simply does not comprehend the problems created by cybernetics and by a mass society in which individual initiative is not an adequate basis for success. Further, the general assumption that America is an affluent society makes it difficult for many even to accept the fact that a real poverty problem exists. I recently lectured on poverty to a women's society of the Riverside Church in New York. Later, one woman was overheard to say to another, "That man is enthusiastic, but isn't he an awful liar." In short, in a land of opportunity, every man can be a success. Perhaps a few do fail, but that is clearly their fault.

USE OF FALSE NORMS

If part of the problem for the churches lies in ideological assumptions that no longer have much validity, this situation is compounded by the tendency to apply norms and expectations to the poor, and in particular to the Negro poor, which simply do not make sense. For most members of religious communities, whatever may be their motives for participation or their confusion about their actual commitments, it is quite clear that religious nurture is essential for children and an important responsibility of the family. The Sunday School, developed on a massive basis, may turn out to be

the biggest fraud in history. But it has been supported and maintained as the ultimate *raison d'etre* for the church. It teaches
"ethical values to children."

Thus, deeply committed to his family and its nurture, the white
Protestant often looks at the Negro family with something akin to
disgust. He looks at the present patterns without any recognition
of the fact that until a hundred years ago no Negro was allowed
to function as a responsible father in a family, and since then more
often than not has had difficulty finding an economic basis for
support. Even as sophisticated an urban expert as Moynihan seems
unable to comprehend that there might be some legitimacy in the
Negro response to the report he prepared for the Department of
Labor (March, 1965). Accurate as Moynihan's statistics may be,
the whole frame within which the report was placed brought an
inevitable distortion which an historical perspective does not
warrant.

Another illustration of the frequent distortion of reality that is
part of the present scene is the fear of Protestant parents toward
permitting high school and even college children to work in inner
city neighborhoods. The concern is often focused on anxiety about
the daughter being molested. Clearly, the image in the white mind
has been implanted by mass media and other sources until the
fears are very real. One simple statistic indicates the unreality of
much of white concern. At present, in New York and New Jersey
state prisons, approximately 75 per cent of the inmates are Negro
and Puerto Rican, while 85 per cent of those in prison for any
kind of sexual attack on women are white. Such a statistic is
simply preposterous to the middle class white Protestant mother.

Finally, the churches are almost totally unprepared to deal
with such a concept as "black power." Granted this phrase can
be employed in a variety of forms, one basic intent of its use is
simply to declare that black men are going to seek to concentrate
whatever power they possess or can amass in gaining their legitimate share in American society. In this sense, black power is in
no way different from Irish power or trade union power. But the
coupling of these two words, as I have found in many confrontations with church groups, provokes an antagonism of response that
is overwhelming. The reaction suggests that white Christians in
large numbers do not in fact accept the reality of the black man
as a brother, unless he becomes in effect ideologically a white

Christian American. I have yet to encounter any significant white group that was even able to comprehend why Adam Powell is precious to Harlem. The Negro poor know only too well that their spokesmen have almost universally been presented to them by the white community, and that the upper mobile middle class Negro is not about to identify with or provide leadership to the great mass of northern Negroes in urban ghettos.

ANTI-URBAN BIAS

Protestants for the most part have become suburban in mentality and commitment. Indications seem also to point to a similar movement out of central cities by Roman Catholics and Jews, but the reality is not so complete. In New York City, for example, if the entire population of nearly 8 million were classified by religious heritage, the figures would be something like 50 per cent Roman Catholic, 32 per cent Jewish, and about 18 per cent Protestant, at least half of whom would refuse any such designation. Of the remaining Protestant 9 per cent, nearly two-thirds are Negro and Puerto Rican. Thus, the WASP population of New York City is less than 5 per cent. The white Protestant has moved out to suburbia as though the city had the plague, there to nurture his family in the good life, at the price of commuting and in the context of an almost antidemocratic homogeneity of community life. Efforts to evoke from this suburban Protestant any effective concern for the central city where he usually earns his living have been minimal in spite of a variety of attempts. Apparently when he steps on the 5:02 commuter train, the one thing he wishes to do is forget all about the life of the city.

Whatever the compound that makes up the suburban mystique, it clearly has an unbiblical ring. The God of the Bible calls men to live in community, to take responsibility for their history, and to give expression to their faith in Him through their commitment to create a society wherein human values are encouraged. The suburbanite rejection of significant public responsibility for urban society is a real denial of faith. No better illustration is at hand than is implicit in Jane Jacobs' *The Death and Life of Great American Cities* (1961). Exaggerated though her thesis may be, she is certainly right in pointing to the pattern that has developed mammoth low income public housing projects without giving any real attention to what kind of housing will encourage human life. Public housing in many ways mitigates against the human in seeking to meet the animal needs of man: garbage disposal, elevators, fresh air. In theory it is clear that the task of Christian and Jew alike is to uphold in society the importance and meaning of human life, to insist that institutions be for man and not against him. But the churches at no time had even the slightest notion that public housing was part of their business or that they had a vital part to play in affirming the need to build housing that families would like and that would encourage human life. Rather, the churches thrust themselves into the act only to demand ample reimbursement for any of their buildings that were destroyed in the process of demolition and to learn where middle class families might be moving in order to build new churches in the choice locations.

REVERSALS IN THEOLOGY

The integrity of the churches is clearly at stake in their ability to meet the challenge of poverty in American life. Only a fool would predict such tradition-bound institutions will have the capacity for the radical changes required by such response. However, the implicit basis of the churches does provide for continuing reformation which may demand the breaking off of sectarian elements, the emergence of new forms of church life, the development of a remnant of the faithful. In this section, I want to point to the theological changes that are altering the climate in which new vitality may arise and that require the churches to reverse much present understanding and operation. Not for one minute do I suggest that such patterns are becoming or likely to become normative for the institution but only that they point to the direction in which new life and viability lie.

PATERNALISM TO PARTICIPATION

The Christian posture toward the deprived has generally been a genuine concern for the less fortunate, for the victims of cruel circumstance, for the "deserving poor." At best, those who had been given the love of God wanted to share their largesse with those outside the fold. Implicit in much of Christian social concern, charity, and benevolence has been the attitude of those blessed toward the outsider, an attitude that bears an almost inescapable tendency to paternalism. The Christian is the lifeguard, standing in the door of his church and throwing out life rings to drowning men, but without any real risk to himself. He goes down to the slums to help in a settlement house; he is a big brother to kids in trouble. He shares his affluence with others. As Monsieur Vincent was quoted as saying, "When you give alms to the poor, don't expect gratitude. Be grateful if they don't hate you." The Christian, far too often, has expected gratitude. No longer can the Christian operate from a position of strength over against the weakness of others and expect to get away with it.

In the inner city, white suburbanites are almost universally resented and unacceptable, except at one point. They are still viewed as useful in remedial and tutorial programs, for when all is said and done, no matter how helpful the tutor from outside, it is the child himself who does the learning and gets the credit. The fact that such a helping role is still possible points, of course, to the clue in the whole matter. What is happening is an understanding that Christian concern is never paternalistic in any sense, but comes through a pattern of "solidarity with sinners," with the poor and broken, that allows for no sense of superiority. This is, of course, thoroughly biblical. Jesus is often called "the man for others." His uniqueness involved his continual participation in the common life of Palestine, freely living with all manner of men, willing to identify with the outcasts, and refusing to set himself as a Godly man over against anyone. In theological terms, this pattern of participation or "presence" in the common life of the world is expressed in the word "incarnation."

Many a young clergyman, struggling to relate to the world of the inner city, has had to discover the hard way that only through genuine participation patterned after the incarnation of Jesus can he hope to bridge the tremendous cultural barriers that have been created. He must literally jump into the common life of the community, one man with others, struggling against the common torrents of life. He is not the lifeguard on the bank, but one drowning man with others, not more virtuous or "saved" or set apart in any way other than through his confidence that God's will shall be done.

SOCIAL WELFARE TO A COMMITMENT TO JUSTICE

The churches are presently bereft of much of their own rationale for service. Throughout much of Christian history, they have borne the concern for charity, developed hospitals, provided schools, produced a myriad of forms of social service. And now, not only in welfare state societies but also in the developing nations, they find their services either taken over by the state or stripped from them.

In this situation, often viewed by traditionalists as a crisis, the only authentic response is "Thank God!" Now the issues before the community of faith become clear. The time has come to limit the passion for acts of individual benevolence and welfare services for the sake of a fundamental commitment to justice for all men. Biblical faith ought to be political through and through. Contemporary Christians like to use Aristotle's definition of politics as the art of making and keeping men truly human, and then transpose this meaning into the definition of the church's own task. God has called men to faith precisely to do justice and to love mercy. Christians are "God's politicians," who by their very nature ought to participate fully in the structures that maintain a society and in doing so urge the polity in the direction of justice and opportunity for all men. In an almost cliché phrase, the number one item on God's agenda for the church is the problem of poverty. Not alms for the poor, now, but commitment to the fundamental social changes that will enable all men to share fully in the benefits of an affluent society.

The inevitable conflict and the necessary compromises which arise whenever men struggle for social change find the churches woefully unprepared. The strong emphasis upon love and reconciliation has made conflict per se something to be eschewed as evil, in spite of all biblical evidence to the contrary. The witness of Jesus again is striking. He created a situation of conflict by his commitment to the truth. Early Christians at one point were referred to as troublemakers (the literal Greek means "pests"). In short, willingness to expect and accept conflict is an essential part of the reversal of theological self-understanding.

SALVATION STATUS TO MISSIONARY VOCATION

Part of the problem of paternalism which plagues the church arises from the misunderstanding of faith as primarily a matter of attaining salvation. The incredible preoccupation of Christendom with this problem accounts in part for the Protestant Reformation. It also accounts for the primary impetus given to the missionary expansion of the churches in the nineteenth century and subsequently. The reality of Christendom as an all embracing reality in Western Europe led inescapably to the notion that God intends all men to be Christian and that the task of the church is to bring all men to a saving knowledge of Jesus Christ before they are cast into outer darkness or the fires of hell. Although contemporary theology has much tempered the older missionary urgency, the fact still remains that most Christians view church participation as somehow the guarantee of "salvation." There is no doubt that the scriptures are concerned about this matter, but in no way that justifies the preoccupation of Christians to the exclusion of other central aspects of faith.

In the face of the realities of secular culture and the challenge of urban problems, a number of churchmen, both Catholic and Protestant, are now prepared to argue that to be a Christian is primarily a matter of accepting a missionary vocation and only indirectly a matter of any salvation implications. God has work to be done and for this purpose he called upon Israel and the New Israel, a peculiar people, marked by no special virtues, but enabled by divine grace to get on with the task of service and witness in his name.

The implications of this concept are significant. On the one hand, it implies that Christians need not be concerned about converting anyone. That is God's business. He calls men to faith. A corollary to this is the recognition that men who do not know Christ as Lord or confess the God of Abraham may still attain to full humanity, that is to salvation or wholeness. In a word, what the church possesses is not a passport to salvation, but the knowledge of what human life is all about and a commitment to share this knowledge in word and deed with all men—but without one coercive or ulterior motive.

The second implication also demands a radical alteration in traditional Christian thinking. Now Christians are content to view themselves as humanitarians, nothing more, but also nothing less. The gospel is the good news for all men that: (1) this is God's world and He cares for man; (2) human history is important, it is going somewhere, and men are called in freedom by God to give it shape and direction; (3) we see described in the flesh what true human life looks like in the person of Jesus of Nazareth; and (4) to fulfill one's own true humanity, one needs to discover and express the meaning of freedom and responsibility.

All of this is tremendously important for the churches as they seek to meet the challenges of today's urban scene. Here is a clear calling to participation without institutional self-interest, freedom to work with secular instruments of justice, and the acceptance of the needs of men as adequate justification for participation. For many of us over the years who have flinched under the challenge, "What you are doing is nothing but social work, or pure humanitarianism," this is a freeing work. Christians are called to be nothing else than humanitarians, for Christ's sake.

SUCCESS TO TRUST

Finally, the churches today are called to overcome their preoccupation with institutional success and accept their proper role as a minority group in what some writers now speak of as "the new diaspora." Commitment to God's work, not acceptance of some creedal position or institutional membership must be the test. This conception goes against the grain of traditional ecclesiastical thinking, preoccupied with "church extension," evangelistic crusades (e.g. "scalp-taking raids"), and the maintenance of the present structures. But the reversal of faith suggests that the focus must be on obedience to God's claim to participation in public responsibility and involvement at the points of human need. A key text, often cited today, is the story in Matthew 25 of the last judgment. In this parable of the kingdom, Jesus makes it quite clear that concern for neighbor is the one test of faithfulness.

One illustration will underline this point. In East Harlem, a major problem has been narcotics addiction. For many years, addicts could find no help in any social agency, doctor's office, or church. They were dope fiends, to be handled only punatively. A Protestant parish undertook a ministry in this field, struggling for several years first to understand something of the problems of the addict and then seeking means of help. After three years, and the expenditure of funds at an annual rate of $50,000, there were no new church members, only a handful of men not using narcotics, and a lot of knowledge about what did not work in helping addicts. Any rational or prudential investment of church funds would have proscribed a rapid end of the program and the deployment of resources where they would pay off more significantly. But the church felt in this case a real commitment to the addict. Trust in Christ means the commitment to human need, without counting the cost or depending on results as the final arbiter.

INSTITUTIONAL IMPLICATIONS

The contemporary theological "reformation" just described makes the task of the church quite clear: it exists to share in God's work of shaping history for the sake of human life. It is the mission of the church to share in transforming, redirecting, and making manifest the possibilities for all men in a technological society which makes poverty both unnecessary and a denial of God's concern for the good of all men. Such a theological position creates the tension between institutional maintenance and the fulfillment of primary purposes which explicitly renounce such self-interest.

Due in part to this tension, the present climate in the churches is very ambiguous. The defection from ordained ministry in both Roman Catholic and Protestant churches is increasing at an astonishing rate. The confusion over function and emphasis is clearly a severe clergy problem. This situation involves nothing very new, for the Blizzard studies ten years ago underlined clearly the role dilemmas of the urban clergy (1956, pp. 508-10). What is new is the feeling on the part of clergy that the job is not worth sorting out, the dilemma not worth resolving, the local congregation an irrelevant base for effective urban ministry. Priests and ministers are moving out of ecclesiastical positions into a variety of secular vocations (not least of all jobs in various poverty programs) in a degree unthinkable in such other professions as law or medicine.

For the layman, the theological reformulations and proposals that see the church primarily as a servant body in the world also present severe problems of acceptance and readjustment. He has tended to see the purpose of the church in some such guise as: (1) a place that services his "religious" needs, (2) a center of instruction on moral values for children, (3) a fellowship of the saints to whom God has granted "salvation." These categories are not to be taken as definitive, but they serve to indicate that for most church members, involvement is for the sake of what they get out of it, not something which challenges them to responsible love of neighbor and nurtures them for the struggles made inevitable by social change. Thus, to suggest to the average congregation that the number one item for them on God's agenda is the elimination of poverty is met with a response of incomprehension or rejection. Yet, in an age growing increasingly secular in its orientation and rapidly losing interest in ecclesiastical validation for its patterns, the churches must either recover their sense of mission or retreat into insignificant enclaves, a vestigial remnant of Christendom in the secular city.

The present stage of ecclesiastical life needs a brief historical footnote. For Roman Catholicism, of course, the developments of Vatican II are the key. For Protestants, a more extended word is required. At the time of formation of the World Council of Churches at its first formal assembly in Amsterdam, 1948, it was determined to make a major study emphasis of the topic "The Evangelization of Man in Modern Mass Society." It was all too apparent, save in North America, that in the emergent industrial-urban world of the last half of the twentieth century the churches were in for real trouble. The alienation of the working classes and urban residents from church participation was almost complete. The study sought to make use of social sciences in its analysis of mass society and to gain helpful insights into the object of "evangelism." But by the end of six years, at the second general assembly of the World Council, those responsible for the study urged a second stage. Even as some understanding of modern society began to penetrate their thinking, the study leaders were made acutely aware of the wide disagreement as to what evangelization was all about. The fact that churches in common membership in the World Council of Churches could find no agreement on such a basic concept of the church's life was more than a little distressing.

The second phase of the study was, therefore, devoted to the search for a common definition of evangelism. What is the purpose of the churches in relation to mass man: To take his scalp, to save his soul, to help him find personal meaning in a depersonalizing world, or what? In this period from 1954 to 1960, a great deal of creative theological study was produced that sought to come up with the answer to this question. A wide degree of consensus emerged across the full ecclesiastical spectrum from sectarian type churches to Roman Catholicism among those who now affirmed the essential purpose of the church as missionary and defined this term primarily as accepting the gift of faith as a mandate for service and responsibility in the world. Since the early 1950s this theme has been widely introduced to theological students and clergy troubled about their ministry. A whole shelf of books pushing this ecumenical theological consensus has been produced, including such works as Hendrik Kraemer, *Theology of the Laity* (1959); George MacLeod, *Only One Way Left* (1956); Arnold Comme, *Agents of Reconciliation* (1961); E. R. Wickham, *Church and People in an Industrial Society* (1957); Ernest Southcott, *The Parish Comes Alive* (1956); together with a great deal of material in *World Council* and other ecclesiastical journals.

Despite these efforts, the basic patterns of church life, certainly in the United States, have been impervious to this new theology. A generation of young clergy, filled with mission theology and determined to transform their introverted congregations into missionary bodies, has met with frustration and defeat. The phrase "morphological fundamentalism" was coined to describe the rigidity of present ecclesiastical structures to which Christians tend to cling as though they were given, and not contingent on their historical development. Since the Third General Assembly of the World Council in New Delhi in 1961, the main attention in evangelism studies has thus been devoted to the question: "The Missionary Structures of the Congregation." What structures are required if the churches are to fulfill their legitimate mission in the present world and how can the requisite changes be brought about? This study has proved to be a very fruitful project for the churches, but has led in many more directions than its originators could possibly have anticipated.

In North America, the study was embraced as eagerly by denominational bureaucracies as by beleaguered young clergy. Here was to be a fundamental attack on the question of "church renewal." Only gradually did the real implications of the study become all too apparent to the conservative of mind. The normative character of the residential congregation was severely challenged. When the primary question for the church is this: "What does God's mission demand of Christians in this time and place?" it becomes obvious that new forms of Christian presence and community are required that go far beyond the reformation or renewal of traditional congregational or parish patterns. In blunt form, it would not be enough to renew and reorient all the present congregations of this country for effective mission. A multiplicity of new forms would still be required if the work of Christians is to be effective. This is not the place to describe the internecine warfare in ecclesiastical circles which the study has created. But for our purposes, the relation of the churches to the problem of poverty provides the context for reflecting on the possibilities of significant change in ecclesiastical structures.

The Missionary Structure Study has underscored for the churches the "reversals" of theological thinking outlined in the previous section of this chapter. Renewal will not be accomplished by focusing attention on building up the institution, but by seeking to discover and fulfill the missionary task for which the institution exists. At present, as the churches seek to respond in this way to the problems of poverty, a variety of new forms and structures are emerging, even as traditional congregations seek to discover their own "missionary" structure and potential.

CHURCHES AND POVERTY: THE SEARCH FOR NEW STRUCTURES

By the summer of 1967 it is possible to point to a number of specific patterns which are taking shape within the Protestant churches as they seek to respond as institutions to the problems of poverty. This is not to suggest that any large realignment of priorities has taken place, but to indicate the kind of roles that are being assumed. They are signs of hope, parables of change and responsibility that may point the way for whatever renewal will occur in the churches. Six characteristics can be detected in these Protestant efforts in relation to poverty and they provide here a framework by which to describe their scope and diversity.

EXPERIMENTAL IN CHARACTER

"We shall not know what we shall not do" has become a challenging phrase that has led to significant experimentation in the churches. The Division of Christian Life and Mission of the National Council of Churches has just undertaken a quite new pattern of operation, not as a kind of natural evolution, but as a significant response to the need to use the structures of united Protestantism not so much to serve the denominations as to serve the world. The impetus for this reorganization came about in 1963 from the necessity of responding to the crisis of civil rights. The structures of the National Council, up to that point, were designed to assist the denominations, even as the denominational offices existed to assist the local congregations in their work, the purpose of which was to send the individual Christian into the fray. A reversal of this whole pattern was essential if any effective corporate response were to occur within Protestantism with sufficient strength and focus to respond to the problems of civil rights and poverty.

As a result of the new pressures, the National Council is now reorienting much of its operational pattern in terms of task forces and functional units that seek to bring to bear the concern of the churches as a whole on particular issues or problems. For example, in February, 1964, the General Board of the National Council of Churches authorized an Antipoverty Task Force. And in Chicago, the City Missionary Society, an agency with many years of service to the problems of the city largely through the support of settlement houses and inner city churches, has gone so far as to change its name (summer 1967) to The Community Renewal Society. As such, it is seeking large new funds to support the efforts of Christians to renew the city, rather than to maintain the churches.

Where parish churches and the traditional residential congregations are finding new effectiveness, they have emerged with a new freedom to ask the question, "What are the problems in our community which demand our attention?" But in such situations, the ability of a congregation to deal with any very controversial issue is extremely low. Parish clergy are coming here and there to recognize that their role is to feed their best laymen into task forces or community groups, dealing with hot issues, rather than to fight the useless battle of involving the congregation as a body in any such issue.

Pluralistic Patterns

In a pluralistic society, a variety of forms of church life will be required. European sociologists have recently suggested that the parish concept can be replaced by the notion of "zonal structures," or the variety of ecclesiastical forms that will enable Christian presence, witness, and service, to take shape in the various worlds in which modern man lives and works. In a community or city, then, one would expect residential congregations to accept part of the task, but no longer to be the normative pattern. Alongside such gatherings of Christians are emerging industrial missions; task forces on housing, race relations, and poverty; cell groups in factories and offices; house churches; new ministries to crisis situations, such as narcotics addiction and the plight of migrant workers; chaplaincies to particular vocational groups; and various forms of Christian community participation in militant social action, such as community organization or politics. In a community like East Harlem, for example, Christians may receive communion as part of a Christian community in a regular church building, on the desk of the reception office of Exodus House (a program for the rehabilitation of drug addicts), on the kitchen table of a home where a house church cell gathers weekly, or in the small chapel of an ecumenical action center.

Given the traditional dogmatism of the churches, one hard lesson demanded by pluralism is a willingness to accept the fact that pluralistic structures may even express a legitimate contradiction. In New York City, a conservative minister develops a program for addicts that on both theological and operational grounds is in radical contradiction to a church program in East Harlem. All too often, such programs find themselves spending a diversionary amount of effort in challenging each other. In fact, both may have demonstrable effectiveness and deserve support. Either one may be able to reach a particular segment of the addict community with significant help, yet could not hope to have any impact on those aided by the other group.

USING EXISTING SOCIAL STRUCTURES

In much of its involvement in the fight against poverty the church has shown the wisdom to avoid building duplicate and perhaps competitive structures to existing secular agencies. A church organization is justified in developing its own structures of social action only when it faces a social problem which society has ignored or when some unique contribution is clearly possible (Webber, 1964, ch. 7). In most cases, the religious community should be a seedbed for troops, which because of their faith, are committed to public responsibility.

Many illustrations of the church's present role come to mind. In supporting the community organization attempts under the Industrial Areas Foundation, the churches have supplied a great deal of money and manpower. In Rochester, the Council of Churches was partly responsible for bringing Alinsky forces to the community, putting up a great deal of the money through denominational and local congregation grants but making no effort to determine direction or policy for the local organization, known as FIGHT. Elsewhere, congregations are beginning to require that their members make a commitment to join one community organization working for justice or brotherhood, as a symbol of their religious commitment and faith.

At issue at once is the question of the unique or particular contribution which the Christian can make in a secular organization. Does he bring any competence or insight? Actually, the religious illiteracy of most Christians is such that they are unable to establish connection between their faith and their secular role, making a current phrase, "the secular relevance of the Gospel," quite meaningless. But Christians are often driven back to ask what insight or relevance they do bring, and this initiates for the first time a genuine study of their faith and a confrontation with the demands for obedience which a biblical faith lays upon them. Much of the theological ferment in the churches today arises as laity and clergy, challenged to live responsibly in relation to social problems, discover the poverty of their religious understanding.

Ecumenical Necessity of Structures

Some part, perhaps most, of the modern movement toward church unity arises from common threats to ecclesiastical institutions. Many mergers grow out of weakness. But authentic ecumenism means simply the necessity for common action in mission. Contemporary theological emphasis on the church in mission, and defining mission in terms of witness as service rather than in gathering souls into church membership, makes common action among denominations both easier and a necessity. Many of the most creative efforts of the churches today result in part from their ecumenical character. In Harlem, for example, Catholics and Protestants have developed common poverty programs under the Ministers' Interfaith Association. Summer programs in the community have evolved with shared use of facilities and staff. In the summer of 1967, Protestant and Catholic seminarians worked together on the staff of a Roman Catholic parish. Similar ventures have developed in many cities across the country. On a national level, such a program as Urban America is an example of interdenominational cooperation in the housing field.

A major point of concern for the churches has been in this latter area. Churches here and there are getting into the nonprofit housing business in part because the field is not replete with unavoidable conflict, but also because Section 221D(III) of the National Housing Act is really an open invitation to participation in developing urban housing. The report on Metro North in *The Reporter* magazine (November 17, 1966) provides one illustration of a notable success involving cooperation among a Catholic parish, a Protestant church, and a secular neighborhood house.

Powerful and Powerless Structures

The role of the churches in antipoverty programs has demanded a new recognition of the power that the churches do possess. It has also demanded a willingness to focus this responsibility and at the same time devise structures that are inconspicuous and powerless. In a grape strike in Delano, some clergy can play an aggressive role in support of the unionization efforts, seeking on a national level to mobilize church support. The major commitment of the National Council of Churches and various denominations to the Delta Ministry Project has led to severe conflict not only with Southern politicians, but also with church leaders and members. The Presbyterian support of Alinsky-type community organizations all over the country, a major commitment of home missions funds, has led to several law suits from disgruntled Presbyterians who did not wish to see their benevolence money so used.

The church is an institute with power although powerlessness is also a characteristic of church structures. Power, moreover, is a problem for an institution that takes its starting point from the ministry of Jesus. To a unique degree, however, the church is challenged to use its power without obvious self-interest. Perhaps its real power arises precisely in so far as it in fact achieves this goal of disinterested concern for human problems and, thus, serves the society in a quite unique capacity. Countless projects have been undertaken by the churches to aid the victims of poverty who can expect little help from the "war on poverty" in time to do them any good. Remedial reading projects are only one illustration, although on a rather vast scale, of the church programs undertaken in recent years.

LAY STRUCTURES AS ESSENTIAL

Part of the current dilemma of the clergy arises from the elementary fact that the work of ministry in our day will fall largely to laity. The ordained clergyman simply cannot pretend he is the learned man in the community, holding a central role in its life, as in colonial days. If witness and service are to be performed, the clergy must accept a secondary role, for the most part, as staff rather than line officers. Their role is to prepare and equip the laity for the work of mission, from which they themselves are largely disqualified by the very fact of being paid Christians. Where the faithful gather to reflect on their faith, determine their commitments, and plan for their mission, there is a place for a theological specialist, traditionally an ordained clergyman. But in the actual work of mission in the world, the burden in a secular society falls almost exclusively on non-ordained men and women. Where clergy take the lead in action groups or poverty programs, from Leon Sullivan in Philadelphia to Cecil Williams in San Francisco, they are functioning in effect as laymen who happen along the line to have been to seminary and gotten themselves ordained.

Industrial missions in Detroit and Boston indicate the role of the clergy. They are theological consultants to men in industry, concerned about human values in a technological society, and eager to assume as much responsibility as possible. Only as biblical faith can authenticate itself in terms of providing understanding and perspective in the concreteness of such testing does it merit commitment.

One other phenomenon is worth mentioning. Increasingly, men with theological training, convinced of the irrelevance and intractability of present ecclesiastical structures, are undertaking secular employment but seeing this as a ministry. The biblical picture of Paul, earning his own way as a tentmaker, has led them to speak of this action as a modern "tent-making ministry." Perhaps such patterns suggest the one way in which creative experimentation can emerge without expecting the institute to pay the bill. The best illustration on a substantial scale is under way in a program in Philadelphia called MAP (Metropolitan Associates of Philadelphia). If the large number of men, now evacuating from parochial responsibilities, can be seen by the churches as breaking valuable new ground rather than as defectors, and if the men can be kept from bitterness, then the kind of freedom and opportunity from which renewal may be bred could emerge from this trend.

THE GOSPEL AND THE POOR

Jesus began his ministry by announcing that he had been sent to preach the good news to the poor. As institutions, the churches are making some responses to the problems of poverty through a wide range of structures and programs. We have indicated something of the scope of these in the preceding section. But one final issue remains to be articulated. What is the word of gospel, of good news that the churches have always claimed they possessed for all men, and yet which in the New Testament is underlined with special emphasis for the poor? It is more than a calling to Christians to give special heed to the plight of the poor. Jesus seems to imply that the poor have a peculiar advantage in relationship to the kingdom of God.

The gospel, at its heart, is concerned with enabling men to discover and express their authentic humanity. For the poor and powerless in our time, buffeted by the claims of an affluent society, the need to establish their own identity as human beings is urgent. What the churches of our time are called upon to announce is the fact that all men are brothers endowed with the right to live with meaning and fulfillment and to give credence to this claim by their identity with the deprived. To the urban poor, the gospel must come in the form of a community which, in the words of Adolph Harnack, is "as wide as human life itself and as deep as human need." In this community, the fundamental requirements of human life can be met: the need to establish identity, to have a history, to have a future and a purpose. All men need this, but most of all the urban poor and the Negro in America.

The gospel comes in a community which offers men an identity as sons of God, a history in the story of Israel and the church, and a community of brothers in which all human barriers are shattered. But the gospel goes a second step. Just as man needs identity to be human, so also he needs to accept responsibility for his life and for his world. The gospel is also the challenge to live responsibly for one's neighbor. Again and again in urban slums, men come to live not because their problems have been solved, but because they are learning to accept responsibility for social change. Perhaps most men in our time will discover this lesson for themselves, if it will be learned at all. For the Christian, it is the essence of his gospel that in losing one's life for others, one finds the meaning of life.

References

AUTHOR'S NOTE: *In addition to works referred to in the text, the references given below include other materials relevant to the study of the urban church and the issue of poverty.*

BERGER, PETER. *The Noise of Solemn Assemblies* (Garden City, N. Y.: Doubleday, 1961).

BLIZZARD, SAMUEL. "The Minister's Dilemma," *The Christian Century*, 73 (1956), pp. 508-10.

COMME, ARNOLD. *Agents of Reconciliation* (Philadelphia: Westminster Press, 1961).

COX, HARVEY. *The Secular City* (New York: Macmillan, 1964).

FRIEDEN, BETTY. *The Feminine Mystique* (New York: Norton, 1963).

Glock, Charles Y. "Afterword: A Sociologist Looks at the Parish Church," in Walter Kloetzli (ed.), *The City Church: Death or Renewal* (New York: Muhlenberg Press, 1961).

Godin, Abbe. *France, Pagan?* (London: Sheed & Ward, 1949).

Herberg, Will. *Protestant-Catholic-Jew* (Garden City, N. Y.: Doubleday, 1955).

Hoekendijk, Hans. *The Church Inside Out* (Philadelphia: Westminster Press, Random House, 1961).

Illich, Ivan. "The Vanishing Clergyman," *The Critic*, 25, No. 6 (June-July, 1967), pp. 18-27.

Jacobs, Jane. *The Death and Life of Great American Cities* (New York: Random House, 1961).

Kraemer, Hendrik. *A Theology of the Laity* (Philadelphia: Westminster Press, 1959).

Lenski, Gerhard. *The Religious Factor* (Garden City, N. Y.: Doubleday, 1961).

MacLeod, George. *Only One Way Left* (Glasgow: The Iona Community, 1956).

Marty, Martin. *The New Shape of American Religion* (New York: Harper and Brothers, 1958).

McLoughlin, William G. "Is There a Third Force in Christendom?" *Daedalus*, 96, No. 1 (Winter, 1967), pp. 43-68.

Metcalf, George R. "Metro North Moves Mountains," *The Reporter* (November 17, 1966), pp. 24-29.

Moynihan, Daniel P. *The Negro Family: The Case for National Action* (Washington, D. C.: U. S. Department of Labor, Office of Policy Planning and Research, March, 1965).

Southcott, Ernest. *The Parish Comes Alive* (New York: Morehouse, 1956).

Stringfellow, William. *A Private and Public Faith* (Grand Rapids: Eerdmans, 1962).

Underwood, Kenneth. *Protestant and Catholic* (Boston: Beacon Press, 1957).

Webber, George. *The Congregation in Mission* (Nashville: Abingdon, 1964).

Wickham, E. R. *Church and People in an Industrial City* (London: Lutterworth Press, 1957).

Wieser, Thomas (ed.). *Planning for Mission* (New York: National Council of Churches, 1966).

Wilcox, Preston R. "The Church and the War on Poverty," unpublished manuscript delivered to Diocesan Conference, Pennsylvania, October 8, 1965.

Williams, Colin. *What in the World* (New York: National Council of Churches, 1964).

———. *Where in the World* (New York: National Council of Churches, 1963).

Winter, Gibson. *The New Creation as Metropolis* (New York: Macmillan, 1963).

———. *The Suburban Captivity of the Churches* (New York: Macmillan, 1962).

World Council of Churches. *The Church for Others* (Geneva, 1967).

Part III

POVERTY AND POWER

The Role of the Poor in Urban Politics

Introduction

THE preceding eight chapters of this volume have suggested how the situation of the poor—indeed, how poverty itself—reflects the interaction among several main sets of variables: economic, sociological, and political. Each set, in a sense, constitutes a spectrum of "givens" for the other; yet each is subject, at least theoretically, to some degree of conscious and deliberate change. Adequate low income housing, for example, would be neither so scarce nor so segregated today if relevant policy and action in the public and private sectors had been of a different character during the last decade. The same can be said of inadequacies in medical care, consumer protection, legal services, and the other basic requirements of humankind. Although it is true that the proposed changes would not have greatly increased the gross national product nor radically transformed the stratification patterns of American society, they could have substantially reduced absolute, and even relative, poverty for many millions of disadvantaged people. That this did not happen is unfortunate but understandable. For those with the power to authorize and implement major modifications in existing public and private institutional policies and practices have tended to constrain the pressures for change, if not to resist them outright.

In the face of this seeming rigidity in the system, some now argue that the poor must become more powerful before they stand much chance to become less poor. Others, however, retort that people in our kind of society are not likely to acquire power until they have climbed or been lifted out of poverty. Historically, as we are well aware, the political perspective has yielded a variety of images of the poor: they have been seen as the manpower for constructive social movements; as a potential mob to be used for purposes other than their own or to be kept under tight control; and as the helpless victims of intentional or inadvertent exploitation and brutalization. Currently, with the passage of the national antipoverty act and the inauguration of the "war on poverty," the political perspective has assumed new prominence. More and more it seems that meaningful change in the status of the poor is not likely to come about—except very slowly, indeed—through the benevolent paternalism or good will of the majoritarian society. In the face of this situation some see no real alternative to the mobilization and exercise of power by the poor themselves.

It is to this perspective that the five chapters in this section direct their attention. The first three discuss the promise and limitations of the community action component of the "war on poverty" and the problems involved in activating the poor. Each in its own way makes explicit the need for political action and participation by the disadvantaged if significant progress is to be made in the nation's efforts to eradicate poverty. The remaining two chapters provide a comparative view to the American scene by training their sights on two of the developing areas of the world. Together, the five contributions produce not one, but alternative, answers to the question: Is the power of the poor a variable that should be taken as a given or viewed as subject to significant, deliberate manipulation?

The outstanding innovation of the Economic Opportunity Act was the provision for "maximum feasible participation of the poor" in community action programs. It has also proved to be one of the most controversial aspects of the "war on poverty." Attacked, on the one hand, by local officials and the welfare bureaucracy as a threat to their control and, on the other, by some of the poor themselves as only a token gesture, the provision has traveled a rocky road. In Chapter 9 Sanford Kravitz examines the origins of this participatory concept, the manner in which it has been interpreted by policy-makers and administrators at the various levels of government, how it has been implemented, and the impact it has had.

Kravitz regards the community action programs—which serve as the vehicle for operationalizing the concept of participation—as neither great successes nor utter failures. Like Shostak, he believes that they have been a critical factor in awakening communities to the deep-seated social, economic, and physical dimensions of poverty. Hidden issues have been given visibility, the development of indigenous leadership stimulated, and important new services brought to many poor people. Three years of CAP operations have, in his view, established the principle of participation by target area residents at least in some communities. They have also brought about some changes in the power alignments around the coordination and distribution of social services. As for the impoverished, more and more of them have learned that participation and action can sometimes affect public and private welfare programs and procedures.

At most, however, the gains have been modest. The traditional structure of power at the community level, although challenged and forced to make some accommodations, remains substantially unchanged. And the grand promise of the Economic Opportunity Act with its image of a massive "war on poverty" has failed to materialize. Part of the disillusionment with the poverty program can be traced to its own rhetoric which pictured it as much more than it actually was and promised much more than it could deliver. Kravitz emphasizes the frequently overlooked fact that OEO has only a small part of the responsibility for dealing with an immense problem which involves all sectors of the society in one form or another. He correctly points out that programs to address poverty at the local level through concerted community action and resident participation are not likely to show significant gains unless they are matched by several major national commitments. These include income redistribution, a large scale, publicly-subsidized employment effort, and a vastly expanded program for low-income families. Without these major program elements, structural reorganization of the American community to meet the needs of the poor will remain more a matter of hope than reality.

Chapter 10 also deals with the community action program, reprinting the interpretative analysis prepared for the Senate Subcommittee on Employment, Manpower, and Poverty by Howard W. Hallman, director of the poverty study staff which investigated the CAP agencies and operations in 35 communities, 24 of them urban. The study's purpose was "to determine not what the community action program ought to be . . . but rather what it actually is in various communities." Against the historical background and evaluative overview provided by Kravitz, some of Hallman's descriptive generalizations take on particular interest and emphasis: a predominant commitment to the strategy of giving power to the poor complete with confrontation of and conflict with "the establishment" obtained in only three communities; most emphasized improving services to the poor relevant to more effectively meeting their pressing needs for jobs, social services, better education, shelter, health care, and the like. Community leaders in about half the places studied saw the cause of poverty as residing mostly in the poor themselves and, therefore, sought ways to help the poor as individuals and families break out of the "cycle of poverty"; the other half also emphasized the failure of society and its institutions and about a third made institutional change a major function.

Hallman emphasizes the diverse beginnings of CAP agencies, followed by the emergence in each community of a governing coalition, seldom monolithic and sometimes torn by conflict; how conservative it is clearly affects the degree of institutional change sought through OEO programs. At least a third of the members on all of the boards of directors are "representatives of the poor," but they tend to be non-poor residents of poverty areas; and on only 9 of the 35 boards did such persons constitute half or more of the membership. In some communities resident participation also has been encouraged with respect to the boards of delegate agencies and through neighborhood councils, but to what degree depends importantly upon the policies set for the CAP staff by the board coalition and the freedom staff enjoy to encourage and facilitate such participation. Especially in urban areas, established agencies have often resisted even modest efforts at innovation and coordination in programs for the poor, but federal directives themselves have sometimes restricted or disrupted fruitful beginnings.

Like Shostak and Kravitz, Hallman concludes that real remedies for poverty "will be costlier and much more difficult than the limited efforts which are now underway." The community action program could be built into something effective; at the moment it is "a pitiful start."

In Chapter 11 Warner Bloomberg, Jr. and Florence W. Rosenstock provide a more detailed look at the effort to engage the poor as participants in the decision-making that helps to shape the antipoverty program in each community. They note that the underlying reasons for seeking such participation range from doctrines about participative democracy to the purely pragmatic generalization that the poor know a lot about poverty. More important, however, is whether or not low participation is seen as essentially a consequence of poverty that will change only when the status and related culture of the poor are changed, or is viewed as one of the reasons the poor have not achieved redress of their grievances —increasing participation then being one of the available means, perhaps an essential one, for forcing establishment of more effective antipoverty programs by middle and upper class community decision-makers. Bloomberg and Rosenstock accept the latter view as the more valid.

However, they note that direct involvement in community decision-making, except for elections, is rare even among the broad middle strata. If participation by the poor is to have major impact on decisions that shape the "war on poverty," then the poor must become, relative to most of the more affluent segment of society, "over-participators." After comparing two approaches to generating such participation—the "social action–social protest model" and the "community development model"—the authors conclude that both can be applied effectively in programs to elicit participation by poor citizens but each may appeal more strongly to different types of poor people. The techniques engendered by the action-protest model frequently produce an effective counteraction by the majoritarian community, and this may limit or reduce the gains to be made by the poor as participators. Bloomberg and Rosenstock, therefore, suggest that the community development model may often provide more effective strategies for increasing participation by the poor. But, echoing the judgment of the preceding authors, they conclude that the potential for participation can never be realized with the meager resources now devoted to this effort, and that few institutions are contributing what they could.

The last two chapters in this section shift our attention to nations where the urban poor are a much larger and a much more deprived segment of society. If poverty was an absolute condition and politics a function only of numbers, we might expect the poor of the cities in underdeveloped areas to be both more belligerent and more effective than their counterparts in the United States. But no such simple pattern obtains. Much more complex lessons must be learned from the comparison.

Chapter 12 focuses on the urban poor in Africa, principally in Nigeria and Kenya. Peter C. W. Gutkind builds his discussion around urban unemployment, one of the most serious problems of the developing nations and a prime determinant of poverty. As Gutkind shows, every newly-independent African state is faced with the imbalance between its resources and the demands of its people for new means of earning a living. Caught up in the technological revolution and the web of a competitive international economy, the emerging nations find they cannot turn their back on the *extensive* use of labor-saving devices and the *intensive* use of manpower. Thus, while production is increasing, the size of the work force in many sectors of the economy has remained steady or even declined. The consequences of this phenomenon are not difficult to surmise. For one thing, the capacity of these countries to absorb the rapidly growing labor pool—the product of rapid population increase and widespread migration from the villages—is exceedingly limited, whatever the speed of their economic development. For another, as migrants enter the urban center their expectations and demands increase but their prospects for fulfillment, if anything, diminish.

The American reader will find both similarities and differences here between the experiences of his own country and those of the new African states. At times he will be reminded of earlier periods in American history when the Horatio Alger dream predominated, when job competition among ethnic segments of the population was common, when the labor movement lacked political muscle. At other points, he will almost feel that the contemporary domestic scene is being described as he reads of the growing gap between the poor and the more affluent members of the society, of the seeming insensitivity of the governmental and private elite to the needs and aspirations of the disadvantaged, of the lack of adequate instrumental channels for the deprived to express and obtain redress for their grievances.

Gutkind shows that although the urban unemployed have all the potential of becoming an important pressure group, they have thus far failed to create any organizational structure which is cohesive and coherent enough to generate collective action. What associations they have formed have lacked skilled leadership and have been torn by internal dissension. He also shows that although unemployment in the cities is extremely high, certain factors have acted as safety valves to prevent any serious explosion. One of these is the refuge and support—the traditional mutual aid—that the unemployed urbanite can still find among his extended kin group and his friends. Another is the belief of the deprived that jobs will eventually become available and that the privileges which the affluent enjoy may one day be theirs.

It is clear, however, that the social and political pressures are mounting and will continue to do so as awareness increases that the present course of national development is bringing major benefits to the few at the expense of the many, as the ostentatious life of the elite ceases to appear as a possibility to the poor, as the employed find it increasingly burdensome to support their unemployed kin and friends, and as the impression grows that local or national political leaders do not have the interest or inclination to help the disadvantaged. Africa's unemployed stand today, in Gutkind's words, "as a monument to the unfinished revolution which a few short years ago swept the continent into the rough waters of a dubious sovereignty." The day may be approaching when the poor will insist that the revolution be completed.

William Mangin's portrayal of the urban poor of Latin America provides a number of striking contrasts to the African scene. Instead of new nations, many of whose leaders are still of the generation that won independence, the political context in South America is that of long established sovereignties largely controlled by business and landed elites who have often supported autocratic and militaristic regimes. Even if they have not been "de-tribalized," many of the urban African poor seem to have been "politicized" by the movements for independence to a far greater degree than the urbanized ex-peasants of Latin America. The latter move toward political relevance, not through associations of the unemployed such as Gutkind has described, but through a "squatters' communities" movement that is unique in its character and tactics.

Mangin argues with great force that both the apathy and the action of the urban poor in South America must be understood in terms of the interplay between peasant cultural persistances and the social, psychological and structural consequences of impoverishment. Obviously, then, other variables than peasantry and poverty must be used to explain why some of the slum dwellers of such cities as Lima, Rio de Janeiro, Bogotá, and even Brasilia seize the initiative and subsequently some of the city's land, while others remain in apparent apathy and despair. Once more we encounter some familiar variables: organizational skills, a clear perception of need, some political sophistication—these and other requisites for effective self-help projects are more likely to be found among the more urbanized, more literate, more secure of the poor. If their appearance in turn leads to any notable degree of successful action, the result is a shift away from the attitudinal themes denoted by such concepts as "the image of limited good" and "the culture of poverty." But the new patterns are rooted and emerge from the same cultural base of potentialities as the old. Once again there is evidence that generalizations about the cultural inadequacies of the poor serve better to rationalize than to explain the persistence of impoverishment.

Mangin provides many revealing details on how "squatter's invasions" are organized and carried out, and on the subsequent development of these *barriadas*. He also describes the resistance to such actions by established authorities and their blindness to the lessons taught by the relative success of many such communities. Revealing, too, are some brief comparisons with the situation of the urban poor in the United States, where there is no longer either the open land or the openness in the system that seems essential for an effective squatters' movement.

Mangin's conclusions are similar to those of the other contributors to this section and suggest a generalization which, subject to some interpretation for each society, may be trans-cultural. Without the organized participation by the poor in the political life of the urban community, progress toward alleviating, if not eliminating, poverty is likely to be far from the maximum possible. At the same time, politically relevant action by the poor, whatever its form and content from one society to another, is not likely to produce by itself much more than situations of uncertainty and new possibility. The poor themselves do not have and are not likely to acquire the power to transform established institutions in ways which would substantially reduce poverty in a relatively short time. Hypothetically, others with such power might respond to these situations of uncertainty and new possibility in ways that would be truly effective in bringing about such institutional change. But there is little evidence that they are likely to do so.

—*W. B. Jr. and H. J. S.*

9

The Community Action
Program in Perspective

SANFORD KRAVITZ

☐ THE IDEA OF COORDINATED COMMUNITY ACTION to relieve human
distress and poverty has been present in American towns and cities
for almost 100 years (Bruno, 1957; Pumphrey and Pumphrey, 1961).
The growth and spread of the various forms of local community
coordinating structures started to take shape in the first decade of
this century when social service organizations began to struggle
with the requirements for coordination of the services spawned
by large scale immigration and industrialization.

ORIGINS OF COMMUNITY ACTION

Two parallel efforts for relief of the distress of the poor had
taken firm root in American communities during the last two
decades of the nineteenth century: the Charity Organization Society movement and the Settlement movement. These two streams
of social welfare, both with their roots in England, had engaged
the philanthropic public. In the process they had become involved
in an ideological struggle over the same issue which still divides
present efforts to attack poverty. The Charity Organization Societies saw the answers to poverty in retraining the indigent, improving
his moral standards, removing him from the influences of depraved
family life, and subjecting him to the knowledge and counseling
skill of an experienced worker or skilled upper class volunteer. The
Settlement movement, primarily concerned with environment and
the effects of the social structure, concentrated its efforts on reconstructing neighborhood life, on improving facilities and resources
in a single geographical area, and on the stimulation of one program

participant by another through group effort. It was the Settlement movement that led the fight for shorter working hours for women and for child labor laws.

An effort was instituted in 1889 (Warner, 1889, pp. 183-203) to apply scientific principles to determining the causes of poverty; it concluded by finding both individual and environmental bases. These findings did not affect the split and by 1899, the Charity Organization movement and the Settlement movement were vying for the allegiance, service support, and the gifts of American philanthropy.

Pressure for increased resources from the philanthropic public, the growth in the number of service agencies, and increased interest in improved management as well as in rationalizing the array of programs for the poor encouraged the spread of the new coordinating agency form, the council of social agencies. These embryonic action programs usually emerged in a community as it achieved a particular level of economic development. The "Council" movement was entirely voluntary, reflecting the nature of practically all of the welfare services of the period. The movement was given substantial impetus during World War I as national and local community war fund campaigns highlighted the need for coordination and unified effort. By the early 1920s, federated fund raising—the Community Chest idea—had spread rapidly through the country. The Community Chest needed procedures by which it could evaluate the budgets of agencies that were presented to it for funding. It required planning if it could speak on the priorities of competing community demands. The councils, in turn, needed support to pay for their planning and coordinating activities. Thus marriage was called for, and increasingly, across the country, community planning and voluntary federated fund raising were joined together.

The councils were made up of representatives of the member social agencies which benefited from the Community Chest. Their task was to influence the decisions to be made in the allocation of the Chest's funds and to be alert to new and emerging community needs. The capacity to meet new need was always to be governed by the availability of resources after distribution to existing approved services.

The Council of Social Agencies, or the Welfare Council, as they later were called, was a social work institution. It oriented itself toward a view of community problems in terms of the professional disciplines and agency capability to deal with such problems. It organized itself into a casework division, a group work division, and a health division. Family problems were casework problems, health problems were the responsibility of visiting nurses or private physicians and hospitals.

The rapid growth of governmental services after 1930 placed strains on the welfare councils to become more inclusive in their membership and to widen their concern with social problems. Until the 1960s, they appeared unable to make any major breaks from the form and function that had governed their early beginnings. Some large councils struggled to find scientific means to determine community needs and priorities. Others attempted to engage public agencies and to plan for public services.

Councils for the most part had only modest funds for planning. Their research efforts were largely statistics on utilization of services which would be helpful to the Community Chest in its campaign. To be sure, discussions went on among the professional workers and the councils as to the latter's role in generating social action. However, fear of jeopardizing tax exempt status generally put a damper on most efforts of these bodies to enter the public arena. Their main concern during most of this forty-year period was to balance community resources so as to meet the capacity of the Community Chest to raise money.

Councils, moreover, were circumscribed by the independent actions of health agencies that raised their funds in separate campaigns and by their own failure to engage the growing numbers of public services in the social welfare area. They had, in fact, little or no influence on the allocation of public health and welfare resources and their impact on public programs was minimal. The coordinating-structure mode of organization under which they operated and their reliance on the business and social elite for key leadership gave them a stance that was directed at social services and their refinement, not social problems and their causes. In short, social planning councils, the major community vehicle present in American communities for collective attention to social problems, were mainly concerned with coordination and efficiency, not innovation or structural deficiencies in the community. There was thus no major mechanism fully prepared to engage the critical problems of poverty in urban America.

THE EMERGENCE OF NEW FORMS

American communities passed through the 1950s with only mild awareness of the growing numbers of problems that were impinging upon them. Urban renewal agencies sprang up across the country following the passage of the Housing Act of 1949. Their programs brought physical change to the center of the city, but the agencies were either unable or more often generally disinterested in coping with the social problems of the poor that large scale clearance activities both uncovered and generated. The welfare councils at the same time were attempting to deal with the proliferation of health care agencies and the growing problems of suburbia. Little or no attention was given to the alarming rise in unemployment. In 1953 unemployment stood at 3.5 per cent; it rose to 3.8 per cent in 1956 and to 5.5 per cent in 1959. In 1940 Negro unemployment was 20 per cent higher than that of whites. In 1953 the differential had risen to 71 per cent and by 1963 to 112 per cent (Marris and Rein, 1967). During the 1950s, 1,400,000 Negroes left the South and migrated North and West to the urban and industrial centers to replace the two million whites who had fled to the suburbs. Planning agencies faced suburbia, or talked about regional problems or metropolitan government.

The lack of action or direction in local communities was mirrored in the inaction of a conservative administration in Washington. The grand promises of decent housing for all made by the Housing Act of 1949 were converted to tokenism by the action of Congressional appropriations committees. The amendments to the Social Security Act of 1956 authorized social services to families on welfare, but a reluctant Congress once again failed to appropriate funds. And the Civil Rights Act of 1957 was another dismal disappointment.

The situation was no different with respect to education. The elementary and secondary school systems of the nation were beset by the Sputnik challenge and with demands for improved education of the talented and with a concern for academic excellence. Most urban school systems, as well as their critics and supporters, seemed unaware of the growing crisis in the inner city schools.

Public welfare programs for the very poor had expanded greatly since the passage of the Social Security Act. They were, however, operated across the country with varying degrees of skill and enlightenment. Attitudes toward public welfare were particularly characterized by a harsh and punitive attitude on the part of the public, reflecting a more general feeling that indeed the poor make their own poverty.

THE FORD FOUNDATION
GRAY AREAS PROGRAM

The first substantial departure from the drift which had characterized the 1950s came with the development of the Ford Foundation Gray Areas Program in 1961 (Marris and Rein, 1967, p. 11). In the late 1950s the Foundation had invested in a series of experimental programs in metropolitan planning and in aid to education in the inner city and in urban renewal. These efforts had not produced startling results for a variety of possible reasons. Big city mayors, predominantly Democratic, were not interested in sharing power and authority with the burgeoning suburbs that were predominantly Republican. Urban renewal had been unable to deal effectively with the social backlash of its business district development efforts. The few inner city school efforts had been fragmented approaches to innovation, i.e., team teaching, preschool programs, home visitors, and the community-centered school. While these were innovative concepts, they were dispersed through school systems that demonstrated little capacity or inclination to make any fundamental changes in the total system in order to reach more effectively the child living in poverty.

Cognizant of this state of affairs, the Public Affairs Department of the Foundation sought a bolder and more comprehensive approach, an approach which would be broader than efforts to effect one subsystem, the inner city school, but smaller, more manageable, and more capable of producing action than efforts to achieve metropolitan governmental and regional planning. The Foundation started this new program with the allocation to each chosen city of what were considered, for that time, to be enormous development funds. These funds were to be used for coordinated programs in such areas as youth employment, education, and expanded social and community services. The Foundation also pressed for the establishment of new community agencies which presumably would be uncommitted to the existing service structure. It was believed that such new agencies would be more readily prepared to experiment and to use their funds as leverage for change. The first grant in the new program was made to Oakland, California, on December 28, 1961. This grant was followed by subsequent allotments to New Haven, Boston, Philadelphia, Washington, D. C., and to a statewide agency in North Carolina (the North Carolina Fund).

THE PRESIDENT'S COMMITTEE ON JUVENILE DELINQUENCY

In September, 1961, almost coincident with the development of the new Ford Foundation program, the Congress passed the Juvenile Delinquency and Youth Offenses Control Act of 1961. The Act provided funds for demonstration projects and training efforts with the objective of launching a new national and comprehensive attack on the problem of juvenile delinquency and youth crime. The language of the legislation, which had been prepared by the new President's Committee on Juvenile Delinquency, focused attention specifically on the social antecedents of juvenile crime, youth unemployment, poor housing, poor health, inadequate education, and the alienation of lower-class communities and neighborhoods.

The development of the new legislation had been in large measure guided by the theories of Cloward and Ohlin (Cloward and Ohlin, 1960). Their recently published book had viewed the origins of delinquency among lower-class youth as mainly a failure in the opportunity structure. The administration of the Act was placed in a special office of Juvenile Delinquency and Youth Development in the Department of Health, Education and Welfare. The bill mandated that the grants to be allocated by HEW be made with the advice and final approval of the President's Committee. This committee consisted of the Attorney General, the Secretary of Labor, and the Secretary of the Department of Health, Education and Welfare. It was given the assignment of coordinating interdepartmental support for the new program.

The new law, as interpreted by the administration, was a mandate for major strategic investments in comprehensive local community attacks on delinquency. The conceptual base in "opportunity theory" allowed a wide scope of relevant action.

The President's Committee viewed the conventions of institutional practice as their principal reform targets. The new program was thus characterized by a requirement for innovation, by its intellectual and theoretical underpinnings, and by its general anti-bureaucratic stance. Criteria for effective programs stressed certain critical elements:

(1) the recognition of the strong interrelationship of social problems;

(2) remedies that would focus on change in the opportunity structure rather than on changes in the behavior of an individual or redirection of personality;

(3) the requirement that communities undertake a rational analysis of their social problems and propose solutions consistent with the problem definition (the solutions were assumed to be capable of integration); and

(4) the recognition of the necessity for substantial participation of public agencies and the political executive arm of government in the efforts to be undertaken.

On the basis of what was believed to be general understanding of these principles, 17 demonstration projects were chosen in 16 cities. One project received action funds almost immediately. This was Mobilization for Youth in New York City, where the planning phase had been completed under an earlier grant from the National Institute of Mental Health. The remaining 16 received funds to undertake the planning of the programs. In most cases, the planning grant was for a one-year effort.

IMPACT OF THE NEW PROGRAMS

Despite the relatively small size of the programs and limited geographical coverage of the projects, these new efforts very quickly jolted the communities in which they were inaugurated. The new programs and the new planning structures also spread shock waves throughout most of the medium-sized and larger communities of the nation. Their advent challenged existing planning structures such as welfare councils and other established agencies which had traditionally controlled a particular terrain of human services.

The new programs almost coincidentally emerged at a critical moment in American social history. Along with the civil rights revolution, the worsening problem of youth unemployment, concern over automation and its impact on the unskilled, they highlighted the failures of existing planning mechanisms and of the educational and welfare institutions. They talked in terms of problems, not organizations, they acknowledged the power of professional politicians, they called for public responsibility in addressing the problems of the inner city, and they urged a rededication to serving the poor.

Both the Ford and the HEW funded programs aroused strong feelings among professionals in welfare and in the related human service fields such as education and employment. To those who were dissatisfied with the *status quo* of programs and of organizations, they became shining symbols of what might be done. On the other hand, to a broad group who sharply disagreed with their central assumptions, they represented a monstrous compound of evil, waste, and disrespect for experience.

Despite the mixed success of some of the projects and the outright failure of several others, the experience threw a national spotlight on the following problems:

(1) Many voluntary "welfare" programs were not reaching the poor.

(2) If they were reaching the poor, the services offered were often inappropriate.

(3) Services aimed at meeting the needs of disadvantaged people were typically fragmented and unrelated.

(4) Realistic understanding by professionals and community leaders of the problems faced by the poor was limited.

(5) Each specialty field was typically working in encapsulated fashion on a particular kind of problem, without awareness of the other fields or of efforts toward interlock.

(6) There was little political leadership involvement in the decision-making processes of voluntary social welfare.

(7) There was little or no serious participation of program beneficiaries in projects being planned and implemented by professionals and elite community leadership.

The program contribution in each community of these two demonstration efforts was mixed, but the fact of their development —and even the criticism and attacks they sustained—escalated long-festering problems into wide public view. As a consequence, discussion of them as critical national issues could no longer be evaded. Thus, a seedbed, however imperfect, was provided for the central conceptual elements in the later Community Action Program (CAP)—the program that was to become a major pillar in the Economic Opportunity Act of 1964.

DEVELOPMENT OF THE CONCEPT OF COMMUNITY ACTION IN THE ECONOMIC OPPORTUNITY ACT

Any set of proposed solutions to the central problem of poverty must deal with the individual problems that are faced by the poor in their own communities—problems that are beyond the provision of direct financial assistance and beyond the provision of employment through the usual market place. The Social Security measures of the 1930s and subsequent amendments were relatively effective in dealing with a large sector of the problem, but a substantial gap remained in both the local and national capacity to reach the poor effectively.

The problem confronting the planners of the war on poverty in the winter and spring of 1964 was something of this nature: Poverty is a complex social and economic issue; it is rooted in an extensive array of social and individual causes; what kind of program therefore can be developed to permit a counterattack across the total spectrum of need at the local community level?

The inability of existing and emerging welfare, education, and manpower-retraining programs to achieve their full potential was seen as continuing unless effective ways could be found to (1) diagnose the problem of poverty within a local community and (2) apply the specific remedies in a coordinated fashion.

The planners placed great faith in the capacity for coherent, rational action at the local community level. They argued that the availability of new large sums of money for planning and program assistance would reform the existing institutions or would create new agencies that would assume the necessary responsibility. The focus on the local community was in fact part of a growing pattern of federal aid in which assistance was provided to local efforts on the basis of local appraisal of local needs rather than the traditional grant-in-aid by state formula for specified programs.

A conceptual model of a community action effort calls for careful diagnosis of needs and subsequent application of all appropriate program and organizational solutions. It implies central local authority to exert influence on and make decisions about the critical program components, the involvement of major institutions, and, above all, the power to control allocation of resources. With some modest (and some major) concessions that are contrary to the model—e.g., de-emphasis on planning and increased emphasis on the development of a consensus structure—the Community Action Program emerged as a major weapon in the war on poverty.

The experience of the Juvenile Delinquency program indicated that year-long planning efforts had neither been well administered nor sympathetically accepted at the local community. Great impatience was generated while the community waited for the professional staff to produce action or service projects. This impatience was reflected in key members of the Congress, and thus the term "planning" became euphemistically "program development." The idea that the entire local community program, even unto its discrete parts, must be theoretically linked, was tabled in favor of a slow putting together of relevant pieces. This latter was described by staff as the "building block" approach. It also was a realistic avenue to the modest funds that were to be made available for an all-out "war on poverty."

The willingness of the early programs to directly confront the major institutions and to be prepared to engage in combat over principle was sidetracked in favor of a consensus structure for policy-making in which the relevant actors were (1) the political structure, (2) the social agency, civic organization structure, and (3) the residents of the areas to be served.

The community action program concept was still sketchy, but was a more fully developed model than most of the other programs included in the Economic Opportunity Act. It also provided means for a local community focus for other titles to the Act. The Neighborhood Youth Corps would be locally operated and recruitment and post-training placement could be handled by the local community action agency. VISTA volunteers would be assigned to work on local projects. The CAP concept, developed largely around an urban model, was tested on problems of rural poverty, Indians, and migrants. The open-ended nature of the organizational design provided a framework within which a breadth of program activities could be carried on and nationalized; it could serve all ages; and it could provide an umbrella for the diverse and discrete phenomena identified as the many faces of poverty, both rural and urban (Grossman, 1966, p. 16). Thus it became an all-purpose program.

MAXIMUM FEASIBLE PARTICIPATION

One of the outstanding innovations, with import far beyond the expectations of the bill's drafters, was the requirement for the participation of the program beneficiaries in policy development, planning, and implementation. During the short span of three years, Title II-A in its development of a new array of actions or at least a rearrangement, in its focus on problems, and in its precise emphasis on the poor, has wrought some changes in the interests, the power alignments, the leadership, and the social welfare programs of most communities that have felt its impact.

ORIGINS OF CONCEPT

There will be continuing efforts to trace the origins of the concept of "maximum feasible participation" and the full history is not yet written (Rubin, 1967). They were present to a degree in the delinquency projects in the form of a general concern for the development of community competence. Few precedents existed in other programs and none in federal legislation. There had been discussions for several years at the federal level about creating new job opportunities for the poor. There had also been discussions about greater citizen participation on advisory boards in projects affecting public welfare and urban renewal, but participation of the poor was rarely an issue and had never before been legislatively mandated as a program requirement.

Even in the Economic Opportunity Act, although the words were present, a clear legislative intent was absent. The bill stated that a Community Action Program must be "developed, conducted and administered with the maximum feasible participation of residents of the areas and members of the groups served. . . ." The inclusion of this requirement brought little or no attention from the Congress during the 1964 hearings. Attorney General Robert Kennedy was the only witness to mention the concept in his testimony. It is true that a democratic and socio-therapeutic intent drawn from the tradition of community organization and community development existed in the minds of some of the staff members of the President's Task Force on Poverty. This intent was in part drawn out of the failure of established welfare programs to reach the most needy of the poor. It was felt that if poor people help to plan services in their own behalf, they will plan services that are relevant to their immediate needs. It was also felt that their needs would be given increased attention and their competence as full participating members of the community would be enhanced. It was further felt that with participation of the poor, programs were more likely to be utilized by the beneficiaries.

Richard Cloward has stated an additional idea that only took on meaning and broader acceptance several years after the poverty program was under way. In his words:

> the anti-poverty program, precisely because of its mandate to involve the poor, can help to bring about political preconditions for major economic changes: but this can happen only if the forms of involvement lead to new bases of organized power for low income people. Economic deprivation is fundamentally a political problem and power will be required to solve it . . . The possibility that the anti-poverty program can contribute to the growth of low-income power lies in delivering to the poor and their leaders control over the programs and the funds to be funneled into their slums and ghetto communities (Cloward, 1965, pp. 55-56).

David Grossman, a member of the President's Task Force on Poverty and later a key leader in the administration of the Community Action Program, ties the participative concept to the passage of the Civil Rights Act.

> The Civil Rights Act . . . opened up opportunities for Negroes and other minorities to claim long overdue rights; the Economic Opportunity Act was intended to make the exercise of these rights more than a theoretical possibility for the vast proportion of the nation's minorities who were trapped in poverty. The civil rights movement carried with it overtones of participatory democracy

that had been dormant in much of American life for decades. This legislative combination clearly had much to do with the way the maximum feasible participation phrase was interpreted by Negroes, and to a lesser extent Puerto-Rican, Mexican-American and other minority groups (Grossman, 1966, p. 18).

MEANING OF "PARTICIPATIVE" PHRASE

The issue of the precise meaning of the phrase "maximum feasible participation" has been with the Community Action Program from the very beginning. It has been extensively discussed at all levels of national life from the neighborhood to the White House. The Office of Economic Opportunity has generally insisted on local solutions and local interpretations within reason. Jack Conway, the first director of the Community Action Program and later the deputy director of OEO speaking during the summer of 1964, described a local community action program as a "three-legged stool." By that he meant that the local CAP agency rested on three foundations: participation by the public officials of the community, both elected and appointed; participation by voluntary agencies and institutions; and participation by representatives of the poor. Local programs were not to be the tools of politics— but Conway felt that the programs would be doomed without effective support from city hall or a county government. He did not see the local programs as simple extensions of Health and Welfare Councils or settlement houses, but he felt that a large and influential part of the community would be alienated without effective support from such groups. Neither did he ever imply that local programs be controlled by the poor; however he would add that without an important role for the poor, the program would be scorned by the very people it was designed to assist. At one point Sargent Shriver stated that community action was not federal action, it was not state action, it was not city hall action, it was not health and welfare council action, it was not action by business or labor, it was not action by the poor—instead, it was to be *community* action.

Community consensus was clearly a main thread running through all this thinking. Community action was supposed to be the way in which all important segments of the community would mobilize all available resources to deal with poverty. This conception, much to the surprise of the OEO staff, thrust the program into the midst of local politics and controversy.

The notion that the poor should be actively and effectively involved in policy-making led directly into this controversy. It raised critical questions, such as the number of poor who must serve to guarantee effective representation, how they would have to be selected, who would select them. The issue became primarily joined around numbers. At its base were gnawing problems and ambivalence regarding whether inarticulate, uneducated poor people with low self-esteem and without skill in parliamentary procedure could share power and decision-making with the representatives of more powerful community interests (Rubin, 1967, p. 11).

Administrative Handling of Requirement

The intensity of this form of politics caught the OEO staff off balance. The evolution of the administrative handling of the "maximum feasible participation" requirement is the best illustration. For the first few months of the program, when only a handful of communities were preparing draft applications, the small Washington staff would sit down with community representatives—usually sent because the mayor had put together a small group of influential local leaders—and ask them, among other questions, whether representatives of the poor had participated in developing the proposed program. Usually the answer was, "Well, not very much, but about as much as would be feasible. We need to move fast." For a few short months, this answer satisfied the OEO staff, and they would admonish the delegation to expand its committee as soon as possible once the program was under way.

This "happy" situation did not long persist. Soon telegrams began to arrive, usually on the day on which a grant was to be signed, addressed to Mr. Shriver, to Senators, to the President, protesting the lack of participation by the residents of the area. By this, the sender usually meant that some existing organization had not been consulted. (One such group—typical of many—was called the "Cleveland Committee For A More Effective Action Program.") New local organizations began to form and demand a voice in the poverty programs. OEO staff would urge the mayor's committee to sit down with such groups and try to work things out—usually by expanding the size of the CAP committee. A new pattern began to emerge as these activities increased. After weeks and sometimes several months of negotiations, the "mayor's committee" would usually offer not only a place on the governing board, but one of the top staff jobs—frequently the staff directorship—to the head of the protesting committee. If he decided to participate, he would often be accused by his followers of having "sold out." With these concessions made by the local "establishment," OEO then began to terminate negotiations and fund local programs despite the protests.

Through this painful and prolonged process of many months duration, a local "consensus" structure would finally emerge. In the meantime, the local headlines proclaimed the "mess" and denounced "delays" in Washington, and mayors and Congressmen were angered. Through this process, the press and members of Congress became, in effect, part of the negotiating process. If one group did not get what it wanted, it took its problem to the newspaper or to its Congressman. It was an extremely difficult task to communicate at both the Washington and community levels that participation by the poor was an objective attainable in more than one way and that to find the best path for any one community was a complicated and not necessarily peaceful undertaking.

Several cities tried the election approach. The results were so disappointing that Mr. Shriver nearly forbade the use of federal funds to finance any future "poverty elections." New York City tried the community convention approach—with delegates to the neighborhood conventions representing any existing organization, from churches to schools to settlement houses to protest groups. The conventions then elected representatives to sit on a community council and on the city-wide antipoverty board. Selection by the mayor was used in some cities. Techniques that worked well in some places, did not work in others (Rubin, 1967, p. 11).

The administrators of the CAP program took an experimental attitude toward the problem. They did not specify any fixed percentage which the poor should have on local governing boards of community action agencies, preferring instead to leave this to be worked out as part of the local community consensus. There were great variations from community to community, with national averages running about 27 per cent at the end of the first year and about 30 per cent at the end of the second. In the 1966 amendments to the Economic Opportunity Act, the Congress specifically established minimum requirements and ordered that after March 1, 1967, at least one-third of the members of the governing boards of local community action agencies represent the poor.

From the perspective of some critics of the program, the controversial requirement for maximum feasible participation was seen as a plan for social and political revolution, stimulated by legislation, paid for by the taxpayers, and implemented by an application to Washington. The Conference of Mayors devoted an entire day of its 1965 annual meeting to a hostile discussion of Community Action Program suggestions regarding implementation of the requirement for maximum feasible participation (U.S. Conference of Mayors, 1965).

Eventually, in the medium-sized and larger cities, many mayors worked out accommodations that made it possible to live with varying degrees of comfort with the statutory requirement. In 1967, under the leadership of Representative Edith Green of Oregon, a coalition of big-city Congressmen and Southern conservative Democrats, succeeded in further amending the Economic Opportunity Act to provide for political control of local community action agencies. The amendment was termed the "boss-boll weevil" amendment by the Republicans (Wofford, 1967).

Although there are some communities in which residents of poverty target areas have developed considerable political capability and a few in which they have wrested almost complete control of the local community action agency, these examples are not part of any long term trend. And although the case has been made for resident participation, the direction for community action programs seems to be clearly toward increasing bureaucratization and rapid absorption into the governmental system.

The passage of the Economic Opportunity Act in the House of Representatives in November, 1967, was only achieved after administration representatives corralled the necessary Southern Democrat votes through the amendment mentioned above. Final control of the local community action agency was transferred to local public officials.

EVALUATION OF CONCEPT

Cloward and Piven have commented with respect to the "participative" concept:

we see no evidence that involvement of the poor by government will generate a force for social change by nurturing the political capabilities of the poor. Rather, governmental programs for the poor are likely to diminish whatever political vitality the poor still exhibit. Future prospects for social change will be increasingly shaped not by low income influence, but by the expansionist forces of public bureaucracies. If the emerging programs successfully impart competitive skills, the bureaucracies pursuing their own enhancement may thereby succeed in raising low income people into the middle class. In this way the clients of the bureaucracies can, one by one, join the middle class political majority, and government involvement can indeed be said to have increased their political influence (Cloward and Piven, publication pending).

In examining the concept of maximum feasible participation it is not necessary or accurate to assume either of the polar positions, i.e., it has been extraordinarily successful or it has failed. The concept of participation in program operation and decision-making by the residents of target areas, once thought to be completely unworkable, has become an accomplished fact in many communities. Prior to this development, social welfare could be adequately characterized as a noblesse oblige responsibility of one group for the less fortunate. In the three years of operation of the Community Action Program, major changes have been wrought in the interests, leadership, and power alignments around coordination and distribution of social services. There is a still to be completed democratization of social welfare that has seen a generation of change in 36 months. This change has impacted the social elite leadership of social welfare, the social work professionals, educators, and public officials, so that there can never again be a retreat to positions held before this program concept was introduced in those communities where it has taken some hold. It has affected nationwide thinking on the subject. The changes have been more than therapeutic on participants as more and more organized poor have learned that action and participation and having representation *can* affect voluntary and public programs and procedures. The growing awareness of the requirements for power to affect change can be attributed, in part, to both the successes and failures of this aspect of the Economic Opportunity Act.

Maximum feasible participation can mean providing local people with a stake in their community. It is an extremely important process for dealing with the pervasive urban problem, the alienation of large numbers of poor from the political process. Unfortunately, the belief has been generated that poverty itself can be overcome by this process, whereas it is in fact only a means of achieving the power to control the events that shape the lives of poor people. Some believe that this is a necessary antecedent to the elimination of poverty; it is not, however, the equivalent of the elimination of poverty. As Haggstrom has written:

> . . . for the first time poor people have been told by legislative mandate that they are capable of taking a hand in their affairs. They have been called upon to speak on their own behalf, to assess their needs, and to join in the design and implementation of programs to meet those needs. In some communities more militant groups have organized independently to alleviate their distress— and succeeded. . . . each victory generates confidence in self . . . a necessary precondition to action—and confidence in the efficacy of organization to correct the gnawing grievances that plague their lives (Haggstrom, 1965, pp. 205-23).

RESULTS OF THE COMMUNITY ACTION PROGRAM

In three years over 1,000 communities have been organized for the purpose of providing more effective programs and services for the poor. This accomplishment might be compared with the 45-year period it has taken to organize about 500 welfare planning councils. For many of these 1,000 communities, the goal of a truly comprehensive poverty program is not even in sight, even if understood. The tasks of ascertaining needs, planning programs, coordinating services, and maximizing all relevant resources are well beyond the present capability of most of these programs. For a few communities with skill and competence, the process is well under way. Many are embarked on a handful of useful projects but their range is limited and their relevance to providing any basic long-term solutions to the problems of poverty is a gnawing question.

As for other indirect accomplishments, the story of participation of the poor has already been described. The Head Start idea has exposed over one million children to a preschool experience. The necessity for an early childhood development experience has become an accepted part of national policy with overwhelming support from the Congress. The field of early childhood development has received a massive infusion of interest, money, and new ideas.

The notion of new careers for the poor in the so-called helping professions was rooted in the concept of maximum feasible participation. A resolution in the acceptance of this approach to employment has occurred. The administration and the Congress are heavily committed to press ahead in the broad application of this principle in the public services. The teaching profession, the social welfare field, and the health professions, all of which were strong centers of resistance in 1964, have begun slowly to embrace the idea. It is possible that this change may create for the poor hundreds of thousands of new jobs that are stable and not subject to the shifts in an economy linked to military crises.

Cited above as an issue which triggered concern for a poverty program was the inadequacy of services reaching the poor who needed them most. Since 1964, over 800 neighborhood-based, multiservice centers have been organized to deal with this specific problem. The issue of the adequacy as well as the relevancy of services is still an extremely critical one, but the fact of the movement toward decentralization of service programs cannot be ignored.

At the start of the Community Action Program, a handful of institutions of higher education, a few foundations, and a few concerned educators were worrying about the loss in talent and energy to the nation due to the failure of talented children from poor families to get into college, a failure due in large measure to the quality of their elementary and secondary education. Today, over 40,000 high school students with the help of 300 colleges are involved in the Upward Bound program. Many of these are co-sponsored in the form of a loose linkage to a local community action program.

At the start of the Community Action Program, very little community effort could be discerned in the area of reorganizing medical services for the poor. The enormous disparity in the health care of the poor was a regular topic for discussion among a small group of concerned physicians and laymen, but little progress had been made toward evoking national concern. After several years of demonstration program development, the concept of the comprehensive neighborhood health centers which provide one-door, personalized quality health service for the poor is rapidly spreading. This concept is widely supported in the Congress and has even been endorsed by officers of the American Medical Association.

Prior to the passage of the Economic Opportunity Act, the Congress had only passed one bill to aid migrants in 15 years. Community action programs for those in this category are currently supporting new literacy programs, health projects, housing efforts, employment training, and child care in migrant centers across the country. It is estimated that about 150,000 migrants have been touched in some way by these efforts.

At the start of the antipoverty program, aid for Indians living in poverty came through the work of the Bureau of Indian Affairs or the scattered efforts of church missions. Three years of development has seen the organization of well over 100 community action programs on reservations that are run by Indians, for Indians, and with Indians.

THE PROMISE AND THE CRITICISM

In the three years since its inception, the Community Action Program has been a critical factor in awakening many communities to the deep-rooted social, economic, and physical problems of poverty. Important new services have been brought to hundreds of thousands of poor people. By focusing attention on doing things in a new way, by involving poor people in programs as planning participants rather than solely as program beneficiaries, some narrowing of the gap between the poor and the rest of the community has occurred. The Community Action Program has proved to be a catalyst for the development of leadership among those regularly excluded from this role. And hidden issues lying dormant for years have been given visibility.

Critics of the program were awaiting the problems even before it was launched. The accumulated years of structure and tradition do not shift easily and without trauma. Yet, the rapidity with which the Community Action Program moved its projects out across the country sparked visions of an ever increasing attack on poverty. Local communities were led to expect substantially increased resources in successive years of the program. These expectations were heightened by a campaign of "maximum feasible public relations." But the high expectations failed to materialize. The image of a massive "war on poverty" has instead become just the "poverty program." From the grand promise of the Economic Opportunity Act, funding and organizational difficulties have educed a series of specific programs aimed at selected areas of the poverty spectrum. In almost every instance these have been allotted only a small portion of the funds required to really attack the problem.

The poverty program has actually been the victim of two enemies. The first has been its own rhetoric, in part created by the desire of all associated with it to believe that it was more than it was, and thus in turn to promise too much. It was not, as some envisioned, an income redistribution program, it was not a large scale public employment program, and it contained only modest program elements to engage in a structural reorganization of the American community to serve the poor more effectively. It had only a small part of the responsibility for dealing with an immense problem that crisscrosses federal, state, and local responsibility and bridges both public and voluntary responsibility. The Office of Economic Opportunity and the Community Action Program have had limited responsibility to deal with these problems.

The second major difficulty has been the series of local organizational problems which mirror those of the federal effort. The Community Action Agency is a local agency, locally organized with varying degrees of power and delegated decision-making capacity from local government, voluntary social agencies, civic organizations, and residents of poverty areas. These subgroups are not and cannot be immune to the shifts and vagaries of local leadership. There is, moreover, no master organizational plan and no clearly mandated program. Local efforts have suffered from (1) lack of skilled professional leadership; (2) the conflicts over resident participation; (3) mismanagement of funds by persons unskilled in program administration; and (4) the inability of the various service programs to bring about change in the large bureaucratic health, welfare, education, and employment structures which draw the bulk of their resources independently of the Office of Economic

Opportunity. The concept of community action ignores the first three problems in this group and assumes that the last is resolved through a combination of good will, recognition of the rightness or goodness of the mission of the Community Action Agency, and the skillful use of its federal dollars.

The Community Action Agency has within it (as most institutions do) certain bureaucratic tendencies which have already been demonstrated in a number of cities. One such is a tendency toward an "inversion of purpose" which manifests itself when a growing organization becomes preoccupied with its organizational maintenance functions and forms alliances for self-protective purposes. In the process, it is likely to oppose initiative, or imagination, or independence of groups that may be critical of its efforts.

WHAT CAN THE FUTURE HOLD?

Through each session of the Congress, the fate of the Community Action Agency hangs regularly and precariously in the balance. At the same time, the Congress has sanctioned a modest new version of community action called "Model Cities" under the auspices of the Department of Housing and Urban Development. HUD has built a stronger planning element into the program than the Community Action Agency and has tied social development to physical renewal of the city. The program is also directly tied to local political authority. It is reasonable to assume, however, that these variations will make only a minor difference in the experience of this new venture as compared to that of the Community Action Agency unless several new steps are taken.

Programs to address poverty at the local level of government must first of all be matched by several major national commitments. These are only briefly described here and will not be fully discussed. The first of these is a national income redistribution program which brings new dollar resources directly into the hands of poor people. Such financial relief would very directly remove from program and service concern those individuals and families among the poor who are perfectly able to cope with life except for the absence of money. The second is a large-scale, publicly subsidized program, locally administered, to assure employment at a decent wage for all those willing and capable of working.

The third effort must be in the area of housing. It has been recognized that to meet the current housing needs of the poor, the nation requires five million new low-income dwelling units as soon as it can get them. Such a program must be nationally organized even though it can be effectively administered at the local level. Major efforts in this direction would remove the presence of the most ubiquitous environmental hazard that the poor face, the place they live in. For every person needs a livable physical environment if he is to thrive and be productive.

Given these national efforts, the concept of concerted community action has a chance of surviving and making a significant contribution toward the reduction of poverty and poverty-producing conditions. To carry on this task, two conditions will be required:

(1) The community action agency must strengthen its central planning capability. It must gain increased technical capacity for diagnosing need and applying the appropriate programmatic interventions. It must gain increased control over the allocation of resources in all the relevant areas of its program. Without such control, planning can become largely an intellectual exercise with no consequent capacity for implementation.

(2) To assure its vitality and responsiveness to need, new and courageous efforts must be undertaken to decentralize all appropriate responsibility to smaller community units. The Community Action Agency must contribute to the production of responsible leadership for meaningful community programs by developing and enlarging the competence of residents of poverty neighborhoods to manage their own projects. This approach is vital for two reasons. The first is the necessity of finding new ways to combat the increasing alienation of poverty area residents as they encounter the service bureaucracies. The second is the strong requirement for improved centralized planning and resource allocation.

Given these conditions there is a possibility that the high purpose of the Community Action Program might be fully realized. In more specific terms, this means that it could perform the following very vital tasks relevant to a really serious war on poverty:

(1) link low-income people to critical resources, e.g., education, manpower training, counseling, housing, and health;

(2) increase the accessibility of available critical services that the poor still often find beyond their reach or blocked off from them by the manner in which their need has been defined;

(3) create competent communities by developing in and among the poor the capacity for leadership, problem-solving, and participation in the decision-making councils which affect their lives; and

(4) restructure community service institutions to assure flexibility, responsiveness, respect, and true relatedness to the problems faced by the poor.

Just as the problem of poverty has many causes, so too, does the Community Action Program have many limitations. The problems, as we have seen, have been conceptual, financial, and organizational. None of these has yet proved fatal. Unless, however, they are positively attacked, the probability of the program's survival is not promising.

References

Bruno, Frank J. *Trends in Social Work* (New York: Columbia University Press, 1957).

Cloward, Richard, and Lloyd Ohlin. *Delinquency and Opportunity* (New York: Free Press, 1960).

Cloward, Richard. "The War on Poverty: Are the Poor Left Out?" *The Nation* (August 2, 1965).

Cloward, Richard, and Frances Fox Piven. *Politics, Professionalism and Poverty.* (Publication pending.)

Grossman, David. "The Community Action Program: Innovation in Local Government" (1966, unpublished ms.).

Haggstrom, Warren C. "The Power of the Poor," in Frank Riessman, J. Cohn, and A. Pearl (eds.), *Mental Health of the Poor* (New York: Free Press, 1965), pp. 205-23.

Marris, Peter, and Martin Rein. *Dilemmas of Social Reform* (New York: Atherton Press, 1967).

Pumphrey, Ralph E., and Muriel W. Pumphrey (eds.), *The Heritage of American Social Work* (New York: Columbia University Press, 1961).

RUBIN, LILLIAN. "Maximum Feasible Participation: The Origins, Implications and Present Status," *Poverty and Human Resources Abstracts*, II (November-December, 1967).

WARNER, AMOS G. *Publications*, American Statistical Association, New Series I (November 5, 1889), pp. 183-203.

WOFFORD, JOHN G. "Administration of the Community Action Program: An Exercise in Local Responsibility" (1967, unpublished ms.).

UNITED STATES CONFERENCE OF MAYORS. "City Problems of 1965," *Annual Proceedings of the U. S. Conference of Mayors, 1965* (Washington, D. C.: U. S. Conference of Mayors, 1965).

10

The Community
Action Program

An Interpretative Analysis

HOWARD W. HALLMAN

☐ OF ALL THE PROGRAMS AUTHORIZED by the Economic Opportunity Act, the community action program is the most complex. It has many facets and many forms around the nation. It is the most controversial, and it is probably the most misunderstood. This being the situation, the study staff concluded that a major focus of the evaluation and examination of the poverty program should be an effort to gain a greater understanding of the community action program. Such a study would seek to determine not what the community action program ought to be (and on this topic there are many views) but rather what it actually is in various communities. Thus, the study would be basically descriptive.

BACKGROUND

This concept crystallized in February, 1967 as the resolution authorizing the subcommittee's total study was making its way through the Senate's procedures. A major challenge was to devise a

EDITOR'S NOTE: *This analysis was prepared for the Subcommittee on Employment, Manpower, and Poverty of the Committee on Labor and Public Welfare of the U. S. Senate, and appears in* Examination of the War on Poverty: Community Action Program—Volume IV *(Washington, D. C.: U. S. Government Printing Office, 1967), pp. 8, 97-915. The author was the Director of the Poverty Study Staff of the Senate Committee on Labor and Public Welfare.*

method for collecting information in the very short time which would be available. The solution adopted was to seek in each of the seven administrative regions of the Office of Economic Opportunity a qualified consultant who could conduct case studies in a representative sample of communities. Some, but not all seven consultants had been lined up by February 20 when the Senate approved the authorizing resolution, and soon thereafter the list was complete.

REGION AND CONSULTANT

Northeast: Institute of Public Administration, New York, N. Y.

Mid-Atlantic: Community Action Associates, Inc., Pittsburgh, Pa.

Southeast: Institute of Government, University of Georgia, Athens, Ga.

Great Lakes: Center for Urban Studies, University of Chicago, Chicago, Ill.

North Central: Institute for Community Studies, Kansas City, Mo.

Southwest: Texas Social Welfare Association, Austin, Tex.

Western: Marshall Kaplan, Gans & Kahn, San Francisco, Calif.

A tentative study outline was drawn up and discussed at a meeting of informed persons on March 7. A week later, on March 13, representatives of the consultants assembled in Washington to review the proposed outline, to raise questions, and to agree on the procedure to be followed. This was quickly followed by a revision of the study outline, which was mailed to the consultants, who then plunged into their assignment with a deadline of May 31.

Each consultant agreed to study five communities and one state technical assistance agency. Since there was neither time nor assembled data to draw a national sample, selection of the communities and states was left to the consultants. They were requested to choose communities in which the community action program had been conducting programs beyond initial planning for at least a year so that the study would be about actual operating experience. Each consultant was encouraged to include two rural communities in its sample and to select a group which ranged from harmonious and successful to controversial and failing, as far as could be determined in advance from informed observers.

Of the 35 communities so selected, 24 were urban and 11 were rural. Thirteen of the urban communities have programs covering an entire county, and of these at least five have significant pockets of rural poverty. The distribution by size was as follows:

	Number of Communities	
Population	Largest City or Town	Total Area
Over 500,000	7	10
250,000 to 500,000	7	11
100,000 to 250,000	7	7
50,000 to 100,000	3	5
Under 50,000	11	2
Total	35	35

Of the rural areas, all but one had more than one county, including two which encompass eight counties. As can be seen, the 35 communities represent a fair cross-section of community size with two exceptions. Cities between 50,000 and 100,000 and small counties which have their own community action agencies are underrepresented, but both of these tend to be places which have been slow to initiate community action programs and thus not as many were in operation long enough to be studied. The complete list, identified by the name of the largest city or town, follows.

In these 35 communities, the consultants interviewed more than 1,000 persons, including CAP staff and board members, public officials, social agency personnel, and persons served by the poverty program.

FINDINGS

A review of the 35 case studies reveals that the community action program in its dominant form is a new kind of service program, with services directed primarily to individuals rather than to families or other groups. These services are often, though not always, different from those previously provided to poor people (how they differ is important and is discussed later). To be sure, the community action program in many communities has other features than services, as we shall see, but the most universal pattern is the presence of service in some form or other in every community studied.

TABLE 1

COMMUNITIES STUDIED BY REGIONAL CONSULTANTS

Largest City or Town	Population (1960)	Number of Counties	Total Population (1960)
Urban:			
Philadelphia, Pa.	2,002,512	(1)	2,002,512
Detroit, Mich.	1,670,144	——	1,670,144
Cleveland, Ohio	876,050	1	1,647,895
Washington, D.C.	763,956	——	763,956
St. Louis, Mo.	750,026	1	1,453,558
San Francisco, Calif.	740,316	(1)	740,316
New Orleans, La.	627,525	——	627,525
Denver, Colo.	493,887	(1)	493,887
Phoenix, Ariz.	439,170	——	439,170
Newark, N.J.	405,220	——	405,220
Oakland, Calif.	367,548	——	367,548
Oklahoma City, Okla.	324,253	1	439,506
Honolulu, Hawaii	294,194	1	500,409
Wichita, Kans.	254,698	1	343,231
Syracuse, N.Y.	216,038	1	423,028
Jacksonville, Fla.	201,030	1	455,411
Worcester, Mass.	186,587	——	186,587
Gary, Ind.	178,320	1	513,269
Corpus Christi, Tex.	167,690	——	167,690
Fresno, Calif.	133,929	1	365,945
Chattanooga, Tenn.	130,009	1	237,895
Charleston, W. Va.	85,796	1	252,925
Pontiac, Mich.	82,233	1	690,259
Binghamton, N.Y.	75,941	1 .	212,661
Rural:			
Rock Hill, S.C.	29,404	4	169,712
La Grange, Ga.	23,623	8	163,054
Washington, Pa.	23,545	2	256,695
Sikeston, Mo.	13,765	6	162,027
Eagle Pass, Tex.	12,094	3	40,971
Cleveland, Miss.	10,172	1	54,464
Russellville, Ark.	8,921	8	99,362
St. Johnsbury, Vt.	6,809	3	49,012
Tell City, Ind.	6,609	4	60,892
Hazard, Ky.	5,958	4	93,366
West Plain, Mo.	5,836	6	80,219

(1) City and county are coterminous.

Conversely, except for a very small number of communities, the community action program does not involve a predominant commitment to the strategy of giving power to the poor, of deliberate confrontation with established powers, of purposefully created conflict. This is a stereotype placed on CAP in its early days by a few articulate advocates of this approach and echoed ever since by journalists, who have not examined what is actually going on. Yet, this approach is found only in San Francisco, Syracuse, and Newark of the 35 communities studied. All three were included in the sample because of the controversy surrounding them, but this writer does not know of any other communities where this approach predominates. To be sure, resident participation is the major theme in Philadelphia and Washington, but not in the confrontation-through-conflict style which characterizes the first three. Contrary to the hopes of a few and the fears of many, CAP is not social revolution. However, in a number of places CAP is using less radical means to produce significant institutional change.

Thus, variation found among the communities does not reflect a choice between services and citizen organization. Those who follow the most activist approach to resident participation also provide services, and many but not all of those with effective service programs pursue certain forms of resident participation. The crucial difference is the approach to institutional change and to planning and coordination, two topics which are further considered below.

Those who have firsthand acquaintance with poor people, their needs and aspirations, would not find the service emphasis surprising. What the poor want most is concrete results. For example, Marshall Kaplan, Gans and Kahn report that in a survey of the West Oakland poverty area, residents perceive the following as their priority problems: "First, the lack of jobs and sustained income; second, the weakness inherent in the educational systems; and third, the lack of community facilities." Only as they gain experience as subprofessionals and neighborhood leaders, and perhaps absorb some social theory, do they become concerned with such abstractions as "decisionmaking" and "power." In referring to those who have so advanced, the same consultants report: "They see [the CAP] as creating an articulate community, one able to have some control over the development of their area, and able to participate equally in decisionmaking processes concerning allocation of local resources." But first come the basic needs of life—food, clothing, shelter, personal health and safety—and the services which assist in satisfying these needs. Thus, the service emphasis is a natural focus for the community action program.

SERVICES

But what are the services? Here, the uniqueness of CAP begins to show up, and the sameness as well.

The OEO national emphasis programs are the most universal of all CAP components. Every community studied has Head Start and the Neighborhood Youth Corps. Most have neighborhood service centers, and they even use the word "neighborhood" in rural areas where settlement is sparse. During the first year of the program, education received the major emphasis, but this declined when the Elementary and Secondary Education Act of 1965 began to channel funds to local schools serving poverty areas and when OEO in November, 1966 placed education on its low priority list. Manpower programs have been gaining although they tend to be funded from other sources than Title II of the Economic Opportunity Act, which authorizes the basic program. Table 2, showing the allocation of CAP funds throughout the nation since the program began, suggests the relative emphasis although there is plenty of variation among communities.

Head Start illustrates the way CAP services can be different. First, Head Start provides a combination of educational, health, child care, and family services whereas in an age of specialization such services tend to operate separately in most communities. Second, Head Start offers a new approach to the role of parents and other citizens. In a few locales this is not much more than service to parents, although most are providing parents employment opportunities in the program. In a growing number of communities, parents and other citizens are acting in a policy advisory capacity, and in a few instances, the residents are completely in charge through a delegate agency which they control (such as in Bolivar County, Miss.). Third, Head Start is being used to modify the practices of existing institutions, particularly elementary schools. Where this occurs, the money invested in actual services pays dividends by favorably influencing the way in which other funds are spent. Fourth, Head Start uses a considerable number of volunteers, thus broadening the degree of community participation. And

TABLE 2

FEDERAL EXPENDITURES FOR COMMUNITY ACTION PROGRAM THROUGH
APRIL 21, 1967

	[In Millions]
Major program components:	
Child development, including Head Start	$ 393
Education	220
Neighborhood centers, including social service	131
Health	41
Employment	40
Neighborhood organization	38
Legal services	36
Homemaking, food, and clothing	26
Cultural and recreation	25
Housing and community facilities	20
Economic development	12
Consumer programs	4
Subtotal	$ 986
Other expenditures:	
Administration, including evaluation	91
Technical assistance and training	46
Research and demonstration	36
Local program development	34
Subtotal	$ 207
Grand total	$1,193

fifth, Head Start focuses upon opportunity and prevention, thus seeking to break the cycle of poverty.

In addition to such differences, which permeate many of the CAP components, a number of communities have used CAP funds to introduce program innovations: a neighborhood health center in Denver; a program hiring elderly persons as library aides in Northeast Kingdom, Vermont; Project Retains, a summer program for potential junior high school dropouts in South Carolina; the legal services program in Washington, D.C.; the comprehensive manpower system developed in St. Louis; the multiservice neighborhood center in Detroit; and a rural version in 27 locations in the eight Arkansas counties served by ARVAC. Many of these innovations are gaining widespread applications, such as legal services, comprehensive health services, and most of all the neighborhood services centers.

The latter are found in many locations, in many forms. Their emphases differ as widely as the community action agencies which sponsor them. Mostly they consist of a common gathering place for a few decentralized programs and a point of referral to other services. But some communities, such as Detroit and Phoenix, use them as a major means for linking services so that they work together as a concerted whole. A few others, such as San Francisco and Syracuse, use them as a base for neighborhood organizations aimed at building a power bloc among the poor. Occasionally, different centers in the same city will play different roles, such as in Worcester where one sponsor operates four centers emphasizing only services and two other sponsors have centers with the additional thrust of citizen involvement. Yet, in all communities studied, services were offered through the neighborhood centers regardless of other emphases.

But by no stretch of the imagination can all the services offered in the 35 communities studied be said to be innovative. The consultants' descriptions of component programs indicate that the number of truly innovative programs is exceedingly small when placed in a national perspective even though for a particular community a component may be new. But this could be expected, for "there is nothing new under the sun" (a statement recorded in the third century B.C., probably not for the first time). Creativity tends to come more in variations and in new combinations of old approaches rather than in something startlingly new. Such creative synthesis characterizes the most effective community action agencies.

Types of Community Action Agencies

It is what they are doing in addition to providing services which distinguishes various types of community action agencies. Reasoning backward from their performance, one finds that the variations can be explained in part by the different assumptions, usually unstated, which the agencies make about the causes of poverty. By inference, several basic premises can be ascertained.

An emphasis upon services to individuals implies that one of the causes of poverty is the nature of the poor themselves. Help an individual overcome his shortcomings and he will be able to escape from poverty. Teach him to read and he will get into occupational training. Teach him an occupational skill and he will get a job. Give him part-time work so that he can stay in high school and he will graduate and be employable. Give him a decent preschool experience and he will succeed in school. Improve his health and solve his legal problems and he will be able to break the cycle of poverty.

This personalized explanation of poverty seems to be extended to provide a rationalization for citizen involvement as well. The poverty program is seen as dealing with "underdeveloped" people, as is foreign aid. Resident participation enhances personal development. Being on the board of the community action agency or participating in an advisory committee for Head Start, a neighborhood center, or a health program helps individuals to identify with the program, to gain a better opinion of the service agency, to make more use of the services, to be better motivated and less alienated.

Although the consultants' reports lack clear and comparable findings on the theoretical underpinnings of the programs studied, reading between the lines this writer judges that about half of the 35 communities conduct programs which indicate that they see the cause of poverty mostly in the poor themselves. They tend to start by providing services directed toward helping poor people ameliorate their present conditions and begin an escape from poverty. About one-fourth seem to be at this stage. As they gain experience, they become more concerned with forms of resident participation which stress self-help, and another one-fourth are at this second stage.

The other half of the communities studied also share the belief that one cause of poverty is in the individuals themselves, but they see another major cause as the failure of society and its institutions. These communities fall into three groups of approximately equal size.

The first group consists of those who are concerned about the failure of social institutions to provide the services in sufficient quantity and quality to respond to the needs of the poor. They also believe that present services are too fragmented and do not deal with the whole person. This being the analysis, the remedy is a planning process and coordination procedures which link services to one another. If necessary, they are also willing to initiate new services and to organize new institutions. An urban example is Jacksonville, Florida, where the community action agency has established its credentials sufficiently for the mayor to designate it for a major planning and coordinating role in the model city program. By and large the best of the rural programs would fall into this category: the four counties in eastern Kentucky, the South Carolina program, ARVAC in Arkansas, and Northeast Kingdom, Vermont. Since these rural areas have such a lack of organized services, the community action agencies rarely encounter opposition from other agencies. In rural areas the need for institutional change is not as great as the need for institutional development.

Not so in the cities though. There, those community action agencies which see institutional failure as a major cause of poverty are confronted with significant agency resistance to change. This leads a second group of CAA's to adopt another strategy: an all-out attempt to force institutions to change their current practices. Since September, 1965, after a year's struggle for control, the San Francisco Community Action Agency has placed heavy emphasis upon neighborhood organization designed to build strength to confront the established agencies with citizen power. During the past year both Syracuse and Newark have altered course to pursue this approach with vigor. In Syracuse the change occurred after a new executive director was appointed. Newark, always leaning in this direction, had previously placed greater emphasis upon building new institutions controlled by the poor, particularly neighborhood boards. In the District of Columbia, the opposite trend has occurred. During 1965-1966, Washington's United Planning Organization (UPO) established a number of city-wide, special interest action committees, each focused upon the work of a particular agency, and these committees began to exert citizen pressure until so much resistance developed in powerful places that UPO was forced to pull back. It then switched to the development of community corporations, new institutions governed by neighborhood residents.

In Philadelphia and Oakland heavy pressure for institutional change has been applied through hybrid public agencies, curious organizational forms with great instability. In Philadelphia, the CAA as a public corporation has been dominated by a bloc led by the vice-chairman, an ally of the mayor, and the representatives of the poor on the governing board; this bloc has exerted some pressure for institutional change. In Oakland the staff is on the public payroll in a municipal department under the city manager, and the governing board is a private, non-profit organization which since January, 1967 has had a majority selected by the poverty neighborhoods. The instability of these two CAA's is reflected in events occurring since the consultants made their visits in April. Philadelphia has been forced by OEO to reorganize, and the executive director of Oakland has resigned. But the very nature of the strategy of institutional attack inevitably means continuous controversy until CAA retreats, as UPO did, or until the community's governing coalition gives in, which has not happened yet in any of these places.

The third pattern of institutional change is where the governing coalition itself provides the leadership or at least allows an agency on its fringe to initiate change. Communities following this approach have the most complete program, combining a broad array of services, planning and coordination, and resident participation, although the latter is under certain restraints so that it does not lead to open confrontation. An approach of this breadth is found in Detroit where the community action agency is part of a city administration committed to change; being close to the mayor, the CAA is in a position to work for institutional change from within. In Phoenix, the CAA is also situated within city government where it can promote change, but it is not in as strong a position as Detroit's agency to accomplish broad planning and coordination. Although the New Orleans CAA is a private, non-profit agency, it can be considered part of that city's governing coalition, but it is an avowed advocate of institutional change. The CAA in Corpus Christi is similarly situated and seems to be pushing for change. The St. Louis CAA is halfway between these two pairs, being a private non-profit corporation with the majority of directors selected by the mayor; from this position it stresses building effective service systems as its main strategy for change, most noteworthy in the manpower field.

All the places where the community action agency is working for institutional changes from within have a high quality of leadership in some key spot: in Detroit, the mayor; in Phoenix, the mayor and city manager; in New Orleans, the CAA's executive staff; in Corpus Christi, the board of the CAA; in St. Louis, the board chairman and executive director. Certain other communities are less fortunate, and the community action program is floundering or of such small scale as to be of little significance: Cleveland, Worcester, Chattahoochee area in Georgia, and the delta area in Missouri are examples. In these communities, the leadership lacks the capacity to put into action a program proportional to the needs, or it is so divided that the resources of the community cannot be effectively mobilized.

Origins and Control

This leads one to ask: Who started the community action agencies and who controls them now? According to the consultants' reports, in at least 13 of the 35 communities studied an elected official was the prime initiator—usually the mayor in cities and the county commissioner (supervisor, judge) in rural areas, although in one situation state legislators seemed to have played this role (South Carolina) and in another instance a Congressman (Lake County, Indiana). In six communities the voluntary social welfare coordinating body (health and welfare council, united fund, and so forth) took the initiative. In three communities, the mayor and the health and welfare council joined together, and in two other places the health and welfare council combined with other agencies to organize the community action agency. In two locales the city manager provided the leadership, and in two others an economic development commission performed that role. Two of the community action agencies evolved from youth development projects, whose origins are not recorded in the reports. Two multicounty community action agencies were formed by merger of previous separate county CAA's, and how the latter got started is not reported. In the other three communities, the initiative was provided by the school superintendent and business leaders, by a push from civil rights organizations, and by the director of the Neighborhood Youth Corps. In virtually all cases, the community action agency was organized by a leadership group and not by grass-roots organizations in the poverty areas. However, in at least eight instances, the pressure from civil rights organizations was a major spur for the community leaders to act—sometimes to prevent federal funds from going to these civil rights groups.

As the community action agencies were formed, the governing board almost always reflected a broader base than that represented by the initiators. The most dramatic change was the inclusion of representatives of the poor as OEO enforced this aspect of "maximum feasible resident participation." A variety of other interests not initially represented were also added to the board, in part because of the desire of the originators and in part because OEO pushed for representation from public agencies, private social agencies, and key interest groups, such as business, labor, civil rights, and religious. During the first year of the program, organizational issues dominated the dealings between the communities and OEO. By and large, this period has passed, leaving the CAA's with governing boards which are more broadly representative than almost any other organization in their communities. In most communities these boards operate as part of or at least in harmony with the governing coalition.

As used in this report, "governing coalition" refers to an alliance of leaders who have power and influence in community decision-making. Its function is to govern. Persons participate in the coalition because they hold a public office or represent an influential organization or interest, and participation changes over time. Within the coalition, continuous bargaining occurs, and relative strength varies with the issue. In sum, the governing coalition is a dynamic alliance. To this writer, the term is more descriptive of the true situation in most communities than the terms "establishment" or "power structure," which are now in vogue but which suggest more of a monolith than actually exists.

In only three of the 35 communities studied is the community action agency dominated by a majority who are not part of the governing coalition: Syracuse, Newark, and San Francisco. In each of these, this majority consists of representatives of the poor and minority group leaders. Two other cities, Honolulu and Oakland, have boards with similar majorities, but at this stage they operate within the context of the governing coalition, not against it. This occurs in Oakland because the staff is part of city government. In Honolulu the board is merely a subcommittee of the council of social agencies, which has ultimate control.

But there is disharmony in other places even though the CAA is not completely independent of the governing coalition. The Winter Garden Tri-County Committee in Texas is in conflict with two of the three county governments even though the governing coalition, including the county judges, has a majority on the board. Similarly, in Wichita governing-coalition people have majority control, but there is no clear community consensus about the role of the community action program, with neighborhood representatives and perhaps staff, too, pressing for a more militant, change-oriented role. Denver has gone through a period of tension and struggle for control but seems to be stabilizing. Bolivar County, Mississippi, experienced a period of competition which was resolved by organizing a broadly representative CAA which in turn delegates significant operating responsibilities to an agency controlled by Negro citizens. Since the latter now have a majority of registered voters in the county, a new type of governing coalition is emerging—biracial, somewhat incohesive, but at least providing a new position of influence for the Negro population.

In some communities, a very conservative coalition has kept tight reins on the community action program so that little is happening beyond the introduction of some new services to the poor. This is the case in Cleveland and Worcester. In Oakland County, Michigan, the CAA is controlled by a labor-social-welfare-neighborhood group which so far has had little cooperation from local government although no major conflict. In Lake County, Indiana, and Fresno, California, the CAA's have been limited mostly to a services approach and have been kept out of action which might produce institutional change.

On the whole though, more harmony exists than disharmony, and most of the struggles for control have been resolved, usually through compromise among varied interests rather than overbearing domination by one segment of the community. In other words, the term "community" can properly be emphasized in describing the community action agency. Not that CAP can be expected to be a docile program, for it cannot if it is to make progress in changing the social conditions which perpetuate poverty. Rather, in most places the program has entered the realm of social bargaining, which is the process through which a democracy solves many problems.

Boards of Directors

As to the formal organization, in all but three of the 35 communities studied, the CAA's are private, non-profit organizations. The other three, Detroit, Phoenix, and Philadelphia, are public agencies, but the latter is now being reorganized as a private, non-profit agency. In Oakland, the board is private, but staff services are provided by a municipal department. In a number of other places, the CAA is private but was set up by and is close to city government so that in effect it is a quasi-public agency, such as in St. Louis.

The boards of directors are fairly large. The median membership is 39, and the distribution is as follows:

NUMBER OF DIRECTORS:	Number of CAA's
20 and under	2
21 to 30	9
31 to 45	14
46 to 60	9
61 and over	1

There is considerable use of executive committees, as might be expected with boards of this size. Some of the CAA's also use task forces and program committees to deal with special topics.

The regional consultants were not requested to supply a list of board members so that a complete analysis of board composition is not possible from their reports. However, it appears that the elected chief executive of local government is either on or appoints his personal representative to somewhat less than half of the boards, but in a number of other instances he appoints members at large. The extent of cooperation between the CAA and local government is not totally correlated with having the mayor represented on the board. For example, in Newark the mayor is honorary chairman and the Winter Garden Tri-County Committee (Texas) has representation from the county judges, but conflict with local government is quite evident. Nonetheless, harmonious relations with local government seem more likely to be occurring where the chief executive is represented. But harmony may not always be to the best interests of the program, such as in Cleveland where the mayor is chairman of the board but an ineffective city government smothers the community action program.

All of the boards of directors also include representatives of a variety of other agencies and interests, as required by OEO regulations. These representatives tend to be selected by the organizations. In the multicounty rural areas, a common pattern is for particular agencies to get together and name one of their number, such as the school superintendents, the ministerial alliance, and others. However, there are examples of persons being named at large, either by the mayor or by the other members of the board.

Representation of the poor was, of course, the most controversial organizational issue during the first year of the program, but this matter has been resolved in most places and is no longer a major point of contention. As required by Congress in the 1966 amendments, all of the community action agencies have at least one-third of the board chosen by "residents of the area or members of the groups served." Some have more, as follows:

Per Cent of Board, Representatives of the Poor:	Number of communities
33⅓	16
34 to 49	10
50	4
51 and over	5

The four with exactly one-half are Northeast Kingdom, Vermont; Leslie, Knott, Letcher, and Perry Counties, Kentucky; delta area, Missouri; and Fresno, California. The five with representatives of the poor in a majority are Syracuse, Newark, Oakland, San Francisco, and Honolulu.

In a majority of the communities, representatives of the poor are selected by neighborhood boards or area councils. These in turn are chosen by neighborhood residents, usually in open meetings but occasionally through elections by ballot or voting machine. In other words, the usual pattern is for indirect selection of representatives of the poor through the intervening action of a neighborhood board or area council. In a small number of communities, these representatives are chosen at large through some type of election process, and in a few others, part of the representatives are chosen at large and the others by area boards or neighborhood councils.

The consultants' reports do not furnish much information on the characteristics of those selected to represent "residents of the areas or members of the groups served." Apparently some are poor and some are not. Among those served by the program, there is division on this issue. Some believe that the best spokesman for their interests should be selected, regardless of current income, while others believe that only a person who himself is poor can adequately express the feelings of the poor. Left without specification, the tendency is for non-poor persons to be selected, for many of the same qualities which produce leadership also lead to job success and thus make those individuals less likely to be poor even though they reside in a poor area.

It is apparent that after two years of experience, representatives of the poor are beginning to be influential on the governing boards. Several of the consultants indicate that at first these representatives did not understand board proceedings and were inarticulate, but in recent months they have been more expressive and more forceful in their participation. This seems to have come about mostly through "on-the-job" learning, for most communities have not offered leadership training opportunities. One exception though, is Oakland County, Michigan where the United Auto Workers have assisted in leadership development.

RESIDENT PARTICIPATION

Board membership, though, is by no means the only method of resident participation. The use of professional aides is universal. As statistical studies conducted by OEO consultants have shown, the majority are women, pay is just above the poverty level in most places, and there is little opportunity for advancement. These findings are confirmed by the regional consultants. In other words, a major breakthrough in creating new career opportunities in human service occupations has occurred, but further gains are needed.

As has been noted earlier, resident participation has been the main theme of the program in San Francisco, Syracuse, Newark, Philadelphia, and Washington. In none of these have the results equaled the expectations of the local founders or the social theorists who advocate "power for the poor." Several consultants are quite sympathetic with this approach and plead for more time before a final judgment is made. They may be right, too, for in Washington even though UPO had to pull back from a fairly aggressive use of citizen action, the city is undoubtedly better off because of enlarged resident participation throughout the inner city. San Francisco probably has also gained from the actions of its CAA, but the control by neighborhood boards has prevented an effective city-wide mobilization of resources. In Newark, the Institute of Public Administration found great in-fighting among the leaders of the poor and unresponsiveness from city hall. Its report in late May concluded by saying:

The whole problem of the relationships between the city government and the community action agency needs reexamination, although at present this may not be possible . . . . But one suspects that things will get worse before they get better.

In all of these cities—possibly with the exception of Syracuse—city government has performed ineptly in responding to the needs of the poor. A maximum commitment to citizen action has been one of the few strategies available to the community action agency. The limited success so far probably represents as much the total community's failure as the shortcoming of the resident participation approach. Yet, had civil leadership been more competent, the program would have been better balanced, with resident participation but one of several complementary strategies.

This has been the case in Detroit and Phoenix where the CAA's are public agencies. These cities feature neighborhood multiservice centers with resident advisory boards. Some of the staff engage in neighborhood organization activities but operate under certain constraints in keeping with their affiliation with the governing coalition. The New Orleans CAA contracts with the Social Welfare Planning Council for neighborhood organization services and is willing to accept picketing of its own board meeting. Corpus Christi has just recently hired staff to perform neighborhood organization. Wichita has been engaged in this process longer, and neighborhood extension aides have assisted a number of citizen action groups.

A number of the communities stress self-help in their approach to the poor, and the techniques of community development, best known for application in places like Puerto Rico and India, are utilized. For example, Community Action Associates describe what is done in eastern Kentucky: "The community development aides in the outreach program spark community projects, and bring to the agencies the urgent needs of communities, and various representations are made to local and State and national agencies." The CAA itself plays the role of "mediator" between the poor and established agencies.

As was pointed out in discussing selection of board members, neighborhood boards and area councils are widely used. Newark has developed the use of neighborhood boards to the greatest extent. Oklahoma City, Chattanooga, and Denver have active neighborhood councils. Oakland County, Michigan, has two residents groups organized in geographic areas and a large, third one for senior citizens. One of the dilemmas of these neighborhood councils, though, is whether to include all the residents of a poor neighborhood or to concentrate only on those who are poor. In Charleston a previous all-inclusive approach with small groups in rural hollows was replaced by larger area councils only for the poor, and the consultant concludes that more was lost than gained. The general tendency is to be all inclusive.

ARVAC in rural Arkansas makes wide-scale use of program advisory committees in which persons served are represented. Some of the other rural areas, such as Lincoln Hills, the Ozark and delta areas in Missouri, and the rural parts of Broome County, New York, have less extensive efforts of resident participation, due in part to distances which make transportation, communications, and organization difficult.

Contained within the topic of resident participation is the issue of race, for in three-fourths of the communities studied minority groups constitute a major portion of the poverty population. Thus, participation of the poor and participation of minority groups in community affairs becomes intertwined—in North and South alike. In both regions, the community action program has contributed substantially to intergroup relations, and particularly so in the South where community action agencies are the most widespread biracial boards. As the Institute of Government of the University of Georgia observed in its study of the South Carolina project:

> Both Negro and white citizens say that the program, through its county advisory committees and target area organizations, has improved communications between the races. There is some evidence also that the program is establishing better understanding of the conditions of poverty in the counties.

On the issue of political action—a question sometimes raised in connection with resident participation—the consultants were able to discover virtually no improper use of the community action program. In the delta area of Missouri, some politicians had used the CAA for patronage purposes for a period, but that practice had been halted through the intervention of OEO's regional office and the General Accounting Office. But elsewhere the CAA's seem to have stayed clear of partisan politics, and political leaders have not attempted to take over the community action program. To be sure, many of the citizen groups assisted by the community action agencies take public positions on program issues, but rarely has this had partisan connotations.

As has been mentioned several times, the role of staff in resident participation is a crucial matter. A major concern of a number of agencies is that staff serve as an enabler to help people help themselves rather than merely doing things for the residents. This philosophy also is a way around the question of whether staff should participate in direct action, for it is the residents, not staff, who are the actors. There is a wide range of practices, but except in a half dozen or so communities staff operates under some constraints. In at least four places—Georgia, the Winter Garden area in Texas, Oklahoma City, and Lake County, Indiana—VISTA workers have greater freedom of action than CAA employees.

The conclusions of the Institute of Community Studies (Kansas City) indicate where resident participation stands at this stage:

> Many representatives of the poor express dissatisfaction with their advisory role and want more meaningful participation for the poor. This suggests on the one hand that residents who have been drawn into the program are a new element in community affairs and are closer to the hard core than the representatives of traditional agencies. On the other hand these criticisms suggest that OEO and local CAP staffs have succeeded in imparting the philosophy of community action to a significant number of people.

THE ESTABLISHED AGENCIES

But what of these traditional agencies? They too are involved. Typically, one-third of the board of directors consists of representatives of public agencies, such as the board of education, welfare department, and public health agency, and of private groups, such as the health and welfare council, the family service society, and others. Beyond that, there is extensive use of existing agencies to operate programs through subcontracts from the community action agency.

Although no statistics are available it appears that more than half and perhaps as much as two-thirds of the community action funds are channeled to these delegate agencies. But there is wide variation. New Orleans and Denver started by delegating almost every program, but recently both have taken on responsibility for neighborhood centers which they perceive as key tools for coordination. Other CAA's are also retaining control of the central staff of neighborhood centers. Philadelphia delegates most programs but not resident participation. Detroit has channeled large sums to the public and parochial schools, and elsewhere public schools are frequently used as delegate agencies. There is a small but growing trend to use new agencies which are operated by persons served. Newark and San Francisco have done so from the beginning, and Washington, D.C., has been shifting in this direction. In the Northeast Kingdom, Vermont, the CAA has turned Head Start over to autonomous boards with a majority of poor persons.

By and large the CAA's in rural areas tend to operate more programs directly than do their urban counterparts. This is true in Washington and Greene County, Pennsylvania, Lincoln Hills, Indiana, the four-county area in eastern Kentucky, and the four counties in South Carolina. This happens mainly because there are almost no other agencies with the capability of running such programs, reflecting a major difficulty in mounting the poverty program in rural areas. The new community action agencies provide a capacity which did not previously exist. One part of their new role is to serve as a vehicle for planning and program coordination.

PLANNING AND COORDINATION

Although resident participation has had the most public attention of the original requirements of the Economic Opportunity Act, a parallel phrase in the authorizing legislation describes a community action program as one which mobilizes and utilizes public and private resources in an attack on poverty. This is a mandate to plan and coordinate, but neither OEO nor most community action agencies have given this requirement as much attention as resident participation. Nonetheless, there is a growing body of experience with planning and coordination.

A number of cities actually began organizing and planning before the Economic Opportunity Act was passed. In places like Washington, Charleston, St. Louis, Oakland, and Syracuse, previously existing agencies, established to administer funds from the President's Committee on Juvenile Delinquency or the Ford Foundation, were in a position to prepare applications for grants under this new program. Elsewhere, the more alert cities got an organization going before Congress completed its work on the act, such as in Detroit and Denver.

The rural areas and smaller communities, though, were less able to initiate programs quickly, for they lack the financial resources, the staff talent, and the organizational structure to move fast with new programs. OEO helped them in two ways. First, a series of program development grants were funded. Second, grants were made to states to establish technical assistance agencies, which could assist in the organization of community action agencies. Although only about a third of the rural areas reviewed in this study were given major organizational assistance by these state agencies, the total pattern across the country more likely would show a majority so aided. (For this study, communities were chosen if they had action programs going for at least a year, and this tended to be rural communities which had sufficient local initiative to get going on their own without the longer time period required for the route of program development plus state technical assistance.)

But regardless of the form, almost all of the early planning for the community action program was focused on meeting the OEO requirements for an application. Only communities where the CAP was part of a wider effort did this planning have a broader orientation, such as in Detroit where the CAP came out of the community renewal program and in Washington where the CAP was assigned to an organization originally established to do united planning. Elsewhere the tendency was to string together a series of projects some of which were included because they were pet projects of members of the sponsoring coalition. Long-range planning seldom was a major concern of the newly founded community action agencies.

Coordination, though, proved to be a challenge which many of the CAA's soon had to face. At a minimum, they were required to coordinate the various component programs which they were funding. And since widespread use has been made of delegate agencies, the new CAA's have had to develop working relationships with these established agencies. About one-half of the community action agencies studied used this necessity as an opportunity to embark upon a broader effort to coordinate—perhaps orchestrate would be a better term—the total community's effort to eliminate poverty, at least in the field of human resource services.

This has been easiest in the rural areas, and the clearest examples are there: Northeast Kingdom, Vermont; South Carolina; Washington and Greene Counties, Pennsylvania (described as a "catalyst"); the four counties in eastern Kentucky (described as a "mediator"); ARVAC in Arkansas. About the latter, the regional consultant wrote:

> The ARVAC staff states that a new philosophy is emerging which is that they are getting away from the individual aspect of service to new directions in a group-type situation. This has involved ARVAC in more of a coordinating role as well as a role to mobilize other resources. . . . This shift from a direct service agency to a role of planning and coordination is similar to the function of a Community Welfare Council in many cities in the United States. This does not involve the same problems as it would in an urban community since in a rural area it is the only planning agency.

Indeed, competition has made it difficult to achieve broader planning and fuller coordination in the cities. In several places, the community welfare council initiated the community action program. But soon the child grew bigger than the parent, and a new organization had to be established, such as in Oklahoma City. And as the new agency moved into fields traditionally beyond the scope of the community welfare council, such as employment and education, the child challenged the parent. But in these new fields it also posed a potential threat to other agencies. Thus, the attempt to coordinate in cities is perpetually bumping into resisting agencies.

Yet, there are a few CAA's so situated within the governing coalition that they are able to accomplish significant coordination: Jacksonville, New Orleans, and Detroit, for example. Some are able to go part way, such as Oakland County, Michigan, which sees "community mobilization" as a major responsibility even though local government does not fully recognize this role for the CAA. In contrast, the three CAA's with the strongest commitment to resident participation outside the governing coalition—San Francisco, Syracuse, and Newark—are precluded from a coordinating role.

Manpower programs offer the best illustration of the need for and the difficulties of coordination, for these programs are among the most fragmented of all service programs affecting the poor. Where effective manpower coordination exists, it is usually the community action agency which has brought it about, such as in St. Louis and Detroit. In Oklahoma City, manpower coordination is being achieved through a combination of the CAA and CAMPS (Comprehensive Area Manpower Planning System, a new device promoted by the Labor Department to coordinate MDTA programs with other manpower activities). The CAA director is chairman of the CAMPS committee, but even so there is potential conflict between CAMPS, which includes only agency representatives, and a CAA manpower task force, which includes laymen—businessmen, labor leaders, and the poor, unless the efforts of the two structures are closely linked. Elsewhere such linkage would be even harder, such as in Wichita where the CAA and the state employment service have been in contention. Newly emerging is a dispute between the CAA and recent efforts by mayors to form their own manpower coordinating instruments, and this came to the fore recently in San Francisco, Oakland, and Newark in the planning of the concentrated employment program.

Yet, even where the local agencies can get together, there is no assurance that their wishes will be respected by federal agencies. For example, in Oakland County, Michigan, the CAA and the state employment service worked arduously to develop a joint program only to have it rejected by the federal agencies which were asked to fund it. Over and over again, the consultants came across instances where local initiative was blocked and local responsibility was curtailed by action of federal agencies.

By last fall a number of the abler community action agencies were getting into a position where they could initiate long-range planning in order to more fully mobilize resources and to achieve a more comprehensive approach to the elimination of poverty. Such planning would be based upon the assumption that the locality would have a say in the allocation of resources, particularly community action funds. But then Congress chose to earmark all but a small portion of these funds, and OEO established nationwide priorities for the spending of the balance. Out the window went local planning efforts. Ironically, this came just at the time when local capability was developing sufficiently to take greater responsibility for planning and coordination.

Institutional Change

For during the two and one-half years since the community action program commenced a substantial amount of new local capability has developed. Most noteworthy, a new local institution concerned with the needs of poor people—the community action agency—has come into being. As has been noted several times, such institutional building has been particularly significant in rural areas which suffer for the lack of an effective agency structure.

In the cities, though, the situation is somewhat different. There one finds a plethora of agencies. The difficulty lies in their failure to serve the poor adequately: social work agencies using casework techniques which are more applicable to middle class persons; schools in poverty areas failing to teach children to read; manpower programs taking only the cream of the crop; municipal housekeeping departments having a double standard of service with quality correlated to neighborhood income; housing inspection agencies lacking vigor in dealing with slumlords; welfare departments using methods which destroy human dignity; hospitals providing impersonal clinics and highly fragmented medical services for the poor; and so on. What these situations urgently demand is institutional change.

As was pointed out earlier, about one-third of the agencies studied view institutional change as a major function, but a number of the others become so involved in minor ways. Almost everywhere the introduction of non-professional workers hired from the neighborhoods served represents a major innovation in the personnel practices of agencies such as schools and social welfare agencies. The decentralization of services to the poverty areas is a significant change for such agencies as the state employment service and the legal services agency, and when this is combined with outreaching recruitment by neighborhood workers, another new technique is introduced. The presence of poor people on governing boards, not only of the community action agencies but also some of the delegate agencies, is a new approach, and the small but growing trend of using corporations governed by neighborhood residents modifies the existing pattern while building a new institution.

Most of the institutional change which has occurred has been brought about through negotiation and persuasion, often sweetened by the money which the community action agencies receive and disburse. In some of the cities where the CAA's are controlled by the governing coalition, they are able to use their position to influence other agencies; for example, they might have the backing of a change-oriented mayor or the support of decision-makers who control the united fund. In other cities where the CAA is fighting the governing coalition, the techniques of neighborhood organization and social protest have to be relied upon. In both situations, though, legal action to assure the rights of individuals have been utilized, especially in relation to such agencies as the housing authority and the public welfare department, which have administrative regulations susceptible to challenge.

In the opinion of this writer, the community action agencies which are accomplishing the most are those which have an effective working relationship within the community's governing coalition but at the same time are pressing vigorously for institutional change. This is not to make a blanket condemnation of those who are pressing for institutional change from the outside, for that may be the only course available in a community at a particular time. But since the function of the governing coalition is to make decisions about the allocation of community resources and the conduct of various public and voluntary programs, it is much better to be a part of that decision-making process rather than always fighting from the outside.

The challenge to the Office of Economic Opportunity is to stimulate and encourage those agencies showing little interest in institutional change to embark upon this strategy of action. OEO's role in the communities where conflict exists might be that of a mediator, which seeks a middle ground between the more militant persons who run the community action agency and the more conservative persons who control the governing coalition. Here and there the regional consultants found OEO playing such a mediating role, but their findings suggest that this is not a deliberate choice or a strong feature of the OEO regional offices. But this is a most difficult role to play and perhaps too much to expect from a new agency.

CONCLUSION

There are no adequate measures of success or failure of the community action program. The seven regional consultants found both strengths and weaknesses in the programs they studied. These are recorded in the consultants' summary chapters. On the whole, their conclusion was that the program has achieved considerable results in its beginning years and that despite occasional difficulties it should be continued and strengthened. They found the functions of service, resident participation, planning and coordination, and institutional change all to be required even though sometimes conflicting. For, as the Center for Urban Studies, University of Chicago, stated: "Our case studies suggest that the participation of the poor, delivery of services, and service innovation are mutually reinforcing in the development of antipoverty programs."

The administration's original congressional presentation on the Economic Opportunity Act stated that the causes of poverty are complex and interrelated and so also must be the solutions. That statement also summarizes the community action program as it exists today: complex with interrelated parts. Almost everywhere it is providing useful new services for the poor. At its best it is truly achieving the congressional purpose—to provide stimulation and incentive for urban and rural communities to mobilize their resources to combat poverty through community action programs.

Yet, these studies report only the beginning. Since they were made, major riots have erupted in two of the case cities: Newark and Detroit. On the one hand, the community action program in Newark was found to be troubled with internal and external conflict in spite of some successes with neighborhood boards and manpower programs. On the other hand, Detroit was found to have one of the most effective programs of those studied, with strong leadership from city hall and substantial citizen support.

Since both cities had riots, this writer is drawn to the conclusion that even at its best the community action program and related reforms are barely beginning to remedy the social injustices which corrupt the American society. The irrational drives which spark and fuel the riots are far stronger and far deeper than we have been willing to admit. The remedies will be costlier and much more difficult than the limited efforts which are now underway.

Compared to the total need, then, the community action program is a pitiful start. But it is a start. It can be a firm foundation upon which larger and more effective programs are built.

11

Who Can Activate
The Poor?

One Assessment of "Maximum
Feasible Participation"

WARNER BLOOMBERG, JR.
and FLORENCE W. ROSENSTOCK

☐ WHATEVER ITS ORIGINAL AUTHORS INTENDED it to convey, the
phrase, "maximum feasible participation" of the poor, has become
a troubling and troublesome ideological projective test for social
scientists and social critics, as well as for planners and protesters.
To some it has been read as simply one of several pieties included
in the legislation for the "war on poverty" and applicable to only
one of its titles, an exhortation not subject to any very precise
policy prescriptions. In sharp contrast, militant activists, whose
contemporary strategy and style are best expressed in the direct
mass action techniques of certain civil rights groups such as SNCC,
heard it as an unequivocal call for a modern populism of the poor,
the beginning of a political reconstruction that would eventually
institutionalize participative democracy as the form and process
of the urban polity. Many local officials in city halls and community
chest agencies reacted with predictable anger and alarm, some of
the more paranoid among them suspecting that this was but one
more ploy in federal expansionist gamesmanship, others fearing
a possible increase of independent political power on the part of
the people of the central city ghetto (Graham, 1965). Adminis-

AUTHORS' NOTE: *This is a revised version of a paper originally presented
to the joint session on "Poverty and Progress" of the American Sociological Association and the Society for the Study of Social Problems, San
Francisco, August 29, 1967.*

trators in the Office of Economic Opportunity, especially in regional branches, in sheer self-defense often sought to shove such basic issues at least temporarily into the background by reducing them to questions of percentage representation of the poor, however selected, on the local boards or commissions that review and provide overall supervision of OEO projects, tending to urge one-third as a kind of *ad hoc* numerical embodiment of social justice. That effort failed as the 1967 Congress combined the "one-third poor" formula with other stipulations that would emasculate the authority of the board on which the poor sat.

However future historians may assess the significance of all this, enough intriguing and seemingly paradoxical patterns have emerged to merit serious and extensive attention by social analysts. For example, in a number of cities clergymen, who have been characterized in the past by timidity, a penchant for accommodation with the worldly *status quo,* and almost unparalleled political incompetence, have become partners with the Industrial Areas Foundation, whose guiding spirit, theoretician, and proprietor, Saul Alinsky, displays a brash and secularist rhetoric, a flair for clever but not consistently successful manipulation of conflicting interests, and a compulsive antagonism to anything that can be identified as part of "the establishment." Again, some local politicians who normally seek access to every source of fiscal irrigation for their frequently patronage-parched urban domains, actually attempted to sandbag and seal off the funding of community action components for the "war on poverty." Finally, more notable successes in eliciting and facilitating effective participation of the poor have occurred (largely unnoticed by such cosmopolitan types as big newspaper journalists and big university social scientists) in certain rural areas and within some smaller cities and towns than in the troubled metropolises with their impacted ghettos.

The following attempt to think through and beyond current confusion over the participation of the poor in programs to alleviate and eliminate poverty is directed to the following questions:

(1) What do we want people to participate in, and why? Should the poor display a different pattern of participation than those who are not poor?

(2) What determines whether non-participators begin to participate, vis-à-vis that in which they ought to participate, and

what conduces to continuity in participation? Are the poor a special case in this regard?

(3) Assuming that some kinds of participation by the poor are especially desirable and can be elicited and facilitated, what organizations and groups can best contribute to the development of that participation?

The first question obviously involves major normative considerations. The remaining two focus on empirical problems requiring application of such behavioral concepts and theory as are available and appropriate. The first will be dealt with quite briefly, the latter two more extensively. Conclusions are necessarily tentative, resting on a much too "thin" data base. Forthcoming studies will hopefully permit more solid and certain generalizations in the near future.

PARTICIPATION: IN WHAT AND FOR WHAT?

The phrase, "maximum feasible participation" has to do with the involvement of people in decisions that will affect in fairly direct ways their own lives and well-being, decisions shaping the policies, programs, and specific projects undertaken by private welfare agencies and by local governments with the purpose, or at least the alleged goal, of enabling the poor to overcome some of the most debilitating effects of poverty and to enjoy increasing opportunities to move out of poverty. Thus, the concern is for *political* participation, taking "political" quite broadly.

Why this persistent emphasis on the poor participating in associations and offices relevant to decision-making that affects their own lives and place in the social arrangements of the community? In part it reflects the Jeffersonian tradition in American idealism, epitomized by Percival and Paul Goodman's assertion that "to make positive decisions for one's community . . . . is one of the noble acts of man" (Goodman and Goodman, 1960, pp. 10-11). In part, it results from an emphasis on the distinction between formal and effective freedom, which leads contemporary philosopher Lawrence Haworth to argue that the good city must necessarily be one whose very institutions motivate and facilitate, rather than merely permit, extensive self-rule through broad citizen participation (Haworth,

1963). For the right to choose whether or not to participate in community decision-making affecting one's own life is an empty one unless means are available to enter into the political process as well as to withdraw from it or stay outside of it (a choice which often is not permitted in totalitarian societies). Such views also are nicely congruent with the emphasis on the worth and dignity of the individual embodied in the "social gospel" doctrines of some Christian churches and their analogues in others and in liberal Jewish social theory.

However, much of the push for participation by the poor derives from more immediate and pragmatic concerns (though these are compatible with the idealistic social and political theories just mentioned). First, there seems to be at least a crude correlation between the degree of participation on the part of any given segment of a community in politically relevant associations and in community decision-making roles and the extent to which the private and public agencies of the community serve the interests and meet the perceived needs of that segment; and the poor have been both the least organized and the least evident in such roles (Bloomberg, 1966). Second, effective participation by the poor on behalf of what they believe to be their own interests and needs is seen as an antidote to the derogatory view of the poor as either undeserving or self-defeating held by a majority of Americans, a view which either relieves the rest of the community of responsibility for poverty or provides a rationale for emphasizing and reinforcing the dependency of the poor (Miller and Rein, 1966). Third, the experience of power through relevant association and participation in decision-making and the concomitant development of relevant organizational and political skills have been proposed as a necessary "therapy" for the alleged alienation of the poor, which is said to be derived from their powerlessness and in turn reinforces it in a continuing vicious circle of causation (Haggstrom, 1964). Fourth, the poor can contribute much from their own experience to the formulation of programs and projects to alleviate and reduce poverty. These arguments lead directly to the conclusion that the poor, like the Negroes in the active core of the civil rights movement, must become, relative to the middle class majority, "overparticipators" in politically relevant associations and campaigns. Unless the poor thereby manage to create an effective and expanding core constituency for the innovative and reformist components of the "war on poverty," only the support of certain sympathetic groups, such as the liberals in organized labor and religious institutions, can prevent it from being almost wholly co-opted to the interest of established political and welfare organizations and agencies (Miller and Rein, 1965; Miller, 1964a; Miller, 1964b).

PARTICIPATION: CORRELATES AND CAUSES

What, then, determines whether or not people participate in politically relevant associations, organize on behalf of one or another institutional or community decision, and seek access to the actual decision-making roles? In attempting to answer this question, first for the American population in general and then with respect to the poor in particular, it is important to remember that we are considering unusual rather than typical behavior (Bloomberg, 1966). Contrary to a fairly popular stereotype, the majority of American citizens belong to only one or two organizations, if any, and for the most part are passive members rather than part of the active core of any associations to which they belong. Moreover, only a small proportion of those associations are normally relevant to or in any way affect the kind of decision-making with which "maximum feasible participation" is concerned; usually they serve other individual and institutional goals, most often those having to do with religion, job security, and recreation and sociability. And when actual involvement in roles most directly concerned with making community decisions apart from elections is examined, the proportions drop below the 10 per cent level. As Dahl has said, "The first fact, and it overshadows almost everything else, is that *most citizens use their political resources scarcely at all*" (Dahl, 1961, p. 276).

The point has already been made that the poor are least evident, by any of the usual indices, among the minority who are "participators." It should be added that the correlation of participation with education, income, and other generally valued characteristics is probably curvilinear, with a rapid increase in memberships, politically relevant activity, and participation in direct decision-making roles as the shift is made into what we usually refer to, albeit somewhat vaguely, as the "upper middle" and "upper" strata. But the meaning of the available correlations is far from clear.

Three Theoretical Models for Participation

Many, especially schoolmen and educational psychologists, seem to conclude that any group's place on the socioeconomic class ladder determines the extent of their political participation. They hold that this is true at least in part because the relevant cultural patterns themselves are associated with social level. Therefore, eliciting extensive and continuing social action from the poor becomes a practical goal only if segments of the poor can be "leapfrogged" upward along some of the status continua, or if changed cultural patterns can somehow be developed among people whose locations in the social structure remain relatively fixed. In short, since political participation is believed to derive from social structural and cultural variables, it is not itself a means of changing the place of the poor in society or the values and action norms which the poor display. Education and other means of deliberate cultural change may be used to affect the latter, and programs such as those which relocate people a number of jumps upward in employment status may be used to begin to break up the "status crystallization" of the poor.

Unfortunately, a majority of the adult poor are not employable, or continue to be chronically underemployed, given current standards and institutional patterns (Morgan, *et al.*, 1962; Sokol, 1965; Zeisel, 1964). Job retraining and placement programs inevitably have had only limited impact. Efforts to remake the subcultures of the slums or of individual poor families through educational and training programs have been meager, but their results have been so negligible that one must doubt the utility of such projects, unless truly massive resources could be brought to bear. As a result, those who believe the most evident correlations actually denote causal factors for participation, who use cultural and social structural patterns to *explain* the absence of participation by the poor, tend to emphasize programs for children and youth. "Compensatory education" is proposed as a means both for developing values and overt behavior norms that depart from the parental models and for creating skills that will leapfrog high school or job corps graduates into good jobs.

A second model, shared in large part by a variety of reformers and organizers of what might best be called the "social action–social protest school," in effect reverses the direction of causation associated with the frequently reiterated percentages and correlations (Alinsky, 1946, 1957, 1962; Alinsky and Sanders, 1965a; Alinsky and Sanders, 1965b; Anderson, 1966; Haggstrom, 1964; Riessman, 1965, 1966; Wakefield, 1960). Those who lack money income also rank low on all the other status hierarchies, according to this view, precisely because they have no other power resources with which to enforce claims for more goods and services, better neighborhoods, and access to other kinds of opportunities and pleasures associated with the American version of the "good life." Most aspects of what we have been calling the "culture of poverty" are seen as reflections of this powerlessness, the habits inculcated by being continuously subject to others' decisions and the emotional adjustments and rationalizations that make this condition as bearable as possible for people who also learn from the larger society that dependency and helplessness among adults are signs of personal worthlessness.

Only the experience of individual and group potency through organization on behalf of their own needs and interests and through the exercise of power against those who have excluded and exploited them, will enable a majority of the poor, especially the most deprived, to break through the "bind" of their own cultural and psychological patterns at the same time that they break down the institutional barriers that are the sources of their impoverishment. An inevitable part of this "sociotherapeutic" process, and a necessary component for its full success, is the clarification of the conflict between the poor and the presently powerful and affluent segments of the society, and the mobilization of the emotional and intellectual energies of the poor around this frequently concealed but now fully revealed nexus of antagonistic interests and purposes.

A third model, the "community development" approach, largely disregards the usual correlations and does not impute any special and especially entrenched incapacities for action to any segment of the population (King, 1965; Ross, 1967; Taylor, 1956; United Nations, 1955). It assumes that there are enough capacities for leadership and action distributed among all, or almost all, human communities or subcommunities to make possible development of effective self-help programs and projects. Though these are to be based in the locality, they may be developed cooperatively with supralocal agencies and organizations that are part of "the establishment." To elicit action organizers must enable residents with leadership and activist capabilities to articulate the needs felt by themselves and the others in their community, to understand what can be changed and how such changes can be brought about, and to realize the resources that they do have and how their resources can be expanded so as to be able to effect desired changes. The problems of a cultural nature confronting the organizer are not so much those of alienation in the face of opportunity and apathy in the face of perceived needs, but patterns of evaluation that produce contentment with the *status quo* and habitual interpretations that prevent understanding or acceptance of available means for successful problem-solving, such as new technology or formal procedures for political and legal action.

Community development personnel, therefore, see education techniques as useful, not to change the "basics" of a culture or subculture, but to inculcate cognitive and judgmental patterns, especially in selected leadership personnel, that are specifically relevant to a definite project to be undertaken, whether it is to clean up a well in a village in an underdeveloped nation or to petition and create political pressure for a road in an Appalachian hollow or a park and recreation center within an urban slum. These particular patterns of perception and evaluation may link into and therefore elicit change in more basic cultural components, but that is not necessarily a goal and there may even be some concern for preserving as much of the old culture as is compatible with meeting the people's perceived needs in their present historic circumstances. However, educational techniques depart drastically from the typical and fairly formal classroom procedures of most American programs of adult education. They are intermixed and interwoven with the ongoing projects and the organizer-educator often participates directly in the project. He also may act as an intermediary between those whom he serves and those with whom they must deal, usually local decision-makers, until his "clients" gain the necessary skills and understanding to do so themselves.

Some Implications of the Alternative Models

These three statements of theory and strategy are, of course, only "models." Actual projects and organizations may and do combine elements from more than one. Nevertheless, each has a certain logic which is likely to affect both who utilize it and the scale and locale of its most effective utilization.

For example, the first approach, seeking to change the habits of enough individuals or families to amount to an alteration of culture and trying to promote a forced-draft movement of a great many poor persons up some one or two relevant status dimensions, such as employment or school achievement, requires very large resources unless it is to be merely a research experiment or another pilot demonstration. Programs such as Head Start, Job Corps, and Manpower Retraining usually require substantial plant, professional staff, large organizational structures, and relatively substantial allocations of money. There is a tendency for them to be undertaken on at least a ghetto-wide, if not city-wide, basis; to be developed through existing institutions that already have some staff, buildings, and so on; to require federal or foundation fiscal support; and to have "successes" contingent upon decision-makers in other institutional sectors or at least outside of the direct influence of those in the business of changing habits and achievement skills: Head Start gains tend to be washed out unless relevant reforms take place at subsequent grade levels; job training programs do not succeed in "leapfrogging" the impoverished unless both initial placements and subsequent opportunities for advancement make this possible. Finally, the focus on individuals and families, as has already been pointed out, is largely irrelevant to other kinds of changes in community and institutional patterns that presently contribute to dependency and deprivation.

While both the social protest–social action model and the community development model address themselves directly to issues involving the institutional *status quo* in the community and to overcoming conditions of dependency, their respective logics can yield quite different action strategies and to some degree different resource and personnel requirements. The social action–social protest model is embodied in the work of SNCC in the South and in IAF developed and influenced organizing efforts in some Northern slums. The community development approach has been most evident in rural areas and smaller cities and towns.

Social action theory assumes the existence of a profound but often disguised conflict between a class and/or racial-ethnic minority and a majority who support or acquiesce in the existing institutional regime, the "establishment" in each institutional sector.

Cooperation and collaboration with most existing agencies is, therefore, likely to confuse rather than clarify this underlying conflict. Authentic cooperation, from this viewpoint, would be possible only if the poor could approach the established political and private welfare institutions from positions of power and thereby bargain with them on behalf of aims and projects proposed by the poor themselves. Organizers, therefore, must use every opportunity to bring latent conflict to the surface, to intensify it, and to aid the poor in developing and using whatever power resources can be developed by those who have little money: the capacity to disrupt the community's "peace and tranquility," to develop bloc voting, to investigate and disclose practices disadvantageous to the poor, to consolidate such economic power as the poor can muster through action such as boycotts, and to obtain from sympathetic supralocal sources of community funds, such as the federal government, conditions to the granting of those funds.

Frequently, some "quick and easy" victories are sought in order to give the poor initial experience and to overcome their sense of impotence and helplessness before "the establishment." The dramaturgy of conflict which the organizer seeks to create and maintain around these often minor initial demands is a necessary part of this "sociotherapy." Any who seek to organize the poor or develop projects meeting their needs through means which neglect or bypass this "sociotherapeutic" process of protest, conflict, and the direct experience of power are seen, at best, as digressive and in the long-run ineffective, and, at worst, as part of "the enemy," albeit inadvertently. Efforts, therefore, may be made to eliminate or co-opt "competing" organizations.

Finding starting points for the generation of protest is the way this form of social action usually begins, often with a handful of angry and determined people and their organizer. They can be living in a housing project, or located within a few city blocks in a metropolitan slum, or inhabiting the shacks along a dirt road in the southland's agrarian, tenant-farmer black belt. Initial smallness of scale does not necessarily reduce the effort to a research or demonstration project, for a sequence of organization-building actions is assumed. Only modest physical and monetary resources may be required, at least at first. Frequently, these resources are obtained only as programs develop and by such means and in such locations as the poor themselves can manage, though they may be aided by sympathetic private or public agencies that are supralocal and, therefore, not part of the community "establishment" that is increasingly being identified as "the enemy." Except for a few organizers, or even just one, no professional staff is required and little or no formal organization. It is anticipated that eventually a large-scale organization of the poor, perhaps an "organization of organizations," will be developed, but it will be largely self-staffed by indigenous personnel who have acquired new skills.

As Frank Riessman has pointed out, there are important differences between Alinsky's IAF and the "New Left," and these should not be neglected even though they may usefully be seen as variants within this social action–social protest type (Riessman, 1965). The IAF will utilize any and all existing organizational bases actually located within poor communities and willing to be consolidated into (and in decisional terms merged with) the new organization; the New Left tends to involve only the poor themselves, to develop among them a thoroughly new leadership, and to try to reach the most alienated. Since participation is an end as well as a means, those operating within the framework of the New Left ordinarily would not sacrifice "democratic process" for a desired "product," that is, an immediate victory; IAF organizers seek to develop an indigenous leadership capable of planning and carrying out successful action, but they use many techniques of manipulation and control within the developing organization to make sure that "right decisions" are made, sometimes asserting that local leaders can have their own way only when they can "pay the bills." Alinsky and his orthodox followers are rather anti-ideological and determinedly unromantic, emphasizing and normally approving of whatever works to build a lasting local organization which can get what its members and their constituents want by the usual exercise of interest-group power politics within the local polity; the New Left is oriented to a rather unsystematic ideology stressing a "new society" utopianism built up around humanistic values, a militant rejection of the upper-strata and older-generation cultural *status quo*, and a rather romantic view of the powerless and exploited— the poor and racial minorities ("the hope is in the proles"). The most ambitious effort to bring these two variants together into a single approach was Warren Haggstrom's effort in Syracuse and his writings partake of parts of both perspectives.

The community development model leads to action strategies which are in some ways more pragmatic than Alinsky's even though reflecting an idealism as intense and often as naive as the New Left's. Once the client population (which may be but does not have to be the poor or minority groups) has, with the aid of the professional organizer, arrived at its own goals and set some realistic priorities, any legitimate means for achieving those goals may be utilized so long as it does not negate the development of a more and more participative and competent citizenry. Anyone may help who can accept the means and ends required for such community development; so can any agency, private or public, that is acceptable to the participating personnel and amenable to the imperatives and constraints of community development. Conflict is not sought as a necessary part of the process, but its possible or even probable emergence is recognized and accepted as one of the "facts of life." No special dramaturgical procedures are prescribed for therapeutic purposes, and the first projects undertaken often are of the "self-help" variety that neither engender emotional demonstrations nor bring into the open hostility from or toward other segments of the community. Indeed, there may be some effort to avoid conflict until the developing organization has gained internal strength and greater competence and self-confidence through completion of initial projects.

Community development theory is rooted in the communal utopianism of the eighteenth and nineteenth century, but it draws easily upon the jargon of contemporary sociology and anthropology. Its proponents do not, as is the case with so many in the New Left, view academic social scientists as corrupted servants of the various establishments; nor do they reject them as sissified quasi-liberals who panic and run for home when the going gets rough, which is Alinsky's usual portrayal of them. Involvement of social scientists in community development projects is often sought where their skills seem relevant to the undertaking. As with the social action–social protest model, initial organizing efforts may be small in scale (this is probably typical) without rendering the effort ineffective. Each project should enable the organization to develop greater skills among its participants and to add new participants. As organizational size and competence increase, the scale of operation can expand. Eventually projects of very substantial scope intended to bring more and more basic changes to the community may be undertaken, and an increasingly participative local democracy is continuously sought as a deliberate by-product. But no unified overall organization is necessary and no effort is envisioned to launch a social movement or build an institutional structure supra-local in its boundaries and impact.

IN SEARCH OF MORE CLUES TO CAUSATION

The differences among the three models of explanation and action just described have very practical consequences for any university whose leadership, like that at the University of Wisconsin, has asserted a commitment to making the institution relevant to an authentic "war on poverty." For the resources a university can actually assign to such efforts are very limited, and the role it can play through an equally limited number of relevant and willing faculty also is normally constrained by political considerations as well. For example, if alienation were a major cause of citizen inaction, requiring the sociotherapy of the social action–social protest model, then members of the faculty would have to be involved mainly on their own time as volunteers. If differences between subcultures and one's place in the social structure were the main determinants, then only large-scale efforts involving much greater commitments of university personnel than could be realistically anticipated, in conjunction with institutions providing elementary and secondary education, vocational training, and employment, would have meaningful impact on existing patterns. But if participation were significantly linked to variables subject to change through the techniques and strategies of community development, such as perception of needs and the skills and competences for action, then even a few university personnel might make consequential contributions through their professional roles.

In spring and summer of 1964 students and faculty of the Department of Urban Affairs undertook an extensive study of "Northtown A," a fifty-block area within Milwaukee's "inner core north," the segment of the inner city which includes the Negro ghetto and the areas of transition produced by the movement of Negroes north and northwest and the exodus of whites along the ghetto's expanding periphery. A questionnaire survey included many items dealing with the perception of neighborhood and community problems by respondents and forms of participation that were or could be relevant to taking action on those problems. Special emphasis was placed on determining, to the extent that survey procedures permitted, the correlates of participation within this particular population.

The area sampled was particularly useful for this inquiry because it included census tracts with many deprived neighborhoods characterized by low income, a large proportion of Negroes (some representing mainly an influx between 1950 and 1960), substantial unemployment, a large proportion of low-income families, many unskilled workers, many broken homes, and less than average education; while those on the periphery of the ghetto were still predominantly middle class and white with social pathology indicators similar to or less than those of the city as a whole (see Table A in the Appendix).

The dependent variable, political participation (with a broad interpretation of "political"), was indexed by a crude but serviceable "action score" indicating how many of the following kinds of participation each respondent claimed for himself.

1. Registering complaints about community or commercial services, politics, or civil rights.

2. Requesting assistance from an alderman.

3. Attending meetings or public hearings.

4. Belonging to a neighborhood committee, civic group, or improvement association.

5. Voting in local elections.

The matrix of correlations among these kinds of participation is shown in Table 1.

TABLE 1

	Complaining	Requesting Assistance	Attending Meetings	Belonging to Groups	Voting
Complaining	1				
Requesting Assistance	.12	1			
Attending Meetings	.13	.21*	1		
Belonging to Groups	.23*	.10	.17	1	
Voting	.02	.13	.12	.05	1

* Significant at .05 level.

All correlations are, not surprisingly, positive; but all are low enough (though two achieve statistical significance) that one can feel comfortable about treating the items as separate dimensions of participation. Each respondent could, therefore, receive an action score ranging from 0 to 5. As can be seen in Table 2, about two-thirds of the respondents reported engaging in either none or only one of these forms of participation. Only about 15 per cent could be considered strongly oriented to action, reporting three or more types of participation. This pattern is compatible with other studies of participation and political action by the general citizenry.

TABLE 2

NUMBER OF RESPONDENTS RECEIVING EACH ACTION SCORE

Score	Number	Per Cent of Total Sample
0	45	27.6
1	66	40.4
2	28	17.3
3	11	6.7
4	7	4.3
5	6	3.7
	163	100.0

Nineteen variables were assessed as determinants of greater or lesser action tendencies among the persons in the sample. Those used to indicate place in the social structure and probable involvement in any related subcultures include race, age, education, family income, financial dependency (indexed by the number of kinds of financial aid being received), and occupation. Those which seemed to have the most direct relevance to the assumptions about causes of participation built into the social action–social protest model included feelings of personal political efficacy, group potency, alienation, perceived commonality of discontent, and personal potency in family relationship during adolescence. Those most related to causes of participation as posited by the community development model included perceived need for improvement of the neighborhood and community, political competence, home ownership, length of residence in the neighborhood and desire to stay in the neighborhood, and preference for neighborhood as against more distant sources of means of decision-making. (Table B in the Appendix presents the matrix of correlations among all of these variables.)

Within this sample, social structural variables were correlated in the usual way, though the relatively small size of the correlations (except for age and dependency) indicates less status crystallization than suggested by stereotypes of inner core populations held by those whose image of the ghetto is shaped more by journalism and fantasy than by personal familiarity or research. Race was not correlated significantly (the highest correlation is .13) with any of the other social structural variables, reflecting both the poor whites, mainly older people, "trapped" in the slum, and a disproportionate representation of middle-income Negroes who tend to be found in the expanding fringe areas of the ghetto and who have more education, better jobs, and higher income than is characteristic of the Negro population as a whole.

Variables relating to sociotherapeutic needs of the sort posited by the social action–social protest model were indexed by responses to questionnaire items taken directly or derived from relevant published research. (Items are summarized in the Appendix.) Except for the correlation between doubts about personal political efficacy and alienation (.50), all correlations are quite low.

The variables suggested by the community development model fall into two main categories. Four of them—home ownership, length of residence, desire to remain in the neighborhood, and preference for neighborhood decision-making—were intended to index what might be thought of as a kind of neighborhood-level "localism" which in turn might be conducive to participation on behalf of improving conditions in the area. The other category included an index of perceived need for improvement and one of political competence relevant to participating in action on community problems. The two highest correlations among these variables, not surprisingly, were between length of residence and home ownership (.46), but other correlations were relatively low.

The simple correlations of each of all 19 variables with action score are arrayed in Table 3. Nine of the eleven most highly correlated variables were selected for inclusion in a computation of multiple correlation and multiple determination coefficients, as

TABLE 3

Simple Correlations With Action Score

Competence	.49	Decision locus	—.15
Perceived need	.33	Adolescent freedom to complain	.14
Income	.25	Political efficacy	.10
Home ownership	.24	Desire to remain	.09
Length of residence	.24	Perceived commonality	.09
Financial dependency	—.20	Adolescent family influence	.08
Group potency	.20	Race	.06
Alienation	.18	Adolescent decision success	.03
Education	.17	Age	.01
Occupation	.16		

shown in Table 4. Because of the correlations among income, financial dependency, education, and occupation, only income and education were included as indicators of "place" in the social structure; financial dependency designates a rather small set of sampled families and many of the multiple aid cases are on old age assistance (thus the high correlation—.47—with age).

Table 4 emphasizes most of all how little—about one-third—of the variation in participation, at least as it is indexed in this study, can be statistically accounted for by the variables considered

TABLE 4

Relative and Cumulative Effectiveness of Nine Variables as Predictors of Action Score

Variable	Multiple Determination Index (R^2)	Correlation With Action Score (R)
Competence	.25	.50
Felt need	.30	.54
Home ownership	.32	.57
Group potency score	.32	.57
Income	.33	.57
Residence length	.33	.57
Decision means	.33	.57
Alienation	.33	.57
Education	.33	.57

here, mainly by those relevant to the community development model. Other combinations (see Tables C, D, and E in the Appendix) continue to emphasize perceived need and political competence as the two most important variables in accounting for action. Both are presumably subject to change by experience and continuing formal education. Competence is positively correlated with present income and education (combined correlation of .43), which may be taken as indicators of opportunity or deprivation with respect to the development (up to the time of the survey) of relevant cognitive skills and actual experiences.

The following conclusions seem warranted by this study:

1. In Milwaukee the patterns of participation in politically relevant activities by residents of the area known as inner city north tend to reflect the perception of problems and their discontent over them, on the one hand, and the political understandings and organizational experience they already have, on the other hand.

2. However, independence or dependency, in terms of available income and its source, operates as an important constraint on or facilitation of such participation: those with less income tend to be less likely to participate, but this withdrawal from or avoidance of participation is more pronounced when income is derived from assistance, especially in families with more than one type of assistance.

3. Social psychological variables such as alienation and belief in personal efficacy or in group potency may to some degree reduce or increase participation beyond what one would expect given the perceived needs, action competences, and income-dependency statuses of any group of category of adults.

4. So much of the variation in participation among these people remains unexplained that no one model or theory can be held exclusively as doctrine on how to activate the poor among them and facilitate their continuing and "maximum feasible" participation.

WHO CAN "ACTIVATE" THE POOR?

The study just reported seemed to indicate that a university could effectively aid at least some of the poor to become more active on behalf of their own needs and interests, if only those poor who are able would become more articulate about these needs and priorities and gain in relevant skills through the kinds of programs a university could properly provide. A university could not change the employment situation, welfare policies, or school system in Milwaukee or any other big city, nor could it undertake political organization and action such as proposed and stimulated by the IAF or groups identified with the New Left. This would seem to exclude those non-participators whose attitudes, psychological resources, and competences would be changed only by either sociotherapeutic experiences of the sort developed and facilitated through social action–social protest techniques of organizing or by the resocializing experiences that would accompany a substantial change in economic well-being and independence. Yet, this would appear to leave a very substantial proportion of the poor, those who would be responsive to community development techniques.

Experiments With University Involvement

As a first test of this hypothesis, a seminar on neighborhood problems was developed in the fall of 1964 for a nearly defunct neighborhood organization in one of the poorer areas of Milwaukee's ghetto. Held at a neighborhood church, its format followed that of the problem-centered workshop with participants determining their own interests and priorities. Besides providing initial leadership for both discussion and early attempts at organizational action, the university personnel also provided some of the emotional leadership of the group, generating enthusiasm and representing to the participants an image of them as people capable of planning and carrying out effective projects.

Early attempts to survey each family in the neighborhood and to hold block meetings proved ineffective. The seminar was used to analyze reasons for failures. The group did conduct a successful effort to increase the turn-out of ghetto voters for a school board election in which racial segregation was a key issue. A grievance committee concerned with property problems developed sophistication with respect to the details of the building code and enforcement procedures and skill in dealing with personnel in the health and building departments and in tracking down owners through the Department of Deeds and Records. As a result of their work, some absentee-owned houses were torn down and others were improved.

Though the members became a more effective group, they failed to expand the membership or their range of activities. In part, this reflects the preoccupation of some of its more active members and leaders with the development of a separate and much larger organization that subsequently produced, directly or indirectly, rehabilitation work on nearly a hundred homes in the area, had about one hundred members with a sizable active core, attempted to obtain public funding for its projects, initiated a large summer program for youth in its 20-block area, conducted several large cleanup campaigns, sought to develop a tenant program, and attempted to encourage new multi-unit residential development. Occasionally its tactics resembled those of the social action–social protest type of organization, as when members "decorated" the exterior of city hall with rats caught and killed during a cleanup campaign. But most of the time its methods have reflected the "respectable" character of the majority of its members, many of whom are ghetto homeowners, and its temporary tie-in with a private developer. It has since diminished in size and activity, and its active core is now seeking to revive its thrust along more reformist and less property-oriented lines.

The next year (1965-1966) the same educational and training procedures were used with a much larger group of participants: 35 representing eleven already existing block, community, and special interest groups of inner city resident, some poor and some not poor at all. The results were quite mixed. A majority of the participants represented property preservation and improvement associations and remained very cautious about either expanding their purposes or utilizing new techniques of action.

However, a subgroup concerned with the problems of youth, whose members were mainly women and who were from or close to impoverished families, undertook two effective projects. The first involved a six-lane arterial, constructed to carry traffic from the temporary terminus of an incomplete expressway into the downtown area, running directly in front of a public housing project whose children must cross the arterial to get to school. The participants, after careful investigation followed by fruitless petitions for a stoplight, decided to utilize direct action techniques, stopping traffic at the end of the school day and conducting the children across the arterial. Since this went beyond the kind of activity with which the university would normally be associated, the project ceased to be based in the seminar and was taken over by an organization of mothers in the housing project. After traffic was stopped twice a stoplight was installed at the corner nearest the project, accompanied by brief dedicatory remarks by the traffic engineer and the alderman for the ward. This "victory" in turn stimulated another neighborhood group to demand and demonstrate for an overpass for pedestrians, which was provided by the City at a cost of $36,000.

The subgroup on youth then turned its attention to the problems of children who could not study at home because of crowded conditions or other family difficulties. After studying and analyzing the situation, and the inadequacy of after-school study hall projects in institutional settings such as church basements, they obtained the use of livingroom space in 20 ghetto homes for over 100 children divided into small groups—three, four or five—and aided by volunteer college students.

These two experiments made it clear that a university could elicit and facilitate participation by the poor in both self-help and action projects, with certain limitations. First, unless a university is prepared to go far beyond even a liberal interpretation of its role as teacher, researcher, and demonstrator, there is a point at which the poor have to proceed through their own organizations independent of any formal ties with the university in order to carry out needed action. Second, while many of those in poverty areas who are not poor and who own property identify with the poor and will participate effectively in action projects clearly relevant to the problems of the impoverished, small improvement associations dominated by resident property-owners are likely to be quite limited in the extent to which they can expand and change either their purposes or their methods, and therefore provide the most easily recruited but least effective vehicle for university efforts to increase the participation of the poor themselves. Finally, the techniques just described probably would facilitate development of a fairly large organization of the poor, but this would require a much more substantial, continuing commitment of university resources.

Another experiment was conducted during 1966-1967 in Racine, Wisconsin, where the School of Education and the Department of Urban Affairs at UWM joined with the Racine Unified School District to create a year-long N.D.E.A. Institute for teachers of the disadvantaged. One project involved the development of more effective participation in school affairs by parents who are among the economically deprived. Active committees in six schools ranged from half a dozen to 15 members, but they drew upon and represented a much larger group; over 150 attended the one "mass meeting" called, in spite of the fact that it was the evening of the February blizzard that buried Chicago and severely affected Racine. The committees developed lines of inquiry and action to affect school practices in the areas of report cards, homework, and discipline. It remains to be seen how successful they will be in achieving their initial objectives and whether or not this organization of inner city parents will persist without continuing university staff support.

These small efforts may be contrasted with that undertaken at Syracuse University under the leadership and direction of Dr. Warren Haggstrom. (The following account is based on documents from the Syracuse project, journalistic accounts, and data from local informants—both participants and bystanders. Every effort has been made to avoid gross errors in this necessarily brief and simplified report, but a definitive and authoritative report must come from Dr. Haggstrom.) An OEO demonstration, training, and research grant funded the Community Action Training Center in the School of Social Work as a vehicle to demonstrate that both social work and "war on poverty" goals could be achieved most effectively given development of means whereby the poor themselves could decide on needed forms of institutional change in the community and could bring about such change by social action–social protest, and to a lesser degree self-help, methods. Though Saul Alinsky served as consultant and lecturer for the CATC and Fred W. Ross, formerly West Coast director and long-time organizer for the IAF, became its field director, the CATC approach reflected a modification of Alinsky's tactics on the basis of Haggstrom's own theory and experience. At the outset alliances with other community institutions and groups were minimized, and the interests and involvement of the poorest of the poor were emphasized. To secure the developing organization's independence from possibly constraining university influences and interests, the Syracuse Community Development Association was created to stimulate the formation, development, and growth of "completely autonomous, self-directed, democratic" neighborhood organizations composed of persons in low-income areas. It also would seek to create an "equally autonomous, self-directed, democratic" overall organization that would be based upon the neighborhood organizations but also would include churches and other community organizations interested in the problems of low income persons. SCDA, with a board of trustees including professionals and clergymen that could solicit and administer funds but could exercise no control over decisions by individual organizations, was to carry out the organizing in the community while the CATC trained professional organizers and carried on the related research. Since their respective staffs were essentially the same persons, the legal distinction between the two was often considered irrelevant by the community, the rest of the university, the federal government, and even those within the project.

Organizing focused on predominantly lower-income Negro neighborhoods, including four public housing projects. In the first month of organizing 115 house meetings were held, indicating the scale of the operation. These were followed by neighborhood meetings and the formation of six larger organizations, four in housing projects and two in residential neighborhoods. Committee structures were built up around problem areas identified by members. Later a joint action committee was formed as a step toward an "organization of organizations." Initial accomplishments were fairly typical of successful action groups: improvement of leases for public housing tenants, increased police protection, and accelerated and more extensive replacement of stoves and refrigerators. A voter registration campaign also was conducted throughout the inner city.

Two elements of the IAF version of social action–social protest organization were much in evidence in Syracuse. One was the focus on and intensification of issues which created or brought to the surface conflict between the poor and one or another of the institutional "establishments," with extensive use of such dramaturgical techniques as demonstrations, protest pamphleteering, and the like. The second was a close control over and manipulation of organizational decision-making by the professional organizers until such time as the members displayed the skill to win the victories needed for building organization and for their own "sociotherapy," for developing personal and group potency by the experience of wielding power in matters of real concern to them.

The reaction of the conservative larger community and of the political and institutional leadership, in particular, was predictable, intense, and effective. The local press mounted a campaign of hysterical red-baiting. The university administration experienced heavy pressure from conservative patrons and alumni, and the Syracuse project became a center of political controversy involving the OEO with local politicians, especially mayors, in a number of cities, who already held the CAP component of the "war on poverty" suspect. SCDA escalated its own militancy, launching a "people's War Council Against Poverty" and holding a "national convention of the poor." In the end both the university administration and the OEO capitulated to the pressures. Federal funding was denied to the SCDA unless they applied through the Syracuse Crusade for Opportunity, the political-welfare establishment's mechanism for developing and controlling OEO-funded projects in Syracuse. Though some funds were temporarily continued for the CATC's training and research component, it was clear that it would not be carried on in the form and with the spirit Haggstrom originally had created.

However, the neighborhood organizations and an Organization of Organizations continue to function in Syracuse, and the latter is obtaining some private funding. Moreover, former CATC staff moved into the positions of executive director and director of field operations in the Crusade for Opportunity, and a Crusade membership meeting in January, 1967, produced a "floor rebellion" through which representatives of the poor gained 60 per cent of the seats on the Crusade's board of directors. The battles which once raged between it and the CATC-SCDA are now being waged within the crusade organization and between it and the business-welfare establishment (Senate Subcommittee on Employment, Manpower, and Poverty, 1967a). While the final outcome is uncertain, it is clear that the use of social action–social protest techniques have produced organizations of the poor and a substantial and sustained increase in political participation by the poor. It is equally clear that for political reasons most universities may not be able to provide a base from which to launch and maintain such efforts. Nevertheless, the School of Social Welfare at the University of California, Berkeley, has established an Urban Community Development Center in Oakland for relatively autonomous organizing work among the poor.

MORE ACTION AND FURTHER INTERPRETATION

Because some successful efforts by organizers using the social action–social protest model (Haggstrom in Syracuse, IAF in Chicago and Rochester, and the like) have received so much publicity, there has been a tendency, as Frank Riessman has pointed out, to overlook the failures produced by this approach. Perhaps more important is the failure of both theorists and policy-makers to be adequately cognizant of successes achieved by others whose programs and projects are much more oriented to the community development model. Two examples will provide the basis for some concluding argument about the possibilities of greatly enlarging the participation of the poor, about who can carry this out, and about what "maximum feasible participation" may best be understood to mean.

Northcott Neighborhood House, a settlement house originally located in a public housing project in the poorest section of Milwaukee's Negro ghetto, provided the base from which its director, Lucius Walker, Jr., developed a "grass-roots" community organization. (This account is based on information provided by Mr. Walker, others on his staff, and participant observers.) Under his direction, staff contacted residents of the area wherever they could find them, including in taverns and pool halls. After building up a sense of trust and identity with the residents, the staff then involved them in formulation of agency programs and subsequently in service on the board of the agency itself. In September, 1964, the board approved a program for an extensive community organization effort in the deeply impoverished inner area of the Negro ghetto. A residents' poverty advisory council was created for Northcott, and under Walker's direction its eight members read and discussed background literature such as Harrington's *The Other American* and May's *The Wasted Americans*. They also studied carefully and in detail the Economic Opportunity Act itself.

At this time, OEO-funded programs were being developed in Milwaukee without any meaningful participation by the poor. After two months of such study, the council contacted half a dozen existing neighborhood associations in the area, presented what they had learned, and on the basis of initial reactions went on to create an "Organization of Organizations" made up of 21 neighborhood associations. "Triple O" then challenged the existing set-up for administering federal antipoverty funds. Its public campaign opened in June, 1965, with a representative of Triple O being ejected from a meeting of the Social Development Commission, an agency designed by the mayor of Milwaukee to engage in social welfare planning for the metropolitan area that subsequently had been accepted by OEO as the umbrella organization to screen proposals for antipoverty funds in Milwaukee County. At this time its membership included two representatives each from the city government, the county government, the school board, the vocational school board, and the united fund organization. Triple O's campaign ended more than a year later with the SDC enlarged to include seven representatives of the poor, two from organized labor, and two from the clergy. Prior to this a compromise strategy by SDC produced a 35-man "Economic Opportunity Board" with broad community representation, including 16 residents of poverty areas. The EOB screened proposals to OEO but the SDC retained veto power over its decisions. Now the only veto power rests with the governmental bodies at city and county level.

Throughout this campaign the professionals in Triple O concentrated on sustaining and building alliances with sympathetic groups throughout the community at the same time that they continued their organizational efforts in the ghetto. These allies were helpful when Triple O's case was carried to the regional and national offices of the OEO, and aided in soliciting support from Congressmen and Senators in the face of bitter opposition by the mayor. A number of leaders came from existing neighborhood organizations, but few were from the civil rights and school segregation protest organizations. Although mass rallies were held, the rhetoric of the campaign was relatively restrained and a generally sympathetic press developed. The SDC itself split when several of its leading members, who were acquiring some respect for the representatives of the poor with whom they dealt, opposed a final ploy by the mayor to have the representatives of the poor named by a "recruitment and certification board" made up of heads of agencies that deal with poverty problems. Subsequently the mayor created a means for as graceful a retreat as possible by the appointment of a "select committee" to study the reorganization of the SDC.

The member organizations of Triple O at one time increased to over 60. Proposals for action projects most often originated with either individuals or member organizations. A variety of efforts, many fairly successful, dealt with problems involving management of housing projects, law enforcement, retail business practices, and welfare agency services. But no major change in ghetto conditions has been accomplished.

At first most of the continuing work of Triple O was handled by a steering committee that met once a week and referred its decisions to the body of delegates, which met once every two weeks. When the delegate group became increasingly apathetic and inclined to rubber-stamp the work of the steering committee, the latter was abolished and weekly delegate meetings (usually attended by 35 to 40 people) were used to shape all decisions and handle all business, however complex. Indigenous leaders increasingly related to Northcott's professional staff only for technical assistance and eventually broke with them altogether over strategies for the use and administration of a $36,500 grant from OEO to expand community organization and further develop indigenous leadership among the poor of the ghetto. Northcott remains a delegate agency only for funding purposes and Triple O has shown little capacity for further innovation and major growth "on its own."

It is clear that in Milwaukee the role of the poor in decision-making relevant to them was transformed from passivity and powerlessness to increasing participation in less than two years. Throughout that period Triple O emphasized the development of relevant knowledge among its leaders and the increase of their operational skills, while seeking all possible allies on each separate project or campaign, working with and through established agencies whenever possible. They avoided rhetoric and tactics that would force others, who might at times be allies, to take a permanent position "for or agin'." It remains to be seen how well the organization will function having demanded and achieved full independence from the professional organizers who did so much to create it. Its more recent drift toward the social action–social protest mode and style has been accompanied by greater internal bickering and less rather than more participation from the neighborhoods.

Another example of the success of community development techniques can be found in the "hollows" around Charleston, West Virginia. (Most data for this account were obtained from AAY–CD staff, especially Mr. Gary Wilson.) There the Action for Appalachian Youth–Community Development agency has helped to bring into effective existence 18 community associations. The individual and collective activities of these organizations of the poor (including some of the poorest of American poor) have ranged all the way from independent self-help projects such as construction of recreation areas and repair of roads, through establishing an agricultural producers cooperative and—with the AAY–CD as the institutional vehicle—area centers for welfare services, to mass picketing and protest marches outside of the building housing the state road commission. However, the militant actions have been undertaken only after a substantial period of organizational development, not as part of the initial building up of the organizations; and such militancy subsides with the individual issue. The creation of these organizations followed the community development model even more closely than did the initiation and expansion of Triple O in Milwaukee.

AAY–CD's first organizers were bright college graduates who, though middle class, evidenced real concern for the problem of poverty and a capacity for relating to people in the field. Their in-service training program emphasized the special problems of Appalachia along with classical community development procedures. An organizer would spend six weeks or more getting to know the people in a hollow; trying to assemble the needs they felt, which he helped them articulate, into some sense of community rather than individual problems, keeping the focus on problems; and holding off from action or even organization until enough of them seemed ready to move effectively in this way. Thus, joint meetings of households would eventually produce a committee or larger group to work on a specific problem; typically, by three months or so after organizing started, a number of such committees would be meeting. Since these separate committees frequently represented not only different projects, but also differences in kinship, political affiliation, or church membership, combining these committees into a single organization for the hollow was often not only the next, but also the most critical, step to be taken. Legal considerations inevitably required incorporation, which in turn led to more formal organization and thence to programs to train the officers and to develop needed but new forms of organizational support among their constituents. County-wide training sessions were developed for each office, which both prevented domination by the professional organizer and aided in building connections between individual community organizations.

Most of the hollows repeated past efforts to obtain action on what for them were their most pressing problems: roads, which mean access to stores, jobs, and even the mail; and school assignments and busing arrangements for their children. A first year of failures was experienced by most of the hollows, which generated, not apathy and despair, but increasing hostility toward the refractory governmental bodies and increasing readiness to undertake new and more militant techniques for the first time. The push in this direction came from school-age children and youth who had been in Appalachian Freedom Schools, on the one hand, and from those who had been the most apathetic previously, the adults over 45, who compared their efforts much more to union models (the Mineworkers) than to the civil rights movement. The separate community organizations have begun to support each other in these efforts, and the AAY–CD encourages and facilitates all possibilities for intercommunity cooperation and organization, spreading projects developed in one hollow to the others and promoting joint meetings, committees, and the like.

There is every reason to believe that the success of these 18 functioning community organizations will continue. There are signs that, having largely overcome the sometimes deep cleavage between the employed and the welfare families within each hollow (along with political, religious, and kinship factionalism), they might be able to begin building genuine bridges of associational cooperation between the Negro and white poor in the Charleston area. And they are increasingly trying to act as change agents for welfare, school, and government institutions. While the organizations' projects grow very slowly in scope and sophistication, the AAY–CD continues to seek and utilize whatever support it can obtain for each project from any and all sources. In spite of militant actions against "the establishment," the agency works with the authorities in all ways possible, keeps its political fences in as good repair as it can, and obtains at least small amounts of funds or other material support from the local united fund as well as from both county and federal levels of government.

On the other hand, lack of funds remains a critical problem, and along with the preoccupation with the neighborhood unit this has produced a program lacking in breadth, scope, and innovative thrust. The establishment of area centers by OEO fiat, short-circuiting the traditional community development process, has elicited participation mainly from the non-poor of the hollows (Subcommittee on Employment, Manpower, and Poverty, 1967b).

These two examples make it clear that the kinds of organization and consequent gains advocated by proponents of the social action–social protest model can in large part be obtained by strategies and tactics derived from or compatible with classical community development techniques. The place of conflict and related, dramatic actions in the developmental sequence clearly is different. Conflict itself is more a consequence and less a means, and polarization of the larger community is avoided whenever and wherever possible. This, we suspect, makes the long-range prospects for successful organizations of the poor created through community development more hopeful than those created through social action–social protest strategies. For once the various institutional establishments have "contained" the latter, which they have been able to do in every case, further major gains then require overcoming exactly those new barriers or shifting into new areas and modes of action. Thus, the Woodlawn Organization (TWO) in Chicago, as it seeks to develop programs dealing with job training and employment and with education, looks more and more like organizations oriented to community development, especially since the latter also may and do use militant tactics to deal with situations of unavoidable conflict with the managers of the community *status quo*. But it also must be kept in mind that community development strategies also have failed to produce large scale organizations militant and effective enough to achieve substantial changes in local institutions rather than staying at the level of "successful" projects.

SOME CONCLUDING THOUGHTS ON "FEASIBLE" AND "MAXIMUM"

The evidence presented thus far would seem to indicate that a good many of the poor in both urban and rural settings can participate extensively and effectively in organizations and activities directly relevant to shaping and administering the "war against poverty." Other changes in their place in the social structure are not necessary antecedents of such participation, any more than upward mobility necessarily produces middle class activists. If there is a "culture of poverty" that constrains political participation, then many of the people of the hollows and the ghettos seem able to move out of it with alacrity given effective efforts to bring them within the influence of either social action–social protest or community development organizations. Indeed, one would doubt that attitudes and patterns of overt behavior that are so poorly "rooted" deserve the name of "culture" at all (Gans, 1967).

We may, therefore, dismiss change of status as a prerequisite for political participation where many of the poor are concerned. At present one cannot, of course, assert that it is not prerequisite for some. But one could just as well assert that being forced into downward mobility is a "prerequisite" for bringing some middle class people into political activity, as was the case during the depression of the 1930s. The question is not how to bring *all* of the poor into participatory roles, but how to fill such roles with a large enough number of the poor that they are "overrepresented" in decision-making to the degree necessary to enable a distressed minority to have much greater impact on decisions affecting its welfare than its numbers and wealth would otherwise make possible in our political system.

It also seems possible to reject with confidence any assertion that a large proportion of the poor can be brought into effective action only by the strategy and tactics of the social action–social protest approach, or that there is some major segment of the poor, such as the very poorest or impoverished Negroes, who can be reached and activated only in this manner. Such "sociotherapeutic" experience may indeed be essential for certain individuals among the poor, or at least will work best in recruiting them. But this also is probably true of the non-poor. The white middle class citizen whose political alienation and apathy are in part rooted in a sense of powerlessness, even though it has not been attended by material deprivation, also is probably the sort of person who may be activated by conflict-oriented organizations and movements that provide a maximum of dramaturgical accompaniment for actions taken, such as antifluoridation campaigns and extreme right-wing associations.

While the techniques used by IAF organizers and by Haggstrom in Syracuse may indeed recruit some individuals who otherwise would not be drawn into an association and its efforts, it seems likely that they also serve to keep some out. Perhaps more important, by polarizing the community and hardening the opposition to the movement and the organization, they may actually diminish the number of decision-making roles in community structures into which the poor can move, at least relative to the number that would be made available by techniques and developmental sequences such as those employed by Triple O in Milwaukee and AAY–CD in the Charleston area. But this must not be read as a prescription for avoiding militancy and conflict. Any such conservative and "neutralist" version of community development doctrine generally will neither maximize the participation of the poor nor produce needed institutional change.

In short, a realistic and meaningful interpretation of "maximum feasible" must rest upon some theoretical and practical judgments about, not only how many of the poor can be motivated to seek participation and can become competent in political action, but also how much room those who manage the establishments can be made to yield to them given various types of pressure. To believe that maximum gains will accrue to strategies that maximize resistance may be quite romantic. It is equally unrealistic to assume that maximum resistance already pre-exists any and all efforts by the poor wherever they may be located, as it pre-exists efforts by Negroes in some of the areas of the "deep south," thereby justifying social action–social protest strategies and tactics from the outset. Initial use of organizational procedures which maximize conflict and the dramaturgy of conflict, thereby maximizing resistance, may all too easily create the situation of the self-confirming hypothesis. The community development approach has the advantage of first testing for and seeking to locate and utilize all the "give" and "open spots" in the existing structure of decision-making, saving the more militant, conflict-oriented, expressive techniques for those times and places where the existence of a pre-existant and implacable opposition has been clearly ascertained. At the same time, it is clear that a doctrinaire refusal to engage in the building of militant protest groups and even mass movements may very well prevent organizations of the poor from moving past small-scale projects toward instigating major institutional change.

Organizers oriented to both models have demonstrated beyond any doubt whatever that participation by the poor can be substantially increased. How large a cadre of activists can be built up among the poor is a question which can be answered with assurance only by empirical demonstration. One thing is clear: we will never know what "maximum" might be unless there is a maximum effort to find out. Thus far, pitifully few resources have been devoted to activating the poor to participate in the "war on poverty."

Many different agencies and institutions could and ought to be involved. Every university should devote an increasing proportion of its extension resources to enabling the poor to perceive and articulate their needs more effectively and to the development of relevant competences among them. Every welfare agency, private and public, should utilize the participation of the poor in all ways possible—as non-professionals, in "third force" agencies such as Frank Riessman has sought to create, on advisory and evaluative committees (when they are authentic and not spurious facades), and so on. All such efforts can add to and benefit from vigorous and continuing efforts to develop relevant, independent, large-scale organizations of the poor themselves—both through community development techniques and through conflict-oriented protest movements where they are pragmatically requisite. In the absence of such organizations other contributions are likely to exercise only a vernier adjustment on the existing low level and often ineffective participation by the poor. Only if all of these approaches are used in concert will we have maximized the possibility of achieving that "overrepresentation" of the poor in community decision-making necessary for a new measure of social justice and political democracy in our cities and hinterlands.

Appendix

THE NORTHTOWN-A SURVEY

FOR THE SURVEY of Northtown-A a random cluster sampling procedure was used with the household as the sampling unit. Blocks were selected using census data and households were ascertained through use of the city directory. Letters were sent to household occupants prior to initial personal contact by interviewers, and the project was "legitimized" by publicity in local newspapers and on the radio. Interviewers varied hours of contact between 9:00 A.M. and 9:00 P.M., and respondents were selected within households to assure representativeness in terms of sex, age, and household status. When the respondent and the interviewer were of different races at the initial contact, an appointment was made for the interview itself and an interviewer of the same race as the respondent conducted the actual interview, a procedure employed for about 15 per cent of the completed interviews. Approximately 80 per cent of the initially designated sample clusters were represented in the 163 usable interviews.

Table A, based on census data, compares the census tracts of the Northtown-A area and, where possible, the area as a whole, with the city of Milwaukee.

Whether or not individuals perceived greater or lesser need for improvement in their neighborhoods was indexed by five questions: (1) In general, would you say that you are satisfied or dissatisfied with this neighborhood? (2) Are there any particular problems which you think are facing this neighborhood, or any changes which you think are needed around here? (3) Are you satisfied with the say you have about how things are run in the community, or do you wish you had more influence in community affairs? (4) In general, do you think this is a safe neighborhood to live in? (5) In general, do you think this is a good place to raise children?

Political competence was interpreted as relevant knowledge and experience in organizational activity. Respondents were asked: Who should someone go to if he wanted to get something done about (a) community services such as police or fire, (b) commercial and recreational services such as stores and restaurants, (c) political affairs and civil rights? Each correct answer was given a score of 1, so that three points could be gained for this type of knowledge. Respondents also were asked: Which of the following are elected by the people in Milwaukee? (a) Mayor's coordi-

TABLE A

Selected Characteristics of the City of Milwaukee and "Northtown-A"

(All entries are rounded percentages except median education)

	Race		Income: Family-1960						Residential Stability	Unskilled Employed		Unemployment			Divorced, Separated		Children Under 18	Education
	1950 Non-White	1960 Non-White	Under 3,999 All	Non-White	4,000-7,999 All	Non-White	Over 8,000 All	Non-White	In Home Less Than 7 Years	Male	Fe-male	Males White	Non-White	Fe-male All	Male	Fe-male	Not Living With Both Parents	Median for Persons 25 or Older
City of Milwaukee	4	8	17	40	50	46	33	15	60	13	20	4	12	5	4	5	12	10.4
Tract 30	79	88	48	47	48	49	4	4	69	24	62	0	13	9	18	21	30	8.7
Tract 34	8	62	42	44	45	43	13	13	73	15	33	7	10	12	9	13	20	8.9
Tract 35	41	87	39	38	46	48	15	14	67	27	51	4	15	11	12	18	33	8.5
Tract 53	9	73	39	38	43	43	18	19	67	25	45	10	10	12	9	12	28	8.9
Tract 33	3	47	37	45	43	40	20	15	67	18	26	6	10	15	6	10	20	8.7
Tract 54	0	53	27	24	50	52	23	25	64	18	41	4	10	18	6	9	30	9.7
Tract 60	0	12	27	30	49	50	24	20	55	19	25	5	9	2	3	6	15	9.5
Tract 55	0	14	23	—	54	—	22	—	58	19	30	6	—	4	3	6	15	9.5
Tract 61	0	1	17	—	54	—	29	—	54	14	20	5	—	3	3	5	12	9.5
Northtown-A	55	45	—	—	—	—	—	—	62	20	34	6	11	9	7	5	22	9.1

nator of economic development. (b) Alderman. (c) State assembly-man. (d) School board member. (e) City manager. Four or five correct answers yielded another point. A point was given for belonging to one or more organizations apart from neighborhood improvement and civic groups (used in index of participation), and another for holding office in one or more organizations. Thus, the competence index ranged from 0 to a possible 6.

Feelings of personal political efficacy were estimated by scoring from 0 to 5 for disagreements with the following statements: (1) People like yourself actually don't have any say about what government does. (2) Public officials don't care much about what you are thinking. (3) Voting is the only way you can have any say about how the government runs things. (4) Sometimes politics and government seem so complicated that a person can't really understand what's going on. (5) There's little use writing to public officials because they aren't really interested in your problems.

Belief in group potency was indexed by responses to the following items: People disagree about how much influence community groups— say, just ordinary groups of citizens—can have. Do you think such groups can do a great deal, something, or hardly anything at all about (a) improving the schools, (b) helping increase employment, (c) organizing a neighborhood cleanup campaign, (d) getting taxes lowered in Wisconsin, (e) getting stoplights or stopsigns installed around here, (f) changing the plans for location of a new expressway? These items were designed to represent a wide range of probable impact by "an ordinary group of citizens" and were so perceived by respondents. Scoring provided a possible range from 0 to 12.

Alienation was indexed by agreement or disagreement with four items that were among the six weighing most heavily into a factor (derived by factor analysis of 68 test statements) indicating resentment, apprehension, and feelings of rejection: (1) It's hardly fair to bring children into the world with the way things look for the future. (2) These days a person doesn't really know who he can count on. (3) Nowadays a person has to live pretty much for today, and let tomorrow take care of itself. (4) In spite of what some people say, the lot of the average man is getting worse, not better.

Whether or not people believe their feelings and judgments about community problems isolate them from other residents or constitute something they share with others, a sense of "commonness," was indicated by their response to this item: Which one of the following statements comes closest to your own sentiments? (a) I think I am pretty much alone in my way of thinking about problems in this community. (b) Although not alone, I feel that only a small minority of people think

TABLE B

	Perceived need score	Action score	Competence score	Political efficacy score	Group potency score	Alienation	Home ownership	Residence length	Desire to stay	Perceived "commonness"	Decision means	Adolescent influence	Feelings about complaining	Success of influence attempts	Race	Age	Education	Income	Financial aid
Action score	.33																		
Competence score	.20	.49																	
Political efficacy	.11	.10	.26																
Group potency	.12	.20	.23	.00															
Alienation	.03	.18	.32	.50	.08														
Home ownership	.13	.24	.19	-.05	.09	.02													
Residence length	.29	.24	.20	-.06	-.01	-.01	.46												
Desire to stay	.19	.09	-.06	.00	.07	.09	.07	.09											
Perceived "commonness"	-.06	.09	.00	-.07	-.05	-.15	.04	.01	.01										
Decision means	-.10	-.15	-.02	.13	-.06	.21	.04	.03	-.11	-.01									
Adolescent influence	-.01	.08	.03	.04	.22	-.04	.08	-.03	-.12	-.02	.11								
Feelings about complaining	-.04	.14	.01	.14	.17	.16	.01	-.04	-.02	-.00	.12	.51							
Success of influence attempts	-.09	.03	.01	.11	.07	-.02	.03	-.10	.02	-.12	-.10	-.02	.49						
Race	.13	.06	.07	.28	.30	.29	.16	.14	.11	.06	-.17	.06	.25	.55					
Age	.10	.01	.06	-.12	-.28	-.11	.22	.51	-.20	-.04	.09	-.04	-.14	.15	.20				
Education	.05	.17	.32	.36	.17	.45	-.09	-.09	.01	-.06	-.02	.27	.09	-.17	-.04	-.33			
Income	.07	.25	.33	.25	.15	.23	.28	.09	-.01	.03	-.12	.18	.01	.18	.27	.14	.24		
Financial aid	.01	-.20	-.06	-.04	-.15	-.16	.05	.18	-.23	-.19	.09	-.06	-.06	.13	-.14	.12	-.22	-.35	
Occupation	.18	.16	.13	.03	.10	.17	.03	.10	.03	-.16	-.14	.05	.06	.01	.01	.09	.30	.23	.05

the same way I do about problems in this community. (c) I feel that most people think the way I do about problems in this community. (d) I feel that just about everybody in this community thinks the way I do about its problems.

To see if there might be some fairly obvious linkage between present feelings of alienation or personal potency and earlier experience with family authority, respondents were asked what they recalled from when they were "growing up"—"when you were around 16"—about (a) influencing family decisions, (b) freedom to complain about decisions they disliked, and (c) effectiveness of any such complaints. Correlations among the three were fairly high—around .50—and each was tried separately against the other variables.

Desire to remain in the neighborhood was indicated simply by asking if the respondent would want to move assuming ability to rent or buy a house elsewhere. Orientation toward neighborhood decision-making was indexed by preference among the following as sources of decisions affecting the neighborhood: (a) a vote of people in the neighborhood, (b) neighborhood leaders, (c) experts in the field and/or the mayor and the common council.

The complete matrix of correlations is displayed in Table B. About 2 per cent of the respondents were in their 20s, 18 per cent in their 30s, 21 per cent in their 40s, 23 per cent in their 50s, 16 per cent in their 60s, and the remainder in their 70s and 80s. Of the 42 per cent whites, about 42 per cent were 60 or older, while only about 33 per cent of the Negroes were above 60. On the other hand, about 41 per cent of the whites had at least a high school education, compared with 30 per cent of the Negroes. Because so many of the older whites had low incomes, there was little correlation between income and race; about 20 per cent of the sample had annual incomes under $3,000, another 24 per cent between $3,000 and $4,999, and only about 22 per cent above $7,500. About 8 per cent were retired and about 12 per cent unemployed.

Tables C, D, and E (next page) display some of the alternative combinations of variables used as predictors of "action scores."

TABLE C

RELATIVE AND CUMULATIVE EFFECTIVENESS OF SIX VARIABLES
AS PREDICTORS OF ACTION SCORE

Variable	R^2	R
Competence	.25	.50
Felt need	.30	.55
Income	.31	.56
Group potency	.31	.56
Political efficacy	.32	.57
Race	.32	.57

TABLE D

RELATIVE AND CUMULATIVE EFFECTIVENESS OF SIX VARIABLES
AS PREDICTORS OF ACTION SCORE

Variable	R^2	R
Felt need	.11	.33
Income	.17	.41
Assistance	.25	.50
Education	.27	.52
Age	.28	.53
Race	.29	.54

TABLE E

RELATIVE AND CUMULATIVE EFFECTIVENESS OF EIGHT VARIABLES
AS PREDICTORS OF ACTION SCORE

Variable	R^2	R
Felt need	.11	.33
Income	.17	.41
Desire to stay	.19	.44
Home ownership	.20	.45
Residence length	.21	.46
Age	.22	.47
Race	.22	.47

References

ALINSKY, SAUL. *Reveille for Radicals* (Chicago: University of Chicago Press, 1946).

——. "From Citizen Apathy to Participation," paper presented at the Sixth Annual Fall Conference, Association of Community Councils of Chicago, October 19, 1957 (Chicago: Industrial Areas Foundation, 1957).

——. "Citizen Participation and Community Organization in Planning and Urban Renewal," paper presented to Chicago Chapter of the National Association of Housing and Redevelopment Officials, January 29, 1962 (Chicago: Industrial Areas Foundation, 1962).

—— with MARION K. SANDERS. "The Professional Radical," *Harper's*, 230 (June, 1965a), pp. 37-47.

—— with ——. "A Professional Radical Moves in on Rochester," *Harper's*, 231 (July, 1965b), pp. 22-29.

ANDERSON, PATRICK. "Making Trouble is Alinsky's Business," *New York Times Magazine*, 6 (October 9, 1966), p. 28.

BLOOMBERG, WARNER, JR. "Community Organization," in Howard S. Becker (ed.), *Social Problems: A Modern Approach* (New York, John Wiley & Sons, 1966), pp. 387-90.

DAHL, ROBERT A. *Who Governs?* (New Haven: Yale University Press, 1961).

GANS, HERBERT J. "Poverty and Culture: Some Basic Questions About Methods of Studying Life-Styles of the Poor," paper presented to the International Seminar on Poverty, University of Essex, England, April 3-6, 1967. (Mimeograph.)

GOODMAN, PERCIVAL, and PAUL GOODMAN. *Communitas: Means of Livelihood and Ways of Life* (rev. ed.; New York: Random House Vintage Books, 1960).

GRAHAM, ELINOR. "The Politics of Poverty" and "Poverty and the Legislative Process," in Ben B. Seligman (ed.), *Poverty as a Public Issue* (New York: Free Press, 1965), pp. 231-71.

HAGGSTROM, WARREN C. "The Power of the Poor," in F. Riessman, J. Cohen, and A. Pearl (eds.), *Mental Health of the Poor* (New York: Free Press, 1964), pp. 205-23.

HAWORTH, LAWRENCE. *The Good City* (Bloomington, Indiana: Indiana University Press, 1963).

KING, CLARENCE. *Working With People in Community Action* (New York: Association Press, 1965).

MILLER, S. M. "Politics, Race and Poverty," in Irving L. Horowitz (ed.), *The New Sociology* (New York: Oxford University Press, 1964a), pp. 290-312.

———. "The Politics of Poverty," *Dissent,* 2 (Spring, 1964b), pp. 212-18.

——— and MARTIN REIN. "The War on Poverty: Perspectives and Prospects," in Ben B. Seligman (ed.), *Poverty as a Public Issue* (New York: Free Press, 1965), pp. 311-16.

——— and ———. "Poverty, Inequality, and Policy," in Howard S. Becker (ed.), *Social Problems: A Modern Approach* (New York: John Wiley & Sons, 1966), p. 426-516.

MORGAN, JAMES N., M. H. DAVID, W. J. COHEN, and H. E. BRAZER. *Income and Welfare in the United States* (New York: McGraw-Hill, 1962).

RIESSMAN, FRANK. "A Comparison of Two Social Action Approaches: Saul Alinsky and the New Student Left," unpublished manuscript. (Mimeographed, 1965.)

———. "Self-Help Among the Poor: New Styles of Social Action," *Transaction* (September/October, 1966), pp. 32-37.

ROSS, MURRAY G. *Community Organization* (2nd ed.; New York: Harper & Row, 1967).

SOKOL, PHILIP. "Providing for the Dependent," in R. M. MacIver (ed.), *The Assault on Poverty: and Individual Responsibility* (New York: Harper & Row, 1965), pp. 9-19.

SUBCOMMITTEE ON EMPLOYMENT, MANPOWER, AND POVERTY OF THE COMMITTEE ON LABOR AND PUBLIC WELFARE, UNITED STATES SENATE. "The Community Action Program in Syracuse, New York," *Examination of the War on Poverty: Community Action Program—Vol. IV* (Washington, D. C.: U. S. Government Printing Office, 1967a), pp. 988-1005.

———. "Report on the Community Action Program of Charleston-Kanawha County, West Virginia," *Examination of the War on Poverty: Community Action Program—Vol. V* (Washington, D. C.: U. S. Government Printing Office, 1967b), pp. 1325-81.

TAYLOR, CARL C. "Community Development Programs and Methods," *Community Development Review,* International Cooperation Administration, Washington, D. C., No. 2 (December, 1956), pp. 34-42.

UNITED NATIONS. *Social Progress Through Community Development* (New York: United Nations, 1955).

WAKEFIELD, DAN. *Revolt in the South* (New York: Grove Press, 1960).

ZEISEL, JOSEPH. "A Profile of Unemployment," in Stanley Lebergott (ed.), *Men Without Work* (Englewood Cliffs, N. J.: Prentice-Hall, 1964), pp. 115-29.

12

The Poor In Urban Africa

A Prologue To Modernization, Conflict, And The Unfinished Revolution

PETER C. W. GUTKIND

Tell the world that the unemployed are in real want.
I have nothing to eat, no house and no clothes.
This life is punishment to me.

(*Daily Telegraph* [Lagos], May 20, 1966).

☐ IT IS, I THINK, FALSE TO ASSUME that change and modernization are contingent upon urbanization and industrialization. The preconditions for modernization seem to depend heavily on "The Will to be Modern," a gradual or sudden rejection of the *ancien régime*.

AUTHOR'S NOTE: *The research on which this paper is based was carried out between May and October, 1966 and supported with grants from the following: The Canada Council, The Wenner-Gren Foundation for Anthropological Research, The Social Science Research Council (USA), The Research Fund from the Social Science and Humanities Division, McGill University and the Centre for Developing Area-Studies, McGill University. The views expressed in this paper are wholly those of the author and are not endorsed by any of the above named organizations. Invaluable comments were received from Professors Robert Armstrong, Oniteri, and members of the staff of the Nigerian Institute of Social and*

In this manner modernity means to be scientific, to achieve change through rational and dynamic ideas. For traditional societies which are thus changing, modernization results in a shift of political power to those new political groupings which, in the eyes of their members, can obtain for them new demands (Blanksten, 1963). Of course, in some special cases, modernization has been brought about by the consolidation of traditional or neo-traditional sources of political organization and power (Apter, 1960; Apter, 1961). In such instances a traditional political elite has been helped along by a colonial system which favors the retention of a king or chiefs while it tries at the same time to adapt their functions to modern conditions. However, whether it is a question of continuity over time or a radical break with the past, almost everywhere in Africa change and modernization are being expressed in terms of the involvement of an ever larger number of people in the political process (Almond and Coleman, 1960; Finkle and Gable, 1966). Yet, it would restrict our analysis of modernization considerably if we viewed this great transformation entirely as a shift of political power, although this has been, no doubt, the most obvious facet to the outsider. We must not ignore an equally important aspect of change and modernization which is found in the realignment and the restructuring of the social position of individuals and groups as evidenced by their occupational and social mobility, or lack of it.

Modernization, both as a process and an ideology, seems to manifest itself in a vastly increased range of new choices confronting individuals (Apter, 1965, p. 10) and in the chance to sever old

Economic Research, Ibadan University. In Lagos I had the benefit of constant consultation with Professor T. M. Yesufu and Senior Civil Servants of the (then) Federal Government of Nigeria. I am particularly grateful for the help rendered by the Officers in Charge of various Labour Exchanges both in Nigeria and Kenya. In the latter country I benefited greatly from my conversations with Dr. Peter Marris and members of the Institute of Development Studies, University College, Nairobi. I would like to thank Mr. A. T. Brough, Ministry of Economic Planning and Development, Government of Kenya, for his support, and the Senior Civil Servants of the Ministry of Labour for their guidance. Finally, much of the data were collected by my research assistants in Lagos, Mr. Adelosoye, Mr. Aralu and Mr. Nwobi, and in Nairobi, Mr. Waiyaki and Mr. Owur.

relations and forge new ones (Smelser, 1966; Mair, 1963). Thus, Apter suggests that modernization in non-industrial societies might be analyzed as "the transposition of certain roles . . . and the transposition of institutions supporting these roles." However, he adds that because "social organizations are more chaotic and confused . . . . politics become the mechanism of integration, and authority is the critical problem confronting the leaders." Thus, different roads to modernization lead to different patterns of authority expressed variously by different groups whose objectives and socio-economic and political base will vary considerably (Apter 1965, pp. 1-122; and Apter, 1964).

What changes a traditional society to a modernizing one? The immediate response to this question is that the range of agents, both internally and externally generated, is so vast that no single factor analysis could ever provide a satisfactory explanation of an inherently very complex set of processes and events. Clearly much depends on who the "modernizers" are, what their position is (or will be) in the total fabric of national life, what their "ideology" of modernization is, and how they expect to effect change. Yet our minds immediately turn to the "elites" and to the youth of the new nations as spearheading the drive to change and modernize (Apter, 1964, pp. 28-30). But it is false to assume that only the privileged elites or those with some secondary or primary education are spearheading the agitation, the demands, and the welter of ideas— all of which contribute to political uncertainty and create the foundations of incipient revolution, apparently the main consequences of the de-colonization era. As the national life of the new nations of Africa and the older countries of Latin America becomes more differentiated, and as individuals and groups are torn ever more from their traditional economic, social, and political moorings, their actions and ideas are not marked by any large measure of consensus on how the good life is to be achieved. While the elites have consolidated their power, new groupings have arisen at a lower level of the social order. The foothold of the latter, however, is less secure, their loyalties are undergoing change, and they are exposed to all the complexities and iniquities inherent in the transition from kin-based and small scale societies to a larger national unit held together in a most precarious manner (Blanksten, 1963).

FACTORS AFFECTING POLITICAL AND SOCIAL DEVELOPMENT

Today, every newly independent African nation, whatever its political structure and ideology, and whatever its economic foundation, finds itself in the tight grip of the imbalance between its resources, its limited technical and administrative skills, and the demands of its people who are determined to find new means of earning a living. Our understanding of the implications of these conditions has, thus far, been limited because we appear to have basically underestimated the consequences of several important factors which have a direct bearing on the possible course of political and social development in Africa.

The first underestimation relates to the fact that most African nations are faced with the pressure of meeting the basic subsistence needs of their growing populations. Seen in terms of a ratio between population and suitable agricultural land (if not of high quality), a good many African countries are indeed "underpopulated." Given the possibility of some changes in agricultural productivity, coupled with measures to arrest erosion and to extend irrigation and the use of fertilizers, many of them could, if they considered this to be the path of their development, find room for their increasing populations. But the question is not whether a country suffers from over or under population, nor whether a "Back to the Land" movement holds any real promise for the future—which, in my view, it does not—it is that even a relatively small population makes demands which few African governments are able at present to meet.

Whatever the projected or the actual rate of economic growth, if the picture is seen in the context of political and economic agitation and demands, we might conclude that most African governments, given minimal resources and their intelligent use, would be better able to close the gap between expectations and available resources when dealing with a smaller rather than a larger population. The truth is that the present generation of unemployed and underemployed in virtually all of the new African states has little or no prospect of obtaining regular work in either agriculture or in manufacturing or industry. The outlook for future generations is even bleaker. Although it is true that 100 years ago in Europe and North America an upward birthrate was considered vital to radical economic transformation based on labor intensive methods, today the evolution of technology has put an end to such a strategy (Dumont, 1966).

Second, we have underestimated the consequences of the technological revolution for all the low-income and newly independent countries whether in Africa, Asia, or Latin America (Edgren, 1965). We normally do not associate this revolution with non-Western states which are still predominantly agricultural and where industrialization and urbanization are still minimal. However, whatever the ideology of development, i.e. how an African government intends to diversify the economy of its nation, there is no turning back the clock. The African economies are now more than ever part and parcel of a world network of trade dominated by the economically powerful who expect to exchange their produce under highly competitive conditions. This presents the African nations with a clear challenge to produce their own products in the most competitive manner possible, that is, through the utilization of the most competitive technology both in agriculture and industry. Labor intensive methods are not generally geared to the reduction of the cost of units produced. For example, the Minister of Works, Communication, and Power of the government of Kenya told the House that his Ministry was not considering building more roads with hand labor because the cost was more than double that of using machines (*East African Standard* [Nairobi], November 14, 1963).

Although a number of African governments have given emphasis to and experimented with extensive labor utilization, the results have generally not been successful. It is true that small-scale cash crop farming and certain plantation economies (such as the tea and coffee industries) will continue to make extensive use of labor, but most developments point to the fact that employment opportunities in the future will be very limited. Productivity will increase, albeit slowly, but either with a reduced or non-expanding labor force. Copper production in Zambia, to cite one example, rose approximately 11 per cent in 1964 while the mine labor force increased by only 2 per cent (Copper Industry Service Bureau, 1964).

In the non-agricultural sector employment opportunities even now are severely restricted. This situation is not the result of unwillingness to make use of the vast labor reservoir available in the towns but rather to the fact that primary and consumer commodities, to be competitive with imported products, must be produced in large quantities and in the cheapest possible way. Faced with such pressures, few governments can afford to turn their back on the extensive use of available technological innovations. These pressures are reinforced by the vital importance for national development of certain industries which are highly sensitive to the almost immediate utilization of technological innovations such as the building industry, public works, petro-chemical complexes, and the manufacture of many consumer commodities. To this we must also add that the construction and maintenance of such rapidly expanding public services as electric supplies and communication systems are subject to some of the most far-reaching technological achievements in the field of electronics (Ardant, 1963; Ardant, 1964; International Labour Organization, 1965). In short, the capacity to absorb labor in the non-agricultural sector is exceedingly limited whatever the speed of economic development and however diversified the economies are likely to be in their primary, secondary, and tertiary sectors.

Both Table 1 and Table 2 lend support to the observation that wage-earning employment has been unable to absorb the available manpower in virtually all sectors of the African economy. In fact, the Kenya data, as shown in the latter table, indicates quite clearly a decline of over 10 per cent of Africans in paid employment between 1960 and 1965.

The third underestimation, at least until very recently if judged by the belated appearance of literature on the subject, pertains to the consequences of the educational revolution, perhaps the most far-reaching of all the developments. This is a revolution which stands in direct relation to modernization, conflict, uncertainty, dependency, and the creation of such new groupings as the involuntary urban unemployed. Its impact is not to be measured solely in terms of improved literacy rates or classroom attendance. Were this the case, perhaps no more than 30 per cent of Africa's total population could be characterized as strongly influenced by the desire to break away from the past and seek a different life for themselves and their children. Rather, the educational revolution, as the evidence indicates, is taking place outside the classroom and in particular among those young people, mostly unschooled and hence unskilled, who have migrated to the towns.

TABLE 1

PERCENTAGE OF AFRICAN POPULATION IN WAGE-EARNING EMPLOYMENT
(Figures in parentheses are based on Unofficial Population Estimates)

	1948	1952	1957	1958	1959	1960	1961	1962
East Africa								
Kenya	7.4	7.6	7.7	7.2	7.1	7.1	6.6	6.3
Uganda	3.2	3.7	3.7	3.6	3.5	3.5	3.3	3.1
Tanganyika	5.3	5.6	4.5	4.4	4.4	4.6	4.5	4.3
Central Africa								
Zambia	9.1	12.0	9.4	8.9	8.3	7.9	7.3	7.0
Malawi	—	—	(6.1)	(6.0)	(5.7)	(5.4)	(5.1)	(4.6)
S. Rhodesia*	(17.2)	20.8	20.0	19.9	19.3	19.0	17.7	16.8
West Africa								
Nigeria	1.2	1.0	1.4	1.4	1.3	1.4	1.1	1.4
Ghana	(6.2)	(4.0)	(4.4)	(4.5)	(4.8)	4.9	5.0	4.9
Gabon	—	—	10.2	9.1	9.8	9.7	9.4	—
Cameroon	—	—	—	(3.4)	(3.2)	(2.5)	(2.6)	2.2

* Includes large numbers of Africans from neighboring territories.
SOURCE: ILO Year Book of Labour Statistics.

TABLE 2

NUMBERS IN PAID EMPLOYMENT, REPUBLIC OF KENYA, 1960-1965

(1964 = 100)

	1960	1961	1962	1963	1964	1965
Agriculture	130.5	121.0	117.9	105.5	100.0	100.6
Private Industry & Commerce	114.3	103.3	101.2	94.6	100.0	99.4
Public Service	92.9	96.1	96.1	90.6	100.0	102.5
African	112.7	106.5	105.3	96.2	100.0	101.1
Asian	111.0	109.9	104.9	106.7	100.0	97.8
European	151.0	145.1	129.4	115.7	100.0	93.8
Total Employment	113.7	107.8	105.9	97.4	100.0	100.7

SOURCE: Republic of Kenya, Economic Survey 1966, Nairobi, June, 1966, p. 60.

Formal education is not the only generator of new ideas and needs. The urbanite, of whatever length of residence and irrespective of his economic position, is thrown into a social situation which demands that he respond aggressively and competitively. His "reference model" stems from the demands of a money economy whereby he must offer his services in return for the rewards which the society holds out before him. Although some measure of formal education might make a migrant to the urban area more employable, this advantage is not invariably perceived by those with no qualifications whatever. The unskilled and the unemployed strongly believe that they are entitled to work and to earn a living in a more rewarding area than agriculture. Whether among men who have been to school or not, the view is widely held that opportunities are identified with non-agricultural activities (Chaplin, 1961; Fogg, 1965; Anderson, 1966; Koff, 1966; Heijnen, 1966; Griffiths, 1966), or that urban-based wage earning is an indispensible supplement to agricultural earnings (Elkan, 1960, pp. 75-96).

Thus, while we are now well acquainted with the problems faced by the unemployed primary and junior secondary school leavers in Africa (Callaway, 1962, pp. 220-38; Callaway, 1963, pp. 351-71; Kamoga, 1965, pp. 5-18; Christian Council of Kenya and the Christian Churches' Educational Association, 1966; Peil, 1966, pp. 7-16), it would be most unwise to assume that only those will protest whose education has brought them neither opportunities nor rewards. Both the schooled and the unskilled express a clear feeling of frustration, bitterness, and hostility. Both groups define their objective—to obtain rewarding work—in practically similar terms, although the unschooled see their position as even more hopeless than the primary school leaver in the never fulfilled search of white-collar employment. A large number of interviews, in Lagos (120) and Nairobi (120) during the summer of 1966, indicated that while those with a little education have refined their objectives somewhat more precisely and are less willing to lower their sights, the unschooled are by no means prepared to latch on to "opportunities" which they evaluate as being of limited worth. This attitude is characteristic of many young and unemployed men in Lagos. A response from one of them, selected at random, makes this very clear:

> Yakobo, an Ibibio from southeastern Nigeria, had left home three years ago. He was one of eleven children of whom only five had managed to obtain some primary education, but Yakobo was not one of them. Until he was seventeen he had helped his father look after his land. But he became dissatisfied and decided to join his oldest sister and her husband who were resident in Lagos. Soon after his arrival in Lagos he was lucky to find work as a labourer with the Municipal Council of the City of Lagos. He held this job for about eight months but then was dismissed by the foreman for, so he claims, not paying his "due" to him. Then followed a period of almost five months without work during which time he regis-

tered with the Employment Exchange and otherwise tried to find work by going from one factory gate to another in the industrial areas of Lagos. Finally he was lucky when he was offered work as a sweeper in a small factory. He claimed that he was actually reluctant to accept this work had it not been for the pressure from his sister and brother-in-law who were getting tired of having to look after him. His reluctance was based on the following view:

"Work like that [as a sweeper] does not help you to get better work. I have met many men who have done work like that and they are still doing this work. They will never do anything else. I think that I can do better than that. . . . I see all those here in Lagos who have been to school and who are waiting to get good work. I have not been to school and I cannot read or write but I think that I shall wait and not take another position like a sweeper because I would then always be a sweeper. . . . I think that those who have been to school are lucky and they know what they want. . . . Perhaps it is better to wait until I can get work which will give me a greater chance to earn more money. . . . There are other people who do not mind being sweepers or scavangers [i.e. night soil men] . . . As long as my sister does not tell me to leave her house I will stay here and try to find better work in an office as a messenger perhaps" (Gutkind, 1966).

Thus, modernization and change become linked to the search for a different and better life with greater and more rewarding opportunities. In this sense, modernization is not just a release from stultifying tradition. After all, tradition may mean relative security for an individual whereas modernization makes a man stand alone and seek his own salvation. The modern African state seems quite unable to help him in this quest.

SOME HISTORICAL PERSPECTIVES

The colonial governments, both in Nigeria and Kenya, had become aware of the problem of unemployment in the middle 1930s and certainly by the early 1940s. Thus, in 1935 "a test count was made of the unemployed in Lagos by a Committee appointed to inquire into the question of unemployment;" it found "3,944 persons registered as unemployed" (Federal Government of Nigeria, 1944). In 1942, the Annual Report of the Department of Labour, Nigeria, reported that "some unemployment remains in Lagos and other big towns" while the report for the year 1944 recorded that "though there are more men in paid employment than ever before there are also more unemployed men in the towns, who are being maintained by their friends and relations and who appear to be content to remain idle indefinitely waiting for jobs which may never materialize." The report went on to say:

> . . . unemployment due to people crowding into towns with no particular employment in view is a growing evil and it is unnecessary to emphasize the harm it does . . . if the unemployed remain unemployed for long they will tend to become unemployable, and to form discontented groups of useless hangers-on to society. They sever their connection with the country, but never succeed in establishing themselves in town (Federal Government of Nigeria, 1944, p. 5).

In Kenya, too, the Department of Labour reported in 1941 that the "number of idlers and unemployed in Nairobi is unduly large . . . the number of loafers is excessive, forming a problem which is in urgent need of attention" (Colony and Protectorate of Kenya, 1941, p. 3). Although a concern was expressed by the two labor departments in 1948, the Kenya report claimed that "there is little or no unemployment in Kenya in the accepted sense, i.e. involuntary. There is work for all who seek it" (Colony and Protectorate of Kenya, 1948, p. 7). Likewise the Nigerian report suggested

> From all parts of the country Labour Officers report that there is virtually no unemployment in the generally accepted sense of the term. This is easily understandable in the light of the fact . . . that regular wage-earning employment affects only a very small proportion of the total population. Another relevant circumstance is the cohesion of the Nigerian "family" unit, the good or bad fortune of each member of which is primarily the concern of the whole, as a result of which destitution and begging are almost unknown (Federal Government of Nigeria, 1950, p. 9).

Yet the latter report goes on to say that "nevertheless, comparatively small numbers of genuinely unemployed persons may be found in Lagos. . . ." and by the end of 1949 some 5,341 registrations were still outstanding at the main Lagos Employment Exchange (Federal Government of Nigeria, 1950, p. 9). The number of registrations had no doubt been kept down because of a Restriction Order passed in 1944 prohibiting employers from entering into contracts with persons with less than six months' residence in Lagos and other major towns. The Labour Department readily admitted the difficulties in enforcing this Order.

With the rescinding of the Restriction Order for Lagos in 1952, the registration of unemployed in the city rose from a total of 5,599 adults in March, 1952 to 19,263 fresh registrations of adults 12 months later. By March 1954, the number of new registrations for Lagos had risen to 27,644 adults and 5,221 juveniles. Commenting about the latter group in the Annual Report for 1953-1954 (and doing so for the first time), the Labour Department concluded that:

> . . . many young people seem prepared to wait indefinitely for a particular type of employment on which they have set their hearts (usually clerical) rather than accept any alternative. For this parents seem largely to blame. The unfortunate effects which are often produced by any extended period of unemployment, immediately following the end of a young person's school life are too often disregarded or minimised (Federal Government of Nigeria, 1953-1954, pp. 7-8).

The same theme is taken up again in the report for 1955-1956 but this time in more pressing terms:

> The increasing number of primary school leavers is beginning to create a problem. This is particularly so in the urban areas such as Lagos, where most of the school leavers have no agricultural background. It seems to be no answer to their employment problems therefore that there is always the alternative to "to go west" into agriculture (Federal Government of Nigeria, 1955-1956, p. 10).

In the same report the Labour Department also recognized (for the first time) that unemployment is somehow linked to the patterns of economic development and other policy changes. As it stated:

> Transitional unemployment has however become a feature accompanying the large development and constructional programmes throughout the Federation. The completion of a major work or the suspension of activity in another often heralds the disbanding of large numbers of employees. Thus the curtailment in January 1956 of development work by the Cameroons Development Corporation led to the dismissal of over 4,000 workers (Federal Government of Nigeria, 1955-1956, p. 10).

Other examples of employment setbacks were noted in subsequent years.

The problem of unemployment was, however, further aggravated by the immediate implementation of one of the recommendations of the Kaine Board of Inquiry that the Ogbette Coal Mine [in the Eastern Region of Nigeria] should gradually be closed down. Consequently the services of a further 1,700 workers, in addition to the 2,500 previously retrenched, were dispensed with (Government of Nigeria, Quarterly Review, Vol. 1, No. 1, 1960, p. 61).

Another important occurrence was the decision of many expatriate firms to withdraw from the retail trades, a decision which led to retrenchment of many workers. The introduction of new processes and the shortage of capital in some branches of industry were other causes of unemployment observed during the quarter (Government of Nigeria, Quarterly Review, Vol. 3, No. 5, 1962, p. 99).

In the period 1959-1960, the governments of both Kenya and Nigeria seem to have come to the recognition that they were faced with a serious problem. Thus, the Annual Report of the Kenya Department of Labour speaks of the fact that "throughout 1960 Labour supply was greatly in excess of demand, and it became clear that unemployment in the wage-earning sector of the economy was rapidly becoming a major problem" (Colony and Protectorate of Kenya, 1961, p. 3). Throughout Kenya (there were 28 Employment Exchanges by 1960) some 73,871 adult Africans (male and female) had applied for work but only 22,006 had been placed in employment.

Likewise, in Nigeria, the Annual Report for 1959-1960 observed:

> It seems however clear that unemployment, as opposed to underemployment (which tends to be characteristic of an under-developed economy) has now reached substantial proportions in towns. Retrenchment of workers . . . was mainly of persons who had for many years been in paid employment . . . The consequent problem of juvenile employment has now become acute, engaging the serious attention of the [then] four Governments of the Federation. . . . All the Employment Exchanges in Western Nigeria, for example, recorded increases in the number of unemployed persons during the year (Federal Government of Nigeria, 1963, pp. 5-6).

In June, 1959 the (then) Federal Nigerian Minister of Labour and Welfare referred to the "acute unemployment or rather underemployment in the capital city of Lagos and other towns [which] persists" (Government of Nigeria, Quarterly Review, Vol. 1, No. 1, 1960, p. 3); and in June, 1964 the Ministry of Labour reported that "with large numbers of illiterate, unemployed persons in and around the urban centers, the general problem of unemployment is assuming disturbing proportions, especially in the face of increasing numbers of primary and secondary school leavers" (Government of Nigeria, Quarterly Review, Vol. 1, No. 7, 1964, p. 81).

THE UNEMPLOYED IN LAGOS AND NAIROBI

Despite obvious concern, few African governments have any precise idea of how extensive unemployment is today, how the unemployed live, or what their political sentiments and attitudes are. Since the achievement of independence in many African countries, governments have attempted to get an idea of the measure and nature of unemployment, but what information they have obtained has generally been kept under lock and key. Some sample surveys indicate that from 10 to 35 per cent of the male population of most African towns with populations over 20,000 are classified as unemployed. Thus, in the Federal Territory of Lagos, with an estimated population of 600,000 in 1964, approximately 65,000 persons, almost all males, were said to be actively seeking employment although less than 10 per cent of them had registered at the Lagos Employment Exchange. When the very densely settled contiguous areas of Mushin, Shomulu, and Agege are added, we obtain a population total of over one million and an estimated percentage of urban-resident unemployed of approximately 22 per cent for the Federal Territory of Lagos and its surrounding peri-urban region. In Abeokuta, a town 50 miles north of Lagos with a population of approximately 125,000 people in 1963, it was estimated that 34.6 per cent of the male population over the age of 14 (the potential labor force) was unemployed, while in Kano, in 1963, with a population of 192,500, only 5.7 per cent of the potential force was said to be actively looking for work. In Zambia, although no precise data exist, observers have suggested that possibly as much as 40 per cent of the potential labor force resident in the copper mining towns are seeking employment. While copper productivity has greatly increased, the labor force has remained steady.

In Nairobi, where no recent sample surveys have been carried out, it is difficult to determine the exact extent of unemployment among the African residents (Segal, 1965, pp. 17-21). The East Africa Royal Commission Report, 1953-1955, concluded: "Taking the East African economy as a whole there is no evidence of unemployment as that is commonly understood." A few lines later it added in apparent contradiction: "It is known, however, that in urban areas persons who are in employment sometimes have to support friends and relatives who have come in search of work without succeeding in obtaining it," yet "the extent of actual unem-ployment and underemployment cannot be measured on the basis of the available data but there is general agreement that it is con-siderable" (East Africa Royal Commission, 1953-1955 Report, 1955, p. 147). In 1962, the Statistical Division of the Government of Kenya estimated that out of an African (and small Somali) popu-lation in Nairobi of 156,000, approximately 22,000 African males (about 14 per cent) over the age of 15 were seeking employment. By mid-1966, the African population was estimated at 164,000 and the numbers seeking employment was thought to stand at 26,000. However, the Nairobi case is a special situation as those seeking work also include large numbers of Africans, primarily Kikuyu, living in the rural areas outside of the city limits who come into the city almost daily in search of work but return in the late afternoon to their rural homesteads (Dalgleish, 1960, p. 20). A random sample survey of 100 men registered at the Nairobi Employ-ment Exchange, during August, 1966, revealed that 64 were Nairobi residents of more than nine months' duration and 36 had come from outside the city limits.

During the Tripartite Agreement in Kenya (1964-1965), which was designed to reduce unemployment by means of an agreement between government, the employers, and the trade unions (by which employment was to be increased 10 per cent in the private sector and 15 per cent in the public sector in return for a one year moratorium of wage increases and strikes), some 205,000 persons registered at Employment Exchanges, only about 10,000 of whom had previously been registered. The Agreement was effective from February, 1964 to April, 1965. During this time, some 55,821 per-sons (47,499 men and 8,322 women) registered in Nairobi. These registrations were drawn from residents within the city limits and the surrounding areas. However, two factors need to be taken into account. First, the extensive publicity given to the Tripartite Agreement resulted in the registration of many rural underemployed Africans; and second, it was estimated that approximately 20 per cent of those who registered were at the time in wage employment but did not reveal this information in the hope of obtaining better jobs (Government of Kenya, Manpower Branch, Ministry of Labour and Social Services, 1965, pp. 94-98).

Nevertheless, despite the absence of various statistical measures, it is virtually certain that the dimensions of unemployment will steadily increase when we take into account the high population growth (at least 2.5 per cent per annum both in Nigeria and Kenya —as of course elsewhere in Africa), and the ever larger number of African children who enter primary school and manage to successfully complete at least six or seven years of schooling. Thus, at the end of 1963, there were almost three million children in Nigeria's 15,090 primary schools, of whom 107,552 were in 126 such schools in the Federal Territory of Lagos. It has been estimated that there are approximately 500,000 primary school leavers per annum in Nigeria of whom no more than about 12 per cent will go on for further secondary education. While others continue in technical or secretarial schools and some find employment as apprentices (Callaway, 1964, pp. 1-18) in commerce, industry, the public services, and the civil service, at least 50 per cent of the primary school leavers (and increasingly also among the junior secondary leavers) look for work in the non-agricultural sector. As enrollment increases, probably at the rate of 10 per cent per year, the pool of unemployed school-leavers will rapidly increase particularly in view of the factors cited earlier.

In Kenya the situation, while on a somewhat smaller scale, is equally serious. In December, 1964, 103,400 children had completed primary school and taken the Kenya Preliminary Examination (KPE). Forty-six per cent continued in further education including technical and commercial schools (this figure also includes 25 per cent who repeated primary school in order to obtain higher passes), 6 per cent obtained wage employment, 12 per cent returned to work on the family farm or became self-employed, and 36 per cent were unable to find employment (of these, 26 per cent were rural residents without work and 10 per cent urban unemployed). In absolute numbers approximately 38,000 primary school leavers out of 103,400 could not be absorbed into the economy of the country as producers of commodities or services (Christian Council of Kenya, 1966, p. 95).

The statistical evidence while lacking in precision is, nevertheless, an indication of both the current position and, possibly, of future trends. Although almost every African government has attempted various schemes to reduce the level of unemployment few, if any, have succeeded with any measure of success. Thus, Youth Service Corps, Workers Brigades, Agricultural Settlement Schemes, and efforts to get young men back to the land have been started in many countries (Hodge, 1964, pp. 113-21). However, some governments have discovered that Youth Service Programmes have all the potential of becoming centers of competitive political and ethnic-centered power (Lloyd, 1967, p. 241). Some governments have opted for labor intensive measures in their public works projects (taking as their guide recent International Labour Organization studies) only to find that this approach is not competitive with capital intensive techniques. Preference has been given to the employment of primary school leavers whenever suitable vacancies have occurred. The political leaders have promised to bend their energies to create an economy which can absorb all available manpower and have championed the principle of the right to work. At the same time they have condemned laziness and the unwillingness of primary and secondary school leavers to work on the land (Nyerere, 1967, pp. 72-79).

THE POLITICAL DIMENSION: ASSOCIATIONS OF UNEMPLOYED

The study of new groupings and categories within the African population provides us with a point of departure for the analysis of economic, social, and political change. These new categories usually coalesce and crystallize into (new) politically-oriented interest groups which reflect the needs of people compelled to deal with new circumstances and the demands made by them for more equitable economic and social conditions. The way these new groups perform their political functions varies according to a wide variety of historical and contemporary circumstances. In most cases they operate in the context of incipient modernization while at the same time maintaining a major foothold in the traditional system.

This straddling position not infrequently makes the articulation of their various new functions, interests, and demands less effective because of their often uncertain multipurpose performances. Blanksten has suggested that such groupings express political loyalties which initially might produce a "central lack of political integration" in the plural societies which make up the new national states of Africa. Conflict almost invariably results between these "ascendant interests" and the traditional and established elites as a greater degree of socioeconomic differentiation and a greater specialization of functions materialize, a development which weakens the political power of some groups and increases that of others. Blanksten has skillfully described the conditions which determine positive or negative responses to the ascendant groups (1963).

ORGANIZATIONAL EFFORTS

The urban unemployed in Africa constitute one of the ascendant groups. To promote their interests they have at times attempted—mostly unsuccessfully thus far—to organize. The various associations which they have formed have as yet been able to do little to advance the interests of their membership. Most of them have lacked skilled and powerful leadership and have been torn by internal dissension. Because of this inability to organize themselves and develop a sense of corporateness, many unemployed have participated in the pre- and post-independence political movements, serving the leaders of these movements whenever called upon for mass rallies and demonstrations. (Their role in post-independence election struggles still remains to be documented [Lloyd, 1967, p. 252].) In this respect they were part of the general mobilization of the African urban populations in the anticolonial struggle, a part that is clearly indicated in the life histories of several Lagos men between the ages of 23 and 28. Typical is the following account by a Yoruba who had come to Lagos in 1958 after completing primary school at Oyo:

> When I arrived in Lagos in January 1958 I first stayed with an uncle who looked after me while I tried to get work. I eventually found a job as a time keeper with a construction company. This

work lasted eight months until I lost my work because I became ill
and when I returned my work had been given to some other person. For four months I was unable to get work until an organizer
for the Action Group approached me with the offer of trying to
help me out. I joined the party and found that a large number of
other unemployed men had done the same. I was not given a
regular wage for my work but I was given shelter and food by the
organizer. My work was to run messages and to try to get others
to join. When we had big street meetings it was my duty to bring
people to the meeting. I sometimes washed cars for the organizers
or distributed papers. When Nigeria became independent Awol-
owo thanked me for my work and asked whether I wanted to have
a job in the party. But I declined because I wanted to earn a
better wage. I again registered with the Employment Exchange
and eventually found work again as a time keeper with the Lagos
City Council (Gutkind, 1966).

Many of the younger unemployed men formed the core of the
various "youth wings" of the parties which rallied them in very
large numbers. These age-homogeneous movements produced their
own "band" leaders and acted as political socialization structures
for the membership. In the absence of alternative channels for the
expression of economic, social, and political grievances, they attracted a good deal of support from many unschooled and schooled
unemployed. However, a sense of disillusionment over lack of
achievement by mere membership also set in very quickly, particularly as political instability increased and political parties were
restricted in their activities.

Although the unemployed have formed a distinct strata in the
economic structure, they have yet to become a major political force
in Africa. It is perhaps remarkable that no political leader in the
post-independence era has as yet attempted to organize them into
a vocal political pressure group. The few leaders who have tried
to do this have risen from among the unemployed. Generally, the
response by government to this leadership has been to treat it as
potentially subversive, or to "offer" employment to those attempting
to organize the unemployed.

Interviews conducted in Lagos and Nairobi revealed the conviction held by many of the unemployed, particularly those who
had been without regular work for more than one year, that local
or national political leaders had neither the interest nor the inclination to help them. In Lagos, in the summer of 1966, after the first
military coup in January of that year, 27 out of 120 unemployed

respondents expressed very hostile and cynical views about the efforts made to assist them in finding work. All but 17 explained that it was necessary to bribe government officials, political leaders, foremen, and supervisors in an effort to generate an interest in their plight. One man put it this way:

> In our country every man must pay the politician if he wants any favour. It is part of our custom but every year the price is higher of the bribes we must pay. Because we are without work, we have no money and our relatives and friends are reluctant to give us their money. Our only way to interest our leaders in our problems is to organize ourselves. We cannot rely on our leaders, they are only interested in money and in their own power. Our leaders have let us down but soon they will have to remember us again (Gutkind, 1966).

Why have the unemployed not become a more powerful political community? In part the answer lies in the fact that the unemployed person is still able to find refuge and support among his kin and friends in both the urban and rural areas. Yet, those fortunate enough to have regular employment are steadily voicing their clear opposition to the pressure brought upon them by (unemployed) members of the extended kin group and friends. Some political leaders have expressed the view that the demands by the unemployed on their kin and friends are an impediment to economic progress which, evidently, will rest more and more on the shoulders of the elite. Thus Mr. Tom Mboya expressed this view in September, 1966:

> Growth depends on initiative and initiative can be badly stifled if the individual who makes the effort is required to share the reward with many others whose claims can only be justified on moral grounds.

> In every part of East Africa one can witness the undesirable situation in which a member of a family whose income increases is suddenly and constantly besieged by demands for support from a large number of distant relatives.

> This continues to be part of our lives. It holds true of the small shopkeeper and the trained professional man. In social terms, such a man contributes to society in accordance with the patterns of an economy based on individual initiative but his rewards are severely limited by the traditions of a collective system at family level (*East African Standard* [Nairobi], September 19, 1966).

The *East African Standard,* in paraphrasing Mboya's speech, went on to say:

> This was a deterrent to productive effort and was especially costly at a time when East Africa needed its own indigenous entrepreneurial ingenuity. In short, the system was a drag on initiative because it provided everybody with automatic but considerable insurance against want, thereby diminishing mobility, thrift, and entrepreneurial drive.
>
> However, as the State gradually assumed increasing responsibility for social security and health and medical care, the individual would be relieved of many of his present extended family obligations and would be able to retain more of his income for his immediate dependents (*East African Standard* [Nairobi], September 19, 1966).

Although views such as these are not new, there is clear evidence that the unemployed are very much aware of the burden they create for hosts who are willing to look after them often for many months and even years. Many unemployed men indicated that their benevolent hosts were treating them more like servants than close kin. They also pointed to the increasing frequency of conflict between themselves and their hosts which has led many of them to leave one home and take up residence in another. I have described elsewhere this process of circulating from one relative or friend to another (Gutkind, 1967). The data from Lagos and Nairobi indicate that there is progressively less economic and social elasticity which allows for the maintenance of the wholly dependent person as a legitimate member of traditionally-based kin groupings.

POLITICAL SOCIALIZATION

Faced with such a situation, the unemployed are forced to deal with their economic and personal predicaments in their own terms. It is at this point of breakdown of traditional mutual aid that the unemployed, both individually and collectively, redefine their place in the social order in more political terms. Indeed, it appears that only when they are conscious of their exposed social and economic position do they become aware of the existence of large numbers of other men whose situation does not differ greatly from their own. Although in the early weeks or months of their job hunting they tend very much to keep to themselves and not reveal to others the opportunities they hear about, after months of looking for work they will register at the Employment Exchange (not having done so initially since they had heard that few people obtain work by referral from the Exchange, an agency which the majority of private employers refuse to use in any case). Here they come into contact with a large number of other men and here their political socialization takes place as they sit outside the offices of the Exchange passing the time in conversation. It is, therefore, not surprising that associations of unemployed have come into being as a result of acquaintances first made at the Lagos and Nairobi Exchanges. The case of Paulo S., a Luo from Western Kenya, who had been searching for office work for 15 months, provides an insightful look at this development:

> Paulo was 25 years of age and had successfully completed Primary School in 1959. He then returned to help his family farm their land but in 1963 decided that he should try and obtain more lucrative work so that he could help his younger brothers who needed money to pay their school fees. When he arrived in Nairobi early in 1964, he stayed with his paternal uncle, a foreman in the Public Works Department, who looked after him for seven months. During this time Paulo wrote 47 applications, copies of which he had filed away, to potential employers and claims that he visited at least another 50 offices in government departments, factories and commercial houses. Finally in November 1964 he was successful in obtaining employment in a small office but left after six weeks because he resented the authoritarian manner adopted by the chief clerk, an Asian, who allegedly insulted him. When he returned home that night, his uncle started to quarrel with him and accused him of being a burden on his family. He advised him to return home to his father and offered to pay his bus fare. Paulo was not prepared to accept this suggestion and instead moved that night seeking shelter with a relative on his mother's side.

> About a week later Paulo registered at the Employment Exchange. He went three times a week using the other two workdays to visit offices and write more applications. He did this for almost five months during 1965. He records in his interview how he became progressively more depressed over finding employment. One day he went to the Exchange and while waiting from seven in the morning to three in the afternoon he talked to a lot of other men, something which he had not done much before, to find out from them "how they managed to live without work and pay." He then records his experience as follows:

> "I learned that a great many men were living in the same poor way that I was living. Their relatives and friends were not looking

after them the way they should. They told me that most of them had to work everyday for their brothers or uncles or others. They did not get enough to eat and they often had fights and bad words with their friends. I also found out that many of them had been evicted from their place where they were sleeping. I did not like to hear what I heard and I thought that somebody should tell our leaders about our suffering."

A few days later Paulo met a young Kikuyu, one Samuel G. and an older man, a Gishu from Uganda. As they exchanged ideas, while drinking tea in a huge barn attached to the Nairobi Employment Exchange where the men waited to be called, Paulo discovered that both of them shared his ideas that their suffering should be brought to the attention of the government. There and then:

" . . . we decided to form an Association of Kenya Unemployed and to lay our case before the Minister of Labour. We drew up a petition asking the Minister to see us so that we could lay our case before him on behalf of all those who signed the petition. We managed to get some 89 signatures."

Collecting the signatures caused a certain amount of commotion in the barn. Some of the officers working in nearby offices appeared in the barn to find out what was taking place. When the men saw the Labour Officers they at first assumed that some of them might be called to visit a potential employer. But when they learned that this was not so they responded with shouts and cat-calls as the Labour Officers tried to find out what was taking place. Paulo, who had been appointed President of the new Association, stepped forward and in a reasonable manner explained that "we had formed an Association of Kenya Unemployed and wished to present a petition to the Ministry of Labour in view of the fact that it was useless to come here every day because many hundreds of men come but you can't give us work." One of the Labour Officers persuaded Paulo to see the Supervisor, which Paulo did. When he stayed in the office of the Supervisor for longer than was thought appropriate by the men waiting outside, some of them looked in the windows and started an argument with the Supervisor and some of the Labour Officers. The Labour Officers were unable to restrain the men from shouting and withdrew into an inner office while some of the men who had looked into the open windows now climbed into the building. The Supervisor who feared trouble called the police. Hearing this most of the men dispersed so that when the police arrived they had either left the Exchange or had returned to the barn. The police talked to some of those who had stayed behind and also to Paulo whose explanation appeared to satisfy them. However he also announced that his Association would hold a press conference two days later either in the barn or outside the Exchange.

The press conference took place as planned with a number of reporters present. Paulo and his two companions were to be the speakers. Fewer than the normal number of men were present that day partly because, so Paulo suggested, they were "afraid of the police and that there might be arrests." The press conference lasted less than ten minutes after which time Paulo and one of his companions, the Kikuyu, were detained by the police and taken to the station for questioning. They were released after half an hour during which time Paulo laid before the police his complaint about the working of the Employment Exchange. This was of no interest to the police who merely warned him not to disturb the peace.

Eventually the petition was presented to the Ministry of Labour which acknowledged its receipt but took no further action. The Association of Kenya Unemployed held further meetings in the barn and dispatched several letters to various Ministers of the Government and some political leaders. Eventually the membership lost interest in further participation and the Association disbanded (Gutkind, 1966).

ASSOCIATIONS IN THE LAGOS AREA

Associations of the unemployed have a long history in the Lagos area. As early as 1929 an Association of Work Seekers was formed by one Israel Obi, an Ibo from Aba in Eastern Nigeria. The declared objective of this group was to "bring to the attention of His Excellency the Governor the plight of those unable to obtain work" since it "was not in keeping with the idea that we all are children of God that some of us should suffer because we are prevented from earning our living." The Association claimed a membership of 137 "duly registered and honest members whose qualifications are on our files." In 1934 another group emerged under the name of the Association of Disabled and Hungry Workers of Lagos and Agege. Their leader appears to have been an Ibibio who, in a document which is badly faded, called upon "The King and Government" to give each man at least "ten shillings a month until such a time . . . to prevent pestilence . . . and lest it befall an honest person to become a thief."

In more recent years, particularly after World War II when returned African veterans made many efforts to organize themselves as political pressure groups, associations of unemployed were conceived as readily as they disappeared. Thus in 1951, a Tiv from the Middle Belt of Nigeria attempted to organize an Association of Nigerian Unemployed in Lagos with a branch in Jos. And in 1955 an Ibo managed to sustain the activities of an Unemployed Workers Council for a period of approximately four months by means of promising jobs to them if they followed his "divine leadership."

In 1963, a spontaneous "rebellion," allegedly organized by a dismissed Efik painter who had formed a Workers Demand Party took place outside the Lagos Employment Exchange. The "rebellion" took the form of job applicants abusing the Labour Officers, some stones were thrown, the police arrived, the alleged ringleaders were interviewed at the police station and later released, and all returned to normal. In July, 1966, the *Morning Post* (Lagos) reported on the projected activities of yet another association.

> The Lagos branch of the Labour Unemployed Association, comprising more than 1,000 members, have indicated their intention to stage a peaceful demonstration anytime from now in protest against what they describe as the "favouritism" and "tribalism" at the Labour Exchange (July 11, 1966).

Police interviewed the organizers, and no demonstration took place but a petition was handed to the Ministry of Labour and Social Welfare.

REASONS FOR ASSOCIATIONAL FAILURES

As can be seen from the above, few, if any, of the numerous attempts to form associations of unemployed men have had any staying power. The reasons for this are complicated since they are rooted in the very complexity of the yet imperfectly understood change and modernization processes. However, there are several possible explanations. First, to be effective such associations must cut across ethnic lines in order to avoid extensive fragmentation of the political effort and for the sake of concerted action. Instead, the unemployed use their ethnicity, as members of tribal associations, as an instrument of competition for employment. Secondly, no association can operate effectively without an established organizational structure which has continuity over time and whose officers are wholly committed to the activities and objectives of the group. Such a body requires financial support from the membership and skilled, i.e. educated and trained, organizers. Neither of these conditions have been met in the various associations.

Even if these handicaps could be overcome—which is at present unlikely—other difficulties would still remain. African governments have generally reacted with extreme sensitivity to the activities of associations of unemployed. Whenever they become aware that such an association has been formed and has for the moment succeeded in developing some measure of leadership, they generally treat the movement as an open challenge to the government and have the leaders questioned by the police or "found" jobs, thus undercutting or stifling further action by the group.

More fundamentally, however, associations of unemployed will only become self-sustaining when they develop into protest movements with objectives closely related to the establishment of a more equitable economic and political order. At present many unemployed men believe that jobs will eventually become available and their individual efforts rewarded. Many believe these opportunities will arise at the moment political leaders representing their ethnic groups come to power, or at such a time when they have established a personal contact with a political leader or a civil servant. Few unemployed men understand that the barriers to their sought after opportunities spring from economic and technological characteristics of modernization rather than from their inability to cultivate political relations with members of the elite.

THE UNEMPLOYED AND THE TRADE UNIONS

The unemployed in urban Africa reflect the cleavages and conflicts that accompany political and economic change. As a group they are rejected by most of the other modern groupings that have come into being. As a new and increasing category of the urban population they are a manifestation of the breakdown of modernization (although there are some observers who would suggest that the unemployed represent a hopeful sign that African economies are being transformed along twentieth-century lines). To the political parties, the unemployed, particularly in the urban areas, represent a potentially disruptive political element and a possible challenge to the authority of the new political elite. The elite generally view the unemployed as backward and as basically unemployable, while the latter view the elite as arrogant and exploitative. In the midst of this confrontation stand the trade unions which aim to bridge the gap between the workers and the elites.

In Nigeria, where the trade union movement is generally more developed than in East Africa (with the possible exception of Kenya), many unemployed men until recently looked to its leaders for political support. This applied to those who had at one time been members of a union and also to many who were new to the labor market but had taken note of the efforts by the unions to obtain better conditions of employment for their members. However, considerable disillusion now exists among the unemployed. Out of 120 men interviewed in Lagos, 51 expressed views very similar to the following:

> When I was a construction worker [said a 26 year old Ijaw who had been unemployed for seven months], the union leaders worked for us. If we paid our dues . . . they did what we wanted. The union I belonged to obtained better wages for us but we did not see our leaders very often. Like all of our leaders they ride in big cars and live in big houses.
>
> When I lost my work I could no longer pay my dues but I thought that the Nigerian Trade Union Congress would help me and find new work for me. But I was wrong. I went to see them many times but they always asked for my dues first. I explained to them that I could not pay because I had no work. I asked them why they could not help and they said that only workers who pay dues can get help from the union.
>
> One day at the office of the Congress they told me that unemployed men are rough and make work for the union more difficult. They warned me not to take any work unless I was paid the minimum wage. On another day a union organizer came to the house of my neighbour and asked him whether I had found work. He told him that I had not found work yet. When I heard about this I returned to the union office but was told again not to take any work for less than the minimum wage. I became angry and they told me to leave (Gutkind, 1966).

Role of Trade Unions

The trade unions in many of the new nations of Africa have yet to become major foci of political power tied intimately to a major political party (or parties), even though they have often shown themselves to be a vital factor in the post-independence struggles. Today, the roots of their power lie in their contact with the labor force, although they must compete with the ethnic associations, political parties, cooperatives, and other groups for this grass-roots loyalty (Berg and Butler, 1964, pp. 340-81). However, many of the unemployed men, both in Lagos and Nairobi, take the view that the trade unions are not the same as the political parties (which had forsaken them) because their function is to represent the interests of the working men. As one young Kikuyu put it: "They should not be interested in politics but only in us."

Millen seems to give support to this view:

> The labor leaders in the main provide a counterweight to forces in the society which seek to organize power around traditional religious, caste, tribal or linguistic groups. Because the general thrust of trade union effort is toward modernization, it is a valuable adjunct to the modernists who are trying to build new social, political and economic structures.
>
> . . . the labor organizations have been in a strategic position to articulate the demands, not only of their own membership, but also of people who lacked other advocates (1963, p. 55).

Faced with mounting unemployment, the trade union movement has been placed in a difficult position. Many unemployed men feel that its leaders have erected political and economic barriers designed to protect the interests of the few, of those who have work, while using the unemployed when it suits them. Thus, in the widespread strike in Nigeria in June, 1964 it was said that the unemployed were in the vanguard of the rioters at Port Harcourt and that the trade union leaders were prepared to let the blame fall on them for the damage done and the tensions which were generated. Likewise, in the Congo (Brazzaville), Ivory Coast, Dahomey, Tanganyika, and the Central African Republic, the trade unions have been identified with attempts to overthrow African governments, often using as their spearhead the urban-resident unemployed.

However, more fundamentally, the trade unions view the large pool of unemployed as a constant threat to their bargaining position. Small-scale employers in the construction industry, for example, are ever ready to hire the unemployed at wages well below the statutory minimum. Sometimes when unemployed men assemble outside factory gates or building sites, employers will ask them whether they are or ever were members of a union. On two occasions, in Lagos in July, 1966, fights broke out at a building site and outside a factory between those willing to work for lower pay and those who insisted on the minimum wage.

The trade union movement is committed to protecting the privileges of their (working) membership. When men lose their jobs the trade unions show little interest in them. However, Davies reports that the Union Marocaine du Travail (UMT), when it was formed in 1955, "organised unemployed workers as well as the employed, and of its 600,000 members more than half were unable to pay their dues because they were either underemployed or unemployed altogether" (1966, p. 122). He likewise found that recently the Ghana Trade Union Congress had "more dues-paying affiliates than there were [registered] wage-earners" (p. 125). Whether this was due to a large number of unemployed who maintained their "membership" is now impossible to determine.

EMPLOYMENT EXCHANGES

Even before the end of World War II, Employment Exchanges were established in both Kenya in 1944 and Nigeria in 1943 (Government of Nigeria, 1944). Initially, many men availed themselves of the registration and search facilities which were provided (Dalgleish, 1960). In more recent years, however, men have come to feel that the best way of obtaining employment is by individual effort, primarily by cultivating friendships with those in important political positions. Today, many men take the view that the Employment Exchanges are to be treated as the last resort, or at best as no more than a supplement to their own efforts. Few men trust the honesty and integrity of the Labour Officers and many applicants go to great extremes to bring pressure to bear on the former on the basis of ethnicity, a remote kinship connection, common village residence, town or district residence, or friendships made during school days or in some other context. It is not unusual for an applicant to appear at the home of a Labour Officer and offer his services as a servant saying that all he requires is food and shelter. Nor is it unusual for registered applicants to pass letters or money wrapped in paper to the Labour Officers as they enter or leave their offices.

These matters must have been of considerable concern to the Nigerian government as evidenced by the establishment in 1960 of an Advisory Committee on the Eradication of Employment Corruption. However, the actions of the Committee to encourage employers to make more use of the Employment Exchange seem to have been of little avail as the Ministry of Labour reported in March 1961:

> The result of discussion with a number of employers on the possibility of filling their vacancies through the Exchange were not encouraging. As long as employers found little or no difficulty in obtaining the types of labour they required without the assistance from the Exchange it was unlikely that approaches to them in this respect would yield much satisfactory result (Government of Nigeria, Quarterly Review, Vol. 2, No. 2, 1961, p. 11).

These efforts have not been entirely negative, and in June, 1964, the Ministry was able to record that not all employers had decided to ignore the Employment Exchanges:

> In the Sapele Employment Exchange there was a remarkable increase in the number of industrial workers registering for employment. The increase was as a result of the decision of the Site Engineer of an indigenous construction company to recruit his labour through the Employment Exchange only (Government of Nigeria, Quarterly Review, Vol. 1, No. 7, 1964, p. 89).

Dissatisfaction with the Employment Exchanges on the part of the unemployed has been common. In Lagos an association of "The Applicants of the Federal Ministry of Labour" filed the following petition which highlights their grievances:

The Labour Officer,
Federal Ministry of Labour,
Ikeja.

COMPLAINTS

Dear Sir,

With humble and due respect we beg to forward this our Complaints before your consideration and assistance.

Here are undermentioned Complaints we put forward before you for Consideration and assistance.

(1) *Employment at Gate.*

We have investigated and found that some factories and departments in Ikeja are do [sic] employ through the back-door without the Consent of the Labour Officer. People are being employed at the gate even without labour cards, e.g. factories like. . . .

(2) *Applicants turned back.*

Some applicants after directing them by the Labour Officer to certain factories they are being turned back for unknown reasons.

(3) *Method of Approach.*

We then appealed to the Labour Officer to see that the misgrossed [sic] management by certain factories be forced to a standstill and apply the Labour Code. We feel that this will bring a great helping hand to teach the Ministry of Labour and the applicants to solve the mass unemployment and also in checking of bribery and corruption now facing the superior young Republic of Nigeria.

(4) *Appeal to the Labour Officer.*

We hereby appeal to the Labour Officer to help us go round the offices . . . to find out where vacancies exist and also investigate how people are being employed in offices without the Consent of the Labour Officer.

(5) *Tribalism within the offices.*

We beg also for the tribalism and nepotism that some personnel Manager used to play with the applicants whenever they are being called for interview. This act happens everytime within these offices here.

We shall be grateful if much consideration will be given to the above raised points by the applicants.

Thanks

your obedient applicants,
(Signed by 3 officers)

Aside from the refusal of many private employers to use the Exchange, a major factor contributing to the growing political discontent is that men in high position use their offices to dispense

jobs as a form of patronage. Thus in March, 1964 the *East African
Standard* (Nairobi) reported:

> . . . a spokesman for the Ministry of Labour said . . . the Min-
> istry was disturbed by allegations that personnel officers in some
> firms were demanding bribes before they took on individual work-
> ers as a condition for their acceptance for a job (March 9, 1964).

Yet, two years later the Kenya government became aware that its
own civil servants were not free from unethical practices in this
regard. In April, 1966, a delegation of unemployed men, resident in
Nairobi, registered a strong complaint with the Minister of Labour
charging that jobs in the public services were filled by those who
had friends in influential places. These allegations led the Ministry
of Labour to issue a statement, on May 10th, 1966, condemning
such practices (Ref. C. 47/01, entitled "Sponsoring of Candidates
for Employment").

ETHNICITY AND UNEMPLOYMENT

The relationship between unemployment and interethnic conflict is close and an important stimulant to growing political awareness which in turn is exploited by political leaders (Lloyd, 1967,
pp. 299-303). The tensions which are generated by interethnic
competition among the unemployed almost invariably find expression in an increased sense of ethnic solidarity both among the
unemployed and the workers (pp. 239, 296). Thus, tribal associations, whose role in African political development (particularly
in pre-independence days) has been very considerable, have come
to the aid of their unemployed members (p. 198). Indeed, some
leaders of these associations have argued that this new mission
has given their organizations a new *raison d'être* for their activities.
However, unemployed members of these associations have been
viewed as a disruptive element by that section of the membership
unwilling to give shelter and support to their less fortunate members. This latter attitude was described by the President of the
Aba [Ibo] Improvement Union in Lagos in these words:

> Some of our members complain that we are responsible for a
> lot of men who are lazy and don't want to work. Some of our

> members have refused to help because they say that our first duty
> is to help our people back in Aba and to collect money for students
> who must go to school or for higher training. At our last meeting
> several members said that they could no longer give money because
> they needed it for themselves. They made many complaints about
> how difficult it is for them. Several members abused me because
> I told the membership that one Ibo must help another even if all
> of us must give up some of our money (Gutkind, 1966).

When visiting beer halls, bus parks, markets, squatters' settlements, and highly congested areas generally, it is not unusual to
witness fights between members of various ethnic groups who have
accused one another of "stealing" jobs. Thus, in Lagos, non-Yoruba
(particularly those from the smaller tribes) are frequently accused
of taking work away from the dominant Yoruba. Likewise in
Nairobi fights, which can be traced to frustration built up while
seeking work, often break out on housing estates between Kikuyu
and others. And these are not easily forgotten.

> The brand-new youth centre built by the Kenya Y.M.C.A. in
> Shauri Moyo [Nairobi] serves one of the most overpopulated quar-
> ters. But the main point of attraction for the African is not recre-
> ation, games and leisure time activities, but the continuously
> vague hope for a job (East African Standard [Nairobi], February
> 18, 1966).

The economic and social problems faced by the urban-resident
unemployed are, of course, accentuated by the uncertain conditions
which prevail in Africa's urban areas. As the migrant enters the
urban system his expectations and demands increase while his
prospects of fulfillment diminish—circumstances which heighten his
political and economic awareness and strengthen his position, albeit
but slowly. Millen has summarized this position as follows:

> Many of the unskilled in Africa and Asia on leaving their
> villages to join the urban labour force have cut some or all of their
> ties with rural forms of "social insurance" that the extended family
> system provides. The loss of this security makes them receptive
> to political appeals and, usually, susceptible to political manipula-
> tion. The job and pay framework within which the urban worker
> functions is only one of the influences that contributes to his sus-
> ceptibility. The overcrowded cities . . . make their impact. All
> around him he finds squalor, disease, crime, alcoholism, prostitu-
> tion and inhuman competition in the job market (Millen, 1963, pp.
> 59-60).

THE UNEMPLOYED AS A DIVERSE
COMMUNITY

Although the unemployed have all the potential of becoming an important political pressure group, the perception they have of their plight has yet to be translated into a corporate organizational structure which is coherent enough to generate collective action. The awareness of their political power will increase as the gap between them and the active workers, and the managerial and professional elite, increases. Their ideological persuasion is uncrystallized because of the low level of their political socialization and the total absence of effective and sustained leadership.

In the total urban system they represent one of many groupings which make up the old and new cities and towns of Africa. They are highly dispersed throughout the urban area so that it is possible to find unemployed men living in favorable circumstances in the home of a close kin or friend in a well set-up neighborhood. It is just as possible to find them sleeping in the streets, in markets, in bus parks, under bushes and in creeks and, of course, in the congested areas of the town. If seen as an economic and social category of the population, its members have little in common beyond the fact that all of them are looking for some kind of employment. If seen as a group, there appears to be little to hold them together. They are internally highly fragmented and divided along ethnic, age, and educational lines. While the school-leavers are generally young (i.e. under 18 and unmarried), the unschooled are generally older with family responsibilities. What percentage of the unemployed are under 14 is not easily determined but conversations with some of these youngsters in both cities left no doubt that they considered themselves as of working age. They held such occasional jobs as washing cars, carrying loads, watching market stalls, looking after younger children, hawking combs, pencils, cigarettes, or cloth, and generally picking up whatever casual work they could find.

Socially, there are those who are wholly dependent on relatives, friends, and others whose very casual work allows them to live within inches of mere subsistence but who have maintained a remarkable measure of independence. Again there are those who go to great efforts to obtain work and those who make little such effort, preferring to be kept by their hosts. And while many school-leavers systematically refuse to accept any work not seen as commensurate with their education, others with less or no schooling will accept virtually any employment offered to them.

Social-psychologically too, the range is enormous. While many seem to show little adverse effects as a result of prolonged periods of unemployment—with absolutely nothing to do—others express clear signs of frustration and bitterness. Again, while many strongly express their determination to resist participating in antisocial behavior, others have taken to petty criminal activity.

THE UNEMPLOYED AS A POLITICAL COMMUNITY

Although the unemployed lack much needed political leadership, they are the first significant manifestation in contemporary African society of incipient economic, social, and political stratification along class lines. They highlight the enormous differences between the elite and the poor and exhibit a real difference of life style from the rest of the society, a difference which is particularly obvious in the urban areas. For many their style of life is dominated not merely by severe poverty but also by a total lack of upward mobility and the real fear that they are forever "fixed" in the incipient class system. Although they actively compete for work, they lack the education and skills which could give them the initial anchorage and "push" they desire. Particularly in West Africa, personal and social aspirations are high, fanned by a large degree of political involvement and an extensive and articulate group of politicians able to exploit grievances. Yet the life style of the unemployed has progressively removed them from the bulk of the population about whose predicaments and aspirations they know little. As such, all the manifestations of class conflict exist. Exclusive recruitment from the elite categories diminishes economic opportunities for all, while at the same time educational opportunities and standards are on the increase. While the elites are the economic and social "pace-setters," the aspirations of the poor remain high. Peter Lloyd writes:

> Many are certain to be frustrated in their attempts to achieve goals by methods which are new and but poorly understood. Lack of success may be attributed either to one's personal insuffi-

ciency or, as we have seen to be common in West Africa, to the machinations of others, through witchcraft, sorcery or corruption. Slowly personal aspirations will become more realistic. But as the ostentatious life of the elite ceases to appear a possibility for oneself or one's children, so opposition to it is likely to grow. Hopes of entertaining the elite change to demands that it be shorn of many of its privileges (Lloyd, 1967, p. 309).

Thus, the mainspring of political activism for the urban-resident unemployed stands in direct relation to the manner in which their demands for work and upward mobility are satisfied. Up to now they have given frequent but unorganized expression to these demands. What activism has been shown has been restricted to a peripheral participation in pre- and post-nationalist political agitation rather than as an organized group of unemployed with their own platform of demands. But in the years since independence, a larger number of unemployed men have increasingly come to recognize that the political parties have shown progressively less interest in the economic circumstances of the mass of the population. Urban conditions have deteriorated and popular sentiment is beginning to crystallize. The absence of leadership among the unemployed is merely a reflection of the general shortage of this commodity at all levels of political affairs.

The emergence of political groupings designed to express popular discontent is, of course, restricted in the context of current African political structures. In the one-party African state, it is assumed that all categories of the population will bend their energies and support toward the party of "national integration." The activities by any group of men that impedes this objective are viewed with suspicion and hostility. It would not be surprising, therefore, that those who demand work are likely to look to more revolutionary ideologies and, initially, to express their demands in uncoordinated attacks against the government and the politicians. The cynical attitude expressed by many unemployed men is channelled into an increasing political awareness that the present course of national development has brought major benefits to the few at the expense of the majority.

But the poor lack the instrumental channels to express their grievances. What channels they have, such as ethnic and voluntary associations, do not provide the ideological and political framework required to press the urgency of their case. Instead, these groups concentrate their political efforts along traditional and ethnic lines. Lloyd summarizes the argument as follows:

> . . . the institutionalized channels for the expression of . . . grievances are becoming less effective, so that protests are not directed against the structure of society by organized political movements. Instead individual frustrations are expressed through charges of tribalism and corruption, of witchcraft and sorcery. Action lies in developing one's own relationships with influential patrons and in seeking from supernatural agencies protection against evil forces and support in one's aspirations. Outbreaks of aggressive behaviour tend to lack coherent leadership or organization, to be without any class ideology or goal—save a general attitude of destruction directed against those with wealth, power or property (Lloyd, 1967, p. 317).

Furthermore, so long as the unemployed are dependent on their close and far kin and friends, and as long as they can, if they wish, return to the rural areas to (try to) obtain a living from the land, they remain immune to the intensive social and economic pressures which might make them a more active political community. Thus, political parties and politicians, such as the Eastern Nigerian-based Socialist Workers and Farmers Party, have not yet been able to develop a strong sense of class consciousness among the disadvantaged urbanites and to place class loyalty above tribalism or regionalism. Not only do these safety valves retard class consciousness but this is:

> . . . minimal when movement from the underprivileged into the privileged class is believed to be easy and frequent [in Nigeria in particular]. Men are rarely apt to oppose privileges which, they believe, may one day be shared by themselves. West African society is still seen as an open society. The chances which a farmer's son has of obtaining a good education and a well paid office are . . . far less than he imagines them to be. But most of the successful elite are still identified with their home areas, serving for the youth as models of possible achievement. So many men have graduated when nearer forty years of age than thirty, that others in their twenties still assiduously prepare for university entrance examinations, ever postponing the age when they will have to admit that they have lost the chance. It is significant that those who aspire to elite status are the skilled manual workers, the junior clerks and teachers—the very people one would expect to find active in radical political and protest movements; revolutionary leadership has rarely been drawn, anywhere in the world,

from the most depressed and poverty-stricken groups (Lloyd, 1967, pp. 315-16).

Lloyd's view that artisans, clerks, and teachers are "the very people one would expect to find active in radical and protest movements" is open to question since these are established middle income groups, jealous of the elite status enjoyed by the few, and unlikely to support revolutionary or protest movements which, in their view, would not help them reach the elite level. Although class-consciousness is still incipient, *Présence Africaine* has warned that: "If there is no real class consciousness at the moment it could be born by the crying inequalities that are obstinately practised by our governing bodies" (Vol. 25, No. 53, n.d., pp. 247-51).

THE BASIS OF CONFLICT AND CONFRONTATION

The predicaments faced by the urban-resident unemployed (and nothing has been said in this chapter about the rural-based underemployed and the place they are likely to have in the political matrix), must be seen as one graphic manifestation of a complex set of political, economic, and social conditions which has engulfed the new nation states of Africa. There are those who argue that the new African nations must first rid themselves of those traditionalist institutions which do not promote progress toward a modern society. This would require, for all intents and purposes, a total transformation of these societies and the rapid adoption of a Western style of life, of Western institutions, habits, and ideas brought to life by rapid and extensive industrialization—a forlorn and, perhaps, basically undesirable objective.

Others have suggested a less radical, more gradual, but perhaps also less dynamic, procedure. This approach is based on the progressive development of local entrepreneurship and the gradual transformation of a traditional institutional structure to serve modern functions. Essentially it relies heavily on the small African elite being instrumental in this transformation. But, as observers of the African scene have noted in recent years, the elite's perception of its innovative and transformative role reflects its privileged position and its progressive isolation from the mass of the population. While the elite intellectually supports the need for national unity and stability, it has not, with some rare exceptions, readily supported ideologies that are likely to threaten its privileged position.

Thus, the stage is set for a political confrontation springing from conflict generated by the unequal distribution of wealth and power. In more practical terms, there is substantial evidence to support the observation that the unemployed will progressively become more frustrated in their search for minimal security as the employed find it impossible to bear the burden of supporting their unemployed kin and friends. When this stage is reached, the unemployed person will be totally dependent on the state or on charity. Even now, many of those who seek work in towns refuse to be dependent on kin or to return to rural areas from which they are basically alienated, although they still attach considerable importance to their ethnic origin and anchorage.

Such a development clearly produces a situation of incompatibility of interests—a major conflict based on the pursuit of different goals. These goals (of the elite and of the poor) require that each side lay their hands on the machinery of political power and hold on to it. Hence, as each group jostles for influence, authority, and dominance, conflict becomes the essential lubricant of political and economic relations. If this is true, then the unemployed will stand in the forefront of the political arena. Hobsbawm, writing about Latin America, has suggested that the unemployed will engage, sometimes in partnership with the workers, in anticonstitutional activities to be met by "massacre as a permanent political institution" (Hobsbawm, 1963, p. 737).

Africa's unemployed, and those who are today underemployed but tomorrow join the pool of the work seekers, are part of the debris of modernization and exploitation. More significantly, they stand as a monument to the unfinished revolution which a few short years ago swept the continent into the rough waters of a dubious sovereignty.

As Stanley Diamond writes:

Millions of Africans, radically disengaged from their own traditions, are being rapidly proletarianized in both rural and urban areas, and are being forced to substitute a mere strategy of poverty and survival for authentic cultural expression. Put another way, they are being rapidly converted into marginal producers and marginal consumers on the remotest fringes of contemporary industrial society (Diamond, 1963, p. 178).

References

AUTHOR's NOTE: *In addition to works referred to in the text, the references given below include other materials relevant to the study of the poor in urban Africa.*

ALMOND, G. A., and J. S. COLEMAN (eds.). *The Politics of the Developing Areas* (Princeton, N. J.: Princeton University Press, 1960).

ANDERSON, J. E. "The Teenager in the Rural Community," Conference on Education, Employment and Rural Development, University College, Nairobi, September, 1966.

APTER, D. E. "The Role of Traditionalism in the Political Modernization of Ghana and Uganda," *World Politics*, 13 (October, 1960), pp. 45-68.

———. *The Political Kingdom of Uganda* (Princeton, N. J.: Princeton University Press, 1961).

———. *Ideology and Discontent* (New York: The Free Press, 1964).

———. *The Politics of Modernization* (Chicago: University of Chicago Press, 1965).

ARDANT, G. "A Plan for Full Employment in the Developing Countries," *International Labour Review*, 88 (July, 1963), pp. 15-55.

———. "Automation in Developing Countries," *International Labour Review*, 90 (November, 1964), pp. 432-71.

BARYARUHA, A. *Factors Affecting Industrial Employment: A Study of Uganda*, (Nairobi: Oxford University Press, 1967).

BERG, E. J., and J. BUTLER. "Trade Unions," in J. S. Coleman and C. G. Rosberg (eds.), *Political Parties and National Integration in Tropical Africa* (Berkeley: University of California Press, 1964), pp. 340-81.

BLANKSTEN, G. I. "Transference of Social and Political Loyalties," in B. F. Hoselitz and W. E. Moore (eds.), *Industrialization and Society* (Paris: Unesco-Mouton, 1963), pp. 175-96.

CALLAWAY, A. C. "School Leavers and a Developing Economy" in R. O. Tilman and T. Cole (eds.), *The Nigerian Political Scene* (Durham: Duke University Press, 1962), pp. 220-38.

———. "Unemployment among School Leavers," *Journal of Modern African Studies*, 1 (September, 1963), pp. 351-71.

———. "Nigeria's Indigenous Education: The Apprentice System," ODU (University of Ife Journal of African Studies), 1 (July, 1964), pp. 1-18.

CHAMBERS, M. "Jesus of Oyingbo," *New Society*, 80 (April, 1964), pp. 13-15.

Chaplin, B. H. G. "School Attitudes to Agriculture," *West African Journal of Education,* 5 (October, 1961), pp. 94-96.

Christian Council of Kenya and the Christian Churches' Educational Association. *After School What? Further Education, Training and Employment of Primary School Leavers* (Nairobi, March, 1966).

Colony and Protectorate of Kenya (later Republic of Kenya). Annual Reports, Department of Labour, Nairobi, 1941-1961.

Colony and Protectorate of Kenya. Unemployment, Sessional Paper No. 10 of 1959/60 (Nairobi: Government Printer, 1960).

Copper Industry Service Bureau. *Copperbelt of Zambia Mining Industry Year Book 1964,* Kitwe (Zambia), 1964.

Dalgleish, A. G. *Survey of Unemployment, Colony and Protectorate of Kenya* (Nairobi: Government Printer, 1960).

Dalton, J. H. "The Predicament of African Development," *Social Science,* 36 (October, 1961), pp. 239-46.

Davies, I. *African Trade Unions* (Harmondsworth: Penguin African Library, 1966).

Deutsch, K. W. "Social Mobilization and Political Development," *American Political Science Review,* 55 (September, 1961), pp. 493-514.

Devauges, M. R. "Urban Unemployment in Africa South of the Sahara: Unemployment in Brazzaville," *Bulletin Inter-African Labour Institute,* 7 (May, 1960), pp. 9-48.

Diamond, S. "Modern Africa: The Pains of Birth," *Dissent,* 10 (1963), pp. 169-79.

Dumont, R. *False Start in Africa* (New York: Praeger, 1966).

East Africa Royal Commission. Report 1953-1955, CMD 9475 (London: H.M.S.O., 1955).

Edgren, G. "The Employment Problem in Tropical Africa," *Bulletin of the Inter-African Labour Institute,* 12 (May, 1965), pp. 174-90.

Eisenstadt, S. N. "Changes in Patterns of Stratification Attendant on the Attainment of Political Independence," *Transactions of the Third World Congress of Sociology,* 3 (1956), pp. 32-41.

———. "Sociological Aspects of Political Development in Underdeveloped Countries," *Economic Development and Cultural Change,* 5 (April, 1957), pp. 289-307.

Elkan, W. *Migrants and Proletarians* (London: Oxford University Press, for East African Institute of Social Research, 1960).

Epstein, A. L. *Politics in an Urban African Community* (Manchester: University Press, for Rhodes-Livingstone Institute, 1958).

Federation of Nigeria. *Report on Employment and Earnings Enquiry, December, 1962* (Lagos: Federal Ministry of Labour, 1962).

FINKLE, J. L. and R. W. GABLE (eds.). *Political Development and Social Change* (New York: John Wiley & Sons, Inc., 1966).

FOGG, C. D. "Economic and Social Factors Affecting the Development of Smallholder Agriculture in Eastern Nigeria," *Economic Development and Cultural Change*, 13 (April, 1965), pp. 278-92.

FRANK, A. G. "Urban Poverty in Latin America," *Studies in Comparative International Development*, 2 (1966), pp. 75-84.

GOLDRICH, D., R. B. PRATT and C. R. SCHULLER. "The Political Integration of Lower-Class Urban Settlement in Chile and Peru," *Studies in Comparative International Development*, 3 (1967-1968), pp. 1-22.

GOVERNMENT OF KENYA, MANPOWER BRANCH, MINISTRY OF LABOUR AND SOCIAL SERVICES. "Kenya: Report on the Tripartite Agreement on Measures for the Immediate Relief of Unemployment," *Bulletin Inter-African Labour Institute*, 12 (February, 1965), pp. 94-98.

GOVERNMENT OF NIGERIA. Annual Reports, Department of Labour, Lagos, 1942-1962.

——. Quarterly Review, Ministry of Labour and Social Welfare, Lagos.

GRAVES, D. R. "The Agrarian Problem in West Africa," *Orbis*, 6 (Spring, 1962), pp. 119-36.

GRIFFITHS, V. L. "The Education of the Young in Rural Areas," Conference on Education, Employment and Rural Development, University College, Nairobi, September, 1966.

GUTKIND, P. C. W. Field Notes, Lagos and Nairobi, 1966.

——. "The Energy of Despair: Social Organization of the Unemployed in Two African Cities: Lagos and Nairobi. A Preliminary Account," *Civilisations*, 1, 2, 3 (1967) and 4 (in press).

HEIJNEN, J. D. "Results of Job Preference Test Administered to Pupils in Standard VIII, Mwanza, Tanzania," Conference on Education, Employment and Rural Development, University College, Nairobi, September, 1966.

HOBSBAWM, E. J. "The Most Critical Area in the World," *The Listener*, 2 (May, 1963), pp. 735-37.

HODGE, P. "Ghana Workers Brigade, a Project for Unemployed Youth," *British Journal of Sociology*, 15 (June, 1964), pp. 113-21.

INTERNATIONAL LABOUR ORGANIZATION. *Year Book of Labour Statistics* (Geneva, 1946-1964).

——. *Why Labour Leaves the Land: A Comparative Study of the Movement of Labour out of Agriculture*, Studies and Reports, New Series, No. 29, Geneva, 1960.

——. "Economic Development, Employment and Public Works in African Countries," *International Labour Review*, 91 (January, 1965), pp. 14-46.

——. "Technological Changes in the Construction Industry and their Socio-Economic Consequences," *Ekistics*, 19 (April, 1965), pp. 229-40.

KAMOGA, F. K. "Future of Primary School Leavers in Uganda," *Bulletin Inter-African Labour Institute*, 12 (February, 1965), pp. 5-18.

KEIR, SIR D. L. *Survey of Technical and Commercial Education in Northern Rhodesia*, Kitwe, September, 1960.

KILSON, M. "African Political Change and the Modernization Process," *The Journal of Modern African Studies*, 1 (December, 1963), pp. 425-40.

KOFF, D. "Education and Employment Perspectives of Kenya Primary Pupils," Conference on Education, Employment and Rural Development, University College, Nairobi, September, 1966.

LERNER, D. *The Passing of Traditional Society: Modernization in the Middle East* (Glencoe, Ill.: The Free Press, 1958).

LLOYD, P. C. *Africa in Social Change: Changing Traditional Societies in the Modern World* (Harmondsworth: Penguin Africa Library, 1967).

MAIR, L. P. *New Nations* (London: Weidenfeld and Nicolson, 1963).

MILLEN, B. H. *The Political Role of Labour in Developing Countries* (Washington, D. C.: The Brookings Institution, 1963).

MITCHELL, J. C. and A. L. EPSTEIN. "Occupational Prestige and Social Status among Urban Africans in Northern Rhodesia," *Africa*, 29 (January, 1959), pp. 20-40.

NYERERE, J. "Education for Self-Reliance," *Africa Report*, 12 (June, 1967), pp. 72-79.

PEIL, M. "Middle School Leavers: Occupational Aspirations and Prospects," *Ghana Journal of Sociology*, 2 (February, 1966), pp. 7-16.

PRESENCE AFRICAINE. "About the Class Struggle in Negro Africa," 25, No. 53 (n.d.), pp. 247-51.

RAY, R. S. *Labour Force Survey of Tanzania, Ministry of Economic Affairs and Development Planning* (The United Republic of Tanzania, Dar es Salaam, January, 1966).

REPUBLIC OF KENYA. *Economic Survey 1966* (Nairobi: Government Printer, June, 1966).

SEGAL, A. "The Problem of Urban Unemployment," *Africa Report*, 10 (April, 1965), pp. 17-21.

SMELSER, N. J. "The Modernization of Social Relations," in M. Weiner (ed.), *Modernization: The Dynamics of Growth* (New York: Basic Books, 1966), pp. 110-21.

TOBIAS, G. *High-Level Manpower Requirements and Resources in Tanganyika 1962-1967* (Government Paper No. 2 of 1963), Government of Tanganyika (Dar es Salaam: Government Printer, 1963).

TOURAINE, A., and D. PECAUT. "Working-Class Consciousness and Economic Development in Latin America," *Studies in Comparative International Development*, 3 (1967-1968), pp. 71-84.

13

Poverty and Politics in Cities of Latin America

WILLIAM MANGIN

☐ WHAT IT MEANS TO "BE POOR" obviously varies with place and time. The Siriono Indians of Eastern Bolivia spend most of their time hustling to get enough to eat, as do the Bushmen of the Kalahari desert; yet the members of neither culture think of themselves as poor nor are they very much like each other. They own practically nothing but, of course, there is practically nothing to own where they are and all the members of each society are more or less in the same situation. They have just about equal access to what there is and, until fairly recently, they had little contact with outsiders. They are poorer than the poor in affluent societies but there are no rich groups with which to compare themselves in their own societies.

Culturally prescribed reactions can vary, even to extreme scarcity situations: both of these people are constantly engaged in difficult food quests, yet the Siriono are suspicious of each other, selfish, and use food to exploit each other, while the Bushmen enjoy each other, share food and cooperate. Other groups in other places could be included in such comparisons to show that primitive, peasant, rural, and urban poverty can most usefully be defined in terms of *relative deprivation*, but that people in apparently similar situations of impoverishment also behave quite differently. Moreover, such comparisons could be made with respect to relative deprivation over time. The poor of London 200 years ago, the poor of New York 80 years ago, the poor of Calcutta 20 years ago, are all different from the poor of those cities today and from each other.

THE RESPONSE TO IMPOVERISHMENT

Clearly, then, how people respond to deprivation does not reflect simply different absolute amounts of wealth. Miller and Rein (1964) say of poverty:

> It is a moving escalator, reflecting the values of a society. . . .
> The recent tendency in American society has been to raise the
> absolute level while increasing inequality. The percentage of the
> total pie going to the bottom 20% has slightly declined in the post-
> World War II period.

Poverty as "a way of life" seems to need the fact of exploitation of one group by another to exist. Slums, ghettos, or whatever poor peoples' neighborhoods are called vary tremendously among themselves in terms of organization, morale, and internal cultural integration. They can be predominantly people on the way up the social ladder, as I will suggest for squatter settlements in Latin America, or people staying at the bottom. Stokes (1962) and Turner (1967) have referred to slums of hope and slums of despair. I think that the high end of the scale is associated with availability of models and the possibility of success in either the general society or in the slum subculture, or both. In some cases both routes have been open to at least a few members of the slum group.

The studies of a Boston Italian neighborhood 20 years apart by Whyte (1943) and Gans (1962) indicate a remarkable cultural persistence accompanied by the possibility of choosing local or city-wide routes to cultural success. The re-creation of the shtetl in the Eastern European Jewish ghettos (Zborowski and Herzog, 1952) provided fewer opportunities for movement in the general society but considerable satisfaction within the local cultural setting. The voluminous literature, including hundreds of excellent novels and stories, from all over the world on the adaptation of agricultural peasant groups to urban and industrial life, shows again remarkable persistence of peasant village patterns, cultural values and beliefs—many of them functional rather than dysfunctional—for two, three or even four generations after the initial migration away from the peasant community.

The same variables of relative deprivation and relative opportunity may also apply to hinterland communities' response to the influences of urbanization, however they are spread to the villages. In non-European, American Indian peasant communities, such as Tusik in Yucatan (Redfield, 1941) or Vicos in Peru, the majority of the people are poorer than the poor of Merida, Lima, or Mexico City; but they do not have the immediate, everyday experience with better off reference groups. They are relatively in the same position as other Indian communities they see, and some are able to gain certain desirable posts in their internal politico-religious systems.

URBANISM AND THE PEASANT

Obviously there is no neat and necessary sequence of stages in cultural development. Nevertheless, the tribal village of Tusik, the Mayan peasants of Chan Kom, the town of Dzitas and the capital city of Merida have their counterparts in the valley of Mexico and in other parts of Latin America. While it is possible for an illiterate tribal Indian to become literate in a few months and to move to a large city and become a factory worker or, in a few rare cases, to move to New York or Paris and become a graduate student, shorter social moves are much more common. Even taking into account the sudden appearance of roads and factories in formerly remote areas, the fact that there is contemporary change, and also the individual exceptions which seem to be rather numerous, it is still possible to say that communities such as Tusik and Vicos are primarily Indian and "represent" or retain more cultural traits from an earlier historical period than peasant communities from the same regions of Yucatan and Peru such as Chan Kom, San Luis (Tumin, 1952), or Huaylas (Doughty, 1967). They, in turn, stand in similar relationship to district capital towns such as Dzitas, Huancayo (Tschopik, 1947) or even Tepoztlan (Lewis, 1951). At the opposite end of the complexity scale stand the capital cities.

Not that all individuals in such cities lead more complex lives. Some do, some do not; but obviously more patterns are present to choose from. Indeed, there are folk people in the cities just as there are literate secular people in small mountain villages. Moreover, stimuli for change may be provided by foreign or national tourists, as in the lake region of Guatemala and Cajititlán, Mexico

(Nuñez, 1963), as well as by factories and roads. The return of labor migrants, army veterans and travelers bring in the outside. Anthropologists do their part. Vicos has changed because of the Cornell-Peru Project. It has received worldwide attention through the UN, *Reader's Digest*, newspapers, and so on; and the Peace Corps volunteers stationed there between 1962 and 1964, to their dismay, signed in hundreds of visitors.

Integration, community solidarity and morale are not always figured into evolutionary or developmental scales used in measuring change. But they are patently significant for the political life of communities and subcommunities, and thus may have a good deal more to do with change, albeit indirectly, than rather static sequential models would suggest. Two approaches to such variables have attracted attention in recent years: Foster's hypothesis of "the image of limited good" (1965b) and Lewis' hypothesis of a "culture of poverty" (1961). Each helps to explain some of the behavior of the urban poor in Latin America; each displays certain shortcomings in this regard. Both will, therefore, be examined before detailing the data concerning the political activity of some of the impoverished inhabitants of certain cities in South America.

The "Limited Good" Orientation

In a series of articles Foster has presented a consistent and original view of peasant interpersonal relationships in Mexico (Foster, 1961; 1963; 1965a) and in general (Foster, 1965b). He says that contractual relationships outside the nuclear family are "dyadic," that is, between two persons, whether of equal or unequal status. These dyadic contracts operate in the framework of a cognitive orientation he calls "The Image of Limited Good."

Foster says:

> I mean that broad areas of peasant behavior are patterned in such fashion as to suggest that peasants view their social, economic, and natural universes—their total environment—as one in which all of the desired things in life such as land, wealth, health, friendship and love, manliness and honor, respect and status, power and influence, security and safety, exist in finite quantity and are always in short supply, as far as the peasant is concerned. Not only do these and all other "good things" exist in finite and limited quantities, but in addition there is no way directly in peasant power to increase the available quantities (1965b, p. 296).

The system is seen as closed so that "an individual or a family can improve a position only at the expense of others" (Foster, 1965b, p. 297). Particularly in the economic sphere there is only a limited amount of wealth, and progress of one is usually at the expense of another.

Thus, Foster asserts, extreme individualism is chosen over co-operation in preserving peasants' security because cooperation assumes leadership, with peasants who accept leadership being vulnerable to criticism and sanctions from envious neighbors. He concludes by saying:

> Viewed in the light of Limited Good peasant societies are not conservative and backward, brakes on national economic progress, because of economic irrationality nor because of the absence of psychological characteristics in adequate quantities. They are conservative because individual progress is seen as—and in the context of the traditional society in fact is—the supreme threat to community stability, and all cultural forms must conspire to discourage changes in the status quo (Foster, 1965b, p. 310).

I have been impressed with how the scheme fits my own experience in Peru in both mestizo and Indian communities and with migrants from the mountains to Lima. It also fits numerous other situations described in the highland literature, particularly in the field of community development and in the introduction of technological change. But I have reservations about applying the idea too generally. It seems to me that it fails to deal sufficiently with the impact of outside forces on the peasant community and the position of peasants in relation to more powerful members of their society. In Vicos, for example, many Indians were willing to change their agricultural technology but were blocked from doing so by middle class Peruvians. They were unable to buy fertilizer or crop spray because they were Indians. They had no access to the government's extension service for the same reason. Once such resources became available through the intercession of the Cornell-Peru Project, many Vicosinos willingly improved their economic position.

In other parts of Peru where there was no outside protection Indians have found that if they acquired too many animals or too much land, it would be stolen from them. The novels *Broad and Alien is the World* (Alegría, 1941) about Peru and *Huasipungo: The Villagers* (Icaza, 1964) about Ecuador were not overdrawn when written 30 years ago. Peasants' abuses of each other cannot compare with the abuse of peasants by outsiders. The case reported by Harris (1964) is illustrative. Merino sheep much better than the local variety were introduced to the Indians in an Ecuadorian community. When suspicion was overcome and the sheep were accepted by the local Indians, wool production improved so much that the local mestizos came and stole all the sheep.

In Lima squatter settlements, Rotondo and I both noted that a large number of poor migrants to the city, with few possessions and a most tenuous hold on economic security, nevertheless asserted other people envied them. As Rotondo points out (1963), envy and feeling that others are envious is very common among the migrants. But we also noticed considerable pride in and support for local leaders. The squatter invasions around Lima show evidence of planning, cooperation and leadership of the highest quality; yet many of them were organized by men and women only a few years out of peasant communities (Mangin, 1963; 1967b). That these leaders are often involved in subsequent squabbles and are often accused of misappropriating funds would tend to bear out Foster's idea. However, in about an equal number of the cases I observed, the leaders were not involved in serious squabbles and accusations. The same is true of peasants and children of peasants in migrants' regional associations (Mangin, 1959). In the land invasions by Indian peasants in the Peruvian sierra the leaders are increasingly from the communities and seem to be typical men and women rather than especially charismatic individuals.

But more information on the invasions and on the rapidly spreading peasant syndicates throughout the Andes is needed to make sure that global ideas do not produce caricatures of reality. Despite such general works as Foster's and many armchair speculations on the "soul" of Mexico, Peru, Colombia, et al., there have been very few studies of personality. Rotondo and his associates in Peru (1963) have done significant work with highland migrants to Lima and the Sullivan Institute of Psychoanalysis staff worked for three months interviewing Vicosinos and has extensive data on personality formation (unpublished). There are chapters on child training and family in many monographs, some rather detailed. However, different investigators come up with different pictures. Moreover, the same investigator often notes great differences in neighboring communities with the same underlying culture.

Nash (1964) describes differences in the economic systems and world views of Cantel, Guatemal and Amatenango, Mexico, setting forth historical and social reasons for the differences. He also (p. 302) mentions in passing that a neighboring community of Amatenango with the same general culture, Aquatenango, ". . . is much more acculturated, much more receptive to Ladinos, works in closer harmony with the Instituto (a Mexican government bureau), and in general is a less defensive and hostile community in relation to the outside world." Bunzel describes markedly different drinking routines and patterns of social personality in two towns with similar cultures (Bunzel, 1940), and Viquiera and Palerm (1954) show dramatic differences in alcoholism, suicide, and witchcraft in two neighboring Mexican towns. The Cornell Project studies in highland Peru and the ILO studies around Puno reveal great variation between local communities. The "progressive" Indian communities of Muquiyauyo (Adams, 1959), and Sicaya (Escobar, 1947) of the Mantaro Valley in Peru can be matched by very different kinds of Indian communities in the same valley (Tschopik, 1947; my own personal observations in the area) where large numbers of the young men have gone to Lima or to Huancayo (the provincial capital) and nothing much is happening economically or politically.

Of course, these reported variations may reflect personality differences among investigators, but in most cases I believe that such personality differences lead to tapping existent themes in the communities, all "true." Differences between neighboring communities with the same culture are another facet of the same phenomenon. Certain economic, political, or historical-accidental events lead to an accentuation of already existent themes in the cultures of the communities. If the local value system is such that the aspirations of most of the members of a community can be realized through local resources and with little threat from the outside, then change does not always appear attractive. Many highland peasant communities are, to some extent, in that situation. The aspiration level is relatively low compared to middle class, upper class and even lower class urban dwellers, and many important rewards are available in the fiesta system and in holding local political office.

If some factor such as encroachment on land by outsiders, a natural disaster, or overpopulation enters to make the desired goals unavailable, or if some local or outside leader or some planned or chance exposure to new ideas makes a different set of aspirations seem more desirable than the old ones, then change can seem attractive. In fact, such negative and positive events occur together; and peasant communities are constantly subject to pressures and are constantly changing. A common response to pressure is migration to a plantation or a city. Another, sometimes accompanying migration, is to draw back as the Indians do in Alegría's novel (1941); but, unfortunately, the dogged resistance he describes often gives way to disorganization and resignation as, for example, in Carcas, Peru (Castillo, Castillo and Revilla, 1964) or among the Otomi in Mexico (Wallis, 1953).

A third response is to acculturate strategically by developing new ways of coping, often based on old ways presented in a new, and sometimes distorted, form, as in nativistic movements. There have been no large scale nativistic movements in Latin America but there have been many social bandits and primitive rebels who frequently had small scale milennia in mind (Hobsbawm, 1965). Indians and Cholos still sing of the brigand band of Atushparia in Ancash, Peru; and two guerrilla bands operating in the central Andes of Peru in 1965, made up largely of white, Negro and mestizo university students, took the names Tupac Amaru and Pachacutec after a leader of a rebellion against the Spanish in Cuzco and a highly successful Inca imperialist. They were unable to attract large numbers of Indians but the syndicates in the south have attracted thousands. Personalism plays a large role in mobilizing highland peasants but, as Hobsbawm shows for peasant movements in Andalusia and Sicily (1965), political organization and strategy are less common than manipulative charisma and anarchistic appeals based on long standing and usually merited distrust of all governments.

Foster takes account of the potentialities for change that inhere in existing themes in peasant culture:

> Those who have known peasant villages over a period of years have seen how the old sanctions begin to lose their power. . . . The problem of the new countries is to create economic and social conditions in which this latent energy and talent is not quickly brought up against absolute limits, so that it is nipped in the bud.

This is, of course, the danger of new expectations—released latent *n* achievement—outrunning the creation of opportunities (1965b, p. 310).

It is obviously not only a problem in "the new countries," but in practically all countries, particularly in highland Latin America.

I agree with Foster that a change in cognitive orientation can alter behavior and economic and political productivity, and even effect apparent personality changes in individuals, without extensive "deep" changes in personality or culture, as he says, "at the mother's knee." But I doubt that the "image of limited good," with its fear of individual progress and personal envy is more important in retarding change than external economic and political conditions.

THE CULTURE OF POVERTY

I would take a similar position in relation to Lewis' culture of poverty. Lewis says:

> The culture or subculture of poverty comes into being in a variety of historical contexts. Most commonly it develops when a stratified social and economic system is breaking down or is being replaced by another, as in the case of the transition from feudalism to capitalism or during the industrial revolution. Sometimes it results from imperial conquest in which the conquered are maintained in a servile status which may continue for many generations (Lewis, 1961, p. xxv).

He also sees it as, ". . . a way of life, remarkably stable and persistent, passed down from generation to generation along family lines" (1961, p. xxiv).

Lewis describes this in Mexico (1961, pp. xxvi-xxvii), where he believes at least the lower third of both urban and rural populations live in a "culture of poverty." For these people life expectancy is lower than average, the death rate higher, education and literacy low, and child and female labor common. Even in the heart of Mexico City they remain marginal to the modern urban society, not participating in labor unions or political parties, not using many of the major commercial and service institutes of the city, often not even obtaining welfare assistance and social security benefits. They cannot afford doctors, mistrust hospitals, and rely upon herbs, home remedies, and local curers and midwives. Though they pray to images of saints and make pilgrimages to popular shrines, they are critical of priests and alienated from them. Lacking skills and thus steady, adequately paid employment, they acquire neither material nor cash reserves, cannot obtain credit from banks, and often must depend upon local and frequently exploitative merchants and moneylenders.

In the crowded quarters of their slum homes privacy is minimal, violence common, the solidarity of marriages and families idealized but uncertain. Resigned and fatalistic, the people are oriented to the present with little capacity to delay gratification or plan for the future. In such a milieu expression of *machismo*, the cult of masculinity, shifts from a middle class emphasis on sexual exploits and the Don Juan complex into a focus on heroism and lack of physical fear; and drinking becomes less a social amenity and more a way to forget troubles, to build up confidence to meet new difficulties, and simply to prove one's ability to drink. Hatred of police, mistrust of government, and cynicism about even the church are also dominant attitudes. Interwoven with all of the foregoing are the remnants of beliefs and customs of diverse origins.

Lewis omits "primitive" peoples in the culture of poverty because their ". . . backwardness is the result of their isolation and underdeveloped technology and whose society for the most part is not class stratified. Such peoples have a relatively integrated, satisfying, and self-sufficient culture" (1961, p. xxiv). By the same logic we can question the inclusion of closed, corporate Indian communities with internal prestige systems so long as they do not use outsiders as reference groups. An element of choice is involved. Poverty implies involuntary deprivation in relation to some known standard. A mestizo in Marcara can be living in poverty by his own and the society's definition while a Vicosino with much less can be considered well off by himself and his fellows and not be considered at all by the general society.

In dealing with urban migrants, however, it is a rare case when the type of limited aspiration level encountered in the closed community can continue for more than a generation. Even in many of the rural closed communities most of the people are well aware of the disparities in wealth that exist in their areas and they have deep resentment toward local patrons and officials. For example, deprivation is so great in the Peruvian sierra that migrants to urban areas, although appearing to be in an appalling economic state, are often pleased with the relative improvement in status. The realization of certain goals such as acquiring property in a squatter invasion, getting children into school, or, above all, getting steady work, can more than overcome substandard living conditions, low pay, poor quality education, and the like, at least for a time. There are data supporting this from Peru (Mangin 1967a; Turner, 1963), Mexico (Butterworth, 1962), Chile (Herrick, 1966) and all over Latin America (Mangin, 1967b), as well as in many other parts of the world (Turner, 1967). The children and grandchildren of the migrants will and do have higher aspiration and will not be satisfied with the same conditions.

Migrants often exhibit, in addition to the traits enumerated by Lewis, the envious behavior Foster attributes to the image of the limited good. But, as in the case of Foster, blocked access to opportunities would seem to account for all of these attitudinal patterns as much as any passing down of a culture of poverty. As Turner and I, and many Peace Corps volunteers, noted in Lima, when community organizing increased access to opportunity and presented new possibilities for gaining power, communities responded by widespread participation. Nor did it matter whether the organizing originated inside or outside of the community or from political, religious, foreign or domestic groups. New leaders arose, internal fights crystallized, cooperation occurred, morale improved, and people acted. What appeared to be entrenched apathy often turned out to be simply a strong, resentful feeling that there was no chance.

The organizing moves frequently were short-lived, eventuating in failure. Sometimes they left the communities more divided and alienated. But at other times they had the reverse effect. The difference in morale between squatter settlement dwellers and slum dwellers in Lima is impressive even to casual visitors. It seems to me to be largely due to the fact that the squatter settlements were formed by organized invasions, have internal community organization with elections, and reward talent, initiative and courage. The slum dwellers are basically the same kinds of people in regard to status characteristics, that is, many of them are rural migrants mainly from the mountains, mainly young, and the like, but they do not see the future the same way and they exhibit more depression and alienation.

Squatter Settlements in Peru

Nowhere is the potentiality of the urban poor to display behavior contradictory to the "culture of poverty" and "image of limited good" concepts more evident than in the "squatter communities" of South America. Such settlements have expanded greatly around large cities in rapidly urbanizing countries since the end of World War II. The various colorful names given them—*favelas* in Brazil, *bidonvilles* in North Africa, parachutists, mushrooms, clandestine or phantom settlements in parts of Spanish America— all have the local connotation of "shantytown." All of them begin as shantytowns; some remain so, at least in part. But the term obscures the fact that most squatter settlements are constantly improving their environments and that they represent a tremendous social and political investment in community organization as well as a multimillion dollar investment in house construction, the development of services, and the creation of small businesses. They are self organizing communities that grow up outside of, and often in the face of active opposition from, national governments. They are prime examples of the sort of popular initiative sought and so seldom encountered by leaders of community action programs in the United States. In hundreds of cases, thousands of people have taken matters into their own hands, gone beyond the inadequate, slow, and inefficient national and international welfare and aid programs, and created their own communities in and around large urban centers.

In spite of this, however, they are generally referred to as "disgraceful," "shameful," "festering sores," and the like, and both the benevolent and punitive official positions start with the removal of the squatters. "Eradication" is the most commonly used word in "solutions to the squatter settlement problem." Hostility and misunderstanding characterize the prevailing local attitude toward squatter settlements in most countries. The upper and middle class urban population sees their city invaded by undesirable and potentially revolutionary country people whose most visible manifestation seems to be the unsightly shantytowns. Architects and planners see what they regard as costly and wasteful use of urban land. Police and political leaders see them as defiance of law and order since they are illegal and are formed by invasions. Many citizens are genuinely frustrated by the lack of official efforts to cope with the housing and other social problems reflected in the creation of the settlements and think that if it only wanted to, the government could eradicate them and build new housing. It is also apparent that many members of the power elites of the countries involved find it uncomfortable and threatening that so many people have taken action and accomplished something without their help and direction, in fact, in the face of their opposition.

MYTH AND REALITY

A number of myths have arisen about the settlements, surprisingly similar in widely separated areas, and they persist in the face of accumulating contrary evidence. The nature of these myths varies somewhat from country to country but essentially they are the same, as indicated by comparing my study of the *barriadas* of Peru, the work of Leeds in Brazilian *favelas*, and Turner on a worldwide sample of squatters. The myths were created and reinforced by newspapers, government agencies, United Nations and US-AID missions, social scientists, travelers, and the majority of the middle and upper class populations of the countries involved. They are so pervasive that they often influence the attitudes of the squatters about themselves and about other squatters. They certainly have helped determine governmental policies toward the squatters with the increasing visibility of the settlements since World War II.

The myths in Peru say that the squatters are of rural origin and that they are recently arrived, Quechua-speaking, mountain Indians. They are, supposedly, disorganized, uneducated, unambitious, and an economic drag on the nation. Consistency being no requirement in mythology, they are also thought to be highly organized political radicals ready to descend on the city to communize and destroy. The references to the *barriadas* of Lima as "breeding grounds of communism," "red seedbeds," "ripe for agitators," etc., are even more numerous than the frequent references to them as centers of crime and delinquency, broken homes, and abject poverty. Some are all or several of these things but the "outside agitator" myth is as popular in Peru as it is in the United States. Not only do many see the *barriadas* as centers of revolution, but some see them as formed by agitators, usually communists;

and certain Peruvian, Brazilian and United States officials have even blamed rural-urban migration on communist agents.

The *barriadas* first came to my attention while I was working in the mountains of Peru in 1952. Many of the people I knew in the mountains had friends and relatives living in *barriadas* in Lima, and when I visited them I was frequently surprised by the difference between the way they lived and saw themselves and the way people outside thought they lived and saw them.

After ten years of study of *barriadas* in Peru, my own data show that the *barriada* people have resided in Lima, on the average, for about nine years before coming to the *barriada;* that they are largely literate, with a higher educational level than the general population; that, although they originally come from the mountain provinces and many are native Quechua speakers, the vast majority of them speak Spanish and are far removed from traditional, rural Indian culture; that families are relatively stable compared to city slum areas and rural provinces; that delinquency and prostitution are rare in *barriadas* but high in city slums; that, although many are marginally employed, most total family incomes are well above the poorest level, and the security of a rent-free house makes *barriadas* much more attractive than the high rent, unpleasant slums from which most of the residents come. The data also indicate that they are highly organized, politically sophisticated, strongly nationalistic and patriotic, and relatively conservative in aspirations for change. They reflect neither Oscar Lewis' culture of poverty, although they are poor, nor Franz Fanon's spontaneous, revolutionary urban lumpenproletariat, although they are spontaneous and revolutionary in the way they acquire and defend their land.

The prevailing view, both popular and that of reporters and social scientists, also asserted that migrants from the mountains had a difficult time adjusting to the city and that the *barriadas* constituted the most visible and the worst consequence of the disruptive effects of rural-urban migration. My original impression may have been an overreaction to the differences between rumor and reality, but I am still impressed with the capacity for and evidence of popular initiative, self-help and local community organization. There is tremendous poverty. There are unbelievable inequalities in the administration of justice, tax laws, protection under the law, and distribution of wealth. Class tensions run high. Migrants suffer from all kinds of health and sanitation problems, inadequate schools, lack of public services, and general discrimination if they are "Indian" in appearance, as many of them are. I was caricatured in a leading Lima newspaper as a Yankee anthropologist who affirmed happiness in *barriadas* and saw them as Paradise Lost, because, in a talk, I stressed the integrative aspects of *barriadas* and did not say that they were "festering sores." Only a very naive observer could ignore the poverty, underemployment, sickness, lack of sewage disposal facilities, and the colossal waste of human resources reflected in *barriadas*. When the local people say, as they so often do, "We are abandoned, living in infra-human conditions," they are speaking part of the truth. There is, however, another story. Both they and most of the outside observers neglect the fact that they have provided a solution to a most difficult problem of housing and community organization in a rapidly urbanizing country where the small controlling elite has been uninterested, or in the few instances where interested, manifestly unable to take effective action.

How "Barriadas" Originate

I will try here to describe something of the way Lima's *barriadas* are formed, how they develop and become part of the city, and some of the consequences of their formation and the national reaction to them. The *barriadas* of Lima have about 450,000 residents. Lima has always grown through migration from rural areas, mostly the Andean provinces, and a large percentage, probably over half, of the city's adults came from there. Most of the *barriada* children were born in Lima, but over 80 per cent of the adults were provincial born, again mostly from the mountains. Since Lima has two million people and Peru in total about thirteen million, the *barriada* population of Lima constitutes a good part of the nation. Still another 400,000 live in *barriadas* around other large cities.

At first glance the *barriadas*, clinging to steep, rocky hillsides or clustered along the banks of the Rimac River, appear to be planless hodgepodges of straw shacks. In fact, most of them have plans, often made in consultation with architectural or engineering students, and most of the residents convert their original straw houses to brick and cement as fast as they can afford to. The recently invaded area of El Agustino hill is mainly straw construction. The 20 year old central part of San Martin now has a paved main street and the houses are mainly of brick and cement. The paving of the street came after many years of construction of houses and stores, and was followed by the installation of elegant fronts on stores, banks, movie houses, plus the painting of many house fronts. The residents had been holding off because of the dust from the unpaved street.

The history of a *barriada* can be studied both by observing, or reconstructing, the experience of one community and by comparing *barriada* communities started at different times. It can also be seen in any one *barriada* at any given time by comparing the old settlers with the newcomers. Some of the hillsides present an historic panorama with the oldest brick and cement houses on the relatively flat streets at the foot, and the newest straw houses on rocky platforms carved out of the steep banks. Benavides was formed by invasion in 1954 and continued to grow until 1959 or 1960. By that time the hillsides were practically full, and most of the new residents of the last few years have been mainly replacements through resale or rental. The Benavides population appears quite stable when comparing a 1956 San Marcos University census and our census of 1959, and I was able to find practically all of the sample families when I returned in the spring of 1966.

The large-scale invasions that have formed most *barriadas* are necessitated by the opposition of the government and the forcible prevention or removal of those squatting on vacant land. A few families would have no chance. Large numbers can be, and have been forcibly removed with considerable injury and loss of life, but they stand a better chance against the police. The calculated, and often verified, position of invasion organizers is that no government is strong enough to attack openly invading families, including women and children, particularly after public attention has been centered on the incident. As a matter of fact, invaders have been attacked, women and children beaten and killed, and meager household goods, gathered at great cost, burned or otherwise destroyed; but the invaders have returned as many as four different times to one place and have, in the end, been allowed to stay.

The organizational work involved in planning and organizing an invasion includes alerting newspapers, one of which can always be assumed to be antigovernment and willing to feature any embarrassing news, and calling for help from, or at least the blessing of, some prominent political or popular figures—for example, a bishop or the president's wife. These are last minute details that top off long months of secret planning and organizing. Some of the early invasions were probably spontaneous and involved trial-and-error learning. Now the pattern is fairly well established.

There are some men and women, motivated by personal compassion in some cases, by personal gain or political advantage in others, who have helped organize several such actions. One man who had been involved in at least three major invasions told me that he did it because he enjoyed the excitement and the activity. Some leaders have been in political parties and some have become involved in *barriada* land speculation; but most have been people seeking a new place to live where they can have a roof of their own. Of the many *barriada* leaders I have met, a few have been charlatans, a few incompetents; but most have been highly intelligent, articulate, calculating, courageous, tough people. The nominal leader is a man, but women are always active in the organization and, in many cases, the second position named is the secretary of defense who is often a woman. (The title probably comes from labor union organization where the secretary of defense is an important post, but there are also provincial clubs where the position exists.)

The association is defensive from the beginning. Its recruitment from among those dislocated by urban renewal, co-workers, people from the same province living in Lima, neighbors and friends, stresses contacting "persons of confidence." The preparations must be secret because if the proposed location is known the police will guard it. Lima is located on the coastal desert and the land not irrigated by the Rimac River is rocky and arid and not in use. Some *barriadas* have recently invaded some cultivated areas north of Lima but mostly they have entered barren land. A search is made by lawyers or near-lawyers, both in oversupply, to check on the title to the desired piece of land. My own impression over the years has been that practically any plot in Peru has at least two titles, and that much of the arable land is in litigation; but some reasonable claim to the piece by some public agency, preferably the national government, is the rule in *barriada* invasions. The place is marked out with rocks, usually at night, and the lots are assigned. Certain lots are set aside for schools, churches, clinics, plazas, etc., and streets are allowed for on the level parts. Much discussion goes on about who is going where, but the original invasion is generally orderly.

Considering the lack of similar examples of initiative, cooperation and efficient organization in the national life, it is all the more remarkable that hundreds of people—in a few invasions over a thousand—can secure their own transportation in taxis, trucks, buses and large tricycles, get to an appointed location at approximately the same time after coming from all sections of a crowded city, gather the materials to construct straw houses on a given plot of land and have them ready, and behave in a consistently courageous, disciplined, yet non-provocative manner in the face of armed attack by the police. In the past 20 years it has happened over 100 times. During the present Belaunde regime the emphasis has been on preventing the invasions and they have not been met with excessive violence when they have occurred. The relative numbers, however, have stayed about the same under the dictatorship of Odria, the elected term of Prado, the military takeover of 1962-1963, and the present liberal administration.

SUBSEQUENT DEVELOPMENT

The invaders are generally married couples under 30 with their children. Childless couples are rare in *barriadas* and single adults not part of a larger household are usually barred from invasion groups and excluded from later residence, where possible, by the *barriada* association. As the population ages the number of adolescents obviously increases and families begin to send for and otherwise accumulate older relatives, often directly from the provinces. Grandparents can be very useful as baby sitters, allowing the wife to work. They also can tend the stores that so many families operate in their front rooms and assist with the many menial tasks that are necessary in a community where water has to be carried, sewage disposed of, fuel gathered, small animals tended, and houses watched.

Except for the largest *barriadas*, where there is considerable local employment in construction, marketing, and general manual labor, most of the men and many of the women work in various parts of the city. This has given rise to dozens of private bus cooperatives and multiple passenger taxi lines (*colectivos*), as well as expansion of the established bus companies' service. Occupations vary, with most concentrated in service work, many in factory work and marketing, a good number in white-collar work including police and military, and a few professionals. There is a men's club in the *barriada* area of Comas that has among its members a medical doctor, a bank branch manager, a police lieutenant, four lawyers, several businessmen, and two Peace Corps volunteers. Anxiety about loss of employment or not having steady employment was the most obvious source of insecurity noted in our interviews, and many respondents said that they, or their husbands, were envied because they had steady work. *Barriadas* do create jobs, particularly in construction work, and many families supplement or gain most of their income from stores, bars, or shops operated in their homes.

As the *barriada* becomes more permanent, the electric company of Lima begins to sell service. For years prior to that time individuals buy generators and run lines, often crisscrossing each other, to their own clients. One man in Benavides who had such a generator with a number of customers, also bought a TV set on time and charged admission to watch, making enough to meet the payments. Water and kerosene, the major fuel, come in by truck, bicycle, and carried on backs, and are sold in quantities ranging from 50 gallon drums to Inca-Cola bottles. The number of entrepreneurs in *barriadas* is very large. We estimated that about one-third of the households of Benavides offered something for sale. Elaborate credit arrangements are set up and it is possible to buy as small an item as a bottle of hair tonic on time from an itinerant peddler.

After the invasion the residents are all "owners" of their lots. All of the units are dwellings, although some double as stores and restaurants. The nuclear family of husband, wife and children is by far the most common household unit. As time goes on, renting becomes more frequent, and many individuals sell, trade, lend or lease their lots and houses to others, using beautifully made titles with numbers, seals, lawyers' signatures, and elaborate property descriptions, but also with very dubious, or in most cases no, legality. Extra relatives arrive and some families take in boarders. Some build structures intended for stores, hotels, or other commercial ends. Disputes over land begin and are taken to the association, the National Housing Authority, the city government, the police, and the courts. Decisions are usually reached but there is little consistency and, along with most of the national legislation, they have a "provisional" character.

After the passage of the Law of Barriadas in 1957, five years passed before land titles were given out. In late 1962, taking advantage of the preoccupation of the military junta with other matters, a group of engineers and architects in the National Housing Authority passed out land titles to a few hundred families in two of the oldest *barriadas*. Even these few titles, to people who had been living on the sites for ten years, were clearly marked "provisional." I have seen birth certificates stamped "provisional."

The association leaders are, at first, the invasion leaders, but they either run for office or give way to new candidates who run, normally within a year. *Barriadas* hold elections about once a year and, although the campaigns are spirited, the results are respected. Local elections have been a rarity in Peru. Limited ones have been held under the present government for the first time in over 60 years. Unofficial *barriada* elections have been among the few examples of popular local government in the intervening time. Since the elections are unofficial it is not always possible for the association to enforce its rules. They do manage to collect dues from most members, screen most new applicants, prevent some land speculation, resolve most land disputes, and, perhaps most importantly, organize cooperative projects and act as broker between the *barriada* and national ministries, city government, and international organizations such as the Peace Corps and the UN. Individual personality factors plus kinship and regional loyalty play the largest part in the elections, but national political parties do intervene and generally play a role. The original leaders sometimes move out but may retain some influence. Factionalism develops and, following a time honored Peruvian tradition cutting across all social classes, accusations of misappropriation of money lead to serious splits. As the *barriada* becomes more a part of the city and less under attack, and as local factionalism increases, the association loses power. Associations have also lost power in the two largest *barriada* areas, once encompassing over 40 different *barriadas*—Pampa de Comas and San Martín—with the official election of a mayor and town council in each of the two areas in the 1963 elections.

Outside contact is quite frequent. Police stations in adjoining neighborhoods of the city are used for complaints about petty thievery and wife and child beating, but only on rare occasions do the police do more than register the complaint. Papers are needed for voting, registering births, deaths and marriages, testifying to military status; the numbers on the voting book are used on receipts, employment applications, and the like. Many individuals left the provinces before getting any documents and many need new ones for marriages and other official matters, so trips are made to the town hall in the municipality where the *barriada* is located. Since the *barriadas* are not all officially recognized and town clerk behavior is highly particularistic and whimsical, some of the quests for documents are truly heroic. Many people are also involved with government agencies petitioning for services, jobs, medical care, social security, unemployment insurance, and the like, and still others have outside contacts with church groups, provincial clubs, social clubs, unions, and schools. There are grammar schools in some *barriadas* but in many the children are sent outside to school; and in all some children are sent outside to church and private schools. High school and university students commute to the city from the *barriadas*.

An important outside agency for *barriadas* is the National Housing Authority, the JNV. JNV has legal power to decide on land use and funds to help with plans, technical assistance, and, in some cases, with construction. For a few years there were two agencies, one reflecting a past regimè and the other the present government. The rivalry had a few advantages but proved costly. It was resolved, and one agency created, the JNV. A conflict has arisen, however, between the powers of the newly elected local mayors in the several municipal divisions of Greater Lima and the JNV. The acceptance of the JNV varies with its accomplishments. In some *barriadas* it is cheered, in others it is stoned. In some areas it has facilitated building and services. In others it has failed because of the inability of the central office to delegate authority or because of too many plans and not enough action.

As of now *barriada* people are suspicious of large scale projects and, like most rural Peruvians, wary of entering into any loan or mortgage arrangements involving their property. They are quite aware of the insurance value of their squatters' houses in the event of an emergency such as illness, loss of employment, or the need to travel. One man stated the position quite clearly, "I can build my house when I can afford it. If I have overtime work on construction one week, I can buy bricks and cement, and food and beer for my brother-in-law to come and help. If I have no work, or I spend, as when I had to travel to the sierra for my mother's funeral, I don't work on the house, and I don't pay rent." Another insurance factor leading to community stability is that if a man abandons his wife in a *barriada*, he leaves behind his house and the woman becomes a better remarriage risk, being a property holder.

Our data from the questionnaires and the ethnographic material show that, in spite of many complaints, the aspiration levels of most of the adults are relatively low and many of them feel that they have achieved more than they thought possible when they have more or less steady work, a house of their own, and their children in school. They overwhelmingly agree that their present *barriada* situation is preferable to what they had in the provinces and, even more so, to what they had in Lima before the invasion. The data do indicate that they have very high aspirations for their children. If mobility is blocked and the children are not able to go on to secondary schools and move up the occupational ladder, from all indications the most likely course of events, then the political climate of *barriadas* could very well change. As of the present, they seem mobilizable only in defense of their homes.

Eviction and eradication of *barriadas* involve great monetary cost and are politically disruptive and dangerous. There seems to be an increasing realization that migrants come to cities for economic and other good reasons, and that they stay. Another consequence of the passage of time is an inevitable loss of the initial enthusiasm and feeling of belongingness brought on by the sense of achievement in accomplishing the invasion and the *esprit de corps* resulting from being under attack. Bickering becomes common and class distinctions arise. People begin to identify themselves and others as Indians, Cholos, Mestizos, Negroes, Mountaineers, Coastal People, city people, country people—in short, the divisions in the larger society begin to divide the community. People still call each other "neighbor," and say, "Here we are all paisanos," but the status characteristics of the general society begin to assert themselves. Along with this, however, personal networks of godparents, friends, relatives, people from the same region, local clubs, local commercial associates, begin to develop. Mutual aid on public projects continues, cooperative work groups keep on working on houses, and the community generally stays able to rally in the face of outside threats.

For people who have achieved so much on their own, the *barriada* residents are remarkably unaware of their accomplishments and their potential, and they see the "solution" to their problems as coming from outside. In our own sample in Benavides, and in countless personal experiences, people answer that the government, the municipality, or some outside agency should provide the answer. Few see that they can play any part in the solutions. In one sense they are right, particularly in the case of expensive capital improvements such as water supply facilities, sewers, and paved streets. Similarly, for services such as police, clinics, and schools, the people can go only a short way without assistance from the government. They have shown, however, that in house construction and land development they can do as well as the government at much less cost. In fact, it can be said that they do better than the government. They have succeeded in part because the government did not intervene to help at least in the customary manner of government "help." In the cases where the state has tried housing projects for poor people they have had very little success. The administrative costs and the bureaucratic restrictions on loan qualifications, coupled with the high construction and material costs when the government has done the contracting, put the housing out of range of the economic means of the potential clients.

Yet it seems that any official encouragement or recognition, such as paving a street or even tax collection, is a welcome sign in a *barriada* and leads to increased activity in self-improvement. Without painting an overly-optimistic picture, it appears that most *barriada* residents are non-alienated, eternally hopeful, yet properly cynical, individuals. Over the past several years I have talked with foreigners who have visited, or stayed a time, in *barriadas,* mainly anthropologists, Peace Corps volunteers, and college students. Most of them remark on the amount of construction and home and community improvements, the number of small businesses, the degree of organization, the lack of help from the government, and the friendliness of the people. Most of them also remark on the lack of resentful action on the part of the *barriada* residents in the face of the difficult conditions under which they live. The *barriada* rhetoric to outsiders is loaded with, "We are humble people," "Here we live in our honest humility," "We are abandoned," "We work hard," and with calls for outside help from the government, the ministry, or some "they"; but it is strikingly non-resentful, and not very revolutionary.

"SOLUTIONS" TO THE "PROBLEM" OF SQUATTERS

My major point has been that the squatter settlements represent a solution to a complex problem of rapid urbanization and migration, combined with a housing shortage. The "problem" is that this solution is unacceptable to many in positions of power. Their reactions tend to fall into two main categories.

THE "ERADICATION-DEPORTATION SOLUTION"

A common view, not popular in print but frequently expressed by planners and decision-makers, is to eradicate the settlements and send the squatters back to the farms they came from. This might be called the "festering sore–hard nosed" view. So far it has led mainly to talk. In Peru in the early 1950s a law was introduced requiring all those intending to migrate from the provinces to Lima to get permission from the prefect of the department. Since many people did not know about the law, many did not know about the prefect, and those that did could not find him because prefects spend most of their time in Lima, the law was never implemented.

At least one source from every country surveyed said that the squatters were more satisfied with their present housing and economic situation than what they had had in the rural areas and small towns, and in the central city. This includes even the Argentine situation (Germani, 1961) where the squatters are of a somewhat different character. Herrick (1966), referring to migrants to Santiago, and not exclusively *callampa* residents, said that return movement was rare. "Of these migrants, all of whom had moved to Santiago within the last ten years, only one-seventh knew anyone who had come to Santiago to live and who had subsequently returned to his place of origin for any reason." In my study of a *barriada* in Peru, only two families from the sample moved out in two years, one to return to the mountains, one to go to a house in the city. I heard of very few families going back to the country. The city growth and the squatter settlements are there to stay.

As a matter of political reality, the possibility of shipping hundreds of thousands of people back into a hinterland to which they would not voluntarily return seems remote, short of the application of force on a scale that would approximate bloody civil war But the consideration of such a possibility indicates a predisposition on the part of some planners and governmental officials that cannot help but affect their approach to other ways of meeting "the problem."

If put in the context of regional development and decentralization programs, "deportation" might have some effect on migration of new people to cities; but I doubt that it would much affect squatter settlements. In a small jungle colonization program in Peru in which the government and the Great Plains Wheat Foundation financed some *barriada* residents to move to the upper Amazon region, the squatters simply "sold" their homes to others. Brasilia and Ciudad Guayana, Venezuela, are spectacular attempts to decentralize, and have been more or less successful, but squatter settlements had formed in both places before the cities were even constructed!

THE "ERADICATION-RELOCATION SOLUTION"

Many who would consider themselves "liberal" and "progressive" also advocate eradication of the squatters' settlements. Schulman (1966) notes that "Msgr. Ruben Isaza, Bishop Coadjutor of Bogotá, has called them 'malignant tumors that have grown on my city' and, along with others of his countrymen, is working for their displacement and for the betterment of the social and economic factors which have created them." This might be termed the "festering sore–bleeding heart" view. It is the most popular one in print and can be found in all of the countries. When acted upon it generally results in housing projects and satellite cities that turn out to be too expensive for the dislocated squatters, as well as unsatisfactory in many other ways, very much like urban renewal projects in the United States.

The report by Wagner, McVoy, and Edwards (1966) showed that the Rio satellites were too far away from work and residents complained of losing jobs because of transportation problems. No local enterprise grows because of zoning and planning regulations. Salmon (1966) points out that the mortgage payments are too high, particularly if some emergency comes up, since people are so close to the margin economically. He also cites some ex-*favelados* reporting that they felt safer on the streets of the *favelas* because there were more people around and they knew everybody. Lance Belville, in *The New York Times* (Nov. 21, 1965), reports identical feelings in another satellite city near Rio, Vila Aliance, and quotes a resident who formerly lived in a *favela* overlooking Botafogo Bay, close to his work, as saying,

> I hate it here . . . they brought me to this place in handcuffs.
> . . . it's too far from my work . . . My old shack had plenty of
> room for me and the family . . . and the shack didn't leak . . . I'm
> too far from the beach to go find crabs . . . Sometimes I just can't
> make the payments on the house . . . The house can wait. My
> children cannot wait.

Safa (1964), studying matched samples in shantytowns and public housing in Puerto Rico, found that management by bureaucrats had taken over control of neighborhood affairs which are in the hands of local men in shantytowns. In the projects it was considered up to "management or the police to settle disputes between neighbors or to reprimand a delinquent youth," replacing former informal sanctions. "The maximum income level imposed by project regulations discourages the man from improving his socio-economic position." "The result is that the comparatively wide range of incomes found in the shantytown is sharply reduced in public housing." Women find friends in both places but men do not. One man said (of the housing), "Here one can die and there is no one to do you a favor. There is no brotherhood or good neighbors." Men also felt that the avenues of cooperation open to them in shantytowns were not open in housing. They "do not even have a place to get together in the project, since the local *cafetin* and pool parlor have been eliminated."

Oscar Lewis (1966), in an excerpt from *La Vida* subtitled, "Portrait of a Puerto Rican Family—from deprivation in the slums to disaster in a housing project," quotes a woman to very much the same effect. She left the squatter settlement because she did not want to upset her social worker who had been good to her. She found the project dead and said, "I hated to go out because it's hard to find your way back to this place even if you know the address." "Listen, I'm jittery, really nervous, because if you fail to pay the rent even once here, the following month you're thrown out." The squatter settlement she left was more expensive (she was renting) but she could decide on how much electricity and water to use and she had many legal and illegal avenues to make money there that were blocked in the project.

In Venezuela, where the resources are vast, the housing projects, *Superbloques,* have hardly touched the housing need. Turner (1967) says that even with the thousands in the Superblocks, they have not had any effect on migration to Caracas or *rancho* population expansion. The satellite cities of Ventanilla (Lima), Ciudad Kennedy (Bogotá), and Vila Kennedy and Esperanca (Rio), heavily subsidized joint national government-AID housing programs, have turned out to be still too expensive for poor people. They have met the needs of some of the more affluent working class and white-collar members of the population, but have had little effect on the housing shortages experienced by masses of city dwellers.

SOLUTIONS WITHOUT "ERADICATION"

The general dissatisfaction with large scale housing projects in Brazil, Argentina, Venezuela and Colombia, has led to more interest in rehabilitation of existing situations, both on the part of national governments and AID. Peruvian officials are well aware of the controversy and may avoid costly mistakes made in the "satellite cities" and "Superblocks" of other countries. Experiments are being initiated with credit cooperatives, low cost loans with optional technical assistance, and by providing services and letting the owner do his own contracting. These may be expanded in the future.

Providing land, sewers, water and technical assistance, and possibly house shells, and allowing people to build at their own pace, has worked at least once in Valdivieso, Lima (Turner, 1963). In that case, however, it was unoccupied land that was used and did not involve eradication. However, real success with this approach is likely only if planners and officials can be made more cognizant of the values and needs of the people and both governmental and private agencies at least a little more honest and effective.

The lack of familiarity with the style of life and the desires of lower class clients has already led to some serious design and priority problems. People need the land, the walls and the roof immediately. They can wait for other things. They also prefer to buy electricity ahead of bathrooms, although, if they can afford it, they want both. But many institutions will not lend money on houses without bathrooms. The settlers want flat roofs and strong foundations so that they can add a second story. They want yards to raise guinea pigs and chickens and front rooms that can be used as bars and stores. But project architects want center pole and shell construction, residential zoning, and so on.

In the non-construction area, many lending institutions require marriage certificates. Estimates run as high as 60 per cent for the number of common-law marriages. If the couple decides to get married to qualify for the loan they find the need for birth certificates. It is next to impossible to get one if you are over three months old. And so it goes. And even many of those qualifying for the countless provisional lists for middle class and blue-collar housing give up and invade *barriadas* when they are passed over for the third time in favor of someone's cousin or some government official. Moreover, Latin American rural people are so familiar with being cheated and dispossessed by banks and mortgage holders that the very concept of a bank loan or a mortgage is suspect. As John Turner, an architect with many years experience in Peru, has pointed out, if people are sold land and allowed to do their own contracting and building with optional technical assistance and control, the costs go down for both the clients and the government. The many proponents of eradication always assumed an investment of almost nothing in straw and scrap construction instead of the investment of millions of dollars in labor and, as they put it, "noble materials" actually present in most of the settlements. Yet the AID report of Wagner, *et al.* (1966), says, "Generally speaking, the cost of upgrading the *favelas* will be less than the cost of relocation of *favela* dwellers in new housing construction."

"Many favelas have schools, meeting houses, churches, stores, and small shops; they also have self-help-constructed water and electricity distribution systems, and in some instances sewer systems. Small industries operated by individual owners or as family enterprises are scattered throughout most favelas. A good many houses are of perfectly sound construction." (See also, *N.Y. Times,*

August 12, 1966, Juan de Onis). The same reasoning is documented in detail by Helio Modesto and Charles O'Neil (Leeds, 1966). In Peru this approach has been suggested by some middle level planners. Usandizaga and Havens (1966) point out pride in achievement and suggest rehabilitation rather than eradication in Barranquilla. The O'Neil article (*Ibid.*) and another in the same series on eviction in a *favela*, by Smith, point out some of the political and social difficulties of eradication.

But so far the president and most leading architects have decided in favor of large construction programs involving high rise apartments (*Time*, March 12, 1965). O'Neil also points out, aptly for other countries as well as Brazil, that national political decisions about United States aid, creation of income opportunities through contracts, purchases, new government jobs, and so on, are all involved in the decisions about rehabilitating or eradicating. Unfortunately, there are more opportunities for all of those items in eradication and big project construction. Agencies in governments tend to survive, once created, whether or not they are effective in their avowed purpose; and agencies for eradication and housing project construction are already established.

Yet it is increasingly obvious that national governments, even with United States aid, can not provide housing, and that people are going to go somewhere. There are also small signs that some governments are beginning to think that popular initiative is more productive to work with than to fight against. The solution at least being *considered* in Peru, Brazil, Colombia, Venezuela and Chile, is to check new squatter settlements by providing cheap land and services for those who want it and to rehabilitate rather than eradicate most existing squatter settlements.

As Turner (1963) shows, the governments of Peru, Chile, and Colombia have in fact experimented with housing cooperatives, credit programs and minimal aid programs with some success on a very small scale. Meanwhile, thousands of people continue to apply what he calls the "unaided self-help solution."

SOME COMPARISONS AND CONCLUSIONS

Lewis' description of a culture of poverty is correct for some squatters' settlements and for many city slums. But most *barriadas* and other squatter settlements in other countries (Mangin, 1967) cannot be categorized as being part of the culture of poverty. Adversity and hostility are handled by their inhabitants with remarkably little breakdown. Along this line, Robert Coles (1967), Erik Erikson (1966) and others have pointed out the strength, self-discipline, and endurance of impoverished Negroes in the civil rights movement in the United States—men, women and children under extreme stress. The South African situation has produced equally dramatic examples. Neira (1964) and I have pointed out similar strength on the part of poor people in the land invasions in rural and urban Peru.

As yet no government has taken advantage of these qualities in any conscious way. Indeed, the idea may present us with a paradox. With a few minor exceptions no modern state—capitalist, communist, or whatever—has allowed large groups of poor people to work out their own definitions of problems and their own solutions. It may be too disruptive and I am not suggesting it as an all-purpose solution. It may be structurally impossible for a state to support conflict against itself. But the conflict comes anyway, even in benevolent systems. If the hand that is feeding you is the zoo keeper's, you probably have to bite it, particularly if it is not feeding you much. In the countries where large squatter developments have taken place the governments were not feeding anybody much of anything. That may be the best situation for emergence of effective community action by the poor, a necessary though certainly not sufficient condition.

The kind of community action represented by the squatters may only be possible in a national state where the government is not in full control. In many of the cases the land squatted on was public land or land in dispute. Building trades unions, which would prevent such action in this country, are in most of the underdeveloped countries, especially in Latin America, either non-existent, or small and weak, or under the control of the governments, or militant and not interested in stopping people from building their own homes. Many construction workers live in squatter settlements and make extra money or build mutual aid capital by working on neighbors' homes. Zoning and housing code laws may exist in some of the countries but they are seldom enforced.

Repressive police forces exist, and are used, but few of the countries with squatters are sure of the loyalty of all branches of the armed forces and few are willing to risk a full-scale attack on hundreds of families in full view of press and TV. Also, in spite of the authoritarian nature of many of the regimes, a certain amount of looseness is tolerated as long as it is not in an area of behavior that directly threatens the economic interests and power of the ruling groups. There is no large middle strata majority with a vested interest in law and order and the possibility of earning income from every piece of property and every business and labor contract. Interestingly enough, the squatters themselves often adopt extreme versions of nineteenth-century capitalism, begin selling things to each other, and make all kinds of restrictive rules about how new members can be admitted to the community. Once they have broken the law and seized their own land they turn out to be conventional, non-revolutionary, tractable members of the society. But without the looseness, disinterest, and general lack of control, they would never have had the chance.

In the United States there seems relatively little opportunity for poor people outside of the traditional channels, and many of these are no longer viewed as unqualified pathways of opportunity. There is even some questioning, particularly among the younger generation, of conventional notions of "desirable" goals. Yet Negroes are publicly urged by all of the media, as by the schools and by those in authority, to use the traditional channels "like everyone else did." No wonder that Carmichael's statements about the United States being a racist society meet with little objection among Negroes, even though his plans for changing it do not always elicit the same approval.

Yet the black poor sound very much like the white poor and even the white middle class majority have sounded at times in the face of apparently arbitrarily blocked opportunities. The solution to white opposition to black voting in Mississippi offered by Malcolm X (1965) is thoroughly "American":

So we here in the Organization of Afro-American Unity are with the struggle in Mississippi 1000 per cent. We're with the efforts to register our people in Mississippi to vote 1000 per cent. But we do not go along with anybody telling us to help non-violently. We think that if the government says that Negroes have a right to vote, and then some Negroes come out to vote, and some kind of a Ku Klux Klan is going to put them in the river, and the government doesn't do anything about it, it's time for us to organize and band together and equip ourselves and qualify ourselves to pro-

tect ourselves. And once you can protect yourself, you don't have
to worry about being hurt . . .

I have heard versions of that all of my life and they have always
been an available line in the American culture, along with the
"work hard, send your kids to school, paint your porch, be patient"
theme. In thousands of stories, movies and TV shows (cowboy,
war, and others) "the American way" is to try the latter, but with
resort to the former when the promised pay-offs for "good conduct"
are withheld. If both lines of action are blocked, then many manifestations of the culture of poverty appear.

But there seems to be evidence, as I have said, that the culture
of poverty is more of a "quasi-culture" in that it can be thrown off
so fast with changes in economic or social opportunities. The
changes may be in a constructive manner, such as those brought
about by the squatters' movements, in which case they break down
the "image of limited good" and "culture of poverty" inhibitions
to development. Or they may be in a destructive mode if no other
avenues are open, as in the case of the Watts and Detroit property
destruction and fighting.

Change from the top is probably necessary in the United States
because the top is so powerful and is backed by a relatively satisfied, enormous middle majority with a vested interest in the *status
quo* and with varying degrees of racial prejudice. Yet precisely for
that reason, there seems little likelihood of much change coming
from the middle and the top. The technical and financial problems
of poverty in the United States could probably be largely solved
with half of what we spend on the Vietnamese war. But the solutions would take a recognition of crisis and an acceptance of fundamental changes in our political, economic, and value systems. That
is asking a lot.

Culture is, however, a repository of possible patterns of behavior
and we have in our repository many patterns that do allow for
change and do support equality of opportunity. This remains a
source of hope for the United States. But such patterns are not as
salient in the Peruvian cultural repertory (and much of what I
have said of Peru applies to highland Latin America and to a lesser
but still large extent to most of the rest of Latin America). There
is no strong tradition that one man should have the same opportunity as another. There is no strong feeling, and certainly little

validation, for the idea that ability and hard work are related to success. There is some indication that the urban squatter invasions and the land invasions in rural areas, as well as the large number of internally and externally fostered development programs (Adams, 1967), are beginning to open up new possibilities, and may create some kind of a balance of power with the extremely powerful, foreign-backed, upper classes. This may manifest itself in Vargas or Peron type populist dictatorships, perhaps more left than right because of cold war pressures, or in social and christian democratic movements such as those of Frei in Chile or Belaunde in Peru. Counter moves can be expected from entrenched upper class military and middle-class, "Nasserist" military. Certainly, there seems to be no particular reason to think that there will not be millions of Latin Americans living in absolute and relative poverty for as long as we can foresee, with continuing political consequences for these nations in general and for their cities in particular.

References

ADAMS, RICHARD N. *Muquiyauyo: A Community in the Andes* (Seattle: University of Washington Press, 1959).

——. *The Second Sowing: Power and Secondary Development in Latin America* (San Francisco: Chandler Publications, 1967).

ALEGRIA, CIRO. *El Mundo es Ancho y Ajeno* (New York: Farrar and Rinehart, 1941).

BUNZEL, RUTH. "The Role of Alcoholism in Two Central American Cultures," *Psychiatry*, 3 (1940), pp. 361-87.

BUTTERWORTH, DOUGLAS S. "A Study of the Urbanization Process Among Mixtec Migrants from Tilantongo in Mexico City," *America Indigena*, 22 (1962), pp. 257-74.

CASTILLO, HERNAN, *et al. Carcas: The Forgotten Community* (Ithaca: Cornell Press, 1964).

COLES, ROBERT. "Civil Rights is also a State of Mind," *New York Times Magazine*, May 7, 1967, pp. 32-34.

DOUGHTY, PAUL. "La Cultura, la Bebida y el Trabajo en un Distrito Mestizo Andino," *America Indigena*, 27 (1967), pp. 667-87.

Erasmus, Charles J. "Upper Limits of Peasantry and Agrarian Reform: Bolivia, Venezuela and Mexico Compared," *Ethnology,* 6 (1967), pp. 349-80.

Erikson, Erik H. "The Concept of Identity in Race Relations: Notes and Queries," *Daedalus,* Vol. 95 (Winter, 1966), pp. 145-71.

Escobar, Gabriel. *Sicaya, una Comunidad Mestiza de la Sierre Central del Peru* (Peru: University de Cuzco, 1947).

Foster, George. "The Dyadic Contract: A Model for the Social Structure of a Mexican Peasant Village," *American Anthropologist,* 63 (1961), pp. 1173-92.

———. "The Dyadic Contract in Tzintzuntzan, II: Patron-Client Relationship," *American Anthropologist,* 65 (1963), pp. 1280-94.

———. "Cultural Responses to Expressions of Envy in Tzintzuntzan," *Southwestern Journal of Anthropology,* 21 (1965a), pp. 24-35.

———. "Peasant Society and the Image of Limited Good," *American Anthropologist,* 67 (1965b), pp. 293-315.

Gans, Herbert. *The Urban Villagers* (New York: Free Press, 1962).

Germani, Gino. "Inquiry into the Social Effects of Urbanization in a Working-Class Sector of Buenos Aires," in Philip M. Hauser (ed.), *Urbanization in Latin America* (New York: International Documents Service, 1961), pp. 206-33.

Harris, Marvin. *Patterns of Race in the America's* (New York: Walker Paperback, 1964).

Herrick, Bruce H. *Urban Migration and Economic Development in Chile* (Cambridge: The M.I.T. Press, 1966).

Hobsbawm, E. J. *Primitive Rebels: Studies in Archaic Forms of Social Movements in the 19th and 20th Centuries* (New York: Norton, 1965).

Icaza, Jorge. *Huasipungo: The Villagers* (Carbondale: Southern Illinois University Press, 1964).

Leeds, Anthony (ed.). "The Favelas of Rio," manuscript for a projected book based on papers presented at Americanists' meeting in Argentina, 1966. (Mimeo.)

Lewis, Oscar. *Life in a Mexican Village: Tepoztlan Revisited* (Urbana: University of Illinois Press, 1951).

———. *The Children of Sanchez* (New York: Random House, 1961).

———. "Even the Saints Cry," *Trans-Action,* 4 (November, 1966), pp. 18-23.

Malcolm X. *Malcolm X Speaks,* edited by George Breitman (New York: Merit Publishers, 1965).

Mangin, William. "The Role of Regional Associations in the Adaptation of Rural Population in Peru," *Sociologus,* 9 (1959), pp. 21-36.

———. "Urbanization Case History in Peru," *Architectural Design,* 33 (August, 1963), pp. 366-70.

———. "Squatter Settlements," *Scientific American,* 217 (October, 1967a), pp. 21-29.

———. "Latin American Squatter Settlements: A Problem and a Solution," *Latin American Research Review,* 2 (Summer, 1967b), pp. 65-98.

MILLER, S. M. and MARTIN REIN. "Poverty and Social Change," *The American Child,* 46 (March, 1964), pp. 10-15.

NASH, MANNING. "Capital Saving and Credit in a Guatemalan and a Mexican Indian Peasant Society," in R. Firth and B. S. Yamey (eds.) *Capital, Saving and Credit in Peasant Societies* (Chicago: Aldine, 1964), pp. 287-304.

NEIRA, HUGO. *Cuzco: Tierra y Muerte* (Lima: Problemas de Hoy, 1964).

NUNEZ, THOMAS A., JR. "Tourism, Tradition, and Acculturation: *Weekendismo* in a Mexican Village," *Ethnology,* 2 (1963), pp. 347-52.

REDFIELD, ROBERT. *The Folk Culture of Yucatan* (Chicago: University of Chicago Press, 1941).

ROTONDO, HUMBERTO. "Baltazar Caravedo and Javier Mariategui," *Estudios de Psiquiatria Social en el Peru* (Lima: Ediciones del Sol, 1963).

SAFA, HELEN. "From Shantytown to Public Housing: A Comparison of Family Structure in Two Urban Neighborhoods in Puerto Rico," *Caribbean Studies,* 4 (1964), pp. 3-12.

SALMON, LAWRENCE. "Report on Vila Kennedy and Vila Esperanca," mimeographed report distributed by COHAB, 1966.

SCHULMAN, SAM. "Latin American Shantytown," *New York Times Magazine,* January 16, 1966, pp. 30-38.

STOKES, CHARLES J. "A Theory of Slums," *Land Economics,* 38 (August, 1962), pp. 187-97.

TSCHOPIK, HARRY, JR. *Highland Communities of Central Peru,* Publication No. 5 of the Institute of Social Anthropology (Washington: Smithsonian Institute, 1947).

TUMIN, MELVIN. *Caste in a Peasant Society* (New Jersey: Princeton University Press, 1952).

TURNER, JOHN et al. "Dwelling Resources in South America: Conclusions," *Architectural Design,* 33 (August, 1963), pp. 389-93.

———. "Barriers and Channels for Housing Development in Modernizing Countries," *Journal of the American Institute of Planners,* 33 (May, 1967), pp. 167-81.

USANDIZAGA, ELSA and EUGENE A. HAVENS. *Tres Barrios de Invasion: Estudio de Nivel de Vida y Actitudes en Barranquilla.* Ediciones Tercer Mundo (Bogotá: Facultad de Sociología, March, 1966).

VIQUIERA, CARMEN and ANGEL PALERM. "Alcoholismo, Brujeria y Homocidio en dos Comunidades Rurales de Mexico," *America Indigena,* 14 (1954), pp. 7-36.

Wagner, Bernard, David McVoy, and Gordon Edwards. "Guanabara Housing and Urban Development," Program Report and Recommendations by AID Housing and Urban Development Team, July 1, 1966. (Mimeo.)

Wallis, Ethel Emilia. "Problemas de Aculturación Implícitos en la Educación Indígena del Otomi del Mezquital," *America Indigena*, 13 (October, 1953), pp. 243-58.

Whyte, William Foote. *Street Corner Society* (Chicago: University of Chicago Press, 1943).

Wolf, Eric. *Peasants* (Englewood Cliffs, N. J.: Prentice-Hall, 1966).

Zborowski, Mark and Elizabeth Herzog. *Life is with People: The Jewish Little-Town of Eastern Europe* (New York: International University Press, 1952).

Part IV

KNOWLEDGE, POLICY, AND POVERTY

Introduction

L OCAL, state, and national officials in both public and private institutional sectors are often charged with ignoring the findings of the behavioral sciences in making and executing policy affecting the urban social order. Some observers explain this failure as a consequence of the "lag" between what social science researchers have learned and what the "conventional wisdom" portrays as true. Other critics maintain that policy-makers frequently disregard expert judgment and the evidence on which it is based because they see the conclusions as posing a threat to their established interests. To raise this general issue, however, is also to raise the question of how complete and secure knowledge actually is in the area of poverty and how easily and directly this knowledge translates into relevant policy. The five chapters in this concluding section of the volume are relevant to this question. They deal with some of the key issues in theories about poverty and the implications these theories have for policy in both the United States and other nations.

As previous chapters have already pointed out, the rapid growth of urban population in the developing countries has been accompanied by an increase in the scale and intensity of poverty-related problems in their cities. In Chapter 14, Gerald Breese examines some of these problems and the dilemmas which policy-makers face in attempting to cope with them. Like Gutkind, Breese stresses the crucial nature of the labor market, a market characterized not only by the existence of widespread unemployment but by massive underemployment as well. Comparative studies and the advance of knowledge about these factors are severely handicapped, as Breese shows, by the lack of adequate and reliable data.

Breese, like others in this volume, reminds us that poverty in the newly developing nations is, both absolutely and relatively, much more severe and massive than what we normally call poverty in Western society. Governmental policy relevant to situations where large segments of the population are barely above, and in many cases even below, subsistence levels is not likely to be the same as that required in countries where the problem is more one of growing inequality between a comfortable majority and a deprived minority than one of sheer survival. Moreover, emphasis in the developing states is on nation-building, and this orientation influences policy-making in many profound ways. For example, investment in housing and community facilities and in undertakings that will develop long-range job opportunities often receives second priority to projects designed to enhance the prestige or image of the government in the international community. But, as Breese points out, policy decisions affecting poverty in the modernizing societies are inevitably connected with other interests and goals held by those in power. This creates a variety of dilemmas for decision-makers that research can help illuminate but by no means remove.

Chapter 15 shifts the scene from the developing nations to the "mature welfare states" of Europe and to their policies concerning the urban poor. The impression has long persisted in many circles that the United States has much to learn from its European counterparts about dealing with poverty. This belief, however, has been based more on impression and journalistic accounts than on rigorous comparative research. Steven Pflanczer examines the question of knowledge transference in the light of history, current practices, and the requirements of social science research. His contribution serves to put the question in better perspective.

After pointing out the methodological and empirical difficulties of making valid international comparisons, Pflanczer traces the major general conditions—demographic, social, and political—within which the welfare systems of Europe evolved. Dividing the states into Eastern and Western blocs, he shows how the development of welfare and social security programs in each sector reflects economic, political-ideological, and national-cultural differences. He suggests that the problem of urban poverty can best be viewed from two complementary research perspectives. The first looks at urban welfare programs simply as localized expressions of overall objectives set for the total social system as represented by the nation-state. The second views them within the context of local social systems that display certain kinds and degrees of autonomy within the framework of the larger national system.

Pflanczer points out that the difference in welfare programs among states cannot be explained solely by the variables of urbanization and socioeconomic development. He repeatedly emphasizes that the causes and cures of urban poverty, whether in Europe or elsewhere in the world, are implicit in a multiplicity of political choices made at many different times and places. Welfare programs, in other words, are integral parts of the continuous search for uniqueness and autonomy in shaping and maintaining a certain way of national life. Hence, to select some institutional component of European welfare policy from the complex context in which it evolved and attempt to transplant it into the socio-cultural system of American urban centers assumes, as Pflanczer says, "a kind of knowledge and skill we cannot as yet claim to possess."

Chapter 16 is a critical response to much of the theorizing about poverty in the United States. While the preceding two authors assume a concern for both economic and non-economic variables in diagnosis and prescription relevant to the problem of poverty, Gordon Sutton focuses specifically on the way in which economic definitions of poverty tend to disregard or disguise certain essential sociological characteristics of the poor. He argues for the need to widen the sociological conceptions of poverty as a public issue and to inquire into the functions of poverty for the total social system. His discussion once again points up the critical need both to utilize extant knowledge of poverty and to increase our understanding of it through meaningful research if we are to devise sound policies and effective strategies in the war against poverty. It is pure speculation, he notes, to assume as many seem to do that money alone from the affluent sector of society is the simple answer.

Examination of certain non-economic dimensions of poverty indicates, according to Sutton, that an important segment of the American poor are so separated from the socio-cultural mainstream of society that programs aimed mainly at economic factors, such as unemployment, have limited potential. Using low income as evidence of poverty but not its definition, he divides the poverty aggregate into two major categories: transitional and non-transitional. The first consists of those for whom poverty is largely an economic problem—such as the aged and infirm—and for whom solutions may be characterized in terms of income needs. The second is composed of those who are born into poverty—such as the culturally disadvantaged children of the ghetto—and whose expectations of leaving it have been minimal. For this latter group the conventional programs and strategies designed to alleviate poverty are largely irrelevant and inappropriate. Sutton's observations illustrate the inescapable implications of theory for practical policy, whether policy-makers recognize them or not. Unless we are prepared to utilize and further develop our knowledge and expertise in this field, we may merely be spinning our wheels and working our way deeper into the ruts. The sometimes strident demand for less study and more action, recently heard in certain governmental and political circles, needs to be replaced by a call for much more study conducted in concert with such increases in action programs as have been and will be mounted.

Warren Haggstrom, the author of Chapter 17, is highly critical of the direction taken by the "war on poverty." He argues that current efforts to materially alleviate poverty have largely failed and asserts that present policies ignore historical antecedents and the strategies which behavioral theory and experience dictate. Along with other contributors to this volume, he maintains that neither charity nor traditional welfare methods have the potential for eliminating poverty. The achievement of this goal is possible only if authentic and adequate support can be generated for the development of a social movement among the poor oriented to self-help goals and strategies. Such a movement remains unlikely so long as those in charge of the "war" remain preoccupied with conflict-avoidance strategies such as (1) providing a stake in the poverty war to groups primarily because they might otherwise oppose new programs, (2) stifling or discrediting opposition while avoiding intellectual discussion of the issues, and (3) refusing to develop programs which threaten to alter existing practices.

What Haggstrom is saying is that a social force must be created and brought to bear on government to change the political context in which it functions before meaningful progress in eliminating poverty can be expected. More specifically, he is saying that the only way the nation's chief poverty agency, the OEO, can achieve the freedom and resources to initiate meaningful programs is to mobilize the poor as its natural political constituency. Such mobilization, however, cannot take place unless the OEO seriously seeks to induct the poor into full participation in American society. Efforts in this direction would inevitably be marked by controversy since a war on poverty based on full societal participation by the poor would threaten entrenched agencies and their conventional programs along with many other kinds of vested interests. Thus, if the policy-makers for the OEO were determined above all else to make a significant impact on poverty, they would not seek to avoid controversy—as they have consistently done, according to Haggstrom—but would "endeavor to mobilize a sufficient political force to ensure its [OEO's] own continued effective operation in the midst of inevitable controversy." Yet, few are sanguine that we will move in this direction in the foreseeable future.

The last contributor to this section, Phillips Cutright, also concludes that needed policy changes in the United States are not likely to be implemented "unless (1) the political leadership necessary to push new legislation emerges and (2) the poor and near-poor population can be mobilized to support these efforts." He reaches this conclusion by way of an analysis that draws together many of the preceding concerns by examining simultaneously economic, political, and sociological variables as they affect the amount of income inequality and efforts to redistribute income through social security programs in both developed and underdeveloped societies. Although his generalizations are stated in modest rather than global terms, and qualified by the cautions appropriate to scientific inquiry, Chapter 18 provides an example of how far available data, with all its shortcomings, can carry us when sophisticated techniques of analysis are skillfully utilized. It also reinforces the point made in varying ways by the other four chapters: that greater knowledge about the problem of poverty is more likely to clarify than to resolve the dilemmas faced by policy-makers.

Cutright begins with a theoretical model that uses four variables as predictors of inequality in the distribution of income between various employment sectors of the society: (1) level of economic development, (2) the degree to which political institutions tend to be representative, (3) the proportion of the labor force still separated from the urban power centers as farmers or farm laborers, and (4) policies affecting use of national wealth in capital formation, foreign trade, and military forces. Data from 44 non-Communist and 8 Communist nations, with the former first taken together and then stratified according to level of economic development, reveal the pervasive importance of both development per se and political representativeness for explaining tendencies to produce greater or lesser inequality among a citizenry. At the same time some policy decisions affect different types of nations rather differently, though both sides of the "cold war" clearly sacrifice possi-

bilities for decreasing income inequality to the maintenance of
large-scale military enterprises.

Because the initial analysis neglects the impact of income redistribution through social security programs, and thereby may seriously underestimate the "disposable" (as against "gross factor")
income of lower strata, Cutright next examines the extent to which
gross national product is allocated to national social security expenditures. He attempts, with notable success, to predict this
allocation on the basis, once again, of political, economic, and
sociological variables: per cent of population voting in national
elections, per cent of the labor force in industry, and the cumulative
development of a social security bureaucracy. On the basis of
these variables, the social security expenditures of the United States
are about what one would expect.

Seen from this perspective, the "war on poverty" problem
becomes one of devising and implementing strategies either for
rapidly changing some of these underlying patterns or else for
making the United States a "deviant case." Haggstrom emphasizes
political participation and Sutton the sociological gulf that separates some of the poor from the rest of society, a separation
epitomized by their virtual exclusion or self-isolation from the
mainstream of both employment and politics. But Pflanczer would
seem to caution against drawing conclusions about workable strategies until we explain the patterns now evident in this country. Why
did we get such a late start in social security programs? Why is
political participation lower here than in so many urban-industrial
nations in the West? Do such explanations as we have bode well
or ill for hopes of contriving new kinds of social security assistance
to the poor, as well as increasing the old, fast enough to reduce
inequality well beyond what Cutright's initial independent variables would predict?

Finally, Cutright's work underscores what the previous chapters
by Gutkind, Mangin, and Breese indicate: what we call "foreign
aid" can all too easily promote the interests of an established elite
without reducing either income inequality or political instability.
On its international front, as on the domestic front, an American
"war on poverty" may be foredoomed to failure, no matter how
arduous, extended, and costly its campaigns, so long as those who
make policy believe they cannot or must not challenge established
political and sociological patterns.

Present knowledge concerning causes and cures of poverty has many gaps, many inadequacies. But it is clear that we know enough, now, to recognize some of our most chronic exercises in futility for what they are. It is not lack of knowledge that prevents new departures by those who make policy.

—W. B. Jr. and H. J. S.

14

Some Dilemmas in Poverty, Power, and Public Policy in Cities of Underdeveloped Areas

GERALD BREESE

☐ IN NEWLY DEVELOPING NATIONS OF THE world the day never ends without an increase in their urban population. Or to paraphrase, the sun never sets on the persistent daily growth of population in urban areas of the Third World. Even more significant, there appears to be no possibility of anything other than the continued growth of urban settlements in such countries for many years to come. Responsible urban officials can awaken every morning with the uncomfortable knowledge that the problems of their cities are larger than they were the day before and will again be larger the next day. The tide never recedes; it only comes in.

The present chapter endeavors to bring a world perspective to this volume's consideration of power, deprivation, and urban policy. As the reader will have observed, only several of the chapters have moved outside the Anglo-European context. This focus, however, should not obscure the fact that African, Asian, and Latin American nations are experiencing a surge in urbanization which gives every promise of increasing in the near future.

It is impossible to dismiss casually the half-billion people in the cities of these sections of the world. On the other hand, it is also impossible to discuss them fully in a score or so of pages. This chapter obviously cannot be comprehensive; it selects a few crucial aspects for consideration and focuses mainly on large cities for lack of space and data to deal with others. An attempt will be made to touch upon several topics covered in earlier chapters for comparison sake, even if necessarily briefly.

To understand urbanization in newly developed countries one must know the context, even if only in the most general terms. Hence, we first turn to a consideration of the scale and pace of urbanization in these nations. Our presentation of these matters must necessarily be abbreviated, with the details to be gleaned from other readily available sources (Davis, 1965; Breese, 1966; and Breese, 1968).

MAJOR CHARACTERISTICS OF URBANIZATION IN NEWLY DEVELOPING COUNTRIES

Certain background factors must be kept in mind in discussing the scale and rate of urbanization. However poorly named, the well-known population "explosion" is a reality. As the United Nations' Demographic Yearbooks point out, the net growth of the world population approximates 180,000 persons every 24 hours, well over 64,000,000 each year. Concurrently, there has been an utter collapse of efforts to control in-migration to cities, even in the case of the strict measures taken in Communist China. Almost everywhere, urbanization is taking place at accelerated rates.

SCALE AND PACE

Kingsley Davis notes that urbanization must be carefully defined (1965). He refers to it as "the proportion of the total population concentrated in urban settlements, or a rise in this proportion." He makes it clear that we must distinguish between urbanization, as defined above, and the growth of cities, since if there is an equal concurrent growth in rural population, cities can grow without any increase in urbanization. As Davis says, "The process of urbanization is a change that has a beginning and an end, but the growth of cities has no inherent limit."

According to a provisional study reported in a recent United Nations conference paper:

> The number of the world's inhabitants has risen from about 1,860 million in 1920 to 2,069 million in 1930, 2,297 million in 1940, 2,517 million in 1950 and 2,994 million in 1960. The estimated increases in successive decades were by 209, 228, 220 and 477

million, respectively. . . . In terms of the present tentative estimates, the world's *urban* population (localities of 20,000 and more
inhabitants) has grown from 253 million in 1920 to 753 million
in 1960, a three-fold growth in 40 years, or a net addition of
roughly 500 million urban residents. . . . Absolute increases in
urban population, in the successive four decades, were by an estimated 75, 99, 105 and 221 million, respectively. . . . In relative
terms, the *world's* population grew by 11 per cent in the 1920's,
11 per cent in the 1930's, 10 per cent in the 1940's, and 19 per cent
in the 1950's. . . . *Urban* population in each of these four decades
increased by 30, 30, 25 and 42 per cent; the city population
(100,000 and over) increased by 35, 33, 25 and 46 per cent; the
successive increases in big city population (500,000 and over)
were by 41, 32, 28 and 57 per cent; and those in multi-million
cities (2.5 million and over) by 61, 36, 27 and 65 per cent (United
Nations, Bureau of Social Affairs, 1966b).

It may also be interesting in this connection to compare the
data in Table 1 (Breese, 1966, p. 19).

TABLE 1

TOTAL WORLD POPULATION AND WORLD URBAN POPULATION: 1800-1960

Year	Total World Population Millions	Population Living in Localities of 20,000 Inhabitants or More		Population Living in Localities of 20,000 to 100,000 Inhabitants		Population Living in Localities of 100,000 Inhabitants or More	
		Millions	% of World Population	Millions	% of World Population	Millions	% of World Population
1800	906	21.7	2.4	6.1	0.7	15.6	1.7
1850	1,171	50.4	4.3	22.9	2.0	27.5	2.3
1900	1,608	147.9	9.2	59.3	3.7	88.6	5.5
1950	2,400	502.2	20.9	188.5	7.8	313.7	13.1
1960	2,962	803.2	27.1	213.1	7.2	590.0	19.9

SOURCE: Kingsley Davis and Hilda Hertz, "Patterns of World Urbanization for 1800-
1950," as reproduced in United Nations Secretariat, Bureau of Social Affairs, in coopera-
tion with the International Labour Office, Food and Agriculture Organization, of the
United Nations, United Nations Educational, Scientific and Cultural Organization, and
World Health Organization, Report on the World Social Situation Including Studies of
Urbanization in Underdeveloped Areas (New York: United Nations, 1957), p. 114,
Table 1. The 1960 data are based on Homer Hoyt, World Urbanization: Expanding
Population in a Shrinking World (Washington, D. C.: Urban Land Institute, 1962), p.
31, Table 3; 1960 data are approximately comparable with those for 1800-1950.

In the discussion that follows, the availability of data makes
necessary a focus on large cities, defined for our purposes as those
having 500,000 or more population. Some exceptions and variations

can be expected in the characteristics of smaller places, but no attempt is made to point out or speculate upon these distinctions here.

SOURCE OF INCREASE

The first questions pertaining to this tremendous surge in urbanization are where the increase comes from, and who the migrants to urban areas are. Turning attention first to the question of where the increase comes from, it is quite clear that the bulk of it is derived mainly from migration to the urban area. However, we should not overlook the fact that the increase in growth of cities also arises partly from the surplus of urban births over deaths.

The reasons that impel the migrant to move from the village or rural area into the city are not entirely clear. It is very difficult to determine the precise causes and their relative importance. What has come to be known as the "push"-"pull" constellation of factors may throw some light on the question. "Pull" refers to the attraction the city has for the rural dweller and is not difficult to specify. Concerning "push," however, there is considerable confusion, particularly as to the effect of circumstances over which the rural dweller has little or no control and the manner in which they influence him to move toward the city. Among the "push" factors which affect migration to urban areas are progressive fragmentation of land holding or ownership, primogeniture systems that leave the younger sons little alternative, over-population, too little opportunity for securing land that can be worked to produce a living, limited opportunities in local administration, and insecurity related to various types of destruction and disorganization incidental to wartime and political changes. The recognition among rural residents that perhaps they are suffering a kind of relative deprivation as compared with city folk is an additional variable not to be overlooked.

The "pull" factors, on the other hand, include reports likely to have been circulated by "successful" earlier migrants to urban areas who have returned to the village and spoken highly of the many advantages of city life. If things have been going badly in the country area and the reports indicate that things are better in the city, there is little doubt as to what the rural dweller will be inclined to do; if possible, he will migrate city-ward.

CHARACTERISTICS OF MIGRANTS

Little conclusive evidence is available concerning the characteristics of migrants to urban areas. Except in the case of certain countries of Latin America, there appears to be more migration of males than females. No evidence exists indicating that only the best educated and the most highly motivated, the most ambitious, migrate from rural to urban areas. Indeed, there is some speculation that "rural rejects," so-called, may be among the large numbers who move to urban areas as an escape from censure arising from lack of success in the rural situation. Some also may go to escape caste limitations. We do know that migration occurs predominantly among people in the low age brackets of the labor force, namely 15 to 45 (Breese, 1966, page 73 ff.).

Where do these migrants to urban areas go? The available evidence suggests that initially they move primarily into what has been called "uncontrolled urban settlement," more popularly known as squatter settlements (Turner, 1966). Given the circumstances of their arrival at the city, it should occasion no surprise that the alternatives force most migrants into urban settlements of this type. One of the subjects we know least about, incidentally, is just how important to the morale and ultimate "success" of the inhabitants are the grindingly low conditions of these squatter areas.

These, then, are some of the givens against which the phenomena of poverty, power, and urban policy in newly developing countries must be discussed.

URBAN SOCIOECONOMIC CONDITIONS INVOLVING POVERTY, POWER, AND URBAN POLICY

The definitions of poverty usually employed in the more developed nations cannot be applied to newly developing countries. For example, the "poverty" (or deprived) top income level expected to be $7,000 in 1970 for a family of 5 in the United States of America, in most newly developing nations would provide a very comfortable existence. Such a definition is a hollow mockery to the destitute plight of inhabitants of central slums and peripheral squatter warrens of cities in Asia, Africa, and Latin America.

Hard data concerning the characteristics and extent of urban poverty in newly developing countries are difficult to secure. Probably the most nearly comprehensive data for any one country are incorporated in the socioeconomic surveys begun in 1954 under sponsorship of the Research Programmes Committee of the Planning Commission of India. There are about 35 reports published, but unfortunately most contain information only for the period 1954 to 1956 (Lackdawala *et al.*, 1963; cf. India, February, 1964, especially Table 3.21) and thus are not useful for current analysis. Furthermore, these studies are difficult to make comparable for purposes of intracountry examination and thus permit safe national generalizations. Even more difficult, if indeed not impossible, is the task of making studies of this nature comparable across national boundaries. The visual evidence, however, is readily at hand; even a blind person knows that the stench rising from the hovels of densely packed "uncontrolled urban settlement" can be associated only with the grossest impoverishment.

Concomitants of Poverty

Urban poverty under newly developing country circumstances is clearly many cuts below the touchstones of poverty in Western society, since it involves incomes barely above subsistence levels, or even below. It has been suggested that the city equivalent to "subsistence agriculture" is "subsistence urbanization" (Breese, 1966, pp. 5, 99-100, 143) and with similar results, namely, poor diet, poor health, poor housing, poor clothing, and poor life chances. This is poverty which generally has as its concomitants lack of occupational mobility, indebtedness, exploitation by others of more secure status, strains on family solidarity, and in its most abject states: frustration, futility, and resignation.

Poverty under such circumstances comes to mean that level of income which precludes the worker and his family from securing decent shelter, clothing, and food, a condition most closely related to the individual's ability to secure regular and adequately remunerative employment. For these people, the "revolution of rising expectations" becomes "the revolution of un-met expectations."

The kinds of demands placed on the urban worker make it extremely difficult for him to escape the poverty trap. He must support himself under circumstances marked by high living costs and inflation, and he does not have the joint family to act as a buffer in bad times. He must support his immediate family and often his relatives, whether in town with him or in the village. Usually, also, he must send back part of his earnings to the village. Once established in the city, he must provide traditional hospitality and aid to townsmen newly arrived to the urban settlement. If possible, he must save funds for occasional visits to his home village. The desperate efforts to meet these obligations under adverse conditions have a circular effect since they leave the individual with reduced capacity to be more productive, thus inducing a further downward spiral.

The misery of poverty has much company in cities of newly developing countries. The fact that large numbers of the urban population are desperately poor is hardly an ameliorating factor in the situation. Under such duress, consumption norms drop to dead levels for all and grounds for comparison among the poor cease to exist. What is "expected" tends to sink to very low levels, if not the minimum, and all are close to being in the same condition.

If the poor so resignedly view themselves, how does the remainder of the population look upon them? In cities of newly developing nations it appears that, unless their official position so requires, the somewhat more financially secure segments of the population, and particularly the affluent, devote scarcely any attention to the poor. It is as if the poor were considered to "deserve" their condition, as if they were in too large numbers to do much about their plight, and as if they were invisible or in another world. Everywhere the commitment of others to the deprived appears to be minimal except in times of civil disturbances.

The problems related to the gaps between income and expenditures, and level of living, are not matters just recently noted. They have been pointed out in detail in UNESCO studies of *Urbanization in Asia and the Far East* (Hauser, 1957), *Social Implications of Industrialization and Urbanization in Africa South of the Sahara* (International African Institute, 1956), and *Urbanization in Latin America* (Hauser, 1961), as well as in various reports of the United Nations in 1957, 1963, and 1965 in particular, under the title, *Report on the World Social Situation* (United Nations Economic and Social Council, 1957, 1963, and 1966).

"Minimum" Living Standards

Man throughout his experience has struggled to maintain himself at "minimum living standards" or better. The fact that different
conditions alter what is "minimum" presents great difficulties in
broad-scale definition, measurement, and comparison of minimum
living standards. Just how complicated this is can be noted in a
recent review of the problem by N. N. Franklin who examines the
question in terms of examples from Kenya, India and Latin America
(1967). Franklin draws a distinction between physical needs and
social necessities. Considering poverty as "the negative counterpart
of the term minimum living standards or the satisfaction of human
needs," he defines the concept of minimum human needs as including not only physical requirements—i.e., those necessary to stay
alive and to maintain working capacity—but also conventional or
social needs related to the customs of the community as, for example, in some societies the necessary wearing of shoes to preserve
human dignity. He points out that a family should "not be obliged
to live in a manner that sets it apart from other families in the
social group to which it belongs and that makes it unable to live
according to the established customs of the community." He reminds us, incidentally, that the distinction between physical and
social needs is not always clear.

The major concerns of the poor, in other words, are not limited
to sheer survival or physical well-being. They include, among other
wants, the improvement of status, personal satisfaction, and the
rewards of stimulation expected from the city. The urban migrant,
moreover, is anxious to prove success to those back in the village,
and to achieve an autonomy that provides freedom from traditional
constraints.

THE CRUCIAL NATURE OF EMPLOYMENT IN CITIES OF NEWLY DEVELOPING COUNTRIES

It appears that the single most important determinant of standard of living, as well as the likelihood of poverty, its extent and
characteristics, is employment (International Labour Organization,
1961 and 1964). Our interest here in international comparisons of

employment plunges us at once into serious difficulties. Economists face such problems constantly (Merritt and Rokkan, 1966; Morgan-stern, 1963). More and better international indices are urgently needed; some have been attempted and proven useful, as in the case of Ginsburg's *Atlas of Economic Development* (1961) and Bruce Russett *et al., World Handbook of Political and Social Indicators* (1964). It remains true, however, that substantial restraint and care must continue to be applied to the use of existing international indices and series.

Securing useful cross-national statistics on detailed aspects of employment has proved particularly difficult. As might be expected, matters of definition and concept loom large (Islam, 1964) and have received detailed attention from the International Labour Organization (hereafter ILO) at successive conferences on this subject since 1923 (International Labour Organization, 1959). The twenty-sixth issue of the ILO's *Yearbook of Labour Statistics* (International Labour Organization, 1967), for example, provides series on general levels of employment, unemployment, unemployment by industrial or occupational group, hours of work in non-agricultural activity and manufacturing, wages, and consumer prices over 10 year periods. Unfortunately, even such data from a distinguished source have limited analytical value since there are so many external, internal, direct, and indirect forces determining them and changes within them. A recent article by Samuel Baum (1967) discusses the labor force and its industrial distribution, and other articles in the *International Labour Review* and elsewhere consider additional aspects of this subject.

It is impossible to present here in any depth the few known details of international employment. Among the interesting questions that arise is to what extent urban employment is affected by primarily urban factors, as compared with how much the transfer of underemployment from the villages inflates the urban statistics (United Nations, 1957, p. 129). Furthermore, the statistics are affected by factors highly variable among countries as, for example, the age at which children enter the labor force, the participation of women in the labor market (Lefaucheux, 1962; Collver and Langlois, 1962), how long adults remain in the work force, the comparative qualifications of migrants for entering the labor force (their skills, experience, and the like)—subjects too large for consideration in detail here.

The requirements of the labor market invariably control whether people end up employed, unemployed, or underemployed. One thing is clear for every newly developing country—the employment scene is characterized not just by *un*employment, but also by massive *under*employment. High as unemployment is in developing countries, the visible unemployment seems less than might otherwise be expected because of the "disappearance" of the labor force in large numbers into the underemployment category, especially into the low-production services sector.

Unemployment and Underemployment

One of the most perceptive summaries of employment, unemployment and underemployment trends and problems has been prepared by the ILO (1964). Much of the discussion that immediately follows is based on this report. The ILO study indicates that from 6 to 12 per cent, and sometimes even up to 20 per cent, of the rural and urban labor force in newly developing countries is likely to be unemployed. Other studies reported in the *International Labour Review,* for example (International Labour Organization, 1962, 1963 and Harewood, 1960) support such estimates in the case of many South Asian and West Indian countries:

> Unemployment in the developing countries is concentrated primarily in urban areas. According to recent surveys, in India and Ceylon the rates of urban unemployment were respectively 7 per cent and 14 per cent; similar rates appear to prevail in the large cities of Latin America and Asia. Urban unemployment is, however, fed by an in-flow, dangerously rapid in many cities, of underemployment and impoverished peoples from rural areas. In many developing countries the majority of the urban unemployed are young persons. The unemployment rate among young persons is usually much higher than among other age groups. In India, for example, the same survey shows that in urban areas about 17 per cent of the labor force in the age group 16 to 21 were unemployed compared with about 5 per cent in the age groups 27 to 56.

The 1964 ILO study also notes that "The conceptual and practical problems of defining and measuring unemployment pale into insignificance compared to those surrounding the concept of underemployment," and "There is no general agreement as to how to go about measuring or even defining underemployment" (International Labour Organization, 1964, pp. 24, 25). It goes on to say:

Underemployment exists when persons in employment who are not working full time would be able and willing to do more work than they are actually performing, or when the income or productivity of persons in employment would be raised if they worked under improved conditions of production, or transferred to another occupation, account being taken of their occupational skills. Underemployment appears in various forms, some of which can be measured with reasonable accuracy by means of statistical inquiries. The following major categories of underemployment may be distinguished:

(a) Visible Underemployment, which involves shorter than normal periods of work and which is characteristic of persons involuntarily working part time;

(b) Invisible Underemployment, which is characteristic of persons whose working time is not abnormally reduced but whose earnings are abnormally low or whose jobs do not permit full use of their capacities or skills (sometimes called "disguised" underemployment), or who are employed in establishments or economic units whose productivity is abnormally low (sometimes called "potential" underemployment).

Even the above report is scarce in, and conservative about, the representativeness of its data concerning underemployment in urban areas. Statistics given include 29 per cent of all employed urban workers in Ceylon averaging less than 40 hours per week while approximately 10 per cent of all persons working in urban areas were underemployed; and in Indonesia the urban figure was about 12 per cent. Virtually every newly developing country reveals underemployment, large numbers engaged in "trivial underproductive tasks." The prospect appears to be more, rather than less, of such utilization of labor. The problem is accentuated in its long-term aspects by the necessity of absorbing annual increases as well as existing workers into employment. The galloping differential between number of jobs available and increases in the age groups most needing work but generally lacking skills and training is viewed with great concern as, for example, in the statement:

Employment problems and policies call for dispassionate and objective analysis and discussion. But behind the abstractions of which such analysis and discussion must make use—"investment ratio," "surplus labor" and "structural change," "labor mobility" and the rest—are human needs and human problems. Action that is needed may not be taken or may not be taken vigorously enough, unless there is also a sense of the urgency of many of the problems discussed in this [ILO] report—the frustration, hopelessness, misery and poverty accompany long spells of unemployment anywhere; the acute hardship, extending even to destitution and starvation, to which it may lead in less developed countries; the prospect that millions of young people in countries with high birth rates and falling death rates may waste the formative years of their lives in idleness and uselessness. Next only to keeping the peace, these problems may well be felt to present the greatest social challenge of our age (International Labour Organization, 1964, p. 2).

Wage Differentials

In addition to unemployment and underemployment, there are also substantial wage differentials in whatever urban employment exists. Expected differences between wages in rural and urban areas, the latter being generally the highest, are to be expected. Within the city there are predictable differentials among unskilled, skilled, and administrators. For example, "A recent estimate taken in East Africa showed that the senior civil servant earns 10 to 12 times as much as the artisan and 25 times as much as a laborer; invariably the peasant earns even less than a laborer" (United Nations, Bureau of Social Affairs, 1966a, p. 30).

Other studies indicate that wage differentials may be increasing as, for example, between manual and non-manual workers (Taira, 1966). In one troublesome aspect, however—the double standard (higher for foreigners) in wages paid for the same work—the situation is more promising. With increases in staffing by nationals, these differences are likely to be less and less common. Another relevant area, whether there are significant wage differentials for the same work from city to city within a country, has not yet been adequately explored.

Here and there minimum wages have been established, as in the case of Africa (United Nations, Economic and Social Council, 1957, p. 154) but in practice they do not apply to migrant or short-term labor. There is some evidence, in any case, that the influence of minimum wages in raising the standard of living is more circumscribed in developing than in developed countries (Smith, 1967).

Measures of changes in wage levels are very unsatisfactory, since wages may be shown to have increased but subsequent inflation may have totally, or more, wiped out the increase. The United Nations *1963 Report on the World Social Situation* (pp. 84-86) indicated that money wages rose in percentage more than consumer prices in virtually all the countries reporting (including 24 developing nations), but "One must, however, beware of giving these facts greater importance than they deserve, bearing in mind that in a number of developing countries wages are very low at the beginning of the period and, generally speaking, still are despite the considerable percentage increase in certain cases." In brief, for most residents of cities in newly developing countries, even if they are employed, the prospects for escaping poverty are dim.

Income and Needs

The poverty level is observable not only in income levels, but also in what income can buy, and what the city offers as compared with the countryside. Urban health conditions, for example, are minimal but still better than in most rural areas. This has not always been the case, as the *1957 Report on the World Social Situation* points out: "Prior to the twentieth century, health conditions in cities throughout the world as reflected in general and infant death rates were worse than in rural areas," partly as a result of such factors as overcrowding and contamination of food and water supply (p. 134). Subsequently, major improvements in health have appeared, but the poor still live in surroundings threatening to their health, particularly in urban squatter areas.

Housing needs related to poverty are enormous (Abrams, 1964; Breese, 1966, pp. 127 ff.; United Nations, Department of Economic and Social Affairs, 1962). In addition to the sheer deficit in housing for poverty levels and others, the existing housing in squatter areas is often badly located regarding place of work, weak in supporting community facilities such as water supply and sewerage, over-crowded, and costing too high a percentage of income. It is estimated that in urban Africa only 50 per cent live in decent housing, in urban Asia and the Far East only 60 per cent, and in urban Latin America only 60 per cent.

The consumer price index during the period 1950 to 1960 showed a median rise for the world as a whole of 41 per cent, while the figure was 46 per cent for Africa, 47 per cent for Europe, 33 per cent for Asia and 31 per cent for America (United Nations, Economic and Social Council, 1963, p. 83; International Labour Organization, 1967). Prices for food, in particular, were high due to large mark-up between producer and middleman, middleman and shopowner, shopowner and retail customer, as well as from waste due to spoilage and deterioration. Rises in consumer prices are catastrophic for those at the poverty level since food and shelter consume such large percentages of total income. Under these circumstances it occasions little surprise to read the estimate that about half of Asia, for example, suffers from malnutrition (Sukhatme, 1961).

There are other dysfunctional consequences of insufficient buying power. One in particular bears mention. When the gap between income and expenditure widens it is easy for an individual or family to fall into debt, a trap from which escape is highly improbable. At subsistence levels the vicious cycle is seldom broken. The psychological, not to mention the physical, consequences of this condition are well known.

In presenting some excellent data on incomes gained by inhabitants of Latin American marginal settlements, Anatole Solow (1966) is forced to conclude that:

> The majority of urban families can be characterized as marginal in terms of their low income, low educational level, underemployment and other social and cultural characteristics which limit their ability to integrate into the urban economic, industrial and political structure of the city.

The question of whether the poverty-ridden have, can have, or can be expected ever to have prevailing middle-class values under such circumstances becomes almost academic (Rodman, 1965).

For the poverty-ridden the course toward disillusionment must be direct, quick, and bitter. The expectation in the move from rural to urban is that income and level of living will rise. The quantity of disillusionment about this after migration is colossal. The revolution of rising expectations is usually matched by frustrations. The revolution of unmet expectations, the differential between hopes and aspirations referred to earlier, may in fact develop into a "revolution of rising discontents" (Abrams, 1964, p. 283).

OTHER ASPECTS OF THE EMPLOYMENT PICTURE

A few still untouched aspects of employment, unemployment, and underemployment can only be referred to here, though they are in themselves major subjects. The first concerns a special kind of "poverty"—the unemployment and underemployment of the university-educated in such countries as India. For a complex of reasons which cannot be detailed here, such persons presently comprise an unemployable and miserable amalgam of frustration, prestige-hunger, insecurity, and rootlessness. A different kind of poverty—more than just economically unrewarded—harasses such graduates. As W. Arthur Lewis points out, similar problems often also confront those who have completed secondary—and even primary—school levels (1966, p. 78). It is a mystery to many that these people have not, as yet, expressed their frustrated expectations in political unrest, for it appears that a long period will elapse before the middle-range and administrative roles for which they may be fitted will be developed.

The much discussed "critical manpower shortages" of newly developing countries cannot by any stretch of the imagination be expected to offer hope for the poverty-ridden (Harbison, 1962). The current population growth inexorably yields larger and larger surpluses of labor without correspondingly rapid gains in employment opportunities. The gradual introduction of heavy-duty construction machinery, prefabrication of housing—which may be necessary if any substantial dent in the housing deficit of these countries is to be made—other labor-saving devices, and related developments suggest the situation will worsen before it gets better. It is widely believed that modernization in traditional sectors of the economy, including rural areas in particular, will be necessary before any substantial alleviation of these problems will be possible (Harbison, 1967; Lewis, 1966, pp. 80 ff., and Zschock, 1967).

POWER

The subject of power need not be discussed here in detail since it is treated extensively in other chapters of this volume. It should be noted, however, that the massive political inertia induced by poverty in cities of newly developing countries may derive partly from traditional resignation of the poor to being poor. One cannot help but wonder what the poverty-stricken may be expected to do when they are no longer resigned to their plight. News of the explosive political dynamite of Hong Kong, Singapore, Calcutta, and Djakarta cannot be long in reaching other ears. Surely, it must become clear eventually that those in such poverty have little to lose by revolt. One cannot expect the newcomers to the city, in particular, to be totally insensitive to contrasts between their own poverty and the highly visible affluence of some others, a contrast that must eventually become corrosive. As W. Arthur Lewis emphasizes in his study of *Development Planning: The Essentials of Economic Policy:* "the unemployed are . . . . the shock troops of political discontent, their presence intensifying all the social tensions which are endemic to new and rapidly growing communities" (1966, p. 86).

In searching for clues as to why the unmet needs of the poverty-ridden in these cities do not move them to political action it may be worth remembering that, for all practical purposes, the impoverished are not *disenfranchised;* rather, they are for all practical purposes *unfranchised* in modern society, and especially in a large city. There the individual counts for almost nothing. He must act, if at all, by way of group pressure; and the rural migrant recently come to the city is not adept at this. He does not possess the requisite skills, organization, and financial resources for such action; he does not have the knowledge of which channels to follow; furthermore, he has no tradition of participation in decision-making of the sort required in the urban context.

For the poverty-ridden, at least, there must appear to be no readily available, tested means to sharpen issues, organize support, and bring pressure to bear in effective ways over the long run. The poor learn readily how quickly sheer violence is repressed by the Establishment.

Unfortunately, it is also true that the striving middle classes and the prestigious or responsible government officials are seldom inclined to join hands in action with the much more numerous poor. These parties are, perhaps, afraid—and quite justifiably so—of the Pandora's Box they might open in the process.

The fact that poverty may well be the central political issue of urban areas in newly developing countries is not very helpful to the victims, for they are ill-equipped to know how to use this fact effectively for their own betterment. In this respect, the city in newly developing countries is not yet fully the theater of political action. However, there are signs that it may become such in the near future, especially if it and its inhabitants continue to receive so little attention.

SOME POLICY DILEMMAS

Meanwhile, the emphasis and attention in most newly developing countries is on nation-building in general. The process is all-consuming and even compulsive. Judging from the evident eagerness to secure them, it appears that a new nation in order to be "self-respecting," must have, at the earliest possible moment, not only a national flag and representation at the United Nations but also a military force—preferably including an air arm with jets— a national airline; a hydroelectric scheme; modern sea and airport facilities; land reform; complexes for steel-aluminum-oil production; a skyscraper; at least a few miles of superhighway including a cloverleaf; television; and, in more recent times, a contraceptive program; an automobile assembly plant; and the possibiilty of atomic power!

Although many of these items could redound to the benefit of a nation's cities—or city—and thus presumably in one way or another favorably affect the economy by also providing jobs for the burgeoning urban population, the competition for scarce financial resources creates trouble, since not all desired ends can be secured. Inevitably, priorities must be established. A fact of life for newly developing countries in particular is that the scarcer the resources the more crucial is an allocation which takes into account both short-run and long-run benefits.

Priority confrontations abound with dilemmas and require cost-benefit calculations exceedingly difficult to make (Paukert, 1965). Not all of the dilemmas are financial in focus. For example, a newly developing country must decide how much emphasis it is going to place on greater popular participation in government, as compared with efforts to avoid public "interference" in decision-making (or to avoid perhaps even revolt). In some countries, it is feared that allowing an urban public to have a heavy hand in establishing priorities might result in disproportionate attention and funds being given to the provision of goods and services customarily expected by city dwellers as opposed to rural dwellers, and especially in those cases where the city dwellers constitute a minority, however vocal and visible, of the national population (Pye, 1962).

Given the circumstances that pertain in a newly developing nation neither the residents of the city nor those of the countryside, and perhaps not even a sufficient number of responsible national officials, will be apt to understand fully the high degree of interdependence of the city, its hinterland, its larger region, and its entire tributary nation. It does not necessarily follow, on the other hand, that what is good for the city must be good for the countryside. Precautions must invariably be taken to see to it that even though urban problems are highly visible and of a magnitude to become national problems, they must not be viewed from the demands of sheer expediency to solve them in such a way as may damage the larger national interest.

Such considerations necessarily elevate the city's problems to the realm of national problems, where they take a seat beside other categories of need. The fragility of accommodation among various national objectives and interests in newly developing countries is complicated by a circumstance that looms much more important than in the case of more nearly secure and developed nations—namely, the extent to which forces outside the control of the country affect it. For example, the opening or closing of the Suez Canal has always had ramifications for Bombay; or, the American development of synthetic fibers suitable for making bags may profoundly threaten the jute industry in the tinder box that is Calcutta. "Lightning" may strike a newly developing country from the most unexpected sources and with little or no warning.

Such circumstances are further complicated by another dilemma faced by these countries, namely, the alternative of desired self-sufficiency versus accepting the assists in development assumed to derive from cultivating foreign investment and foreign loans to meet capital investment needs or resolve emergency conditions such as food shortages. Whatever the choice in such a dilemma, it early becomes apparent that national development seems invariably to require urban areas. To make these areas viable thus involves allocation policy decisions by national government. The ceaseless growth of cities in newly developing countries necessitates, among other things, corresponding growth in job availability and suitable accommodations for the old and new residents. At the same time, pressure exists to establish the prestige and demonstrate the capacity of a new nation to both indigenous and foreign populations, pressures which may, more often than not, be met by the erection of a magnificent presidential palace and a skyscraper for use by the bureaucracy. Investment in undertakings that will develop long-run job opportunities, and investment in housing and community facilities, not infrequently receive second priority.

Related lessor dilemmas include such matters as whether to clear slums in squatter areas and replace them with government housing at prices the same people can afford, or whether to provide these substandard areas with an injection of such amenities as sewerage systems and water taps. The resolution of these dilemmas is hardly hastened by the fact that experts strongly disagree as to which is the most desirable course under the circumstances.

A more basic, and difficult, dilemma involving the urban affairs of a developing state is whether national policy should aim to strengthen a very few cities (or in the case where there is only one, the primate city) or whether in both the long-run and the short-run the best interests of the country will be served by providing the needed infrastructure for a larger number of urban centers. The purpose of the latter policy would be partly to help these new communities grow and attract industry and people to decentralized locations, and partly to relieve the pressures on the most populated city or cities. As in the preceding instances, expert opinion on the question is divided, reflecting the duress of given scarce total resources and the absence of pertinent precedents testing the comparative viability of the alternatives.

These examples by no stretch of the imagination exhaust the dilemmas of newly developing countries vis-à-vis cities. They do suggest, however, why responsible parties who have to act in such dilemmas can be criticized for whichever course they elect to follow. Whatever the choices, each has its proponents; and the decision-makers are condemned if they do and condemned if they do not make a particular decision.

For reasons that should be clear to all, the policy decisions regarding cities in any newly developing country are of interest and relevance to the international community within which such nations must operate and to which they must relate. In the last analysis, the resolution of problems pertaining to poverty and power in the urban areas of any country will have repercussions on cities elsewhere, for modern society appears to thrive best in the urban context. The problems of cities are correspondingly of universal importance. For strange as it may seem, the man rummaging through garbage cans in Singapore has much in common with his counterpart in Chicago, and a thousand other cities across the globe.

References

ABRAMS, CHARLES. *Man's Struggle for Shelter in an Urbanizing World* (Cambridge, Massachusetts: The M.I.T. Press, 1964).

BAUM, SAMUEL. "The World's Labor Force and Its Industrial Distribution, 1950 and 1960," *International Labour Review*, 95 (January-February, 1967), pp. 96-112.

BREESE, GERALD. *Urbanization in Newly Developing Countries* (Englewood Cliffs, N. J.: Prentice-Hall, Inc., 1966).

—— (ed.). *The City in Newly Developing Countries: Readings on Urbanism and Urbanization* (Englewood Cliffs, N. J.: Prentice-Hall, Inc., 1968, forthcoming).

COLLVER, ANDREW, and ELEANOR LANGLOIS. "The Female Labor Force in Metropolitan Areas: An International Comparison," *Economic Development and Cultural Change*, 10 (July, 1962), pp. 367-85.

DAVIS, KINGSLEY. "The Urbanization of the Human Population," *Scientific American*, 213 (September, 1965), pp. 41-53.

FRANKLIN, N. N. "The Concept of Measurement of Minimum Living Standards," *International Labour Review*, 95 (April, 1967), pp. 271-98.

GINSBURG, NORTON S. *Atlas of Economic Development* (Chicago: University of Chicago Press, 1961).

HARBISON, FREDERICK H. "Human Resources Development Planning in Modernizing Countries," *International Labour Review*, 85 (May, 1962), pp. 435-58.

——. "The Generation of Employment in Newly Developing Countries," in James R. Sheffield (ed.), *Education, Employment, and Rural Development* (Nairobi, Kenya: East Africa Publishing House, 1967), pp. 173-93.

HAREWOOD, JACK. "Overpopulation and Underemployment in the West Indies," *International Labour Review*, 82 (August, 1960), pp. 103-37.

HAUSER, P. M. (ed.). *Urbanization in Asia and the Far East* (Calcutta: UNESCO Research Center on the Social Implications of Industrialization in Southern Asia, 1957).

———. *Urbanization in Latin America* (Paris: UNESCO, 1961).

INDIA, GOVERNMENT OF. *Report of the Committee on Distribution of Income and Levels of Living: Part I—Distribution of Income and Wealth and Concentration of Economic Power* (New Delhi: Government of India, Planning Commission, February, 1964).

INTERNATIONAL AFRICAN INSTITUTE, LONDON. *Social Implications of Industrialization and Urbanization in Africa South of the Sahara* (Paris: UNESCO, 1956).

INTERNATIONAL LABOUR OFFICE. *Employment and Economic Growth*, Studies and Reports, New Series No. 67 (Geneva: International Labour Office, 1964).

———. *Yearbook of Labour Statistics* (Geneva: International Labour Office, 1967).

INTERNATIONAL LABOUR ORGANIZATION. *International Standardization of Labour Statistics*, ILO Studies and Reports, New Series No. 53 (Geneva: International Labour Office, 1959).

———. *Employment Objectives in Economic Development*, ILO New Series No. 62 (Geneva: International Labour Office, 1961).

———. "Unemployment and Underemployment in India, Indonesia, Pakistan, and the Philippines," *International Labour Review*, 86 (October, 1962), pp. 369-87.

———. "Survey of Employment, Unemployment, and Underemployment in Ceylon," *International Labour Review*, 87 (March, 1963), pp. 247-57.

ISLAM, N. "Concepts and Measurement of Unemployment and Underemployment in Developing Economies," *International Labour Review*, 89 (March, 1964), pp. 240-56.

LAKDAWALA, D. T. *et al. Work, Wages and Well-Being in an Indian Metropolis: Economic Survey of Bombay City* (Bombay: University of Bombay, 1963).

LAFAUCHEUX, MARIE-HELENE. "The Contribution of Women to the Economic and Social Development of African Countries," *International Labour Review*, 86 (July, 1962), pp. 15-30.

LEWIS, W. ARTHUR. *Development Planning: The Essentials of Economic Policy* (New York: Harper and Row, Publishers, 1966).

MERRITT, RICHARD L. and STEIN ROKKAN (eds.). *Comparing Nations: The Use of Quantitative Data in Cross-National Research* (New Haven: Yale University Press, 1966).

MORGANSTERN, OSCAR. *On the Accuracy of Economic Observations* (Princeton, N. J.: Princeton University Press, 1963).

PAUKERT, FELIX. "The Distribution of Economic Gains from Economic Development," *International Labour Review*, 91 (May, 1965), pp. 367-92.

Pye, Lucian W. "The Political Implications of Urbanization and the Development Process," in *United Nations Conference on the Application of Science and Technology for the Benefit of the Less Developed Areas, Geneva, 1963, United States Papers* (Washington, D. C.: U. S. Government Printing Office, 1962), pp. 84-89.

Rodman, Hyman. "The Lower Class Value Stretch," in Louis A. Ferman, Joyce L. Kornbluh and Alan Haber (eds.), *Poverty in America: A Book of Readings* (Ann Arbor, Michigan: University of Michigan Press, 1965), pp. 270-85.

Russett, Bruce M. *et al. World Handbook of Political and Social Indicators* (New Haven: Yale University Press, 1964).

Smith, A. D. "Minimum Wages and the Distribution of Income with Special Reference to Developing Countries," *International Labour Review*, 96 (August, 1967), pp. 129-50.

Solow, Anatole A. "Housing Conditions of Urban Low Income Families in Relation to Levels of Social and Economic Development in Latin America," in Publications Series in Public and International Affairs (Pittsburgh, Pa.: University of Pittsburgh, Graduate School of Public and International Affairs, March, 1966).

Sukhatme, P. V. "The World's Hunger and Future Needs in Food Supplies," *Journal of the Royal Statistical Society*, Series A, General, Part 4 (1961).

Taira, Koji. "Wage Differentials in Developing Countries: A Survey of Findings," *International Labour Review*, 93 (March, 1966), pp. 281-301.

Turner, John F. C. For United Nations Center for Housing, Building, and Planning, "Uncontrolled Urban Settlement: Problems and Policies," Working Paper No. 11 prepared for Inter-Regional Seminar on Development Policies and Planning in Relation to Urbanization (Pittsburgh, 1966).

United Nations, Bureau of Social Affairs. "Urban Growth and Social Development in Africa," Working Paper No. 5 prepared for Inter-Regional Seminar on Development Policies and Planning in Relation to Urbanization (Pittsburgh, 1966a).

United Nations, Bureau of Social Affairs, Population Division. "World Urbanization Trends, 1920-1960" (an interim report on work in process), Working Paper No. 6 prepared for Inter-Regional Seminar on Development Policies and Planning in Relation to Urbanization (Pittsburgh, 1966 b).

United Nations, Department of Economic and Social Affairs. *Report of Ad Hoc Advisory Group of Experts on Housing and Urban Development* (New York: United Nations, 1962).

United Nations, Economic and Social Council. *Report on the World Social Situation* (New York: United Nations, 1957, 1963, and 1966).

Zschock, Dieter K. *Manpower Perspective of Colombia*, Research Report Series No. 110, Princeton University, Industrial Relations Section (Princeton, N. J.: Princeton University, Industrial Relations Section, 1967).

15

Poverty, Urban Policy, and the Mature Welfare States of Europe

STEVEN I. PFLANCZER

☐ THE GENERAL PURPOSE OF THIS ESSAY is to explore a significant question of international urban research: What can be learned from the policies aimed at the urban poor by the mature welfare states of Europe? Obviously, such a question calls for a fairly broad sweep of considerations. Realistically, however, one must recognize and understand the problems which American urban affairs specialists or policy-makers encounter whenever they attempt systematic studies of policies concerning the urban poor of Europe. Whether objective socioeconomic indices or politically successful value positions are looked upon as the determinants of social, welfare, and urban policies, Europe as a whole—a pluralistic system of independent nation-states—does not lend itself to study as easily as the United States. In view of the "war on poverty" and the attendant interest in the problems of the urban poor, the question of what can be learned from the mature welfare states of Europe is timely; this, however, does not make the answer any easier.

There are several reasons for the difficulties which attend this question. First of all, those who ask it are usually making assumptions which, under close scrutiny, are largely unfounded. Foremost among these is that our knowledge of European countries is such that their problems and policies concerning the urban poor can readily be identified and examined within the context of Europe's social and welfare policies in general. Secondly, to make direct and systematic comparisons of American and European policies assumes that the political and scientific issues of European urban poverty are indeed comparable to those of the United States.

Finally, while an answer based upon "some international comparisons" may eventually flatter the Swedes or anger the Albanians, one cannot automatically assume that it is of value to urban policymakers in the United States.

The generally recognized difficulties of international and cross-cultural research need no detailed exposition here. Programmatic exhortations notwithstanding, work along these lines by American scholars proceeds at a rather modest pace. Some of the more obvious reasons are linguistic barriers, the lack of systematic data, or the non-comparability of data that are available. Furthermore, the efforts needed for mastering the historical development and structural peculiarities of individual European countries add to the difficulties of making international and cross-cultural studies. As a result—although the Soviet Union claims a fair amount of specialized research interest in the United States, and American urban affairs specialists have easy access to the work of British and Scandinavian social scientists—Europe as a whole is very unevenly studied in matters of social, welfare, and urban policy. Beyond journalistic accounts and impressionistic insights of visiting experts (Kraft, 1965), the social welfare policies and programs of European countries tend to be examined and reported incompletely and in piecemeal fashion.

The classic literature of urban poverty such as the seminal works of Charles Booth, Benjamin Seebohm Rowntree, William Beveridge or, for that matter, the writings of Marx and Engels, are not unknown in the United States. They enable their American readers to grasp the urban consequences of the Industrial Revolution in Europe. London and Berlin, however, were not the only urban centers afflicted with problems of poverty, even though they represent two different types of cities in the sense that London was compelled to adjust to the Industrial Revolution whereas Berlin developed more or less as a consequence of it. The point is that historico-sociological studies of Southern and Eastern European urban problems have yet to find their way into the literature of American urban studies. Even more importantly, there is a general need for adequate and systematic base line data on the urbanization of all countries in Europe. Rigorous comparative studies of social and welfare policies in general and urban policies in particular are virtually impossible to conduct without them.

PREREQUISITES FOR STUDYING THE OBJECTIVE DETERMINANTS OF POLICIES

At the present time, relatively heavy investments of time and energy are needed to obtain even modest generalizations about the most obvious background factors of urban policy in Europe. A good case in point is the necessity of tracing the process of urbanization through the "urbanites in the great cities" (*Grossstaedte, les grandes villes*) of Europe, since no other systematic data can be obtained for *all* of the cities. What follows here is offered merely as an illustration of the types of information that are necessary for formulating specific problems of international urban research. It is hoped that the relevance of this material is obvious for deciding where to look for the urban poor in Europe before attempting to find out what is done for or about them. Discussion of the difficulties encountered in developing these data and reservations about them are indicated in the Appendix to this chapter.

Europe: Where and When?

The internal socio-political transformations of Europe tended to be too swift and frequent in the past to allow suggesting with confidence an historical time span within which systematic data should be made available. However, the Congress of Vienna (1814) and the European order of its day seem an appropriate starting point for reviewing the periodic changes in the map of Europe upon which the great secular processes of industrialization and urbanization took place. These processes provided the major general conditions for the development of social welfare systems which —in Europe as in the United States—provide the principal line of defense against poverty today.

At the time of the Congress of Vienna, the political map of Europe was divided by a conspicuous band of territorial jurisditions from the Two Sicilies northward to Denmark, the predecessor-states of Italy and the Germanies of today. Belgium and the Netherlands were one country; Norway and Sweden to the north were the Kingdom of Sweden, while to the east Finland and Poland were part of the Russian Empire. The Mid-Danube Valley was surrounded by the Austrian Empire, and to the south and southeast of it the Turks dominated the rest of Europe with the exception of parts of Greece.

About a century later, just before World War I, the political map of Europe was considerably different, displaying as full-fledged nations Belgium, the Netherlands, Norway, Sweden, Germany, and Italy. Nothing had changed in the east. The Austro-Hungarian Empire was still masking the territory of the future Czechoslovakia, while the dissolution of the Ottoman Empire had already made possible the emergence of Rumania, Bulgaria, Albania, and parts of the future Yugoslavia.

The territorial boundaries of Europe's nation-states were rearranged again at the end of World War I. Finland; the three Baltic States of Estonia, Latvia, Lithuania; and Poland became independent of Russia's successor-state, the Soviet Union. The Austro-Hungarian Empire was disassembled into Austria, Hungary, and Czechoslovakia; and the Balkan States also took their approximate shape of today.

The inter-war years, an era of dictatorships, brought only minor territorial adjustments. So did World War II. However, two of the major consequences of the latter have direct bearing upon the central concern of this chapter: first, the politically significant division of Europe into Western and Eastern blocs; and second, the various attempts to achieve a "United Europe" within the so-called Western bloc. With regard to both, the general character of the social systems within the two divisions has immediate relevance. For it seems that pervasive socioeconomic planning, on the one hand, and attempts at the coordination of social policies by sovereign nation-states, on the other, have set the frame of reference within which "learning from the mature welfare states of Europe" may or may not occur.

BASE LINE DATA OF POPULATION GROWTH

Both the population of Europe and of its great cities (100,000 people or more) increased during the eighteenth century by approximately 50 per cent. In 1800, the 22 cities of this class contained about 3 per cent of Europe's total population of about 120 million, while none of the 5.3 million inhabitants of the United States was living in a city of 100,000 or more. The next 160 years brought those spectacular increases in the total population, the population of the great cities, and the number of such cities in both Europe and the United States that index the evolution of "mature," industrial-urban societies.

As shown in Tables 1 and 2, population grew by over 200 per cent in Europe and 1,081 per cent in the United States between 1800 and the 1890s, a consequence of the Industrial Revolution and its demographic concomitants: high birth rates and steadily declining death rates. To specify only one of the contributing factors of growth, the typical range of birth rates was about 30 to 40 per 1,000 population in most of Europe, and Russia's birth rate of approximately 50 per 1,000 was matched by that prevailing in the United States (United Nations, 1965a, p. 151). The relative growth rates of Europe and the United States were achieved, of course, amidst the wars of a turbulent century in the history of Europe and a steadily increasing flow of immigrants to the New World.

TABLE 1

Population of Europe and the United States, 1800, 1890s, 1960s
(In Millions)

	1800	1890s	1960s
Western Bloc Countries		199.8	309.5
Eastern Bloc Countries		164.2	277.0
Europe	120.0	364.0	586.5
United States	5.3	62.6	179.3

Source: See Appendix.

TABLE 2

Growth of Population of Europe and the United States 1800-1890s, 1890s-1960s
(In Per Cent)

	1800-1890s	1890s-1960s
Western Bloc Countries		54.9
Eastern Bloc Countries		68.7
Europe	203.3	61.1
United States	1,081.3	186.4

Source: See Appendix.

Bearing in mind the tentative character of the data, it can be seen that the population of the 1890s living in the territories which now belong to the Western bloc countries was almost 200 million as compared to the 164 million people residing in what is now the area occupied by the Eastern bloc nations. By the 1960s, the population of the Western bloc had grown to over 309 million, while the total population of the Eastern bloc had increased to 277 million. Thus, the last 70 years have seen a population increase of more than 60 per cent in Europe and 185 per cent in the United States.

Urbanization and the Great Cities of Europe

Both in Europe and the United States this rapid growth of population occurred concurrently with urbanization. According to Weber, urban growth in Europe "has very generally taken place since 1850" and was well under way by the 1890s, although England (between 1820 to 1830) and the United States (between 1840 to 1850) were the first countries to experience rapid concentration of people in their great cities (Weber, 1967, p. 150).

As shown in Tables 3 and 4, between 1800 and the 1890s the population in the great cities of Europe grew from 4 to 43 million, almost 34 million of this number in the West and more than 9 million in the East. The United States, which did not have any cities of over 100,000 in the first year of the nineteenth century, had almost 10 million people living in such cities by 1890. Between

TABLE 3

POPULATION IN THE GREAT CITIES OF EUROPE AND THE UNITED STATES 1800, 1890s, 1960s
(In Millions)

	1800	1890s	1960s
Western Bloc Countries		33.8	74.4
Eastern Bloc Countries		9.3	64.2
Europe	4.1	43.1	138.6
United States	0.0	9.7	50.7

SOURCE: See Appendix.

the latter date and the 1960s the population of the great cities of Western Europe increased by 120 per cent to over 74 million, while those in what is now the Eastern bloc territory increased by 590 per cent to 64 million. During this same period, the population in the major cities of the United States increased almost 423 per cent— to about 51 million—approximately twice as fast as in all the great cities of Europe taken together.

TABLE 4

GROWTH OF POPULATION IN THE GREAT CITIES OF EUROPE AND THE UNITED STATES, 1800-1890s, 1890s-1960s
(In Per Cent)

	1800-1890s	1890s-1960s
Western Bloc Countries		120.1
Eastern Bloc Countries		590.3
Europe	951.2	221.6
United States	—	422.7

SOURCE: See Appendix.

Thus, both Europe and the United States have experienced spectacular growth of their total population as well as that of their large cities during the past 160 years. It is worth noting, however, that urban growth in the Eastern bloc countries was much faster between the 1890s and the 1960s than the rate in either the United States or the Western bloc countries.

The increase simply in the number of great cities in Europe as well as in the United States provides yet further evidence of the secular process of urbanization. European cities of over 100,000, as shown in Tables 5 and 6, increased in number almost three and one-half times between the 1890s and the 1960s, while an even more pronounced growth occurred in the United States. And as

TABLE 5

NUMBER OF GREAT CITIES IN EUROPE AND THE UNITED STATES, 1800, 1890s, 1960s

	1800	1890s	1960s
Western Bloc Countries		102	281
Eastern Bloc Countries		33	187
Europe	22	135	468
United States	—	28	130

SOURCE: See Appendix.

the Tables also reveal, a still greater rate of increase in the number of large cities took place in the Eastern bloc nations during this same period.

TABLE 6

GROWTH OF THE NUMBER OF GREAT CITIES IN EUROPE AND THE UNITED STATES, 1800-1890s, 1890s-1960s
(In Per Cent)

	1800-1890s	1890s-1960s
Western Bloc Countries		175.5
Eastern Bloc Countries		466.6
Europe	513.6	246.6
United States	——	364.3

SOURCE: See Appendix.

By 1960, as a result of the relatively faster urban growth in the Eastern sector, approximately the same proportion of the total population was living in great cities in both the Western (24 per cent) and the Eastern (23.2 per cent) bloc countries. These urbanites accounted for 23.6 per cent of Europe's total population as compared with 28.3 per cent in the United States (see Table 7).

TABLE 7

POPULATION IN THE GREAT CITIES AS PER CENT OF TOTAL POPULATION OF EUROPE AND THE UNITED STATES, 1800, 1890s, 1960s

	1800	1890s	1960s
Western Bloc Countries		16.9	24.0
Eastern Bloc Countries		5.7	23.2
Europe	3.4	11.8	23.6
United States	0.0	15.5	28.3

SOURCE: See Appendix.

URBANIZATION AND SOCIOECONOMIC DEVELOPMENT IN EUROPE

Thus, the forces underlying urbanization have operated in Europe without much regard for the political boundaries of nation states. But until fairly recently, Eastern Europe lagged behind the Western bloc in number of large cities and the proportion of the total population contained within them. If policies affecting urban poverty were mainly reflections of national cultural differences, we would expect many distinctive programs as a consequence of the persistence of so many distinctive nation-states in Europe. And if urbanization were the determining variable, we would expect to find Eastern and Western blocs looking more and more alike, with the former still developing programs and policies dealing with urban poverty of the sort that had obtained for some time in the West. But if the degree to which economics were socialized and state planning practiced made the difference, then it might be the West whose welfare provisions for the urban poor were "catching up" with the longer and more thoroughly "socialized" Eastern bloc. However, we know that urbanization and industrialization, though substantially correlated over the long run, do not proceed at equal rates over shorter time periods. Since national productivity obviously has something to do with the amount of poverty, including urban poverty, policies concerning the urban poor might well vary with degree of socioeconomic development.

To illustrate, a crude procedure of calculating the average rank of European countries based upon a six-point scale of 13 socioeconomic indicators used in a study of fertility trends (United Nations, 1965a, pp. 137-40) has produced the following groupings of socioeconomic development. The Eastern bloc country of Albania, according to this calculation, was in a class by itself at the lowest level of development. Next came Yugoslavia, Rumania, Bulgaria, and Poland, on the one hand, and Portugal, Spain, and Greece, on the other. The third group consisted of the Soviet Union, Hungary, and Czechoslovakia among the Eastern bloc countries, and of Italy, Finland, Ireland, and France among the Western bloc. Finally, the highest level of development appeared to have been reached by East Germany and by the remaining Western bloc nations of Austria, Belgium, Norway, Luxembourg, Netherlands, Switzerland, Denmark, Germany, the United Kingdom, and Sweden. Although this grouping may seem plausible on an impressionistic basis, whether or not it is correct is less important here than its intended purpose of illustrating the need for a reliable classification of European countries in terms of general socioeconomic development. Since urban policies in general, and those concerning the poor in particular, are more likely to be contingent upon national social policies than on autonomous reactions to local conditions, their determinants cannot be identified through an *ad hoc* or indiscriminate use of cross-sectional data or even time series of relevant policy variables. The need for a standardized, composite index of national socioeconomic development appears to be obvious.

One immediate use for such a standardized index is suggested by the probable differences between the social skills of the rural in-migrants who are steadily moving into the great cities of Europe. Assuming that the patterns of social life in these cities are relatively system-free, in the sense that they represent a *sui generis* form of living, namely urban, which is the same everywhere—whether in Subotica (Yugoslavia) and Cartagena (Spain), in Novomoskovsk (Soviet Union) and Foggia (Italy), or in Zwickau (East Germany) and Derby (United Kingdom)—the question is this: Are the social skills of the rural in-migrants of these cities essentially the same even though they come from social environments representing quite different levels of general socioeconomic development? If not, then the problem of poverty may be quite different in two cities which in other ways seem essentially similar. And policies may reflect these different kinds of urban poverty that are in turn derived from differing national socioeconomic characteristics.

In spite of the broadly programmatic orientation of this chapter, it is recognized that comparative case studies of modest scope are the most realistic means of obtaining preliminary data and propositions. It is also recognized that the selection of cities for such purposes could be facilitated by a standardized index of levels of general socioeconomic development. Finally, it should be added that measures or indices of economic development alone appear to be poor substitutes for the purpose suggested here.

FRAMEWORK FOR THE STUDY OF SOCIAL, WELFARE, AND URBAN POLICIES

The last point referred to above further emphasizes the complexity of our task if we take seriously the suggestion that policy formation affecting urban poverty in the United States might be aided by "what we can learn" from the "mature welfare states" in both the Eastern and Western bloc countries. But the difficulties extend beyond this, for the causes and cures of urban poverty—in

Europe as elsewhere—are implicit in a multiplicity of political choices made at many different places and times. Their discovery requires special effort.

Two Complementary Research Perspectives

The problems of urban poverty in the great cities of Europe can be viewed from two complementary research perspectives. From the point of view of broad social and welfare policies, the problems of such cities are part of the overall objectives set for the total social system represented by the nation-state. Whether specific national urban policies are developed or national policies are primarily geared to urban needs depends upon the actual or desired urban-rural mix of the total population whose resources are required for the realization of overall policy goals. In any event, national social and welfare policies are among the contributory conditions of urban welfare, and their effects can indirectly be measured by the indices of poverty.

The other perspective posits the analytical primacy of the great cities whose needs are identified and met through autonomous efforts which take, however, full advantage of the appropriate provisions of national social and welfare policies. To what extent local social and welfare policies predominate over those of the nation-state depends upon the adequacy of national measures to meet local needs, on the one hand, and upon the uses to which local autonomy is put to the same ends, on the other. In any event, the effects of local and national policies can be measured by appropriate indices of the incidence and prevalence of poverty in the large cities of Europe or elsewhere.

Regardless of how poverty may be defined for purposes of international urban research—a considerable problem in its own right—it will ultimately be understood as a result of the combined consideration of these two perspectives (van Nieuwenhuijze, 1966, pp. 67-72). This consideration, in turn, is not possible until each of the two perspectives is adequately explored and useful typologies of social, welfare, and urban policies devised. The implications of this for "learning from the mature welfare states of Europe" through research are fairly obvious.

The Social and Welfare Policies of Nation-States

As reflected by the general aims of the Western bloc countries which formed the Council of Europe in May, 1949, respect for the civil liberties of the individual, political freedom under the law, and economic and social progress constitute the frame of reference within which the social policies of these countries are shaped (Robertson, 1961, pp. 10-13) and adjusted to the emerging needs of the European Coal and Steel Community, Euratom, and the European Economic Community (Robertson, 1966). The social policies of the Eastern bloc countries, on the other hand, are intimately tied to the Marxist-Leninist doctrines of establishing the material and technical basis of communism through "a planned organization of the social process of production in order to guarantee the welfare and full development of all members of society" (Lenin, 1936, Vol. 6, p. 113).

The distinguishing characteristic of the Eastern bloc countries is the pervasive role played by the central authority of the state, an authority that has the power to dispose of all available national resources and, in fact, does so in an exclusive and programmatic manner. Beyond the quasi-parliamentary forms of political integration controlled by a single party, the exercise of public power involves the development and deliberate use of *direct planning* as a special instrument of policy-making. Under the overall supervision of the Communist Party, academic experts and other state functionaries specify the quantitative targets and appropriate policy instruments of national aspirations (United Nations, 1965b, p. 2). Consequently, the successful pursuit of specific plan targets conditions the realization of such ideologically stipulated major goals as industrialization, socialization, economic independence, full employment, and social welfare.

The somewhat more familiar parameters of social policy in the Western bloc countries are reflected by such major goals as continuous economic growth and expansion, full development and deployment of human resources, area and regional development, and more or less comprehensive systems of social security. The political and social integration of these countries occurs in an historically *ad hoc* and interstitial form of *indirect planning* as the voluntary and free endeavors of individuals, corporate involvement, foundation sponsored programs, and governmental activities coalesce into the "created harmony" of social order (Myrdal, 1960, p. 80). Or to use slightly different language, individual contributions, corporate giving, foundation money, and tax revenues represent the major resources, and their use involves a continuous interplay of competition and cooperation between private and public organizational structures peculiar to just about each and every social unit—including the great cities—that one may wish to examine (Owen, 1964).

The relevance of the general character of the Western and Eastern bloc countries for the specific problems of urban poverty is obvious only in the sense that both types of social systems must meet a certain range of the proximate needs of all their members regardless of the different ways in which overall system goals are stated or in which the means and priorities of their implementation are determined. In the West as well as in the East, the poor are those members of the social system whose proximate needs are not met, presumably for the general reason that they cannot cope with the practical consequences of the metasociological assumptions about the nature of the institutional order. The implementation of system goals produces such basic patterns of social life that some people cannot effectively participate in them and thus are shortchanged by the very system which is the only one they could call their own. If and when any system-wide measures are taken to correct this state of affairs, the system may be said to have a general welfare policy as opposed to social policies in general. Although both social and welfare policies are, so to speak, cut out of the same cloth of national strivings and aspirations, it is useful to maintain a distinction between them.

Indeed, scholarly and not-so-scholarly arguments about the welfare state tend to hinge upon perceived and stipulated preferences for the development of broad social rather than welfare policies. It seems, however, that a welfare state makes deliberate use of its organized power for purposes of meeting a certain range of its members' basic needs which are not met as a consequence of its broad social policies. Whether it maintains minimum levels of income, meets certain common social contingencies, or provides an agreed upon range of social services (Briggs, 1965), a welfare state can be identified through welfare policies and programs which are *national* in scope. By welfare programs is meant here those designed to provide attitudes, goods, and services to individuals and families whose capacity for procuring them through their own efforts has been impaired, interrupted, or has not yet reached maturity (Gordon, 1963, p. 4).

Although this definition applies equally to public and private programs, statutory or public welfare programs provide the most convenient indicators of national welfare policies in Europe. As elsewhere in the world, such programs are known as systems of social security and usually include social insurance, social assistance, and public services. In general, social security systems are concerned with the long- and short-term risks involved in the impairment, interruption, or maturing of the abilities of individuals to take care of themselves. Again, in general, social insurance programs are compulsory and contributory rather than publicly financed schemes and provide benefits commensurate with contributions rather than with needs. Social assistance programs, in turn, tend to have a residual character in the sense that they are usually financed out of the general revenues of government as a substitute for, or supplement to, the social insurance benefits of those who are eligible by law for such assistance. Finally, public services tend to be provided directly by public authorities from general revenues, regardless of benefits which may accrue to individuals through social insurance or assistance.

European Social Security Systems

A survey of social security systems shows that all of the 27 countries of Europe considered in this chapter can appropriately be called welfare states: all have extensive social security systems of relatively long standing. Regardless of whether Bismarck's Germany (1883) or the British (1945) should be praised or blamed for being the first to work out the general pattern of programs which characterize the modern welfare state, the use of the term appears appropriate with regard to all of these nations. Based upon the length of legislative and administrative experience with social welfare programs of national scope, the typical (average) European country:

has had a work injury program since 1905;

has provided sickness and maternity benefits since 1912;

has paid old age, disability, and survivors benefits since 1918;

has distributed unemployment compensation since 1923; and

has had a program of family allowances since 1945.

The exceptions are the corporatist state of Portugal, on the one hand, and the Eastern bloc countries of Albania, Bulgaria, Czechoslovakia, Poland, Rumania, and the Soviet Union, on the other. The latter do not have unemployment compensation programs, but they do have all of the other programs listed (Social Security Administration, 1964).

The systemic character as well as the structural diversity of the programs in effect today are functions of the general political experience, evolving institutional makeup, and cultural traditions of the individual countries during the past 25 years or so. This could hardly be otherwise, for the welfare programs of Europe's nation-states are integral parts of the continuous search for uniqueness and autonomy in shaping and maintaining a certain way of life (Haas, 1964, p. 465). Nevertheless, these are national variations on what seems increasingly to be a single broad line of institutional evolution in urban-industrial societies. Dating from the reconstruction years following World War II, the major trends of recent developments appear to be the following throughout Europe:

(1) extension of eligibility rights and contingent benefits beyond the labor force;

(2) more comprehensive protection of the population against all major social risks;

(3) modification of the relationship between contributions and benefits in recognition of the need for more effective redistribution of national incomes; and

(4) standardization and centralization of the management of various programs.

Space does not permit any detailed review of how national social security systems or specific programs in Europe differ from each other in terms of traditional categories of analysis, i.e., criteria of eligibility, nature and amount of benefits, methods of financing, and administrative organization (Burns, 1949). In addition to calling attention to the major trends of recent developments, it is more important to note here that the program coverage of the social security systems of Europe is such that they are among the most complete in the world. The most obvious difference between the European systems and that of the United States is the absence of family allowances in the latter—a fact that merits the attention of policy-makers.

The completeness of program coverage and the relatively high levels of benefits (and costs) achieved by the social security systems of Europe are related to the age of their component programs (Aaron, 1967). This factor tends to lead to more or less intricate "patchworks" of legislative measures and administrative structures —which are very much in evidence in Europe as in the United States—without serious proposals to radically alter or replace them by a new system. In any case, neither the creation nor the continued operation of Europe's welfare programs can satisfactorily be explained by the basic ideological orientation and political character of the regimes which continue to support and develop them in both the Western and Eastern bloc countries (Cutright, 1965).

While differences in national ethos may explain the social-situational roots of legislative intent concerning the social security systems of the Soviet Union and the United States, the actual operation and development of these systems is ultimately guided by the requirements of effective social organization and national needs (Rimlinger, 1965). Finally, the often quoted and generally unfavorable comparisons between relative proportions of national income spent on social welfare by the United States and by some of the European countries provide, at best, a political argument; the "superiority" of some European social security systems and the adequacy of that of the United States must be established on technical grounds of performance—and international studies of urban poverty are one of the ways to do just that.

The Urban Policies of the Great Cities

In the preceding discussion, the system referent of Europe's social and welfare goals was seen as the nation-state inasmuch as (1) *social policies* concern the discrepancies between actual and desirable conditions throughout the entire institutional network of national life, and (2) *welfare policies* do the same for a specific institutional sector of it. To focus upon *urban policies,* in turn, is to take a new system referent into consideration—in this case, the great cities of Europe's nation-states. Although it seems unlikely that such cities themselves could play a larger role in the reduction of urban poverty than national governments, American urban affairs specialists generally prefer the research perspective of examining local points of view and efforts within broad national contexts rather than the other way around. The reasons for this orientation can be stated in different ways; all tend to boil down, however, to the culturally conditioned preference for "as little government intervention as possible" through vigorous and jealously guarded exercise of local autonomy, and this may be a significant factor with regard to international comparisons. Be that as it may, urban poverty cannot adequately be defined and studied without also taking into consideration specifically urban policies, i.e., the social and welfare policies of the great cities. In a full analytical perspective, urban poverty reflects the failure of the social and welfare policies of the nation-state and of the cities themselves. Unfortunately, there are simply no adequate data for systematic intercity comparisons; we can only note what we could expect to learn given adequate studies.

The social policies of the great cities in general, and their welfare policies in particular, are functions of their autonomy with regard to the nation-state. And while the major cities of the Eastern bloc countries are more or less autonomous agents of the welfare state, those of the Western bloc countries and the United States are to a greater or lesser degree partners of it. The fact that Hungary's great cities, for instance, have the same rights as its intermediate politico-administrative units (*megye,* county, *département*) denotes a form of competitive home-rule or autonomy which may be different from similar arrangements, say, in Switzerland or in the United States. Just how different the local autonomy of the large cities is with regard to their respective nation-states in Europe may well be one of the by-products of studies which concern themselves with the question of what the inhabitants of those cities consider to be their share of responsibilities for the poor among them. The point is that specific field studies rather than a priori classification of the cities in terms of autonomy appear to be the most fruitful way of discovering the fundamental issues of urban policy-making.

If it were possible to conduct field studies of urban poverty in the Eastern bloc countries of Europe, only "public" social and welfare policies of the great cities could be studied there. The major goal of socialization, i.e., public ownership and control of all significant national resources so persistently and effectively pursued in that part of Europe, eliminates the major cities of the Eastern bloc countries from consideration as centers of "private" initiative and related localism in the shaping of urban policies. Amidst radical transformation of the entire social structure, only the physical features of these cities remind the urban specialist from the West of the most obvious problems of urban life (Fisher, 1962). However, policy alternatives for solving them tend to reflect the competing views of *apparatchiki* and other technical experts rather than of different and independent social groups. The absence of free enterprise and of the attendant welfare structures of "bourgeois philanthropy" in such countries is, nevertheless, not without interest in the sense that the study of functionally equivalent arrangements can shed light upon alternative forms of social organization. That is, a comparative study of the urban policies concerning the poor, say, of Prague (Czechoslovakia) and Warsaw (Poland), on the one hand, and of Glasgow (United Kingdom) and Copenhagen (Denmark), on the other, could yield revealing results.

The study of urban policies in the Western bloc countries and the United States, on the other hand, must cope with the quasi-public character of institutional and associational forms of social organization which involve the actual exercise of para-political power. Beyond ideological disputes, the roles of free enterprise and private welfare must be made empirically explicit with regard to the social and welfare policies in the large cities where a plurality of problem-solving groups attempt to find and maintain stable and mutually compatible solutions to such problems—among others—as urban poverty. In addition to government's role, welfare related endeavors concern the voluntary contributions of individuals, private corporate involvement, and the activities of foundations. But the fundamental issue is not whether or to what degree the urban centers of the Western bloc countries have extensive programs based upon private efforts similar or analogous to the work of Community Chests, United Funds (Seeley *et al.*, 1957) and the activities of American philanthropic foundations (Andrews, 1956);

comparative studies are ultimately interested in the relative efficiency of the social and welfare policies of the great cities with regard to urban poverty. Briefly, structural inventories of the system components of such cities represent only a very challenging beginning; the aim is to invade the largely unchartered territory of testing extant policies.

Whether American specialists are ready to undertake the testing of the social and welfare policies of large cities within a framework of international urban research is—to say the least—an open question. Eminently qualified experts, who are aware of the systemic complexity of the general problem of poverty, tend to view the past accomplishments of social scientists as rather modest. Systematic testing of policies in general appears to be a newly recognized need and challenge (Lampman, 1966, pp. 228-29). Be what it may with regard to national policies concerning poverty, comparative studies of the social and welfare policies of cities in the United States can be considered reasonable prerequisites for venturing into the field of international comparisons. At the present time, only broad outlines of inquiries rather than specific working models are available to guide such international studies. Indeed, perhaps *Poverty and Progress, Social Mobility in a Nineteenth-Century City* (Thernstrom, 1964) comes closest to being a model for case studies of urban poverty. If so, there is then plenty of work to be done before the social and welfare policies of the great cities of Europe and the United States can be comparatively tested.

One can hope such work will proceed. The large cities of the Eastern bloc countries could provide an ideal setting for the study of urban poverty where the public policies of the nation-state predominate over and against local views and efforts to implement them within a centrally-planned social system. The cities of the Western bloc, on the other hand, could lend themselves to the study of urban poverty from the perspective of localism, that is, the interplay between private and public efforts to formulate social and welfare policies in the urban communities themselves in order to supplement the policies of the nation-state.

SOME TENTATIVE CONCLUSIONS

This chapter began with the question: What might the United States learn relevant to its own "war on poverty" from the policies

484 □ Power, Poverty, and Urban Policy

aimed at the urban poor by the mature welfare states of Europe?
One is tempted to answer: very little unless and until we accomplish the research which would make meaningful, systematic, and
thus fruitful comparisons possible. Most so-called "comparisons"
available to American policy-makers have in fact focused on a few
current programs or provisions in one or another European country,
and these are taken as "examples" of what we could or should be
doing in the United States. Yet it is quite clear that European
social policies are the result of complex historical experiences,
political and social value preferences, and improvisations to deal
with immediately pressing problems of national scope. To successfully select some institutional component from the complex context
in which it evolved—e.g., the "ombudsman"—and to attempt to
transplant it into the socio-cultural systems of our own urban
centers assumes a kind of knowledge and skill we cannot as yet
claim to possess. But the comparative research which would yield
such prerequisite knowledge would itself throw much new and
needed light on the nature of the poverty problem in the United
States, as well as in other countries, and on the relative efficacy of
different solutions in alternative national contexts.

For these reasons, this chapter has repeatedly indicated the
need for such "disaggregated and correlated, panpolitical and
future-oriented, urban social indicators concerning people, families,
and institutions" in the great cities of Europe as Moynihan has
recently advocated for use in the United States (1967, pp. 159-77).
So, also, has it emphasized the concomitant use of two research perspectives that should be understood as complementary: the one
viewing urban welfare programs simply as localized examples of
national goals and policies; the other focusing on the generation
of conditions and actions within a local social system that displays
certain kinds and degrees of autonomy. Until such adequate research is available, the findings of case studies in the United States
and modest comparative efforts concerning a few great cities of
Europe and the United States ought to replace the *ad hoc* and
eclectic policy recommendations which are occasionally gleaned
from the experiences of the more mature welfare states of Europe.

Acknowledgment of the limitations of our knowledge does not
preclude suggesting some generalizations based on the material
covered by this chapter; it simply serves to emphasize how very

tentative such generalizations must be. With this caveat, the following are noted.

First, the existence of extensive social security systems with broad similarities among virtually all of the European nations clearly reflects the supranational, transcultural force of urbanization and industrialization. We can say with some confidence, though we have yet to explain it satisfactorily, that the urban-industrial society—at least as we know it—will be a "welfare society," with the role of the state per se subject to important variation. There is no evidence to suggest that some kinds of social policies (such as those affecting rate of economic growth) might eliminate the need for extensive welfare policies and provisions.

Second, in dealing with poverty, the greatest emphasis on social rather than welfare policy, in conjunction with socializing the economy, has been mainly in the Eastern bloc countries where, for example, unemployment compensation as such does not exist. This emphasis seems to be essentially a political-ideological choice since, as has been indicated, there are nations which are Western bloc counterparts of the Communist states of Eastern Europe in terms of urbanization and socioeconomic development.

Third, the United States provides an example of a nation, continental in scale with major regional differences in urbanization and socioeconomic development, in which national social policies dealing with poverty have been minimal until fairly recently, while welfare has been largely the province of state and local public and private agencies, with the private sector more developed in the welfare field than in other countries. It is, moreover, the only nation in the West with no family allowances. Clearly, these differences from Europe's Western bloc cannot be explained by the variables of urbanization and socioeconomic development. Once again we must turn to political and ideological, and even particular cultural and historical, variables in trying to establish explanations. Only comparative studies, however, will enable us to determine what has produced the American welfare system as we now know it. And only when we have this kind of understanding will we be able to consider borrowing selectively from the European experience an effective intellectual and programmatic tactic.

Appendix

For this chapter, "Europe" refers to a land area of approximately 10 million square kilometers which includes, in addition to 25 other countries, the territory of Iceland and the European segment of the Soviet Union. It excludes, however, such small countries as Monaco, Andorra, and Lichtenstein, and also such small islands as Cyprus and Malta, which are technically part of Europe. (Note that the territory of the United States is approximately 9.4 million square kilometers.) As to the major divisions of Europe, Western bloc countries refer here to Austria, Belgium, Denmark, Finland, France, West Germany, Greece, Iceland, Ireland, Italy, Luxembourg, Netherlands, Norway, Portugal, Spain, Sweden, Switzerland, and the United Kingdom; the Eastern bloc nations are Albania, Bulgaria, Czechoslovakia, East Germany, Hungary, Poland, Rumania, Yugoslavia, and the Soviet Union. Use of the cold war terminology of "blocs" may not be the best, but such nomenclature seems better than that of "capitalist-socialist" or "communist-noncommunist" countries. The other definitions and related data offered here are likewise not authoritative or final; their intended purpose is to invite improvement and to point to research needs.

The population data for Europe in the 1890s were derived from national enumerations between 1881 and 1897; the majority of such counts were, in fact, conducted in the 1890s (*The Statesman's Year-Book, 1901*). Since few countries of Europe had at that time the same territorial boundaries as their name-sake successor-states have in the 1960s, the population figures of the territorial equivalents of today's Western and Eastern bloc nations and the growth rates derived from them are, at best, approximate. The attempt to show the development of Europe's urbanization beyond the 1890s is based upon the data of cities of 100,000 or more ("the great cities") since no other systematic data could be assembled for all Europe. Inasmuch as members of the Institute of International Studies at Berkeley, California, were unable to reach their goal with regard to the Eastern bloc countries of Europe, let alone the world, an ambitious and praiseworthy effort to identify metropolitan areas throughout the world was only partially successful (International Urban Research, 1959). Indeed, even with exceptional resources, a study of the growth of Europe's metropolitan areas in some historical depth may present almost insurmountable difficulties. Yet, while direct comparisons between Europe and the United States in terms of urbanites in the great cities may appear somewhat unsatisfactory, they are not without relevance inasmuch as urban poverty tends to be a "city proper" phenomenon of the metropolitan areas of the United States. But it remains true that the extent to which these findings may be affected by the use of population data of "city proper" rather than that of "agglomeration-conurbation-metropolitan" areas cannot be determined with precision, since the unreliability of the latter forced the use of the former data for purposes of systematic comparisons. More than that, the "city proper" data for the Soviet Union are mere estimates.

The two principal sources of the data appearing in the tables were:

(1) Keltie, J. Scott (editor), the *Statesman's Year-Book*, Statistical and Historical Annual of the States of the World for the Year 1901 (New York: Macmillan, 1901); and

(2) United Nations, Statistical Office of the United Nations, Department of Economic and Social Affairs, *Demographic Yearbook 1964*. Special Topic: Population Census Statistics III. UN Sales No. 65.XIII.1 (New York: United Nations, 1965), Table 1, pp. 97, 105-6, 110; and Table 7, pp. 173-75, 183-87, 188-89.

The Tables consist of more than mere compilation of existing data since operational judgments had to be made about the definition of Europe and the major distinction between Western and Eastern bloc countries, particularly with regard to the 1890s. For purposes of identifying the great cities in the European part of the Soviet Union, the conventional dividing line between Europe and Asia was taken to mean the Ural Mountains and the northwestern boundaries of the Soviet Socialist Republic of Khazakstan. Whether the European segment of the Soviet Union defined in this manner was the same as that for which population data were available in both sources could not, of course, be determined. Similarly, a number of decisions had to be made in order to obtain the approximate population totals of the Eastern bloc countries in the 1890s. To that end, parts of the Austro-Hungarian Empire were used to reconstruct Czechoslovakia (Silesia, Moravia, Bohemia), Poland (Galicia), Rumania (Bukovina), and Yugoslavia (Carniola, Coastal Land, Dalmatia). The population of Eastern Germany, on the other hand, was obtained by dividing the total population of the German Empire of the 1890s in proportion to the division of the two Germanies of the 1960s. Depending upon carefully considered needs, more precise data could be assembled through specialized efforts—the data of this chapter are approximate and show only crude, major trends of urbanization. *The Growth of Cities in the Nineteenth Century* by Adna Ferrin Weber— whose calculations did not go beyond the data of the 1890s—represents the type of work that ought to be emulated and up-dated by the urban specialists of today.

Much more also should be attempted to establish the needed base line studies of welfare systems—the necessary data for the years following the end of World War II are well within reach. The various source books and studies published by the United Nations, the publications of the International Labour Office (ILO, *International Labour Review,* monthly) and of the International Social Security Association (ISSA, Bulletin, monthly) as well as improved census data and related statistics provided by the European countries themselves appear to make such studies possible. As to projects of more limited scope, Denmark, Finland, Iceland, Norway, and Sweden have issued comparative social welfare statistics since 1948 (Statistical Reports of the Northern Countries, 1964). Similarly, the Council of Europe and the European Economic Community are providing a certain amount of relevant systematic data.

References

AARON, HENRY. "Social Security: International Comparisons," in Otto Eckstein (ed.), *Studies in the Economics of Income Maintenance* (Washington, D.C.: The Brookings Institution, 1967), pp. 13-48.

ANDREWS, F. EMERSON. *Philanthropic Foundations* (New York: Russell Sage Foundation, 1956).

BRIGGS, ASA. "The Welfare State in Historical Perspective," in Mayer N. Zald (ed.), *Social Welfare Institutions* (New York: John Wiley & Sons, Inc., 1965), pp. 37-70.

BURNS, EVELINE M. *The American Social Security System* (Boston: Houghton Mifflin Co., 1949).

CUTRIGHT, PHILLIPS. "Political Structure, Economic Development, and National Social Security Program," in Mayer N. Zald (ed.), *Social Welfare Institutions* (New York: John Wiley & Sons, Inc., 1965), pp. 123-40.

FISHER, JACK C. "Planning the City of Socialist Man," *Journal of the American Institute of Planners,* 28 (November, 1962), pp. 251-65.

GORDON, MARGARET S. *The Economics of Welfare Policies* (New York: Columbia University Press, 1963).

HAAS, ERNST B. *Beyond the Nation-State* (Stanford: Stanford University Press, 1964).

INTERNATIONAL URBAN RESEARCH. *The World's Metropolitan Areas* (Berkeley and Los Angeles: University of California Press, 1959).

KELTIE, J. SCOTT (ed.), *The Statesman's Year-Book,* Statistical and Historical Annual of the States of the World for the Year 1901 (New York: The Macmillan Co., 1901).

KRAFT, IVOR. "Impressions of Social Welfare in Eastern Europe," *The Catholic Charities Review,* 49 (May, 1965), pp. 4-10.

LAMPMAN, ROBERT J. "Ends and Means in the War on Poverty," in Leo Fishman (ed.), *Poverty Amid Affluence* (New Haven and London: Yale University Press, 1966), pp. 212-29.

LENIN, V. I. *Collected Works,* Cooperative Society for Foreign Workers in the Soviet Union (Moscow, 1936).

MOYNIHAN, DANIEL P. "Urban Conditions: General," *The Annals of the American Academy of Political and Social Science,* 371 (May, 1967), pp. 159-77.

MYRDAL, GUNNAR. *Beyond the Welfare State* (New Haven and London: Yale University Press, 1960).

VAN NIEUWENHUIJZE, C. A. O. *The Nation and the Ideal City* (The Hague, Paris: Mouton & Co., 1966).

OWEN, DAVID. *English Philanthropy 1660-1960* (Cambridge, Massachusetts: The Belknap Press of Harvard University Press, 1964).

RIMLINGER, GASTON V. "Social Security, Incentives, and Controls in the U.S. and U.S.S.R.," in Mayer N. Zald (ed.), *Social Welfare Institutions* (New York: John Wiley & Sons, Inc., 1965), pp. 102-22.

ROBERTSON, A. H. *The Council of Europe* (New York: Frederick A. Praeger, Inc., 1961).

———. *European Institutions* (New York: Frederick A. Praeger, Inc., 1966).

SEELEY, JOHN R., et al. *Community Chest, A Case Study in Philanthropy* (Toronto: University of Toronto Press, 1957).

STATISTICAL REPORTS OF THE NORTHERN COUNTRIES. *Social Welfare Statistics of the Northern Countries 1960 (1960/61)* (Stockholm, 1964).

THERNSTROM, STEPHAN. *Poverty and Progress; Social Mobility in a Nineteenth Century City* (Cambridge: Harvard University Press, 1964).

UNITED NATIONS, DEPARTMENT OF ECONOMIC AND SOCIAL AFFAIRS. *Population Bulletin of the United Nations No. 7—1963* with special reference to conditions and trends of fertility in the world, Doc. No. ST/SOA/Ser. N/7, UN Sales No. 64. XIII.2. (New York: United Nations, 1965a).

UNITED NATIONS, SECRETARIAT OF THE ECONOMIC COMMISSION FOR EUROPE. *Economic Survey of Europe in 1962, Part 2, Economic Planning in Europe,* Doc. No. E/ECE/493/Add. 1, UN Sales No. 65.II.E.4. (Geneva: United Nations, 1965b).

UNITED NATIONS, STATISTICAL OFFICE OF THE UNITED NATIONS, DEPARTMENT OF ECONOMIC AND SOCIAL AFFAIRS. *Demographic Yearbook 1964.* Special Topic: Population Census Statistics III. UN Sales No. 65.XIII.1. (New York: United Nations, 1965c).

UNITED NATIONS, STATISTICAL OFFICE OF THE UNITED NATIONS, DEPARTMENT OF ECONOMIC AND SOCIAL AFFAIRS. *Statistical Yearbook 1965,* UN Sales No. 66.XVII.1. (New York: United Nations, 1966).

U. S. DEPARTMENT OF HEALTH, EDUCATION, AND WELFARE, SOCIAL SECURITY ADMINISTRATION. *Social Security Programs Throughout the World, 1964* (Washington, D.C.: U.S. Government Printing Office, 1964).

WEBER, ADNA FERRIN. *The Growth of Cities in the Nineteenth Century* (Ithaca, New York: Cornell University Press, Cornell Paperbacks, 1967).

16

Policy Implications of Some Non-economic Dimensions of Urban Poverty

GORDON F. SUTTON

☐ THIS CHAPTER DEALS WITH THREE related points of concern which, though stated theoretically and abstractly, in fact have consequences that are thoroughly tangible for the poor themselves. First, it will examine the current economic "definition" of poverty and note the deficiency of it from a sociological perspective. This will be followed by an attempt to state a priori an approach to a sociological analysis of poverty, distinguishing between *transitional poverty,* which refers to the lifeways of those who will not spend their entire lives in poverty, and *non-transitional* poverty, which refers to the lifeways of those whose expectations of leaving poverty are minimal. Third, some of the implications which these distinctions have for antipoverty programs will be noted.

POVERTY AS A LACK OF MONEY

The frequently quoted exchange between Ernest Hemingway and F. Scott Fitzgerald, in which the former spoils Fitzgerald's attempt to say that the two of them are different from the rich, hinges on Hemingway's quip that the rich merely have more money.

AUTHOR'S NOTE: *An earlier version of this chapter was presented at the annual meetings of the American Sociological Association, San Francisco, California, August, 1967, in a joint session with the Society for the Study of Social Problems. The views set forth in it are those of the author and do not necessarily represent those of the Office of Economic Opportunity, with which he is associated.*

Whatever the philosophical or rhetorical merits of Hemingway's notion, it is less than satisfactory as a guide to social policy in the United States. To try to construct a scheme to do something about poverty in this country that is founded simply on a notion of quantitative economic differences—the poor are only those with less money —is seriously to understate and even misstate the nature of poverty as it has appeared to occur in Western literature over the last 200 years. Yet, in a sense, we have become committed to just such an idea in the current pursuit of antipoverty efforts.

The argument presented here is that it is not sufficient to define poverty, for purposes of social policy, by saying that poverty is people without as much money as most others in the society. It is, however, useful to begin by saying that poverty has to do with poor people and their relationship to the society.

The economist's view of poverty tends to derive from consideration of the flow of personal or family income within a specified current time period. This line of thought defines a population in poverty as those located on an income scale below a given point; hence, those on the lower end of a continuous income distribution. In this definition, there is no *formal* recognition of qualitative distinctions between the poor and non-poor, although it is possible to bring these distinctions in by looking at the differential qualitative characteristics of the income-defined populations.

Although not in fundamental disagreement with the economist's view as sketched above, I should like to develop a line of reasoning which begins, rather than concludes, with this continuous and time-limited conception. It will then be possible to move from this position toward one which emphasizes certain sociological dimensions of poverty.

Let us start by accepting the Orshansky scheme, known otherwise as the Social Security Poverty Index (economy model), to determine the size and characteristics of the population "in poverty." The operations which define poverty along these lines take into account current family income required to keep body and soul together, adjusted for family size and age differences, according to minimum schedules of costs for food, housing, medical services, and other living requirements. One arrangement applies to the farm population and another to the non-farm. The results of the application of rules derived from these principles to the United States population surveyed in March, 1966, are set out in Table 1.

It seems to me that we do not need to worry at this time about the quality of the Social Security Index as a means of identifying the initial population target in the national antipoverty effort. Just as this index represents an improvement over the fixed-dollar threshold of the Council of Economic Advisers used earlier by the federal government, further useful modifications could be made. At this point, however, the differences in size and characteristics are likely to be small. But even more important than this, further fiddling with this particular identification apparatus is likely to place too much weight on the importance of the dollar income factor as the prime element in the orientation of approaches aimed at a solution of the problem. Nevertheless, it is convenient for purposes of analysis to establish the "population in poverty" (which will be termed here the "poverty aggregate") by applying Social Security criteria to national population data. We can then turn away from the problem of the procedures for identifying the poor and ask what the resulting aggregate looks like from the viewpoint of poverty as an affliction of both the impoverished, as arbitrarily defined above, and the larger society. As a first step, let us sort out some of the components of this population.

POVERTY IN A DYNAMIC FRAMEWORK

The major weakness in the "cash" approach to poverty, that of the Social Security Index described above, arises in the unmanageable character of the population aggregate generated by such a scheme; that is, unmanageable in sociological terms. It is quite possible for the sociologist to work with the population generated by a "cash" apparatus; but it turns out to be very difficult to move forward until a definition of what poverty is or what it is about is made in sociological terms—in terms of social structure, of roles, of institutional systems.

If low income is evidence of poverty, though not its definition, a useful initial sorting of the poverty aggregate is that which separates those impoverished for some short run, as a transitional state, from those who are born and die in poverty and whose lifeways have provided the conventional poverty stereotype. Such a distinction between transitional and non-transitional poverty focuses upon the cross-generational experience of individuals and families.

TABLE 1

POVERTY AND LOW-INCOME STATUS OF NONINSTITUTIONAL POPULATION IN 1965: NUMBER AND PER CENT OF PERSONS IN HOUSEHOLDS WITH 1965 INCOME BELOW SSA POVERTY OR LOW-INCOME LEVELS, BY AGE, RACE, AND FAMILY STATUS*

[Numbers in Thousands]

Age and Family Status	Total Persons					White					Nonwhite				
	Total¹	Poor		In Households With Low Income Poor and Near Poor²		Total¹	Poor		In Households With Low Income Poor and Near Poor²		Total¹	Poor		In Households With Low Income Poor and Near Poor²	
		Number	%	Number	%		Number	%	Number	%		Number	%	Number	%
All persons	191,535	32,669	17.1	47,256	24.7	168,853	22,362	13.2	34,250	20.3	22,681	10,308	45.4	13,007	57.3
Unrelated individuals	12,132	4,830	39.8	5,643	46.5	10,476	4,007	38.2	4,708	44.9	1,655	824	49.8	936	56.6
Members of family units	179,403	27,839	15.5	41,613	23.2	158,377	18,355	11.6	29,542	18.7	21,026	9,484	45.1	12,071	57.4
Children under age 18³	69,639	14,282	20.5	20,373	29.3	59,522	8,652	14.5	13,477	22.6	10,117	5,630	55.6	6,896	68.2
Under 6	24,163	5,252	21.7	7,652	31.7	20,366	3,121	15.3	4,995	24.5	3,798	2,132	56.1	2,658	70.0
6-13	31,749	6,630	20.9	9,325	29.4	27,276	4,038	14.8	6,202	22.7	4,472	2,591	57.9	3,121	69.8
14-17	13,728	2,400	17.5	3,396	24.7	11,880	1,492	12.6	2,278	19.2	1,848	908	49.1	1,118	60.5
Persons aged 18-24⁴	19,669	2,769	14.1	4,087	20.8	17,305	1,901	11.0	2,922	16.9	2,364	869	36.8	1,164	49.2
Unrelated individuals⁵	1,158	465	40.2	557	48.1	1,011	389	38.5	464	45.9	146	76	52.1	92	63.0
Members of family units	18,511	2,304	12.4	3,530	19.1	16,294	1,512	9.3	2,458	15.1	2,218	793	35.8	1,072	48.3
Head	3,050	571	18.7	812	26.6	2,713	410	15.1	614	22.6	338	162	47.9	199	58.9
Wife	4,885	601	12.3	966	19.8	4,438	456	10.3	747	16.3	447	145	32.4	219	49.0
Never-married children⁶	7,794	857	11.0	1,296	16.6	6,794	489	7.2	812	12.0	1,000	368	36.8	483	48.3
Other	2,782	275	9.9	456	16.4	2,349	157	6.7	285	12.1	433	118	27.3	171	39.5

Persons aged 25-54	67,659	7,700	11.4	11,642	17.2	60,382	5,242	8.7	8,375	13.9	7,276	2,458	33.8	3,271	45.0
Unrelated individuals	3,770	822	21.8	967	25.6	3,000	554	18.4	655	21.8	770	269	34.9	312	40.5
Members of family units	63,889	6,878	10.8	10,675	16.7	57,382	4,689	8.5	7,717	13.4	6,506	2,189	33.6	2,959	45.5
Head	30,844	3,633	11.8	5,507	17.9	27,615	2,428	8.8	3,917	14.2	3,229	1,205	37.3	1,591	49.3
Wife	28,062	2,568	9.2	4,176	14.9	25,625	1,833	7.2	3,149	12.3	2,437	735	30.2	1,027	42.1
Other	4,983	677	13.6	992	19.9	4,142	428	10.3	651	15.7	840	249	29.6	341	40.6
Persons aged 55-64	16,923	2,640	15.6	3,758	22.2	15,392	2,072	13.5	3,011	19.6	1,529	567	37.1	746	48.8
Unrelated individuals	2,524	851	33.7	990	39.2	2,198	688	31.3	801	36.4	326	163	50.0	188	57.7
Members of family units	14,399	1,789	12.4	2,768	19.2	13,194	1,384	10.5	2,210	16.8	1,203	404	33.6	558	46.4
Head	7,490	912	12.2	1,385	18.5	6,820	683	10.0	1,069	15.7	668	228	34.1	315	47.2
Wife	5,647	671	11.9	1,092	19.3	5,231	541	10.3	914	17.5	416	130	31.2	179	43.0
Other	1,262	206	16.3	291	23.1	1,143	160	14.0	227	19.9	119	46	36.7	64	53.8
Persons aged 65 and over	17,645	5,279	29.9	7,397	41.9	16,252	4,494	27.7	6,466	39.8	1,394	786	56.4	933	66.9
Unrelated individuals	4,679	2,692	57.5	3,129	66.9	4,268	2,376	55.7	2,786	65.3	411	317	77.1	345	83.9
Members of family units	12,966	2,587	20.0	4,268	32.9	11,984	2,118	17.7	3,680	30.7	983	469	47.7	588	59.8
Head	6,895	1,521	22.1	2,446	35.5	6,348	1,245	19.6	2,103	33.1	547	276	50.5	344	62.9
Wife	3,514	749	21.3	1,285	36.6	3,338	649	19.4	1,164	34.9	176	100	56.8	120	68.2
Other	2,557	317	12.4	537	21.0	2,298	224	9.7	413	18.0	260	93	35.8	124	47.7

[1] Noninstitutional population.

[2] Families in poverty and families above poverty but below low-income index.

[3] Includes never-married own children of head and all other never-married relatives under age 18. Excludes 346,000 children under age 14 who live with a family of nonrelatives.

[4] Includes heads, wives, and other never-married relatives under age 18.

[5] Includes 93,000 unrelated individuals aged 14-17 of whom 90,000 had incomes below SSA poverty level in 1965 and 2,000 were above poverty but below low-income level.

[6] Aged 18-21.

* This table is reproduced from "The Poor in 1965 and Trends, 1959-65," Research and Statistics Note (U. S. Department of Health, Education, and Welfare, Social Security Administration), Note No. 5-1967.

SOURCE: Derived from special tabulations by Bureau of the Census from the Current Population Survey for March, 1966.

For example, the cumulative impact of family and neighborhood milieus are emphasized in assigning most of the aged poor to the transitional group and most of the "culturally disadvantaged" children of the ghetto to the non-transitional category.

Transitional Poverty

As an illustration of the transitional state, those who have become poor as a consequence of age and infirmity may be joined with the graduate student of small means and the mentally and physically ill-equipped. The important point here is that there are people occupying positions reasonably well integrated in the society who are poorer than the majority of the community and to whom we may wish to address one or several programs to assure them shelter, food, and some undefined set of other necessities and comforts over the short run. This is the group for whom poverty is largely an economic problem, entailing solutions that may be characterized in terms of income needs.

If we hold such a view of the problem, in effect we postulate that the assumption of a continuous welfare distribution as evidenced in a current income measure may be suitable in dealing with those who are in this state of transitional poverty. Such an assumption, it should be noted, is implicit in the "cash" measures mentioned earlier. For purposes of considering ways out of poverty, this means that income distribution is treated as isometric with the welfare distribution, which in turn implies that (1) the welfare distribution is of the form of an interval scale, and (2) marginal income increments cumulate to transform conditions of poverty to conditions of non-poverty for any individual.

The purpose of pushing to the fore these implications of the Social Security Index is not to urge its abandonment, but to make clear the difficulties which may accompany efforts to use it in developing antipoverty policies and programs. The Index can still have utility, for example, for such tasks as identifying program recipients, providing a rough measure of the extent of poverty within the country, and evaluating program effectiveness.

The degree of "marginality" of impoverished populations with respect to the mainstreams of the social system is an important key to explaining the deprivation they endure, whether they fall into the transitional or non-transitional category. When we consider those who fall into the former category, we are looking at the situation of people whose lifeways are oriented toward the major social and cultural themes of the society and whose behavior displays that orientation. Those so afflicted are hardly in a group apart, even though through age, temporary setback, "deferred gratification," or personal defect they have become marginally effective participators in the society, at least in terms of generating income.

The discussion of measures to modify income distributions so as to reduce income inequality is directed meaningfully toward this transitional category. Jobs and training may be discussed in the context of antipoverty "solutions" for this group. In addition, the discussion includes income-maintenance schemes and provision of services. The aged and the physically and mentally handicapped may require special environmental arrangements, to say nothing of adequate housing. Impoverished students have been and can be provided with income supports which might be returned at a later date, directly through payments on loans or indirectly through taxation, viewing this training period as a worthwhile expense to society.

As a major point of departure from the past, those in this transitional category might well be provided assistance as a right rather than as a charity (demeaning or otherwise), with commensurate legal protections for this right. The care of this transitional group would thus appear to require actions to construct a social and economic "floor" below which these persons might not fall.

NON-TRANSITIONAL POVERTY

Non-transitional poverty, on the other hand, involves situations and conditions pointed to by many of the stereotypes of the poor. In essence, but not in detail, these are the conditions and situations which afflict the group David Matza has called the "disreputable poor," with or without additional handicaps taken from those characteristic of the transitional category (1966). Indeed, the continuous welfare assumption simply does not provide an adequate framework for explaining the deprivation of the non-transitional poor. Rather, it is postulated that a *social discontinuity* exists such that these persons are identified not only as being poor on a welfare index but also, from the point of view of the organization of the community, as being located, as it were, in the interstices of the social system. These are the rejects of the society just as their housing, transportation, social services, jobs, and neighborhoods are the leavings from an earlier social life.

Those in the non-transitional set represent by far the more difficult problem of poverty, in part because their condition does not have a time limit and may be regenerative through families and handed down from generation to generation. Viewing the part played by the kinds of social differentiation and problems of interdependence which come to exist in developed societies, the non-transitional poor stand only marginally integrated within the society characterized by organic solidarity. Yet the functional requirements of the social system may well demand their presence. Everett Hughes has said:

> Poverty might be the thing that destroys some social systems, but certainly many societies have maintained their equilibriums for centuries with higher rates and greater depths of poverty than we have in our society. Poverty may indeed have been a necessary condition of many social systems (1965, p. 76).

What, then, are the *social benefits* of poverty? This is the question to which we must come after exploring more fully the matter of discontinuity in our social system.

POVERTY AND SOCIAL DISCONTINUITY

Matza has reviewed the historical aspects of those stereotyped as the "disreputable poor." The lumpenproletariat, the déclassé, the paupers of several generations of Western society are a kind of out-caste, a group which is referred to by Gunnar Myrdal as the "underclass" (1965, pp. 404 ff). This is the group for which such full-employment strategies as are found in England, Denmark, and Australia, among others, may be irrelevant and inappropriate in the search for solutions. Those in the non-transitional state of poverty place before us questions of socialization and participation with respect to the community and the problem of the right of free choice or, as Duncan has recently put it, "freedom of full participation" (1967, p. 86).

The presence of such a set of conditions as non-transitional poverty and the presence of a social discontinuity raise questions of a different order in an appreciation of the analysis of the organization of the community. That is, with regard to this group, poverty refers to separable and somewhat different problems for the society and for those afflicted with the condition of poverty.

Taken together in its various components, the poverty population is clearly an aggregate rather than a group, in structural terms, and it is thus unmanageable without partitioning. That is because sociological theory talks in terms of groups and not aggregates. The non-transitional component, when separated out, does, however, tend to be visible as a geographically and socially clustered aggregate which is separated from the community, viewed both as a social system and as a geographical arrangement. The non-transitional component is likely to be only marginally aroused by the programmatic derivatives from the assumption of the continuity of the welfare distribution, i.e., the assumption that this subpopulation is only quantitatively different in relative "command over resources" (money).

Non-transitional poverty, then, is here viewed as a condition of a discrete aggregate in the society. Even though the income distribution or a welfare distribution of the total United States population may not immediately supply evidence of such a discontinuity, it is hypothesized that this break exists in terms of the patterns of role differentiation and interdependence within the society. Operationally, alienation with respect to the larger society, diminished labor force participation, and the prevalence of jobs without future expectations, careers, or security are featured in the role descriptions of the population in this aggregate.

How this disjoint class comes to exist can be dealt with in the framework of social change. Rapid social change and, particularly, associated migration which creates cultural disinheritance are of some interest in the development of a causation thesis which might underlie the hypothesis of an underclass—those in the non-transitional state of poverty. Radical cultural disruption and accompanying social disorganization, as discussed by E. Franklin Frazier and more recently by Daniel Patrick Moynihan, clearly relate to this issue (Frazier, 1951; Moynihan, 1965). The study of the impact of the urban environment upon previously rural populations in the current period is less clearly developed, but should be considered in the same or a similar frame.

Non-transitional Poverty: A Social-Cultural View

Let us try to place some of these ideas into a frame of reference, or at least attempt to associate these ideas with other lines of reasoning in order to further explicate this approach. First, we are involved with something of a structural analysis of poverty in that the direction of the analysis calls for explanation in terms of the processes, the forces, and the systems of the larger society. Apart from looking at the poor themselves, this approach goes more toward discussing poverty as an epiphenomenon of society.

Herbert Gans has recently remarked:

> If the prime purpose of research is the elimination of poverty, studies of the poor are not the first order of business at all; data on the extent of poverty, the kinds of poverty and of the life styles of the poor are much less important than studies of the economy which relegates many people to underemployment and unemployment, and of the society which leaves teenagers and older people without viable economic and social functions (1967, p. 5).

I do not agree with Gans' further assertion that "many if not most of the problems of most poor people can be solved by providing incomes and jobs" primarily because of the existence of the converse and alternative assumption, equally well-founded, that if the problems of poor people are solved, most will have income and jobs. However, I would happily join with him in imploring students of the problem of poverty to construct a test of that assertion as an hypothesis. Quoting Gans again:

> Those who argue that jobs and income are the major policy measures for the elimination of poverty are not much interested in culture, but they do make a cultural assumption; that the culture of the poor will not interfere in their adapting to economic opportunity. They take a *situational view* of social change; they suggest that people respond to the situations—and opportunities—available to them, and change their behavior accordingly. But there is an opposite conception, or set of conceptions, the cultural view of social change, which suggests that guaranteeing jobs and income are necessary but not sufficient to eliminate

poverty. This point of view argues that poverty and the lowly position of the poor leads to a separate and independent lower class culture . . . or culture of poverty . . . sometimes making it impossible for poor people to develop the behavior and value patterns needed, say, to take a job (1967, p. 6).

Although Gans' remarks state very nicely the distinction which is, in my view, crucial in sensing the difference between transitional and non-transitional poverty, they carry an implication—one not necessarily endorsed by Gans—which must be immediately disavowed in considering non-transitional poverty. This is the implication that there is a culture of poverty.

In the place of a culture of poverty, let us postulate the idea of a disaffiliated lower class which has as a property something of an "anti-culture"; that is, while the non-transitional class of the poor does display *common behavior* as a response to *common environment*, the normative characteristics of this population—the mores, values, and beliefs—are not of one culture or subculture as distinguished from the culture of the larger American society. This use of the term "anti-culture" is not intended to refer to culture as a formal concept, but to describe behavioral aspects of those in the non-transitional class with regard to what one might expect to find on the basis of general descriptions of American culture, what we often call "middle class culture." I believe there is support for this view in Robert Merton's conception of cultural differentiation within the society (1957, pp. 131 ff.).

What I am suggesting here is that the situational and cultural views described above are not necessarily polar opposites. The character of cultural inculcation is at the heart of the matter: the plight of the poor who are here categorized as non-transitional is rooted in lack of development and "incorrect" or aberrant socialization within the lower class with regard to the broad cultural patterns.

PARTICIPATION AND THE "DISREPUTABLE POOR"

The distinction between transitional and non-transitional poverty also is reflected in the development of participation. Several studies have suggested a direct correlation between money income and participation in formal organizations and political activity, as well as in regular occupations which have career characteristics (Axelrod, 1956; Matza, 1966, pp. 326-36; Zimmer, 1955). For example, examination of the occupational role and the underlying experiential foundation upon which it is based is crucial in considering participation of individuals and families in community organization. Thus, while some merit may accrue in getting "jobs" for the poor, such an activity is increasingly viewed as more than a matter of jobs-mean-income and the associated implication of non-poverty. Occupation is more than mere work (i.e., a "job") in an economic exchange, as most economists would be the first to admit.

But this line of analysis almost immediately discloses problems as we try to formulate operational efforts to state something about the levels of involvement in the community. How much should be brought within the "participation" rubric; how comprehensive should it be? It is not clear, for example, just what aspects of informal relationships should be included. Again to what degree should we take account of such "symptoms" of involvement as awareness of events which occur in the community and in the more immediate neighborhood and attitudes expressive of responsible concern for these events?

The non-transitional poor are, in terms of participation and involvement, non-participators. Some opinion suggests that even involvement with social agencies is inadequate so that direct public assistance, often thought of as the distinctive credential of the destitute, is frequently not provided. Possibly the relief rolls are more for those in transitional poverty. Matza notes:

> The disreputable poor are probably the only authentic outsiders, for modern democratic industrial life, contrary to romantic opinion, has had a remarkable capacity for integrating increasingly larger proportions of the population (1966, pp. 310-39).

A researchable question of considerable importance here is that of the differences in the characteristics of recipients and the non-recipients of public assistance among those who are eligible. Or, more broadly, the difference between those who are "disreputable," those who are eligible, and those who are recipients.

The non-transitional poor display other forms of non-involvement and non-participation. These poor are of the class in which labor force participation, in both quantity and quality, is at its lowest. Where such persons are in the labor force, they are in occupation-less jobs, that is, jobs with no skills, no security, no contractual expectations beyond the few hours of the present day, hours for which cash is paid on a daily basis. The pay for this work is low, the size of the wage rate perhaps in inverse proportion to the size of the casual labor pool which waits on informally designated street corners.

SEGREGATION AND NON-TRANSITIONAL POVERTY

Of some programmatic interest is the current focus upon the segregated poor in large urban places, in the so-called ghettos of our cities. Much more sophistication is needed in examining the socio-geographical process of the sorting of population, with respect to differing characteristics, by residence. While segregation by race may be more pronounced for Negroes than segregation by income, this may not be the case at all for those in non-transitional poverty.

A primary distinction to be made among families in the segregated, non-transitional category is between farm and non-farm backgrounds. The residence history of these "disreputable" poor can assist in appraising the consequences of changes in kinds of community of residence (e.g., by size of place). Such an appraisal could tell us more about the extent to which failures in participation are due to (1) recency of urban residence, or (2) classically, the lack of urban social and occupational skills of less recent migrants who grew up in rural areas, or (3) cultural disruption in a more pervasive sense. These alternative conditions indicate possible variations in immediately remedial approaches aimed, as were the efforts of many settlement houses of an earlier era, at assimilation.

For those whose life as adults and as children has been within the city, and whose parents were similarly impoverished, a different set of circumstances may prevail. These are perhaps the permanent settlers of the poverty areas of the city, the leftovers from the process of fractional selection discussed by Matza in which some get out and some do not (1966, pp. 336-38).

When people in the city ghetto, then, are viewed in the aggregate, two components may be discerned. One consists of those who are mobile, recently arrived, and soon (in months or years) to leave, having successfully experienced adjustment to the urban setting.

Another is made up of those who are "caught up in the cycle of poverty" and who, barring the intercession of the larger society, show little sign of leaving. It has been said that it takes 40 years to convert a peasant to a city worker. Mass communication developed since that was written may be reducing this interval somewhat.

With respect to the downwardly mobile, Duncan and Cowhig suggest that counts of these have been routinely underestimated in the public discussions concerning antipoverty instruments (1966, p. 131). Philip Hauser has recently likened current programs to attempts to mop up the poverty floor while the spigot is still running. The move to poverty, as previously indicated, may have been recent or perhaps in an earlier generation. We might prefer a rule of thumb which states "the shorter the duration of poverty, the easier the return to non-poverty." At any rate, it is important that we learn much more about this duration-of-stay feature of the downwardly mobile.

ANTIPOVERTY PROGRAM IMPLICATIONS

What does it mean to talk, as did Hughes in an earlier quotation, of the "social benefits" of poverty? What can be learned about poverty conditions and society by examining the question of the functional significance of poverty, that is, poverty viewed as a phenomenon which underlies necessary organization properties and processes of the social system as presently constituted?

At the present time, only the Community Action Program takes a diffuse approach to encouraging "maximum feasible participation" by the poor. Otherwise, little attention has been focused on ways to eliminate poverty roles (as against poverty incomes) and poverty-related conditions of social organization.

Consider these examples of issues which might be addressed:

(1) The social and economic significance of low wage occupations related to structural features of the community: to what degree do the poor play a role in bearing costs of certain industrial and service activities in the community? It may be argued that in the case of increasing costs of hospitalization since World War II, for example, part of the burden has been shifted from persons

occupying low-wage roles (dishwashers, orderlies, nurses, and so on) to insurance pools and consumers of such services. Consider, moreover, occupations in domestic services and in a number of so-called manual occupations. To what degree are such occupational functions essential in the society and who should pay the costs of sustaining such activities?

(2) To what degree do the poor contribute to the support of potentially idle urban real estate? To what degree do current private practices and public policies encourage further blight of such areas? Is there a social and physical maintenance floor, parallel in intent to the idea of income maintenance for persons and families, which could be constructed and below which individual neighborhoods cannot fall?

(3) More general implications of the hypothesis that non-transitional poverty is qualitatively different from poverty in general and is perpetuated by presently obtaining organizational requirements of the society: such poverty may not be amenable to treatment by contemporary antipoverty programs.

POVERTY AS A SOCIAL PROBLEM

Merton has suggested that in order for a social problem to exist, there must be a belief within the population that the society has the power to control the problem or to bring about changes related to it (1966, pp. 779-99). In a sense, some agreement has come to exist within Western developed societies that poverty is such a social problem. In the "war against poverty," for example, we have seen slogans asserting that poverty will be eliminated within the United States in the foreseeable future. On the other hand, however, debate is going on among people interested in antipoverty efforts as to whether we have the tools to do away with poverty. One school of thought asserts that we do, indeed, know what poverty is (poverty is being poor) and that it may be eliminated by providing everyone with an adequate income. Such an income would be provided by jobs and job-training for the many, and by income-maintenance together with assorted social services for the disabled, the aged, and the residual poor.

A more sophisticated view in the debate asserts that although the immediate programmatic requirements may call for jobs, training efforts, and the like, there is serious doubt about the validity of that "understanding" of poverty which sees it as a soluble problem in the society we now know. This line of thought suggests that our antipoverty slogans do not differ greatly from others that have appeared over the last 150 years. Further, it regards as pure speculation the implication that money alone from the affluent sectors of society can and will make the effective difference from the attempts of the past.

CONCLUSION

This chapter has attempted to explore the need to widen the sociological conceptualizations of poverty as a public issue and to rough out a few categories which might provide fruitful lines for more intensive analysis. A sociological dimension, built up around the distinction between transitional and non-transitional poverty has been suggested, to be added to the more prevalent individualistic dimension with its emphasis on income.

The chapter further suggests that the social benefits of poverty constitute a subject of critical importance. These benefits are not to be sought out in order to justify the present scheme of social arrangements; rather, understanding them will aid our attempts to anticipate some of the social consequences (and, on the other side, some of the useful antipoverty strategies) involved in the reduction of poverty in the United States.

References

AXELROD, MORRIS. "Urban Structure and Social Participation," *American Sociological Review*, 21 (February, 1956), pp. 14-18. This article is also reproduced in Paul K. Hatt and Albert J. Reiss, Jr. (eds.), *Cities and Society* (rev. ed.; Glencoe, Ill.: The Free Press, 1957), pp. 722-29.

DUNCAN, OTIS DUDLEY and JAMES COWHIG. "Social Background and Occupation Commitment of Male Wage Workers in Agriculture," *Agricultural Economics Research*, XVIII, No. 4 (1966).

DUNCAN, OTIS DUDLEY. "Discrimination Against Negroes," *Annals of the American Academy of Political and Social Science*, I (May, 1967), pp. 85-103.

FRAZIER, E. FRANKLIN. *The Negro Family in the United States* (rev. and abr. ed.; New York: The Dryden Press, 1951).

GANS, HERBERT J. "Poverty and Culture: Some Basic Questions About Methods of Studying Life-Styles of the Poor," prepared for the International Seminar on Poverty, April 3-6, 1967, University of Essex, Colchester, Essex, England.

HUGHES, EVERETT G. "Comment on Sociological Analysis and Poverty," *American Journal of Sociology*, LXXI (July, 1965).

MATZA, DAVID. "The Disreputable Poor," in Neil J. Smelser and Seymour M. Lipset (eds.), *Social Structure and Economic Development* (Chicago: Aldine Publishing Company, 1966), pp. 310-39.

MERTON, ROBERT K. *Social Theory and Social Structure* (rev. ed.; Glencoe, Ill.: The Free Press, 1957).

———. "Social Problems and Sociological Theory," in Robert K. Merton and Robert A. Nisbet (eds.), *Contemporary Social Problems* (2nd ed.; New York: Harcourt, Brace, and World, 1966).

MOYNIHAN, DANIEL P. *The Negro Family: The Case for National Action* (Washington, D.C.: U.S. Department of Labor, Office of Policy Planning and Research, March, 1965).

MYRDAL, GUNNAR. *Challenge to Affluence* (New York: Vintage Books, 1965).

ORSHANSKY, MOLLIE. "Counting the Poor: Another Look at the Poverty Profile," *Social Security Bulletin* (January, 1965), pp. 3-10.

ZIMMER, BASIL G. "Participation of Migrants in Urban Structures," *American Sociological Review*, 20 (April, 1955), pp. 218-24. This article is also reproduced in Paul K. Hatt and Albert J. Reiss, Jr. (eds.), *Cities and Society* (rev. ed.; Glencoe, Ill.: The Free Press, 1957), pp. 730-38.

17

On Eliminating Poverty

What We Have Learned

WARREN C. HAGGSTROM

□ Two conditions are necessary for the emergence of a social movement—one powerful enough to result in social change—in a disadvantaged population. First, there must be communicated vividly to such population a vision of a relative paradise which it is led to expect that it can inhabit. Second, the disadvantaged population must have available to it instrumentally effective social structures for undertaking the social journey into the paradise which it seeks. When the first, but not the second, of these conditions is met, the level of frustration within the population rises and is often discharged in various collectively irrational ways. Since 1964, this is precisely the situation which has existed in the United States with respect to the poor.

With the proclamation of a War on Poverty in 1964, President Johnson led the poor to anticipate entering the paradise (in this case a world of status and luxury) which is televised to them daily. At the same time, however, the federal government has not matched presidential rhetoric with the structures to implement it, a prime necessity since within areas of poverty there are few effective social structures (e.g., action or work organizations) through which the poor can act. As a consequence "New Left" and civil rights organizers have entered low income areas with agitational rhetoric but with little analysis of what is required to develop and wield power.

Since 1964, therefore, conditions have stirred low income areas from their traditional slumber, but without widely available realistic definitions for collective action. The result has been urban rioting, the legitimation of revolutionary appeals, and the creation of a number of otherworldly sects, some of which use the rhetoric

of black power. These irrational, self-destructive collective manifestations have tended to polarize American society and to mobilize
an affluent and powerful racist majority against a divided and
helpless minority which lacks access to those resources and institutions through which it might defend itself. The war on poverty
has thus come to elicit a war *on* the poor, so much so that one can
now take literally the designation of low income neighborhoods as
target areas.

How did it happen that sophisticated political strategists arrived
at such a disastrous unanticipated outcome? It will be my argument in the following pages that through a preoccupation with
evading or escaping from conflict, the Office of Economic Opportunity has also avoided politically feasible, inexpensive strategies
which could have minimized or eliminated collective violence,
reduced individual violence, and made marked progress toward
the abolition of poverty in the United States. Let us begin by
considering the background of the idea of the "maximum feasible
participation" of the poor in antipoverty programs.

APPROACHES TO THE PROBLEM OF POVERTY

The major tradition of the affluent helping the poor is rooted in
the giving of alms to beggars by religious organizations. When
separate professions of helpers began to appear, the simple giving
of alms gave way to more systematic and equitable programs
(usually marked by a means test), and the alms became supple-
mented with services intended to ensure that the poverty was
temporary. Since it was feared that people would get in the habit
of receiving money while languishing in idleness, work relief had
to be invented as a first service designed to prevent avoidable
relapses into permanent dependency.

Traditional "Welfarism"

In this century, the buying power of alms has been greatly
increased and social services for the poor have proliferated. Settlement houses provided cultural programs to extend to the poor
advantages generally available to their social betters. The recrea-

tion movement attempted to create a healthy environment for poor children. Information exchanges were created—when it began to be recognized that a single family might need services of many kinds—to coordinate services to multiproblem families. Public welfare not only gave alms, it gave them through social workers who were expected also to help recipients with their problems. Aggressive casework (for hard-to-reach families) developed, and intensive psychiatrically-sophisticated programs were inaugurated to help poor families overcome psychological disabilities and enter affluent neighborhoods within a period of years. Public housing similarly was intended to enhance upward mobility, and urban renewal made it impossible for the poor to continue to inhabit their aging neighborhoods. Social workers were supported in all these efforts and were expected to make referrals, to teach housekeeping, to help in problem-solving.

As time passed, it gradually became clear that the poor were evading these maneuvers. Additional money bought additional goods but did not affect the fact that in clearly defined rural and urban areas large groups of people remained outside the major economy, apparently unable to function adequately in the larger society. The various services whose installation had been accompanied by glowing accounts later came to symbolize a realization that nothing appeared to have helped transform the low income populations even though a small minority of persons and families were doing much better than before.

At first it was believed that the intractable poor are generally inferior and therefore could not be expected to participate fully in society. On this hypothesis large numbers of people in the United States have been sterilized; some physicians even seriously advocated genocide. Gradually it became known that intelligence tests did not measure genetic abilities. There was then no further reason to doubt that under appropriate conditions the poor could become able. Helpers began to believe that the deprived only lacked enough knowledge and skill to be successful. They delved into and adapted theories of psychoanalysis and "deepened" their services. They plunged into the lore of anthropology in order to understand, and thereby affect, an alleged culture of poverty. They embraced the social sciences, learning about roles, social structures, the family as a social system, and similar constructs. Eventually, when these approaches did not appear to work, research became the watchword: if we do not know how to help the poor, the methods of science will enable us to develop the necessary skills.

Unfortunately, most of the poor stayed poor, while the professions serving and researching them flourished. Neither the natural processes of the abundant society, nor the alms-and-service professions, nor the expert fact finders appeared able to end poverty. The federal government next escalated the several attacks into a full blown war which was to tackle the problem from many directions simultaneously and with enough resources to do the job.

Within the agency created to conduct the war on poverty, the Office of Economic Opportunity, a recognition existed that not all the programs to help the poor had failed. Social insurance, for those who were eligible, interest rate adjustments, income tax exemptions, and other measures which did not single out the poor as a presumably inferior group seemed more successful. From these and other facts it was deduced that middle class helpers are ineffective in direct relationships with people who are officially defined as poor and who are recipients of money and services determined by the helpers. It was supposed possible that middle class persons simply did not know enough about poverty and, therefore, that their services tend to be inappropriate. Or the relationship of superior to inferior may stigmatize those receiving help: the stigma and related adverse consequences for the poor would then cancel out much of the benefit otherwise to be gained from the money and services. In either case the problem presumably would be solved if the poor helped to design and administer their own programs. This innovation in the kinds of program which otherwise had already shown promise, buttressed by the broad support of the federal government, gave rise to confidence in an eventual antipoverty victory.

The Tradition of Self-Help

There was also a different tradition—one with major successes— the tradition of self-help, on the basis of which it might be assumed that the poor should participate extensively in programs designed to help them. Arnold Toynbee has generalized a similar doctrine to apply over long historical periods to entire societies. A community is faced with a challenge; it manages through its own efforts to overcome the challenge and goes on to flourish in many other ways as well. For example, the emergence of a tiny country in the Netherlands as a great world power came about after its people had succeeded in building long dikes to hold out the sea. Cooperative Israeli settlements and communal Indian tribes in the southwestern United States managed to flourish in areas normally closed to settlement. The Hutterites prospered whereas North Dakota farmers, who received much more outside help, were going broke. The Black Muslims were alleged to have transformed through a self-help doctrine some of the most deprived inhabitants of the black ghettos. The Chinese and Japanese settlements in the United States, originally in poverty, plagued by racial discrimination, and with little outside assistance, managed to prosper. And the cooperative movements transformed many areas of rural poverty. Communities incorporating some version of a self-help ethic have, in other words, often moved out of poverty while those who have received much help from outside have frequently tended only to need more. Shouldering the White Man's Burden helped the white man but appeared to do little for the colonial populations.

Revolutions have usually been self-help enterprises. The Egyptians were presumed incapable of running the Suez Canal until they became independent—then it was discovered that they could operate the canal quite nicely. The proverbial poverty, starvation, and filth in Chinese villages were succeeded by enough food, increasing education, and no flies after the landlords and their allies were violently thrown out. India, with less of a challenge in becoming independent and no revolution against landlords, showed only a temporary revival before subsiding again toward its previous condition.

Revolutions may be considered extreme cases of social movements directed to secure social change. Less spectacular social movements, however, have also helped poor people. Farm subsidies did not keep farmers solvent, but the Grange, the Non-Partisan League, the Farmer-Labor Party, the Canadian CCF, the rural Progressive LaFollette movement, the Farmer's Union, and the National Farm Organization have provided a vitality and force working in the direction of economic development in rural communities, characteristics which were not conspicuous where such organizations were not strong. We also know the shortcomings of the paternalistic company stores and dwellings for factory or farm laborers as compared with the outcomes of union movements by which various categories of the poor levered their way out of poverty.

There has been most celebration, however, of the long continued autonomous striving of individuals. Samuel Smiles' famous book, *Self-Help*, published in dozens of editions, praised the virtues of the person who eventually succeeds to fame and fortune after long and patient struggles in poverty. Emerson wrote about "Self-Reliance," and the Horatio Alger stories popularized similar ideas. The value of self-responsibility is almost universally appreciated. The upwardly mobile man who makes a fortune is impressive as a man; his grandchildren who live off the fortune often appear to be relative nonentities.

It is true that self-help might often have been brought in ex post facto as a convenient interpretation of chance successes. However, the very fact that it has so consistently been used as an explanation for success could be taken as an indication of the presumed value of a person who helps himself and the presumed inferiority of one who does not. Since social valuations are directly or indirectly the primary basis for self-esteem, a personality trait central to motivation, and since the poor are often believed to have been disabled through a negative self-image, the engagement of the poor in self-help activities would appear to be advantageous in inducing psychological motivation and objective economic benefits.

It is also true that many self-help efforts have failed. Community development projects have typically left only a school house or a latrine to mark the death of a transient communal effort, while most social movements of the current poor in the United States have given rise only to feeble organizations. Relatively few individuals among the poor have been upwardly mobile through their own efforts.

On the other hand, it does appear that under some conditions self-help efforts have worked better than assistance extended to the poor from above. With resources of the war on poverty available, one might assume that appropriate conditions could be created. Those who are able to benefit from individual self-help could advance by means of training and literacy programs, Head Start, and similar projects. And the benefits from collective self-help could be achieved by participation of the poor in directing the war on poverty.

IMPEDIMENTS TO PARTICIPATION
BY THE POOR

One of the major weaknesses in the present war on poverty is that the Office of Economic Opportunity—and the same would be true of any analogous agency—has no political constituency with a vested interest in supporting its programs. It lacks, in other words, the kind of support on which the Department of Agriculture or the Department of Labor can count. If, on the other hand, the poor were able to mobilize through a social movement, their support could free the federal government to initiate programs which would otherwise be politically impossible. This is what occurred when the civil rights movement acquired the political support that allowed federal administrators to reduce or eliminate racially discriminatory practices in their agencies.

Thus vaguely rationalized, the expression "maximum feasible participation" had very little definition when it was incorporated into the antipoverty legislation. Its meaning was to be worked out in the crucible of concrete programs which would embody legislative intent in a variety of ways. These, it turned out, covered a spectrum that ranged from the creation of powerful democratic organizations of the poor in a Syracuse demonstration project to the small bands of hand picked "worthy" poor rather condescendingly allowed to sit on advisory committees to some community action programs in many other cities.

It was soon clear that beneath the virtuous antipoverty rhetoric of "community leaders" lay political forces which would seek to shoulder the poor aside from significant participation in the war on poverty. The lawyers, businessmen, politicians, and college professors did not really believe that uneducated failures could be entrusted with money or would become responsible in the exercise of political power. Politicians knew that funds and organizations in the hands of the poor could make their own position more precarious, while the same resources in their own hands could be used to help their friends and discourage or coopt political opponents. Barriers of all kinds against Negroes, against the uneducated, against the deprived, would be threatened if the poor suddenly obtained control of effective organizations and large sums of money. Unions "protecting" apprenticeship programs, businesses "protecting" employment standards, universities "protecting" admissions standards: all had a stake in keeping the war on poverty out of the hands of the poor.

The tenuous idea of maximum feasible participation thus came to create conflict and controversy in antipoverty programs everywhere. Organizations of the poor used the phrase as a slogan to legitimate attempts to compete with established interests for control of the new programs. And where control by the poor was most nearly significant the struggle waxed most fiercely.

The Syracuse Case

The Syracuse experience provides a notable example of controversy generated by the participative principle. In 1965, the Community Action Training Center (CATC) of Syracuse University (of which I was the Director) conducted a demonstration project intended in part to help low income people to create powerful, autonomous, democratic organizations through which to work on their various collectively defined problems. Before the first organizer was employed, however, CATC was the object of bitter attacks by local politicians, social agencies, and newspapers. By June, 1965, after about four months of organizational work, one of the two Syracuse daily newspapers published on its front page the following comments concerning the CATC organizational drive in public housing:

> The Syracuse Housing Authority says it has been vainly battling "organized gangster tactics"—but to no avail. Law and order in many cases, the Authority says, have broken down. . . . The Authority charges there is a class war going on in the Marxist tradition. . . . The problem appears hopeless to the Syracuse Housing Authority . . . The police seem powerless in the face of what McGarry describes as hit-and-run tactics reminiscent of guerilla warfare. The Housing Authority has asked the federal government for understanding, even warning of the consequences of organized lawlessness, anarchy and vandalism. . . . Besides the personal intimidation of tenants, reports to the Authority revealed alleged immoral acts committed in some of the hallways of the projects. There are cases of urinating and defacating in the hallways, the

Authority reveals. But more substantial are these reports of wide-spread destruction. Smashed windows. Damaged elevators. Ransacked laundry rooms. Splintered doors. Uprooted fences. Destroyed dry wells. Hatcheted shrubs and trees. Excessively damaged vacant apartments. . . . McGarry says 75 per cent of the housing residents are . . . being and have been harassed, smeared, badgered and intimidated. . . . This is perhaps one of the most diabolical acts ever perpetrated on a community by an institution of higher education . . . McGarry says (*Syracuse Post-Standard*, June 22, 1965, pp. 1 ff).

Not only did the newspaper fail to contact any representative of the Community Action Training Center concerning these allegations, but it was impossible for the Center Director even to get to talk with relevant members of the newspaper staff.

The Office of Economic Opportunity responded to controversy and threats of controversy concerning maximum feasible participation by continuing to support the idea in public statements while covertly depriving the poor of any effective participation in its programs. For example, in November, 1965, following pressure from the White House, Sargent Shriver directed that OEO support for the Syracuse organizational effort be phased out within 90 days, thus ensuring that the newly created fledgling organizations of the poor could not survive. However, his actual directive to CATC was disguised to give the appearance that the organization was merely being referred to the local community action program for further funds. In response to inquiries about this decision, Mr. Shriver sent the following telegram to concerned persons and groups within and outside the United States:

DEEPLY REGRET YOU WERE APPARENTLY MISINFORMED BY ERRONEOUS REPORTS REGARDING THE CURRENT AND FUTURE STATUS OF GRANT TO THE COMMUNITY DEVELOPMENT ASSOCIATION OF SYRACUSE.

HERE ARE THE FACTS: FUNDS HAVE NOT, REPEAT, NOT BEEN DISCONTINUED FOR THIS PROJECT. IN FACT, OUR ACTION OF DECEMBER 1 EXTENDED THAT GRANT FOR THREE MONTHS WITH FUNDING OF $111,000 FOR THAT PERIOD. AT THE SAME TIME WE URGED THIS ACTION GROUP TO APPLY FOR AN ADDITIONAL TWELVE MONTHS GRANT THROUGH THE COMMUNITY ACTION AGENCY OF SYRACUSE. THIS DECISION WAS MADE AS A RESULT OF OUR STRONG CONVICTION THAT THE ORGANIZATION HAS CREATED AVAILABILITY AND

REACHED ESTABLISHED MATURITY SUFFICIENT TO ENABLE IT TO APPLY FOR COMMUNITY ACTION FUNDS AS OTHER GROUPS HAVE SUCCESSFULLY DONE IN OTHER CITIES. IF THE LOCAL COMMUNITY ACTION AGENCY SHOULD PROVE TO BE UNFAIR OR ARBITRARY AS SOME FEAR IN JUDGING THIS APPLICATION, THE COMMUNITY DEVELOPMENT ASSOCIATION MAY APPLY DIRECTLY TO OEO AT THE REGIONAL OR NATIONAL LEVEL FOR DIRECT FUNDING AS IN THE PAST. THREE MONTHS WILL BE AMPLE TIME FOR ONE, OR IF NECESSARY, BOTH PROCEDURES TO BE FOLLOWED.

I MET PERSONALLY ON WEDNESDAY WITH A DELEGATION FROM SYRACUSE TO DISCUSS THEIR PROJECT AND ALLAY MISUNDERSTANDINGS. THERE HAS BEEN NO CUT-OFF OF FUNDS TO THE SYRACUSE PROJECT, BUT RATHER AN EXPRESSION OF OUR CONFIDENCE IN ITS VALIDITY AND AN EFFORT WITHIN ITS LOCAL COMMUNITY TO ADHERE TO NATIONAL POLICY.

APPRECIATE YOUR CONTINUED INTEREST IN THE PROJECT AND ASSURE YOU OF OURS.

During the following March, when there were no further federal funds for organizational work in Syracuse, Mr. Shriver announced the premature and unplanned reduction and termination of the CATC training and research program. He described this action as *further* OEO *support for* the Syracuse University antipoverty program (Long, 1966).

CONFLICT-AVOIDANCE STRATEGIES

Grandiose rhetoric and the avoidance of conflict became identifying characteristics of the war on poverty everywhere. It had originally been announced by President Johnson in March, 1964, as a Great Society program which was to have as its objective "total victory" to be secured by "total commitment" of all the energy of the nation and not merely of the government. The President urged that we "bring to the challenges of peace the same determination and strength which has brought us victory in war."

But the war on poverty turned out, from the beginning, to be peculiar. Traditionally the poor have conducted their own wars on poverty, and conducted them against real enemies. For example, A. C. Townley of the Nonpartisan League once commented, "If you put a lawyer, a banker and an industrialist in a barrel and roll it downhill there'll always be a son-of-a-bitch on top." But where was the enemy in the new war on poverty? One can search the speeches of Sargent Shriver without finding any clear reference to real enemies in the war which he presumably has led. The grand rhetoric of Lyndon Johnson gave rise to a series of exceedingly modest programs cautiously designed to avoid antagonizing any group except the poor.

Let us illustrate this latter point. One strategy to avoid the threat of conflict has been to provide a stake in the war on poverty for groups that otherwise might oppose new programs. Thus, federal antipoverty funds have become fixtures in the budgets of agencies that are presumably concerned to help the poor. Large corporations have been enlisted to run Job Corps Centers (G.E., IBM, Xerox, IT&T, U.S. Industries, Burroughs). Middle class volunteers have been drawn into VISTA and Women in Community Service. The traditional business, political, and professional elites of local communities dominate the boards of community action programs. Powerful professions, such as law and medicine, have been drawn into service programs for the poor. Universities have received grants to conduct training and research into poverty. Visible leaders of the poor have been offered jobs or have been appointed to board or committee positions of high status and little power. Major and minor experts on poverty have found lucrative opportunities for supplementing their incomes through employment as consultants to the Office of Economic Opportunity or to the programs that it has funded.

A second strategy to avoid the threat of conflict has been to stifle or discredit opposition to the war on poverty while avoiding disputation or intellectual discussion of issues being raised by critics. For example, in his speech at Yale in April, 1966, Sargent Shriver did not meet the arguments of those who maintained that the federal government could not carry out the changes that would be necessary to end poverty. He, instead, distorted the views of these critics and charged them with indulging in "intellectual gamesmanship." In the same speech he pointed out that existing agencies and professions have been missing the mark or not reaching the poor, and argued that they would be made more effective by the stimulus of competitors supported through the war on poverty. But, the "competition" to which Mr. Shriver referred has turned out to be mostly a fiction. Jobs for non-professionals are being defined for work that is not now done by professionals or work that professionals prefer to avoid. Educational programs for school dropouts are not very competitive with the traditional programs which remain unchanged for those in school. Teachers, instead, can feel relieved that someone else has now to cope with the dropouts. Martin Deutsch's educational program for two- to four-year-old children is not competitive with Head Starts for older children. If Deutsch turns out to be following a promising lead, Head Start will require extension, not replacement. Mr. Shriver, it would seem, has merely used the language of competition to discredit existing agencies and professionals in order to make legitimate his invasion of their theoretical jurisdictions without, however, threatening their actual practices.

A third conflict-avoidance strategy, that of not developing programs which threaten to alter existing practices, has already been mentioned, but it bears closer scrutiny. Instead of moving in new directions, the programs which have consistently failed in the past are now extended, while innovations appear only as supplements to what has traditionally been done. The domination of community action programs by the local elites who have also dominated the community chest and united fund programs, insofar as these have traditionally been directed to the poor, has ensured the vetoing of any disturbing community action change in pre-existing local programs. Similarly, national antipoverty measures have carefully avoided challenging the traditional employment practices of corporations or the traditional functioning of the schools. And the war on poverty has not helped the unorganized poor to form new labor unions where they have the appropriate skills but are barred from membership in established unions. There have not even been challenges to the illegal and legal practices (denial of access to public housing or of adequate access to public welfare, racial discrimination in employment, failure to provide good housing for families relocated by urban renewal) which directly maintain poverty.

It can be argued that such a description of the war on poverty omits mention of the ways in which realistic and fruitful conflict is indirectly fostered by it. For example, if the board of a community action program is made to include representatives of the poor and civil rights leaders, a conflict process will arise, so it is said, which will result in local programming more sensitive to the poor than would otherwise exist. In practice, however, the minorities of such boards who are leaders of the poor or of civil rights groups lack access to expert knowledge concerning alternatives to current programs, have little or no hope of exercising sufficient influence to secure decisions to make major changes, have no democratic process in neighborhoods of poverty which instructs them and makes them representative of the poor, and are subject to cooptation by their new status and their immersion in board discussions dominated by affluent people. So-called representatives of the poor come to represent the establishment to their neighborhoods rather than their neighborhoods to the establishment. In the words of Leonard Chazen, by the end of 1965 "Entrenched political organizations were in control of local poverty programs, with ornamental poor scattered among the community action boards as an obeisance to the principle of participation" (1966, p. 621). If the poor realistically are to be represented by members of community action boards, there must *first* be viable, broadly based, democratic organizations in areas of poverty which will advise, instruct, and, when necessary, dismiss their representatives in accordance with how well the neighborhoods of poverty are, in fact, being represented.

It might be argued more plausibly that provision of legal services in low income areas will lead to defense of the rights of the poor and to successful confrontations with slum landlords, the police and prison system, public welfare agencies, corporations, and unions. But the history of school desegregation illustrates the fact that litigation has seldom secured institutional changes in American society except very gradually and when buttressed by a supporting social movement. It is true that legal services will increase conflict (and thereby lead to consensus) but primarily among people (as distinct from institutions).

By late 1967, it appeared that the Johnson Administration had abandoned even the pretense of maximum feasible participation and, in a final effort to avoid conflict, was willing to turn the community action programs over to the direct or indirect control of local politicians. The bill enacted in December, 1967, extending the poverty program for another two years, requires that community action agencies become instrumentalities of state or local governments, rather than being autonomous bodies chartered as not-for-profit corporations. It further mandates that one-third of the board members be representatives of state or local government.

It is obvious that the conflict-avoidance strategies of Sargent Shriver averted neither controversy nor violence. In fact, conflict-avoidance strategies often *result in violence,* while conflict strategies often *reduce violence* (see, e.g., Solomon, *et al.,* 1965). To say that there is conflict is only to say that there are two sides, each of which tries to force the other to modify its course of action. It is to say nothing whatever about violence or the prospects for it.

Consequences of Conflict-Avoidance

We have noted several consequences of the federal emphasis on strategies of conflict avoidance. Perhaps the most serious is the way in which such avoidance creates a collapse in morale and initiative of staff members and helpers in antipoverty programs and thereby results in the self-destruction of their effectiveness. For example, in one city a mother, inspired by an OEO program in which her child had been enrolled, wanted to circulate a petition among her fellow public housing tenants appealing for a recreation area for all the children. The local antipoverty officials discouraged the initiative, feeling that the resulting controversy would threaten the possibility of receiving more antipoverty funds. In many cities, moreover, community action agencies employ the poor to do work which seems to everyone involved to be trivial and unimportant—but which has the "merit" of being non-controversial. Unable to give up the income, the frustrated employees are discouraged in virtually all attempts to do something significant, something which might be disturbing to someone who is "somebody."

Inevitably the attempts to organize the poor in accordance with the perspectives of the affluent and at the expense of meaningful involvement result in a decline in motivation in those who are officially "being helped." They are apathetic and often hostile, and they may begin to act in ways that seem to justify the prejudice against them in the community. The structure of authority in the helping programs becomes a structure to control the deprived, not to help them. It does little good for the poor to participate in a program in the sense in which Jews participated in programs organized for them in Nazi concentration camps.

The dissipation of morale among poverty workers and the deprived increases with the recognition of the true nature of the programs, and this condition tends to result in a dissolution of the internal structure of authority. Both the helpers and the poor together become privatized, abandoning all but a listless conformity with the expectations officially held for them or exploding into angry outbursts. The war on poverty thus comes to operate as a collective defense mechanism which permits the majority community to believe, for a time, that the poor are being helped while little in fact is being accomplished.

The problem is complicated by the vagueness of the puff rhetoric of the antipoverty programs. If the war on poverty were popular, a vague rhetoric would be advantageous to its image since different groups of people would interpret it in various positive ways in accordance with their individual perspectives. However, the gap between rhetoric and accomplishment ends by undermining the very popularity of such programs. Vague presentations of a stigmatized program encourage an unnecessarily wide range of negative interpretations throughout the community.

Current antipoverty programs, in fact, tend to corrupt those associated with them. Often the most honest and committed people from the civil rights movement or elsewhere have accepted positions in which they have expected to help the poor. But the structures which they enter inhibit generous motivations until the participants become forced to choose between keeping a steady job and doing good. The poor are similarly corrupted. Even the elections to neighborhood boards constituted entirely by the poor carry much the same significance as elections to high school student governments.

Let us imagine that someone wanted to create a program that would be the greatest possible political liability to its sponsors. He could, perhaps, proceed as follows. First, he would announce the institution of a program which would create apprehension among many people that their interests or values are being threatened. The war on poverty, for example, originally threatened to take money from competing activities which would otherwise have been better supported, and it seemed to threaten change to institutions and practices that had become jealously guarded domains of vested interests. Next, he would make certain that the original grand announcement would not result in an effective program. This strategy would add to critics of the first variety new opposition by original supporters of the program. Finally, he would have the program decline slowly while a great amount of money is gradually wasted. This slow attrition would allow maximum time for a maximum number of enemies to mobilize against the program. Unfortunately for it, the war on poverty has unintentionally nearly followed such a course. Its theorists should not now be surprised by the outcome.

This pathetic and absurd finale to the resounding initial rhetoric of 1964, raises the question whether the federal government can conduct a war on poverty at all (as distinguished from sponsoring programs which may help the poor without affecting poverty). Let us briefly consider the prospects for effective federal action against poverty.

WHAT CAN BE DONE

A new war on poverty would have to contrast sharply and favorably with current programs in order to establish a different and better reputation and induct an increasing level of political support. And the new projects should be carefully designed to elicit a maximum motivation and possibility for the poor to engage in their own struggle to end their own poverty.

Any federal agency creates social structures, the positions of which are occupied by personnel. In a war on poverty, the structures should be located in low income areas and, so far as possible, the positions occupied by the poor. But, it is true that those anti-poverty programs which have created such structures have not been very impressive to date. In my opinion the fault lies with the nature of the structures, not with the nature of the poor.

THE REWARD STRUCTURE

In a work organization which induces high motivation there is likely to be a close relationship between contribution and reward. The employee who contributes less suffers an immediate reduction in reward; the employee who increases his contribution immediately benefits. Informal employee organization can be (although often is not) mobilized to support the formal reward system. Abraham Zaleznik has pointed out:

> Self-esteem is built in large part through intimate experience with the cycle of productivity and reward as the result of the activation of talents. An individual acts and produces; he is evaluated and rewarded. This simple two-step cycle is important for building competence and self-esteem (1966, p. 188).

It is known that the experiences of the poor, their social position, and the stigma attached to this position have combined to assault their self-esteem and to depress their motivation for accomplishment. In this circumstance it is not reasonable simply to provide them with jobs at which they perform ill-defined tasks only loosely related to recognition and reward. It is instead necessary to insist on high standards for performance, to help the poor to meet such standards, and to supply rewards closely related to their contributions.

This requirement leads immediately to another problem. How can such adequate rewards be provided? The federal government cannot merely make careers for the poor out of whole cloth since there is not available enough money and since political opposition to such an alternative would be overwhelming. One can, however, meet this objection in several ways. First, the federal government can choose to sponsor fewer efforts than it now does, but make certain that those which are sponsored meet rigorous standards. No additional funds would be required for this change since the professionals now engaged in antipoverty activities can easily find other work and since the poor who are now employed can be offered better positions in the new programs. Second, the work performed can be significant: to redesign and rebuild the areas which the poor do or will inhabit. Third, the programs can be devised, not merely to provide jobs, but to end poverty, and thus would give substance to the grand vision which is now only words.

A fourth and important additional criterion which might be met is suggested by the history of social movements of the poor. How does it happen that tens of thousands of the poor at various places and times have struggled strenuously over decades, learning as they worked their way out of poverty, *with very little reward?* The answer, I believe, is to be found in an analysis of the nature of organizations. Most work organizations commonly accept as given the relationship between reward and performance which has been established in the majority community. But, in social movements a transvaluation of values occurs. The situation becomes redefined by virtue of the fact that the movement develops a world view alternative to that of the major society. Material objects come to be differently evaluated by how they relate to the collective effort under way. As a result, very limited resources (as these are understood in the affluent community), if correctly selected, can induce high and continued levels of enthusiasm. It would be much less costly to fund the work of a reform movement than it would be to fund a conventional bureaucratic organization to accomplish the same objective.

Need for Better "Symbolism"

Organizations may be regarded as involving both a symbolic system which defines what is to be done, and a system of bodies which does it. The federal government could thus secure a better outcome for its expenditure if the symbolic aspects of its anti-poverty programs were examined. New programs which redefined the situation in carefully understood major ways, whether or not they were also reform movements, would motivate the poor far more effectively than programs now available to them. It is, of course, also true that such new projects would make no difference at all if they were not sensitively related to the present collective orientations in areas of poverty.

The study of social movements also suggests that the stakes in antipoverty programs should be high. Much should be asked of the poor, although over a long enough period of time to enable high levels of accomplishment to develop, and the rewards to them for their effort should be correspondingly great. The rewards should come, not merely for task performance, but also for contribution to the elimination of poverty and the creation of a good community. The result would again verify Martin Buber's observations that:

> there is no way of taking the measure of man's potentialities in a given situation that has to be changed, except by demanding the extraordinary.
>
> the "real" man approximates most closely to the "ideal" just when he is expected to fulfill tasks which he is not up to, or thinks he is not up to . . . it depends on the goal, the consciousness of it and will for it (1960, p. 58).

Thus, it is important not merely to help the poor, but to help them to create a vision of a future community which they find highly compelling and toward which they can proceed by definite and assured steps. To design programs of this capability the federal government would have to get rid of its ballast of information, *status quo* experts, and simplistic economic analyses in order to learn to take into account the process of creation of symbolic systems and social structures which evolve over time and which command enough resources to induct the poor into clearly defined courses of action in relation to precisely understood basic values. Priority should, therefore, be given to maintenance of an intellectual process concerning the development of a good society to which the poor contribute and in which they can and will participate on a basis of equality. The new war on poverty, it follows, would require invitations to dissent and disputation as alternatives to the conditions which now inhibit the employment of reason.

New Careers for the Poor

One could begin a new war on poverty with the establishment of new careers for those who are now poor and employed in antipoverty programs. The new careers should display steps by which increasing levels of ability and contribution by the poor would be automatically and without limit rewarded by corresponding increases in rewards. If such new structures were to lead to a vivid and satisfying future they would elicit high motivation from those being helped. The skills and knowledge required of those assisted should be general rather than special, enabling the poor to transfer to alternative structures in the event that those supporting their current careers were to fail. The time perspective of the program should be decades, not years, and there should be a firm guarantee that no program would be discontinued for any reason except that it is failing to achieve its legitimate and avowed purpose of contributing to the elimination of poverty.

Since such programs would not initially be large, and would be developed at first in only a few places, they could become controversial without jeopardizing continuation of their federal sponsorship, especially if their reputation is also one of soundness and accomplishment. They would not pose immediate threats to powerful national groups. Hence, they would be able to build on the perspectives of the poor rather than on those of the affluent community; they would be able to clarify issues and remain authentic without threat of cooptation of those being helped; and they would be able to unite groups of the poor that would otherwise be irremediably divided. Finally, they would be able to release motivation and create values by projecting otherwise immobilizing hostility onto appropriate targets.

The OEO and Political Mobilization

Implicit in the above suggestion is the assumption that many of the defects of contemporary antipoverty programs are intrinsic to the Office of Economic Opportunity itself, at least with its present form and commitments. They do not result from a lack of money due to the war in Viet Nam since existing funds are so often ineffectively spent. I would estimate that in Syracuse alone more than a million dollars in antipoverty funds have been wasted directly through OEO intervention. Nor do the defects of existing programs stem from gaps in ability and skill of low income people. Recent experience has clearly demonstrated that the lowest income groups can acquire the skill, motivation, and understanding to operate complex enterprises. The defects, moreover, have little to do with maximum feasible participation or the controversy surrounding this provision except in the sense that OEO has avoided mobilizing the poor as its natural constituency. Rather than these factors, the faults of existing programs stem directly from the deliberate failure of the Office of Economic Opportunity seriously to seek to induct the poor into full participation into American society. OEO has been able to imagine nothing more significant than a population slightly better off economically, indefinitely clinging precariously to the under-fringes of our society.

A war on poverty which took seriously the possibility of full societal participation by the poor would pose a substantial threat to all the vested interests that have opposed a broad interpretation of "maximum feasible participation." It would, in fact, threaten established practices and vested privileges of all kinds. Such a war, by its very nature, cannot be otherwise than controversial. Hence, if the Office of Economic Opportunity were to take its mandate seriously it would not seek to avoid controversy. It would, instead, endeavor to mobilize a sufficient political force to ensure its own continued effective operation in the midst of inevitable controversy. To accomplish this, it would have to address itself to the problem of how the poor might be organized for such purpose.

A program of mobilization as envisioned here might proceed along the following lines. The President would create a federally-appointed commission the members of which would be of unquestioned integrity, committed to the extension of democracy, and without partisan political affiliation. This commission would establish an agency to train and employ organizers. The course of training and organizational work would not be determined by the commission but by those whose experience enables them to understand the process. The agency would relate to any organization which it helps to create for only a limited period of time, not more than five years, until such an organization became entirely self-supporting. When the agency decided to assist a low income area to organize, the necessary money would be set aside in advance for the entire period of support to that organization. It would be impossible for the federal government to withdraw such funds unless it were demonstrated in court that the money was being used illegally.

Such an agency should begin on a very small scale and provide from the outset the best possible quality of organizational help. Expansion should be delayed until the inevitable problems of early years are worked out and experience acquired. The pace of expansion should never be such as to reduce the quality of training or of organizational work.

In the context of a general reform movement, an organizational process, such as described above, would be simplified since the possibility of securing major changes would appear to be vivid and immediate. (It does not matter that the poor are a minority, provided they can act collectively as part of a majority.) The sweeping nature of the reform proposals would make the effort expended in the organizational struggle seem worthwhile. The federal rhetoric would then elucidate rather than conceal the course of events, and it would become more possible for the poor to orient themselves appropriately to what is, in fact, in their interest. Since conflict-avoidance strategies would no longer be essential, the enemies of the poor would no longer have an automatic veto by threatening conflict over proposals to which they objected.

The millions of voters from areas of poverty would eventually form organizations as controversial as were those of the new industrial labor unions of the 1930s. Just as the union quickly learned to make political alliances, so the poor would join a potentially winning coalition. And just as happened with labor unions and in the case of Negroes, the party that advocates proposals to extend democracy to new populations is likely to become the political beneficiary of the forces thereby unleashed.

This is an intriguing picture to contemplate. However, I do not believe that the federal government will seriously try in the foreseeable future to induct the poor into American society. The war on poverty will continue to be an inefficient farce to most people, an empty promise to the poor. To be effective today one must begin at an earlier point: the creation of a social force which can be brought to bear on government to change the political context within which it functions.

To sum up: practically no one fears the worthy poor; immobile, apathetic, depressed, permanently chained to life at the bottom, cleaning the houses and the automobiles of the affluent, relegated everywhere to the choice between dirty work and no work. But a great many people, perhaps most, fear the process by which one day the poor could come to full participation in a better society than is ours in 1967.

References

Buber, Martin. *Paths in Utopia* (Boston: Beacon Press, 1960).

Chazen, Leonard. "Participation of the Poor," *Yale Law Journal,* 75 (March, 1966).

Long, Richard F. *Syracuse Herald Journal,* March 19, 1966.

Solomon, Fredric, *et al.* "Civil Rights Activity and Reduction in Crime Among Negroes," *Archives of General Psychiatry,* 12 (March, 1965), pp. 227-40.

Zaleznik, Abraham. *Human Dilemmas of Leadership* (New York: Harper and Row, 1966).

18

The Distribution and Redistribution of Income

Political and Non-political Factors

PHILLIPS CUTRIGHT

☐ SOME OF THE MORE ACRIMONIOUS debate over strategies for the reduction or elimination of poverty in the United States has occurred between those who view the problem as one of economic policy and those who assert the primacy of political reform, usually in the form of "empowering the poor." In a very general sense the same argument has been raised with respect to international poverty, with contentions over the role to be played in the "modernization" process by economic development programs, on the one hand, and the building of effective and stable political institutions, on the other. Such issues are of great theoretical interest at the same time that they present critical implications for policy formation. Lurking behind these questions is an even larger issue: to what degree are the determinants of the amount of poverty realistically subject to control?

AUTHOR'S NOTE: *This chapter draws heavily on and contains extensive quotations from two of the author's articles which have appeared elsewhere. The articles thus drawn upon, by permission, are: "Inequality: A Cross-National Analysis," American Sociological Review, 32 (August, 1967), pp. 572-78, and "Income Redistribution: A Cross-National Analysis," Social Forces, 46 (December, 1967), pp. 180-90.*

My sincere thanks to Professor Bloomberg for his skilled editorial work in blending these two articles into one unit. This chapter would not exist without his aid. He bears, however, no responsibility for the conclusions I have made.

This chapter approaches the problem of poverty within nations by assuming (1) that the degree to which income is distributed equally or unequally will affect the extent to which a population will be both objectively and subjectively defined as poor, and (2) that the effort or lack of effort by governments to provide income security to persons not in the labor force (or otherwise subject to low incomes) through social security programs that redistribute income will also affect national poverty levels. Thus, we view a nation's poverty level, not as a simple function of its per capita income, but as also influenced by inequalities in the distribution of that income and by government programs that redistribute income.

Both the distribution and the redistribution of income are subject to political and non-political forces. This analysis asks to what degree the characteristics of national political systems and varying levels of economic and social development are related to the variations among nations on income inequality and income redistribution. By comparing a number of nations the relative importance of political and non-political forces can be assessed, and conditions in the United States can be viewed in the context of comparisons with nations that are similar to and different from us.

An effort has been made to minimize attention to technical detail and methodological problems that are not relevant to the concerns and purposes of this volume. Readers interested in more detail with respect to the research on which this chapter is based should consult papers by the author published in the *American Sociological Review* and in *Social Forces* (Cutright, 1967a; 1967b). In the following sections theoretical questions are dealt with first, then empirical findings, and finally some implications for policy and strategy.

INEQUALITY AND THE DISTRIBUTION OF INCOME

The "functionalist" school in sociology has viewed inequality in the distribution of income as essentially the product of society's needs (Davis, 1949; Davis and Moore, 1945). The "conflict" theorists see income disparities as reflecting differences in power between groups with competing interests and desires (Dahrendorf, 1959; Mills, 1956; Kolko, 1962).

The Lenski Model

Lenski's synthesis of the "functionalist" and "conflict" theories of the distribution of rewards in societies has cleared the way for empirical research (Lenski, 1966). His theory of social stratification is concerned with the distribution of material rewards and the socioeconomic and political conditions that account for differences in the way the "distributive process" allocates the nation's product.

Both the functionalist and the conflict view of inequality are rejected as incomplete. Lenski accords importance to the functionalist position when he considers societies that do not create a surplus product, but he turns chiefly to the conflict theorist for explanations of inequality in societies at higher levels of economic development. Societies that develop a surplus product are said to allocate that product largely in terms of the distribution of power within the society. The size of the surplus product is largely determined by the level of technology which, in turn, is the prime factor affecting the forms of political and social organization which distribute power within societies.

This generalized scheme to explain differences in "the nature of the distributive system" applies to all types of societies. Given five types—hunting and gathering, simple horticultural, advanced horticultural, agrarian, and industrial—taken in that order, the degree of inequality rises from a very low point in hunting and gathering societies to an apex in agrarian societies, followed by a decline as industrialization takes over. The latter part of this array can be estimated by gross national product per capita (GNP): low GNP nations are largely agrarian, those in the middle GNP stratum are in the early industrialization, a conclusion supported by the theoretical and empirical work of several economists (Kravis, 1960; Oshima, 1962; Kuznets, 1963).

Thus, an increasing level of economic development across the first four types of societies is associated with increasing inequality. Lenski's explanation of the reversal of this trend rests on two changes: (1) the absolute size of the economic surplus, and (2) changes in the distribution of power. As the level of economic development increases, the higher level of technology and declining fertility create a surplus.

The forms of social and political organization that affect the distribution of power also change. So long as the economy is unable to produce a large surplus, the political and economic elite can enforce inequality to ensure the existence of a surplus and their own position of privilege. Populations in industrialized societies will demand equal distribution of the society's product, and, because the amount of the surplus is so vast, the elite can afford to give up some of the surplus and allow the masses to rise above the subsistence level. Societies with high levels of economic development will have an elite willing to make concessions and a population demanding equality. If economic growth is maintained, the elite can continue to take an ever increasing *absolute* (but not relative) share of the wealth produced by the economy.

In Lenski's theory, both "political organization" and the degree of "constitutionalization" are said to affect the degree of inequality. Political structures that facilitate access by the masses to the elite will decrease inequality. High levels of "constitutionalization" will decrease inequality because the power of the many to organize against the few will be guaranteed. Constitutionalization in industrial societies may be measured by the extent to which the society has extended the modern concept of "citizenship" to all segments of the population, and thus identified human as opposed to property rights as the basis of the distributive process. To the extent that citizenship is broadly accepted, the elite will be forced to respond to the claims of the non-elite classes for a greater share of the national product. As political structures increasingly incorporate this modern concept of "citizenship," governments will enter the distributive process and counteract the self-interest of the economic elite. Lenski notes that the operation of the free market without government intervention would lead industrial nations to increasing levels of inequality. Therefore, the role of government is crucial in understanding the reversal of the historical trend of increasing inequality associated with economic development.

SOME MODIFICATION OF THE MODEL

Lenski's model allows for "unknown" factors that may affect the degree of inequality. It seems appropriate to investigate *external* as well as *internal* factors that may influence the distribution of the national product. Two external factors are considered: the allocation of funds to military use, and the dependence of the nation on foreign trade. One internal factor—the level of capital formation—is added. The common characteristic of these three variables is that they are subject to conscious decisions and are, in part, a response by decision-makers to forces beyond their immediate control. The effect that these variables may have upon the degree of inequality within the nation should not be viewed as a desired or expected consequence.

Lenski concluded that high military participation would be related to low inequality in agrarian societies but he was uncertain about the relationship in industrial societies. He cites the work of Stanislaw Andrzejewski (1954) on pre-industrial societies, and notes that the dependence of the modern state on a mass army hastened the extension of universal male suffrage and, therefore, altered the distribution of power in modern societies. Mass suffrage and its resultant political institutions have been with us for some time, however, and there is little reason to think that the amount of military participation will continue to have the same effect on equality it once did. The dependence of the elite on a mass army, is nonetheless, one of the conditions of modern elite existence, and should not be overlooked in examining the conditions that help explain the stability of representative political institutions.

We did not expect that a large mass army would be related to lower inequality in a developed industrial society. The existence of large modern armies requires a vast expenditure of money that could otherwise be allocated more efficiently to speed the rate of economic progress and decrease inequality. We reasoned that military participation would be positively related to inequality in high GNP nations. We were uncertain about the relationship across all types of nations or in the middle and lower GNP strata.

Inequality should be greater in poor nations than in rich nations because poor nations dependent on foreign trade are vulnerable to the economic power of richer nations. Within the lower GNP stratum, those nations dependent on foreign trade should have greater inequality because the exchange process is in the hands of a powerful elite who should prosper relative to the powerless non-elite who produce raw materials. We hypothesized that lower GNP nations would show a positive relation between foreign trade and inequality, while high GNP nations would not be affected because the commercial sector's power would be countered by the power of producers of the exchanged products.

The powerful negative relation between gross domestic capital formation as a per cent of GNP and private consumption suggests that, in the short run, the diversion of funds from private consumption to capital formation (regardless of who determines the level of capital formation) should increase inequality. The higher the capital formation, the smaller the surplus to be distributed. If Lenski's theory is correct, and the power relations among groups in societies are the basic determinants of variation in the distribution of the society's product, it follows that funds for capital formation should be drained away from the relatively powerless. Since these are the same people who are at the bottom of the income distribution, the loss of consumable income to these groups (particularly farmers and the urban poor) should be relatively greater than the loss of consumable income to groups with greater power. High levels of capital formation should be associated with high inequality.

In addition to the allocation of funds to military use, the dependence of the nation on foreign trade, and the level of capital formation, it also seemed important to examine the effect of the size of what might best be called the "powerless labor force." In most nations, the income of the agricultural labor force is lower than the income of people in urban areas. Those in the mass agricultural labor force have been the last to gain literacy, political power, and organizational skills. It is likely that by the time they acquire the skills long before gained by urban populations, their numbers will have diminished, and those who remain in agriculture will still be relatively powerless. The larger the size of this "vulnerable" population, the greater will be the degree of inequality in a nation. It is not possible to deduce whether inequality associated with the size of the agricultural labor force is the result solely of the distribution of power, or simply the result of economic outcomes associated with the generally low value the market assigns to the agricultural product. The truth probably lies somewhere in between. The powerlessness of the agricultural labor force refers to a lack of control over the price of agricultural goods, and a lack of political power that would counteract free market factors. Low reward for agricultural labor is only partially explained by the abundance of this type of labor and "low" productivity. Rural populations lack the educational skills, economic power, and political organization necessary to counteract the claims of the better organized and more powerful urban sectors.

OPERATIONALIZING THE MODEL

All of these abstract concepts must, of course, be represented by available data before the various hypotheses that are combined into this theoretical model can be tested. As indicated previously, the details of the selection of empirical variables and the rationale for each are developed elsewhere (Cutright, 1967a). However, the reader should at least be aware of the kinds of measures actually used in the statistical analysis.

(1) Income Inequality. Adequate data are not available for most nations to provide a comprehensive measure of income inequality that would take account of all sources of income, including government efforts to redistribute income through transfer payments. Instead, use is made of an ingenious measure developed by Kuznets (1963) for "intersectorial income inequality." For each of ten sectors of employment—services, agriculture, mining, construction, manufacturing, commerce, transportation, communications, electricity and gas—the per cent of the labor force in the sector is compared with the per cent of the national product produced by the sector, starting with the sector with the lowest per worker product, and cumulating the percentages. Although measurement error exists, the effect of such errors is to decrease the association of our inequality scores (Lorenz coefficients) with the variables that we expect will account for high or low scores. Both theoretical and empirical checks on the validity of the intersectorial inequality measure have been made and its validity has been found to be adequate. Inequality scores are available for 44 non-Communist and 8 Communist nations.

(2) Economic Development Index. An index for both the size of the surplus and the level of technology was constructed using per capita energy consumption, income converted to U.S. dollars per capita, steel consumption, and the number of motor vehicles

per capita. The level of economic development is empirically a better measure of the size of the surplus than either the absolute or the relative rate of recent economic changes, and this index is obviously a superior measure of technology.

(3) Farm Rental. In the lower GNP nations high farm rental would seem likely to indicate high vulnerability of the agricultural population to exploitation by large landowners, but in high GNP nations it is an indicator of technology in agriculture and of the size of agricultural relative to non-agricultural income, so that it would be negatively related to income inequality. This variable, of course, is not relevant to Communist nations.

(4) Political Representativeness Index. Most of the weight in this index comes from the extent to which there is a parliament and the degree of minority party representation in it, plus the extent to which popular choice could affect the selection of a chief executive. This index thus interprets the distribution of power variable as the extent to which the government is likely to be under effective pressure to take into account the demands of the non-elite population.

(5) Gross Domestic Capital Formation. For most nations the value of residential and other domestic (non-military) construction, machinery, and other equipment and inventories as a per cent of GNP will give the per cent of GNP that Gross Domestic Capital formation comprises. This is one of the "Economic and Security Decisions" which are treated here as "unknown" factors for Lenski's model that may affect distribution of income.

(6) Military Participation Ratio. The proportion of the male population 15 to 64 in military service, as indicated previously, would be likely to deflect money from functions conducive to economic progress and income equality in high GNP nations, though the effect of this type of economic-security decision seemed uncertain for middle and low GNP countries.

(7) Foreign Trade. Amount of foreign trade is influenced by population size as this affects the ability of a domestic market to support an industrialized economy, but foreign trade is always superior to population size as a predictor of inequality, although

the theoretical model posits its effects as unpredictable for the high GNP nations. Data on foreign trade were not available for the Communist countries.

(8) Per Cent of Labor Force in Agriculture. As indicated above, those in the mass agricultural labor force are relatively powerless and fall disproportionately into the lower income categories for both economic and political reasons. In nations with large agricultural populations inequality will be high.

Figure 1 summarizes the conceptual scheme and expected relationship of each indicator to inequality, showing the direction of causality with arrows. The rise in the surplus product has a direct effect on inequality; but it also has an indirect effect because it

Figure 1. CONCEPTUAL SCHEME AND EMPIRICAL INDICATORS

NOTE: "Positive" means that as an independent variable increases, inequality will also increase; "negative" means that as an independent variable increases, inequality will decrease.

forces changes in a nation's political institutions and alters the distribution of power. To make a conservative test of the effect of variation in political institutions (or the power of the propertied class in lower GNP nations), one would want first to remove the variance in inequality that is associated with variation in the size of the surplus product. Therefore, the Economic Development Index is entered first. The Political Representativeness Index (along with farm rental in lower GNP nations) is entered after removing the effects of the Economic Development Index. The order of the remaining variables was determined by our opinion that "Economic and Security Decisions" should be considered prior to the size of the agricultural labor force. Economic and security decisions are made within the framework of the nation's level of economic and political development, and the association of these latter two factors with inequality should be removed prior to entering the decision variables. Furthermore, the size of the agricultural labor force is not likely to affect decisions on national security or the economy (assuming that economic and political factors are controlled), and should be entered last.

Thus, in the "forced" multiple correlation analysis used here the order in which the independent variables are entered is specified on the basis of theory. For example, if per cent of labor force in agriculture, which also is an index of technology and surplus product, were entered first, one would be removing variation in inequality related to both economic and political factors. In the order given by Figure 1, the variance in inequality linked to technology and surplus product is removed first by the Economic Development Index.

FROM THEORY TOWARD REALITY: TEST RESULTS

In general, this theoretical model is strongly supported by our statistical analysis. There are, not surprisingly, some qualifications and modifications suggested by the results of our first test. Table 1 presents an analysis of the 44 non-Communist nations. The approximate dates for each variable are given, along with their means and standard deviations. It also shows the percentage of total variation in the inequality measure that is associated with each indicator, given the order of its appearance in the forced correlation analysis. When entered first, the Economic Development Index accounts for 27 per cent of the variation; the addition of the Political Representativeness Index adds 14 per cent. The three variables measuring current economic and national security efforts contribute very little. All together they add only 6 per cent. We also note that Lenski's view that the size of the agricultural labor force will be related to inequality is confirmed. Even after we control for economic development and four additional variables, knowledge of the size of the agricultural labor force allows us to account for an additional 17 per cent of the variation. A total of 64 per cent of the variation is accounted for.

TABLE 1

MEANS, STANDARD DEVIATIONS, AND PER CENT OF VARIANCE IN INEQUALITY EXPLAINED BY INDEPENDENT VARIABLES IN A GIVEN ORDER: 44 NON-COMMUNIST NATIONS

Independent Variable and Date	Mean	Standard Deviation	Per Cent of Variance	Sign[b]
Economic Development Index, 1953-1955	209.0	34.9	27[a]	—
Political Representativeness Index, 1945-1954	50.1	9.6	14[a]	—
Foreign Trade, 1955	39.1	18.1	4[a]	+
Military Participation Ratio, 1959	1.4	1.8	1	—
Capital Formation, 1950-1959	19.0	6.1	1	+
Agricultural Labor Force, 1951	41.1	22.0	17[a]	+
			64	

NOTE: The measure of inequality was taken for 1951 and has a mean of 19.1 and a standard deviation of 11.2. The variable "Farm Rental" was not included because of missing data in the lowest GNP stratum.

[a] P less than .05, one-tailed test.

[b] A positive sign indicates that as the value of the independent variable increases, the measure of inequality also increases. It is taken from the sign of the beta weight for the variable at the time it is introduced into the analysis.

Although the broad outlines of the major factors related to inequality seem relatively clear, the conceptual scheme contains a number of important qualifications concerning the effect of certain variables on inequality in nations at different levels of economic development. If our model is correct, we would expect that stratification of this heterogeneous group of 44 nations would *increase* the total variance explained (in spite of the loss of prediction we might expect when we drop the Economic Development Index and, in the high GNP stratum, the Political Representativeness Index as well). We expect that the indicators of economic and security decisions will improve our explanation of the variation of inequality within a stratum because interactions among variables are different within the different strata. Also, variables like the Military Participation Ratio and farm rental (not included in Table 1 because of missing data) will be available, and will work in opposite directions within different strata. If this is the case, it follows that when nations are put into "homogeneous strata" these previously suppressed effects will appear.

THE LOW GNP NATIONS

The results for the low GNP nations ($75 to $290 per capita) are displayed in Table 2. In spite of the variation in GNP within

TABLE 2

MEANS, STANDARD DEVIATIONS, AND PER CENT OF VARIANCE IN INEQUALITY EXPLAINED
BY INDEPENDENT VARIABLES IN A GIVEN ORDER: 19 LOW GNP NATIONS

Independent Variable	Mean	Standard Deviation	Per Cent of Variance	Sign
Panel A				
Political Representativeness Index	43.2	7.1	20[a]	—
Foreign Trade	33.6	17.6	14[a]	+
Capital Formation	15.6	5.2	28[a]	+
Agricultural Labor Force	61.6	12.7	23[a]	+
			85	
Panel B				
Political Representativeness Index	43.2	7.1	20[a]	—
Capital Formation	15.6	5.2	40[a]	+
Foreign Trade	33.6	17.6	2	+
Agricultural Labor Force	61.6	12.7	23[a]	+
			85	

NOTE: The measure of inequality has a mean of 26.1 and a standard deviation of 11.9. Farm Rental data were missing for several nations, and the distribution of the Military Participation Ratio did not allow its use in correlation analysis for this stratum.

[a] P less than .05, one-tailed test.

this group, the Economic Development Index makes little contribution to explaining variation in inequality among them and is not included. As expected, nations with higher Political Representativeness scores have lower inequality. The need for further study is underscored by the uncertain relationship between foreign trade and capital formation, whose respective shares of variance shift so sharply when the order of their entry into the calculations is changed (compare Panel A with Panel B). However, both variables have significant effects (in the predicted direction) on inequality. The strong effects of the size of the agricultural labor force *might* be diminished *if* adequate data were available for this group of nations on farm rental and military expenditures, as is the case in the next two strata.

THE MIDDLE GNP NATIONS

TABLE 3

MEANS, STANDARD DEVIATIONS, AND PER CENT OF VARIANCE IN INEQUALITY EXPLAINED BY INDEPENDENT VARIABLES IN A GIVEN ORDER: 13 MIDDLE GNP NATIONS

Independent Variable	Mean	Standard Deviation	Per Cent of Variance	Sign
Panel A				
Political Representativeness Index	51.6	8.2	34[a]	−
Farm Rental	12.4	9.0	13	+
Foreign Trade	42.9	15.9	16[a]	+
Military Participation Ratio	1.1	1.3	7	−
Capital Formation	20.9	5.7	2	−
			72	
Panel B				
Political Representativeness Index	51.6	8.2	34[a]	−
Military Participation Ratio	1.1	1.3	12	−
Farm Rental	12.4	9.0	12	+
Foreign Trade	42.9	15.9	12[a]	+
Capital Formation	20.9	5.7	2	
			72	

NOTE: The measure of inequality has a mean of 15.2 and a standard deviation of 8.5. The per cent of the labor force in agriculture added nothing to the explained variance when inserted either before or after Capital Formation in Panel A.

[a] P less than .05, one-tailed test.

Variation within this stratum on the Economic Development Index is unrelated to inequality. However the Political Representativeness Index accounts for even more of the variation in inequality displayed by the 13 non-Communist nations in the middle strata, with a GNP ranging from $300 to $799 per capita (see Table 3). But capital formation has little effect, and that in the opposite direction than predicted; but only in this non-Communist stratum is capital formation closely associated (.60) with annual growth in per capita GNP. The relationship of farm rental, foreign trade, and the Military Participation Ratio to inequality is similar in both panels.

High GNP Nations

Among the 12 non-Communist nations in the high GNP stratum, with per capita GNP above $800 a year, there is no meaningful difference in Political Representativeness Index scores, so the variable does not appear in Table 4. Variation in the Economic Development Index is not related to inequality, and that measure

TABLE 4

Means, Standard Deviations, and Per Cent of Variance in Inequality Explained by Independent Variables in a Given Order: 12 High GNP Nations

Independent Variable	Mean	Standard Deviation	Per Cent of Variance	Sign
Panel A				
Farm Rental	24.7	18.5	16	—
Military Participation Ratio	1.6	0.7	47[a]	+
Capital Formation	22.4	5.0	26[a]	+
Foreign Trade	43.0	20.1	9[a]	+
			98	
Panel B				
Military Participation Ratio	1.6	0.7	33[a]	+
Farm Rental	24.7	18.5	30[a]	—
Foreign Trade	43.7	18.7	20[a]	+
Capital Formation	26.8	16.6	15[a]	+
			98	

Note: The measure of inequality has a mean of 12.4 and a standard deviation of 4.9.
[a] P less than .05, one-tailed test.

is also omitted. Although the contribution to variation in inequality by each of the independent variables changes depending upon the order in which they are entered (compare Panel A with Panel B), it seems clear that the drain of high defense expenditures on a developed economy is powerfully related to inequality. This ratio, farm rental, and capital formation taken together will account for 89 per cent of the variation in inequality within this stratum.

COMMUNIST NATIONS

Data for some of the variables used in the preceding analyses are not available for the Communist nations; political representativeness scores are identical for all of them and are therefore excluded from the calculations for this stratum. But the three independent variables displayed in Table 5 account for 97 per cent of the variation in our measure of inequality. The Economic Development Index is powerfully associated with inequality. Capital formation is not related to inequality, but, as was also the case

TABLE 5

MEANS, STANDARD DEVIATIONS, AND PER CENT OF VARIANCE IN INEQUALITY EXPLAINED BY INDEPENDENT VARIABLES IN A GIVEN ORDER: 8 COMMUNIST NATIONS

Independent Variable and Date	Mean	Standard Deviation	Per Cent of Variance	Sign
Panel A				
Economic Development Index, 1953-1955	230.6	22.8	68[a]	—
Military Participation Ratio, 1959	2.2	0.9	14[a]	+
Agricultural Labor Force, 1959	47.5	18.2	15[a]	+
			97	
Panel B				
Military Participation Ratio	2.2	0.9	45[a]	+
Economic Development Index	230.6	22.8	37[a]	—
Agricultural Labor Force	47.5	18.2	15[a]	+
			97	

NOTE: The measure of inequality refers to 1959 and has a mean of 33.7 and a standard deviation of 8.4. This measure is similar to, but not directly comparable with, the measure for non-Communist nations. Kuznets, *op. cit.* 1963, discusses differences in Communist and non-Communist national accounting practices that result in comparable inequality measures within, but not across, Communist and non-Communist countries.

[a] P less than .05, one-tailed test.

546 □ Power, Poverty, and Urban Policy

in the middle GNP stratum, capital formation is highly correlated (.93) with annual per capita GNP growth. This correlation may account for the lack of the expected effect. The Military Participation Ratio also makes an important contribution to inequality among these nations that are the "other half" of the cold war; the higher the ratio, the higher the inequality. Also of interest is the strong association of the size of the agricultural labor force with inequality among the Communist nations.

Theoretical Implications

Our analysis leads us to qualify the conceptual scheme offered by Lenski and ourself. Table 1 revealed that 64 per cent of the variance in inequality among the 44 non-Communist nations could be accounted for by our indicators. In that analysis, the size of the surplus product, the distribution of power, and the size of the powerless labor force were relatively powerful predictors, while our measures of economic and security decisions were not. However, the errors of prediction using this model are much greater than the errors of prediction obtained if the nations are broken into strata. When stratified according to their level of per capita GNP, we account for about 85 per cent of the variance in the lowest GNP stratum, 70 per cent in the middle stratum, and over 90 per cent in the high GNP stratum. Over 90 per cent of the variance in the Communist stratum was related to three predictors.

Although the stratification procedure generally controlled the variation in inequality related to the size of the surplus product (and, in two strata, variation in political structure as well), it allowed farm rental to enter and confirm its expected relationship to inequality in the middle and high GNP strata. The Military Participation Ratio also worked as we expected in the high GNP stratum and in Communist nations, and conformed to Lenski's expectations in middle GNP stratum. Foreign trade worked, as we expected, in the low and middle GNP strata, but had the same effect in the high GNP stratum where we did not expect it to be related to inequality. Except for the low and the high GNP stratum, capital formation was found to be a relatively weak variable, and further research is essential in determining and explaining its role. The errors in our predictions, both across and within strata, are shown in Table 6.

TABLE 6

INEQUALITY SCORE AND ERRORS OF PREDICTION: NON-COMMUNIST COUNTRIES
CLASSIFIED BY PER CAPITA GNP, AND COMMUNIST COUNTRIES

Stratum and Country	Inequality Score (Lorenz coefficient)	Across-strata Error	Within-stratum Error
High GNP			
Australia	8	0.1	— 3.2
Belgium	5	— 4.7	0.8
Canada	12	— 4.6	— 0.7
Denmark	13	1.3	2.0
France	22	9.4	0.1
Great Britain	6	1.7	— 1.5
Luxembourg	15	— 4.1	0.7
Netherlands	15	3.2	1.7
New Zealand	11	— 1.5	1.4
Norway	19	7.1	0.5
United States	12	— 0.1	— 2.2
West Germany	11	2.4	0.5
Mean error		3.35	1.27
Middle GNP			
Argentina	20	6.5	— 4.9
Austria	14	4.2	0.6
Chile	23	9.3	7.4
Costa Rica	5	—18.9	—10.6
Finland	9	— 7.7	1.1
Greece	10	— 5.6	— 1.3
Ireland	6	— 8.4	— 3.6
Israel	6	— 2.5	— 0.5
Italy	15	1.1	— 0.2
Jamaica	30	1.4	2.5
Japan	9	2.1	0.4
Panama	21	1.8	7.9
Venezuela	30	0.8	1.2
Mean error		5.40	3.24
Low GNP			
Algeria	39	0.2	0.5
Belgian Congo (L.)	58	15.9	— 0.8
Brazil	29	9.9	6.6
Ceylon	14	—10.4	— 6.1
Colombia	12	— 4.6	— 6.9
Ecuador	20	4.0	— 0.3
Egypt	18	— 6.0	— 0.4
El Salvador	29	2.8	6.9
Honduras	27	— 5.6	— 7.1
India	21	— 4.7	— 0.7
Morocco	41	4.2	8.3
Pakistan	17	—12.9	— 4.1

(Table 6 continued on following page.)

Stratum and Country	Inequality Score (Lorenz coefficient)	Across-strata Error	Within-stratum Error
Peru	45	19.0	1.8
Philippines	16	1.0	5.3
Portugal	19	— 3.1	0.0
Spain	12	— 6.4	5.7
Taiwan	18	0.9	0.2
Thailand	34	2.6	1.9
Turkey	21	— 0.8	— 1.1
Mean error		6.06	3.40
Communist			
Bulgaria	41		— 1.8
Czechoslovakia	27		— 0.0
East Germany	19		— 0.5
Hungary	28		— 1.5
Poland	36		2.1
Romania	41		0.7
USSR	35		1.3
Yugoslavia	43		— 0.2
Mean error			1.01

NOTE: "Across-strata errors" are based on a regression using as independent variables the Political Representativeness Index, Economic Development Index, Foreign Trade, and Agricultural Labor Force. "Within-stratum errors" are based on regressions using Capital Formation, Military Participation Ratio, and Farm Rental in the High GNP stratum; Foreign Trade, Political Representativeness Index, Military Participation Ratio, and Farm Rental in the middle GNP stratum; Agricultural Labor Force, Foreign Trade, Capital Formation, and Political Representativeness Index in the low GNP stratum; Economic Development Index, Military Participation Ratio, and Agricultural Labor Force in the Communist stratum. A positive error means that the nation had higher inequality, i.e., a higher Lorenz coefficient, than was predicted; a negative error means that the nation had less inequality than was predicted. Communist nations could not be included in the across-strata regression because their inequality scores were not comparable to those for the non-Communist nations.

Although different "causes" of inequality are only partially illuminated by our analysis, it seems clear that investigators will obtain different results depending on the type of nation they study and their choice of a causal model. It also appears that the "functionalist" view of inequality (from a macro point of view at least) is supported by our analysis of the latent functions of certain economic and security decisions, while the conflict theorist is supported by our consistent finding that the distribution of power is an important predictor of inequality across all strata and within both strata in which there were differences on the Political Representativeness Index. Finally, the economist may be heartened that his interpretation of inequality as a function of the level of economic development also received solid empirical support.

Implications for Policy

Unfortunately, those who make and implement national policy can only choose to take account of or disregard such knowledge as systematic inquiry makes available. And that knowledge, more often than not, will only clarify, not resolve, the dilemmas that so frequently confront those who must act. For example, our data reveal that for the low GNP nations foreign trade and capital formation are both associated with inequality.

One should not, of course, conclude that a nation should cut back either capital investment or foreign trade. Nations must have capital investment if they are to grow, and they must also trade if they are to reach higher levels of economic development. One can conclude, however, that certain economic decisions will have the latent function of increasing inequality in the short run. On the other hand, if these same actions lead to economic development, the long run effect will be to decrease inequality.

Again, the available evidence emphasizes the importance of increasing political representation if the reduction of inequality in low and middle GNP non-Communist nations is desired. What does this imply for the consequences of "foreign aid" to regimes which repress minority parties, abolish parliaments, and prohibit popular influence in the selection of a chief executive? If such "aid" were to strengthen a self-serving political or military elite and thus retard economic and social development, it would maintain existing high levels of inequality and also stimulate political instability. On the other hand, facilitating the development of representative political structures in concert with efforts to aid social and economic development would appear to represent a maximum strategy for enabling the less developed countries to reduce inequality while also increasing per capita GNP.

Finally, we should note the apparent impact of allocation of men and resources on inequality in the high GNP nations. Once again, it seems clear that hard choices must be made with respect to "guns" as against "butter." Research such as this cannot determine which should be sacrificed for the other, but it can guard us against the temptation to believe that progress in the reduction of inequality in the United States will automatically follow enormous military expenditures.

INCOME REDISTRIBUTION

The analysis up to this point has neglected two important sources of income, resulting in a misleading picture of the shape of the income stratification system. The first is non-family transfer income—this is computed by adding all money and non-money transfers received from sources outside the dwelling unit. With the exception of the well-to-do, who enjoy substantial private insurance programs, non-family transfer income to most families comes from government social security programs. The second source of family income is net intrafamily transfers—this includes any money payments or food and housing donations the unit receives from other members of the family, less any such contributions the unit makes to other members of the family.

When non-family transfers and net intrafamily transfers are added to the "original" gross factor income (and income tax is deducted in the upper income groups), the result is the family's gross disposable income. Since it is gross disposable income that determines the family's ability to consume goods and services, it is likely that gross disposable income is a better measure of the family's income status than is gross factor income.

Data for the United States population clearly show that families with gross factor incomes below $3,000 a year (1959) are helped largely by non-family transfers (Morgan et al., 1962). For example, families with under $500 gross factor income received an average of $709 in non-family transfer income and an average of $314 in net intrafamily transfers. In the $500-$999 interval, the average non-family transfer was $870, compared to $87 net intrafamily income; while in the $1,000-$1,999 interval, the average non-family transfer income amounted to $823, compared to only $12 net intrafamily transfer income.

The power of government programs to alter the shape of the income stratification system is made evident by Table 7. In the United States in 1959 nearly 18 per cent of all adult units had a

TABLE 7

Per Cent of Adult Units in Gross Factor and Gross Disposable Income Intervals: United States, 1959 (N = 3,396 adult units) *

Income Interval	Per Cent by Gross Factor	Per Cent by Gross Disposable	Effect of Transfers and Federal Income Tax
Under $500	17.7	3.2	—14.5
500-999	7.4	8.7	+ 1.3
1,000-1,999	10.6	12.5	+ 1.9
2,000-2,999	8.5	10.7	+ 2.2
3,000-4,999	15.6	22.1	+ 6.5
5,000-7,499	18.2	22.7	+ 4.5
7,500-9,999	10.4	11.3	+ .9
10,000-14,999†	8.0	6.7	— 1.3
15,000 and up	3.6	2.5	— 1.1
Total	100.0	100.4‡	

* An adult unit is a person 18 or older, his spouse if married, and any dependent children living with him.

† Federal income tax responsible for the downward shift in the $10,000 and over intervals.

‡ Total does not add to 100 because of slight errors in estimating from bar graphs in original source. Data adopted from Morgan, et al., op. cit., pp. 314, 317.

gross factor income below $500, but only 3 per cent had a gross disposable income this low. Over 80 per cent of all adult units under $500 gross factor income are moved to a higher income level because of transfer payments. The income status of millions of families is altered by non-family transfer payments, and one effect of this change is to make the distribution of gross disposable income more equitable than is the distribution of gross factor income.

Social Security Programs: A Theoretical Explanation

Social security programs provide the non-family transfer funds that alter the shape of the gross factor income distribution. If the per cent of GNP allocated to social security programs were near zero it is obvious that the distribution of persons to gross disposable income intervals would be very similar to the distribution of persons to gross factor income intervals. A nation with a relatively high per cent of its GNP allocated to social security programs will be a nation in which the income distribution will be strongly altered in an equalitarian direction. Conversely, a nation with a low proportion of GNP devoted to social security programs will be a nation in which the distribution of gross disposable income is very little altered.

How are we to explain the wide variation among nations in the proportion of the GNP that they devote to reducing inequality through income redistribution? First, because social security programs are political acts—legislative acts in fact—we would expect political systems with a strong equalitarian component to have large social security programs (Lenski, 1966, pp. 24-42). Second, the experience of agencies responsible for operating government programs ought to affect security expenditures. A bureaucracy with many years of program experience will have the technical knowledge required to operate a massive program, and it will have the power to implement its internally generated demands for greater coverage of the population by its programs. Further, as programs are initiated, the population becomes a constituency of the bureaucracy, and present and potential beneficiaries are stimulated to act as real or potential pressure groups in support of the bureaucracy's demands for higher benefits and greater coverage.

Third, populations in nations with high levels of modernization have greater control over their environment than do populations in nations low on modernization. Whether or not the former share strongly equalitarian values, the character of life and the hazards associated with industrialization make strong social security programs relevant to the self-interest of major segments of the population. Moreover, people in a modernized society, by experiencing its great control over their environment, learn to expect that "something can be done" about the problems they face. As indicated in the summary of Lenski's theory presented earlier, societies with high levels of economic development are likely to have major segments of their population pressing for greater equality and elites willing to make concessions; such concessions, we expect, will often take the form of social security programs. Thus, the higher the level of modernization, the greater the control by the population over its environment; and the greater the control, the larger the social security expenditures.

This theoretical model, therefore, posits that the degree of political equalitarianism, the experience of the bureaucracy, and the control of the population over its environment will explain the differences in the extent to which governments will or will not operate programs that redistribute income. Although modernization is obviously correlated with per capita GNP, this model makes it clear that "ability to pay" per se is not likely to be a major determinant of legislative acts to reduce income inequality for at least a broad range of nations above the lowest level of economic development. Only as purely economic variables are translated into a form with socio-political relevance can we speak sensibly of their consequence for the proportion of the total GNP, whatever its level, that is deliberately allocated to income equalization through social security programs.

OPERATIONALIZING THE MODEL

Once again it becomes necessary to represent these abstract concepts by available data.

Income Redistribution Through Social Security Expenditures

The dependent variable is the *effort* by government to redistribute a share of the national wealth to persons with low gross factor incomes. This effort will be measured by the per cent of the gross national product allocated to national social security expenditures in 1960. This measure was developed by the United States Social Security Administration and allows us to make comparisons among 40 nations (Social Security Administration, 1965).

Equalitarian Pressure in the Political System

This first independent variable is obviously related to, but not identical with "political representativeness." That variable emphasized the possibilities for non-elite segments of the population to exert demands through a parliament, minority party representation, and impact on the selection of a chief executive. Here we seek a measure more likely to reflect pressures internal and external to government that will affect the redistribution of income. For this we chose the per cent of the voting age population voting in national elections during the 1950s (Russett *et al.*, 1964). We reasoned that regardless of whether the voting is compulsory or not (and both Communist and non-Communist nations have compulsory voting), the level of voting participation should tell us something important about pressures within the political system to reach a certain level of social security expenditures. In systems with forced citizen participation, the government must legitimate its equalitarian ideology through government activity consistent with the ideology. In Communist nations, forced citizen participation is linked to an official ideology of equalitarianism, while in democratic nations, the democratic ideology also demands that, by virtue of their citizenship and shared fate in the social order, the poor and unfortunate be given government aid. A political system that fails to hold elections, or discourages participation by disenfranchising large segments of its population should be one in which neither the full force of a developed equalitarian democratic ideology, nor a developed socialist or communist ideology will be translated into effective government programs involving large transfer payments.

The Experience and Power of the Social Security Bureaucracy

Our measure of the experience and power of the social security bureaucracy is the number of years of social security program experience the nation accumulated between 1920 and 1960. Five types of programs (work injury; old age, invalidity, death; sickness and maternity; unemployment; family allowances) are used (Cutright, 1965; Social Security Administration, 1961). If a nation had only one program in 1920 and added no further programs it would accumulate 41 years of program experience between 1920-1960. If it had all five programs throughout this time period, it would accumulate 205 years of experience. The Social Insurance Program Experience Index (SIPE) for the 40 nations in our sample ranges between 188 (Belgium) and 20 (Ghana). The greater the number of years of program experience, the larger should be the social security expenditures.

Control of the Population over the Environment

Populations in nations with high levels of modernization have greater control over their environment than do populations in nations low on modernization. There are several subtleties involved in analysis of modernization indicators. First, indicators of modernization are intercorrelated, and the choice of one in preference to another does not mean that only one is important. For example, education, the proportion of the population in the industrial labor force, GNP per capita, per cent of the population over 65, and urbanization are all intercorrelated (Russett *et al.*, 1964, pp. 264-87). Each of these indicators taken as an independent variable will show a similar level of correlation against *any* dependent variable—if one is positively related, all will be positively related to the same dependent variable. But the correlations will not be identical, and for prediction purposes one would normally select the one or two modernization indicators that yield the best prediction. The interpretation of the correlation should not, however, ignore the fact that the indicator of modernization yielding the best prediction is itself strongly related to a number of other analytically distinct, but empirically correlated, phenomena. For example, the per cent of the labor force employed in industry yields a slightly better prediction of social security expenditures than do other measures of modernization. This does not mean that the age structure, education level, urbanization, etc., are not contributing to this outcome—they obviously are. We will, however, use the per cent of the labor force that is employed in industry as our indicator of the control of the population over its environment (*Ibid.*, pp. 185-86).

A second subtlety in thinking about indicators of modernization is the multiple conceptual meanings we must ascribe to these indicators. The per cent of the labor force employed in industry is an indicator of economic organization, but it is more; it is an indicator of the probable *vulnerability* of the population to drastic income status change associated with change from labor force to non-labor force status. It is also an indicator of the *sensitivity* of the population to its present and future needs for protection against the hazards of non-labor force status, and its sensitivity to the possibility that *something can be done* about this problem. We do not have to ask whether the population has strong equalitarian values, but we only have to assume that the modernized population can and will act in terms of its present or future self-interest.

Testing the Theoretical Argument

When the three independent variables were entered into a regression equation using all 40 nations, each proved a useful predictor and the multiple R was .93. These nations were then grouped into those above and below $800 per capita GNP because (1) the sample was heavily weighted with high-income nations, and statements about the importance of variables for the total universe might be biased; (2) GNP per capita has little predicting value of itself, but does allow us to group nations into two types that are relatively homogeneous on a number of modernization characteristics; (3) we wanted to see whether the same predicting variables worked in nations at different levels of GNP per capita; and (4) if the same variables worked in the same manner for two strata, the power of the conceptual scheme would be enhanced.

The results are shown in Figures 2 and 3. The multiple R for the group of higher GNP nations was .78 and for the lower stratum it was .89. Figures 2 and 3 provide a visual display of the power of our three predictors to account for the variation among both high and low GNP nations in their effort to redistribute income through social security programs. Although sizable errors exist for a few nations (e.g. West Germany has a much higher effort than we predicted, and Australia is much lower than predicted) the strong relationship between actual expenditures and our predicting variables seems amply demonstrated.

When the social security effort is viewed in the relative terms we are using here, the magnitude of the United States effort, given the late start on such programs in the United States, its low voting participation rate, and its labor force in industry, is predictably low. (Translating the per cent of per capita GNP allocated to social security into dollars per capita spent on social security programs, we can show that Luxembourg, Sweden, and Belgium were spending more dollars per capita than the United States; and Canada, New Zealand, and West Germany were very close.)

Figure 2. ACTUAL AND PREDICTED SOCIAL SECURITY EXPENDITURES FOR NATIONS
ABOVE $800 PER CAPITA GNP

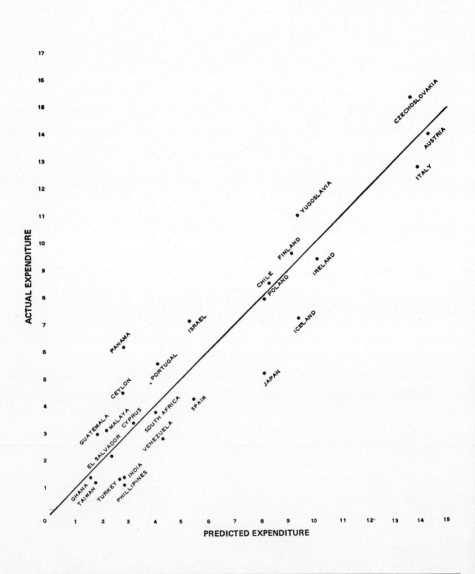

Figure 3. Actual and Predicted Social Security Expenditures for Nations Below $800 per Capita GNP

Table 8 displays the actual social security expenditure data and the errors resulting from the use of a single regression equation for all nations (across strata) and the errors produced by separate equations for each stratum.

TABLE 8

ACTUAL 1960 EXPENDITURES AND ERRORS OF PREDICTION*

Nation and Stratum	Actual Expenditures	Errors of Prediction Across Strata	Errors of Prediction Within Stratum
High GNP			
Australia	7.9	—3.6	—3.6
Belgium	14.2	1.0	0.7
Canada	8.9	0.0	0.7
Denmark	11.1	—0.8	—0.8
France	13.9	1.3	1.1
Great Britain	11.0	—2.4	—2.7
Luxembourg	14.2	2.1	2.2
Netherlands	11.0	—1.3	—1.5
New Zealand	13.0	1.3	1.4
Norway	10.3	—0.8	—0.6
Sweden	12.4	0.4	0.3
Switzerland	7.7	—1.4	—0.2
United States	6.3	—1.1	0.0
West Germany	16.1	3.3	3.0
Mean error		1.50	1.35
Low GNP			
Austria	14.0	1.1	—0.3
Ceylon	4.5	1.3	1.7
Chile	8.5	0.5	0.2
Cyprus	3.3	—0.6	0.1
Czechoslovakia	15.3	3.3	1.6
El Salvador	2.2	0.7	0.0
Finland	9.6	0.7	0.5
Ghana	1.3	0.7	—0.2
Guatemala	3.0	2.2	1.2
Iceland	7.2	—2.5	—2.2
India	1.4	—1.7	—1.5
Ireland	9.4	—0.4	—0.7
Israel	7.1	1.0	1.8
Italy	12.7	0.5	—1.5
Japan	5.2	—3.0	—2.9
Malaya	3.1	0.9	0.9
Panama	6.2	2.3	3.4
Philippines	1.1	—1.8	—1.7
Poland	9.0	—0.3	—0.1
Portugal	5.5	0.9	1.4
South Africa	3.8	—0.5	—0.3
Spain	4.2	—1.4	—1.3

(Table 8 continued on following page.)

Nation and Stratum	Actual Expenditures	Errors of Prediction Across Strata	Within Stratum
Taiwan	1.2	1.0	—0.5
Turkey	1.3	—2.0	—1.4
Venezuela	2.8	—2.3	—1.5
Yugoslavia	11.0	1.6	1.6
Mean error		1.38	1.17

* Actual expenditures are the per cent of total GNP allocated to Social Security expenditures.

A negative sign with an error of prediction means the nation was spending less than predicted, using SIPE, votes, and industrial labor force as independent variables. A positive sign indicates it was spending more. Errors are also in terms of the per cent of GNP.

Interpreting the Results

We have found that the effort to redistribute income is greater in high than in low GNP nations. This is not simply the result of a difference in "ability to pay" (measured by GNP per capita). In both strata, government effort to redistribute income is linked to differences among nations in the pressures for redistribution within the political system (measured by voting participation), the experience of the social security bureaucracy (measured by years of program experience), and the control exercised by the population over its environment (measured by the proportion of the labor force employed in industry). These three variables account for 79 per cent of the variation in social security expenditures in the low GNP stratum, and 61 per cent of the variation in the high GNP stratum. Although an equation using these same independent variables across both strata accounted for 86 per cent of the variation in social security expenditures, the average error of prediction and the standard errors of estimate were slightly smaller when a separate within stratum analysis was used. (See Table 8.)

The analysis within strata also revealed that the addition of each predictor in the low GNP stratum yielded continuous improvement in prediction. In the high GNP stratum the addition of Voting and Industrial Labor Force added nothing after SIPE was used. However, a simultaneous solution yields beta weights of about the same size for each predictor in the high GNP stratum, indicating that all three predictors are contributing to a given outcome. We speculate that the nations in this stratum may be relatively homogeneous now, but past variation in political and economic development accounted for variation in the number of years of program experience—the one variable that can be used as a single predictor in this stratum. We conclude that our model has been tested and found useful.

The effect of large social security programs is to make the distribution of income more equitable. This is true primarily because social security programs distribute income to people with very low gross factor incomes. If one visualizes the national income stratification system as measured by the distribution of gross disposable income, then it is clear that social security programs are having a major impact on altering the shape of the stratification systems in those nations with large programs. Further, our analysis of inequality in the distribution of income in the first section of this chapter indicated that the distribution of gross factor income is more equal in developed than in underdeveloped nations. One must now add to that fact the major finding of this study—government efforts to redistribute income in an equalitarian manner are greatest in the developed nations, the same nations in which the distribution of gross factor income is the most equitable to begin with. Although we lack a comprehensive measure of gross disposable income, we conclude that the distribution of gross disposable income is more equal in developed than in underdeveloped nations.

The impact of income redistribution on the income stratification system in developed nations is probably enormous. (The example of the United States in Table 7 is, after all, taken from a nation in which only 6.3 per cent of the (1960) GNP went to social security expenditures.) The manifest function of these programs (to maintain an acceptable income floor among the poor who are in the labor force, and the dependent population that is out of the labor force) is understood by all. Program planners are also aware of the implications of these programs for maintaining social order, occupational mobility, and economic growth (Cutright and Wiley, 1968). Although the intent of the planners may differ from nation to nation, the political, social, and economic consequences of a more equitable distribution of income may be similar.

A CONCLUDING NOTE

Our study of the political and socioeconomic determinants of social security expenditures reinforces our earlier conclusion that political factors play an important role in explaining national differences on intersectorial income inequality. The importance of encouraging full political representation as a source of pressure to encourage a government to develop programs that redistribute income seems clear; political pressures affect the level of government effort to redistribute income, regardless of whether a nation is rich or poor.

We should, however, emphasize that the *size* of the benefit paid is not only a function of the per cent of the GNP allocated to social security programs, but is also very powerfully affected by the level of GNP per capita. This fact highlights the importance of further economic development in poorer nations, before their available resources will be adequate to eliminate the grosser consequences of abject poverty. Wealthy nations, like the United States, can consider both strategies to shift the distribution of income going to members of the labor force and strategies to increase government action to redistribute income through programs that provide income and certain services directly to the low income population; we must ask which are most feasible, and which type of change is most likely to produce the desired results.

Viewed in cross national perspective, inequality in the distribution of income to earners in the United States seems quite similar to the magnitude of inequality present in other nations similar to our own. The 1951 level of intersectorial inequality in the United States was at the average level for the high GNP nations, and the current level shows a *drop* of 5 points from the earlier figure. Given the nature of the values that validate existing inequalities in the distribution of income to earners it is extremely unlikely that major planned changes in the distribution of income will occur. We conclude, therefore, that a strategy based on changing the distribution of income going to the employed members of the labor force is unlikely to have a major impact on poverty in the United States. But such a change is not necessary!

Poverty in the United States can be quickly and radically reduced by expansion of existing programs that redistribute income and services to low income groups, and by the introduction of new programs. Of the 14 high GNP nations, the United States is lowest in its effort to redistribute income through government programs. What does our study of the determinants of the level of such expenditures tell us about the chances for an increase in redistributive programs in the United States?

I would agree that major changes in social security programs (remember that these programs cover unemployment insurance, family allowances, minimum income programs, medical care, work injury insurance, as well as income programs for the aged and disabled population) *could* conceivably be achieved without "politicization" of the poor and near-poor, but I do not believe this will happen. Nor do I believe that reliance on the effect of the continued cumulation of years of experience by existing bureaucracies is adequate or desirable, especially when we consider the hostile relationship of many of these bureaucracies to their "clients." Changes on our third predictor, the "modernization" of the total population, may or may not effect the *type of program* that will reach those presently poor and not adequately covered by existing programs. A nation can, after all, allocate its social security expenditures through a variety of programs that may or may not make contact with the mass of the low income population. Expansion of programs and expenditures is no guarantee that those presently poor will be helped. To the extent that further "modernization" reaches the poor and the near-poor, their "politicization" becomes more and more likely.

The United States has both the human and the economic resources to move quickly to initiate new programs and expand existing programs that reach the low income population. But it is unlikely that these steps will be taken unless (1) the political leadership necessary to push new legislation emerges and (2) the poor and near-poor population can be mobilized to support these efforts. It is doubtful that the necessary political support will come from the population that is already well off, and since mass support seems necessary if expenditures are to be increased and new programs are to be born, it follows that political support must come from those whose self-interest is directly involved. As is the case for other types of legislation involving special interest groups, the impact of a mobilized interest group can be great, in spite of its relatively small size. This is, perhaps, a hopeful note on which to conclude.

References

Andrzejewski, Stanislaw. *Military Organization and Society* (London: Routledge & Kegan Paul, 1954).

Cutright, Phillips. "Political Structure, Economic Development, 2nd National Social Security Programs, "*American Journal of Sociology*, 70 (March, 1965), pp. 537-50.

——. "Inequality: A Cross-National Analysis," *American Sociological Review*, 32 (August, 1967a), pp. 562-78.

——. "Income Redistribution: A Cross-National Analysis," *Social Forces*, 46 (December, 1967b), pp. 180-90.

—— and James A. Wiley. "Modernization and Political Representation: 1927-1966," Department of Sociology, Vanderbilt University, 1968. (Mimeo.)

Dahrendorf, Ralf. *Class and Class Conflict in Industrial Society* (Stanford: Stanford University Press, 1959).

Davis, Kingsley. *Human Society* (New York: Macmillan Co., 1949).

—— and Wilbert Moore. "Some Principles of Stratification," *American Sociological Review*, 10 (April, 1945), pp. 242-49.

Kolko, Gabriel. *Wealth and Power in America* (New York: Praeger, 1962).

Kravis, Irving B. "International Differences in the Distribution of Income," *The Review of Economics and Statistics*, 42 (November, 1960), pp. 408-16.

Kuznets, Simon. "Quantitative Aspects of the Economic Growth of Nations: VIII, The Distribution of Income by Size," *Economic Development and Cultural Change*, 11, No. 2, Part II (January, 1963).

Lenski, Gerhard. *Power and Privilege: A Theory of Stratification* (New York: McGraw-Hill, 1966).

Mills, C. Wright. *The Power Elite* (New York: Oxford University Press, 1956).

Morgan, James N., Martin H. David, Wilbur J. Cohen, and Harvey E. Brazer. *Income and Welfare in the United States* (New York: McGraw-Hill, 1962).

Oshima, Harry T. "The International Comparison of Size Distribution of Family Incomes with Special Reference to Asia," *The Review of Economics and Statistics*, 44 (November, 1962), pp. 439-45.

Russett, Bruce M., *et al. World Handbook of Political and Social Indicators* (New Haven: Yale University Press, 1964).

Social Security Administration. *Social Security Programs Throughout the World, 1961* (Washington, D. C.: U. S. Government Printing Office, 1961).

——. "International Comparisons of Ratios of Social Security Expenditures to Gross National Product," Research and Statistics Note No. 5 (Washington, D. C.: U. S. Government Printing Office, February 23, 1965).

Epilogue

Shall the Poor Always
Be Impoverished?

S. M. MILLER

and WARNER BLOOMBERG, JR.

☐ FROM TIME TO TIME discussions about the problem of poverty
are embellished by speculation concerning who, if anyone, will be
considered poor in some fabulously affluent future society in which
even those who have least are, by all present standards, well off.
Since the great majority presumably would enjoy what we would
consider a rather sumptuous existence, we might ask the question:
Would not those who had the least—even though that "least" by
then included decent shelter, adequate clothing, fine medical care,
good education, and plenty of the other "necessities"—still consider
themselves to be impoverished and be viewed as such by others?
Though such fantasies as this seem to have little import for con-
tending with contemporary conditions, they underscore the complex interplay between concepts of deprivation, inequality, and
distributive justice which underlie efforts to clarify the nature of
the problem of poverty and to formulate policies that are meaningful as well as workable.

The notion of "relative deprivation" pervades this volume. Mangin points out that some Indians in Latin America do not view
themselves as impoverished even though their lives are a continuous struggle for mere subsistence. Does this mean that we should
refrain from measuring their plight on some general yardstick for
human welfare until they discover how little they have, become
angry about it, and are no longer willing—stoically or even happily
—to expend great effort for the barest existence? Would we, on the
other hand, consider them substantially less impoverished if they
were impressed into forced labor compounds where they received
much more adequate supplies of food, shelter, clothing, and medi-

cal services? Most of the chapters in this book refuse to accept the hidden premise of such a question: that inequitable means for distributing goods and services can regularly and persistently provide an actual distribution that minimizes inequality and thus diminishes poverty understood as relative deprivation. Yet most chapters also accept, if they do not avow, the need for alternative frames of reference with respect to concrete, as against highly abstract, judgmental criteria. We can devise a single yardstick for measuring the respective wealth of nations, but we would not use the same ruler for marking off who is poor in Peru and who is impoverished in the United States.

What makes inter-societal and trans-cultural comparisons and analyses valid, in spite of the difficulties alluded to by Breese, Pflanczer, and others, is not some absolute scale for material well-being, but a set of principles that most of the contributors to this volume implicitly or explicitly assert should be incorporated in every scale we use. Thus, the opening chapter by Haworth and the concluding one by Cutright both require that we consider most of the inequities which may attend the existing patterns of inequality in any society. The total wealth of a nation may set limits on the possible well-being of its citizens, but other factors will determine how that available wealth is distributed among them. Indeed, Haworth from one perspective and Sutton from another explicitly argue that variables other than goods and services must be encompassed within a valid definition of impoverishment. And in terms of both material and non-material criteria, we must consider not only the distance between those who have most and those who have least, but also whether that segment of the population with the least has been left so far behind that it has, in effect, been left out. We can at least imagine societies in which inequality on the various dimensions of citizen welfare does not amount to the virtual exclusion of those who have least (except for individuals and groups who might voluntarily "opt out") from the mainstream of the social order. In such a society the less affluent might still envy those who have more, without considering themselves or being considered "impoverished."

DIMENSIONS OF INEQUALITY

Let us consider, in this regard, six dimensions of inequality. One which has received perhaps the greatest attention is money income. To the extent that well-being must be purchased in the market place, the significance of this variable is apparent and needs little comment. A second is assets; the individual who must subsist on a retirement income is in a far different situation if he owns a mortgage-free home and a late-model car, possesses a substantial supply of creature comforts, and enjoys the cushion of a large savings account than if he begins his exodus from the labor force with none of these assets. A third dimension of inequality is that involving basic services. Roemer and Kisch provide an excellent example of this in their treatment of medical services, forcefully making the point that the organization of medicine as presently constituted has left many people—even many with incomes well above any so-called "poverty line"—deprived of adequate medical care.

These first three dimensions relate essentially to the more tangible side of poverty and affluence. A fourth dimension, education and social mobility, has to do with less material elements in life, although it obviously affects one's ability to obtain income in our kind of society. Education and social level can have a substantial impact on what one seeks and enjoys as the "good things" of life beyond goods and services per se, and especially on the effectiveness with which one is able to use the whole urban environment as a source of both material gratification and good experiences. (It should be added, however, that "schooling" in its present form is often an inadequate source for such education.) A fifth dimension is political participation, a variable whose relevance is underscored in every section of this volume. Even though the United States lags behind other urban-industrial societies in the proportion of its GNP devoted to social security programs, it is nonetheless clear that the distribution of well-being in our society is increasingly affected by political decisions made by those in the governmental apparatus —legislators, executive, administrators, bureaucrats. And the rate of this "politicization" of well-being is likely to increase.

Finally, there is the dimension of social status and self-respect. We have surprising numbers of people in our society whose money incomes seem adequate for at least a moderately decent level of living, but who patently suffer from forms of status anxiety, alienation, and psychologically depriving self-imagery of a character and degree often stereotypically associated with "the poor." Mangin, Haggstrom, and others in this volume have also emphasized that under certain circumstances people who are still materially impoverished may display very positive kinds of self-imagery and self-respect.

The purpose in positing these different dimensions of poverty and well-being in contemporary society is not to deny their very substantial interrelationships. Indeed, strategies for diminishing and perhaps even eliminating involuntary poverty ought to take advantage of such connections. But this is exactly what has not happened. Instead, policies have generally been formulated with little if any regard for the complex of potentiality and constraint that inheres in the interaction between these dimensions. For example, we have barely begun to realize the impact that full provision of needed legal services could have on the situation of the poor city dweller. As the Cahns point out, the protection and implementation of the rights of the poor as citizens and clients in their encounters with various agencies, plus the generation of new conceptions of these rights, could have profound consequences for policy and action in both the public and the private domains. Another example is provided by the relationship between education and material poverty. The actual connection between duration of education and income is much less certain than some of the crudest correlations might seem to suggest. There are too many unemployed and underemployed slum youth who have finished high school and enough cases of dropouts who are making it in the labor force for us to accept the conventional proposition that every year of school can be cashed in at some par value in the employment market. Similarly, if we examine the relationship in the other direction, it is readily apparent that an increase in a family's income does not have an automatic multiplier effect upon the level of formal education the children will attain. Children in families of lower income with parents of higher education tend to go farther in school than those from families in which the parents have less education but enjoy more income. It is essential, therefore, as these examples demonstrate, that we examine the discontinuities as well as the continuities among the various dimensions of poverty and well-being.

As soon as we begin to use such an approach, with all the difficulties in measurement and analysis it obviously entails, we are forced to begin thinking about a mix of programs that would be optimum for meeting the *different kinds* of deprivation which people in our society unnecessarily endure. And since *some* people who have at least minimally adequate money income suffer from *some* of the same kinds of impoverishment as those who lack money income, it becomes possible to imagine and seek to bring into being supporting constituencies for various reforms that at present cannot be coalesced.

This approach also enables us to break away from the preoccupation with "minimum budgets" and to begin to deal more effectively and forthrightly with the question of inequality. We are moved to ask about the extent to which people share in what the society understands to be and is able to provide as "the good life." If one takes 50 per cent of median family income as a standard for defining poverty in the United States it then becomes evident that the percentage of poor families has not declined in the past 20 years. As long as we deal with the income dimension on a budget basis, we will generate programs that deal with the poverty of the past, not the present. Staying within an income and budget framework narrows societal concerns. Systemic changes and institutional reforms—the focus of almost all the chapters in this volume—simply are not stimulated by working and reworking minimum budgets.

Indeed, we need to remind ourselves how much our *definitions* of the poor are implicitly policy statements, especially when we define the poor by the correlates of the population's distribution along a single dimension such as family income. As one lowers the income line, the poor become increasingly different from the rest of the society—more aged, more likely to live in fatherless families, and so on. The tendency then is to see poverty as social pathology rather than societal failure. The level of the poverty line not only determines how many are poor but the characteristics of those who are poor. A broader than income definition of poverty would classify other groups as poor. Methodological procedures and the definitions which they operationalize deeply affect the size and shape of the problem. And there is a world of difference in defining the poor in terms of aged or female-headed families rather than in terms of the employed poor or the welfare poor.

A more adequate, multi-dimensional approach, then, would force us to modify our notions of what it is that concerns us when we worry about poverty and how we should go about measuring it. But this is no mere theoretical exercise since the analyst, whether he likes it or not, today provides much of the imagery and information that feeds into policy decisions. When we talk about paupers or dependents, about clients rather than customers or citizens, about a "culture of poverty" or "the non-transitional poor," we may in no way be biasing our research or weakening our theory but we may be having some important and unwanted effects on how that theory and research is perceived and used by policy-makers. Again, it may be legitimate for social scientists to omit some of the dimensions of poverty from their models for reasons of intellectual or operational convenience; yet when we do so, we should keep in mind that a "non-scientific" consequence of such omission may be that actual human beings get left out of plans and programs intended to bring the whole of our population into the mainstream of life chances in our increasingly affluent society.

SOME IMPLICATIONS OF A MULTI-DIMENSIONAL APPROACH

When we look at the factors listed in the preceding section as *dimensions* of deprivation and well-being rather than as "causes" or "correlates" of poverty, we are forced to evaluate our efforts to reduce impoverishment in terms of outcomes rather than inputs. When only an income measure for poverty is considered, for example, the effectiveness of any "war on poverty" is then likely to be measured by the dollars devoted to it rather than by the distribution of our citizenry along the continua of opportunities and rewards, tangible and intangible.

The import of this is especially evident when we turn to the provision of services. There have been a number of striking examples of the expenditure of large sums in setting up agencies and programs whose actual delivery of services and amenities to the poor has been pitifully small. In most cases the blame is placed on the poor themselves for "their" failure to take advantage of these new opportunities, and all kinds of talk about "under-utilization" arises. Much less discussion, on the other hand, occurs about possible misperception on the part of those establishing such projects as to what is most relevant for the well-being of the poor, and even less consideration is given to the possibility that these programs represent seriously flawed delivery systems. For example, when unfilled openings existed at the beginning of a Head Start program in one major metropolis in 1966, talk about how "the people won't come" started to go the rounds among the professionals. But a study of the situation revealed that of the parents who could have entered children but didn't, 60 per cent hadn't heard of the program, 20 per cent learned about it too late to register, and 20 per cent didn't want to register their children because they felt they should not leave home that early. This sort of thing is by no means unique to our largest cities. In a small city of approximately 100,000 population (with a relatively small ghetto), virtually the same pattern unfolded with a summer Head Start program. Two days before the program was to start, less than half the proposed number of children had been registered. Then a woman who lived in the area, a precinct committee woman who had been hired as a school aide, heard about it and by opening day the class was full.

There are numerous examples of this nature. Agencies that provide legal counsel have no trouble finding poor clients if they provide relevant services, such as handling divorce cases and taking landlords and welfare bureaucrats to court when rights are infringed, and if they are willing to scout the slum neighborhoods for clients who simply may not know how to start talking to a lawyer. But many so-called "legal aid" agencies have not met these two qualifications. Similarly, few programs of consumer education and counseling have been pitched to the problems of the poor rather than of the broad middle class. Viable credit unions have been beyond the reach of the impoverished in terms of required organizational and capitalization bases. Given relevancy and real delivery, ample utilization follows.

Another problem is that a gain on one dimension may require further deprivation on another. More often than not in order to receive the meager cash income provided through most "relief" and "assistance" programs, the individual must submit to conditions and procedures that result in further loss of status and self-respect.

Often the individual must liquidate the few assets he or she may possess apart from such personal property as clothing. To stay in a public housing project may mean not only submitting to a quasi-custodial situation that penetrates into the most private areas of personal conduct, but also giving up chances for employment mobility when a small wage increase would result in losing eligibility to remain in the project. When certain "antipoverty" measures are submitted to this kind of multi-dimensional analysis, we discover that the net gain in well-being is far less than is claimed on the basis of dollar values attached to cash transfers, subsidies, or costs for agency operations.

A multi-dimensional approach to inequality also is conducive to seeing the problem in terms of the "opportunity structures" of the community rather than the "success characteristics" of individuals. This can be well illustrated with respect to jobs as the major source of income. On the one hand, we can take the present structure of opportunities for employment as a given and expend very large amounts of money and personnel resources trying to develop, not just skills, but even attitudes and styles of conduct that are considered necessary to be successful within the system. Those who do not learn these new skills and desired modes of interaction may then be dismissed as "unemployable" and this dimension of opportunity and well-being foreclosed to them. On the other hand, we can say that the labor market is rigid and unwilling to bend its requirements, that employers are unimaginative in terms of new ways of using people, and that government can make better use of some of its money by subsidizing private enterprise, if that is necessary, in order to make it profitable for businesses to employ difficult people. When we posit personal deficiencies as causes, we are then led to programs of social service and amelioration that can at best sustain people above some unacceptable level of material deprivation while the inequality between them and an ever more affluent majority grows greater annually. But when we focus on the provision of opportunities for greater equality for people as they are, then we are forced to consider strategies for changing institutions rather than individuals. In that case, the people whose behavior we would try hardest to change are not the poor but those who make controlling decisions in the various institutional systems which affect the opportunity structure along each of the dimensions of deprivation and well-being.

Much more should be said about employment in this regard. As long as we persist in emphasizing the success characteristics of individuals, given the present structure of opportunity for adequately remunerative employment, we are likely to rationalize what prevails in boom times as "full employment." As a result, the United States accepts a much higher level of unemployment as "normal" than many countries with a lower GNP. We assume that a good growth rate in GNP terms represents full opportunity and therefore "full employment." We do not ask why those at the bottom are not taken up into the labor force even when job vacancies in the aggregate are increasing. We do not ask, for example, if the educational credentials on which we have put ever increasing emphasis in recent decades really have that much to do with successful performance on the job. We have had an inordinate epidemic of "credentialism" in the United States, substituting the inspection of formal evidence of success along one dimension—education—for the more difficult task of determining what a job operationally requires and what opportunity it therefore may provide for one or another individual along the employment-income dimension.

Our experience with the Job Corps illustrates this point. The program, as we know, turned out to be a very expensive approach to developing "success characteristics" among deprived youth. After it had been under way for some time, it became apparent that a noticeable number of the graduates were not getting jobs, or were not getting the jobs they had been trained for. Then another substantial sum of money was spent to induce state employment services to give special attention to Job Corps trainees. Thus a dropout who came in off the street stood at the end of the employment exchange queue; a Neighborhood Youth Corps product moved in ahead of the ordinary dropout; and the Job Corps "graduate" moved to the front of the line. What, then, "explains" the employability of Job Corps products: the new skills and patterns of conduct they learned, the credentials they had acquired—however relevant or irrelevant for the jobs actually obtained—or the influence exerted by the Job Corps as a placement agency on behalf of the youth it claimed to have made "employable"? In any case, such programs for the most part only redistribute the available job opportunities among the jobless; they do not create new opportunities in new kinds of work.

Although assessment is difficult at this early date, one of the most important changes now under way with implications for increasing opportunity and diminishing inequality is that relating to the dimension of political participation. As the chapters by Kravitz, Bloomberg and Rosenstock, and Haggstrom make evident, the demand for "maximum feasible participation" has received only the most equivocal kind of support in the face of some very unequivocal opposition, and extremely little in the way of monetary and personnel resources has been allocated to its implementation. What concerns us here, however, is not any alleged "sociotherapy" or the "power" of the poor, actual or potential. Rather, attention should focus on the initiation of a great, historical political change in the society: the movement in our thinking and policy beyond conceptions of "rights" to conceptions of participation. For "maximum feasible participation" has become the symbolic center of a whole new approach to the political dimension of well-being in our kind of society.

Most of us have long been preoccupied with bringing into existence the policies and apparatus of the welfare state. Now we are beginning to question how such a state functions, how decisions are made within it, the kind of independence and autonomy realized by professionals in the welfare bureaucracy, and the degree and kinds of rights and protection for rights that individuals will have in relation to the welfare state. These issues developed out of a "war on poverty," but they obviously have enormous significance for large numbers of our population whose material well-being has little reduced their apathy, alienation, and often actual helplessness as they confront the governmental apparatus. Proposals for neighborhood councils, resident advisory boards, ombudsmen, effective grievance machinery, and the like are increasingly seen as desirable opportunities for participation on the part of citizens who have not been thought of as "poor." But this only tells us that we have been failing to include the dimension of political participation in our definition of poverty.

This multi-dimensional approach, which helps to draw together the diverse concerns of the chapters in this volume, enables us to develop a new portrayal of "poverty" yielding much broader and deeper conceptions of what we mean when we say people are "impoverished." It leads us to modify our understanding of what "causes" deprivation in its various forms and to strike out in new directions as we seek to extend the conditions of well-being to the whole of the population. Such an approach is implicit in a concern for inequality and is essential for developing policies and programs which can eliminate poverty, in the sense of a "left out" segment of the population, as the inevitable result of inequality.

THIS UNCERTAIN MOMENT

We do not know, of course, that this shall be brought about. It is clearly within the realm of technical and technological possibility. Perhaps because the goal is attainable and yet our progress toward it is presently so halting and uncertain, we are subject to rather wild swings between euphoria and despair. It is particularly essential, therefore, that those whose professional task is research, analysis, and interpretation contribute a continuous focus on main issues and a larger perspective than the annual federal budget. The failure of this volume to provide more that is prospective and prescriptive may thus be a reflection of the current mood and contemporary events preoccupation of so many of the intellectuals who are concerned about the issue of poverty.

We need to remember that only a few years back many social scientists were writing about the poor in the United States, especially the Negro poor, as the most inert in the world. Many of us contemplated the alienation and apathy evident at the moment and concluded that only a long-term commitment by a great number of concerned whites could provide the leadership and numbers adequate for a sustained civil rights movement. Those of us who thought that the Negro would begin to march in the near future and that there would be a great deal of activity and a lot of disturbance were often accused of sentimentalism and unrealism. Indeed, most of the relevant social scientists have been slow in recognizing, accepting, and dealing with these kinds of cataclysmic-crisis nodal points which induce change that only a short time before looked enormously difficult if not impossible to achieve. Why, for example, did most of us fail to anticipate how rapidly Negroes would move to a different outlook in American society? For that matter, having failed to predict the whole development of negritude, of Black Power, of "black is beautiful," how rapidly have we moved to analyze the reasons for this development and for our failure to know it was going to happen?

Uncertainty is not our only hang-up. Not only must we be willing to grapple with our failure to deal with the "unpredictable," but we must also be able to resist demands to simplify the complex and accept the activists' priorities. One can be sure that the multi-dimensional approach suggested here would be attacked as "too theoretical" and "too complicated" for practical application. Such arguments would probably come both from those who sense the magnitude of the implications of such an approach for changing the status quo and from those who equate complexity with inaction. The latter, particularly, would look upon this whole approach as an excuse for detracting from the delivery of money and material to "the poor" while attention is paid to many who are "non-needy." Yet it is absolutely essential that we keep in mind what so many of the contributors to this volume make clear: programs designed narrowly to ameliorate the lot of those who have been left out frequently leave unchanged those structural and systemic characteristics of our society that produce inequalities.

There is hardly an aspect of the problem which will not generate these twin issues of complexity and relevance. One example of this is found in the welter of doctrinaire argument about how to "get the poor organized." The chapter by Bloomberg and Rosenstock could go much further than it does in moving away from simplistic notions of the organizational process and in raising questions about the goals of organization. Some techniques will work with those whom we characterize as the "respectable poor," others with the angriest and most militant, and still others with the most isolated and apathetic. Organizational methods successful with one type are less likely to attract those of the other types. A second aspect relates to the different kinds of goals sought by various poverty programs. In some cases the objective is to achieve material changes which provide amenities directly to the poor. In other instances it is to effect changes in the relationship between the impoverished segment of the community and other groups in society. It is one thing to seek a park for slum children; it is quite another to attempt to place effective members of deprived groups on the park commission. Finally, the differences in cities themselves are important factors, a point suggested but not explored as such in the chapter by Hallman. The Alinsky approach, for example, depends in part for whatever successes it produces on the refractoriness and "stupidity" of established community leadership, much as in the early days of union organization the stupidity of management was one of the organizer's strongest weapons. In this regard we can expect Alinsky to have greater difficulty, say, in Kansas City than in Rochester.

The import of all this is clear: those of us who want to make research and social science analysis relevant to the political dimension must keep in mind the complex interplay between different kinds of goals, different kinds of people, and different kinds of community situations. This position is not likely to be pleasing to those who are on the organizational battlefronts under the banner of one or another doctrine and their reactions will be hard on those of us who may guiltily wish to be judged helpful. But in the end, we will contribute much more to the change process by being in constant tension between relevance and independence of analyses.

To make these observations is not to suggest that social scientists have been completely useless. What we have failed to do, however, is to grapple adequately with the depth of the issues, the new kinds of stratification that are developing, the new goals being generated, the implications over the long term of existing and emerging programs in this country, and the new kinds of indictments of our old behavior. We need hardly be reminded that American society is going through a period of enormous change. All of us, in one way or another, are and will continue to be participants in this process. What we lack is an adequate understanding of these changes and their implications for society. This volume is one effort to contribute to such an understanding. Much, much more is needed. Perhaps the next step is to develop new kinds of relationships between action people and social scientists. We have to learn how to learn from each other.

Supplementary Bibliography

General

ABRAMS, CHARLES. *Man's Struggle for Shelter in an Urbanizing World* (Cambridge, Mass.: The M.I.T. Press, 1965).

AGEE, JAMES and WALKER EVANS. *Let Us Now Praise Famous Men* (Boston: Houghton Mifflin, 1939).

AMERICAN JEWISH COMMITTEE. *The Tyranny of Poverty: A Selected Bibliography* (New York: Institute of Human Relations, 1966).

BAGDIKIAN, BEN H. *In the Midst of Plenty: The Poor in America* (Boston: Beacon Press, 1964).

BREMNER, ROBERT H. *From the Depths: The Discovery of Poverty in America* (New York: New York University Press, 1956).

BRUCE, MAURICE. *The Coming of the Welfare State* (rev. ed.; New York: Schocken Books, 1966).

CHAMBER OF COMMERCE OF THE UNITED STATES. *Concept of Poverty: First Report of the Task Force on Economic Growth and Opportunity* (Washington, D. C.: Chamber of Commerce of the United States, 1965).

CHAVES, ABRAM and R. L. WALD (eds.). *Law and Poverty 1965: Report to the National Conference on Law and Poverty* (Washington, D. C.: National Conference on Law and Poverty, June, 1965).

CHILMAN, CATHERINE and MARVIN SUSSMAN. "Poverty in the United States in the Mid-Sixties," *Journal of Marriage and the Family,* 26 (November, 1964), pp. 391-98.

CLARK, D. "The Poor Identified and Their Prospects Predicted in Context of Poverty War and Housing," *Journal of Housing,* 21 (December, 1964), pp. 578-87.

EDITORS' NOTE: *This bibliography was compiled with the assistance of Mr. Thomas Rose.*

CLARK, HENRY. *The Christian Case Against Poverty* (New York: Association Press, 1965).

COLES, ROBERT. *Children of Crisis: A Study of Courage and Fear* (Boston: Little, Brown, 1967).

CONANT, JAMES B. *Slums and Suburbs* (New York: McGraw-Hill, 1961).

COOK, F. J. *The Welfare State* (New York: Macmillan Company, 1962).

DUNNE, GEORGE H. (ed.). *Poverty in Plenty* (New York: J. P. Kenedy, 1964).

FANON, FRANTZ. *The Wretched of the Earth: A Negro Psychoanalyst's Study of the Problems of Racism and Colonialism in the World Today* (New York: Grove, 1966).

FERMAN, LOUIS A., JOYCE L. KORNBLUH and ALAN HABER (eds.). *Poverty in America* (Ann Arbor: University of Michigan Press, 1965).

FISHMAN, LEO (ed.). *Poverty and Affluence* (New Haven: Yale University Press, 1966).

FORD, JAMES. *The Abolition of Poverty* (New York: Macmillan Company, 1937).

FRIEDMAN, ROSE D. (ed.). *Poverty: Definition and Perspective* (Washington, D. C.: American Enterprise Institute, 1965).

GANS, HERBERT J. "Social and Physical Planning for the Elimination of Urban Poverty," in B. Rosenberg, I. Gerver, and W. Howton (eds.), *Mass Society in Crisis: Social Problems and Social Anthology* (New York: Macmillan Company, 1964), pp. 629-44.

GILBERT, BENTLEY B. *The Evolution of National Insurance in Great Britain: The Origins of the Welfare State* (London: Michael Joseph, 1966).

GLADWIN, THOMAS. *Poverty, U. S. A.* (Boston: Little, Brown, 1967).

GLAZER, NATHAN and DANIEL P. MOYNIHAN. *Beyond the Melting Pot* (Cambridge, Massachusetts: Harvard University Press, 1964).

GORDON, ROBERT A. and MARGARET S. GORDON (eds). *Prosperity and Unemployment* (New York: John Wiley and Sons, 1966).

HENTOFF, NAT. *The New Equality* (New York: Viking Press, 1964).

HERSEY, JOHN. "Our Romance with Poverty," *The American Scholar*, 33 (Autumn, 1964), pp. 525-36.

HUMPHREY, HUBERT H. *War on Poverty* (New York: McGraw-Hill, 1964).

INMAN, BUIS T. "*Rural Poverty: Causes, Extent, Location and Trends* (Washington, D. C.: U. S. Department of Agriculture, 1964).

INSTITUTE OF LABOR AND INDUSTRIAL RELATIONS. *Poverty and Human Resources Abstracts, 1966*, compiled by R. E. Booth, *et al.* (Ann Arbor: Institute of Labor and Industrial Relations, 1966).

JACOBS, PAUL *et al. Dialogue on Poverty* (Indianapolis: Bobbs-Merrill Co., 1967).

JEFFERS, CAMILLE. *Living Poor* (Ann Arbor: Ann Arbor Publishers, 1967).

LEIGHTON, ALEXANDER H. "Poverty and Social Change," *Scientific American*, 212 (May, 1965), pp. 21-27.

LIBRARY OF CONGRESS. *Poverty in the United States: A Bibliography*, prepared by Donna Levine (Washington, D. C.: Library of Congress, 1966).

LUMER, HYMAN. *Poverty: Its Roots and Its Future* (New York: International Publishers, 1965).

MacDONALD, DWIGHT. *Our Invisible Poor* (New York: Sidney Hillman Foundation, 1963).

MacIVER, ROBERT M. (ed.). *The Assault on Poverty and Individual Responsibility* (New York: Harper and Row, 1965).

MEISSNER, HANNA H. (ed.). *Poverty in the Affluent Society* (New York: Harper and Row, 1966).

MENCHER, SAMUEL. *Poor Law to Poverty Program: Economic Security Policy in Britain and the United States* (Pittsburgh: University of Pittsburgh Press, 1967).

MILLER, HERMAN P. (ed.). *Poverty: American Style* (Belmont, California: Wadsworth Publishing Co., 1966).

MORGAN, JOHN S. "The Real Issues in the War on Poverty," *Information*, 14 (April, 1966), pp. 28-32.

ORNATI, OSCAR. "Affluence and the Risk of Poverty," *Social Research*, 31 (Autumn, 1964), pp. 333-46.

———. *Poverty Amid Affluence* (New York: Twentieth Century Fund, 1966).

ORSHANSKY, MOLLIE. "Identification of the Poor," *Monthly Labor Review*, 88 (March, 1965), pp. 300-9.

———. "Recounting the Poor: A Five-Year Review," *Social Security Bulletin*, 29 (April, 1966), pp. 20-38.

PALTIEL, FREDA L. *Poverty: An Annotated Bibliography and References* (Ottowa: The Canadian Welfare Council, 1966).

PARADIS, ADRIAN A. *The Hungry Years: The Story of the Great American Depression* (Philadelphia: Chilton Book Co., 1967).

RICHARDS, LOUISE G. "Consumer Practices of the Poor," *Welfare in Review*, 1 (November, 1965), pp. 1-13.

RIESMAN, DAVID. *Abundance for What?* (Garden City, N. Y.: Doubleday and Co., 1963).

RINGER, PAUL. "Housing and the Poor," *Ontario Housing*, 12 (February, 1966), pp. 10-19.

ROMASCO, ALBERT U. *The Poverty of Abundance: Hoover, the Nation, the Depression* (New York: Oxford University Press, 1965).

SCHLESINGER, BENJAMIN. *Poverty in Canada and the United States: Overview and Annotated Bibliography* (Toronto: University of Toronto Press, 1966).

SCHNORE, LEO F. and HARRY SHARP. "Racial Changes in Metropolitan Areas, 1950-1960," *Social Forces*, 41 (March, 1963), pp. 247-53.

SELIGMAN, BEN B. (ed.). *Poverty as a Public Issue* (New York: Free Press, 1965).

SHONFIELD, ANDREW. *The Attack on World Poverty* (New York: Random House, 1960).

SIMON, ARTHUR R. *Faces of Poverty* (St. Louis: Concordia Publishing House, 1966).

THERNSTROM, STEPHAN. *Poverty and Progress* (Cambridge, Mass.: Harvard University Press, 1964).

Travis, Sophia B. *Refined Poverty Yardstick for Chicago Area* (Chicago: Welfare Council of Metropolitan Chicago, 1965).

Washington Center for Metropolitan Studies. *A Selective Bibliography of Writings on Poverty in the United States* (Washington, D. C.: Washington Center for Metropolitan Studies, 1964).

Will, Robert E. and Harold G. Vatter (eds.). *Poverty in Affluence: The Social, Political and Economic Dimensions of Poverty in the United States* (New York: Harcourt, Brace and World, 1965).

Wyman, George K. *Index of Inadequacy and Indigence in the United States* (Albany: New York State Department of Social Welfare, 1963).

Economic Dimensions
of Poverty

Abel-Smith, Brian and Peter Townsend. *The Poor and the Poorest* (London: G. Bell and Sons, 1965).

Anderson, W. H. L. "Trickling Down: The Relationship between Economic Growth and the Extent of Poverty among American Families," *Quarterly Journal of Economics*, 78 (November, 1964), pp. 511-24.

Ball, Robert M. "Is Poverty Necessary," *Social Security Bulletin*, 28 (August, 1965), pp. 18-24.

Balogh, Thomas. *The Economics of Poverty* (New York: Macmillan Company, 1966).

Becker, Joseph M. (ed.). *In Aid of the Unemployed* (Baltimore: The Johns Hopkins Press, 1965).

Brennan, Michael J. et al. *The Economics of Age* (New York: W. W. Norton and Co., 1967).

Budd, Edward C. (ed.). *Inequality and Poverty* (New York: W. W. Norton and Co., 1967).

Caplovitz, David. *The Poor Pay More: Consumer Practices of Low-Income Families* (New York: Free Press, 1963).

Coleman, John R. (ed.). *The Changing American Economy* (New York: Basic Books, Inc., 1967).

Cummings, Laurie. "The Employed Poor—Their Characteristics and Occupations," *Monthly Labor Review*, 88 (July, 1965), pp. 828-41.

Daniel, Walter G. "The Relative Employment and Income of American Negroes," *The Journal of Negro Education*, 32 (Fall, 1963), pp. 349-57.

Dernberb, Thomas and Kenneth Strand. "Hidden Unemployment 1953-62: A Quantitative Analysis by Age and Sex," *American Economic Review*, 56 (March, 1966), pp. 71-95.

Fisher, Paul. "Social Security and Development Planning: Some Issues," *Social Security Bulletin*, 30 (June, 1967), pp. 13-25.

GALLAWAY, LOWELL. "The Foundations of the War on Poverty," *American Economic Review,* 55 (March, 1965), pp. 122-31.

GOODMAN, LEONARD H. (ed.). *Economic Progress and Social Welfare* (New York: Columbia University Press, 1966).

GORDON, MARGARET S. *The Economics of Welfare Policies* (New York: Columbia University Press, 1963).

GREEN, CHRISTOPHER. *Negative Taxes and the Poverty Problem* (Washington, D. C.: The Brookings Institution, 1967).

GROSSER, C. F. "Community Development Programs Serving the Urban Poor," *Social Work,* 10 (July, 1965), pp. 15-21.

HILDEBRAND, GEORGE H. *Poverty, Income Maintenance and the Negative Income Tax* (Ithaca, New York: New York State School of Industrial and Labor Relations, 1967).

JENNESS, R. A. "Poverty in a Growing Economy," *Canadian Welfare,* 42 (November-December, 1966), pp. 236-43.

KAHN, TOM. *The Economics of Equality* (New York: League for Industrial Democracy, 1965).

KEYSERLING, LEON H. *Progress or Poverty: The U. S. at the Crossroads* (Washington, D. C.: Conference on Economic Progress, 1964).

LAMPMAN, ROBERT J. "Prognosis for Poverty," *Proceedings of 57th Annual Conference of National Tax Association* (September, 1964), pp. 71-81.

——. "Approaches to the Reduction of Poverty," *American Economic Review,* 55 (May, 1965), pp. 521-29.

——. "Ends and Means in the War Against Poverty," in Leo Fishman (ed.), *Poverty Amid Affluence* (New Haven: Yale University Press, 1966), pp. 212-29.

LEBERGOTT, STANLEY (ed.). *Men Without Work: The Economics of Unemployment* (Englewood Cliffs, N. J.: Prentice-Hall, 1965).

LEVITAN, SAR. *Federal Manpower Policies and Programs to Combat Unemployment* (Kalamazoo, Michigan: W. E. Upjohn Institute for Employment Research, 1964).

——. *Federal Aid to Depressed Areas* (Baltimore: The Johns Hopkins Press, 1964).

LIEBERSON, STANLEY and GLENN FUGUITT. "Negro-White Occupational Differences in the Absence of Discrimination," *American Journal of Sociology,* 73 (September, 1967), pp. 188-201.

MARCH, MICHAEL S. "Poverty: How Much Will the War Cost?" *Social Service Review,* 39 (June, 1965), pp. 141-54.

MILLER, HERMAN P. *Rich Man, Poor Man: A Study of Income Distribution in America* (New York: Crowell, 1964).

——. *Income Distribution in the United States* (Washington, D. C.: U. S. Government Printing Office, 1966).

MYRDAL, GUNNAR. *Challenge to Affluence* (New York: Vintage Books, 1963).

OKUN, ARTHUR M. (ed.). *The Battle Against Unemployment* (New York: W. W. Norton and Co., 1965).

ROSS, ARTHUR M. (ed.). *Unemployment and the American Economy* (New York: John Wiley and Sons, 1964).

—— and Herbert Hill (eds.). *Employment, Race and Poverty* (New York: Harcourt, Brace and World, 1967).

Schultz, T. W. "Investing in Poor People: An Economist's View," *American Economic Review*, 55 (May, 1965), pp. 510-20.

Schwartz, Edward E. "A Way to End the Means Test," *Social Work*, 9 (July, 1964), pp. 3-13.

Sexton, Patricia C. *Education and Income: Inequalities of Opportunity in Our Public Schools* (New York: Viking Press, 1961).

Shultz, George P. and Arnold R. Weber. *Strategies for the Displaced Worker* (New York: Harper and Row, 1966).

Smith, A. D. "Minimum Wages and the Distribution of Income with Special Reference to Developing Countries," *International Labour Review*, 96 (August, 1967), pp. 129-50.

Soltow, Lee. *Toward Income Equality in Norway* (Madison, Wisconsin: University of Wisconsin Press, 1965).

Somers, Gerald G. "Retraining: An Evaluation of Gains and Costs," in *Conference on Unemployment Research* (New York: John Wiley and Sons, 1964).

Theobald, Robert. *The Challenge of Abundance* (New York: C. N. Potter, 1961).

——. *Free Men and Free Markets* (New York: C. N. Potter, 1963).

—— (ed.). *The Guaranteed Income* (Garden City, N. Y.: Doubleday and Co., 1965).

Walsh, Mary E. *Marginal Employability* (Washington, D. C.: Bureau of Social Science Research, Catholic University of America, January, 1962).

Weisbrod, Burton A. (ed.). *The Economics of Poverty: An American Paradox* (Englewood Cliffs, N. J.: Prentice-Hall, 1966).

Socio-cultural Dimensions

Back, Kurt W. *Slums, Projects and People: Social Psychological Problems of Relocation in Puerto Rico* (Durham, North Carolina: Duke University Press, 1962).

Bainbridge, John. "The Job Corps," *New Yorker*, 42 (May 21, 1966), pp. 112-18.

Batchelder, Alan. "Poverty: The Special Case of the Negro," *American Economic Review*, 55 (May, 1965), pp. 530-40.

Beck, John M. and Richard W. Saxe. *Teaching the Culturally Disadvantaged Pupil* (Springfield, Illinois: Charles C. Thomas, 1965).

Beiser, Morton. "Poverty, Social Disintegration and Personality," *The Journal of Social Issues*, 21 (January, 1965), pp. 56-78.

Besner, Arthur. "Economic Deprivation and Family Patterns," *Welfare in Review*, 3 (September, 1965), pp. 20-28.

BLOOM, BENJAMIN S., ALLISON DAVIS, and ROBERT HESS. *Compensatory Education for Cultural Deprivation* (New York: Holt, Rinehart, and Winston, 1965).

BURGESS, M. ELAINE. "Some Implications of Social Change for Dependency among Lower Class Families," *American Journal of Orthopsychiatry*, 34 (October, 1964), pp. 895-906.

———. "Poverty and Dependency: Some Selected Characteristics," *Journal of Social Issues*, 21 (January, 1965), pp. 79-97.

CARPER, LAURA. "The Negro Family and the Moynihan Report," *Dissent*, 13 (March-April, 1966), pp. 133-40.

CHILMAN, CATHERINE S. "Child Rearing and Family Relationship Patterns of the Very Poor," *Welfare in Review*, 3 (January, 1965), pp. 9-19.

———. *Growing Up Poor* (Washington, D. C.: Department of Health, Education and Welfare, 1966).

———. "Poverty and Family Planning in the United States," *Welfare in Review*, 5 (April, 1967), pp. 3-15.

COSER, LEWIS A. "The Sociology of Poverty: To the Memory of George Simmel," *Social Problems*, 13 (Fall, 1965), pp. 140-48.

DAVIS, ALLISON. *The Culture of the Slum* (New York: Mobilization for Youth, 1963).

DAVIS, MARY E. "The Misfit—The Involuntary Non-Producer," *Public Welfare*, 23 (October, 1965), pp. 251-58.

DWORKIN, ANTHONY G. "Stereotypes and Self-images Held by Native-born and Foreign-born Mexican-Americans," *Sociology and Social Research*, 49 (January, 1965), pp. 214-24.

FISHER, S. "Essay Review—Negro Life and Social Process," *Social Problems*, 13 (Winter, 1966), pp. 343-53.

FRAZIER, FRANKLIN E. *The Negro Family in the United States* (Chicago: University of Chicago Press, 1966).

GANS, HERBERT. *The Urban Villagers* (New York: Free Press, 1962).

———. "The Subcultures of the Working Class, Lower Class, and Middle Class," in Harry L. Miller and Marjorie B. Smiley (eds.), *Education in the Metropolis* (New York: Free Press, 1967), pp. 136-67.

GITTLER, JOSEPH B. (ed.). *Understanding Minority Groups* (New York: John Wiley and Sons, 1964).

GLADWIN, THOMAS. "The Anthropologist's View of Poverty," in *Social Welfare Forum, 1961*, by the National Conference on Social Welfare (New York: Columbia University Press, 1961), pp. 73-86.

GORDON, EDMUND W. "A Review of Programs of Compensatory Education," *American Journal of Orthopsychiatry*, 25 (July, 1965), pp. 640-51.

GOTTLIEB, DAVID. *Goal Aspirations and Goal Fulfillments: Differences Between Deprived and Affluent American Adolescents* (East Lansing: Michigan State University, 1964).

HABER, ALAN. "The American Underclass," *Poverty and Human Resources Abstracts*, 2 (May-June, 1967), pp. 5-19.

HARE, NATHAN. "Recent Trends in the Occupational Mobility of Negroes, 1930-1960: An Intracohort Analysis," *Social Forces*, 44 (December, 1965), pp. 166-73.

Heller, Celia S. *Mexican-American Youth: Forgotten Youth at the Crossroads* (New York: Random House, 1966).

Henderson, George. "Poor Southern Whites: A Neglected Urban Problem," *Journal of Secondary Education*, 41 (March, 1966), pp. 111-14.

Herzog, Elizabeth. "Some Assumptions about the Poor," *Social Service Review*, 37 (December, 1963), pp. 389-402.

Hess, Robert D. "Educability and Rehabilitation: The Future of the Welfare Class," *Journal of Marriage and the Family*, 26 (November, 1964), pp. 422-29.

Hines, Ralph H. "Social Expectations and Cultural Deprivation," *The Journal of Negro Education*, 33 (Spring, 1944), pp. 136-42.

Honigman, John J. "Psychiatry and the Culture of Poverty," *The Kansas Journal of Sociology*, 1 (Fall, 1965), pp. 162-66.

Hunt, Eleanor P. "Infant Mortality and Poverty Areas," *Welfare in Review*, 5 (August-September, 1967), pp. 1-12.

Hunter, David R. *The Slums: Challenge and Response* (New York: Free Press, 1964).

Irelan, Lola M. (ed.). *Low Income Life Styles* (Washington, D. C.: U. S. Government Printing Office, 1966).

—— and Arthur Besner. "Low-Income Outlook on Life," *Welfare in Review*, 3 (September, 1965), pp. 13-19.

Keller, Suzanne. "The Social World of the Urban Slum Child: Some Early Findings," *American Journal of Orthopsychiatry*, 33 (October, 1963), pp. 823-31.

———. *The American Lower Class Family* (Albany, New York: New York State Division for Youth, 1965).

Keniston, Kenneth. *The Uncommitted: Alienated Youth in American Society* (New York: Harcourt, Brace and World, 1965).

Key, William H. *When People Are Forced to Move* (Topeka, Kansas: The Menninger Foundation, 1967).

Kriesberg, Louis. "The Relationship Between Socio-Economic Rank and Behavior," *Social Problems*, 10 (Spring, 1963), pp. 334-53.

Larson, Richard F., and Sara S. Sutker. "Value Differences and Value Consensus by Socio-Economic Levels," *Social Forces*, 44 (June, 1966), pp. 563-69.

Levinson, P. "Chronic Dependency: A Conceptual Analysis," *Social Service Review*, 38 (December, 1964), pp. 371-81.

Lewis, Hylan. *The Contemporary Urban Syndrome* (Washington, D. C.: Howard University, 1964).

—— and Camille Jeffers. *Poverty and Behavior of Low-Income Families* (Chicago: American Orthopsychiatric Association, 1964).

Lewis, Oscar. *Five Families* (New York: Basic Books, 1959).

———. *The Children of Sanchez* (New York: Random House, 1961).

———. "The Culture of Poverty," *Trans-Action*, 1 (November, 1963), pp. 17-19.

———. *La Vida: A Puerto Rican Family in the Culture of Poverty—San Juan and New York* (New York: Random House, 1966).

Lipton, Aaron. "Cultural Deprivation," *Journal of Educational Sociology*, 36 (September, 1962), pp. 17-19.

LYFORD, JOSEPH. *The Airtight Cage: A Study of New York's West Side* (New York: Harper and Row, 1966).

MACKLER, BERNARD and M. G. GIDDINGS. "Cultural Deprivation: A Study in Mythology," *Teachers College Record,* 66 (April, 1965), pp. 608-13.

McCORMICK, M. J. "Human Values and the Poor," *Social Casework,* 46 (March, 1965), pp. 132-41.

MILLER, HERMAN P. *Poverty and the Negro* (Los Angeles: University of California Institute of Government and Public Affairs, 1965).

MILLER, S. M. and MARTIN REIN. "Poverty and Social Change," *American Child,* 46 (March, 1964), pp. 10-15.

—— and FRANK RIESSMAN. "The Working-Class Subculture: A New View," *Social Problems,* 9 (Summer, 1961), pp. 86-97.

MOLES, O. C., JR. "Training Children in Low-Income Families for School," *Welfare in Review,* 3 (June, 1965), pp. 1-11.

MORRILL, RICHARD L. "Negro Ghetto: Problems and Alternatives," *Geographical Review,* 55 (July, 1965), pp. 339-61.

MOYNIHAN, DANIEL P. "Employment, Income, and the Ordeal of the Negro Family," *Daedalus,* 94 (Fall, 1965), pp. 745-70.

PARSONS, TALCOTT and KENNETH CLARK (eds.). *The Negro American* (Boston: Houghton Mifflin, 1966).

RADIN, NORMA and CONSTANCE KAMLL. "The Child-Rearing Attitudes of Disadvantaged Negro Mothers and Some Educational Implications," *The Journal of Negro Education,* 34 (Spring, 1965), pp. 138-46.

RAINWATER, LEE. "Crucible of Identity: The Negro Lower Class Family," *Daedalus,* 95 (Winter, 1966), pp. 172-217.

——. *And the Poor Get Children* (Chicago: Quadrangle Books, 1967).

RAYMOND, CHARLES. *Up From Appalachia* (New York: Follett Publishing Co., 1966).

RIESSMAN, FRANK. *The Culturally Deprived Child* (New York: Harper and Row, 1962).

——. "Low-Income Culture: The Strength of the Poor," *Journal of Marriage and the Family,* 24 (November, 1964), pp. 417-21.

ROACH, JACK L. "Sociological Analysis and Poverty," *American Journal of Sociology,* 71 (July, 1965), pp. 68-75.

—— and O. R. GURSSLIN. "An Evaluation of the Concept 'Culture of Poverty,'" *Social Forces,* 45 (March, 1967), pp. 383-92.

RUBEL, ARTHUR J. *Across the Tracks: Mexican Americans in a Texas City* (Austin: University of Texas Press, 1966).

SCALES, ELDRIDGE E. "Regional-Racial Differences in Income and Level of Education," *The Journal of Negro Education,* 34 (Fall, 1965), pp. 454-58.

SCHLESINGER, BENJAMIN. *The Multi-Problem Family: A Review and Annotated Bibliography* (Toronto: University of Toronto Press, 1965).

SCHNEIDERMAN, LEONARD. "Value Orientation Preferences of Chronic Relief Recipients," *Social Work,* 9 (July, 1964), pp. 13-18.

SCHORR, ALVIN L. "The Nonculture of Poverty," *American Journal of Orthopsychiatry,* 34 (October, 1964), pp. 907-11.

SCHWITZGEBEL, RALPH. *Streetcorner Research* (Cambridge, Mass.: Harvard University Press, 1964).

Seabrook, Jeremy. *The Underprivileged* (London: Longmans, Green and Co., 1967).

Sexton, Patricia P. *Education and Income: Inequalities in Our Public Schools* (New York: Viking Press, 1961).

———. *Spanish Harlem: An Anatomy of Poverty* (New York: Harper and Row, 1965).

Smythe, Hugh H. and James A. Moss. "Human Relations Among the Culturally Deprived: The Cultural Atmosphere of Depressed Areas," *Journal of Human Relations,* 13 (Fourth Quarter, 1965), pp. 524-37.

Spear, Allan H. *Black Chicago: The Making of a Negro Ghetto, 1890-1920* (Chicago: University of Chicago Press, 1967).

Taeuber, Karl E. and Alma F. Taeuber. "The Negro as an Immigrant Group," *American Journal of Sociology,* 69 (January, 1964), pp. 374-82.

—— and ——. *Negroes in Cities: Residential Segregation and Neighborhood Change* (Chicago: Aldine Publishing Co., 1965).

Thomas, Piri. *Down These Mean Streets* (New York: Alfred A. Knopf, 1967).

Thursz, Daniel. "Social Aspects of Poverty," *Public Welfare,* 25 (July, 1967), pp. 179-87.

Wakefield, Dan. *Island in the City* (New York: Corinth Books, 1957).

Weaver, Robert C. *The Urban Complex: Human Values in Urban Life* (Garden City, N. Y.: Doubleday and Co., 1964).

Weinandy, Janet E. *Families Under Stress* (New York: Syracuse University Press, 1962).

Wetzel, James R. and Susan S. Holland. "Poverty Areas in Our Major Cities," *Monthly Labor Review,* 89 (October, 1966), pp. 1105-10.

Whyte, Donald R. "Sociological Aspects of Poverty: A Conceptual Analysis," *Canadian Review of Sociology and Anthropology,* 2 (November, 1965), pp. 175-90.

Participation and Political Action

Adamic, Louis. *Dynamite: The Story of Class Violence in America* (New York: Viking Press, 1934).

Alinsky, Saul D. "The War on Poverty: Political Pornography," *Journal of Social Issues,* 21 (January, 1965), pp. 41-47.

Besag, Frank. *Anatomy of a Riot: Buffalo 1967* (Buffalo: University of Buffalo Press, 1967).

Brager, John and Harry Sprecht. "Mobilizing the Poor for Social Action," in *Social Welfare Forum, 1965* (New York: Columbia University Press, 1965), pp. 197-211.

Brager, George A. and Francis P. Purcell (eds.). *Community Action Against Poverty* (New Haven: College and University Press, 1967).

BROOKS, MICHAEL P. "The Community Action Program as a Setting for Applied Research," *Journal of Social Issues*, 21 (January, 1965), pp. 29-40.

CARMICHAEL, STOKELY and CHARLES V. HAMILTON. *Black Power: The Politics of Liberation in America* (New York: Vintage Books, 1967).

CLARK, KENNETH B. *Youth in the Ghetto: A Study of the Consequences of Powerlessness and a Blueprint for Change* (New York: Harlem Youth Opportunities Unlimited, 1964).

——. *Dark Ghetto: Dilemmas of Social Power* (New York: Harper and Row, 1965).

COHEN, HENRY. "Community Action: Instrument of Change," *American Child*, 47 (November, 1965), pp. 20-23.

COHEN, JERRY and W. S. MURPHY. *Burn, Baby Burn! The Watts Riot* (New York: Avon Books, 1966).

COMER, JAMES P. "Social Power of the Negro," *Scientific American*, 216 (April, 1967), pp. 21-27.

COSER, LEWIS A. *Continuities in the Study of Social Conflict* (New York: Free Press, 1967).

DAHRENDORF, RALF. *Class and Class Conflict in Industrial Society* (Stanford: Stanford University Press, 1959).

FARMER, JAMES. *Freedom When?* (New York: Random House, 1966).

FARRELL, GREGORY R. *A Climate of Change: Community Action in New Haven* (New Brunswick, New Jersey: Rutgers, The State University of New Jersey, 1965).

FREEMAN, HOWARD E. and CLARENCE C. SHERWOOD. "Research in Large Scale Intervention Programs," *Journal of Social Issues*, 21 (January, 1965), pp. 11-28.

GANS, HERBERT J. "Redefining the Settlement's Function for the War on Poverty," *Social Work*, 9 (October, 1964), pp. 3-12.

GOLD, HARRY and FRANK A. SCARPETTI. *Combatting Social Problems: Techniques of Intervention* (New York: Holt, Rinehart and Winston, 1967).

GORDON, MARGARET S. (ed.). *Poverty in America* (San Francisco: Chandler Publishing Co., 1965).

GROSSER, CHARLES F. "Local Residents as Mediators between Middle-Class Professional Workers and Lower-Class Clients," *Social Service Review*, 40 (March, 1966), pp. 56-63.

HARRINGTON, MICHAEL. *The Politics of Poverty* (New York: League for Industrial Democracy, 1965).

HAYDEN, TOM. *Rebellion in Newark* (New York: Random House, 1967).

HEFFERMAN, JOSEPH. "Social Action and the Poverty Problem," *The Social Worker*, 33 (July, 1965), pp. 169-75.

JACOBS, PAUL. *Prelude to Riot: A View of Urban America from the Bottom* (New York: Random House, 1968).

JANOWITZ, MORRIS. *Social Control of Escalated Riots* (Chicago: University of Chicago Center for Policy Study, 1968).

KILLIAN, LEWIS and CHARLES GRIGG. *Racial Crisis in America: Leadership in Conflict* (Englewood Cliffs, N. J.: Prentice-Hall, 1964).

KING, CLARENCE. *Working with People in Community Action* (New York: Association Press, 1965).

KOLKO, GABRIEL. *Wealth and Power in America* (New York: Frederick A. Praeger Publishers, 1962).

LAING, RONALD D. *The Politics of Experience* (New York: Pantheon Books, 1967).

LEVY, CHARLES S. "Occupational Hazards for Community Organization Workers in Community Action Programs," *The Jewish Social Work Forum*, 3 (Fall, 1965), pp. 61-67.

LIEBERSON, STANLEY and ARNOLD R. SILVERMAN. "The Precipitants and Underlying Conditions of Race Riots," *American Sociological Review*, 30 (December, 1965), pp. 887-98.

MARRIS, PETER and MARTIN REIN. *Dilemmas of Social Reform: Poverty and Community Action in the United States* (New York: Atherton Press, 1967).

MAY, EDGAR. "The Disjointed Trio: Poverty, Politics, and Power," *The Social Worker*, 22 (April-May, 1964), pp. 4-17.

———. "Clients as Participants," *Public Welfare*, 24 (January, 1966), pp. 50-64.

McCABE, ALICE R. "Social Policy Issues and the Family Agency: An Action Oriented Program," *Social Casework*, 46 (October, 1965), pp. 483-89.

——— and DORIS DECORATO. "Helping Disadvantaged Families Learn to Help Themselves," *American Journal of Orthopsychiatry*, 35 (March, 1965), pp. 308-9.

MENDES, RICHARD. *Bibliography on Community Organizations for Citizen Participation in Voluntary Democratic Associations* (Washington, D. C.: President's Commission on Juvenile Delinquency and Youth Crime, June, 1965).

MERRIFIELD, ELEANOR. "Implications of the Poverty Program: The Caseworker's View," *Social Service Review*, 39 (September, 1965), pp. 294-99.

MILLER, S. M. and MARTIN REIN. "Escalating the War on Poverty," *American Child*, 47 (March, 1965), pp. 12-18.

MOGULOF, M. B. "Involving Low-Income Neighborhoods in Anti-Delinquency Programs," *Social Work*, 10 (October, 1965), pp. 51-57.

NELSON, EUGENE. *Huelga: The First Hundred Days of the Great Delano Grape Strike* (Delano, California: Farm Workers Press, 1966).

ORUM, ANTHONY. "Reappraisal of the Social and Political Participation of Negroes," *American Journal of Sociology*, 72 (July, 1966), pp. 32-46.

PECK, SIDNEY M. *The Rank and File Leader* (New Haven: College and University Press, 1966).

PIVEN, FRANCES. "Participation of Residents in Neighborhood Community Action Programs," *Social Work*, 11 (January, 1966), pp. 73-80.

RACHLIS, DAVID. "Voluntary Agencies and Community Action Programs: A Case Example," in *Social Work Practice 1965* (New York: Columbia University Press, 1965), pp. 16-29.

REIN, MARTIN and S. M. MILLER. "Poverty, Policy and Purpose: The Axes of Choice," *Poverty and Human Resources Abstracts*, 1 (March-April, 1966), pp. 9-22.

—— and FRANK RIESSMAN. "A Strategy for Anti-Poverty Community Action Programs," *Social Work*, 11 (April, 1966), pp. 3-13.

REYNOLDS, HARRY W., JR. "Placing the Poor in the Poverty Program," *Midwest Review of Public Administration*, 1 (August, 1967), pp. 87-95.

RIESSMAN, FRANK. "Self-Help Among the Poor: New Styles to Social Action," *Trans-Action*, 2 (September-October, 1965), pp. 32-37.

—— and S. M. MILLER. "Social Change Versus the 'Psychiatric World View,'" *American Journal of Orthopsychiatry*, 34 (January, 1964), pp. 29-38.

—— and MARTIN REIN. "The Third Force: An Anti-Poverty Ideology," *American Child*, 47 (November, 1965), pp. 10-14.

ROSE, ARNOLD M. (issue editor). "The Negro Protest," *The Annals of the American Academy of Political and Social Science*, 357 (January, 1965), pp. 1-126.

RUSTIN, BAYARD. "From Protest to Politics," in Louis A. Ferman *et al.* (eds.), *Poverty in America* (Ann Arbor: University of Michigan Press, 1965), pp. 457-69.

SCHALLER, LYLE E. *Community Organization: Conflict and Reconciliation* (Nashville: Abingdon Press, 1966).

SCHNEIDERMAN, LEONARD. "A Social Action Model for the Social Work Practitioners," *Social Casework*, 46 (October, 1965), pp. 490-93.

SEGAL, RONALD. *The Race War: The World Wide Clash of White and Non-White* (New York: Bantam Books, 1968).

SHIFFMAN, BERNARD M. "Involvement of Low-Income People in Planned Community Change," in *Social Work Practice 1965* (New York: Columbia University Press, 1965), pp. 188-205.

SHOGAN, ROBERT and TOM CRAIG. *The Detroit Race Riot: A Study in Violence* (Philadelphia: Chilton Book Co., 1964).

SHOSTAK, ARTHUR B. "Containment, Co-Optation, or Co-Determination?" *American Child*, 47 (November, 1965), pp. 15-19.

———. "Promoting Participation of the Poor: Philadelphia's Anti-Poverty Program," *Social Work*, 11 (January, 1966), pp. 64-72.

SILBERMAN, CHARLES E. *Crisis in Black and White* (New York: Vintage Books, 1964).

SLAVIN, SIMON. "Community Action and Institutional Change," in *Social Welfare Forum, 1965* (New York: Columbia University Press, 1965), pp. 147-61.

STEINER, GILBERT Y. *Social Insecurity: The Poltics of Welfare* (Chicago: Rand McNally, 1966).

WARREN, ROLAND L. "The Interaction of Community Decision Organizations: Some Basic Concepts and Needed Research," *Social Service Review*, 41 (September, 1967), pp. 261-70.

WASKOW, ARTHUR I. *From Race Riot to Sit-in, 1919 and the 1960's* (Garden City, N. Y.: Doubleday and Co., 1966).

WATERMAN, KENNETH S. "Local Issues in the Urban War on Poverty," *Social Work*, 11 (January, 1966), pp. 57-63.

WEISS, DAVID. "Who Is the Enemy in the War Against Poverty?" *The Social Worker*, 34 (February, 1966), pp. 52-53.

Wickenden, Elizabeth. "What Can a Community Do about Poverty?" *Child Welfare,* 44 (January, 1965), pp. 5-9.

Wilson, Charles R. "The Church and Social Change," *Church in Metropolis,* 7 (Fall, 1965), pp. 19-23.

Woodsworth, D. E. "Community Funds and the War on Poverty," *Canadian Welfare,* 42 (March-April, 1966), pp. 54-63.

X, Malcolm. *Malcolm X Speaks* (New York: Merit, 1965).

Zinn, Howard. *SNCC: The New Abolitionists* (Boston: Beacon, 1964).

Health and Welfare

Anderson, O. W., P. Collette, and J. J. Feldman. *Changes in Family Medical Care Expenditures and Voluntary Health Insurance: A Five Year Resurvey* (Cambridge, Mass.: Harvard University Press, 1963).

Barnhart, Gilbert R. "A Note on the Impact of Public Health Service Research on Poverty," *Journal of Social Issues,* 21 (January, 1965), pp. 142-50.

Bernard, Sidney E. "Providing Comprehensive Medical Care," *Public Welfare,* 25 (October, 1967), pp. 286-300.

Burns, Eveline M. *Needed Changes in Welfare Programs* (Los Angeles: University of California at Los Angeles, Institute of Government and Public Affairs, 1965).

Goffman, Irving J. *Some Fiscal Aspects of Public Welfare in Canada* (Toronto: Canadian Tax Foundation, 1965).

Grant, Murray. "Poverty and Public Health," *Public Welfare,* 23 (April, 1965), pp. 111-15.

Hanft, Ruth S. "National Health Expenditures 1950-1965," *Social Security Bulletin,* 30 (February, 1967), pp. 3-13.

Hollingshead, August B. and Frederick C. Redlich. *Social Class and Mental Illness: A Community Study* (New York: John Wiley and Sons, 1958).

Kagan, Morris. "AFDC A Response to Poverty," *Public Welfare,* 23 (July, 1965), pp. 193-96.

Kahn, Alfred J. "The Societal Context of Social Work Practice," *Social Work,* 10 (October, 1965), pp. 145-56.

Klarman, Herbert E. *The Economics of Health* (New York: Columbia University Press, 1965).

Lepper, Mark H. "Health Planning for the Urban Community: The Neighborhood Health Center," *Public Welfare,* 25 (April, 1967), pp. 141-49.

Lourie, Norman V. "Poverty," in Nathan E. Cohen (ed.), *Social Work and Social Problems* (New York: National Association of Social Workers, 1964), pp. 1-41.

May, Edgar. *The Wasted Americans: Cost of our Welfare Dilemma* (New York: Harper and Row, 1964).

McEntire, Davis and Joanne Haworth. "The Two Functions of Public Welfare: Income Maintenance and Social Services," *Social Work*, 12 (January, 1967), pp. 22-31.

Merriam, Ida C. "Social Welfare Expenditures 1964-65," *Social Security Bulletin*, 28 (October, 1965), pp. 3-16.

———. "Social Welfare Expenditures 1929-67," *Social Security Bulletin*, 30 (December, 1967), pp. 3-17.

Miller, S. M. and Martin Rein. "Change, Ferment, and Ideology in the Social Services," in *Education for Social Work, 1964* (New York: Council on Social Work Education, 1964), pp. 3-26.

Morgan, James N., M. H. David, Wilbur Cohen, and H. E. Brazer. *Income and Welfare in the United States* (New York: McGraw-Hill, 1962).

Muller, C. "Income and Receipt of Medical Care," *American Journal of Public Health*, 55 (April, 1965), pp. 510-21.

Osborne, John E. "Canada Combats Poverty Through Social Policy," *Public Welfare*, 24 (April, 1966), pp. 131-39.

Page, William J., Jr. "Three Dimensions of Expectations of Social Welfare Programs," *Public Welfare*, 25 (April, 1967), pp. 117-21.

Perkins, Ellen J. "Unmet Need in Public Assistance," *Social Security Bulletin*, 23 (April, 1960), pp. 3-11.

Pond, M. A. "Interrelationships of Poverty and Disease," *Public Health Reports*, 76 (November, 1961), pp. 967-73.

Rein, Martin and S. M. Miller (eds.). *Challenge to the Social Services* (New York: John Wiley and Sons, 1965).

Rice, Virginia. "Social Class as a Dimension in Casework Judgment," *Smith College Studies in Social Work*, 34 (October, 1963), pp. 30-48.

Riessman, Frank. "The Revolution in Social Work: The New Non-Professional," *Trans-Action*, 2 (November-December, 1964), pp. 12-17.

———, Jerome Cohen, and Arthur Pearl (eds.). *Mental Health of the Poor* (New York: Free Press, 1964).

Simmons, Savilla M. "Social Services for the Mobile Poor in Urban Areas," in *Social Work Practice 1965* (New York: Columbia University Press, 1965), pp. 162-74.

Suchman, E. A. "Social Factors in Medical Deprivation," *American Journal of Public Health*, 55 (November, 1965), pp. 1725-33.

Therkildsen, Paul T. *Public Assistance and American Values* (Albuquerque: University of New Mexico Press, 1964).

Thurby, Jean A. and Julia C. Attwood. *Public Assistance Medical Care—An Annotated Bibliography, 1958-1963* (Ann Arbor: University of Michigan School of Public Health, 1967).

Webber, Irving L. (ed.). *Medical Care under Social Security: Potentials and Problems* (Gainesville, Florida: University of Florida Press, 1966).

Wedemeyer, John M. "Advancing Equal Opportunity by Changing the System," *Public Welfare*, 24 (April, 1966), pp. 123-31.

Weinandy, Janet. "Casework with Tenants in a Public Housing Project," *Journal of Marriage and the Family*, 26 (November, 1964), pp. 452-56.

Wilner, Daniel M. *et al. The Housing Environment and Family Life: A Longitudinal Study of the Effects of Housing on Morbidity and Mental Health* (Baltimore: The Johns Hopkins Press, 1962).

Yerby, Alonzo. "The Problems of Medical Care for Indigent Populations," *American Journal of Public Health*, 55 (August, 1965), pp. 1212-16.

Zimbalist, Sidney E. "Drawing the Poverty Line," *Social Work*, 9 (July, 1964), pp. 19-26.

Law and the Poor

Allison, Junius L. "Poverty and the Administration of Justice in the Criminal Courts," *Journal of Criminal Law, Criminology, and Police Science*, 55 (June, 1964), pp. 241-45.

Bellow, Gary. *Selected Readings in Law and Poverty* (Washington, D. C.: Office of the Attorney General, 1965).

Cahn, Edgar S. and Jean Camper Cahn. "What Price Justice: The Civilian Perspective Revisited," *Notre Dame Lawyer*, 41 (Symposium, 1966), pp. 927-60.

Caplin, G. M. and Earl Johnson, Jr. "Neighborhood Lawyer Programs: An Experiment in Social Change," *University of Miami Law Review*, 20 (Fall, 1965), pp. 184-94.

Carlin, Jerome E. and Jan Howard. "Legal Representation and Class Justice," *UCLA Law Review*, 12 (November, 1965), pp. 381-477.

———, ———, and Sheldon L. Messinger. "Civil Justice and the Poor: Issues for Sociological Research," *Law and Society Review*, 1, No. 1 (November, 1966), pp. 9-89.

Darsen, Norman (ed.). *Housing for the Poor: Rights—Remedies* (New York: New York University School of Law, 1967).

Doverman, Max. "Today's Legal Revolution: The Reformation of Social Welfare Practice," *Social Service Review*, 40 (June, 1966), pp. 152-68.

Goldfarb, R. L. "Lawyers and the War Against Poverty," *American Bar Association Journal*, 50 (December, 1964), pp. 1152-54.

Grosser, Charles F. and Edward V. Sparer. "Legal Services for the Poor: Social Work and Social Justice," *Social Work*, 11 (January, 1966), pp. 81-87.

Hadl, Robert. "The Supreme Court and the Poor," *The Prison Journal*, 45 (Spring-Summer, 1965), pp. 7-15.

Handler, Joel F. "Controlling Official Behavior in Welfare Administration," *California Law Review*, 54 (May, 1966), pp. 479-510.

Masotti, Louis H. and Jerome R. Corsi. "Legal Assistance for the Poor," *Journal of Urban Law*, 44 (Spring, 1967), pp. 483-502.

Oaks, D. H. and W. Lehman. *A Criminal Justice System and the Indigent* (Chicago: University of Chicago Press, 1967).

Oswald, Russell G. "Poverty and Parole," *The Prison Journal*, 45 (Spring-Summer, 1965), pp. 36-42.

Paulsen, M. G. *Equal Justice for the Poor Man* (New York: Public Affairs Pamphlets, 1964).

Polier, Justine W. "The Invisible Legal Rights of the Poor," *Children*, 12 (November-December, 1965), pp. 215-20.

Pye, A. Kenneth and Raymond F. Garraty, Jr. "The Involvement of the Bar in the War Against Poverty," *Notre Dame Lawyer*, 41 (Symposium, 1966), pp. 860-86.

Reich, Charles A. "Midnight Welfare Searches and the Social Security Act," *Yale Law Journal*, 72 (June, 1963), pp. 1347-60.

——. "Individual Rights and Social Welfare: The Emerging Legal Issues," *Yale Law Journal*, 74 (June, 1965), pp. 1245-57.

Schoshinski, Robert S. "Remedies of the Indigent Tenant: Proposal for Change," *Georgetown Law Journal*, 54 (Spring, 1966), pp. 519-58.

Silverstein, Lee. *Defense of the Poor* (Chicago: American Bar Foundation, 1966).

Sparer, Edward V. "The Role of the Welfare Client's Lawyer," *UCLA Law Review*, 12 (November, 1965), pp. 361-80.

Tenbroek, Jacobus (ed.). *The Law of the Poor* (San Francisco: Chandler Publishing Co., 1966).

Tucker, Edwin W. "The Supreme Court and the Indigent Defendant," *Southern California Law Review*, 37 (Spring, 1964), pp. 149-80.

Wald, Patricia. *Law and Poverty: 1965* (Washington, D. C.: U. S. Government Printing Office, 1965).

The Authors . . .

WARNER BLOOMBERG, JR. is Professor of Urban Affairs and Chairman of the Department of Urban Affairs at the University of Wisconsin–Milwaukee. He received his Ph.D. in sociology from the University of Chicago. He has taught at Syracuse University and was co-director there of the summer workshop on Human Relations and Social Conflict. He has also served as consultant and visiting faculty for a number of institutes dealing with education of the disadvantaged. Among Dr. Bloomberg's publications are *Local Community Leadership*, co-author (University College of Syracuse University, 1960); *Suburban Power Structures and Public Education*, co-author (Syracuse University Press, 1963); and "Community Organization," in Howard S. Becker, editor, *Social Problems: A Modern Approach* (Wiley, 1966). He has also contributed to such journals as the *American Sociological Review, Young Children*, and *Graduate Comment*.

GERALD BREESE is Professor of Sociology at Princeton University. He received his Ph.D. from the University of Chicago. He served as Director of the Bureau of Urban Research at Princeton University from 1950 to 1966. He has held Fulbright and visiting appointments at The American University at Cairo, University of

Natal, and Australian National University. Dr. Breese was research director and contributor to studies published as *Accelerated Urban Growth in a Metropolitan Fringe Area* (1954) and *The Impact of Large Installations on Nearby Areas* (1965). His publications include *Industrial Site Selection* (1954), *Regional Analysis: Trenton-Camden Area* (1954), and *Urbanization in Newly Developing Countries* (Prentice-Hall, 1966). He is also editor of a forthcoming book of readings on urbanization in developing nations.

EDGAR S. CAHN is Executive Director, Citizens' Advocate Center, Washington, D.C. He received his Doctorate in English Literature from Yale University in 1960; and, in 1963, an LL.B. degree from the Yale Law School. Dr. Cahn was formerly employed as Special Assistant to the Director of the Office of Economic Opportunity; Research Associate, Field Foundation; Consultant on Manpower Programs and Community Organization in Venezuela, Agency for International Development; and Special Attorney, Office of Legal Counsel, U. S. Justice Department. He is author of "Zoning Against the Public Interest: Judicial Limitations on Municipal Parochialism" (*Yale Law Journal*, 1962) and of "Beyond the Ken of Courts: A Critique of Judicial Refusal to Review the Complaints of Convicts" (*Yale Law Journal*, 1964). He is also co-author of "The War on Poverty: A Civilian Perspective" (*Yale Law Journal*, July 1964); "What Price Justice: The Civilian Perspective Revisited" (*Notre Dame Lawyer*, 1966); and "The New Sovereign Immunity" (*Harvard Law Review*, 1968).

JEAN CAMPER CAHN is an attorney in private practice and Adjunct Professor of Law at Howard University, Washington, D.C. She is a graduate of Swarthmore College and Yale Law School. She was founder and first director of the National Legal Services Program of the Office of Economic Opportunity. She was formerly employed as International Attorney and Advisor on African Affairs, Legal Advisors Office, U.S. Department of State; Dixwell Neighborhood Attorney, Community Progress, Inc.; and Associate Counsel, New Haven Redevelopment Agency. Mrs. Cahn is co-author of "The War on Poverty: A Civilian Perspective" (*Yale Law Journal*, July 1964); "What Price Justice: The Civilian Perspective Revisited" (*Notre Dame Lawyer*, 1966); and "The New Sovereign Immunity" (*Harvard Law Review*, 1968).

PHILLIPS CUTRIGHT is Associate Professor of Sociology at Vanderbilt University. He received his Ph.D. from the University of Chicago and has taught at Washington State University and Dartmouth College. He worked for the Social Security Administration as Acting Chief of Research Grants and as Social Science Analyst for three years. His most recent paper in cross-national comparisons appeared in the *American Journal of Sociology,* January, 1968, and examines national differences in intergenerational occupational mobility. He is currently at work on a demographic–economic analysis of changing illegitimacy rates in 27 nations during the post World War II period.

PETER C. W. GUTKIND is Associate Professor of Anthropology at McGill University in Montreal, Canada. A graduate of Earlham College, the University of Chicago and the University of Amsterdam, his main interest, since 1953, has been in African Urban Studies. From 1953 to 1959 he was a Research Fellow in Urban Sociology at the East African Institute of Social Research, Makerere College, Kampala, Uganda. He is co-author, with A. W. Southall, of *Townsmen in the Making* (Kampala, 1957) and author of *The Royal Capital of Buganda* (Mouton, The Hague, 1963). More recently he edited (with D. G. Jongmans), and contributed to, *Anthropologists in the Field* (Van Gorcum, Assen, 1967). He has also contributed articles to *Civilisations, Cahiers D'Etudes Africaines, Anthropologica, Human Organization,* and the *Journal of Asian and African Studies.*

WARREN C. HAGGSTROM is Associate Professor and Chairman of the Community Organization sequence at the University of California at Los Angeles. He received his Ph.D. in Social Work and Social Psychology from the University of Michigan, and has taught at Syracuse University. He has worked in a variety of capacities in labor union, farm, political, and community organization. Dr. Haggstrom served as Director of the Community Action Training Center of Syracuse University and has published such papers concerning poverty and community organization as "The Power of the Poor," "Poverty and Adult Education," "Can the Poor Transform the World?" and "Psychological Implications of the Community Development Process."

HOWARD W. HALLMAN lives in Washington, D.C. and is currently a free-lance consultant on community action, manpower, model cities, and other aspects of community development. He received a master's degree in political science from the University of Kansas. During the first session of the 90th Congress, he directed a study of the poverty program for the Senate Subcommittee on Employment, Manpower, and Poverty. He has been associated with housing, urban renewal, and community action programs in Philadelphia and New Haven and is the author of over sixty articles and reports.

LAWRENCE HAWORTH is currently Professor of Philosophy, and Chairman of the Department of Philosophy, at the University of Waterloo, Canada, and is engaged in research at the University's Planning and Resources Institute. He received his Ph.D. in philosophy from the University of Illinois. Prior to taking up his present position in 1965, he was associated with the University of Alabama and Purdue University. Dr. Haworth is the author of *The Good City* (Indiana University, 1963) and of articles which have appeared in *Ethics, Philosophy of Science, American Philosophical Quarterly Supplement, Harvard Business Review, Southern Journal of Philosophy*, and the *Journal of the American Institute of Planners*. He is a consultant to the Urban Affairs Program of the National Institute of Public Affairs.

MILTON J. HUBER is Professor of Consumer Affairs and Director of the Center for Consumer Affairs at the University of Wisconsin–Milwaukee. He is also director of the University's Community Program Center in Milwaukee's black ghetto and a member of the Urban Affairs Department at the University of Wisconsin–Milwaukee. He received his Ph.D. degree from Boston University. A specialist in the socio-economic problems of low-income families, he has served as a consultant to the Community Action Office of OEO and numerous other social agencies, universities and corporations. His most recent writings have centered upon family consumer credit problems and include *A Profile of the Over-Extended Credit Family* (Merrill-Palmer Institute, Detroit) and "Installment-Credit Problems Among Public Welfare Recipients" in *The Journal of Consumer Affairs* (1967).

ARNOLD I. KISCH is Assistant Professor of Medical Care Organization and Assistant Professor of Preventive Medicine at the University of California, Los Angeles. A graduate of Columbia College, he received the M.D. and Master of Public Health degrees from Harvard University where he taught on the faculty. Dr. Kisch, whose chief research interests are in the area of health manpower utilization and modeling of health systems, is the author of a series of case studies on administrative decision-making in the field of medical care. He has served as a consultant to TRW Systems and to the Los Angeles Economic and Youth Opportunities Agency in the development of their health programs. He was co-author of the comprehensive report which led to formation of a unified Department of Health and Hospitals for the City of Boston in 1965.

SANFORD L. KRAVITZ is Associate Professor of Social Planning at the Florence Heller School for Advanced Studies in Social Welfare at Brandeis University. He was formerly the Associate Director of the Community Action Program in the Office of Economic Opportunity responsible for Research, Demonstration, Training and Technical Assistance. As a member of the President's Task Force on Poverty, he played a key role in the initial conceptualization of the Community Action Program. He also served as Program Coordinator for the President's Committee on Juvenile Delinquency from 1962 until 1964. He has worked extensively at the local community level and has written and spoken widely on current urban social problems.

WILLIAM MANGIN is Professor of Anthropology, and Chairman of the Department of Anthropology, at Syracuse University. He received his Ph.D. from Yale University, and has taught at San Marcos University in Peru. He has been Field Director of the Cornell–Vicos Project in Peru and Deputy Director of the Peace Corps in Peru. His most recent publications have been on urbanization and squatter settlements in Latin America (*Latin American Research Review*, Summer 1967) and particularly in Peru (*Scientific American*, October 1967).

S. M. MILLER is Program Advisor in Social Development at the Ford Foundation and Professor of Education and Sociology at New York University. He received his Ph.D. in economics and sociology from Princeton University. A consultant to a wide range of organizations, his basic concern is with social stratification, and social and economic policy. His latest book is *Social Class and Social Policy* (with Frank Reissman). Other publications include *Comparative Social Mobility; The School Dropout Problem— Syracuse* (senior author); *The Dynamics of the American Economy* (co-author); *Max Weber: Readings* (editor), and *Applied Sociology* (co-editor).

OSCAR A. ORNATI is Professor of Management and Director of Project Labor Market at the Graduate School of Business Administration, New York University. He received his Ph.D. in economics from Harvard University. He has taught on the Graduate Faculty of the New School for Social Research (New York), and at Cornell, Harvard and Boston Universities. Dr. Ornati has served as a consultant to the U. S. Department of Labor, the Small Business Administration, and is currently serving as a consultant to the U. S. Department of Commerce. In 1965 and 1966 he was Director of Manpower and Economic Development of the Office of Economic Opportunity. He is the author of *Jobs and Workers in India* (Cornell University, 1955) and *Poverty Amid Affluence* (Twentieth Century Fund, 1966). He has also contributed articles to such publications as *Challenge, Antioch Review, Dissent, Monthly Labor Review,* and *Labor Law Journal.*

STEVEN I. PFLANCZER is currently assistant professor at the School of Social Welfare, University of Wisconsin–Milwaukee. He received his Ph.D. in sociology from Loyola University, Chicago, after studies in Hungary, Rome (Italy), Louvain (Belgium), Strasbourg and Paris (France).

MILTON I. ROEMER, M.D. is Professor of Public Health and Head of the Division of Medical Care Organization at the University of California, Los Angeles, where he is also Professor of Preventive Medicine at the UCLA Medical School. He was Research Professor of Administrative Medicine at Cornell University (Sloan Institute of Hospital Administration) 1957-1962 and Associate Professor of Social and Administrative Medicine at the Yale Medical School 1949-1951. After qualifying in medicine in 1940, he earned the M.A.

degree in sociology and the M.P.H. in public health. From 1943 to 1949 he served in the United States Public Health Service on rural health and federal–state relations tasks. Dr. Roemer serves as consultant to the World Health Organization, U. S. Public Health Service, California State Department of Public Health, Los Angeles County Health Department, and various voluntary health organizations. He is the author of six books and about 150 articles on the social aspects of medicine.

FLORENCE W. ROSENSTOCK is Research Associate in the Center for Social Research in Rehabilitation Medicine of the Albert Einstein College of Medicine in New York City. A graduate of Syracuse University, she received her M.S. in Urban Affairs from the University of Wisconsin–Milwaukee. She is currently engaged in a program of action-research designed to demonstrate new techniques for providing health-care and rehabilitation services in the urban environment.

HENRY J. SCHMANDT is Professor of Urban Affairs at the University of Wisconsin–Milwaukee. He served as Assistant Director of the Missouri State Reorganization Commission, Associate Director of the Metropolitan St. Louis Survey, and Associate Director of Metropolitan Community Studies, Dayton. He is a member of the Southeastern Wisconsin Regional Planning Commission and the Advisory Council to the Wisconsin Department of Local Affairs and Development. Dr. Schmandt is co-author of *Metropolitan Reform in St. Louis* (Holt, Rinehart and Winston, 1961); *Exploring the Metropolitan Community* (University of California Press, 1961); and *The Metropolis: Its People, Politics, and Economic Life* (Harper and Row, 1965). He is also author of *The Milwaukee Metropolitan Study Commission* (Indiana University Press, 1965).

ALVIN L. SCHORR is Deputy Assistant Secretary for Individual and Family Services, Department of Health, Education, and Welfare. He is a graduate of the City College of New York and the George Warren Brown School of Social Work, Washington University, St. Louis. He served in the Office of the Commissioner of Social Security from 1958 to 1965. He was a Fulbright scholar in 1962-1963, studying the planning of government policy in England

and social security and social services in France. His publications include *Slums and Social Insecurity* (Thomas Nelson, London, 1964), and *Poor Kids* (Basic Books, 1966). Mr. Schorr is currently editor-in-chief of *Social Work*, the journal of the National Association of Social Workers.

ARTHUR B. SHOSTAK is Associate Professor of Social Sciences, Drexel Institute of Technology, and a member of the Institute of Environmental Studies at Drexel. He received his Ph.D. in sociology from Princeton University and has taught at the University of Pennsylvania. Dr. Shostak has served as a consultant to OEO, the Philadelphia Anti-Poverty Program, and similar organizations. He has co-edited *New Perspectives on Poverty* (Prentice-Hall, 1965), and is the editor of *Sociology in Action* (Dorsey, 1966). He is also the author of *Blue-Collar Style* (Random House, 1968) and *America's Forgotten Labor Organization* (Industrial Relations Section, Princeton University Press, 1962). Articles of his on poverty matters have recently appeared in *Social Work*, *The Journal of Marriage and the Family*, and *American Child*.

GORDON F. SUTTON is Deputy Chief, Research and Plans Division, Office of Research, Plans, Programs and Evaluation in the Office of Economic Opportunity. He received his Ph.D. in sociology from the University of Michigan. He was previously associated with the Bureau of the Census and the National Center for Health Statistics and has served as lecturer at the University of California, Los Angeles. He is the author of several articles on various topics in demography.

GEORGE W. WEBBER is Director of the Metropolitan Urban Service Training Facility in New York City. A graduate of Harvard University, he received his Bachelor of Divinity Degree from Union Theological Seminary and his Ph.D. from Columbia. He was formerly a member of the Group Ministry of the East Harlem Protestant Parish. He is also currently an Associate Professor of Church and Community at Union Theological Seminary. Dr. Webber is the author of *God's Colony in Man's World* (Abingdon, 1960) and *The Congregation in Mission* (Abingdon, 1964). He is a Kent Fellow.

ALSO AVAILABLE FROM SAGE PUBLICATIONS, INC.

URBAN AFFAIRS ANNUAL REVIEWS   **$20.00 each**

Volume I Urban Research and Policy Planning — edited by Leo F. Schnore and Henry Fagin. Published, 1967.

Volume II Power, Poverty, and Urban Policy — edited by Warner Bloomberg, Jr. and Henry J. Schmandt. Published, 1968.

Volume III The Quality of Urban Life — edited by Henry J. Schmandt and Warner Bloomberg, Jr. To be published in 1969.

Periodicals:

URBAN AFFAIRS QUARTERLY — an interdisciplinary scholarly journal for the urban specialist, published in September, December, March and June.

URBAN RESEARCH NEWS — a bi-weekly newsletter reporting on current developments of interest to urban specialists.

URBAN STUDIES — edited at the University of Glasgow; distributed in the U.S. and Canada by Sage Publications. Published in February, June and November.

THE AMERICAN BEHAVIORAL SCIENTIST — the leading interdisciplinary journal in social and behavioral sciences. Published monthly except July and August.

THE LAW AND SOCIETY REVIEW — published for the Law and Society Association.

COMPARATIVE POLITICAL STUDIES — an interdisciplinary quarterly devoted to the publication of theoretical and empirical research articles by scholars engaged in cross-national comparative study.

DESIGN METHODS GROUP NEWSLETTER — a monthly newsletter of methodology for the solution of large-scale design problems (with particular applications for urban systems).

Other Publications:

EDUCATING AN URBAN POPULATION — edited by Marilyn Gittell. Published, 1967. $7.50 net.

RIOTS, VIOLENCE, AND DISORDER: TURMOIL IN THE URBAN COMMUNITY — edited by Louis H. Masotti and Don R. Bowen. To be published late 1968. $7.95 (tent.).

THE ABS GUIDE TO RECENT PUBLICATIONS IN THE SOCIAL AND BEHAVIORAL SCIENCES — 6,664 annotated bibliographic citations of selected books, pamphlets, and journal articles published during the years 1957-64. $24.95 net. *Annual Supplements are also available at $12.50 each.*

SIMULATION GAMES IN LEARNING — edited by S. Boocock, and E. O. Schild, with a preface by James S. Coleman. Published, 1968. $8.50 net.

Send all orders and requests for further information to:

SAGE PUBLICATIONS, INC. / 275 So. BEVERLY DR. / BEVERLY HILLS, CALIF.

URBAN AFFAIRS ANNUAL REVIEWS

THIS VALUABLE NEW SERIES consists of annual reference volumes designed to present critical analyses of current interest, prepared by experts in various fields of urban studies, and covering—over the years—programs, policies and current developments in all areas of concern to urban specialists. Volumes will be published in March of each year and will be handsomely bound books of about 640 pages in a 6⅛ x 9¼ format. The first volume in this important new series is described at right.

INTERNATIONAL EDITORIAL ADVISORY BOARD

CHARLES ABRAMS, *Columbia University*

HOWARD S. BECKER, *Northwestern University*

ASA BRIGGS, *University of Sussex*

JOHN W. DYCKMAN, *University of California (Berkeley)*

H. J. DYOS, *University of Leicester*

MARILYN GITTELL, *Editor, Urban Affairs Quarterly*

JEAN GOTTMANN, *Ecole des Hautes Etudes (Sorbonne)*

SCOTT GREER, *Northwestern University*

ROBERT HAVIGHURST, *University of Chicago*

WERNER Z. HIRSCH, *University of California (Los Angeles)*

EIICHI ISOMURA, *Tokyo, Japan*

OSCAR LEWIS, *University of Illinois*

WILLIAM C. LORING, *Public Health Service*

MARTIN MEYERSON, *State University of New York (Buffalo)*

EDUARDO NEIRA, *Interamerican Development Bank*

HARVEY S. PERLOFF, *Resources for the Future*

D. J. ROBERTSON, *University of Glasgow*

WALLACE SAYRE, *Columbia University*

P. J. O. SELF, *The London School of Political Science and Economics*

KENZO TANGE, *Tokyo, Japan*

You can still save on future volumes in this important new series by placing a standing order for subsequent annual volumes as they are published. All such standing orders will be shipped upon publication and you will be billed only $17.50 (we pay handling and postage of all standing orders).

Volumes II and III of the URBAN AFFAIRS ANNUAL REVIEWS will be edited by Henry J. Schmandt and Warner Bloomberg, Jr.—both of the Department of Urban Affairs, University of Wisconsin (Milwaukee). Volume II (1968) deals with *Power, Poverty and Urban Policy;* Volume III (1969) with *The Quality of Urban Life.*

Send all orders to:

SAGE PUBLICATIONS, INC. / **275 S. Beverly Drive** / **Beverly Hills, Cal.**

URBAN AFFAIRS ANNUAL REVIEWS

NOW AVAILABLE FOR IMMEDIATE SHIPMENT:

URBAN RESEARCH AND POLICY PLANNING

THE FIRST VOLUME IN THIS IMPORTANT NEW SERIES

URBAN RESEARCH AND POLICY PLANNING is edited by *Leo F. Schnore* and *Henry Fagin*—both of the University of Wisconsin. This first volume of the URBAN AFFAIRS ANNUAL REVIEWS presents a review of research and policy planning during the two decades of the post-war period. Research needs are related to the development of improved planning and policy in several important areas of study.   640 pages $20.00

TABLE OF CONTENTS AND CONTRIBUTORS

An Important Announcement for the Urban Specialist ...

The publisher of *Urban Affairs Quarterly* and the *Urban Affairs Annual Review* series is proud to announce a new publication. In our continuing effort to assist you and your colleagues, we have become convinced of the need for a medium of communication which is published frequently and presents information of immediate interest. Since Monday, November 14th, 1967, we have published (on alternate Mondays) :

URBAN RESEARCH NEWS

A Bi-weekly Newsletter for the Urban Specialist

Urban Research News reports on current developments—personnel, meetings, research projects, publications, etc.—at more than 200 centers engaged in some form of urban research; on the legislative and other activities of governments and governmental agencies; on the foundations, associations, and public and private groups which sponsor and support urban research; on publications—articles, pamphlets, monographs, books and reports—of interest to researchers; on recent and future meetings and other events.

With *Urban Research News* you will be kept informed and up-to-date on people, places, and events in your field; you will know what has happened, what is happening, and what is going to happen in urban research.

Do not miss the current *URBAN RESEARCH NEWS*.
Subscribe NOW!   **$26.00 for 26 issues.**

Please note: all subscriptions are for a minimum of 26 issues—there is *no* single copy rate.

SAGE PUBLICATIONS, INC. / 275 S. Beverly Dr. / Beverly Hills, Cal.